Pro JSP Third Edition

Simon Brown, Sam Dalton, Dan Jepp, David Johnson, Sing Li, and Matt Raible

Apress™

Pro JSP, Third Edition

ISBN (pbk): 1-59059-225-5

Printed and bound in the United States of America 10987654321

Technical Reviewers: Esin Erser, Brad Maiani, Vinay Menon, Kirk Montgomery, Stephen Parker, Steve Reece, Erick Sgarbi, Henri Yandell

Assistant Publisher and Project Manager: Grace Wong

Copy Editors: Mark Nigara, Nicole LeClerc

Production Manager: Kari Brooks

Production Editor: Kelly Winquist

Proofreaders: Linda Seifert, Laura Cheu, Lori Bring

Compositor: Molly Sharp

Indexer: Bill Johncocks

Artists: Neil Lote, Dawn Chellingworth, Paul Grove, Sarah Hall, Rachel Taylor, Pippa Wonson, Joan Howard

Cover Designer: Kurt Krames

Manufacturing Manager: Tom Debolski

Distributed to the book trade in the United States by Springer-Verlag New York, Inc., 175 Fifth Avenue, New York, NY, 10010 and outside the United States by Springer-Verlag GmbH & Co. KG, Tiergartenstr. 17, 69112 Heidelberg, Germany.

In the United States: phone 1-800-SPRINGER, email orders@springer-ny.com, or visit http://www.springer-ny.com. Outside the United States: fax +49 6221 345229, email orders@springer.de, or visit http://www.springer.de.

For information on translations, please contact Apress directly at 2560 Ninth Street, Suite 219, Berkeley, CA 94710. Phone 510-549-5930, fax 510-549-5939, email info@apress.com, or visit http://www.apress.com.

The source code for this book is available to readers at http://www.apress.com in the Downloads section.

Contents at a Glance

Contents

About the Authors

Simon Brown

Simon works in London as a technical architect and has been using Java since its early beginnings, working in roles ranging from developer and architect to mentor and trainer. When not working with Java, he can usually be found speaking or writing about it. In the past few years, Simon has spoken at the JavaOne Conference and has authored or coauthored several books, including his own, entitled *Professional JSP Tag Libraries.* Simon maintains an active involvement within the Java community as a bartender (moderator) with JavaRanch and his open-source JSP custom tag-testing framework called TagUnit.

Simon graduated from the University of Reading in 1996 with a First class BSc (Hons) degree in Computer Science and is a Sun Certified Enterprise Architect for J2EE, Web Component Developer for J2EE, and Developer for the Java 2 Platform.

For information about what Simon is currently up to, you can point your browser to his weblog at http://www.simongbrown.com/blog/.

> *I would like to thank my wife, Kirstie–you're always there for me.*

Simon contributed Chapters 5, 6, 7, and 13 to this book.

Sam Dalton

Sam has worked with Java and related technologies in London for a number of years, and has coauthored two titles, *Professional Java Servlets 2.3* and *Professional SCWCD Certification.* Sam is an active contributor to TagUnit, an open-source custom tag-testing framework (http://www.tagunit.org) and is also pursuing other open-source interests. He has just embarked on the next stage of his career adventure by joining ThoughtWorks (http://www.thoughtworks.co.uk).

Sam graduated from the University of Reading in 1997 with a 2.1 honors degree in Computer Science. He has also achieved various certifications, including Sun Certified Web Component Developer and Sun Certified Developer. Please feel free to e-mail any questions or comments about this book and related topics to books@samjdalton.com.

> *Well here we are again! Who would have thought I would ever be involved in three books? Not me, that's for sure! There are a number of people that I would like to thank for supporting/putting up with me while I was contributing to this book. First of all, as ever, I would like to thank my darling wife, Anne, without whom I would not have the energy to do half of the things that I do. I would also like to thank my Mum and Dad, it means a great deal to me to see how proud my work makes you, thanks! Enjoy the book, and happy reading!*

Sam contributed Chapters 2 and 3 to this book.

Dan Jepp

Dan is currently a senior developer at Dresdner Kleinwort Wasserstein, based in London. He has been working with the Java platform and related technologies for a number of years now and has spoken at several sessions at the JavaOne Conference. Dan has recently authored the title *Professional SCWCD Certification* with coauthor Sam Dalton.

Dan graduated from the University of Kent, in Canterbury, England, where he attained an uppersecond-class honors degree in Computer Science, and has since gained the following Sun Certifications: Sun Certified Programmer, Developer, and Web Component Developer for the Java 2 Platform.

> *Dedicated to my fiancée, Kelly, whose love, support, and encouragement will leave me forever grateful.*

Dan contributed Chapters 1 and 4 to this book.

David Johnson

David is an experienced software developer who has worked in the commercial software development, telecommunications, and Geographic Information Systems industries. David has been working with Java since before the dawn of Java 1.0. Since then, he has been involved in the development of a number of Java-based commercial products including the HAHTsite Application Server, HAHT eSyndication, Venetica's Jasper document viewer, and Rogue Wave's Object Factory IDE. David is also an active weblogger and the original developer of the open-source Roller Weblogger (http://www.rollerweblogger.org) software. David works at HAHT Commerce and lives in Raleigh, North Carolina with his wife and three children.

> *First and foremost, I must thank my beautiful wife, Andi, for giving me the encouragement and time needed to work on this book. She kept my three little boys, Alex, Linus, and Leo, happy and quiet while I toiled away in the back room on my chapters. I should also thank fellow Roller Weblogger developers Lance Lavandowska and Matt Raible. Lance helped me to get started with this project, and Matt helped to improve and perfect my example code. Finally, I would like to thank Bill Barnett and the whole HAHTsite Application Server team at HAHT Commerce for teaching me just about everything I know about web application performance and scalability and for inspiring me to learn more.*

David contributed Chapters 8 and 12 to this book.

Sing Li

First bitten by the computer bug in 1978, Sing has grown up with the microprocessor revolution. His first PC was a $99 do-it-yourself COSMIC ELF computer with 256 bytes of memory and a 1-bit LED display. For more than two decades, Sing has been a developer, author, consultant, speaker, instructor, and entrepreneur. His wide-ranging experience spans distributed architectures, web application and service systems, computer telephony integration, and embedded systems. Sing is a regular book contributor, has been working with and writing about Java, Jini, and JXTA since their very first alpha releases, and is an evangelist of P2P technology and a participant in the JXTA community.

Sing contributed Chapters 9 and 10 to this book.

Matt Raible

Matt Raible is a Montana native who grew up in a log cabin without electricity or running water. After hiking to school a mile and a half every day (and skiing in the winter), he would arrive home to a very loving family. "The Cabin" is a beautiful and awesome place that will always be near and dear to Matt's entire family. Even without electricity, his father, Joseph, connected them to the Internet using a 300 baud modem, a Commodore 64, and a small generator. CompuServe was the name, slow was the game. Matt became inspired by the Internet in the early 1990s, and has been developing websites and web applications ever since. He graduated from the University of Denver in 1997 with degrees in Russian, International Business, and Finance. To learn more about Matt and his life as a J2EE Developer, visit him at http://raibledesigns.com.

I'd like to thank my beautiful wife, Julie, and adorable daughter, Abbie, for their love and support while writing these chapters. Abbie was born three weeks before I was asked to write my chapters, and her smiles and giggles were an incredible inspiration. Chris Alonso, thanks for motivating me to go into computers as a profession and for being such a good friend. Thanks to my dad for passing along his knack for computers and great memory, and to my Mom for giving me a passion for life, happiness, and humor. Kalin–you're the best sister in the world and you make this world a better place with your smiles and laughter. Last but not least, thanks to Matt Good for letting me write Java, and to Martin Gee and Brian Boelsterli for their mentoring.

Matt contributed Chapters 11 and 14 to this book.

Introduction

Welcome to the third edition of *Pro JSP*, designed to help new and experienced Java developers alike discover the power (and even the joy) of creating Java-based server-side solutions for the Web. If you've programmed with JSP before you'll find that the new features in JSP 2.0 make developing JSP pages easier then ever before and if you only know a little Java then this is your chance to add JSP to your toolbox skills.

JavaServer Pages, or **JSP** for short, is a server-side technology that takes the Java language, with its inherent simplicity and elegance, and uses it to create highly interactive and flexible web applications. In today's unsure economic climate, having the Java language behind it makes JSP particularly compelling for business: Java is an open language, essentially meaning it doesn't require expensive licenses and thus JSP solutions can be highly cost-effective.

The founding premise of JSP is that HTML can be used to create the basic structure of a web page, and Java code can be mixed in with it to provide the dynamic components of the page that modern web users expect. If you have an understanding of the concepts of HTML and web pages, JSP provides an unbeatable way to learn about creating innovative, interactive content as well as coming to grips with the popular language of Java. This book will be your guide as you step into this exciting new world.

Who Is This Book For?

This book is aimed at anyone who knows the Java language and core APIs and wants to learn about web programming with the latest versions of the JSP and Servlet APIs.

Familiarity with HTML is required; however, no prior knowledge of server-side Java programming is necessary. Having said that, this book does not claim to be exhaustive in all areas, particularly in relation to other Java APIs such as Enterprise JavaBeans.

What's Covered in This Book

This book covers the latest versions of the JSP and Servlet specifications–versions 2.0 and 2.4 respectively, both of which are new specifications developed through the **Java Community Process** (http://java.sun.com/aboutJava/communityprocess/).

> *It's possible that some small changes might be made before they're finally released; however, any modifications are likely to be minor and the new specifications are already being implemented by a number of products such as Tomcat 5.0.*

Those who have read previous editions of this book will notice that this edition is not a revision of *Professional JSP, 2nd Edition*; rather, it has been "re-coded from the ground up" to address the newest features of Java web development. A lot has changed since the second edition, which was only published back in April 2001!

If you already have some exposure to server Java web development, you should pay attention to any changes in the technologies that are indicated throughout the book, or skip ahead to the sections that interest you the most. On the other hand, if you're new to JSP, servlets, and JSTL, and this is somewhat confusing, you've come to the right place; the early chapters in this book, especially, were written with you in mind.

The book's chapters can be summarized as follows:

Chapter 1, *The Anatomy of a JavaServer Page*, looks at the JSP life cycle, JSP application architecture, and the fundamentals of JSP pages, and provides a feel for where JSP technology fits within the J2EE and other web components such as servlets, tag libraries, and JavaBeans, which exist in the J2EE web tier for providing dynamic web-based content.

Chapter 2, *Servlets and Deployment*, delves into what Java servlets are, and looks at the development and deployment of Java servlets. The Servlet and JSP specifications are developed in parallel, and this chapter is up to date for the latest release of JSP 2.0 and Servlets 2.4 (as is the rest of the book).

We discuss one of the new features of the JSP 2.0 specification in the appropriately named **Chapter 3**, *The JavaServer Pages Expression Language*. The JSP expression language is what you'll be using most often in JSP pages, an intentionally simple language that is, to a large extent, independent of JSP.

Chapter 4, *JavaServer Pages Standard Tag Library*, looks at the reasons for the creation of the JSTL, its details (it is in fact four different tag libraries), and how to install the JSTL and Tomcat 5.0.

Tag Files and Simple Tags is the title of **Chapter 5**. In the same way that the tags contained within JSTL are extremely valuable for improving the readability and maintainability of a JSP page, you can build your own custom tags to enable your own functionality to be reusable and easily maintained. Tag files and simple tags are both new mechanisms for writing custom tags introduced as a part of the JSP 2.0 specification.

Chapter 6, *Classic Tags*, takes a look at the facilities provided by former versions of the JSP specification for writing custom tags. As you'll see throughout the chapter, these previous methods, now called **classic tags**, provide a great deal more flexibility and for this reason are still useful in some scenarios.

Now that you've seen the basics of building custom tags, **Chapter 7**, *Custom Tag Advanced Features and Best Practices*, wraps up your understanding by looking at some more advanced features and the best way to use custom tags.

Chapter 8, *Data Access Options for Web Applications*, discusses how best to access your back-end data from your JSPs and servlets. No matter what type of JSP application you're writing, you'll need to either store the data that is created by your application, or use data from an external source, and this chapter looks at examples using a MySQL database.

In **Chapter 9**, *Introduction to Filtering*, you'll look at filtering, a standard feature of all Servlet 2.4-compliant containers. You'll explore the life cycle of a filter as managed by the container, discuss the very important concept of filter chaining, and then create and deploy two simple filters as a foundation for **Chapter 10**, *Advanced Filtering Techniques.* Chapter 10 acts as a cookbook for the application of filters, as you turn your attention to the more advanced techniques involved in applied filter programming by looking at five examples that can be used as the basis for your own filter implementation.

Chapter 11, *Security in Web Applications*, looks at making your web applications secure and exploring different methods of authentication and authorization.

Chapter 12, *Improving Web Application Performance and Scalability*, is your guide to a number of well-known tools and techniques such as page caching and database connection pooling that you can use to improve performance and stability, even after you've designed and coded your application.

Chapter 13, *Web Application Design and Best Practices*, brings together the techniques covered in the earlier chapters and shows how to build maintainable, extensible Java-based web applications. It looks at the importance of good design and how it can help you build high-quality web applications that are easier to maintain and extend in the future.

In **Chapter 14**, *Using Struts, Xdoclet, and Other Tools*, you'll develop a resume building and viewing (web) application called struts-resume, using a variety of third-party products. All of the products used in struts-resume are open source and help to facilitate and speed up various stages of the development process.

What You Need to Use This Book

The first thing you'll need to use this book is a computer that supports the Java programming language. This includes computers that run Microsoft Windows (including Windows 95, 98, Me, NT, 2000, and XP) or Linux.

We don't use any proprietary software and all code runs on open-source products, available free of charge over the Internet. Consequently, an Internet connection is pretty much essential in order to get hold of this software.

The primary piece of software you'll need is a web container that supports the JSP 2.0 and Servlet 2.4 specifications. Although there are a number of options to choose from, we've elected to use the Jakarta Tomcat web container throughout the whole book because it's the officially designated Reference Implementation. Version 5 is the latest and greatest, which supports the specs we require. You can get the latest release information about Tomcat 5.0 from http://jakarta.apache.org/tomcat/index.html

As you need further software components during the course of the book, we'll indicate clearly where to download them from.

Conventions

We've used a number of different styles of text and layout in this book to differentiate between different kinds of information. Here are examples of the styles used and an explanation of what they mean.

Code has several fonts. If we're talking about code in the text, we use a nonproportional font like this: `for...next`. If it's a block of code that can be typed as a program and run, then it will also appear within a gray box:

```
public java.util.List getDependants() {
  return _jspx_dependants;
}
```

Sometimes you'll see code in a mixture of styles, like this:

```
import javax.servlet.http.*;

public class SessionTracker2 extends HttpServlet {
  public void doGet(HttpServletRequest req, HttpServletResponse res)
```

When this happens, the code with a white background is code you're already familiar with; the line highlighted in gray is a new addition to the code since you last looked at it.

Advice, hints, and background information come in this type of font.

Important pieces of information are placed inside boxes like this.

Bullets appear indented, with each new bullet marked as follows:

- **Important Words** are in a bold type font.
- Words that appear on the screen or in menus, such as File or Window, are in a similar font to the one you would see on a Windows desktop.
- Keys that you press on the keyboard, such as *Ctrl* and *Enter*, are in italics.

1

The Anatomy of a JavaServer Page

The Java 2 Platform, Enterprise Edition (J2EE) has two different but complementary technologies for producing dynamic web content in the presentation tier–namely **Java Servlets** and **JavaServer Pages (JSP)**.

Java Servlets was the first of these technologies to appear and it was initially described as extensions to a web server for producing dynamic web content. JSP on the other hand is a newer technology, but is equally capable of generating the same dynamic content. However, the way in which a servlet and a JSP page produce their content is fundamentally different; servlets embed content into logic whereas JSP pages embed logic into content.

JSP pages contain markup interlaced with special JSP elements that provide logic for controlling the dynamic content. Servlets are built using Java classes that contain statements to output markup code. Of these two different paradigms, JSP pages are preferred for presenting dynamic content in the presentation tier due to their greater readability, maintainability, and simplicity. Further increasing the simplicity and ease of use of JSP pages was one of the main objectives of the JSP 2.0 specification, which includes several new features to make it easier than ever to embrace JSP technology, especially for developers who aren't fluent in the Java syntax.

The inclusion of a new **expression language (EL)** enables JavaScript-style JSP code to be embedded within pages, which makes it much easier for web developers not familiar with the Java syntax to understand the JSP logic. A library of standard actions known as the **JavaServer Pages Standard Tag Library (JSTL)** is also included to provide a host of useful, reusable actions such as conditional statements, iteration, and XML integration to name a few. These actions are applicable in some shape or form to most JSP web applications, and their use will greatly improve the reliability and ease of development for JSP page authors. Custom actions (also known as custom tags) also benefit from changes in the JSP 2.0 specification and it's now possible to write a custom action entirely in JSP syntax instead of Java syntax! These new features will help make JSP pages easier to write and maintain and are discussed in detail in the following chapters:

- The JSP 2.0 expression language (EL) (see Chapter 3)
- The JavaServer Pages Standard Tag Library (JSTL) (see Chapter 4)
- JSP 2.0 Custom Tags (see Chapters 5, 6, and 7)

In this chapter you'll take a look at some of the fundamental concepts based around JSP technology, such as:

- The mechanics of a JSP page
- Typical JSP architectures
- Core JSP syntax
- Tag libraries

The aim of this chapter is for you to gain a grounding in the basics of JSP technology to help you to make full use of the rest of the chapters in this book that build on these basic principles.

Before You Begin

To begin examining the basics of JSP technology it's essential that you have a cursory familiarity with the alternative and complimentary presentation tier web component, Java Servlets. The next chapter will discuss servlets in more detail.

Java Servlets

As mentioned earlier, a servlet can most simply be described as custom web-server extensions, whose job are to process requests and dynamically construct appropriate responses. In practice such responses are usually returned in the form of HTML or XML and are the result of a user making an HTTP request via a web browser. Servlet technology has been an extremely popular choice for building dynamic web applications such as e-commerce sites, online banking, and news portals to name a few, for reasons of simplicity, extensibility, efficiency, and performance over alternative technologies such as CGI scripts.

Some of the most basic advantages of servlet technology are as follows:

- **Simplicity:** Servlets are easy to write, and all the complicated threading and request delegating is managed by the servlet container.
- **Extensibility:** The Servlet API is completely protocol independent.
- **Efficiency:** Unlike CGI scripts the execution of a servlet doesn't require a separate process to be spawned by the web server each time.
- **Performance:** Servlets are persistent and their life cycle extends beyond that of each HTTP request.

Servlets are simply Java classes that inherit from the `javax.servlet.Servlet` interface, which are compiled and deployed inside of a servlet container, which is a Java environment that manages the life cycle of the servlet and deals with the lower-level socket-based communication. The servlet container may be part of an existing Java-enabled web server itself or may be used as a stand-alone product that is integrated with a third-party web server. The servlet Reference Implementation container, Jakarta Tomcat for example, may be used as a stand-alone web server or can be used as a separate servlet container inside a larger commercial web server such as the Apache web server.

Servlets are typically used for returning text-based content such as HTML, XML, WML, and so on, but are equally at home returning binary data such as images or serialized Java objects, which are often used by further servlets to generate some appropriate dynamic response.

JSP Under the Hood

A JSP page is simply a regular text file that contains markup (usually HTML) suitable for display inside a browser. Within this markup are special JSP elements that you'll learn more about later. These are used to provide processing logic that enables dynamic content to be produced on a request-by-request basis.

In JSP terms, any markup that isn't a JSP element is known as template text, and this really can be any form of text-based content such as HTML, WML, XML, or even plain text! Of course the mixture of JSP elements and template text cannot simply be sent to the browser without any form of processing by the server. We mentioned earlier how JSP technology is an extension of servlet technology, and so you probably won't be surprised to learn that each JSP page is, in fact, converted into a servlet in order to provide this processing logic. This servlet is known as the JSP **implementation servlet**.

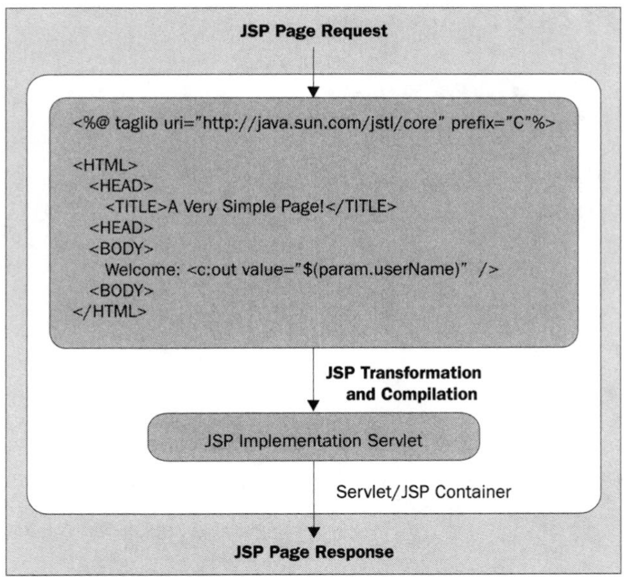

A request for a JSP page is handled initially by the web server, which then delegates the request to the JSP container. The JSP engine will translate the contents of the JSP into its implementation servlet, which it uses to service the request. Usually a JSP container will check to see if the contents of a JSP page have changed before deciding if it needs to retranslate the page in response to a request. This feature can make on-the-spot changes to JSP pages easy since the next request will automatically cause a retranslation and the most up-to-date content will be returned. Compare this with a purely servlet-based approach, which would need the servlet container to be shut down in order to have the necessary changes made, such as recompilation, testing, and finally, a restart!

Let's take a closer look at the process involved in taking a plain JSP text file and turning it into a dynamic web component, also known as the JSP life cycle.

The JSP Life Cycle

As you've just seen, JSP pages don't directly return content to the client browser themselves. Instead, they rely on some initial server-side processing that converts the JSP page into the JSP page implementation class, which handles all requests made of the JSP:

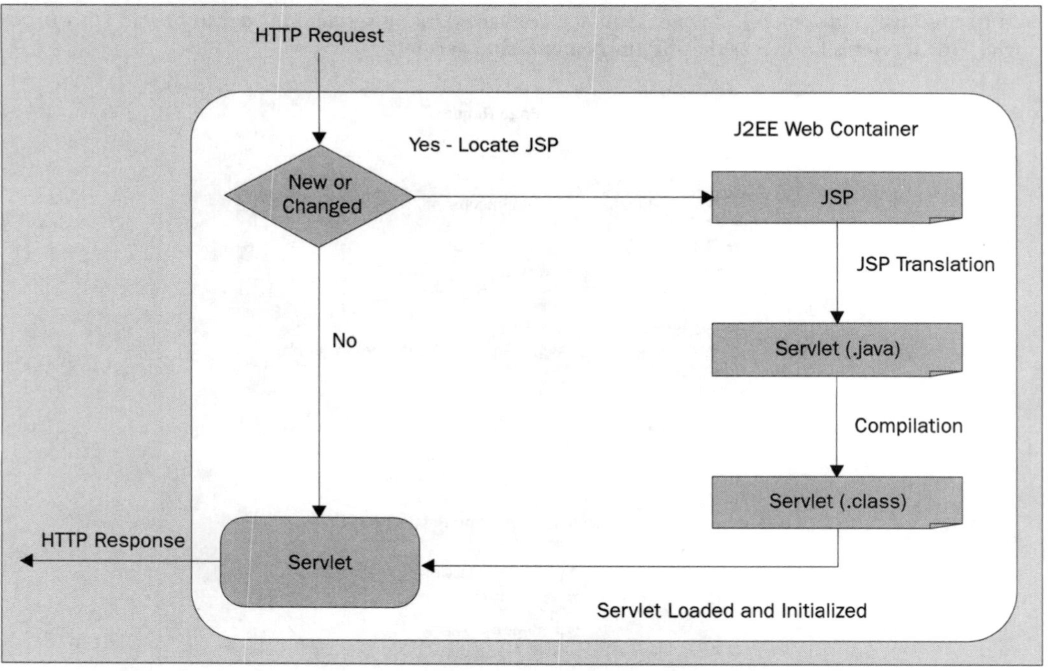

As you can see from this diagram, the JSP servlet container decides whether or not the JSP has been translated before. If not, then the JSP container starts the translation phase to generate the JSP page implementation servlet, which is then compiled, loaded, and initialized and used to service the request. If the JSP container detects that a JSP has already been translated and hasn't subsequently changed then the request is simply serviced by the implementation servlet that exists already inside the container.

The life cycle of a JSP can be further split into approximately four phases to cater for the initial JSP translation right through to the servicing of requests and ultimately to the death of the servlet.

Translation

The first stage in the life cycle of a JSP is known as the translation phase.

When a request is first made for a JSP (assuming it hasn't been precompiled), the JSP engine will examine the JSP file to check that it's correctly formed and the JSP syntax is correct. If the syntax check is successful then the JSP engine will translate the JSP into its page implementation class, which takes the form of a standard Java servlet. Once the page's implementation servlet has been created it will be compiled into a class file by the JSP engine and will be ready for use.

Each time a container receives a request, it first checks to see if the JSP file has changed since it was last translated. If it has, it's retranslated so that the response is always generated by the most up-to-date implementation of the JSP file.

Initialization

Once the translation phase has been completed, the JSP engine will need to load the generated class file and create an instance of the servlet in order to continue processing of the initial request. Therefore, the JSP engine works very closely with the servlet container and the JSP page implementation servlet and will typically load a single instance of the servlet into memory.

As you may or may not be aware, the Java Servlet Specification provides two separate threading models that can be used. The models determine whether single or multiple instances of a servlet can exist. As with servlets, the default threading model is the multithreaded one that requires no additional work for the developer. To select the single-threaded model for your JSP, there's an attribute of the `page` directive called `isThreadSafe` that must be set to `false` to serialize all requests to the implementation servlet behind the JSP:

```
<%@ page isThreadSafe="true" %>
```

Of course such directives must be placed in the JSP so that the JSP engine can make the necessary changes to the page implementation servlet during the translation phase.

Servicing

Once the JSP and servlet containers have completed all of their preliminary work, the initial request can be serviced. There are three important methods that are generated in the page implementation servlet by the JSP engine during the translation phase. These three methods bear a striking resemblance to the `init()`, `service()`, and `destroy()` methods from the `javax.servlet.Servlet` interface. They're the key methods involved in the life cycle of a servlet (as you'll see in Chapter 2).

Each method is explained in greater detail in the following list:

- `jspInit()`

  As the name suggests, this method is used for initializing the implementation servlet in an identical manner to the standard servlet `init()` method, which is used to initialize a servlet. The behavior of both methods can be regarded as identical and each is called exactly once. Although this method is automatically generated during the translation phase, it's possible to override this method in the JSP using a declaration. It can be used for initializing the JSP in order to open a database connection or initialize some session and context variables, for example.

  ```
  <%! Connection conn = null; %>
  <%!
    public void jspInit() {
      try {
        conn = getConnection(...);
      } catch (SQLException sqle){}
    }
  %>
  ```

- `_jspService()`

  This method provides all of the functionality for handling a request and returning a response to the client. All of the scriptlets and expressions end up inside this method, in the order in which they were declared inside the JSP. Notice that JSP declarations and directives aren't included inside this method because they apply to the entire page, not just to a single request, and therefore exist outside the method. `_jspService()` may not be overridden in the JSP.

Destruction

The final method worthy of explanation that is generated as a result of the translation phase is the `jspDestroy()` method. Like the `destroy()` method found in a normal servlet, this method is called by the servlet container when the page implementation servlet is about to be destroyed. This destruction could be for various reasons, such as the server being low on memory and wanting to free up some resources, but the most common reason would be when the servlet container is shutting down or being restarted.

Once this method has been called, the servlet can no longer serve any requests. Like the `destroy()` method, `jspDestroy()` is an excellent place to release or close resources such as database connections when the servlet is shutting down. To do this, simply provide an implementation of this method via a JSP method declaration. For example, to close the database connection you opened inside the `jspInit()` method, you would use the following:

```
<%!
  public void jspDestroy() {
    try {
      conn.close();
    } catch (SQLException sqle){}
    conn = null;
  }
%>
```

JavaServer Pages Best Practices

One of the design goals of this book apart from the obvious introduction to the concepts and mechanics of JSP technology was to teach the best practices learned from experience right from the start. Of all the best practices that have been established around JSP, one of the most important suggests that there should be as little Java code embedded inside a JSP as possible. Experience has shown us that there are three key factors that benefit from this practice:

- Reusability
- Readability
- Maintainability

Let's look at each of these in turn and see how their use can benefit your JSP applications.

Reusability

A common goal associated with using any programming language is that of reuse, whether it involves structuring code inside modules, classes, or some other language-specific construct. Reusing code leads to increased maintainability and productivity, and higher quality since changes to such common functionality only need to be made in a single place. Although the concept of building web-based applications is relatively new, this goal applies equally to building Java-based web applications with JSP.

Web-based applications are typically built up around the pages or screens from which the application is comprised. For example, in an online bookstore, you might build the welcome page first, followed by the page that shows a list of books and then a page that displays the information about a single book. With the ability to embed Java code inside JSP pages, there can be a tendency to simply reuse code on a source-code level by copying and pasting it between JSP pages. While this does achieve some reuse, it brings with it a dramatic decrease in the maintainability of such code as changes and bugs slowly creep in and around the system. Ideally you're looking for reusability at the class or component level.

Throughout this book you'll see many techniques for aiding reusability provided by the JSP specification such as JavaBeans components, custom tags, and tag libraries. A **tag library** (commonly known as a **taglib**) is simply a collection of one or more custom tags that are generally related in some way. For example, the JSP 2.0 specification for the first time includes a standard tag library known as the JSTL. The JSTL's core library contains tags that solve many of the common and recurring problems encountered when building JSP-based web applications. Once the tags are bundled up into a tag library, that tag library can be reused across the following:

- A single page
- The pages of a web application
- Different web applications

The ability to easily reuse custom tags across more than a single page illustrates the true potential of tag libraries to be used as reusable components when building web applications. This is something that you'll be seeing when you examine the best practices for designing and building custom tags in later chapters.

Readability

Another important best practice is that of readability. Embedding too much Java code in the page can easily lead to pages that are unreadable as content (typically HTML) is mixed with JSP tags and Java code wrapped up as scriptlets. In addition to the confusion caused by the various syntaxes that each of these "languages" uses, one clear problem with embedding Java code inside JSP pages is that it's hard to correctly indent your source code. Writing and indenting code is trivial when dealing with regular class files, but trying to correctly indent Java code that is mixed up with HTML and JSP is a different story.

Wrapping up reusable functionality as custom tags or JavaBean components removes this code from the page, therefore making it cleaner, shorter, and more readable. Also, choosing appropriate names for your custom tags can also make a page more readable by page designers–those people that are responsible for the look and feel of a page rather than the mechanics of how it works. This, as you'll be seeing when we talk about some of the best practices associated with custom tags, is very important and often overlooked.

Maintainability

Having a system that promotes reusability and readability is great, but what does that mean in the real world? The maintainability of an application is how well the system can be modified and fixed further on during its lifetime, which for a given application is typically hard to measure. However, in looking at any system, there are several signs that help us to identify whether or not that system will be easy or difficult to maintain. In reality, this is dictated by reuse and the need to ensure that the code is as readable as possible–the two goals that custom tags can help you achieve.

JavaServer Pages Application Architecture

All of these factors mentioned in this chapter are improved by a good design or architecture, therefore it's worth ensuring that sufficient time is taken early on in your project life cycle to select the architecture that best suits your environment and technologies. Although architecture and design can seem a little daunting at first (especially when you're new to the technology and all you really want to do is cut code), with a little effort you'll soon start to understand the benefits that are to be gained by using tried and tested patterns.

As you're no doubt aware, the J2EE presentation tier consists of several different components, which may all be used to create a presentation layer for a web application, such as servlets, JSP pages, tag libraries, and JavaBeans to name but a few. All of these components have their relative strengths and weaknesses, particularly when used in different combinations. Good design is therefore not only concerned with selecting the correct component for a task but is also concerned with ensuring that the component is used in the correct manner.

In recent times there have been two popular web application architectures that have been repeatedly used for web application design, and there are strengths and weaknesses to consider with both. Let's discuss the simpler of these two architectures first.

Model 1 Architecture

The JSP model 1 architecture really is very simple and advocates a web application, thereby providing a number of JSP pages with which a user may interact.

The simplicity of the model 1 architecture is that each JSP page is entrusted to deal with its request entirely by itself, thereby generating a response and sending it back to the client, and for this reason it's often known as page-centric. Usually such JSP pages will make use of some form of **model** to represent the business logic of the application. Usually JavaBean components are used to provide the model so that business logic can be neatly encapsulated for reusability and at the same time keep the amount of processing logic in the page to a minimum.

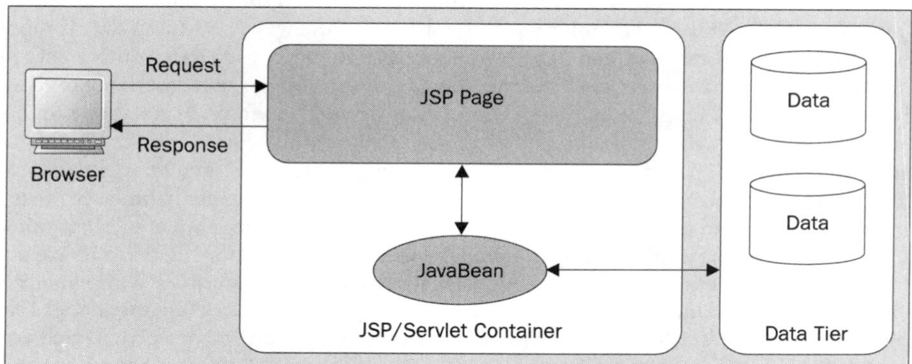

As you can see from this diagram, a JSP page is entrusted with handling a client request and building an appropriate response all by itself, thereby possibly making use of JavaBeans to encapsulate business logic.

Although each JSP page has the potential to contain a lot of processing logic, as long as the application is relatively small with few pages, the model 1 architecture is a good choice because it's very quick and simple to put together. However, such a page-centric architecture can begin to introduce problems when used with larger more complex applications. Some of the more common problems are outlined here.

Maintainability Problems

Because each JSP page is solely responsible for handling a client request, it will often have to directly interact with a business layer. This can result in the application structure being embodied within the pages themselves. This obviously makes the pages more complicated and more likely to contain lots of scriptlet code, which ultimately makes them far harder to maintain.

Reusability Problems

When most of the processing logic is embedded into the JSP pages, it becomes much more difficult to reuse common functionality because it's usually implemented using scriptlets. Often this results in a lot of cutting and pasting of code that isn't only bad from a reusability perspective but is also likely to introduce errors and decrease productivity.

Security Problems

As each JSP page is responsible for handling all of its processing, it's possible that any actions that require a user to be logged in or that access password-protected resources such as databases, could end up exposing sensitive information by embedding it in the page. It's therefore important to make sure that any such logic is encapsulated into JavaBean components or custom actions to prevent this possible security hole.

Of course it would make far more sense to provide such security controls via a single, centralized access point, and you shall see how the next architecture up for discussion does exactly this.

Model 2 Architecture (Model-View-Controller)

As you might expect, the model 2 architecture builds on the model 1 architecture you've just seen, and it overcomes many of the problems identified earlier.

The model 2 architecture is actually a server-side implementation of the popular **Model-View-Controller (MVC)** design pattern. This pattern enforces the separation of the way application data is modeled (hence, the **model**) from the way it's presented (the **view**) and it also requires a separate component to handle the processing in between (the **controller**). Separating these responsibilities into components gives the developer a good opportunity to select the right type of component for each based on its suitability to the task.

As mentioned earlier, JSP pages are best used for presenting content and aren't particularly good for providing complex business processing for reasons of readability and maintainability. Servlets on the other hand are particularly good components for providing business processing, but aren't best suited to generating content. Most applications implementing the model 2 architecture therefore chose to utilize a controller servlet to handle all the request processing and delegate requests to separate JSP components to provide the presentation, thereby making the best use of both technologies. Remember that the model 1 architecture you saw earlier forced the controller and the view to coexist inside the same component, which accounts for a lot of its shortcomings.

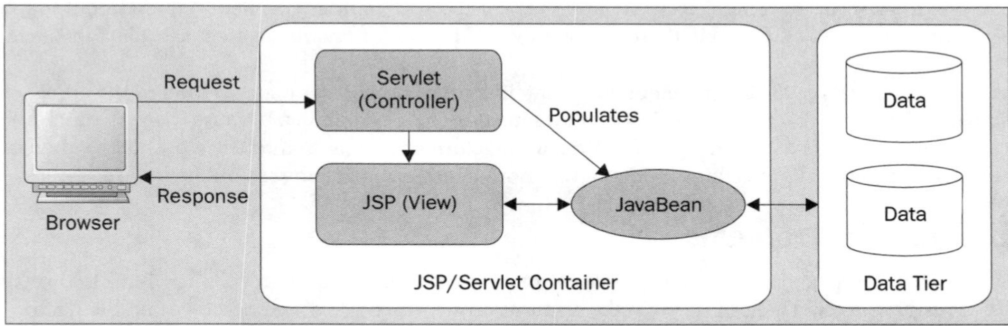

As you can see from this diagram, all requests made of the web application are handled by a single controller servlet. Depending on the type of request received, the controller servlet is responsible for populating the model component with data that it has obtained, usually by interacting with the business layer. The controller then forwards the request to the JSP view component, which constructs a suitable response to the request based around the data stored in the model component.

There are, as always, varying versions of this architecture such as providing multiple controllers to distribute the request-handling functionality across multiple servlets. Although not recommended, it's also possible to provide JSP-based controllers and servlet-based view components; the choice is yours! Remember that the best designs select a component based on its suitability for its job. JSP pages make poor controllers since they're designed to render content, whereas servlets are best suited to request processing and computations instead of generating content.

Whatever components you select, you cannot fail to appreciate how much cleaner this architecture is than the model 1 architecture as each component has a definite, well-defined role.

Let's revisit some of the problems that the model 1 architecture faced and see how this new design helps solve some of them.

Maintainability

Many of the maintainability problems associated with the model 1 architecture were a direct result of implementing a controller and view component as part of the same component: the JSP page. Because all of the business processing as well as the content generation was forced together, the result was messy pages that could be hard to maintain. By separating your application's logic from its presentation by using MVC components, it's far easier to develop cleaner code that focuses specifically on the job at hand, resulting ultimately in a more flexible and maintainable application.

Security

By providing an initial single point of access for potential requests, a servlet-based controller component is an excellent place to provide some form of authentication. If the user making the request can pass the authentication mechanism (perhaps a username or password test) then the controller can continue with the request as normal or alternatively forward it to an appropriate page (perhaps a login page!) where the error can be dealt with.

Due to the fact that the controller component is responsible for handling each and every request, security checks only have to exist in a single place, and of course any changes to the security mechanism only have to be made once. By implementing your security constraints in a single place it's far easier to take advantages of the declarative security mechanisms denoted in the J2EE. Recall that the model 1 architecture required each page to provide similar security checks by itself, which provides a significant security hole if the developer forgets to provide it!

Extensibility

One of the best points about the model 1 architecture is that all of the processing logic is so much more centralized. No longer does such code have to be placed in a scriptlet located deep within a JSP page where it's so much more difficult to access.

This centralization helps to provide a more component-based solution, utilizing JavaBean components and custom or standard actions where software components may be reused and extended, which greatly reduces the chance of making a change that causes a "ripple" effect to other dependent components.

JSP Fundamentals—Hands On

Before you take an in-depth look at the individual components that comprise a JSP page you should have a basic idea how JSP applications are structured and deployed inside a JSP container.

Basic Deployment

While all JSP and servlet containers have their own specific deployment processes, generally the basic techniques are still the same and involve copying your web application (JSP pages, servlets, and static HTML) in a predefined structure into a special deployment directory specified by the container.

The Java 2 Platform, Enterprise Edition (J2EE) specifies a special structure that all J2EE-compliant web applications must take so that J2EE containers know exactly where to find the resources that compose the web application. Most J2EE containers allow web applications to be deployed in one of the following two forms:

- **Expanded Directory Format**

  The web application in its predefined structure is simply copied into the J2EE container's deployment directory.

- **Web ARchive File (WAR)**

  The web application in its predefined structure is archived into a compressed WAR before being copied to the J2EE containers' deployment directory.

The J2EE web application structure defines the exact locations inside your web applications to locate deployment descriptors, HTML and JSP pages, and compiled Java classes as well as third-party Java ARchive (JAR) files that are required by your web applications. We won't go into great detail explaining the intricacies of the web application structure, because this will be covered in far greater detail in later chapters. For now we shall explain the structure of a minimal but fully functional web application that you can use to test the simple JSP examples you shall learn about throughout this chapter.

Because Tomcat 5 for the Apache Jakarta project is the reference implementation of the Servlet 2.4 and JSP 2.0 specifications and will therefore be featured heavily throughout this book, it makes sense to base the deployment introduction around the Tomcat 5 container; but feel free to use the container of your choice.

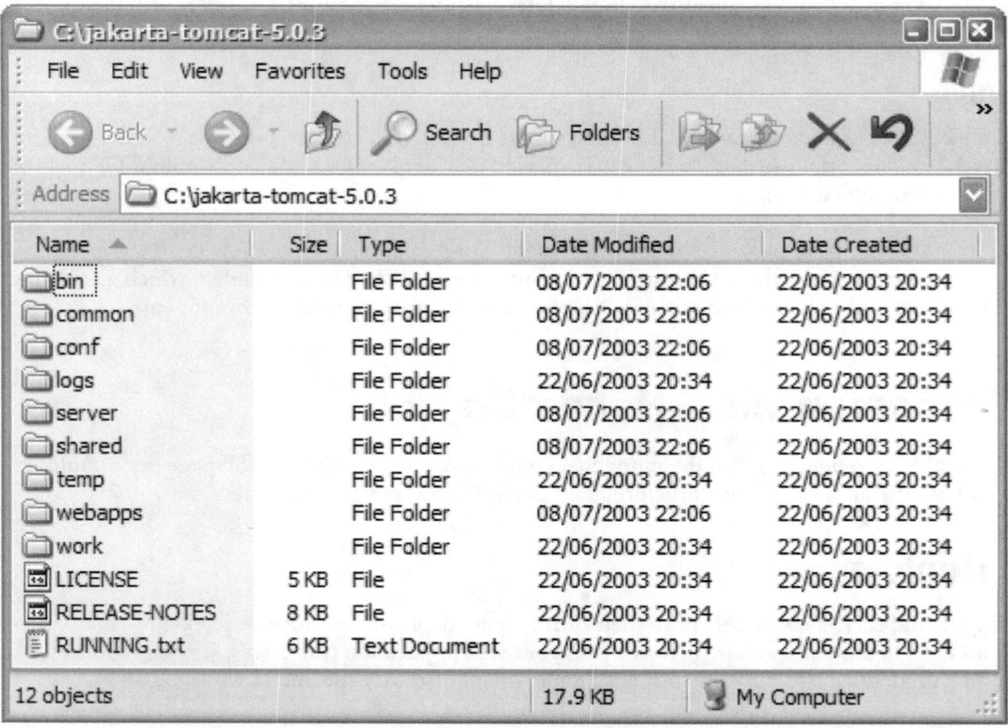

Notice that Tomcat has been installed beneath the `C:\jakarta-tomcat-5.0.3` directory which shall be referred to as the `%TOMCAT_HOME%` directory from now on.

As you can see, there are a fair number of subdirectories and each has a specific purpose. For example, the `bin` directory contains all of the necessary scripts required to start the container and the `conf` directory contains all of the XML-based configuration files used by Tomcat. Don't worry about understanding all the complex configuration files and directory structures because this exercise is designed to get a working web application for you to test the examples you'll see later in the chapter.

We mentioned earlier that most servlet containers have a special deployment directory whereby developers can place web applications as either WAR files or in exploded directory format. You may have guessed by now that in Tomcat it's the `%TOMCAT_HOME%\webapps` directory where you'll be creating the test application ready for deployment. Ignoring the subdirectories that already exist beneath the `webapps` directory (yes, they too are web applications in case you were wondering!), first create a directory to house the web application called `test` and then another directory inside this one called `WEB-INF`. Now you have to following structure:

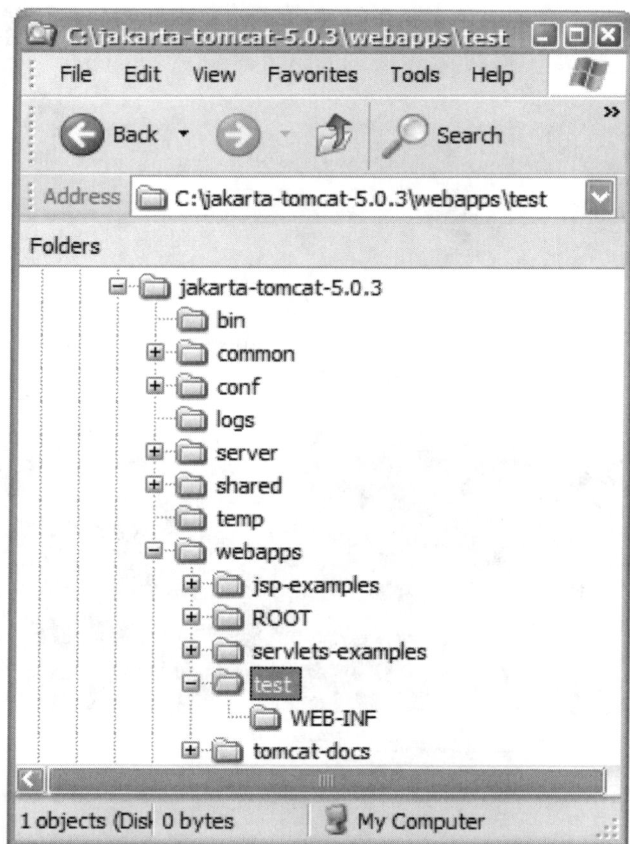

This structure is the standard web application structure that exists inside all WAR files and is known as the exploded directory format. As you may be aware, all web applications must have a deployment descriptor in order to work, and your's is no different. Copy and paste this very minimal deployment descriptor into a file called `web.xml` and save it beneath the WEB-INF directory you just created:

```
<?xml version="1.0"?>

<web-app xmlns="http://java.sun.com/xml/ns/j2ee"
         xmlns:xsi="http://www.w3.org/2001/XMLSchema-instance"
         xsi:schemaLocation="http://java.sun.com/xml/ns/j2ee
         http://java.sun.com/xml/ns/j2ee/web-app_2_4.xsd"
         version="2.4">

</web-app>
```

A point worth remembering is that the name of the `test` directory that you're using to house the web application is known as the **context** of the web application; you'll need to be aware of this context to request the resources of our test web application. You'll see this in action shortly.

Now that you've set up the required web application structure let's create a dynamic web component (that's a JSP to you and me!) that will return the current time of day along with a greeting. Copy the following JSP into a file called `%TOMCAT_HOME%\webapps\test\date.jsp`:

```
<html>
  <body>
    <h2>Greetings!</h2>
    <P>The current time is <%=new java.util.Date()%> precisely
  </body>
</html>
```

Again, don't worry about understanding the syntax of this JSP, you'll learn all about JSP syntax later. Start Tomcat by running the `%TOMCAT_HOME%\bin\startup.bat` (or `startup.sh`) script. When Tomcat is running you should see a prompt with messages like this:

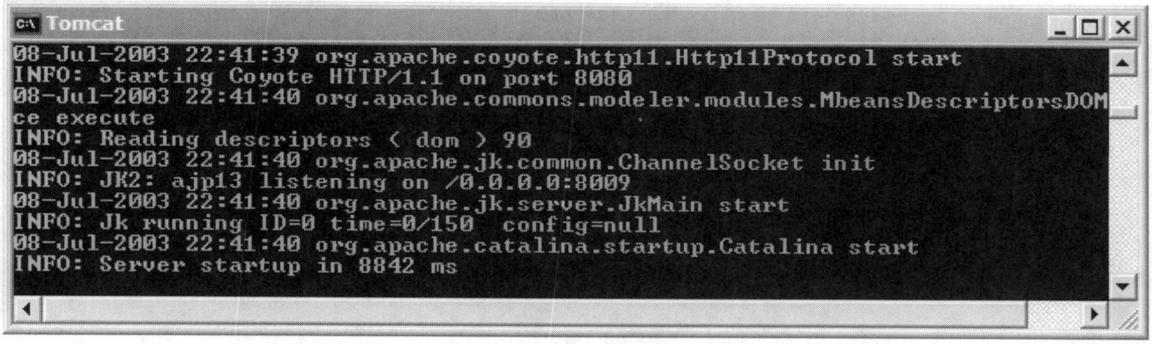

```
Tomcat
08-Jul-2003 22:41:39 org.apache.coyote.http11.Http11Protocol start
INFO: Starting Coyote HTTP/1.1 on port 8080
08-Jul-2003 22:41:40 org.apache.commons.modeler.modules.MbeansDescriptorsDOM
ce execute
INFO: Reading descriptors ( dom ) 90
08-Jul-2003 22:41:40 org.apache.jk.common.ChannelSocket init
INFO: JK2: ajp13 listening on /0.0.0.0:8009
08-Jul-2003 22:41:40 org.apache.jk.server.JkMain start
INFO: Jk running ID=0 time=0/150  config=null
08-Jul-2003 22:41:40 org.apache.catalina.startup.Catalina start
INFO: Server startup in 8842 ms
```

To test that Tomcat is running successfully, let's load the Tomcat welcome page by opening a web browser and typing the following link:

http://localhost:8080

Note that this assumes you installed Tomcat on its default port 8080, so you should change it as needed.

Now you should see the following Tomcat welcome page, which indicates that all is well:

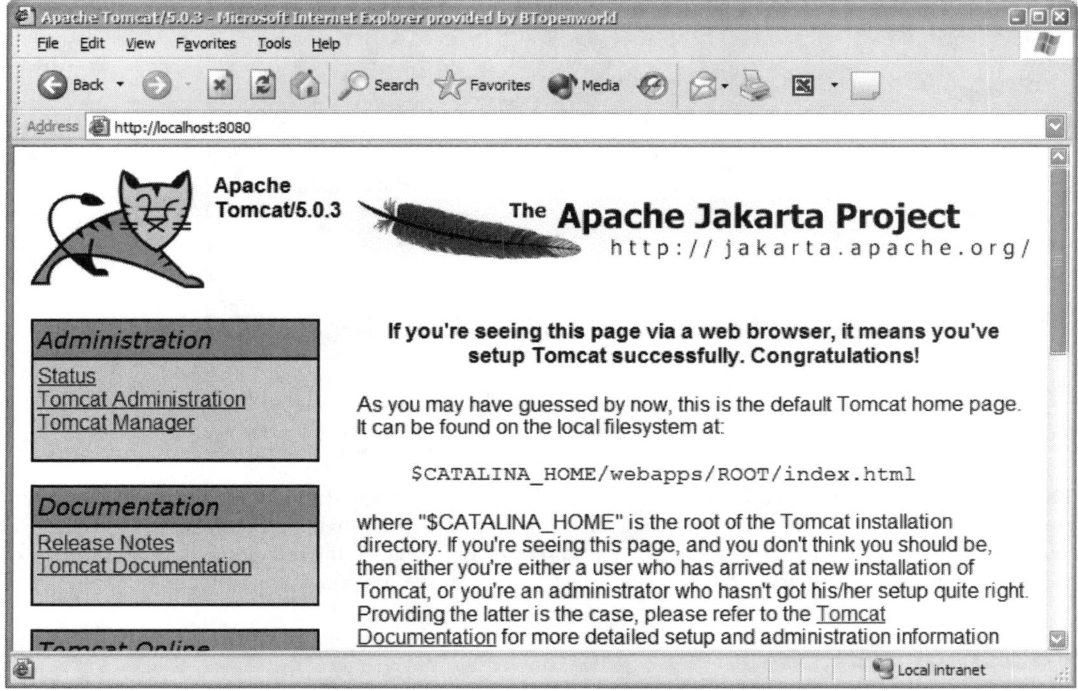

If for some reason you don't see this welcome screen, make sure that you have Tomcat running and are accessing the correct port. Consult the Tomcat documentation if problems persist.

Now you're at last ready to access the test web application. Do this by typing the following URL:

http://localhost:8080/test/date.jsp

Notice how you use the context of the web application (test) to inform the servlet container that it's your application whose `date.jsp` file you wish to access. You should now see some similar (not the same though–remember it's dynamic!) output to the following screen shot:

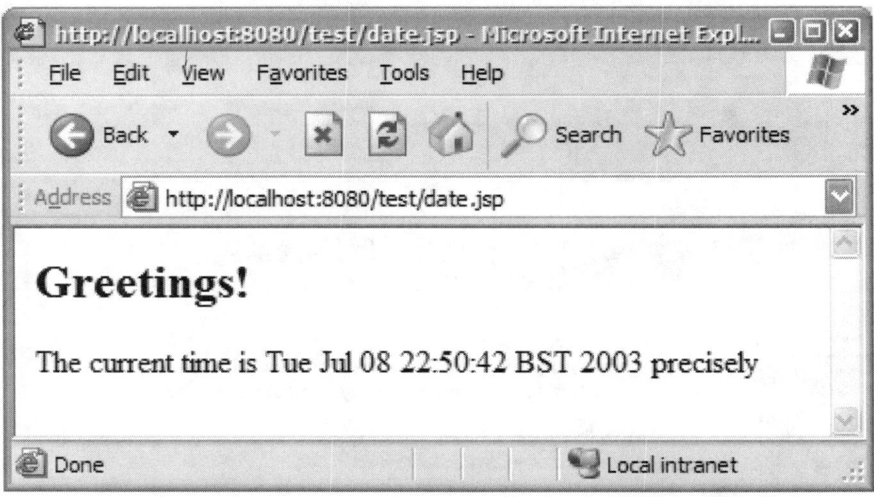

That's it, congratulations! Creating and deploying a JSP web-based application wasn't so hard after all, was it? For the remainder of this chapter you'll see lots of JSP code examples that you're encouraged to copy and paste into JSP files beneath the `webapps\test` directory (and change the link accordingly) to see the code in action. Note that you may need to stop and start Tomcat to see some changes in action.

JavaServer Pages

As mentioned earlier, the sole purpose of JSP technology is to produce dynamic, web-based content. This capability is implemented by embedding programmatic logic among template data (usually markup such as HTML, XML, and so on) which together produces the dynamic content on a request-by-request basis. This programmatic logic may be classified into the following JSP elements:

- Scripting elements
- Directives
- Action elements

In a moment you'll look at each of the elements in turn so you can see how collectively they combine to produce the dynamic content required by today's web applications, but first let's look at the template text.

Template Text

Any non-JSP code located inside a JSP page is known as **template text**. Template text can take any form as long as it's text based. The most common form of template text is markup such as HTML or XML. For example, if your web design team was to develop an HTML page that you were required to convert into a JSP page in order to add some form of dynamic processing, then all of the HTML markup would be referred to as template text:

```
<%@ taglib uri="http://java.sun.com/jstl/core" prefix="c" %>
<%@ page import="com.apress.projsp20.jstl.CalendarBean"%>

<html>
  <head>
  <title>My HTML Example</title>
  </head>
  <body>
    <jsp:useBean id="cal" class="com.apress.projsp20.jstl.CalendarBean"/>
    <c:set var="hour" value="${cal.hour}" scope="request" />

    <c:choose>
      <c:when test="${hour > 0 && hour <=11}">
        Good Morning!
      </c:when>
      <c:when test="${hour >= 12 && hour <=17}">
        Good Afternoon!
      </c:when>
      <c:otherwise>
        Good Evening!
      </c:otherwise>
    </c:choose
  </body>
</html>
```

This is a JSP page that dynamically produces a greeting depending on the time of the day. For now, don't worry about understanding the syntax of the various JSP elements but notice that the highlighted static HTML is referred to as template text. The reason for this term is simply that a JSP can be thought of as a "template" for producing some output. It's the JSP logic embedded inside this template text that is responsible for producing the output based upon this template.

During the translation phase, all of the template text found in the original JSP page is converted into Java statements inside the page implementation servlet that simply output the template text in the correct order as part of the response.

Scripting Elements

Scripting elements are used within a JSP page to manipulate objects and perform computations that enable the generation of dynamic content. Scripting elements can be classified into the following individual elements:

- Comments
- Declarations

- Scriptlets
- Expressions
- Expression language expressions

We shall discuss each scripting element in turn.

Comment

JSP comments are a good way of explaining any complicated logic that may have arisen for whatever reason–perhaps it could be used to flag a piece of scripting code to be simplified at a later date with a custom tag. Alternatively, comments provide non-Java-speaking HTML users or web designers some clues as to what a piece of "magic" JSP code does.

JSP comments may be declared inside a JSP as follows:

```
<%-- This is a JSP comment --%>
```

Comments in JSPs get stripped out during the translation phase and aren't sent to the client as part of the response. HTML comments on the other hand, such as the one shown here, do get sent to a client's browser and any client can view the comments by using the View Source options that most modern browsers provide:

```
<!-- This is an HTML comment -->
```

The fact that JSP comments are stripped and don't form part of a client response is a good thing as it not only keeps the size of the response as small as possible thereby aiding performance, but also removes clues to a potential hacker with regards to the technology used to implement a web-based application the hacker is targeting.

There is of course no reason why JSP and HTML comments cannot work together:

```
<!— HTML comment generated <%= new java.util.Date() %> -->
```

You'll learn the meaning of this JSP expression shortly, but suffice to say the previous comment produces the following in the content returned to a client:

```
<!— HTML comment generated Fri Jan 03 12:37:09 GMT 2003 -->
```

Declarations

JSP pages allow both methods and variables to be declared in a similar manner to the way in which they're declared inside normal Java classes. As with normal methods and variables, once declared inside a JSP page they're available to subsequent scriptlets and expressions and so on for reference.

During the translation phase, any JSP declarations (methods or variables) found inside the page are actually created outside the normal `_jspService()` method in the JSP page implementation servlet and therefore are available to any scripting elements throughout the page.

JSP declarations must be placed between <%! and %> declaration delimiters. The general form of a declaration is shown here:

```
<%! declaration; [declaration;]+...%>
```

For example:

```
<%! Date now = new Date(); %>
```

```
<%!
  private int calculate(int a, int b) {
    ...
  }
%>
```

The previous examples demonstrate two simple JSP declarations. The first generates a `java.util.Date` instance that is available to the rest of the JSP (and therefore to the servlet), whereas the second actually declares a stand-alone method that again is available to the rest of the page.

> **An important note to consider when declaring a page-level variable via a JSP declaration is to ensure that its access is thread-safe. Multiple threads can execute the same servlet (JSP implementation class) simultaneously, and any page-level variables are accessible by each thread.**

Scriptlets

Quite simply, scriptlets are small blocks of source code contained within the <% and %> delimiters that can be used to provide programming-style language functionality around a page's content, thus making their output dynamic.

For example:

```
<%
  User user = (User)request.getAttribute("User");
  if (user != null) {
%>
  Welcome, you have successfully logged in!
<%
  }
%>
```

You can see from the previous example how a very simple piece of dynamic content can be created with a scriptlet. If an object attribute called `user` exists in the request then a welcome message is generated, otherwise one isn't! Admittedly, this piece of dynamic content isn't the most complex but hopefully you can see how scriptlets add logic between the markup of your JSP page to control the output.

The supported scripting languages available for use inside scriptlets are defined by the `page` directive's `language` attribute, which as of JSP 2.0 only supports the use of `Java` as a scripting language. Unlike declarations, all scriptlet code will be inserted into the `_jspService()` method of the generated servlet, which is used to handle the request and generate the response. When multiple scriptlets are included in any page they're included into the compiled servlet in the order in which they appear in the JSP. Unlike JSP declarations, any variables declared in a scriptlet aren't available to the rest of the JSP because they're treated as local variables inside the `_jspService()` method.

When JSP 1.0 first arrived, scriptlets were quickly adopted as the most popular way of adding dynamic features to JSP. Unfortunately, scriptlets became too popular and soon JSP page authors were embedding too much business logic among their markup. This caused several problems.

In multideveloper projects, it's quite common for a web designer with no Java or JSP skills to produce an HTML UI for an application that is then passed to Java developers to convert their work into JSP by adding dynamic content and hooking together business logic along the way. This caused numerous problems in the JSP 1.0 days, whereby delays and frustrations were created due to the dependencies formed between the UI and Java developer. Also problems arose due to the fact that the UI designer would struggle to maintain their pages, as they would need to understand the scriptlet code surrounding their markup properly in order to change it. On top of these difficulties, adding too many scriptlets to a JSP also makes it incredibly difficult to read and hence maintain. Anyone who has had to spend hours debugging a JSP only to find a closing brace is missing will testify how much more difficult it is to fix a page with too many scriptlets on it.

Thankfully, the early experiences of UI and JSP developers haven't been wasted and other methods are now considered better alternatives. For example, using standard JSP actions to manipulate JavaBeans, which contain business logic and encapsulating logic inside custom actions (also known as custom tags), are two alternatives that solve many of the problems mentioned earlier. Most noticeably, both solutions involve the use of XML-style tags that can be used in harmony with the tools of a UI designer.

JSP 2.0 introduces another two candidates that further facilitate scriptless JSP code. The first of these new features comes in the form of the JSTL, which provides a number of standard actions for many of the simple tasks required of a modern dynamic web application. Secondly, for the first time an **expression language (EL)** is available, which can be used to help reduce or even eradicate scriptlets.

As we mentioned at the start of this chapter, further information on JavaBeans, JSTL, and custom actions can be found later in this book where they're discussed in great detail. For now you just need to understand what scriptlets can do along with their limitations.

Expressions

Expressions are similar to scriptlets, but as their name suggests they evaluate a regular Java expression and return a result. This result must be a `String` or be convertible to a `String`, otherwise an exception will be raised during the translation phase or at runtime. Expressions are evaluated by the JSP implementation servlet and are returned to the client as part of the response.

As with the other tag types, expressions must be placed between `<%=` and `%>` expression delimiters so that the JSP engine is aware of the developer's intent to return the value of the expression in the response. The general syntax is as follows:

```
<%= expression %>
```

Two very simple JSP expressions can be seen here. They could be part of any regular JSP that generates nonstatic HTML.

```
<h1>Welcome Back : <%= user.getName() %></h1>

<b>Today's date is <%= new java.util.Date()%></b>
```

Apart from producing dynamic content as part of the client response, JSP expressions can be used to pass request-time parameters and values to other JSP actions that may appear on the page. You'll look at an explanation of this later.

> **Unlike declarations and scriptlets, JSP expressions don't require a closing semicolon (in fact they won't compile with one) as they evaluate the result of a single expression.**

Expression Language Expressions

JSP 2.0, for the first time, introduces an EL based on both ECMAScript and XPath, which has been designed to be simple to use and more user-friendly than Java.

The new EL has built-in support for JavaBean access and manipulation, collections of objects, and automatic type conversion to name but a small part of its extensive feature list. If you're familiar with JavaScript you should have no problem understanding the syntax of the EL, which insists that all expressions must be enclosed within `${` and `}` delimiters.

EL expressions can be used in any attribute that accepts a runtime expression, usually a standard or custom action, or even in plain template text. The addition of the EL further facilitates the writing of scriptless JSP pages; that is, pages that don't contain any Java scriptlets, expressions, or declaration elements.

Although it's the subject of the next chapter, here are a couple of examples to give you a flavor of the new EL:

```
${anObject.aProperty}
```

```
<c:if test="${user.salary > 10000}" >
  ...
</c:if>
```

You can see from the first example mentioned here just how simple it is to access the property of any JavaBean object, with no Java knowledge required at all! The second example demonstrates one of the core actions from the JSTL that is used to provide conditional processing of JSP code. Here an EL expression is used to provide the Boolean test for the action.

JSP Implicit Objects

All JSP scripting elements have access to a number of useful objects provided by the JSP container that are known as implicit objects. Each of these implicit objects are classes or interfaces as defined by either the Servlet or JSP specifications and are described in greater detail in this section.

request

The most notable of the implicit objects is the `request` object, which is an instance of the `javax.servlet.http.ServletRequest` interface. The `request` object provides access to all of the available information about the user request such as request parameters and headers and may be used in exactly the same way as the `HttpServletRequest` parameter is used in the `service()` method of a normal servlet.

Let's consider an example. Imagine a simple JSP that expects a single-request parameter called `userName` and constructs a personalized response to the user.

```
<html>
<head><title>A Simple Example</title></head>
<body>
<h2>Hello<%=request.getParameter("userName")%>, Have a nice day!</h2>
</body>
</html>
```

This simple JSP extracts a request parameter called `userName` from the implicit request object and constructs an appropriate greeting. To send a request parameter to a JSP like the one outlined previously either use an HTML form or add the parameter to the query string of your request as follows:

http://localhost:8080/test/Request.jsp?userName=Dan

response

In a similar manner to the `request` object seen earlier, there's also an accompanying implicit `response` object that represents the current response to be returned to the user. The `response` object is an instance of the `javax.servlet.http.HttpServletResponse` interface. Again, this object can be used in exactly the same way as the `HttpServletResponse` parameter received by the `service()` method of a normal servlet.

out

The implicit `out` object represents an instance of the `javax.servlet.jsp.JspWriter` class that can be used to write character data to the response stream in a similar manner to that seen by the `java.io.PrintWriter` class. While the methods provided by the `JspWriter` such as `print()` and `println()` can be used to write text to the body of the response, it's normally sufficient to rely on plain template text and JSP action elements instead of explicitly writing to the out implicit object.

session

The implicit `session` object provides a reference to an implementation of the client's individual `javax.servlet.http.HttpSession` object, which can be used to store and retrieve session data. While the `HttpSession` can be used explicitly, it should be noted that there are several action elements available that interact with the session that can be used instead.

config

The config object simply provides the JSP developer with access to the ServletConfig object that is used by the web container to configure the JSP and its implementation servlet. The ServletConfig interface is most commonly used to provide access to any initialization parameters that have been configured for either the JSP or its implementation servlet via the deployment descriptor of the web application.

application

The implicit application object provides a reference to the javax.servlet.ServletContext interface of the web application. The ServletContext is used by a web container to represent an entire web application and therefore any data that is stored inside it will be available to all resources included in the application.

Like the session object, several action elements exist that interact with the ServletContext so it may not be necessary to interact directly with the object itself.

page

The implicit page object references an instance of the JSP's page implementation class and is declared of type Object. The page object is rarely used in scripting elements and simply serves as a link between the JSP and its implementing servlet.

pageContext

The pageContext object is slightly different in its functionality from the rest of the available implicit objects. A pageContext instance provides the JSP developer with access to all of the available JSP scopes and to several useful page attributes such as the current request and response, the ServletContext, HttpSession, and ServletConfig to name but a few.

Perhaps the most useful piece of functionality provided by the pageContext variable is its ability to search for named attributes across multiple scopes. Therefore, if you were unsure as to which scope a particular attribute is located, the pageContext can be used to traverse all available scopes until the attribute is found.

The pageContext variable provides this cross-scope functionality due to the fact that it exists at a level of abstraction higher that the lower level JSP implementation classes. The JSP container will create a new unique instance of this class for each request received and assign it to the pageContext variable.

exception

The implicit exception object is only available to those JSP pages that declare themselves as error pages using the following page directive (You'll learn more about directives shortly!).

```
<%@ page isErrorPage="true" %>
```

The application object itself is an instance of a java.lang.Throwable and will represent a runtime error that occurred during the request process.

Any scripting elements inside a JSP page that reference the implicit exception object when that page hasn't been declared as an error page will cause a fatal error at translation time.

JSP Directives

Directives are used for passing important information to the JSP engine. Although directives themselves generate no output, they provide a powerful mechanism for providing page-level information that is typically used during both the compilation and translation phases.

JSP page authors have the following three types of directives at their disposal:

- page directives
- include directives
- taglib directives

Each of these types of directives provides different information to the JSP engine or signifies some required behavior of the generated servlet. The information that is contained inside a directive is totally independent of any user request and is only of use to the JSP engine. All three directive types must be declared between <%@ and %> directive delimiters and take the following form:

```
<%@ directive {attribute="value"}* %>
```

Generally speaking, directives should be placed at the top of the JSP page; however, the include directive, which you'll see later, is an exception to this rule. Let's examine each directive type in turn.

The page Directive

The first directive type is the page directive, which is used to define any page-dependent properties that a JSP page may have, such as library dependencies, buffering, or error-handling requirements to name but a few.

The syntax of a page directive is as follows:

```
<%@ page page_directive_attr_list %>
```

where the page_directive_attr_list is used to define the name of any page attribute along with its value in the form attributeName=attributeValue.

Each page directive applies to the entire compilation unit (that is, the complete JSP plus any included JSP pages) and although multiple page directives may occur it should be noted that each attribute can only occur once in the page with the exception of the import attribute.

A table of the permitted attributes and their possible values as defined by the page_directive_attr_list is given here:

Attribute	Permitted Value	Description
language	"scriptingLanguage"	The scripting language used in scriptlets, expressions, and declarations in the JSP. Currently, JSP 2.0 only supports a value of "Java" and any other value would cause a fatal translation error.
extends	"className"	The name of a fully qualified Java class that will form the superclass of the JSP page's implementation servlet. This attribute should not be used lightly as its use prohibits the JSP container from using its own specially optimized classes.
import	"importList"	Indicates the classes available for use within the scripting environment. Any import values must be fully qualified Java class names and result in a standard Java `import` statement in the page implementation servlet. Note that import attributes may be a fully qualified package name followed by a ".*" or a list of comma-separated classes. The default import list is as follows: `javax.servlet.jsp.*` and `javax.servlet.http.*`
session	"true|false"	Indicates that the page requires an `HttpSession`. If a value of "`true`" is provided, an implicit scripting variable named `session`, which references the current `HttpSession` object, is available to the page. If a value of "`false`" is used, then any references to the implicit session variable will cause a fatal translation error. The default value is "`true`".

Table continued on following page

Attribute	Permitted Value	Description
`buffer`	`"none|sizekb"`	Specifies the buffering model for the initial `JspWriter` used to handle the response generated by the page. A value of "`none`" indicates no buffering is required and all output is written immediately. The size of the buffer can only be declared in kilobytes and the `kb` prefix is required. If a buffer size is specified, then all output is buffered with a buffer not smaller than the one specified. The default value isn't less than 8 KB.
`autoFlush`	`"true|false"`	Indicates whether the output buffer should be flushed automatically when full (specified by a value of "`true`") or whether an exception should be raised indicating buffer overflow (specified by a value of "`false`"). Note that it's illegal to set `autoFlush=true` when `buffer=none`. The result is a translation-time error. The default value is "`true`".
`isThreadSafe`	`"true|false"`	Indicates the threading model to be used by the JSP and servlet container when dispatching requests to the page implementation servlet. A value of "`true`" ensures that the JSP container may choose to dispatch multiple requests to the page simultaneously. A value of "`false`" indicates that the JSP container must serialize multiple requests to the page one at a time. Note that if a value of "`true`" is passed then the JSP page author must ensure that access to any shared variables is synchronized to protect thread safety. The default value is "`true`".
`info`	`"info_text"`	Can be used to provide any arbitrary string, which is returned via a call to the page implementation servlet's `getServletInfo()` method.
`isErrorPage`	`"true|false"`	Indicates whether or not the current JSP is intended to be an error page, which may be referenced by the `errorPage` attribute of another JSP. If a value of "`true`" is specified an implicit scripting variable exception is made available that references the offending `Throwable` from another JSP page. The default value is "`false`".

Attribute	Permitted Value	Description
errorPage	"error_url"	Defines the URL to a resource that any throwable objects not caught by the page implementation are forwarded for error processing. When an error page for a web application is defined in its deployment descriptor (web.xml), the JSP's error page is tried ahead of the one defined by the deployment descriptor.
contentType	"ctInfo"	Defines the character encoding for the JSP page and its response as well as the MIME type of the response. The default value for the type is text/html and for the charset it's ISO-8859-1.
pageEncoding	"peInfo"	Defines the character encoding for the JSP page. The default value is ISO-8859-1.
isELIgnored	"true|false"	Defines whether the EL expressions are evaluated for the JSP page. If enabled any EL expressions are simply ignored by the JSP container. The default value is "false".

The following are some examples of the page directive in action:

```
<%@ page language="Java" %>
```

Here the scripting language to be used on the page is set to Java (the only permitted value):

```
<%@ page import="java.util.Date, java.text.*" %>
```

The java.util.Date class, along with all the classes from the java.text package, are available for use on the page.

```
<%@ page isThreadSafe="false" buffer="20kb" %>
```

Notice that it's possible to provide multiple attributes in the one `page` directive; here the JSP container is advised that multiple requests may not access the page simultaneously and also the page buffer should not be less than 20 KB.

The include Directive

You've just seen how the `page` directive can be used to pass information to the JSP engine during the translation phase to control how the page implementation class is generated. The `include` directive also executes at translation time and enables the contents of a separate resource to be statically merged inside the original page, thus radically affecting the generated servlet.

After translation, the generated JSP servlet contains the content and logic as defined by the two separate resources, in the order that they were specified in the original JSP. This makes it seem as though they were from a single JSP file.

The following is the syntax for the `include` directive:

```
<%@ include file="relativeURL" %>
```

As you can see the directive accepts a single `file` attribute that is used to indicate the resource whose content is to be included in the declaring JSP. The `file` attribute is interpreted as a relative URL; if it starts with a slash it's interpreted as relative to the context of the web application (namely a context-relative path), otherwise it's interpreted as relative to the path of the JSP that contains the `include` directive (namely a page relative path). The included file may contain either static content, such as HTML or XML, or another JSP page.

For example:

```
<%@ include file="/copyright.html"%>
```

As you can see from the previous example, a static HTML file located at the root of the web application context will be statically included into the JSP page that declares the directive. The included file in this case contains important legal copyright information that must be included on all pages of a web application. The `include` directive is an excellent mechanism for reusing a predefined component, such as the `copyright.html` file, to save the duplication of code on each page. This makes the JSP pages smaller, easier to read, and more maintainable, as changes only need to be applied in one place but are reflected throughout the application.

> **Remember when using the `include` directive, the combined contents of the original JSP and all of its included resources are translated into the same implementation servlet. Therefore the original JSP page will share its scripting variables and declarations with those inside the included resources and any duplication of variables or methods names will result in a fatal JSP translation error, because the merged file won't be syntactically correct.**

The include directive is slightly different from the other JSP directives, which are typically declared only once at the top of each JSP page. A JSP page may contain any number of include directives at any position in the page to indicate the exact positions where the content from the included resource should be inserted. Therefore the include directive is well suited to the implement simple template mechanisms that are so commonly used in today's modern web applications. This enables all the commonly used resources of a web application (such as a header, footer, or navigation page) to be encapsulated as separate components (for example, JSP pages or static HTML pages) included throughout the web application.

Let's consider a real-world example of such a templating mechanism that utilizes the include directive to provide a consistent page layout for a web application.

Consider the following two JSP pages:

Header.jsp

```
<html>
  <head><title>A Very Simple Example</title></head>
  <body style="font-family:verdana,arial;font-size:10pt;">
    <table width="100%" height="100%">
      <tr bgcolor="#99CCCC">
        <td align="right" height="15%">Welcome to this example…</td>
      </tr>
      <tr>
        <td height="75%">
```

Footer.jsp

```
        </td>
      </tr>
      <tr bgcolor=" #99CC99">
        <td align="center" height="10%">Copyright ACompany.com 2003</td>
      </tr>
    </table>
  </body>
</html>
```

As you can see, Header.jsp declares the starting elements of an HTML table that is to be 100 percent of the size of the page and has two rows, whereas Footer.jsp simply declares the closing elements for the table. Used separately, either JSP will result in partial HTML code that will look very strange to a user but when they're combined using the include directive it's easy to create consistent pages as part of a web application.

Let's see just how simple this basic template mechanism is to use:

Content.jsp

```
<%@ include file='./Header.jsp'%>
<p align="center">The Content Goes Here...!!!</p>
<%@ include file='./Footer.jsp'%>
```

As you can see, Content.jsp looks like a simple page with only three lines of code; the two include directives and the actual body of the page. Notice how the body of the page is actually between the two directives. This ensures that all of this page's body content is included inside the table declared in Header.jsp.

To run this example simply copy the three files Content.jsp, Header.jsp, and Footer.jsp beneath the test web application directory you created earlier and go to the following URL:

http://localhost:8080/test/Content.jsp

You should see something like the following screen shot:

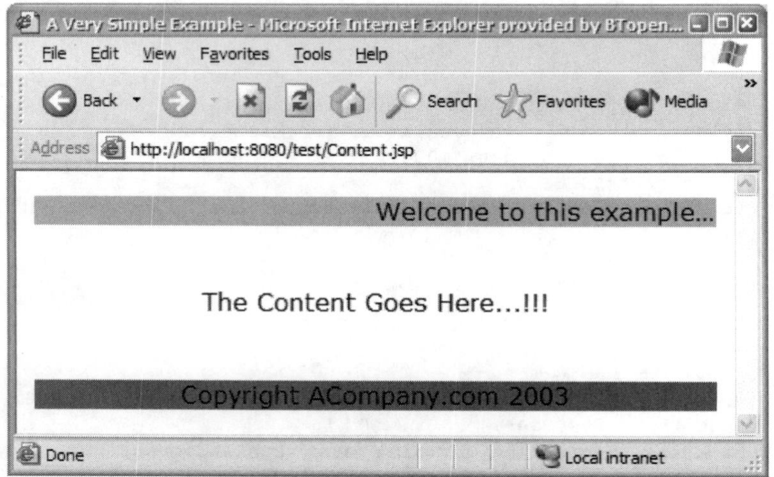

To demonstrate just how effective this basic template mechanism is, let's construct another page (MoreContent.jsp) and see how easy it is to maintain the same look and feel:

```
<%@ include file="./Header.jsp"%>
<p align="center">Here is some more content...!!!</p>
<%@ include file="./Footer.jsp"%>
```

To open it, do exactly the same as you did for the Content.jsp page, only this time point to the URL http://localhost:8080/test/MoreContent.jsp:

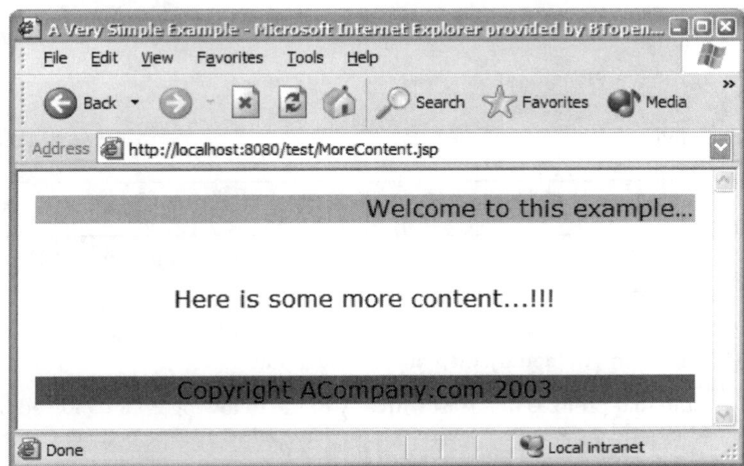

This example should help demonstrate how useful the `include` directive is for constructing component-based web applications that share a consistent look and feel throughout, are extremely maintainable, and do not suffer from related problems caused by code duplication.

The taglib Directives

A tag library quite simply contains a collection of actions (also known as tags) that can be grouped together to perform some form of logic. These actions are XML-based so their use is considerably easier for a non-Java-speaking UI designer. Of course another major benefit is that they can encapsulate large amounts of programmatic logic into a single line of code, which is a much better solution in terms of readability and maintainability and of course reuse, when compared to the ugly scriptlet-based approach you saw earlier.

Tag libraries come in two different flavors these days. The first is custom tag libraries, which have generally been put together by the development team or acquired from another team or project or even the Internet, and as of JSP 2.0, the JSTL, which contains a set of useful actions that are applicable to almost every web application in use today in some form.

To make use of a custom tag library, the web container needs to be made aware of specific information about the library itself. A special file called a **tag library descriptor** (TLD) is used for this purpose. The XML-based TLD file is used to provide general descriptive information about the custom tag library, such as a description of its usage and the JSP version that the tag supports. More importantly, the TLD file contains important information about each of the custom actions or tags that are included inside the tag library, such as which attributes are permitted by which tags, whether the tags accept body content, and so on.

Once the JSP container is made aware of the TLD for a particular custom tag library, the JSP developer can make use of any of the tags declared inside the library. Like custom Java classes (in fact, any class that doesn't reside in the core `java.lang` package), tag libraries must be imported into the page before they can be used. You've seen that Java classes are imported into a JSP page by using a JSP `page` directive, and in a similar fashion, tag libraries are imported using the `taglib` directive.

The syntax for the taglib directive is as follows:

```
<%@ taglib uri="/tagLibraryURI" prefix="tagPrefix" %>
```

The attributes are as follows:

Attribute	Description
uri	Can either be an absolute or a relative URI that identifies the TLD, and therefore, the tag library that is associated with the prefix.
prefix	Indicates a uniquely identifiable string, which is used in the <prefix:tagname> declaration to identify the particular tag in use. Note that prefixes that start with any of the following aren't allowed because they're reserved by Sun: jsp, jspx, java, javax, servlet, sun, and sunw. All prefixes must follow the naming convention as specified in the XML namespaces specification. The current version of the JSP specification doesn't support empty prefixes.

There are, in fact, three different ways that the taglib directive can be used to make a tag library available to JSP page authors, and you'll see each in turn.

Option 1—Absolute URI

The first option for using the taglib directive involves passing an absolute value in the uri attribute that represents the location of the TLD file:

```
<%@ taglib uri="/WEB-INF/tlds/myTaglib.tld" prefix="myPrefix" %>
```

As you can see, the location of the TLD file is explicitly given by the uri attribute. In this example, the WEB-INF/tlds/myTaglib.tld file describes the tag library, and any references to any of the tags inside this library must be prefixed with myPrefix to distinguish the tag from any other tag library that may be available.

For example, if a tag named displayImage was included in the library, then its use may look something like this:

```
<myPrefix:displayImage file="logo.jpg" />
```

The taglib directive is typically used in this form during development, when the locations of resources, such as images and TLDs, haven't been finalized. Perhaps the application hasn't been packaged into a WAR file and still exists in exploded directory format, therefore an absolute value for the TLD file is usually the most convenient.

Leaving your taglib directives in this form after the development process has finished is perhaps not the most flexible option available. Every tag library used in the application would, therefore, have its TLD location hard-coded into the JSP source. If the location of a TLD had to change for some reason, then each JSP page would have to be altered, which could potentially be a long-winded, error-prone exercise.

Option 2—Relative URI

The second form of the taglib directive involves using a relative URI to indicate the location of the TLD file. If a relative URI is to be used, then a relative mapping must be configured in the web application's deployment descriptor using the <taglib> element. Using the earlier example, you can see this in the following example:

```
<webapp>
  <taglib-uri>/myTaglib</taglib-uri>
  <taglib-location>/WEB-INF/tlds/myTaglib.tld</taglib-location>
</webapp>
```

If the deployment descriptor for a web application declared the relative URI as shown previously, then any JSP pages contained in the web application could import the tag library ready for use using the /myTaglib URI:

```
<%@ taglib uri="/myTaglib" prefix="myPrefix" %>
```

As you can see, the taglib directive no longer explicitly declares the location of the TLD file, but instead relies upon the existence of a relative URI mapping in the application's deployment descriptor. This form of the directive is the most popular due to the flexibility it provides. For example, by enabling the relative URI mapping to be set in the deployment descriptor, the location of the TLD files can effectively be set at deployment time, and any changes to the location can be made very simply in the one place.

Option 3—Packaged JAR

The third and final use of the taglib directive involves providing an absolute path to an external JAR file. As the name suggests, a JAR file is simply a way of packaging compiled Java classes and resources into a compressed archive file that can be placed into your application's class path for use. Often when you use a third-party software component it will be distributed as a JAR file. JAR files are created using the %JAVA_HOME%\bin\jar.exe utility. Further information on its usage may be found by simply running the jar command without any parameters.

As mentioned, the taglib directive can accept an absolute value to a JAR file as the value of the uri attribute. This form requires that the JAR file should contain all of the tag handler classes as well as the TLD file, which must be located inside the META-INF directory of the JAR file.

This particular form of packaging is most commonly used when tag libraries are being used from external sources, perhaps when they're purchased from a third party or from another application. It provides a good way to encapsulate all the necessary aspects of a tag library into one distributable component.

Let's have a look at an example:

```
<%@ taglib uri="/WEB-INF/lib/myTaglib.jar" prefix="myPrefix" %>
```

As you can see, the entire tag library is stored in a single component inside the `WEB-INF/lib` directory, where it will be added to the web application's class path, from where it's available.

The one downside to packaging your tag libraries into an external JAR file is that the TLD file is difficult to access. Any changes to the attribute list or similar requires the JAR to be extracted first and then repackaged. Of course, the advantage of this method is that your tag libraries are self-contained and easy to distribute and reuse.

Action Elements

We mentioned earlier how difficult it was to read and maintain JSP pages that are full of scriptlet code. Not only are such pages "ugly" but they're almost meaningless to a web developer unless they also happen to be a Java developer who may have written the scriptlet code in the first place.

A better alternative is to either make use of existing actions (tags) provided by a tag library that encapsulate pieces of functional logic so JSP pages are much cleaner and more readable, and because they're XML tag-based and are usable by a non-Java UI developer. In JSP 2.0 there are three different types of action elements, as you can see:

- Standard actions
- Custom actions
- JSTL actions

Let's take a brief look at each one in turn.

Standard Actions

The JSP standard actions have been in existence since the first release of the JSP 1.0 specification and provide the JSP page author with a (relatively small) selection of useful actions. The majority of the provided functionality is based around the manipulation of JavaBean components as well as the dynamic inclusion of files at request time and URL forwarding.

Let's take a look at some of the more popular standard actions to get a "flavor" of their functionality.

The <jsp:include> Action

You saw earlier how the `include` directive provides a simple mechanism for including the contents of a separate web component to be included into the declaring JSP at translation time. The `<jsp:include>` action also provides a similar facility but with some subtle differences. The `<jsp:include>` action is actually executed at request time, thereby enabling the inclusion of both static and dynamic content and thus providing a more flexible approach.

Another major difference is that the `<jsp:include>` action doesn't include the actual content from the included resource in the same manner as the `include` directive. Instead, the `<jsp:include>` action will include any output generated by the included resource directly to the `JspWriter` assigned to the implicit `out` variable. This means that you can specify any different type of web resource, such as another JSP or servlet, as long as it produces content of the same type as the calling JSP page.

The syntax for using the standard `include` action is as follows:

```
<jsp:include page="relativeURL" flush="true"/>
```

Here you can see the action has two attributes. The `page` attribute is mandatory and contains a relative URL to the resource to be included, in the same way that the `file` attribute was interpreted by the `include` directive. The second optional attribute, `flush`, specifies whether or not the body of the response should be "flushed" or sent to the client browser before the page inclusion. The `flush` attribute is optional and defaults to `false` if not specified.

Due to the fact that the `flush` attribute can cause buffered content to be returned to a client before the included resource is executed, any included resources may not set any response headers.

We mentioned earlier that the `<jsp:include>` action allows static as well as dynamic content to be included, and we hinted that this ability offers flexibility that isn't achievable using the `include` directive. One example of such flexibility is the fact that the page attribute can be specified via a request parameter, because the `<jsp:include>` action isn't executed until the main page is requested:

```
<jsp:include page="${param.nextPage}" />
```

Here you can see how the value of the `page` attribute isn't known until the main JSP containing the `<jsp:include>` is requested and the value is obtained by extracting a request parameter using the JSP 2.0 EL. In other words, it's possible to create dynamic content that is so dynamic, its content isn't known until request time!

The <jsp:useBean> Action

Before any JavaBean component can be manipulated from a JSP page, it's first necessary to obtain an instance of the JavaBean, either by retrieving a preexisting bean from one of the available JSP scopes or by creating a new instance. Either of these options could potentially take several lines of scripting code, especially if the JavaBean needs to be initialized before use, which as you've seen, can clutter the JSP.

The `<jsp:useBean>` action is specifically designed to simplify this process. This standard action associates an instance of a Java object (our JavaBean) that is defined with a given `scope` and `id` and makes it available as a scripting variable of the same `id`. The `<jsp:useBean>` action is highly flexible and its exact functionality is controlled by the attributes passed to the action. When used correctly, this action can greatly reduce the amount of scriptlet code that would otherwise be required.

The syntax for the `<jsp:useBean>` action is as follows:

```
<jsp:useBean id="name" scope="page|request|session|application" typeSpec/>
```

where:

```
typeSpec ::= class="className"                    |
             class="className" type="typeName"    |
             beanName="beanName" type="typeName"  |
             type="typeName" beanName="beanName"  |
                                 type="typeName"
```

Before you see an example of the action at work let's first consider a scriptlet-based alternative that will print out the current time of day (`dateScriptlet.jsp`):

```
<%@ page import="java.util.Date, java.text.DateFormat"%>
<html>
  <head>
    <title>Professional JSP 2.0</title>
  </head>
  <body style="font-family:verdana;font-size:10pt;">
    <%
       DateFormat df = DateFormat.getInstance();
       Date today = new Date();
    %>

    <h2>Today's Date is <%= df.format(today) %></h2>
  </body>
</html>
```

As you can see, this JSP simply imports the `java.util.Date` and `java.text.DateFormat` classes for use and uses a scriptlet to initialize the `Date` and `DateFormat` objects. Some simple template text is used to construct an HTML page and finally a JSP expression is used to format the `Date` object.

Save the code printed earlier into a file called `dateScriptlet.jsp` beneath the `test` web-application folder in the normal manner. Open the following page in your browser, and the output should be similar to the following screen shot, displaying the correct date and time:

http://localhost:8080/test/dateScriptlet.jsp

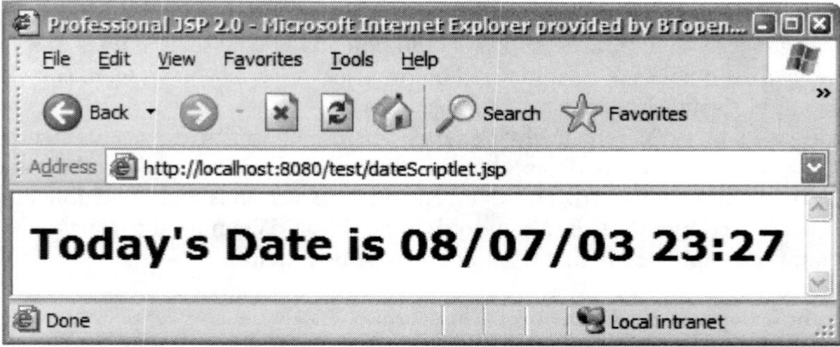

Although the previous example is perfectly functional, you can see the problems a web designer with no Java skills would have understanding even these simple scriptlets. Another possible problem could be that the JSP page won't be compatible with the tools used by the web designer because she's used to XML-type languages. In a more complex example you can imagine how the problem gets worse and worse.

Let's now see how you can encapsulate the previous date-formatting functionality into a JavaBean component and make use of the `<jsp:useBean>` action to solve the problems mentioned earlier:

```
package com.apress.projsp20.ch01;

import java.util.Date;
import java.text.*;

public class DateFormatBean {
  private DateFormat dateFormat;
  private Date date;

  public DateFormatBean() {
    dateFormat = DateFormat.getInstance();
    date = new Date();
  }

  public String getDate() {
    return dateFormat.format(date);
  }

  public void setDate(Date date) {
    this.date = date;
  }

  public void setFormat(String format) {
    this.dateFormat = new SimpleDateFormat(format);
  }
}
```

As you can see, this simple JavaBean component (`DateFormatBean.java`) initializes itself with a default date and format on initialization as well as providing custom methods to set a different date format or time. When all the initialization is completed, the `getDate()` method simply returns the predefined date in the given date format.

Let's take a look at how simple it is to use the `<jsp:useBean>` to initialize an instance of the `DateFormatBean` as opposed to the scriptlet approach:

```
<html>
  <head>
    <title>Professional JSP 2.0 </title>
  </head>
  <body style="font-family:verdana;font-size:10pt;">
    <jsp:useBean id="date" class="com.apress.projsp20.ch01.DateFormatBean"/>

    <h2>Today's Date is <%= date.getDate()%></h2>
  </body>
</html>
```

As you can see in the code (`dateBean.jsp`), the `<jsp:useBean>` creates an instance of the JavaBean class and stores a reference to it in a scripting variable, which is called `date`. All this without a single scriptlet! A simple JSP expression is used to call the `getDate()` method to retrieve the formatted date. It should be no surprise to learn that the output is exactly the same as in the earlier example–only the implementation is different.

The <jsp:getProperty> and <jsp:setProperty> Actions

You saw from the `<jsp:useBean>` action how simple it is to work with JavaBeans from inside the JSP pages. It should probably be of little surprise to learn that there are also standard actions designed to manipulate and retrieve the attributes of these JavaBeans, again without the need for scriptlets or expressions!

As the name suggests, the `<jsp:getProperty>` tag is used to retrieve or access the existing properties of a bean instance. Any bean properties that are retrieved using this tag are automatically converted to a `String` and are placed into the implicit `out` variable, as output.

The syntax for this tag is

```
<jsp:getProperty name="name" property="propertyName" />
```

As you can see, the `<jsp:getProperty>` tag has two attributes, `name` and `property`, both of which must be present. The `name` attribute is used to reference the name of the JavaBean instance on which the `property` attribute exists. This attribute will search all available JSP scopes until the named JavaBean is found. Should the tag fail to locate the requested JavaBean, then a suitable exception will be thrown at request time.

As you can see, this tag is relatively simple in the functionality that it provides, but to make use of it in a JSP, you must ensure that the JavaBean has already been made available to the JSP engine through a previously declared `<jsp:useBean>` tag or a similar. Without the inclusion of this extra tag, neither the `<jsp:getProperty>` nor the `<jsp:setProperty>` tag will function as expected.

While the last example you saw was a great improvement over the earlier scriptlet-based example, you still relied on the use of a JSP expression to access the `date` property from the `DateFormatBean`. You can use the `<jsp:getProperty>` action instead of the expression so that the entire JSP is XML-based.

Let's take a look at the changes to the earlier example that would be necessary (`dateBean_getProperty.jsp`):

```
<html>
  <head>
    <title>Professional JSP 2.0 </title>
  </head>
  <body style="font-family:verdana;font-size:10pt;">
    <jsp:useBean id="date" class="com.apress.projsp20.ch01.DateFormatBean"/>
    <h2>Today's Date is <jsp:getProperty name="date" property="date"/></h2>
  </body>
</html>
```

Again, this is a better solution. Yet you still haven't changed the content returned, just its implementation.

To complement the `<jsp:getProperty>` action, the `<jsp:setProperty>` tag can be used to set the value of an attribute inside a JavaBean. The `<jsp:setProperty>` action is somewhat more flexible and provides the ability to set properties based on request attributes, and so on. In its simplest form the action may be used as follows:

```
<jsp:setProperty name="beanName" property="property" value="value"/>
```

As you can see the name and property attributes are used exactly in the same way as with the <jsp:getProperty> action; the additional value attribute simply indicates the new value to set the JavaBean property to.

Although the <jsp:setProperty> action can be used anywhere within a JSP page, it's often used as a nested action inside the body content of the <jsp:useBean> action. The consequence of this is that the nested <jsp:setProperty> action will only be executed the first time the <jsp:useBean> instantiates a JavaBean. If an existing bean is located in any one of the JSP scopes then the nested action won't be called.

If you recall the listing for the DateFormatBean earlier there were two methods that additionally set the date and the date format properties to custom values. Let's make use of the <jsp:setProperty> action to set the date format to a different value from that in our previous example (shown in dateBean_setProperty.jsp).

```
<html>
  <head>
    <title>Professional JSP 2.0</title>
  </head>
  <body style="font-family:verdana;font-size:10pt;">
    <jsp:useBean id="date" class="com.apress.projsp20.ch01.DateFormatBean">
      <jsp:setProperty name="date" property="format"
           value="EEE, d MMM yyyy HH:mm:ss z"/>
    </jsp:useBean>
    <h2>Today's Date is <jsp:getProperty name="date" property="date"/></h2>
  </body>
</html>
```

If you want to use a compiled JavaBean in a JSP web application, the JSP engine, for example Tomcat, needs to know where to look for it. By default Tomcat (and any other servlet container) checks for classes in the \WEB-INF\classes directory under the web application directory, and any subdirectories of this. So, for our test web application Tomcat would look for JavaBeans in the \webapps\test\WEB-INF\classes directory, and all directories below this.

1. Create the directory structure webapps\test\WEB-INF\classes\com\apress\projsp20\ch01.
2. Then create a new file called DateFormatBean.java and enter the code from earlier in this section and compile it.
3. Next create the dateBean.jsp, dateBean_getProperty.jsp, and dateBean_setProperty.jsp pages beneath the test web application folder, and enter the code (also labeled earlier in this section).

Start Tomcat, open a browser, and run the `dateBean.jsp`, `dateBean_getProperty.jsp`, and `dateBean_setProperty.jsp` pages as you did earlier. Notice that this time, when you use the `dateBean_setProperty.jsp` page, you have changed the date format the JSP generates!

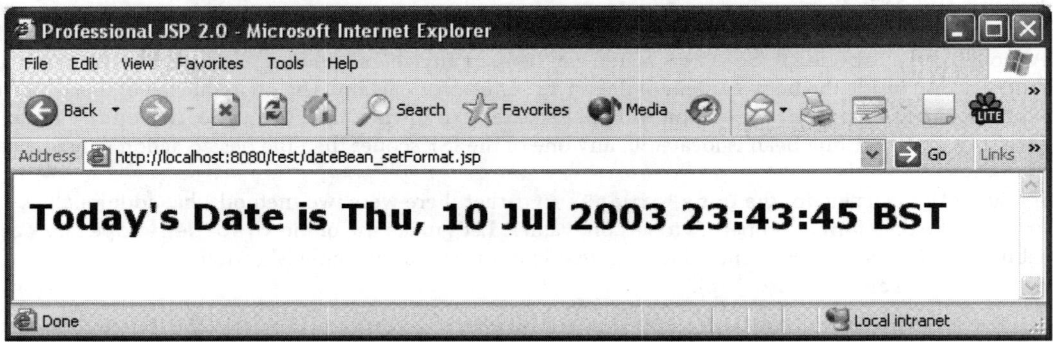

The <jsp:forward> Action

Another very handy action available to JSP page authors is the `<jsp:forward>` action, which not surprisingly is used to forward the current request to another resource such as a static resource, a JSP page, or a servlet in the same context as the containing JSP, for processing.

The syntax for the action is as follows:

```
<jsp:forward page="relativeURL" />
```

Any buffered content that was written before the call to the `<jsp:forward>` action will be ignored. If any buffered content has already been flushed (sent to the client) then the call will result in an `IllegalStateException`.

Note that nested `<jsp:param>` actions may be used in the `<jsp:forward>` action in the same way as with the `<jsp:include>` action to pass additional request parameters to the new resource.
For example:

```
<jsp:forward page="/pages/login.jsp">
  <jsp:param name="userName" value="Dan" />
</jsp:forward>
```

Custom Actions

Earlier you learned about the potential problems created by introducing too much (if any at all!) scriptlet code into a JSP page. Overuse of scriptlets complicates the lives of JSP developers as well as non-Java-speaking UI designers alike.

You've also seen how many of the problems associated with scriptlet code can be alleviated by encapsulating some of the ugly scriptlet code into JavaBean components and manipulating them using some of the standard actions. While this approach is far superior to the scriptlets approach, it's not the only available solution.

Custom actions are another mechanism for encapsulating functionality into reusable components for use inside JSP pages. Unlike JavaBean components, custom actions have full access to their environment (such as the request and session objects), which makes it far easier to provide functionality suitable for a web site. A good example of a custom action could be performing some calculations where the result is locale sensitive, such as being dependent on the language or number format. A JavaBean component has no idea about the environment in which it's run and therefore a developer would have to work a little harder to get the same functionality. That isn't to say that JavaBean components have no advantages. For one, they're by far the best mechanism for representing business objects and storing state, because they don't care about their environment!

Custom actions are packaged together (usually with several similar or complementary actions) into a tag library that must be registered with a JSP container via its TLD file, which advertises the services provided by the tag library. After a tag library is successfully installed inside a JSP container, the library must be imported using the `taglib` directive you saw earlier before any of the action it provides may be used.

The following example demonstrates the use of a custom action called `foo` from a tag library configured by a web applications deployment descriptor called `myTagLib`:

```
<%@ taglib uri="/myTagLib" prefix="myPrefix" %>

<myPrefix:foo>
   ...
</myPrefix:foo>
```

You can see from the previous example how a tag library must be imported before any of the actions it provides (in this case the `foo` action) may be used on the page. Notice how a prefix is used to provide a namespace for actions from one tag library to another.

You'll learn more about creating and using custom actions, including some of the new JSP 2.0 features for simplifying their creation in Chapters 5, 6, and 7.

JavaServer Pages Standard Tag Library Actions

You saw previously how useful the standard actions included in the JSP specification are to page authors; well, the JSTL takes this idea a step further and signifies a new phase for JSP page authors.

The JSTL specification was first released in June 2002 with the sole purpose of making JSP pages easier to write. The JSTL provides four new tag libraries that may be used in a similar manner to the standard tags you saw earlier:

- Core
- Internationalization (I18n) and Formatting
- XML
- SQL

As the names suggest, each library contains a host of useful actions, which are suitable for many of the tasks that JSP page authors are continually having to code manually, such as conditional statements and looping, formatting based on locales, XML manipulation, and database access.

The JSTL also makes use of the new JSP 2.0 EL, which makes the actions even easier to use, especially for a developer unfamiliar with Java syntax. For a more in-depth look at the JSTL and how its tags can be controlled, take a look at Chapter 4.

Summary

Hopefully this chapter has provided you with a general feel for where JSP technology fits within the J2EE and how it fits with regard to the other web components such as servlets, tag libraries, and JavaBeans, which exist in the J2EE web tier for providing dynamic web-based content.

You were also introduced to some of the most popular JSP architectures that are regularly used for designing the modern web application so that you can hopefully see the bigger picture next time you're confronted with design choices. Or maybe this chapter will help you to analyze an existing application.

Lastly, and most importantly, you were introduced to all of the core syntax-level attributes that are available to a JSP page author, including custom actions and the JSTL. Hopefully, this grounding will give you a head start when approaching some of the more complex chapters, which will build on the JSP basics that you've learned so far.

2

Servlets and Deployment

In this chapter, you'll look at the development and deployment of Java servlets. The Servlet and JSP specifications are developed in parallel with a major release of each specification; the current release is Servlets 2.4. Here we'll cover the following areas:

- An introduction to developing Java servlets, including a history of servlets
- Key features of the Java Servlets API
- Developing HTTP servlets
- Deploying Java Servlets 2.4-based web applications

This chapter isn't a definitive guide to Java servlets; instead it provides an overview of the Servlets API and the deployment of applications based on this API.

What Is a Servlet?

As you've learned in the previous chapter, JSP pages are translated into servlets before the web container executes them. This chapter looks at the anatomy of a Java servlet and the Servlet model that supports such servlets, and thus JSP pages.

A servlet is a server-side component that is capable of dynamically processing requests and constructing responses in a protocol-independent manner. This diagram shows the classes that are involved in developing servlets:

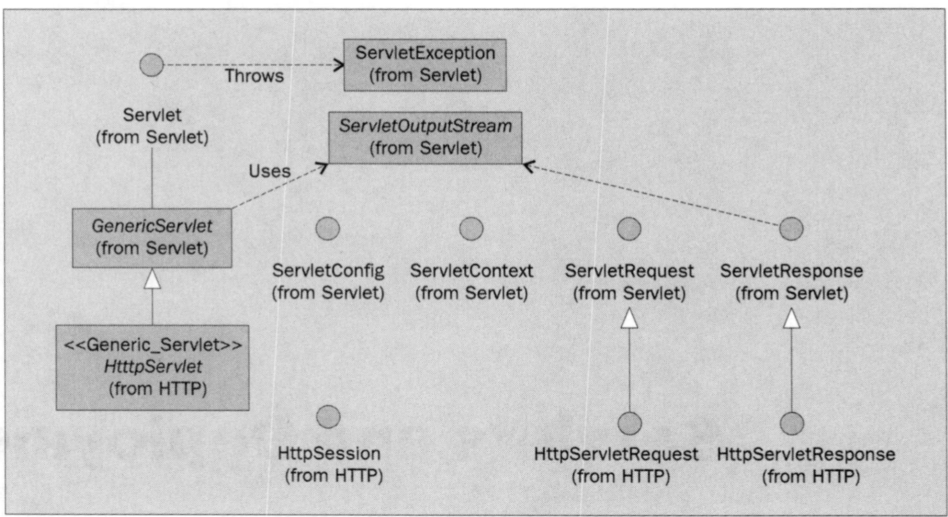

All of the classes and interfaces shown in the diagram are in either the `javax.servlet` or `javax.servlet.http` package. The `javax.servlet` package provides the contract between the servlet or web application and the web container. This allows the vendors of web containers to focus on developing the container in the manner most suitable to them, assuming they provide implementations of the standard interfaces for the web application to use. From the developer's perspective, the package provides a standard library to process client requests and develop servlet-based web applications.

At the center of the package is the `javax.servlet.Servlet` interface. This interface defines the core structure of *all* servlets; however, in developing most servlets you inherit from a defined implementation of this interface (such as `HttpServlet`).

The additional classes and interfaces that you can see in the previous diagram provide additional services to the web-application developer; for example, the web container provides access to the client request via a standard interface. The `javax.servlet` package provides the basis for developing cross-platform and cross-web container web applications without worrying about the implementation of each web container.

Why Servlets?

Why use servlets at all? After all, you have JSP pages, which are far easier to create then servlets. While this is definitely true, there are times when using a servlet is much more appropriate than using a JSP page. One particular occasion in which it is appropriate to use Servlets is in the JSP Model 2 architecture. This was discussed in Chapter 1 of this book.

Servlets are best used in situations where a great deal of programmatic control is required, such as decision making, database querying, or accessing other enterprise resources. If you attempt to perform these types of operations within a JSP page, you'll encounter the following problems:

- **Maintainability:** Since access to resources will be spread over a number of different JSP pages and interspersed with HTML display information, it will be very hard to maintain. The code will also be very hard to read due to the fact that it is interspersed with the HTML code and indentation becomes tricky.
- **Reusability:** When most of the processing logic is embedded into the JSP pages, it becomes much more difficult to reuse common functionality because it's usually implemented using scriptlets. Often this results in lots of cutting and pasting of code that isn't only bad from a reusability perspective but is also likely to introduce errors and of course decrease productivity.

However, there are also many times when using a servlet isn't appropriate. These are primarily in situations when a lot of display formatting is required. For example, it would be best not to use a servlet to present the front page of a website. If you were to use a servlet then it would contain lots of lines such as:

```
out.println("<a href=\"cart.jsp\">Cart</a>");
```

As you can see this is both messy and hard to maintain; every quotation mark must be escaped and you get no feel for the nesting in the page because the ubiquitous `out.println` statements surround everything.

JavaServer Pages Are Servlets!

As mentioned in Chapter 1, JSP pages are translated to servlets before they are run. The web container performs this translation transparently when a user makes a request for a given JSP page. For example, if you were to code the following JSP page and make a request for it, a servlet such as the following would be generated:

```
<html>
     <body>
           This is a very nice JSP page. Todays date is <%=new java.util.Date()%>
     </body>
</html>
```

```
package org.apache.jsp.example;

import javax.servlet.*;
import javax.servlet.http.*;
import javax.servlet.jsp.*;

public final class simple_jsp extends org.apache.jasper.runtime.HttpJspBase
    implements org.apache.jasper.runtime.JspSourceDependent {

  private static java.util.Vector _jspx_dependants;

  public java.util.List getDependants() {
    return _jspx_dependants;
  }
```

```
public void _jspService(HttpServletRequest request,
                        HttpServletResponse response)
    throws java.io.IOException, ServletException {
  JspFactory _jspxFactory = null;
  PageContext pageContext = null;
  HttpSession session = null;
  ServletContext application = null;
  ServletConfig config = null;
  JspWriter out = null;
  Object page = this;
  JspWriter _jspx_out = null;


  try {
    _jspxFactory = JspFactory.getDefaultFactory();
    response.setContentType("text/html");
    pageContext = _jspxFactory.getPageContext(this, request, response,
                  null, true, 8192, true);
    application = pageContext.getServletContext();
    config = pageContext.getServletConfig();
    session = pageContext.getSession();
    out = pageContext.getOut();
    _jspx_out = out;

    out.write("<html>\n\t");
    out.write("<body>\nThis is a very nice JSP Page ");
    out.write(String.valueOf(new java.util.Date()));
    out.write("\n");
    out.write("</body>\n");
    out.write("</html>\n");
  } catch (Throwable t) {
    if (!(t instanceof javax.servlet.jsp.SkipPageException)){
      out = _jspx_out;
      if (out != null && out.getBufferSize() != 0)
        out.clearBuffer();
      if (pageContext != null) pageContext.handlePageException(t);
    }
  } finally {
    if (_jspxFactory != null) _jspxFactory.releasePageContext(pageContext);
  }
 }
}
```

This servlet was generated by Tomcat and was outputted to the `%TOMCAT_HOME%/work/Catalina/localhost/jsp-examples/org/apache/jsp/example` *directory. Locations for these generated servlets will vary among web containers.*

As you can see, the servlet generated performs a whole lot of initialization such as getting hold of the servlet context, session, and page context objects that might be used by your JSP. Once this has been done, it outputs the HTML code from your servlet as a whole bunch of `out.println` statements. If you look at the servlet generated and compare it to the JSP that we wrote, it's easy to see why it's better to write JSPs to perform display formatting operations rather than servlets.

The javax.servlet Interfaces

The `javax.servlet` package is composed of twelve interfaces. The web container implements seven of these interfaces as follows:

- `ServletContext`
- `ServletConfig`
- `ServletResponse`
- `ServletRequest`
- `RequestDispatcher`
- `FilterChain`
- `FilterConfig`

These are objects that the container must provide to the servlets within it. The developer uses the interfaces to develop servlets and the web-container vendors can decide the most suitable way to implement these interfaces. The remaining five interfaces are implemented by the web-application developer to provide the application's functionality:

- `Servlet`
- `ServletContextListener`
- `ServletContextAttributeListener`
- `SingleThreadModel`
- `Filter`

As we have mentioned, the `Servlet` interface is key in developing servlets. This interface defines the life-cycle methods of a basic servlet: initialization, service, and destruction. The interface definition is shown here:

```
package javax.servlet;

import java.io.IOException;

public interface Servlet {

  public abstract void init(ServletConfig servletconfig)
                          throws ServletException;

  public abstract ServletConfig getServletConfig();

  public abstract void service(ServletRequest servletrequest,
                              ServletResponse servletresponse)
                        throws ServletException, IOException;
```

```
    public abstract String getServletInfo();

    public abstract void destroy();
  }
```

As you can see, this interface also provides a method to obtain an instance of the `ServletConfig` interface. The container uses the `ServletConfig` interface to pass initialization information to a servlet. This interface also has a way to get hold of an instance of the `ServletContext` for the current web application (via the `getServletContext()` method). The `ServletContext` interface is the web application's view on the web container. This allows a web application to use the services of the container, such as logging and request dispatching. You can see the `ServletConfig` interface definition here:

```
  package javax.servlet;

  import java.util.Enumeration;

  public interface ServletConfig {

    public abstract String getServletName();

    public abstract ServletContext getServletContext();

    public abstract String getInitParameter(String s);

    public abstract Enumeration getInitParameterNames();
  }
```

The `ServletContext` interface definition is shown here:

```
  package javax.servlet;

  import java.io.InputStream;
  import java.net.MalformedURLException;
  import java.net.URL;
  import java.util.Enumeration;
  import java.util.Set;

  public interface ServletContext {

    public abstract ServletContext getContext(String s);

    public abstract int getMajorVersion();

    public abstract int getMinorVersion();

    public abstract String getMimeType(String s);

    public abstract Set getResourcePaths(String s);

    public abstract URL getResource(String s)
                                throws MalformedURLException;
```

```
  public abstract InputStream getResourceAsStream(String s);

  public abstract RequestDispatcher getRequestDispatcher(String s);

  public abstract RequestDispatcher getNamedDispatcher(String s);

  /**
   * @deprecated Method getServlet is deprecated
   */

  public abstract Servlet getServlet(String s)
                                throws ServletException;

  /**
   * @deprecated Method getServlets is deprecated
   */

  public abstract Enumeration getServlets();

  /**
   * @deprecated Method getServletNames is deprecated
   */

  public abstract Enumeration getServletNames();

  public abstract void log(String s);

  /**
   * @deprecated Method log is deprecated
   */

  public abstract void log(Exception exception, String s);

  public abstract void log(String s, Throwable throwable);

  public abstract String getRealPath(String s);

  public abstract String getServerInfo();

  public abstract String getInitParameter(String s);

  public abstract Enumeration getInitParameterNames();

  public abstract Object getAttribute(String s);

  public abstract Enumeration getAttributeNames();

  public abstract void setAttribute(String s, Object obj);

  public abstract void removeAttribute(String s);

  public abstract String getServletContextName();
}
```

The `ServletContextListener` interface is a life-cycle interface that programmers can implement to listen for changes to the state of the `ServletContext` object. This means that programmers can choose to be informed of events such as the destruction or creation of a `ServletContext` object. This allows the developer to perform application startup and shutdown type functionality (for example, opening or closing database connections) within their web applications. The `ServletContextListener` interface definition is shown here:

```
package javax.servlet;

import java.util.EventListener;

public interface ServletContextListener extends EventListener {

  public abstract void contextInitialized(ServletContextEvent
                                           servletcontextevent);

  public abstract void contextDestroyed(ServletContextEvent
                                         servletcontextevent);
}
```

Implementations of the `ServletContextAttributeListener` interface can perform similar functionality, but the events that they are notified about relate to the modification (add, change, delete) of attributes on the servlet context. This interface definition is shown here:

```
package javax.servlet;

import java.util.EventListener;

public interface ServletContextAttributeListener extends EventListener {

  public abstract void attributeAdded(ServletContextAttributeEvent
                                       servletcontextattributeevent);

  public abstract void attributeRemoved(ServletContextAttributeEvent
                                         servletcontextattributeevent);

    public abstract void attributeReplaced(ServletContextAttributeEvent
                                            servletcontextattributeevent);
}
```

The `RequestDispatcher` interface manages client requests by directing them to the appropriate resources on the server. The developer can use this interface to redirect the application to different pages and servlets. The definition of this interface is shown here:

```
package javax.servlet;

import java.io.IOException;

public interface RequestDispatcher {

  public abstract void forward(ServletRequest servletrequest,
                               ServletResponse servletresponse)
                                      throws ServletException, IOException;
```

```
    public abstract void include(ServletRequest servletrequest,
                                 ServletResponse servletresponse)
                                        throws ServletException, IOException;
  }
```

The ServletRequest interface encapsulates all of the information that is transmitted to a servlet through its service() method during a single client request. A ServletRequest object created by the container provides methods to access any parameter names and values, attributes as well as an input stream. The source for this interface is shown here:

```
  package javax.servlet;

  import java.io.*;
  import java.util.*;

  public interface ServletRequest {

    public abstract Object getAttribute(String s);
    public abstract Enumeration getAttributeNames();
    public abstract String getCharacterEncoding();
    public abstract void setCharacterEncoding(String s)
                         throws UnsupportedEncodingException;
    public abstract int getContentLength();
    public abstract String getContentType();
    public abstract ServletInputStream getInputStream()
                                       throws IOException;
    public abstract String getParameter(String s);
    public abstract Enumeration getParameterNames();
    public abstract String[] getParameterValues(String s);
    public abstract Map getParameterMap();
    public abstract String getProtocol();
    public abstract String getScheme();
    public abstract String getServerName();
    public abstract int getServerPort();
    public abstract BufferedReader getReader()
                                   throws IOException;
    public abstract String getRemoteAddr();
    public abstract String getRemoteHost();
    public abstract void setAttribute(String s, Object obj);
    public abstract void removeAttribute(String s);
    public abstract Locale getLocale();
    public abstract Enumeration getLocales();
    public abstract boolean isSecure();
    public abstract RequestDispatcher getRequestDispatcher(String s);
  }
```

You can access parameters passed to the request via the following methods:

```
  public String getParameter(String name)
  public String[] getParameterValues(String name)
  public java.util.Enumeration getParameterNames()
  public java.util.Map getParameterMap()
```

The getParameter() method will return the parameter value with the given name or null if the parameter does not exist. If this method is used with a multivalued parameter then the value returned will be equal to the first value in the array returned from the getParameterValues() method. The getParameterNames() method is used to retrieve a java.util.Enumeration of String objects containing the names of all the parameters found in the request. If the request does not contain any parameters then an empty Enumeration will be returned. Finally, the getParameterMap() method returns a java.util.Map containing all the parameters found in the request. The parameter names form string-based keys to individual parameter values that are stored as string arrays.

The javax.servlet Classes

In addition to the interfaces that you've seen, there are seven classes contained within the javax.servlet package. They are as follows:

- GenericServlet
- ServletContextEvent
- ServletContextAttributeEvent
- ServletInputStream
- ServletOutputStream
- ServletRequestWrapper
- ServletResponseWrapper

The GenericServlet abstract class can be used to develop protocol-independent servlets and requires only that subclasses implement its service() method. For servlets intended to function in a web context, it's more common to extend the HttpServlet abstract class (which you'll look at in a later section).

The two event classes, ServletContextEvent and ServletContextAttributeEvent, are classes used for notification about changes to the ServletContext object and its attributes.

The ServletInputStream and ServletOutputStream abstract classes provide the ability to read and write binary data from and to the client. Implementations of these classes must provide an implementation of the java.io.InputStream.read() and java.io.OutputStream.write() methods, respectively.

Lastly, the wrapper classes ServletRequestWrapper and ServletResponseWrapper provide useful implementation of the ServletRequest and ServletResponse interfaces. These can be used or subclassed to give developers the ability to adapt the standard behavior of these objects for their own applications' needs.

The Life Cycle of a Servlet

The javax.servlet.Servlet interface defines the methods that all servlets must implement and among others, three methods that are known as **life-cycle methods**:

```
public void init(ServletConfig config) throws ServletException

public void service(ServletRequest req, ServletResponse res)
          throws ServletException, IOException

public void destroy()
```

These life-cycle methods are each called at separate times during the lifespan of a servlet, from the initial creation to the moment it's removed from service and destroyed. These methods are called in the following order:

1. When the servlet is constructed, it is initialized with the `init()` method.

2. Any requests from clients are handled initially by the `service()` method before delegating to the `doXxx()` methods in the case of an `HttpServlet`. This method is responsible for processing the request and returning the response.

3. When the servlet needs to be removed from service, it's destroyed with the `destroy()` method, then garbage collected and finalized. When the container decides to take a servlet out of service it first ensures that any `service()` method calls have completed.

The following diagram shows this sequence of events:

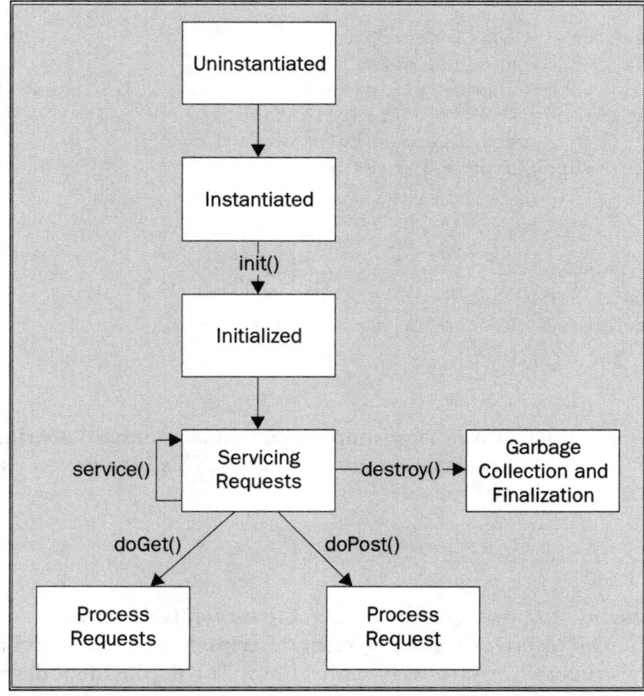

A Simple Servlet

In this section, you'll look at an example of a simple generic servlet. This servlet will extend the class `GenericServlet` that provides a basic implementation of the `Servlet` interface. You'll implement the `service()` method of this class in our subclass, which will do the work of our servlet. You'll also override the `init()` and `destroy()` methods of the `GenericServlet` abstract base class. The code for our servlet is shown here (written as a standard `.java` file):

```
package com.apress.projsp20.ch02;

import java.io.*;
import java.util.Date;

import javax.servlet.*;

public class MyServlet extends GenericServlet {

  public void init(ServletConfig config) throws ServletException {
    super.init(config);
    Date thisDate = new Date();
    log("MyServlet initialized at:" + thisDate);
  }

  public void service(ServletRequest request, ServletResponse response)
                      throws ServletException, IOException {

    response.setContentType("text/html");
    PrintWriter out = response.getWriter();
    out.println("<html><head><title>BasicServlet</title></head>");
    out.println("<body><h2>" + getServletName() + "</h2>");
    out.println("This is a basic servlet.<br>");
    out.println("<hr></body></html>");
    out.close();
  }

  public void destroy() {
    Date thisDate = new Date();
    log("MyServlet was destroyed at:" + thisDate);
  }
}
```

As you can see, this servlet performs a very simple job, that is, it outputs a string of HTML. When the servlet is initialized it will print a message to the servlet log. This is achieved via the `log()` method of the `GenericServlet` base class as follows:

```
log("MyServlet initialized at:" + thisDate);
```

You'll also use this method to print a method when the servlet is destroyed. To deploy the servlet to a web container, you'll need to provide a **deployment descriptor** (`web.xml`) and arrange the files in the appropriate directory structure for Java web applications. The deployment descriptor gives the container information about the components that you are deploying to it. Deployment descriptors are thoroughly explained later on in this chapter. For now it suffices to see the deployment descriptor that will allow you to deploy your servlet:

```
<?xml version="1.0" encoding="ISO-8859-1"?>

<web-app xmlns="http://java.sun.com/xml/ns/j2ee"
    xmlns:xsi="http://www.w3.org/2001/XMLSchema-instance"
    xsi:schemaLocation="http://java.sun.com/xml/ns/j2ee/web-app_2_4.xsd"
    version="2.4">

    <servlet>
        <servlet-name>MyServlet</servlet-name>
        <servlet-class>com.apress.projsp20.ch02.MyServlet</servlet-class>
    </servlet>

    <servlet-mapping>
        <servlet-name>MyServlet</servlet-name>
        <url-pattern>/MyServlet</url-pattern>
    </servlet-mapping>
</web-app>
```

Our files must be arranged in the following manner:

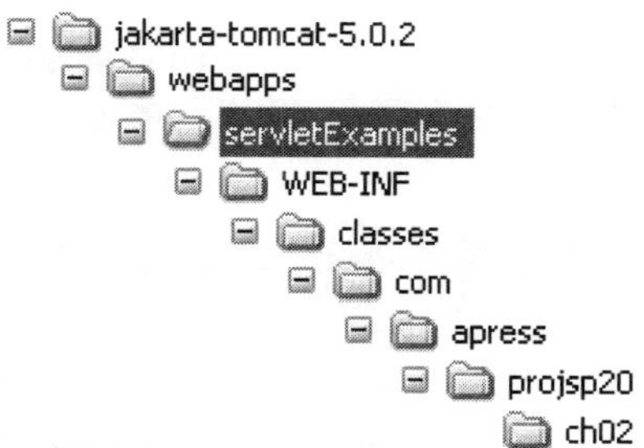

- `servletExamples` is the name for our web application.
- `WEB-INF` is the directory indicating that this is a web application–the directory name is case sensitive.
- `web.xml` is the deployment descriptor, which sits inside the `WEB-INF` folder.
- `classes` is the directory where you store the classes–in appropriate subdirectories for the package structure, for example, `com/apress/projsp20/ch02/` (as shown here) might contain `MyServlet.class` and `MyServlet.java`.

Whereas with your JSP pages the web container will generate the servlet and compile it, you need to compile our servlet. To do this you need the `javax.servlet` packages in your class path. Depending on your web container, these might exist either as a separate Servlet's JAR file or as part of a greater J2EE JAR. In the case of Tomcat 5.0, the file is `servlet-api.jar` located in the `/common/lib` directory.

There are two ways you can deploy a web application into Tomcat:

- Copy your application's files and directories directly into Tomcat's `webapps` directory.
- Create a distributable web application archive (WAR) file.

For simplicity, you'll use the former here, but use the later with your more complete example at the end of this chapter.

So to deploy the application within Tomcat, you can place this directory structure within the `%TOMCAT_HOME%/webapps` directory; the application will now be available at the following URL: http://localhost:8080/servletExamples/MyServlet. You'll get the following page in your browser:

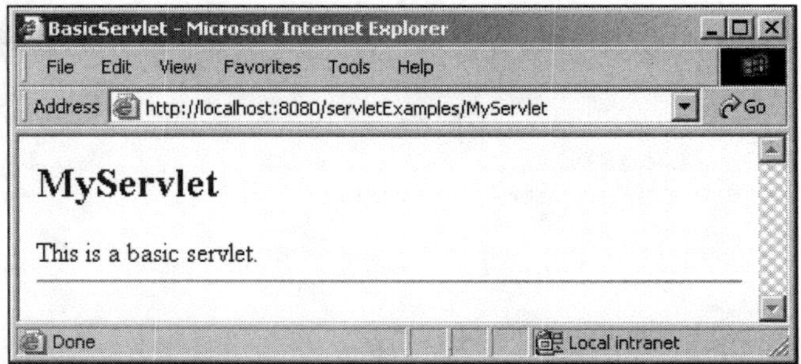

If you were to look at your web container's `log` file (for Tomcat this is located at `%TOMCAT_HOME%/logs/localhost_log.YYYY-MM-DD.txt`) you'll see the following toward the end of the file:

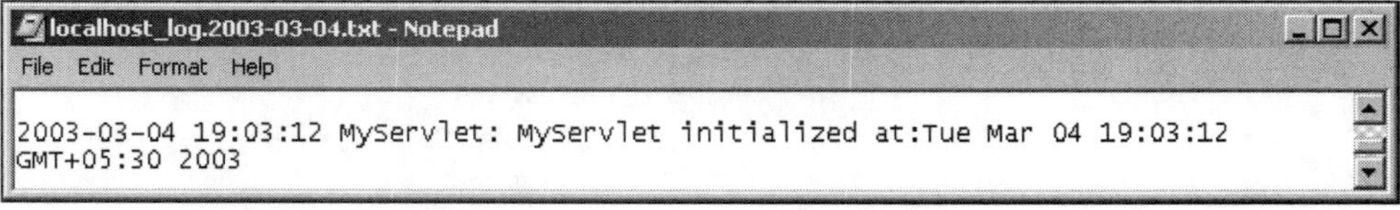

If you now stop the web container and look at the log again you'll see that the servlet has been destroyed and the following text will be present in the log:

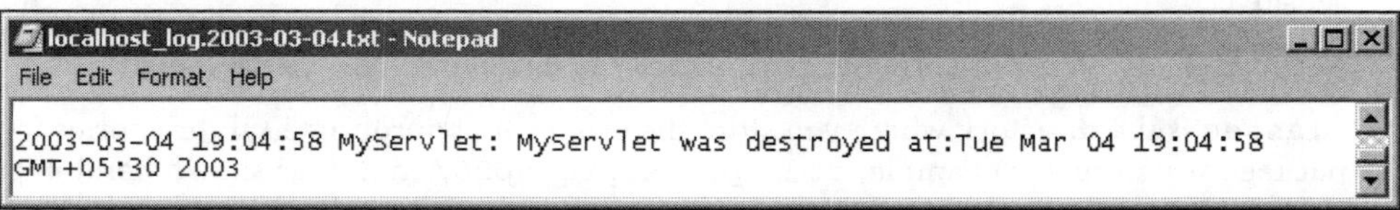

HTTP Servlets

As we have mentioned, the `javax.servlet` package provides generic interfaces and classes to service clients' requests independent of the protocol used. This means that any behavior that is specific to a particular package has to be implemented by the developer within the application. For this reason the `javax.servlet` package is extended to provide a mechanism to handle requests in a protocol-dependent manner. This allows protocol-specific functionality to automatically be provided to the developer.

In this section, you'll look at one such extension: the `javax.servlet.http` package. This package provides classes that can be used and extended to develop servlets that provide HTTP-specific functionality. The main class in the `javax.servlet.http` package is the `HttpServlet` abstract class. This class extends from the `javax.servlet.GenericServlet` class. This means that all functionality provided by this class is available to HTTP servlets. The first thing to note about the `HttpServlet` class is that it provides several new methods that provide protocol-specific functionality. Instead of the single `service()` method as in the `GenericServlet` class, you now have methods such as `doGet()` and `doPost()` that allow your servlet to perform a different task depending upon the manner in which it's being called. However, this very rarely happens in practice.

The request-handling methods that are provided are as follows:

```
protected void doGet(HttpServletRequest req, HttpServletResponse resp)
                          throws ServletException, IOException
```

The `doGet()` method is intended to retrieve an entity from the server as referenced by a request URL.

```
protected void doHead(HttpServletRequest req, HttpServletResponse resp)
                                       throws ServletException, IOException
```

The `doHead()` method is simply a `GET` request that is intended to return only the HTTP header information.

```
protected void doPost(HttpServletRequest req, HttpServletResponse resp)
                                       throws ServletException, IOException
```

The `doPost()` method is intended to allow posting of information (forms and so on) to the server.

```
protected void doPut(HttpServletRequest req, HttpServletResponse resp)
                                       throws ServletException, IOException
```

The `doPut()` method is used to upload a file to a server in a manner similar to the FTP.

```
protected void doOptions(HttpServletRequest req, HttpServletResponse resp)
                                       throws ServletException, IOException

protected void doTrace(HttpServletRequest req, HttpServletResponse resp)
                                       throws ServletException, IOException
```

The `doOptions()` and `doTrace()` methods allow you to override the behavior of HTTP. There is almost no reason to override either of these methods unless the servlet implements functionality beyond the HTTP 1.1 specification.

To handle a request of a given type you simply override the appropriate method.

HTTP Responses and Requests

As well as providing the `HttpServlet` class, the `javax.servlet.http` package also provides HTTP-specific versions of the `ServletRequest` and `ServletResponse` objects. These are named `HttpServletRequest` and `HttpServletResponse`, respectively.

HttpServletRequest

You can use the `HttpServletRequest` interface to find out about the HTTP-specific information of your request to our `HttpServlet` (such as the HTTP request parameters). As this class extends the `ServletRequest` class, you can perform all of the functions of that class as well, such as retrieving request parameters, and so on. Some of the useful operations that you can perform on your request are covered in the following sections.

Retrieving HTTP Request Header Information

HTTP headers store a wide range of information about the user and the request, and they are transmitted between a user (usually a browser) and a web server during each request. HTTP header information is separate from the body of a request and provides some very useful information that can be used by a web component (servlet or JSP page) when constructing a response.

A few of the more common headers are shown here to give you an idea of the information passed between the browser and web server:

Header	Denotes
`Date`	The date and time the request was served
`Accept`	Used to indicate the media types accepted by the client
`Accept-Encoding`	The types of data encoding the browser knows how to decode
`Connection`	Whether the client can handle persistent HTTP connections
`Content-Length`	The length of the body in bytes or `-1` if the length is unknown
`Cookie`	Used to return any cookies sent by servers to the client browser
`Host`	The host and port of the original URL
`Referrer`	The URL of any referring web page
`User-Agent`	Identifies the client or browser making the request

The `HttpServletRequest` interface provides access to the available headers using the following methods:

```
public String getHeader(String name)
public java.util.Enumeration getHeaders(String name)
public java.util.Enumeration getHeaderNames()
public String getMethod()
```

As you can see, the available methods for accessing HTTP headers take a similar form to those methods used for accessing HTML form parameters. The `getHeader()` method is used to access a given header's value while the `getHeaders()` method returns an enumeration of string objects that represent all of the values of a given request header. This method can be used for headers that may have multiple values such as the `Accept-Language` header. Finally, when you are unsure of the available headers, the `getHeaderNames()` method may be used to obtain an enumeration of available header names. Finally, the `getMethod()` method can be used to retrieve the HTTP method used, such as `GET`, `POST`, or PUT.

`HttpServletRequest` also provides a couple of utility methods that can be used to convert the return type of specific header values:

```
public long getDateHeader(String header)
```

The `getDateHeader()` method will return a given header as a long value that represents a `Date` object. This method could be used with the `If-Modified-Since` or `Date` headers:

```
public int getIntHeader(String header)
```

The `getIntHeader()` method returns a given header as an integer value.

Both of these methods will return `-1` if the given header isn't available. The reason to use these over the alternative `getHeader()` method is that you won't have to perform any casting on the value returned. This produces neater and more reliable code.

> **The name of the header passed to the `getHeader()` method isn't case sensitive, like the majority of the `HttpServletRequest` methods such as `getParameter()`.**

Retrieving Path Information

You can also extract a lot of information relating to the path used to request your servlet. The following methods return information about this path:

```
public String getQueryString()
```

The `getQueryString()` returns the query string of a request or `null` if there was no query string. For example, for the following URL, http://localhost:8080/servletExamples/TestServlet?name=sam, the method would return `name=sam`.

```
public String getContextPath()
```

The `getContextPath()` method returns the first part of the URL after the first / after localhost:8080. For the example URL this would return `servletExamples`.

```
public String getServletPath()
```

The `getServletPath()` returns the path to your servlet. In the URL mentioned earlier this would return `/TestServlet`.

```
public String getPathInfo()
```

The `getPathInfo()` returns any additional path information after your servlet path and before your query string. In our example there is no such information present, so `null` would be returned.

```
public String getRequestURI()
```

The `getRequestURI()` returns the complete URI for the request; for example, this would be `/servletExamples/TestServlet?name=sam` for the URL mentioned earlier.

```
public String getRequestURL()
```

The `getRequestURL()` returns the full URL that the client entered into the browser to make the request to your servlet. For example, this is `http://localhost:8080/servletExamples/TestServlet?name=sam`, for the URL mentioned earlier (yes that is correct, it's the whole URL!).

HttpServletResponse

You can use the `HttpServletResponse` interface to provide a response to the request to your servlet. Because this class extends the `ServletResponse` interface, you can perform all of the functions of that class as well. Some of the useful operations that you can perform on your response are covered here.

Setting an HTTP Response Header and Setting the Content Type of the Response

You've seen how the `HttpServletRequest` interface provides methods to access any HTTP headers set by a client's browser when requesting a web resource. Similarly, the `HttpServletResponse` interface provides methods to set headers in the response that is sent back to the browser from the web server. These methods are as follows:

```
public void addHeader(String name, String value)
public void setDateHeader(String name, long date)
public void addIntHeader(String name, int value)
public void setHeader(String name, String value)
public void setDateHeader(String name, long value)
public void setIntHeader(String name, int value)
```

Here you can see two similar types of methods: the `addXxxHeader()` and `setXxxHeader()`. Although very similar in functionality, the two method types have distinctly different behavior. The `addHeader()`, `addDateHeader()`, and `addIntHeader()` methods all simply add a named header value to the response. The result of calling any of these three methods is that multivalue headers can be created in the response.

The `setHeader()`, `setDateHeader()`, and `setIntHeader()` methods will actually check for the existence of a header or headers with the same name already in the response. If the methods find an existing header or headers, they are simply replaced with the new value, otherwise a new header is created.

It's important to note that for any headers to take effect they obviously must be set before the response is committed and sent back to the client.

The `HttpServletResponse` interface also inherits the following two methods from its super class `javax.servlet.ServletResponse`:

```
public void setContentLength(int length)
public void setContentType(String type)
```

The `setContentLength()` method, used for persistent HTTP connections, sets the length of the content body returned to the client. If this value is set too low then the client may stop reading the response prematurely. Likewise, setting this value too high may leave clients hanging around, needlessly waiting for more data. When this method is called from an HTTP servlet, it has the effect of setting the `Content-Length` header.

The `setContentType()` method is used to set the Multipurpose Internet Mail Extensions (MIME, RFC 2045 and 2046) type of the response. The effect of calling this method from an HTTP servlet is that the `Content-Type` header is set accordingly.

In an HTTP servlet that serves HTML content the content type is set as follows:

```
response.setContentType("text/html");
```

`text/html` is the most common type of content returned from servlets. It should also be noted that MIME types are used in many protocols other than HTTP (such as SMTP e-mail) to indicate the type of the response and to show that many different content types exist.

Another method that is worth mentioning in this context is the `setLocale(java.util.Locale)` method that is provided by the `javax.servlet.ServletResponse` interface. This method automatically sets appropriate headers including the `Content-Type`'s `charset` for the appropriate locale.

Acquiring a Text Stream for the Response

The `ServletResponse` interface is responsible for the response that is sent back to a client after the request for some form of resource (HTML, XML, file, and so on). This interface makes a `java.io.PrintWriter` available to any servlet that returns text-based markup such as HTML, XML, or WML to a client.

The `PrintWriter` object enables character data to be sent back to the client. Therefore, the following method is provided by the `ServletResponse` interface:

```
public java.io.PrintWriter getWriter() throws java.io.IOException
```

> **This method returns a `PrintWriter` object that uses the character encoding as specified in the `charset` property of the `setContentType()` method, which must be called before the `getWriter()` method for it to have any effect.**

The `ServletResponse` interface also provides a `flushBuffer()` method, which will force any content stored in an internal buffer to be written to the client. Calling the `flush()` method of the `PrintWriter` will also have a similar effect.

Acquiring a Binary Stream for the Response

As mentioned earlier, servlets do not just have to return character data such as HTML to clients. The `ServletResponse` interface also provides access to a `javax.servlet.ServletOutputStream` object, which can be used for returning binary information such as a GIF image to a client and is obtained with the following method:

```
public javax.servlet.ServletOutputStream getOutputStream() throws
                                                  java.io.IOException
```

The `ServletOutputStream`, as the name suggests, is a subclass of `java.io.OutputStream` so the normal techniques of chaining may be employed: The `ServletOutputStream` is wrapped inside a `java.io.BufferedOutputStream` or `java.io.ObjectOutputStream`.

Calling `flush()` on the `ServletOutputStream` or `flushBuffer()` on the `ServletResponse` will commit the response to the client.

Redirecting an HTTP Request to another URL

It's often desirable for a servlet to redirect the request to another URL. The reasons for doing this are many, for example a user may not have logged in to an application and needs to be redirected to a login page or a site may have moved and users need to be pointed toward an alternative URL.

As the name suggests, the redirect mechanism involves a server informing the client that they must request another URL. Most modern browsers support this functionality automatically and it causes the user only a slightly longer waiting period before their request is served.

It should be noted that there is a distinct difference between redirecting and forwarding a user to an alternative URL. Forwarding is totally invisible to the client and the resource that was forwarded to is returned as if it were the output from the original request. This a very powerful mechanism; generally, forwarding is used to hide the implementation details of components that make up a web application.

The `sendRedirect()` method is provided by the `javax.servlet.http.HttpServletResponse` interface:

```
public void sendRedirect(String location)
```

The location URL passed into the `sendRedirect()` method may be an absolute or relative URL. Absolute URLs must start with a "`/`" and are interpreted as relative to the servlet container root. Relative URLs do not start with a "`/`" and are interpreted as relative to the current request URI.

It's important to note that if the response has already been committed when the `sendRedirect()` method is called, an `IllegalStateException` is thrown.

Another important point to note is that if URL rewriting is being used to maintain client sessions and a redirect is required, then the `encodeRedirectURL()` method of the `HttpServletResponse` interface should be used to add the session information to the redirect URL so that the client's session state is maintained. There are multiple types of redirect headers, which are detailed in the section "Error Pages."

HttpServlet Example

This section will look at a simple example of an `HttpServlet`. This servlet will simply obtain the headers from the `HttpRequest` and respond by outputting these to the requesting browser. Here, you do not implement duplicate functionality in both the `doGet()` and `doPost()` methods, rather you call one from the other (`doPost()` calls `doGet()`) so that the servlet responds identically if it was called by either of these methods. The code for the servlet is shown here:

```
package com.apress.projsp20.ch02;

import java.io.*;
import java.util.*;
import javax.servlet.*;
import javax.servlet.http.*;

public class HttpServletHeaders extends HttpServlet {

  public void doGet(HttpServletRequest request,
                    HttpServletResponse response)
                    throws IOException, ServletException {

    response.setContentType("text/html");

    PrintWriter out = response.getWriter();
    out.println("<html>");
    out.println("<body bgcolor=\"white\">");
    out.println("<head>");

    out.println("<title>Here are the headers</title>");
    out.println("</head>");
    out.println("<body>");

    out.println("<h3>Headers</h3>");
    out.println("<table border=0>");
    Enumeration e = request.getHeaderNames();
    while (e.hasMoreElements()) {
      String headerName = (String)e.nextElement();
      String headerValue = request.getHeader(headerName);
      out.println("<tr><td>");
      out.println(headerName);
      out.println("</td><td>");
      out.println(headerValue);
      out.println("</td></tr>");
    }
    out.println("</table>");
  }

  public void doPost(HttpServletRequest request,
                     HttpServletResponse response)
                     throws IOException, ServletException {
    doGet(request, response);
  }
}
```

You'll deploy the servlet using the following deployment descriptor (see the section on deployment). As you can see it's quite similar to the one you used earlier:

```
<?xml version="1.0" encoding="ISO-8859-1"?>

<web-app xmlns="http://java.sun.com/xml/ns/j2ee"
         xmlns:xsi="http://www.w3.org/2001/XMLSchema-instance"
         xsi:schemaLocation="http://java.sun.com/xml/ns/j2ee web-app_2_4.xsd"
         version="2.4">

  <servlet>
      <servlet-name>HttpServletHeaders</servlet-name>
      <servlet-class>com.apress.projsp20.ch02.HttpServletHeaders</servlet-class>
  </servlet>

  <servlet-mapping>
      <servlet-name>HttpServletHeaders</servlet-name>
      <url-pattern>/HeaderServlet</url-pattern>
  </servlet-mapping>

</web-app>
```

Now compile the servlet file and copy it with the deployment descriptors into the following directory structure under Tomcat to deploy it:

- `servletExamples` is the name for your web application.
- `WEB-INF` is the directory indicating that this is a web application–the directory name is case sensitive.
- `web.xml` is the deployment descriptor, which sits inside the `WEB-INF` folder.
- `classes` is the directory where you store the classes–in appropriate subdirectories for the package structure, for example, `com/apress/projsp20/ch02/` (as shown here) might contain `HttpServletHeaders.class` and `HttpServletHeaders.java`.

You'll see the following when making a request for http://localhost:8080/servletExamples/HeaderServlet:

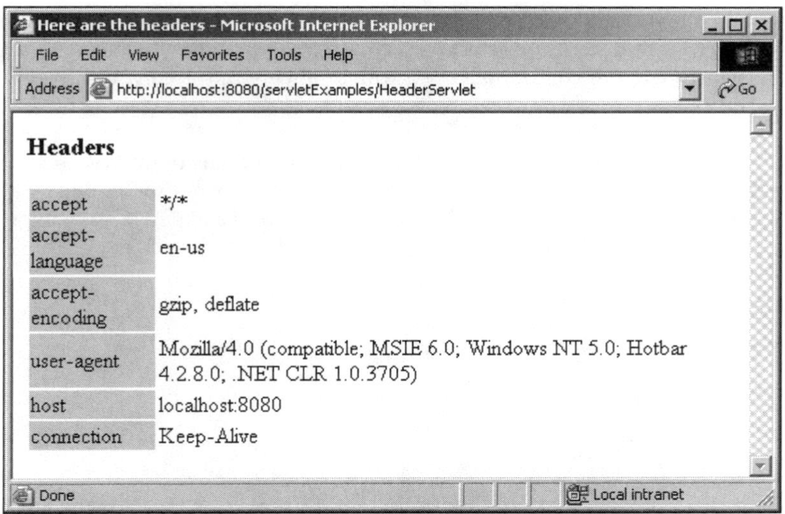

Deploying Java Servlet-Based Web Applications

In this section, you'll look at the deployment of Java servlet-based web applications. You'll focus on the deployment of servlets. You may have noticed the phrase **deployment descriptor** or the file name `web.xml` and wondered what they were. The deployment descriptor (`web.xml`) file is perhaps the single most important item of your web application.

For the deployment descriptor to be valid for web applications using the Servlets 2.4 specification, several things must be true:

- The file must conform to the J2EE Application XML Schema, which is:

```
<web-app xmlns="http://java.sun.com/xml/ns/j2ee"
         xmlns:xsi="http://www.w3.org/2001/XMLSchema-instance"
         xsi:schemaLocation="http://java.sun.com/xml/ns/j2ee/web-app_2_4.xsd"
         version="2.4">
```

- The deployment descriptor must be a well-formed XML file.
- The deployment descriptor must be named `web.xml`.
- The deployment descriptor must reside at the top level of the `WEB-INF` directory of your web application.

Now that you know what a deployment descriptor must be, you may ask what it does. In a nutshell, the deployment descriptor conveys the elements and configuration information of a web application between developers, assemblers, and deployers. All manner of information is defined in the deployment descriptor: from information about the web application itself to information about its constituent parts, and most importantly, how those parts are assembled into a complete web application. This section will discuss the elements of the deployment descriptor that are important for most web applications. The way in which a deployment descriptor is written is often the key to how well a web application fits its purpose. It's simple to write the components of a web application, but how it's assembled is a difficult and often neglected task.

The sections of the deployment descriptor that we are going to focus in on are those that relate to the deployment and configuration of servlets and JSP pages. This does not include the deployment of tag libraries and expression language (EL) functions because these are covered elsewhere in this book. The sections that you'll focus on here are as follows:

- Servlet definitions and mappings
- Servlet context initialization parameters
- Error pages
- JSP configuration elements

To illustrate the parts of the deployment descriptor, we'll show you the following simple (but complete) example and then proceed to explain its constituent parts:

```
<?xml version="1.0" encoding="ISO-8859-1"?>

<web-app xmlns="http://java.sun.com/xml/ns/j2ee"
         xmlns:xsi="http://www.w3.org/2001/XMLSchema-instance"
         xsi:schemaLocation="http://java.sun.com/xml/ns/j2ee/web-app_2_4.xsd"
         version="2.4">

  <display-name>Test Web Application</display-name>
  <description>A test web application</description>

  <context-param>
    <param-name>adminEmail</param-name>
    <param-value>admin@apress.com</param-value>
  </context-param>

  <servlet>
    <servlet-name>Servlet1</servlet-name>
    <servlet-class>com.apress.projsp20.ch02.Servlet1</servlet-class>
     <init-param>
      <param-name>version</param-name>
      <param-value>0.1b</param-value>
    </init-param>
  </servlet>

  <servlet>
    <servlet-name>Servlet2</servlet-name>
    <servlet-class>com.apress.projsp20.ch02.Servlet2</servlet-class>
  </servlet>

  <servlet-mapping>
    <servlet-name>Servlet1</servlet-name>
    <url-pattern>/home.html</url-pattern>
```

```
    </servlet-mapping>
    <servlet-mapping>
      <servlet-name>Servlet2</servlet-name>
      <url-pattern>/AnotherServlet</url-pattern>
    </servlet-mapping>

    <jsp-config>
      <jsp-property-group>
        <url-pattern>*.jsp</url-pattern>
        <el-enabled>false</el-enabled>
        <scripting-enabled>false</scripting-enabled>
        <include-prelude>/header.jsp</include-prelude>
        <include-coda>/footer.jsp</include-coda>
        <page-encoding>UTF-8</page-encoding>
      </jsp-property-group>
    </jsp-config>

    <error-page>
      <exception-type>java.lang.ArithmeticException</exception-type>
      <location>/error.html</location>
    </error-page>

    <error-page>
      <error-code>404</error-code>
      <location>/404.html</location>
    </error-page>

  </web-app>
```

Although the previous deployment descriptor looks very daunting because of its size and use of different, perhaps unfamiliar tags, you'll soon see that it's very simple.

As you can see at the start of the deployment descriptor, there are several tags that are not directly related to servlets, but give information about the web application. These tags occur directly after the <web-app> tag, which denotes the start of the deployment descriptor. These tags are as follows:

```
<display-name>Test Web Application</display-name>
<description>A test web application</description>
```

The <display-name> tag allows you to specify a short name for the overall web application. This tag is designed to allow the name of the web application to be displayed by GUI tools. The <description> tag allows you to provide a short textual description of the purpose of this web application. This is a very simplistic form of documentation for the overall web application.

Now let's move on and look at the parts of the example deployment descriptor that relate directly to servlet deployment.

Servlet Definitions

Looking at the deployment descriptor, you can see that it defines two servlets in the web application. You can see this by looking at the number of unique <servlet> tags. The first of our two servlets is defined here:

```
<servlet>
  <servlet-name>Servlet1</servlet-name>
  <servlet-class>com.apress.projsp20.ch02.Servlet1</servlet-class>
  <init-param>
    <param-name>version</param-name>
    <param-value>0.1b</param-value>
  </init-param>
</servlet>
```

The `<servlet>` tag contains several child tags that give information about the declaration of the servlet. This information includes the unique name that the servlet is registered with in this web application, and the full name of the class that implements the servlet's functionality.

The `<servlet-name>` tag gives the servlet's unique name within the web application. In the case of our first servlet, you can see that it's called `Servlet1`.

The `<servlet-class>` tag gives the fully qualified class name of the class that implements the functionality of this servlet. In the case of our first servlet, you can see that `Servlet1` is implemented in the class `com.apress.projsp20.ch02.Servlet1`.

Looking at the `<servlet>` element for our first servlet, you can see that it contains more than just the name and class of the servlet. It also contains an `<init-param>` tag. This tag allows you to specify initialization parameters for our servlet.

```
<init-param>
  <param-name>version</param-name>
  <param-value>0.1b</param-value>
</init-param>
```

As you can see, our servlet has one parameter set. The `<param-name>` child tag gives the name that the parameter can be accessed by, and the `<param-value>` gives the starting value for the parameter. The parameter can be accessed from our first servlet using the `getInitParameter()` method on the `ServletConfig` object. This method is

```
public String ServletConfig.getInitParameter(String name)
```

So to get access to the parameter defined for our first servlet, you can use the following code within the servlet's class:

```
...
  String version = getServletConfig("version");
...
```

Notice that you don't need to get the `ServletConfig` object explicitly, because the `GenericServlet` class implements the `ServletConfig` interface so that the method is available to you.

You won't be examining the definition of our second servlet in detail, because this is identical to the first servlet. However, the second servlet's definition is simpler because it does not contain any initialization parameters.

Servlet Mappings

Once you've defined your servlet through the <servlet> tag, you need to map it to a particular URL pattern. This is necessary so that the web container knows which requests to send to a particular servlet. You may think, "Why can't I just pass all requests to the servlet with the same name as the end of the URL?" For example, http://localhost:8080/mywebapp/Servlet1 would be routed to the servlet defined with the name Servlet1. This would seem like a logical approach and is in fact the most common way of implementing the mappings between servlets and URLs. However, the approach isn't very flexible. Imagine if you wanted to map more than one URL to the same servlet, which could, for example, check that a user is logged in? This is where the <servlet-mapping> element comes in, and where it illustrates its power.

In the example deployment descriptor, you map servlets to some strange-looking URL patterns. Our first servlet is invoked every time any URL that ends with home.html is encountered. The unique servlet name that you defined in the <servlet> tag (referenced here as <servlet-name>) is mapped to a URL pattern referenced here in a <url-pattern> element:

```
<servlet-mapping>
  <servlet-name>Servlet1</servlet-name>
  <url-pattern>/home.html</url-pattern>
</servlet-mapping>
```

Again, we won't discuss our second servlet, because this is very similar to the first, except that it maps to any URL ending in AnotherServlet.

It's worth mentioning at this stage that servlets can be mapped to more than one URL through the use of wildcards in the <url-pattern> child tag of the <servlet-mapping> tag. For example, the following maps every URL encountered to the same servlet, which allows you to have a central servlet that handles all requests:

```
<servlet-mapping>
  <servlet-name>ValidatorServlet</servlet-name>
  <url-pattern>/*</url-pattern>
</servlet-mapping>
```

You can also have more than one <servlet-mapping> tag per defined servlet. This allows you to map completely disparate URLs to the same target.

Servlet Context Initialization Parameters

Here we'll discuss the application (or servlet context) initialization parameters. You've already seen how to define initialization parameters for individual servlets; now you'll look at defining parameters for the whole web application.

To achieve this, you use the `ServletContext` object. The `ServletContext` is a servlet's view onto the web application that contains it. As such, if a parameter is set in the `ServletContext`, it's accessible from all servlets in the web application.

Through the deployment descriptor, you can provide the `ServletContext` with any number of initialization parameters. You could use such parameters to convey application information such as an administrator's e-mail address. These parameters are available to the servlets in the web application via the `getInitParameter()` and `getInitParameterNames()` methods of the `ServletContext` object:

```
public abstract String getInitParameter(String name)
public abstract Enumeration getInitParameterNames()
```

Note that because this is an interface, all methods are abstract and their implementations must be provided by the web container.

In the example, you define one initialization parameter for your web application using a `<context-param>` element:

```
<context-param>
  <param-name>adminEmail</param-name>
  <param-value>admin@apress.com</param-value>
</context-param>
```

This parameter represents the e-mail address of the application's administrator. This can be pulled into any servlet in the application so that the e-mail address used is consistent throughout the system. To obtain this parameter from any particular servlet, you can use the following code:

```
...
  String adminEmail = getServletContext().getInitParameter("adminEmail");
...
```

Error Pages

In the bad old days of web development, if an error occurred in an application you would see the familiar HTTP error 500, or worse still, a nasty stack trace on the browser. For example, if your servlet performed an operation that resulted in an exception, it was quite common to see the following type of output in the client browser:

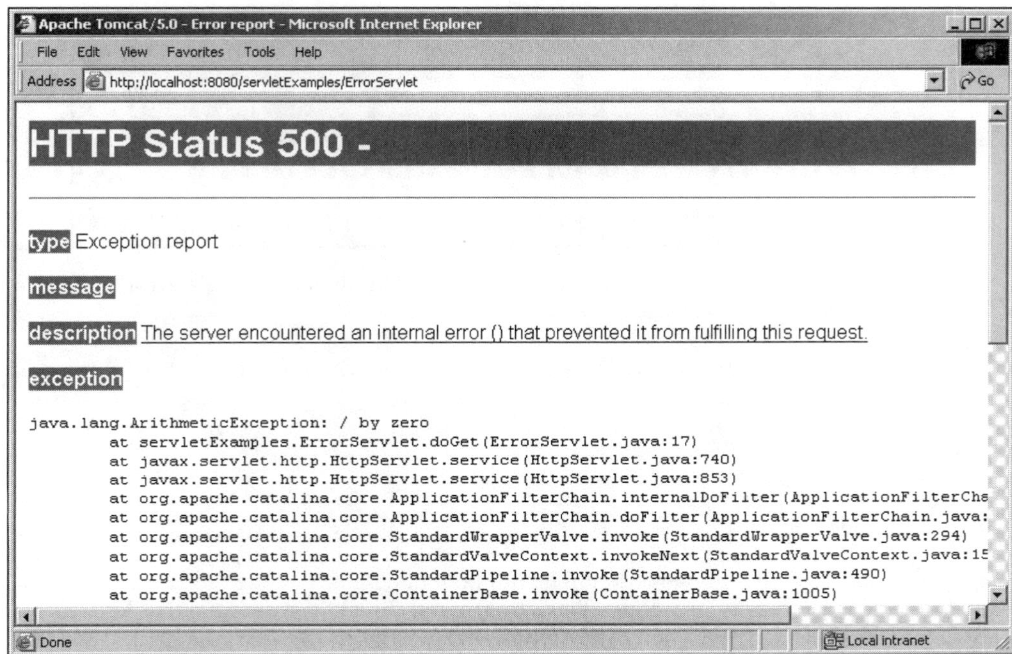

In a production system, this sort of page does not inspire much confidence in the end user of the application! You can prevent such pages from appearing through the use of error pages.

Error pages allow you to respond to problems with custom pages that offer specific information about the trouble at hand. These errors can include Java exceptions as well as HTTP errors (for example, the result of a page not being found).

Our sample deployment descriptor defines two error pages. The first error page is shown whenever the server encounters a `java.lang.ArithmeticException` (as shown previously). The tags to define this are shown here:

```
<error-page>
  <exception-type>java.lang.ArithmeticException</exception-type>
  <location>/error.html</location>
</error-page>
```

As you can see, the `<error-page>` tag has two children: `<exception-type>` and `<location>`. `<exception-type>` defines the exception to catch and `<location>` defines the page or resource to display on encountering the error defined.

After adjusting your deployment descriptor, if you were to run the same servlet that produced the earlier error, `error.html` would be called and displayed instead of the nasty Java stack trace that you saw:

As most users will agree, they would rather be presented with a human-readable error page than a huge meaningless (to some anyway!) Java stack trace.

Your sample deployment descriptor also contains an error-page definition for an HTTP error. This is defined using the following tags:

```
<error-page>
  <error-code>404</error-code>
  <location>/404.html</location>
</error-page>
```

This looks very similar to the previous example, but note the use of the `<error-code>` child tag, instead of the `<exception-type>` child. This `<error-code>` child defines the HTTP error under which the defined error page will be shown. In this example, when the web container cannot find a file requested in the web application, it will show the page `404.html` rather than the server's default error page. For example, when you try to call `WrongServlet`, which is obviously not a real servlet, you should get a customized error page like this:

A list of HTTP error codes and their meanings is given in the following table:

Error Code	Error Type	Error Code	Error Type
100	Continue	404	Not Found
101	Switching Protocols	405	Method Not Allowed
200	OK	406	Not Acceptable
201	Created	407	Proxy Authentication Required
202	Accepted	408	Request Time Out
203	Nonauthoritative Information	409	Conflict
204	No Content	410	Gone
205	Reset Content	411	Length Required
206	Partial Content	412	Precondition Failed
300	Multiple Choices	413	Request Entity Too Large
301	Moved Permanently	414	Request URL Too Large
302	Moved Temporarily	415	Unsupported Media Type
303	See Other	500	Server Error
304	Not Modified	501	Not Implemented
305	Use Proxy	502	Bad Gateway
400	Bad Request	503	Out of Resources
401	Unauthorized	504	Gateway Time Out
402	Payment Required	505	HTTP Version Not Supported
403	Forbidden		

JavaServer Pages Configuration Elements

A new feature of the Servlet 2.4 deployment descriptor is the addition of several JSP configuration elements inside a `<jsp-config>` element. These elements allow you to do the following:

- Control enabling of EL evaluation
- Control enabling of scripting elements
- Indicate page-encoding information
- Automatically include preludes and codas

You can perform some or all of these functions for individual pages or groups of pages. This grouping is controlled by the `<jsp-property-group>` element. This allows you to map URLs to groups of the properties mentioned earlier. As you can see in the previous example , you are applying several properties to *all* JSP pages in the application; this uses the following property group:

```
<jsp-config>
  <jsp-property-group>
    <url-pattern>*.jsp</url-pattern>
  </jsp-property-group>
</jsp-config>
```

Controlling Enabling of Expression Language Evaluation

To enable or disable the evaluation of the EL, you can use the `<el-enabled>` element. This can be used to easily set the `isELIgnored` property of a group of JSP pages. By default, the EL evaluation is enabled for web applications using a Servlet 2.4 `web.xml`. To disable evaluation for all the JSP pages in our application, you can use a fragment similar to the following:

```
<jsp-config>
  <jsp-property-group>
    <url-pattern>*.jsp</url-pattern>
    <el-ignored>true</el-ignored>
  </jsp-property-group
</jsp-config>
```

You can also disable the EL for specific pages using a snippet such as the following:

```
<jsp-config>
  <jsp-property-group>
    <url-pattern>noel.jsp</url-pattern>
    <el-ignored>true</el-ignored>
  </jsp-property-group
</jsp-config>
```

Controlling Enabling of Scripting Elements

To enable or disable the evaluation of scripting elements within a page, you can use the `<scripting-enabled>` element. This can be used to easily set the `isScriptingEnabled` property of a group of JSP pages. By default, scripting is enabled. To disable scripting for all the JSP pages in your application, you can use a fragment similar to the following:

```
<jsp-config>
  <jsp-property-group>
    <url-pattern>*.jsp</url-pattern>
    <scripting-ignored>true</scripting-ignored>
  </jsp-property-group>
</jsp-config>
```

To disable scripting for a specific page, you can use a snippet such as the following:

```
<jsp-config>
  <jsp-property-group>
    <url-pattern>noscript.jsp</url-pattern>
    <scripting-ignored>true</scripting-ignored>
  </jsp-property-group>
</jsp-config>
```

Indicate Page-Encoding Information

Using the `<page-encoding>` element, you can define the encoding for a group of JSP pages. The valid values of the `<page-encoding>` tag are those of the `pageEncoding` page directive. It's a translation-time error to define the `pageEncoding` of a JSP page through one value in the JSP configuration element and then give it a different value in a `pageEncoding` directive, but it's legal to give it the same value. You can use a snippet similar to the one shown here to control the page encoding:

```
<jsp-config>
  <jsp-property-group>
    <url-pattern>*.jsp</url-pattern>
    <page-encoding>false</page-encoding>
  </jsp-property-group
</jsp-config>
```

Automatically Include Preludes and Codas

Through the use of the `<include-prelude>` and `<include-coda>` elements, you can automatically include a page before and after the evaluation of a group of pages.

The `<include-prelude>` element is a context-relative path that must correspond to an element in the web application. When the element is present, the given path will be automatically included (as in an `include` directive) at the beginning of each JSP page in this `<jsp-property-group>`.

The `<include-coda>` element is a context-relative path that must correspond to an element in the web application. When the element is present, the given path will be automatically included (as in an `include` directive) at the end of each JSP page in this `<jsp-property-group>`.

The following fragment shows a file being included at the start and end of every JSP page in the web application:

```
<jsp-config>
  <jsp-property-group>
    <url-pattern>*.jsp</url-pattern>
    <include-prelude>/header.jsp</include-prelude>
    <include-coda>/footer.jsp</include-coda>
  </jsp-property-group
</jsp-config>
```

An Example Web Application

You are now in the position to pull together all of the information in this chapter as a complete web-application example.

This section will cover all of the code required to produce a sample web application. You'll look at all of the code required to put together a simple web application as well as the information needed to deploy the completed application to a web container (in this example, Tomcat 5.0).

The Store

The example used in this section is the ubiquitous web-store application. You'll see a front page, a shopping cart, and a checkout page.

After you've looked at the code for the application, you'll examine the deployment descriptor for the application.

The application will be written in the JSP model 2 style (see Chapter 1 for a detailed description of this), beginning with the controller.

Bear in mind that this is a very simplistic application. Over the course of this book, the examples will grow gradually more sophisticated.

The Controller Servlet

The Controller servlet (`FrontController.java`) coordinates the behavior of our store:

```
package com.apress.projsp20.ch02.store;

import java.io.*;
import java.util.*;
import javax.servlet.*;
import javax.servlet.http.*;

public class FrontController extends HttpServlet {

  public void init() throws ServletException {

    HashMap products = new HashMap();

    Product p = new Product(1, "Dog", "9.99");
    products.put("1", p);

    p = new Product(2, "Cat", "4.99");
    products.put("2", p);

    p = new Product(3, "Fish", "1.99");
    products.put("3", p);

    //Store products in the ServletContext
    getServletContext().setAttribute("products", products);

  }
```

```
  public void doPost(HttpServletRequest request, HttpServletResponse response)
      throws ServletException, IOException {

    // load the action
    String name = request.getPathInfo().substring(1);

    String viewName = "/error.jsp";
    try {
      name = "com.apress.projsp20.ch02.store." + name;
      Class c = getClass().getClassLoader().loadClass(name);
      Action action = (Action) c.newInstance();
      viewName = action.process(request, response);

    } catch (ClassNotFoundException e) {
      e.printStackTrace();
    } catch (InstantiationException e) {
      e.printStackTrace();
    } catch (IllegalAccessException e) {
      e.printStackTrace();
    }

    RequestDispatcher dispatcher = request.getRequestDispatcher(viewName);
    dispatcher.forward(request, response);

  }

  public void doGet(HttpServletRequest request, HttpServletResponse response)
      throws ServletException, IOException {

    doPost(request, response);

  }

}
```

As you can see, this servlet is fairly simple. Its primary job is to receive a request, work out how to process it, delegate the processing to an appropriate class, and forward it on to the next JSP page in the store. This is achieved by reading the request path and attempting to instantiate a class that matches the last part of it. For example, if the request is http://localhost:8080/store/servlet/DummyAction, the servlet will attempt to instantiate a class called `DummyAction` in the current package. Once this class has been instantiated it will call the method process on it, passing in the current request and response objects. This relies on the class implementing a known interface called `Action`. This interface is simple, containing only one method, as follows:

```
package com.apress.projsp20.ch02.store;

import javax.servlet.ServletException;
import javax.servlet.http.HttpServletRequest;
import javax.servlet.http.HttpServletResponse;

public interface Action {

  /**
   * Peforms the processing associated with this action.
```

```
   *
   * @param request     the HttpServletRequest instance
   * @param response    the HttpServletResponse instance
   * @return  the name of the next view
   */
  public abstract String process(HttpServletRequest request,
                                 HttpServletResponse response)
      throws ServletException;

}
```

It is the job of implementations of this interface to process the current request and return the name of the next page to forward it on to. Our store has several implementations of this interface, which will all be shown and explained in this section.

Getting back to the controller, you can see that it also performs another job. The `init()` method of the servlet creates a collection of `Product` objects that are placed into the `ServletContext`. This would not normally be done, because the products would be obtained from somewhere such as a database or configuration file. We have done it this way to avoid cluttering up the code with data-access code. `Product` is just an object that holds the basic data for each item:

```
package com.apress.projsp20.ch02.store;

public class Product {

  private String name;
  private String price;
  private int id;

  public Product(int id, String name, String price) {
    this.price = price;
    this.name = name;
    this.id=id;
  }

  public String getPrice() {
    return this.price;
  }

  public String getName() {
    return this.name;
  }

  public int getId() {
    return this.id;
  }

  public String toString() {
      return "Product:id=" + id + " name=" + name + " price=" + price;
  }

}
```

The Store Actions and JavaServer Pages

Now we have the base for our actions and model, let's flesh it out by combining them with the view.

MainAction

The Main action in our store is implemented (surprisingly) by a class called `MainAction`. This class implements the `Action` interface that you saw earlier. This action, the code of which is shown here, has no other purpose at this time than to forward onto the main page in this site, `main.jsp`.

```
package com.apress.projsp20.ch02.store;

import javax.servlet.http.HttpServletRequest;
import javax.servlet.http.HttpServletResponse;
import javax.servlet.ServletException;

public class MainAction implements Action {

  public String process(HttpServletRequest request, HttpServletResponse response)
       throws ServletException {

    return "/main.jsp";

  }
}
```

The main page for this site, `main.jsp`, is shown here. This page is very simple and displays the list of products available to purchase:

```
<%@ page import="java.util.*,com.apress.projsp20.ch02.store.*" %>

<%
  HashMap products = (HashMap) application.getAttribute("products");

  // List the products, clickable to add to cart
  Iterator it = products.values().iterator();
  out.println("<table>");
  while (it.hasNext()) {
    out.println("<tr>");
    Product product = (Product) it.next();
%>

<td>
 <a href='CartAction?add=true&id=<%=product.getId()%>'><%=product.getName()%></a>
</td>
<td>
 <%=product.getPrice()%>
</td>

</tr>
<%}%>
</table>
```

You display the products by getting the previously created hashtable from the `ServletContext` (this was created by the controller servlet that you read about earlier). You then loop through hashtable, writing each product out into an HTML table row. Each product name is rendered as a hyperlink so that you can add it to the shopping cart that you'll read about next.

This main page has a header and footer included so that you can simply change the style of the page without changing the code that displays products. This is achieved using the `<include-prelude>` and `<include-coda>` subelements of the `<jsp-config>` deployment-descriptor element. The following excerpt shows the deployment-descriptor elements that are required:

```
<jsp-config>
  <jsp-property-group>
    <url-pattern>*.jsp</url-pattern>
    <include-prelude>/header.jsp</include-prelude>
    <include-coda>/footer.jsp</include-coda>
  </jsp-property-group>
</jsp-config>
```

This includes the file `/header.jsp` as the page header and the file `/footer.jsp` as the page footer. These are included for every JSP page within the system.

The header simply contains a basic header and heading, as follows:

```
<html>
    <head>
       <title>The Store</title>
    </head>
    <body>
        <h1>Welcome to the Apress Store</h1>
        <br>
```

While the footer closes the body and adds some navigation links, as shown here:

```
    <br>
        <table>
            <tr>
               <td><a href="CartAction?add=false">Display Cart</a></td>
               <td><a href="CheckOutAction">Check Out</a></td>
            </tr>
    </body>
</html>
```

Cart Action

The cart in your store holds only one type of each product. This is primarily so that you can illustrate error pages for your sample application. The code that implements your cart is another action, `CartAction.java`, and a simple Java class. `Cart.java` is shown here:

```
package com.apress.projsp20.ch02.store;
import java.util.*;
```

```
public class Cart {

  private HashMap items = new HashMap();

  public Cart() {
  }

  public Iterator getItems() {
    return items.values().iterator();
  }

  public void addItem(Product product) throws ItemAlreadyAddedException {
    Integer id = new Integer(product.getId());
    if (this.items.containsKey(id)) {
      throw new ItemAlreadyAddedException();
    }
    this.items.put(id, product);
  }

}
```

The following code shows the Action that handles the web operations on the shopping cart, called `CartAction.java`:

```
package com.apress.projsp20.ch02.store;

import java.io.*;
import java.util.*;

import javax.servlet.*;
import javax.servlet.http.*;

public class CartAction implements Action {

  public String process(HttpServletRequest request, HttpServletResponse response)
       throws ServletException {

    // Check to see if you are adding to the cart or
    // if you want to display the cart
    String adding = request.getParameter("add");

    // Get the cart if it exists
    HttpSession session = request.getSession();

    Cart cart = (Cart) session.getAttribute("cart");

    if (cart == null) {
      cart = new Cart();
    }

    if (adding.equalsIgnoreCase("true")) {
      // Add to it
      addToCart(request, cart);
    }
```

```
      return "/cart.jsp";

    }

    private void addToCart(HttpServletRequest request, Cart cart)
        throws ItemAlreadyAddedException {
      // Get the item to add from the request

      // Get the products from the ServletContext
      HashMap products = (HashMap)request.getSession().getServletContext().
                                  getAttribute("products");

      // Find the one represented by the ID that you passed in
      try {
        String id = request.getParameter("id");

        Product p = (Product) products.get(id);

        System.out.println(p);
        // Add it to the cart
        cart.addItem(p);
        // Add the cart to the session
        request.getSession().setAttribute("cart",cart);

      } catch (NumberFormatException nfe) {
        throw new ItemAlreadyAddedException();
      }
    }
}
```

In this action CartAction performs two tasks: It both adds to the shopping cart and displays the cart.

The first thing done in this action is to retrieve the shopping cart from the user's session. If there is no cart in the session, a new Cart object is created as follows:

```
Cart cart = (Cart) session.getAttribute("cart");

if (cart == null) {
  cart = new Cart();
}
```

Next, this method decides what to do to the cart based on a parameter (called adding) passed to the action in the HttpServletRequest. If the parameter contains the value true then you call the method addToCart(). If the adding parameter is false then you simply redirect to the cart.jsp page. This method looks for another parameter in the HttpServletRequest called id. It then looks for this product in the list of products that you placed into the ServletContext in the initialization, and adds it to the cart object. As mentioned earlier, a cart can only contain one of each product. If the user tries to add more than one of the same item to the cart, an ItemAlreadyAddedException is thrown. As you'll see later, the web container catches this exception and a special page is shown. Once the item is added to the cart (or if the adding parameter is false) the cart is written out to the user's browser by redirecting to the cart.jsp page. This page is shown here:

```
<%@page import="java.util.*,com.apress.projsp20.ch02.store.Cart,
                com.apress.projsp20.ch02.store.Product"%>

<%Iterator items = ((Cart)session.getAttribute("cart")).getItems();%>
    <h1>Current Cart Contents:</h1>
    <table>
    <%while (items.hasNext()) {%>

     <tr>
      <%Product p = (Product)items.next();%>

      <td><%=p.getName()%></td>
      <td><%=p.getPrice()%></td>
        </tr>
    <%}%>

    </table>
```

Checking Out

Obviously, a store is only useful if you can actually buy the products that you put into your cart. In the example store, the CheckOutAction handles this. Obviously, being an example, you cannot really buy the items. The checkout process in our store simply displays the contents of the cart and gives the user a Confirm button. The code for the CheckOutAction is as follows:

```
package com.apress.projsp20.ch02.store;

import java.io.*;

import javax.servlet.*;
import javax.servlet.http.*;

public class CheckOutAction implements Action {

  public String process(HttpServletRequest req, HttpServletResponse res)
          throws ServletException {

      return "/checkout.jsp";

  }
}
```

The action simply redirects the user to the checkout.jsp page as shown here:

```
<jsp:include page="cart.jsp" />

<br>Please Click Confirm to check out<br>
<form action='ConfirmAction'><input type='submit' value='Confirm'></form>
```

This page includes the content of the cart.jsp page to display the cart to the user and presents it with a Confirm button. This will invoke the ConfirmAction.

ConfirmAction

The confirm action in our store simply redirects to a confirmation page. In a real store this might do credit-card processing or any number of other things. The code for this action is shown here:

```
package com.apress.projsp20.ch02.store;

import javax.servlet.http.HttpServletRequest;
import javax.servlet.http.HttpServletResponse;
import javax.servlet.ServletException;

public class ConfirmAction implements Action {

  public String process(HttpServletRequest request, HttpServletResponse response)
       throws ServletException {

    return "/confirmed.html";

  }
}
```

The `ConfirmAction` simply redirects you to an HTML file to tell the user their order has been confirmed. In a real store you would output a receipt or something like it at this stage.

Having seen all of the important code for the simple store application, you'll now look at the deployment descriptor required to deploy this application.

The Deployment Descriptor

Now it's time to deploy the application. The following is the deployment descriptor that you'll be using to do this:

```
<?xml version="1.0" encoding="ISO-8859-1"?>

<web-app xmlns="http://java.sun.com/xml/ns/j2ee"
         xmlns:xsi="http://www.w3.org/2001/XMLSchema-instance"
         xsi:schemaLocation="http://java.sun.com/xml/ns/j2ee web-app_2_4.xsd"
         version="2.4">

  <servlet>
      <servlet-name>FrontController</servlet-name>
      <servlet-class>
         com.apress.projsp20.ch02.store.FrontController
      </servlet-class>
      <load-on-startup>1</load-on-startup>
  </servlet>

  <servlet-mapping>
      <servlet-name>FrontController</servlet-name>
      <url-pattern>/servlet/*</url-pattern>
  </servlet-mapping>

  <jsp-config>
```

```
        <jsp-property-group>
            <url-pattern>/*</url-pattern>
            <include-prelude>/header.jsp</include-prelude>
            <include-coda>/footer.jsp</include-coda>
        </jsp-property-group>
    </jsp-config>

    <welcome-file-list>
        <welcome-file>index.html</welcome-file>
    </welcome-file-list>

    <error-page>
        <exception-type>
            com.apress.projsp20.ch02.store.ItemAlreadyAddedException
        </exception-type>
        <location>/duplicateItem.html</location>
    </error-page>

</web-app>
```

This deployment descriptor contains all of the elements to build the application and allow it to be deployed into any J2EE-compliant web container.

The first thing that you set up is the controller servlet. This servlet processes all requests beginning /servlet that are received by the web application. This is achieved by using two different deployment-descriptor elements, including the `<servlet>` element:

```
<servlet>
    <servlet-name>FrontController</servlet-name>
    <servlet-class>
        com.apress.projsp20.ch02.store.FrontController
    </servlet-class>
    <load-on-statup>1</load-on-statup>
</servlet>
```

and the `<servlet-mapping>` element:

```
<servlet-mapping>
    <servlet-name>FrontController</servlet-name>
    <url-pattern>/servlet/*</url-pattern>
</servlet-mapping>
```

This means that the controller servlet will be requested using a path similar to the following:

http://localhost:8080/store/servlet/ActionName

where `ActionName` is the name of the class that implements the action that you wish to process our request.

Once you've mapped the controller servlet, you declare the pages to be included as the header and footer of each page in the application. This is achieved using the following elements:

```
<jsp-config>
    <jsp-property-group>
        <url-pattern>/*</url-pattern>
        <include-prelude>/header.jsp</include-prelude>
        <include-coda>/footer.jsp</include-coda>
    </jsp-property-group>
</jsp-config>
```

This says that for every page (shown by the `/*` in the `<url-pattern>` element) in the application, you'll include `/header.jsp` at the start and `/footer.jsp` at the end. This allows you to change the appearance of the site at deployment time.

You then have the `welcome` file for the application:

```
<welcome-file-list>
    <welcome-file>index.html</welcome-file>
</welcome-file-list>
```

This index page just ensures that you can direct the user to the `MainAction` without the user having to know the complex URL required.

Next you define an error page for the application. This page is invoked when a specified error occurs in any of the parts of the application. The `<error-page>` element in the deployment descriptor that does this is shown here. More information about this mechanism can be found in the earlier discussion of error codes.

```
<error-page>
    <exception-type>
          com.apress.projsp20.ch02.store.ItemAlreadyAddedException
    </exception-type>
    <location>/duplicateItem.html</location>
</error-page>
```

This definition says that whenever the exception `com.apress.projsp20.ch02.store.ItemAlreadyAddedException` is thrown, the page `duplicateItem.html` is shown. If you recall, we have said that only one item of a specific type can be added to the user's shopping cart. If this constraint is violated, then the previous exception is thrown and the user is presented with a page telling her that she cannot add duplicate items to their cart.

Deploying the Application

Now we'll demonstrate how to deploy the completed and archived application to Tomcat.

The files for this example and the earlier examples, along with the respective WAR files, are available for download from our website.

First you must create a **web application archive (WAR)** file containing the application. A WAR file is just like a JAR file except that the files must be located in specific directories and it's created using the `jar` utility. Therefore, before you can create the WAR file, you must place all the files in the correct directories (this is the same structure that you saw earlier when you deployed directly to Tomcat):

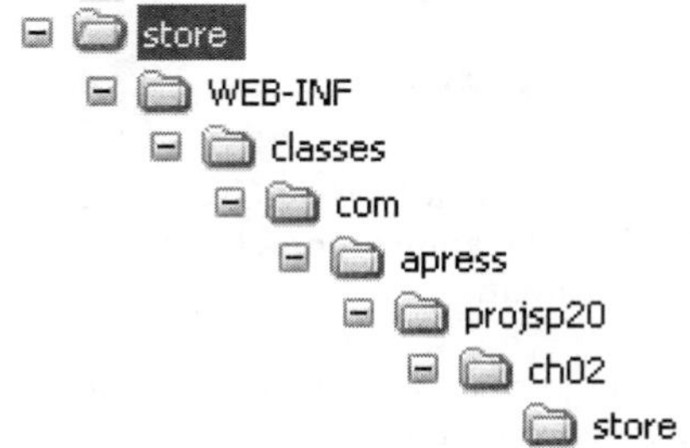

- `store` is the root directory. When you deployed to Tomcat, this was the name of the web application, but when you deploy as a WAR it's the name of the WAR file that becomes the application's name (in Tomcat). Under this directory all the JSP files (`main.jsp`, `cart.jsp`, `checkout.jsp`, `error.jsp`, `header.jsp`, and `footer.jsp`) and HTML files (`index.html`, `confirmed.html`, and `duplicateItem.html`) should be located.
- `WEB-INF` is the directory indicating that this is a web application–the directory name is case sensitive.
- `web.xml` is the deployment descriptor, which sits inside the `WEB-INF` folder.
- `classes` is the directory where you store all of the class files in appropriate subdirectories for the package structure, for example, `com/apress/projsp20/ch02/store/` (as shown here) will contain `Action.class`, `Cart.class`, `CartAction.class`, `CheckOutAction.class`, `ConfirmAction.class`, `FrontController.class`, `ItemAlreadyAddedException.class`, `MainAction.class`, and `Product.class`.

Once the files are in their respective folders, run the following command from the command prompt from the root folder as follows:

```
\store>jar -cvf store.war .
```

This will create a WAR file in the same directory that contains all of the items in the application.

Deploying with Tomcat

Deploying this application with Tomcat is simplicity itself. For basic deployments, all you need to do is copy your WAR file into the `webapps` directory of your Tomcat installation. It's located at `%TOMCAT_HOME%\webapps`. Now restart Tomcat. When Tomcat starts, it automatically detects the WAR file and explodes it, which also creates a `\META-INF` folder with a `MANIFEST.MF` file within it.

To deploy the example in a more advanced way, you can follow these steps:

1. Copy your WAR file to the webapps directory of your Tomcat installation. This step is voluntary, but it's sensible to keep your web-application deployments in the same place.

2. Add an entry to the server.xml file. This file is located in the %TOMCAT_HOME%\conf directory. The line that you should add to deploy the store application is as follows:

```
<Context path="/store" docBase="/store.war" reloadable="true"/>
```

This line declares a context to exist with its base URI being /store (this can be any valid path.) This context is fulfilled by the application at /store.war. You are passing another parameter when creating the context.

If the reloadable parameter is set to true then Tomcat monitors classes in /WEB-INF/classes and /WEB-INF/lib for changes and automatically reloads the web application if a change is detected. This feature is useful during application development, but it requires significant runtime overhead and isn't recommended for use on deployed production applications.

There are many other parameters that can be passed. Most of these are beyond the scope of this chapter, but it would be very useful to enable more control over how your application is deployed. Details of these parameters can be found at http://jakarta.apache.org/tomcat/.

3. Start Tomcat, and your application will be deployed. It can now be accessed at http://localhost:8080/store/. The home page contains a link that passes you through to the main page at http://localhost:8080/store/servlet/MainAction:

4. If you make changes to the application, create a new WAR file, copy it over the old one, and Tomcat will load the new version when restarted.

Summary

This chapter has covered a very large subject area in a very short space. It is intended as an overview and the reader is encouraged to explore more detailed texts on the subjects that it contains. You've seen that the Java Servlet API allows you to build platform-independent server-side Java components to handle user requests. You've also seen that servlets are protocol-independent but that they can be developed for specific protocols, particularly HTTP.

You've also looked at the deployment of servlets-based web applications, with particular attention paid to the deployment descriptor. You've seen how the deployment descriptor describes servlets to the container. You learned about the new deployment-descriptor elements that support the configuration of JSP 2.0 pages, which include the ability to enable and disable the EL and scripting as well as the ability to automatically include other pages at the start and end of a group of JSP pages.

3

The JavaServer Pages Expression Language

One of the new features of the JSP 2.0 specification that you'll be using most often is the **JSP expression language**, an intentionally simple language that is, to a large extent, independent from JSP.

In previous incarnations of JSP, Java code was embedded into JSP pages in the form of scriptlets, for example:

```
<%
  MyBean bean = new MyBean();
  String name = bean.getName();
  out.println(name);
%>
```

This scriptlet creates a new instance of a class called `MyBean`, gets its `name` property, assigns this to a string variable, and then outputs this string to the page. Now you might be looking at this and thinking, "I can achieve the same thing using the JSP standard actions (`useBean` and `getProperty`)."

While this is certainly true, it was previously extremely hard to write a function-rich JSP-based web application without using a number of scriptlets within your pages. In fact, there are many problems associated with using Java code in the form of scriptlets in JSP pages. The first and most obvious of these is that it's very common for non-Java programmers to create the user interface for a system. This is because graphic designers are generally better at creating functional user interfaces than Java programmers! The second problem caused by the use of scriptlets is that of maintainability. Embedding large amounts of code into the user interface of a system makes the interface much harder to change and understand.

For all of these reasons, the JSP 2.0 specification introduces an expression language (EL) that can do pretty much everything that scriptlets can do. This language is far simpler to understand than Java and looks very similar to JavaScript. The following are good reasons for this similarity:

- JavaScript is something that most page authors are already familiar with.
- The EL is inspired by ECMAScript, which is the standardized version of JavaScript.

In fact, both ECMAScript and the XPath EL inspired the JSP EL. The expert groups responsible for the EL were reluctant to design yet another one, but both ECMAScript and XPath fell short in several different areas.

If you've been following the progress of JSP 2.0, particularly the JSP Standard Tag Library (JSTL), you're probably wondering whether the EL used within JSTL is the same as the one in JSP 2.0. Actually, the EL used in JSTL 1.0 is slightly different. However, the JSTL team has agreed that it will be compatible with the JSP 2.0 EL.

In this chapter you'll learn the following:

- The syntax and usage of the EL, including reserved words, disabling scriptlets in a page, and disabling the evaluation of the EL on a page or set of pages
- The operators within the EL, including arithmetic operators, comparison operators, logical operators, and other operators
- Using JavaBeans with the EL
- The implicit objects within the EL
- The declaration and use of functions in the EL

The Syntax and Use of the Expression Language

In this section you'll look at the syntax of the EL, see how to use it on a JSP page, and learn the reserved words of the language. Once you've looked at the basics you'll move on to look at how and why you might disable the EL and Java scriptlets within a page or set of pages.

Basic Syntax

No matter where the EL is used, it's always invoked in a consistent manner, via the construct `${expr}`, where `expr` is the EL expression that you wish to have evaluated.

A simple use of the EL is shown here. This piece of code creates a bean and outputs its `name` property:

```
<jsp:useBean id="bean" class="MyBean"/>

${bean.name}
```

We'll discuss the detailed syntax of the use of JavaBeans later in the "JavaBeans and the Expression Language" section.

Note that in the previous example you used the useBean standard action to create the object. This is the recommended way to do this, rather than instantiating it in a scriptlet.

Literals

Just as in any programming language, the EL provides several literals for developers to use. A literal can be of a Boolean, integer, floating-point, string, or null type. The following are valid values for each literal type:

- **Boolean**: true or false.
- **Integer**: This is limited to values defined by the IntegerLiteral regular expression as follows:

```
IntegerLiteral ::=- ["+"."-"] ["1"-"9"](["0"-"9"])*
```

  This might look rather complicated, but it is in fact very simple. All that this regular expression says is that an integer can begin with a "+" or a "-" symbol, followed by any digit from 1 to 9 followed by any number of digits from 0 to 9. For example, the following are valid integers:

  - \- 102
  - \+ 21
  - \+ 21234

  However, -+ 01 is not a valid integer.

- **Floating Point**: This is defined by the following FloatingPointLiteral expression:

```
FloatingPointLiteral  ::=- (["+","-"])? (["0"-"9"])+ "." (["0"-"9"])*
(["e","E"] (["+","-"])? (["0"-"9"])+)?| (["+","-"])? "." (["0"-"9"])+
(["e","E"] (["+","-"])? (["0"-"9"])+)?| (["+","-"])? (["0"-"9"])+ ["e","E"]
(["+","-"])?(["0"-"9"])+
```

  This expression is significantly more complex. To help you understand this, you can look at some valid and invalid floating-point literals. The following are valid:

  - -1.09
  - -1.003
  - +1.0E10
  - -10.0
  - +0.1

  And the following are invalid:

  - -1
  - +-12.2

- **String**: A string can be represented with either single or double quotes. For example, `"a string"` and `'a string'` are both valid; however, `"as'` and `'as"` are not valid. If you want to represent quotes within a string, then you can use `\"` for double quotes, or `\'` for single quotes. In order to represent a \ in a string you use the escape sequence \\.
- **Null**: You can represent Null by using the string `null`.

Default Values and the Expression Language

Experience suggests that it's most important to be able to provide as good a presentation as possible, even when there are simple errors in the page. To meet this requirement, the EL does not provide warnings, just "default values" and "errors." Default values are type-correct values that are assigned to a subexpression when there is a problem and errors are exceptions to be thrown (and then handled by the standard JSP machinery). An example of such a default value is the value `'infinity'`. This is assigned to an expression that results in a divide by zero. For example, the following piece of EL will display infinity rather than causing an error:

```
${2/0}
```

Using the Expression Language

You can use the EL in the same places as you would have used a scriplet, for example:

- Attribute values for JSP custom tags
- Within template text (that is, in the body of the page)

Using the Expression Language Within Custom Tags

Using the EL within the attributes of a custom tag in a JSP allows you to dynamically specify the attribute values for a custom tag. This is an extremely powerful mechanism. The following code snippet shows how you might dynamically specify an attribute to a custom tag:

```
<myTagLibrary:myTag counter="<%= 1+1 %>">

</myTagLibrary:myTag>
```

In order to achieve this dynamic behavior in the previous version of the JSP specification, you had to use scriptlets. As we've discussed, scriptlets are untidy and cause all sorts of problems with readability and maintainability. With JSP 2.0, you can use the EL to dynamically provide the values to a custom tags attribute. If you were to repeat the previous tag example using the EL, you would see that it was much neater:

```
<myTagLibrary:myTag counter="${1+1}">

</myTagLibrary:iterate>
```

You can see that the value `1+1` is being passed to the custom tag as an attribute named `counter`. The details of the creation of custom tags are discussed at length in Chapters 5 through 7.

You'll look at more advanced use of the language with JavaBeans, arithmetic, and comparisons later in this chapter.

Using the Expression Language Within JSP Template Text

Now that you've seen how the EL can be used to provide the values of custom tag attributes, you'll learn how you can use the EL within the body of a JSP page so that you can produce dynamic content. The following code shows an example of a JSP page with some dynamic content generated by the EL. This page displays the value of a parameter (passed to the page) called `name`. The user is then given a text field in which to enter a new name and a button to submit it back to the page for another greeting:

```
<html>
  <head>
    <title>EL and Template Text</title>
    <style>
      body, td {font-family:verdana;font-size:10pt;}
    </style>
  <head>
  <body>
    <h2>EL and Template Text</h2>
    <table border="1">
      <tr>
        <td>Hello ${param['name']}</td>
        <td> </td>
      </tr>
      <tr>
        <form action="templateText.jsp" method="post">
          <td><input type="text" name="name"></td>
          <td><input type="submit"></td>
        </form>
      </tr>
    </table>
  </body>
</html>
```

In order to run this example, you need to deploy it into a JSP 2.0-compliant web container:

1. Create the directory `%TOMCAT_HOME%/webapps/expressionLanguage/WEB-INF`.

2. Create the `web.xml` file:

```
<?xml version="1.0" encoding="ISO-8859-1"?>
<web-app xmlns="http://java.sun.com/xml/ns/j2ee"
        xmlns:xsi="http://www.w3.org/2001/XMLSchema-instance"
```

```
        xsi:schemaLocation="http://java.sun.com/xml/ns/j2ee web-app_2_4.xsd"
        version="2.4">
</webapp>
```

3. Copy the JSP to a file called `templateText.jsp` and save it in the `expressionLanguage` folder.

4. Start Tomcat, open your web browser, and go to http://localhost:8080/expressionLanguage/templateText.jsp.

You should see a page similar to the following screen shot:

As you can see, this page is a very simple, personalized greeting. You'll look at how the request variable is accessed later on in the section on implicit variables. For now, try entering different values within the text box and clicking Submit Query.

Reserved Words

As with any other language, the JSP EL has many words that are reserved. A reserved word is one that has a special meaning within the language (also known as a keyword). This means that you cannot use it to represent anything else, such as a variable identifier. The reserved words in the JSP EL are as follows:

```
and  eq  gt  true   instanceof
or   ne  lt  false  empty
not  if  ge  null   div   mod
```

It's worth noting that not all of these words are currently in the language, but they may be in the future, and developers should avoid using them.

You'll see examples of using the majority of the reserved words during the course of this chapter.

Disabling Scriptlets

As we've mentioned, the EL is intended to replace the use of Java scriptlets in developing JSP-based web applications. To this end it's possible to prevent the use of scriptlets through configuration parameters. This allows a developer to ensure that no one inadvertently uses scriptlets instead of the EL. This can allow best practices to be more easily enforced.

You can disable scriptlets within a page using the `web.xml` deployment descriptor by choosing to disable evaluation for the following:

- One page
- A set of pages
- The entire application

The tags that you need to add to the deployment descriptor are within the `<jsp-config>` element. The following excerpt shows an example that disables scriptlets for all JSP pages within an application:

```
<jsp-config>
  <jsp-property-group>
    <url-pattern>*.jsp</url-pattern>
    <scripting-enabled>false</scripting-enabled>
  </jsp-property-group>
</jsp-config>
```

The `<url-pattern>` element can represent a single page, for example:

```
<jsp-config>
  <jsp-property-group>
    <url-pattern>/test.jsp</url-pattern>
    <scripting-enabled>false</scripting-enabled>
  </jsp-property-group>
</jsp-config>
```

It can also represent a set of pages, for example:

```
<jsp-config>
  <jsp-property-group>
    <url-pattern>/noscriptlets/</url-pattern>
    <scripting-enabled>false</scripting-enabled>
  </jsp-property-group>
</jsp-config>
```

Disabling the Expression Language

Just as you can disable scriptlets within a page, you can also disable the evaluation of the EL. In previous versions of JSP, the characters `${` had no special meaning, therefore it's possible that people have used them in their JSP pages. If you were to try to deploy these pages on a JSP 2.0-compliant web container, you would get errors. The page overleaf shows the kind of error that you could expect to see:

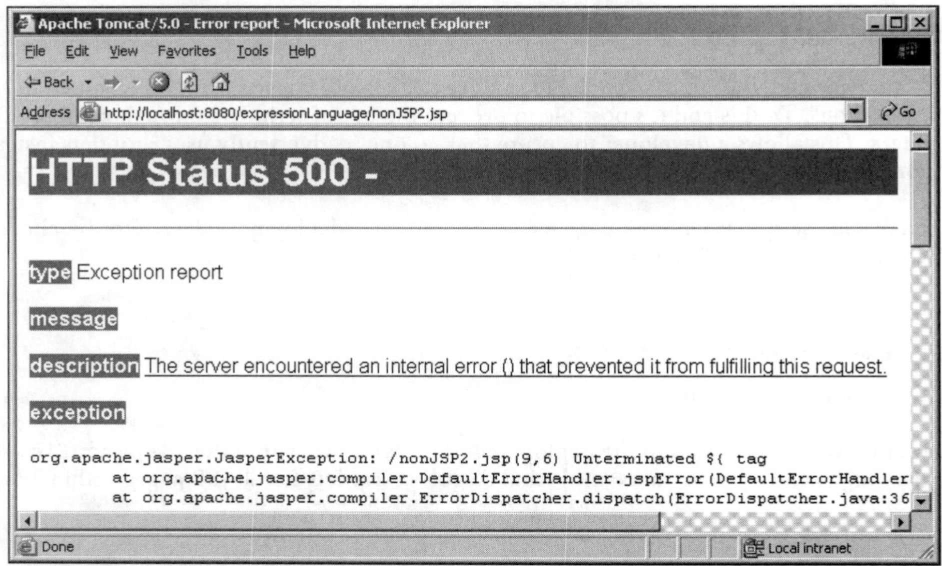

It's worth noting that if a web application is deployed using a Servlet 2.3 deployment descriptor (that is, one that conforms to the 2.3 DTD http://java.sun.com/dtd/web-app_2_3.dtd) then the evaluation of the EL is automatically deactivated. This is to reduce the chance that an error will occur when a web container is upgraded. Conversely, if a web application is deployed with a Servlet 2.4 deployment descriptor (that is, it conforms to the 2.4 XML Schema http://java.sun.com/xml/ns/j2ee/web-app_2_4.xsd) then the EL is enabled by default.

As with the disabling of scriptlets, you can disable EL evaluation in two ways:

- Individually on each page using the page directive
- Within the `web.xml` file by using a JSP configuration element

In order to temporarily disable the EL for a single page it's simplest to use the `isELIgnored` attribute of the page directive in the header of the page:

```
<%@ page isELIgnored="true" %>
```

If you choose to disable evaluation within the `web.xml` file, you can disable for a single page, a set of pages, or the entire application. The following XML example shows how you might disable the EL for an entire application:

```
<jsp-property-group>
  <url-pattern>*.jsp</url-pattern>
  <el-enabled>false</el-enabled>
</jsp-property-group>
```

In order to disable the evaluation of the EL for a single page within the deployment descriptor, you can use an XML fragment similar to the following:

```
<jsp-property-group>
  <url-pattern>noel.jsp</url-pattern>
  <el-enabled>false</el-enabled>
</jsp-property-group>
```

In order to disable the evaluation of the EL for a set of pages within the deployment descriptor, you can use an XML fragment similar to the following:

```
<jsp-property-group>
  <url-pattern>/noel/</url-pattern>
  <el-enabled>false</el-enabled>
</jsp-property-group>
```

If you try to use the EL after you've disabled it, you won't see any errors and the `${expr}` expression within the JSP will appear unaltered in the final output.

Arithmetic Evaluation Using the Expression Language

Now that you've examined the basic syntax of the EL and where it can be used, you'll look at some specific uses of the language. The first of these is using the EL to evaluate arithmetic operations. There are many cases within web-application development where you need to perform some mathematics on a page. This might be to show a number within the text of a page, or it might be to pass to a custom tag to allow it to perform its job. In either case the concepts are exactly the same.

Arithmetic operators are provided to act on both integer (long) and floating-point values. There are six operators that you can use and combine to achieve the vast majority of mathematical calculations with ease. These operators are

- Addition: `+`
- Subtraction: `-`
- Multiplication: `*`
- Exponents: `E`
- Division: `/` or `div`
- Modulus: `%` or `mod`

The last two operators are presented with two alternative syntaxes (both will produce exactly the same result). This is so that the EL is consistent with both the XPath and ECMAScript syntaxes. You can use all of the operators in a binary fashion (that is, with two arguments, such as `2 + 3`) and the subtraction operator to represent the unary minus (that is, `-4 + -2`).

As you would expect, each operator has a precedence that determines the order of evaluation of an expression. This precedence is as follows:

- `()`
- `-` (unary)

- `* / div mod %`
- `+ -` (binary)

You'll update this list when you look at the comparison operators in the next section. You can, of course, use parentheses to change the order of evaluation, as these take the highest precedence.

With operators of equal precedence the expression is evaluated from left to right, for example:

```
1 + 2 + 3 = 6
1 + 2 = 3
```

The following JSP code shows an example of all of the operators in action:

```
<html>
<head>
  <title>Arithmetic</title>
  <style>
    body, td {font-family:verdana;font-size:10pt;}
  </style>
</head>
<body>
  <h2>EL Arithmetic</h2>
  <table border="1">
    <tr>
      <td><b>Concept</b></td>
      <td><b>EL Expression</b></td>
      <td><b>Result</b></td>
    </tr>
    <tr>
      <td>Literal</td>
      <td>${'${'}10}</td>
      <td>${10}</td>
    </tr>
    <tr>
      <td>Addition</td>
      <td>${'${'}10 + 10 }</td>
      <td>${10 + 10}</td>
    </tr>
    <tr>
      <td>Subtraction</td>
      <td>${'${'}10 - 10 }</td>
      <td>${10 - 10}</td>
    </tr>
    <tr>
      <td>Multiplication</td>
      <td>${'${'}10 * 10 }</td>
      <td>${10 * 10}</td>
    </tr>
    <tr>
```

```
        <td>Division / </td>
        <td>${'${'}10 / 3 }</td>
        <td>${10 / 3}</td>
      </tr>
      <tr>
        <td>Division DIV</td>
        <td>${'${'}10 div 3 }</td>
        <td>${10 div 3}</td>
      </tr>
      <tr>
        <td>Modulus</td>
        <td>${'${'}10 % 10 }</td>
        <td>${10 % 3}</td>
      </tr>
      <tr>
        <td>Modulus</td>
        <td>${'${'}10 mod 10 }</td>
        <td>${10 mod 3}</td>
      </tr>
      <tr>
        <td>Division by Zero</td>
        <td>${'${'}10 / 0 }</td>
        <td>${10 / 0}</td>
      </tr>
      <tr>
        <td>Exponential</td>
        <td>${'${'}2E2}</td>
        <td>${2E2}</td>
      </tr>
      <tr>
        <td>Unary Minus</td>
        <td>${'${'}-10}</td>
        <td>${-10}</td>
      </tr>
    </table>
  </body>
</html>
```

In order to run this example you need to deploy it into a JSP 2.0-compliant web container just as you did earlier.

1. Copy the previous JSP sample to a file called `arithmetic.jsp` and save it to the `%TOMCAT_HOME%/webapps/expressionLanguage/` directory.

2. Start Tomcat, open your web browser, and go to http://localhost:8080/expressionLanguage/arithmetic.jsp.

You should see the following output:

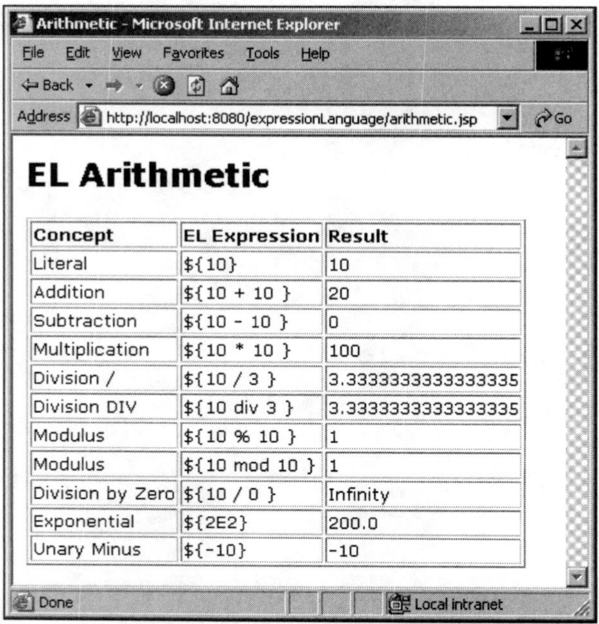

As you can see, all that this JSP does is print out the result of the expression next to the expression itself. It also demonstrates an interesting technique; that of displaying the `${` characters on a JSP page. This is easily achieved using a series of EL escape characters. For example to show the string `${2+3}` on a JSP page, you can use the following expression:

```
${'${'}2 + 3 }
```

You may have read this section and thought that the operators that are provided are not powerful enough. For example where is the square root operator? Advanced operators are deliberately not provided to the JSP developer because advanced calculations should not be done in a page. They should either be done in the controller layer of our application, or by using view-helper components such as custom tags or EL functions (see the section on functions later in this chapter).

Comparisons in the Expression Language

Another useful feature of the EL is the ability to perform comparisons, either between numbers or objects. This feature is used primarily for the values of custom tag attributes, but can equally be used to write out the result of a comparison (`true` or `false`) to the JSP page. The EL provides the following comparison operators:

- `==` or `eq`
- `!=` or `ne`

- < or `lt`
- > or `gt`
- <= or `le`
- >= or `ge`

The second version of the last four operators exists to avoid having to have entity references in JSP XML syntax; however, the behavior of the operators is the same.

In the following example, you can see the comparison operators in use:

```
<html>
<head>
  <title>EL Conditions</title>
  <style>
    body, td {font-family:verdana;font-size:10pt;}
  </style>
</head>
<body>
  <h2>EL Conditions</h2>
  <table border="1">
    <tr>
      <td><b>Concept</b></td>
      <td><b>EL Condition</b></td>
      <td><b>Result</b></td>
    </tr>
    <tr>
      <td>Numeric less than</td>
      <td>${'${'}1 &lt; 2}</td>
      <td>${1 < 2}</td>
    </tr>
    <tr>
      <td>Numeric greater than</td>
      <td>${'${'}1 &gt; 2}</td>
      <td>${1 > 2}</td>
    </tr>
    <tr>
      <td>Numeric less than</td>
      <td>${'${'}1 lt 2}</td>
      <td>${1 lt 2}</td>
    </tr>
    <tr>
      <td>Numeric greater than</td>
      <td>${'${'}1 gt 2}</td>
      <td>${1 gt 2}</td>
    </tr>
    <tr>
      <td>Numeric Greater than or equal</td>
      <td>${'${'}1 &gt;= 1}</td>
      <td>${1 >= 1}</td>
    </tr>
    <tr>
```

```
      <td>Numeric Less than or equal</td>
      <td>${'${'}1 &lt;= 1}</td>
      <td>${1 <= 1}</td>
    </tr>
    <tr>
      <td>Numeric less than or equal</td>
      <td>${'${'}1 le 1}</td>
      <td>${1 le 1}</td>
    </tr>
    <tr>
      <td>Numeric greater than or equal</td>
      <td>${'${'}1 ge 1}</td>
      <td>${1 ge 1}</td>
    </tr>
    <tr>
      <td>Numeric equal to</td>
      <td>${'${'}1 == 1}</td>
      <td>${1 == 1}</td>
    </tr>
    <tr>
      <td>Numeric equal to</td>
      <td>${'${'}1 eq 1}</td>
      <td>${1 eq 1}</td>
    </tr>
    <tr>
      <td>Numeric no equal to</td>
      <td>${'${'}1 != 2}</td>
      <td>${1 != 2}</td>
    </tr>
    <tr>
      <td>Numeric not equal to</td>
      <td>${'${'}1 ne 2}</td>
      <td>${1 ne 2}</td>
    </tr>
    <tr>
      <td>Alphabetic less than</td>
      <td>${'${'}'abe' &lt; 'ade'}</td>
      <td>${'abe' < 'ade'}</td>
    </tr>
    <tr>
      <td>Alphabetic greater than</td>
      <td>${'${'}'abe' &gt; 'ade'}</td>
      <td>${'abe' > 'ade'}</td>
    </tr>
    <tr>
      <td>Alphabetic equal to</td>
      <td>${'${'}'abe' eq 'abe'}</td>
      <td>${'abe' eq 'abe'}</td>
    </tr>
    <tr>
      <td>Alphabetic not equal to</td>
      <td>${'${'}'abe' ne 'ade'}</td>
      <td>${'abe' ne 'ade'}</td>
    </tr>
```

```
    </table>
    </body>
</html>
```

Again, you'll deploy it into a JSP 2.0-compliant web container.

1. Place the previous JSP code sample in a file called `conditions.jsp` and save it to the `expressionLanguage` folder.

2. Start Tomcat, open your web browser, and go to http://localhost:8080/expressionLanguage/conditions.jsp.

You should see the following page:

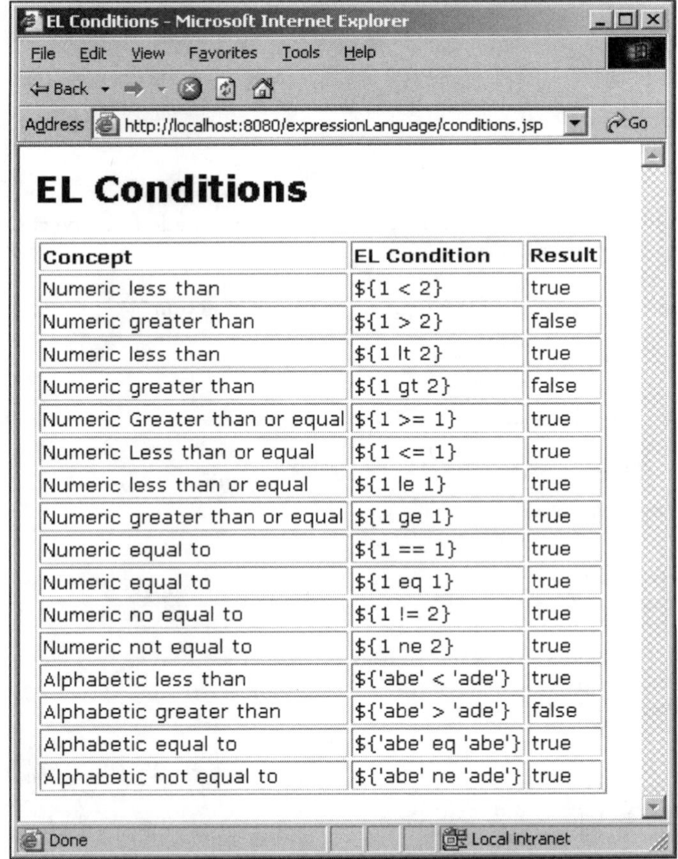

EL Conditions

Concept	EL Condition	Result
Numeric less than	${1 < 2}	true
Numeric greater than	${1 > 2}	false
Numeric less than	${1 lt 2}	true
Numeric greater than	${1 gt 2}	false
Numeric Greater than or equal	${1 >= 1}	true
Numeric Less than or equal	${1 <= 1}	true
Numeric less than or equal	${1 le 1}	true
Numeric greater than or equal	${1 ge 1}	true
Numeric equal to	${1 == 1}	true
Numeric equal to	${1 eq 1}	true
Numeric no equal to	${1 != 2}	true
Numeric not equal to	${1 ne 2}	true
Alphabetic less than	${'abe' < 'ade'}	true
Alphabetic greater than	${'abe' > 'ade'}	false
Alphabetic equal to	${'abe' eq 'abe'}	true
Alphabetic not equal to	${'abe' ne 'ade'}	true

You are now in a position to update your precedence table from the previous section with the comparison operators. Again parentheses can be used to alter the order of evaluation, and identical precedence operators are evaluated from left to right as follows:

- `()`
- `-` (unary)
- `* / div mod %`
- `+ -` (binary)
- `< > <= >= lt gt le ge`
- `== != eq ne`

Logical Operators in the Expression Language

The EL also provides you with the ability to perform logical operations on Boolean arguments. The logical operators are

- `&&` or `and`
- `||` or `or`
- `!` or `not`

Once again, there are alternatives for each of the operators.

If either of the arguments is not Boolean, an attempt will be made to convert them to Boolean; if this is not possible, then an error will occur.

This code shows some examples of the logical operators in action:

```
<html>
<head>
  <title>EL Logic</title>
  <style>
    body, td {font-family:verdana;font-size:10pt;}
  </style>
</head>
<body>
  <h2>EL Logic</h2>
  <table border="1">
    <tr>
      <td><b>Concept</b></td>
      <td><b>EL Expression</b></td>
      <td><b>Result</b></td>
    </tr>
    <tr>
      <td>And</td>
      <td>${'${'}true and true}</td>
      <td>${true and true}</td>
    </tr>
    <tr>
      <td>And</td>
      <td>${'${'}true && false}</td>
      <td>${true && false}</td>
    </tr>
```

```
        <tr>
          <td>Or</td>
          <td>${'${'}true or true}</td>
          <td>${true or false}</td>
        </tr>
        <tr>
          <td>Or</td>
          <td>${'${'}true || false}</td>
          <td>${true || false}</td>
        </tr>
        <tr>
          <td>Not</td>
          <td>${'${'}not true}</td>
          <td>${not true}</td>
        </tr>
        <tr>
          <td>Not</td>
          <td>${'${'}'!false}</td>
          <td>${!false}</td>
        </tr>
      </table>
    </body>
  </html>
```

Once again, you'll run this example by deploying it in a JSP 2.0-compliant web container.

1. Copy the previous JSP sample to a file called `logic.jsp` and save it to the `expressionLanguage` folder.

2. Start Tomcat, go to http://localhost:8080/expressionLanguage/logic.jsp, and you'll see the following page:

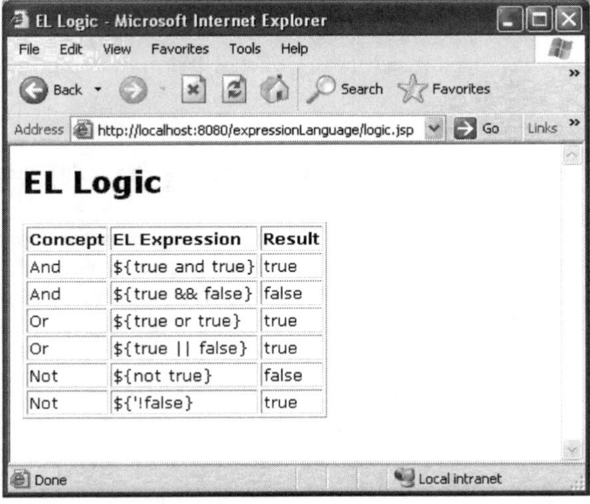

Other Operators

Besides the arithmetic, logic, and conditional operators that you've seen so far, there are several other operators that are available to developers using the EL. These operators are mainly related to objects. A property or method of an object can be accessed using either the `.` or `[]` operator, which is deliberate in order to align the language with ECMAScript. For example, `obj.property` is equivalent to `obj["property"]`.

This allows you to access the items within maps, lists, or arrays. For example to access the item in a map with the key `"sam"`, you could use `myMap["sam"]` or `myMap.sam`.

The final operator that you'll look at is the `empty` operator. The `empty` operator is a prefix operator that can be used to determine if a value is null or empty. To evaluate the expression `empty A`, you first check to see if A is null. If A is null then it returns `true`. If A is an empty string, array, map, or an empty list then it also returns `true`. If it's not null or empty, it returns `false`.

Now that you've seen all of the operators available, you can again update your precedence table to include these new operators:

- `[]`
- `()`
- `-` (unary) `not ! empty`
- `* / div % mod`
- `+ -` (binary)
- `< > <= >= lt gt le ge`
- `== != eq ne`
- `&& and`
- `|| or`

You'll see much more about these operators in our discussion of using the EL with JavaBeans in the next section.

JavaBeans and the Expression Language

So far you've looked at the syntax of the EL. This in itself is not very useful when creating web applications. In this section you'll focus on how to use the EL to read values from JavaBeans to display within a JSP. In previous incarnations of the JSP specification you would have had to use code such as the following to read values from a JavaBean:

```
<jsp:getProperty name="myBean" property="name" />
```

An alternative (and more common) method is to use a scriptlet such as the following:

```
<%= myBean.getName()%>
```

As we've discussed, the use of scriptlets does not represent good practice in JSP development. This may make you ask the question, "If I can use the getProperty standard action, why does any one use scriptlets?" The answer to this question is simple: We developers are lazy! The scriptlet option represents less code and is a lot quicker to type!

To get around this problem, the EL provides a nice way to access the properties of a JavaBean that is in scope within a page, request, session, or application. To achieve the same as the previous code sample, you can use the following expression:

```
${myBean.name}
```

This is a nice neat way to access properties; there are no nasty brackets or any other Java-like syntax present. This brings us to another core feature of the EL: the concept of named variables. The EL provides a generalized mechanism for resolving variable names into objects. This mechanism has the same behavior as the pageContext.findAttribute() method of the PageContext object. Take the following, for example:

```
${product}
```

This expression will look for the attribute named product by searching the page, request, session, and application scopes, and will print its value. If the attribute is not found, then null will be returned. This method is also used to resolve the implicit objects that we'll talk about in the next section.

The following example shows how you can access JavaBeans within a JSP using the EL:

```
<jsp:useBean id="person" class="com.apress.projsp20.ch03.Person" scope="request">
  <jsp:setProperty name="person" property="*"/>
</jsp:useBean>

<html>
  <head>
    <title>EL and Simple JavaBeans</title>
    <style>
      body, td {font-family:verdana;font-size:10pt;}
    </style>
  <head>
  <body>
    <h2>EL and Simple JavaBeans</h2>
    <table border="1">
      <tr>
        <td>${person.name}</td>
        <td>${person.age}</td>
        <td> </td>
      </tr>
      <tr>
        <form action="simpleBean.jsp" method="post">
          <td><input type="text" name="name"></td>
          <td><input type="text" name="age"></td>
          <td><input type="submit"></td>
        </form>
      <tr>
```

```
    </table>
  </body>
</html>
```

Again, you'll deploy this into a JSP 2.0-compliant web container.

1. Create a file called `simpleBean.jsp` in the `expressionLanguage` folder, and enter the previous JSP code sample into it.

2. Inside the `expressionLanguage/WEB-INF` directory, create a directory called `classes`.

3. Create a `com/apress/projsp20/ch03` subdirectory within the `WEB-INF/classes` directory.

4. Create a file called `Person.java` within the `WEB-INF/classes/com/apress/projsp20/ch03` directory with the following contents, and compile it:

```
package com.apress.projsp20.ch03;

public class Person {

    private String name;
    private int age;

    public Person() {
        setName("A N Other");
        setAge(21);
    }

    public void setName(String name) {
        this.name = name;
    }

    public String getName() {
        return name;
    }

    public void setAge(int age) {
        this.age = age;
    }

    public int getAge() {
        return age;
    }
}
```

5. Start Tomcat and your web browser and go to http://localhost:8080/expressionLanguage/simpleBean.jsp.

You should see something similar to the following page:

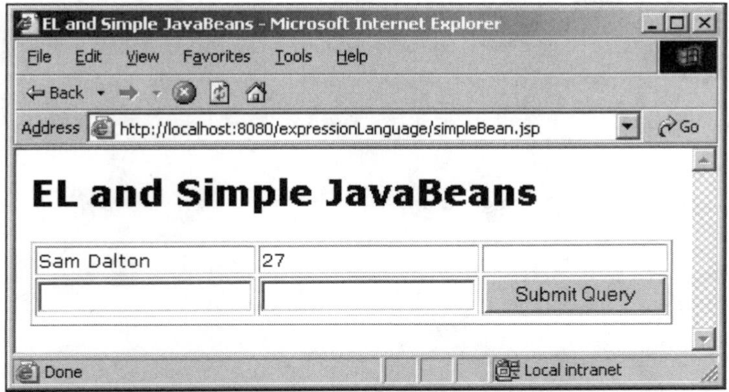

This example creates a JavaBean of type `com.apress.projsp20.ch03.Person` with an `id` of `Person`, and sets its values to values with the same name as the properties that are on the HTTP request. This is achieved with the following code:

```
<jsp:useBean id="person" class="com.apress.projsp20.ch03.Person" scope="request">
  <jsp:setProperty name="person" property="*"/>
</jsp:useBean>
```

The JSP accesses the class via the `id` given to it in the previous `useBean` tag, in this case, `person`. The page then displays the values of the properties of the `Person` bean in a table; this is achieved by the following code:

```
<tr>
  <td>${person.name}</td>
  <td>${person.age}</td>
  <td> </td>
</tr>
```

As you can see the `id` is used to access the JavaBean that you declared with the previous `useBean` tag.

It's worth noting that you could have equally used the following code to access the properties of our JavaBean:

```
<tr>
  <td>${person["name"]}</td>
  <td>${person["age"]}</td>
  <td> </td>
</tr>
```

The following code for the `com.apress.projsp20.ch03.Person` bean is shown here:

```
package com.apress.projsp20.ch03;

public class Person {

  private String name;
  private int age;

  public Person() {
    setName("A N Other");
    setAge(21);
  }

  public void setName(String name) {
    this.name = name;
  }
  public String getName() {
    return name;
  }
  public void setAge(int age) {
    this.age = age;
  }

  public int getAge() {
    return age;
  }
}
```

Try changing the values in the form and clicking Submit Query. You should see your new values in the table. Now that you've seen a very simple use of JavaBeans and the EL, you'll look at a more complex use of the two technologies.

Nested Properties of a JavaBean

The EL provides you with a simple mechanism to access nested properties of a JavaBean. For example you may have the following JavaBean, which has a nested JavaBean property (`Person.java`):

```
package com.apress.projsp20.ch03;

import java.util.Collection;

public class Person {

  private String name;
  private int age;
  private Address address;

  public Person() {
    setName("A N Other");
    setAge(21);
```

```
    this.address = new Address();
  }

  public void setName(String name) {
    this.name = name;
  }

  public String getName() {
    return name;
  }

  public void setAge(int age) {
    this.age = age;
  }

  public int getAge() {
    return age;
  }

  public void setAddress(Address address) {
    this.address = address;
  }

  public Address getAddress() {
    return address;
  }
}
```

As you can see, this JavaBean has a property that is in fact another JavaBean–the `Address` JavaBean (`Address.java`). This JavaBean is shown in exactly the same way as the previous example:

```
package com.apress.projsp20.ch03;

import java.util.Collection;

public class Address {

  private String line1;
  private String town;
  private String county;
  private String postcode;
  private Collection phoneNumbers;

  public Address() {
    this.line1 = "line1";
    this.town = "a town2";
    this.county = "a county";
    this.postcode = "postcode";
  }

  public void setLine1(String line1) {
    this.line1 = line1;
  }
```

```
  public String getLine1() {
    return line1;
  }

  public void setTown(String town) {
    this.town = town;
  }

  public String getTown() {
    return town;
  }

  public void setCounty(String county) {
    this.county = county;
  }

  public String getCounty() {
    return county;
  }

  public void setPostcode(String postcode) {
    this.postcode = postcode;
  }

  public String getPostcode() {
    return postcode;
  }

  public Collection getPhoneNumbers() {
    return phoneNumbers;
  }

  public void setPhoneNumbers(Collection phoneNumbers) {
    this.phoneNumbers = phoneNumbers;
  }
}
```

It's very simple to access these nested properties using the EL. The following JSP snippet shows how you might achieve this:

```
${person.address.line1}
```

The address JavaBean contains a collection of other JavaBeans–`PhoneNumber` JavaBeans (`PhoneNumber.java`). This JavaBean is shown in the following example:

```
package com.apress.projsp20.ch03;

public class PhoneNumber {

  private String std;
  private String number;
```

```
  public String get Number() {
    return number;
  }

  public String getStd() {
    return std;
  }

  public void setNumber(String number) {
    this.number = number;
  }

  public void setStd(String std) {
    this.std = std;
  }
}
```

The EL also provides a simple mechanism for accessing such collections and the properties of their enclosed JavaBeans. The following JSP snippet would access the first phone number for a person's address:

```
${person.address.phoneNumbers[1].number}
```

We can bring this whole discussion together by way of the following example. This is a JSP page that displays all of the details relating to a person and their addresses. Note how we move between the alternative syntaxes for object property access (`complexBean.jsp`):

```
<jsp:useBean id="person" class="com.apress.projsp20.ch03.Person" scope="request"
/>
<html>
<head>
  <title>EL and Complex JavaBeans</title>
  <style>
    body, td {font-family:verdana;font-size:10pt;}
  </style>
</head>
<body>
  <h2>EL and Complex JavaBeans</h2>
  <table border="1">
    <tr>
      <td>${person.name}</td>
      <td>${person.age}</td>
      <td>${person["address"].line1}</td>
      <td>${person["address"].town}</td>
      <td>${person.address.phoneNumbers[0].std}
          ${person.address.phoneNumbers[0].number}</td>
      <td>${person.address.phoneNumbers[1].std}
          ${person.address.phoneNumbers[1].number}</td>
    </tr>
  </table>
</body>
</html>
```

If you were to deploy this to a JSP 2.0-compliant web container in the manner described previously (making sure to also compile the `Address.java` and `PhoneNumber.java` classes) then you would see a page similar to the following:

It's worth noting that this example uses a simple Java servlet in order to set up the information within the JavaBeans. For completeness, the code for this servlet (`PopulateServlet.java`) is here:

```
package com.apress.projsp20.ch03;

import java.io.IOException;
import java.util.ArrayList;
import javax.servlet.RequestDispatcher;
import javax.servlet.ServletException;
import javax.servlet.http.HttpServlet;
import javax.servlet.http.HttpServletRequest;
import javax.servlet.http.HttpServletResponse;

public class PopulateServlet extends HttpServlet {

  protected void doGet(HttpServletRequest req, HttpServletResponse res)
    throws ServletException, IOException
  {

    Person p = new Person();
    p.setName("Sam Dalton");
    p.setAge(26);

    Address a = new Address();
    a.setLine1("221b Baker Street");
    a.setTown("London");
    a.setCounty("Greater London");
    a.setPostcode("NW1 1AA");
    ArrayList al = new ArrayList();
    PhoneNumber ph = new PhoneNumber();
    ph.setStd("01895");
    ph.setStd("678901");
    al.add(ph);
```

```
        ph = new PhoneNumber();
        ph.setStd("0208");
        ph.setStd("8654789");
        al.add(ph);
        a.setPhoneNumbers(al);
        p.setAddress(a);
        req.setAttribute("person", p);
        RequestDispatcher rd = req.getRequestDispatcher("complexBean.jsp");
        rd.forward(req, res);
    }
  }
```

This servlet class should be placed within the WEB-INF/classes/com/apress/projsp20/ch03 folder. You'll also need to modify the WEB-INF/web.xml file to contain the following:

```
<?xml version="1.0" encoding="ISO-8859-1"?>
<web-app xmlns="http://java.sun.com/xml/ns/j2ee"
         xmlns:xsi="http://www.w3.org/2001/XMLSchema-instance"
         xsi:schemaLocation="http://java.sun.com/xml/ns/j2ee web-app_2_4.xsd"
         version="2.4">

  <servlet>
        <servlet-name>BeanTestServlet</servlet-name>
        <servlet-class>com.apress.projsp20.ch03.PopulateServlet</servlet-class>
    </servlet>

    <servlet-mapping
        <servlet-name>BeanTestServlet</servlet-name>
        <url-pattern>/BeanTest</url-pattern>
    </servlet-mapping>
</web-app>
```

The Expression Language Implicit Objects

Within JSP scriptlets you have many implicit objects available to you. These objects allow you to access things such as the request, session, and page context. The EL also provides you with these implicit objects, and a lot more besides. The objects are always available under well-known names and are resolved to objects in the same way as JavaBeans. The implicit objects, along with brief descriptions are as follows:

Implicit Object	Description
applicationScope	This is a Map that contains all applications-scoped variables. The Map is keyed on the name of the variable.
cookie	This is a Map that maps cookie names to a single Cookie object. If more than one cookie exists for a given name, then the first of these cookies is used for that name.

Table continued on following page

Implicit Object	Description
`header`	This is a `Map` that contains the values of each header name.
`headerValues`	This is a `Map` that maps a header name to a string array of all of the possible values for that header.
`initParam`	This is a `Map` that maps context initialization parameter names to their string parameter values.
`pageContext`	The `PageContext` object.
`pageScope`	This is a `Map` that contains all page-scoped variables. The `Map` is keyed on the name of the variable.
`param`	This is a `Map` that contains the names of the parameters to a page. Each parameter name is mapped to a single string value.
`paramValues`	This is a `Map` that maps a parameter name to a string array of all of the values for that parameter.
`requestScope`	This is a `Map` that contains all request-scoped variables. The `Map` is keyed on the name of the variable.
`sessionScope`	This is a `Map` that contains all session-scoped variables. The `Map` is keyed on the name of the variable.

The following JSP code shows an example of how you can use some of these implicit objects (`implicit.jsp`):

```
<jsp:useBean id="sessionperson" class="com.apress.projsp20.ch03.Person"
             scope="session" />
<jsp:useBean id="requestperson" class="com.apress.projsp20.ch03.Person"
             scope="request" />
<html>
  <head>
    <title>Implicit Variables</title>
    <style>
      body, td {font-family:verdana;font-size:10pt;}
     </style>
  </head>
  <body>
    <h2>Implicit Variables</h2>
    <table>
      <tr>
        <td>Concept</td>
        <td>Code</td>
        <td>Output</td>
      </tr>
      <tr>
        <td>PageContext</td>
        <td>${'${'}pageContext.request.requestURI}</td>
        <td>${pageContext.request.requestURI}</td>
      </tr>
```

```
        <tr>
          <td>sessionScope</td>
          <td>${'${'}sessionScope.sessionperson.name}</td>
          <td>${sessionScope.sessionperson.name}</td>
        </tr>
        <tr>
          <td>requestScope</td>
          <td>${'${'}requestScope.requestperson.name}</td>
          <td>${requestScope.requestperson.name}</td>
        </tr>
        <tr>
          <td>param</td>
          <td>${'${'}param["name"]}</td>
          <td>${param["name"]}</td>
        </tr>
        <tr>
          <td>paramValues</td>
          <td>${'${'}paramValues.multi[1]}</td>
          <td>${paramValues.multi[1]}</td>
        </tr>
      </table>
    </body>
  </html>
```

In this example you'll see how to use the request- and session-scope maps, the request parameter map, and the request parameter values map as well as the pageContext object. All the other objects are used in exactly the same manner and are not shown here.

If you deploy this example to a JSP 2.0-compliant web container (as described in the previous sections) and request the page with a URL similar to http://localhost:8080/expressionLanguage/implicit.jsp?name=sam&multi=number1&multi=number2 then you see the following page:

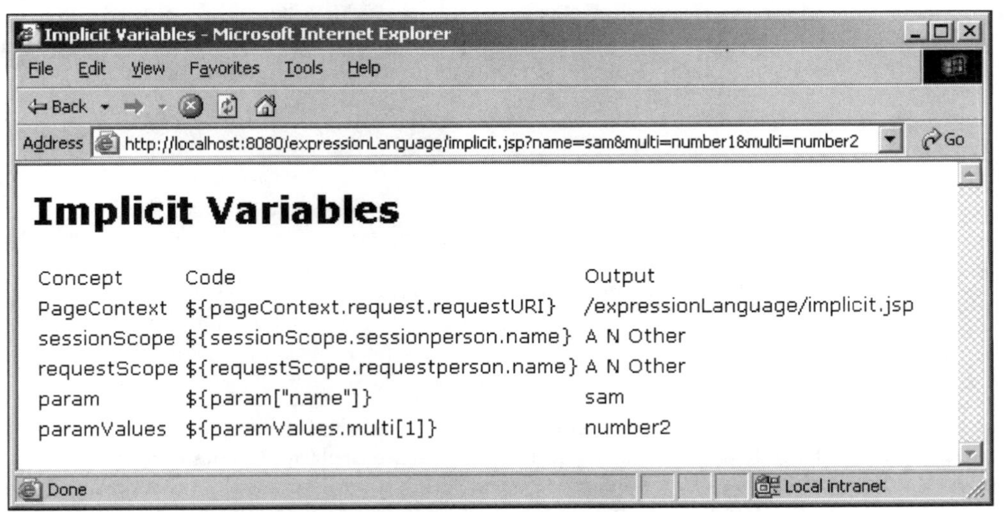

Expression Language Functions

This final section discusses perhaps the most interesting part of the JSP EL: functions. An EL function is mapped to a static method of a Java class. This mapping is specified within a tag library descriptor (TLD) as you'll see later.

As with the rest of the EL, a function can appear either in template text or in the attributes of a custom tag.

A function in EL can take any number of parameters, and these are again declared in a deployment descriptor. Functions are assigned a namespace in a very similar manner to custom tag libraries; for example, the following JSP code invokes an EL function:

```
${MyFunctions:function("param")}
```

The namespace in this example is `MyFunctions`, which is declared using the same code as a tag library with the same namespace:

```
<%@ taglib uri="/WEB-IF/taglib.tld" prefix="MyFunctions" %>
```

You'll see this used in other places in this book to declare namespaces for custom tags; in this chapter you'll use it to declare namespaces for EL functions. Functions must always have a namespace, with one exception: If a function is used within the attribute of a custom tag, then it may omit the namespace as long as it's declared within the same TLD as the custom tag.

A TLD is an XML file that declares a tag library. The TLD contains information relating to the tags in the library and the classes that implement them. The TLD also contains the declarations and mappings of EL functions and each TLD may include zero or more static functions. Each such function is given a name and a specific method in a Java class that will implement the function. The method must be a public static method on a public class. If this is not the case, a translation-time error will occur. Within a TLD, function names must be unique, and if two functions have the same name a translation-time error will occur. You can see an example of the TLD entries used to declare a function here:

```
<taglib>
...
  <function>
    <name>nickname</name>
    <function-class>myPkg.MyFuncs</function-class>
    <function-signature>
      java.lang.String nickname(java.lang.String)
    </function-signature>
  </function>
</taglib>
```

This TLD fragment declares a function called `nickname`, which is intended to return the nickname for a particular user. If you look at the tags, you can see that we declared the name of the function that will be used by the EL using the `<name>` element, the class that implements the function using the `<function-class>` element, and the signature of the function using the `<function-signature>` element. It's this last element that is the most interesting and also the most complex.

The syntax of the `<function-signature>` element is as follows:

```
return_type static_function_name(parameter_1_type,..,parameter_n_type)
```

It's important to note that the parameter and return types must be the fully qualified Java class names. If the declared signature of the function does not match that of the function in the Java class, then a translation-time error will occur.

For more information about the content of TLDs, especially those that relate to custom tags, please see Chapters 5 through 7.

A Simple Function

You are now ready to look at some example functions. The first of these examples outputs a greeting to the user. This greeting is customized depending on the time of the day. So, for example, if it's before midday the greeting will say `Good Morning`; if it's after midday but before 6 p.m. it will say `Good Afternoon`; and finally, if it's after 6 p.m. but before midnight it will say `Good Evening`. You'll first look at the Java class that implements this function (in the `Functions.java` file):

```
package com.apress.projsp20.ch03;

import java.util.Calendar;

public class Functions {

  public static String sayHello() {
    Calendar rightNow = Calendar.getInstance();
    int hour = rightNow.get(Calendar.HOUR);
    int AmPm = rightNow.get(Calendar.AM_PM);

    if (AmPm == Calendar.AM) {
      return "Good Morning";
    } else if (AmPm == Calendar.PM && hour < 6) {
      return "Good Afternoon";
    } else {
      return "Good Evening";
    }
  }
}
```

The TLD for this function is very simple, because it has no attributes (`taglib.tld` in the `tag` folder located under `WEB-INF`):

```
<?xml version="1.0" encoding="ISO-8859-1" ?>

<taglib xmlns="http://java.sun.com/xml/ns/j2ee"
  xmlns:xsi="http://www.w3.org/2001/XMLSchema-instance"
  xsi:schemaLocation="http://java.sun.com/xml/ns/j2ee/web-jsptaglibrary_2_0.xsd"
  version="2.0">
```

```
    <tlib-version>1.0</tlib-version>
    <jsp-version>2.0</jsp-version>
    <short-name>Greeting</short-name>
    <uri>/Greeting</uri>
    <description>
    </description>

    <function>
      <name>greet</name>
      <function-class>com.apress.projsp20.ch03.Functions</function-class>
      <function-signature>java.lang.String sayHello()</function-signature>
    </function>
  </taglib>
```

This declares our function to have the name `greet` and to return a string and take no parameters. You can use this function on a JSP with the following code. Notice how you declare the namespace for your tag library as `Greeting` in the first line, and that the function name is prefixed with `Greeting`:

```
<%@ taglib prefix="Greeting" uri="/WEB-INF/tags/taglib.tld"%>
<html>
  <head>
    <title>Greet</title>
  </head>
  <body>
    <pre>${Greeting:greet()}</pre>
  </body>
</html>
```

To deploy this example, perform the following steps:

1. Edit `web.xml`, so it looks like the following:

```
<?xml version="1.0" encoding="ISO-8859-1"?>

<web-app xmlns="http://java.sun.com/xml/ns/j2ee"
         xmlns:xsi="http://www.w3.org/2001/XMLSchema-instance"
         xsi:schemaLocation="http://java.sun.com/xml/ns/j2ee web-app_2_4.xsd"
         version="2.4">
    <taglib>
        <taglib-uri>
           /chapter3
        </taglib-uri>
        <taglib-location>
           /WEB-INF/tags/taglib.tld
        </taglib-location>
    </taglib>
</webapp>
```

2. Create and compile a file called `Functions.java` within the `WEB-INF/classes/com/apress.projsp20.ch03` directory containing the code sample.

3. Copy the JSP to a file called `greet.jsp` and save it to the `expressionLanguage` folder.

4. Create a folder within the `WEB-INF` directory called `tags` and a file called `taglib.tld` within this folder with the previous TLD file listed as its contents.

5. Start Tomcat, open your web browser, and go to http://localhost:8080/expressionLanguage/greet.jsp.

You should see the following page. As expected, the output of this JSP when viewed after midday but before 6 p.m. is as follows:

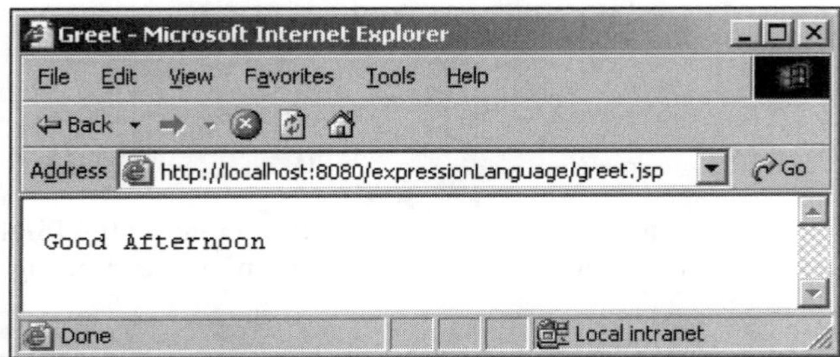

A More Complex Function

Having looked at a very simple function that takes no parameters, you are now in a position to look at a more complex function. This function allows you to view the untranslated source of a JSP page presented in HTML format. Let us take a look at the Java class that implements this function (`Functions.java`):

```
package com.apress.projsp20.ch03;

import java.io.BufferedReader;
import java.io.IOException;
import java.io.InputStream;
import java.io.InputStreamReader;

import javax.servlet.jsp.PageContext;

public class Functions {

  public static String source(String filename, PageContext pageContext)
    throws IOException {
    // use the servlet context to read in the file
    InputStream in;
    BufferedReader br;
    StringBuffer buf = new StringBuffer();
```

```
    in = pageContext.getServletContext().getResourceAsStream(filename);
    br = new BufferedReader(new InputStreamReader(in));
    String line = br.readLine();
    while (line != null) {
      // replace opening and closing tags
      line = line.replaceAll("<", "&lt;");
      line = line.replaceAll(">", "&gt;");
      // writing out each line as we go
      buf.append(line + "\n");
      line = br.readLine();
    }
    br.close();

    // return the contents of the file
    return buf.toString();
  }
}
```

You'll notice that this function makes use of `pageContext` to read in the JSP file to be displayed. This is passed in as a parameter, and as such it must be declared in the function signature. The signature for this function is shown here:

```
<function-signature>
   java.lang.String source(java.lang.String, javax.servlet.jsp.PageContext)
</function-signature>
```

As you can see we've declared the second parameter to this function to be of type `javax.servlet.jsp.PageContext`.

The complete TLD for this function is as follows:

```
<?xml version="1.0" encoding="ISO-8859-1" ?>

<taglib xmlns="http://java.sun.com/xml/ns/j2ee"
  xmlns:xsi="http://www.w3.org/2001/XMLSchema-instance"
  xsi:schemaLocation="http://java.sun.com/xml/ns/j2ee/web-jsptaglibrary_2_0.xsd"
  version="2.0">

  <tlib-version>1.0</tlib-version>
  <jsp-version>2.0</jsp-version>
  <short-name>Source</short-name>
  <uri>/source</uri>
  <description>
  </description>

  <function>
    <name>source</name>
    <function-class>com.apress.projsp20.ch03.Functions</function-class>
    <function-signature>
      java.lang.String source(java.lang.String, javax.servlet.jsp.PageContext)
    </function-signature>
  </function>
</taglib>
```

If you include this tag on a page as follows, it will output the source of the page passed as the first argument, which is obtained from the request parameter called `name`. Notice the use of the implicit `pageContext` variable as the second parameter:

```
<%@ taglib prefix="Source" uri="/WEB-INF/tags/taglib.tld"%>

<html>
  <head>
    <title>Source</title>
  </head>
  <body>
    <pre>${Source:source(param.name, pageContext)}</pre>
  </body>
</html>
```

To deploy this example, follow the steps given for the simple function example, except this time place the previous TLD information in the `taglib.tld` file.

You can see this function at work in the following page; notice how the name of the required JSP is passed in as a request parameter:

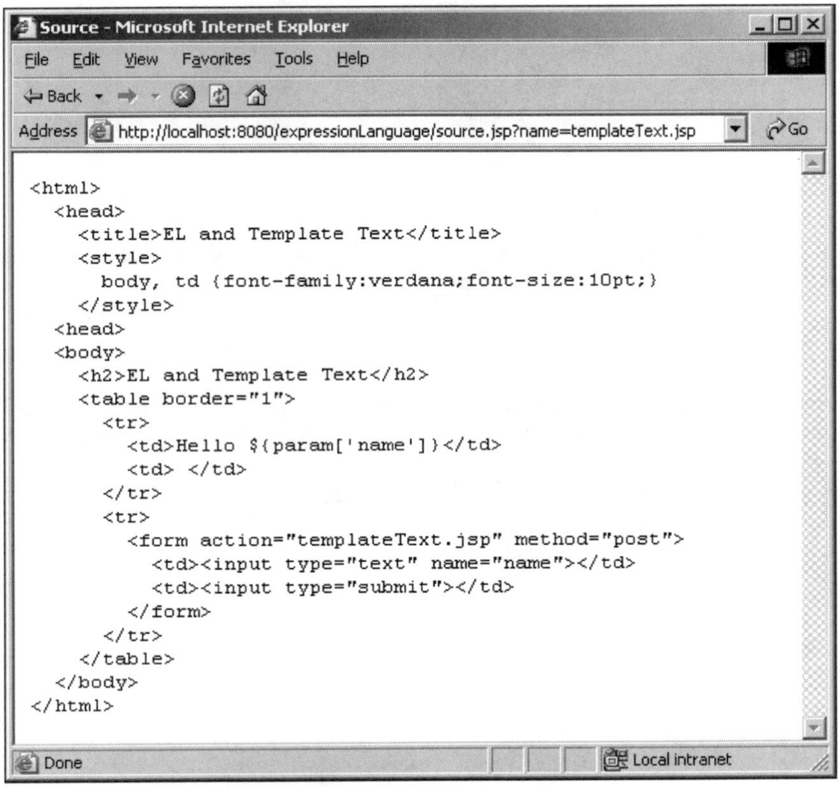

Source - Microsoft Internet Explorer

File Edit View Favorites Tools Help

Address http://localhost:8080/expressionLanguage/source.jsp?name=templateText.jsp

```
<html>
  <head>
    <title>EL and Template Text</title>
    <style>
      body, td {font-family:verdana;font-size:10pt;}
    </style>
  <head>
  <body>
    <h2>EL and Template Text</h2>
    <table border="1">
      <tr>
        <td>Hello ${param['name']}</td>
        <td> </td>
      </tr>
      <tr>
        <form action="templateText.jsp" method="post">
          <td><input type="text" name="name"></td>
          <td><input type="submit"></td>
        </form>
      </tr>
    </table>
  </body>
</html>
```

Done Local intranet

Functions in Tag Attributes

One of the most powerful uses of functions in the EL is to preprocess the attributes passed to a custom tag. In this section you'll look at such a use of the EL. You'll write a function that will convert a custom tag's parameter to uppercase; while this is not a particularly complex function, it should suffice. We don't want to get bogged down in the details of the function's implementation.

Let us first take a look at the Java method that provides this function:

```
package com.apress.projsp20.ch03;

public class Functions {

  public static String toUpperCase(String theString) {
    return theString.toUpperCase();
  }
}
```

As you can see this is an extremely simple function that merely converts its parameter to uppercase. The TLD entry for it is as follows:

```
  <function>
    <name>upper</name>
    <function-class>com.apress.projsp20.ch03.Functions</function-class>
    <function-signature>
      java.lang.String toUpperCase(java.lang.String)
    </function-signature>
  </function>
```

In this example you'll use one of the tags from the JSTL. This tag outputs the value of its `value` parameter to the JSP. The tag takes the following form:

```
<c:out value="a string" />
```

More information about the JSTL can be found in the next chapter. You can place the JSTL JAR files within the `lib` directory of your web application and import them into the page like this:

```
<%@ taglib uri="http://java.sun.com/jstl/core_rt" prefix="c" %>
```

Now that you've seen the constituent parts, you'll look at a JSP that uses a function to preprocess the attribute to the <c:out> tag:

```
<%@ taglib prefix="chapter3" uri="/WEB-INF/taglib.tld"%>
<%@ taglib uri="http://java.sun.com/jstl/core_rt" prefix="c" %>

<html>
  <body>
    <c:out value="${chapter3:upper('a string')}" />
  </body>
</html>
```

In order to deploy this to a JSP 2.0-compliant web container, follow the steps for the other examples in this chapter as well as this additional step:

1. Place the JSTL library files (`jstl.jar` and `standard.jar`) in a directory called `lib` within the `WEB-INF` directory. See the chapter on JSTL for information on obtaining these files.

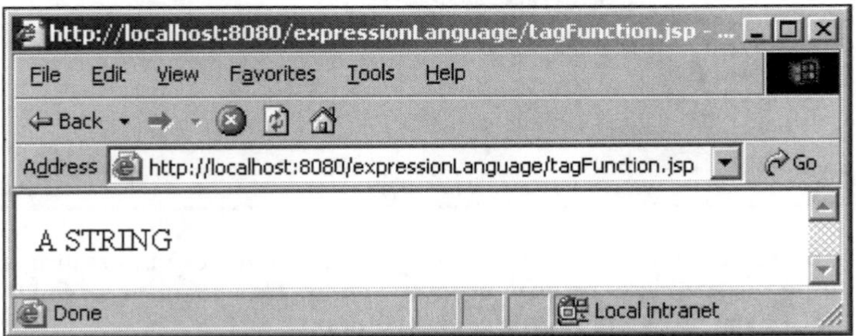

Nesting Functions

Another powerful use of functions is to nest them together. For example, you can use our uppercase function from the previous example to render the source of a page produced by our view source function in uppercase. The following JSP excerpt shows how you might do this:

```
<%@ taglib prefix="chapter3" uri="/WEB-INF/taglib.tld"%>

<html>
  <body>
    <pre>
      ${chapter3:upper(chapter3:source(param.name, pageContext))}
    </pre>
  </body>
</html>
```

This would produce output similar to the following:

```
<HTML>
  <HEAD>
    <TITLE>EL AND TEMPLATE TEXT</TITLE>
    <STYLE>
      BODY, TD {FONT-FAMILY:VERDANA;FONT-SIZE:10PT;}
    </STYLE>
  <HEAD>
  <BODY>
    <H2>EL AND TEMPLATE TEXT</H2>
    <TABLE BORDER="1">
      <TR>
        <TD>HELLO ${PARAM['NAME']}</TD>
        <TD> </TD>
      </TR>
      <TR>
        <FORM ACTION="TEMPLATETEXT.JSP" METHOD="POST">
          <TD><INPUT TYPE="TEXT" NAME="NAME"></TD>
          <TD><INPUT TYPE="SUBMIT"></TD>
        </FORM>
      </TR>
    </TABLE>
  </BODY>
</HTML>
```

Functions can be nested to an arbitrary degree to perform some very interesting and powerful operations. The only restricting factor is your imagination. This encourages small functions that perform very specialized jobs, which is a very positive design point.

Expression Language Functions vs. Custom Tags

As you'll see in later chapters of this book, the JSP 2.0 specification provides a very powerful custom tag mechanism. You might ask why you would use tags over functions and vice versa. There are several factors that can help you to make the choice:

- Is knowledge of the environment required? If the answer is yes, then tags are the way to go. A tag provides easy access to the `pageContext` and other variables; functions do not. In order to access these things within a function, you must pass them in as a parameter.
- Do you require iterative behavior over a body? If the answer is yes, then you should use a tag. Functions do not provide functionality to process a body (they don't have one), whereas tags do.
- Are you trying to provide a small, reusable piece of functionality that acts on one or more arguments? If the answer to this is yes, then you should use a function. Overall, functions are very much simpler to write than tags, therefore they provide a great opportunity to write small self-contained pieces of functionality.
- Would you like to reuse existing Java code in a web context? If the answer is yes, then functions are ideal. As functions are no more than static Java methods, you can easily reuse existing code.

The choice of tags versus functions should be eased by consulting these points, but it's worth noting that the true power of the EL becomes evident when it's combined with custom tags.

Summary

In this chapter you've looked at the JSP EL, which is new with the JSP 2.0 specification. This EL is largely intended to replace scriptlets and be used in combination with custom tags.

You've examined the following areas in this chapter:

- The reasons that the EL has come about, including a look at its history
- The syntax and usage of the EL, including reserved words, disabling scriptlets in a page, and disabling the evaluation of the EL on a page or set of pages
- The operators within the EL, including arithmetic operators, comparison operators, logical operators, and other operators
- Using JavaBeans with the EL
- The implicit objects within the EL
- The declaration and use of functions in the EL, including reasons for using functions over tags and vice versa

In the next chapter, you'll learn about the JSTL and the tags contained within it.

4

JavaServer Pages Standard Tag Library

Despite the popularity of using JSP technology to build the dynamic presentation layers required by today's modern web applications, JSP page authors have repeatedly come up against the same problems.

In all but the simplest of web applications, JSPs have needed to contain some form of logic that is required to tailor the dynamic content, and invariably, until recently, this has been done using JSP scriptlets. Although this solution does produce the required output, using too many scriptlets on a page reduces its readability and therefore its maintainability and generally makes a JSP page look ugly. With scriptlets it's all too easy to forget a closing brace or something equally as trivial, and in a large JSP it can take a significant amount of time to track down the source of the resultant error.

Reduced maintainability isn't the only limitation of a scriptlet-based approach because it also places an assumption on the skill set of the JSP page author developing or maintaining the page. Because scriptlets are written in Java, JSP page authors more or less need to be Java developers or have more than a basic understanding of the language. Often the specific design skills of a web designer cannot be controlled, or they require some assistance to fully embrace JSP technology. A perfect example of the skills mismatch is that a web designer may have his preferred HTML editor or IDE that may not support Java scriptlets because editors are generally designed for XML-type languages such as HTML.

A better approach has more recently been for Java developers to create their own custom actions (often known as custom tags) and make them available to web designers via tag libraries. This solution is far better than the scriptlet-based approach, because the use of a custom tag places no assumptions on the skills of the page author because custom tags are simply XML based. One obvious drawback of custom tags is that they must be coded, packaged, and tested before use, which is a nontrivial task and must be done by a Java developer. This can place time constraints on when web designers can start work and in some cases Java developers have found themselves writing all manner of custom tags for even the simplest of tasks to ensure that no scriptlets are necessary.

The **JavaServer Pages Standard Tag Library (JSTL)** specification 1.0 was first released in June 2002 and its arrival signified a new phase for JSP page authors. The JSTL specification outlines a number of custom actions that are designed to handle the vast majority of common tasks that are needed by JSP page authors. Gone are the days of using ugly scriptlets and thanks to the JSTL, hopefully only more complicated functionality warrants the construction of a custom action.

A few days after the JSTL 1.0 specification was released, the Jakarta Taglibs project from Apache followed up with a reference implementation of the specification ready for use.

Throughout this chapter you'll take an in-depth look at the actions provided by the JSTL. You'll see how actions may be used via examples that will demonstrate just how much simpler it is to build dynamic JSP-based applications with JSTL that avoid many of the problems associated with scriptlets.

To fully appreciate the actions provided by the JSTL it's advisable to be familiar with the syntax of the new expression language (EL)–the subject of the preceding chapter–as you'll assume a basic level of knowledge.

Installing the JavaServer Pages Standard Tag Library

Before you delve too deeply into the details of the tags that comprise the JSTL, it's a good idea to understand what's involved with installing the JSTL into a JSP container that's ready for use. Fortunately, the process isn't too demanding and should only take a few minutes.

To be able to use the JSTL you must have the following:

- At least a Servlet 2.3- and JSP 1.2-compliant container
- An implementation of the JSTL specification

Although any Servlet 2.3- and JSP 1.2-compliant container can be used to develop applications using the JSTL, you'll need to install the JSTL for use inside of the Tomcat servlet container from the Apache Jakarta project. If you're using an alternative container, consult the appropriate documentation for installation instructions. Note that the JSTL installation on other containers may be similar so it's worth reading on!

Originally, the Reference Implementation (RI) of the JSTL was provided by the Apache Jakarta project as part of its Taglibs project, but Sun has since changed the RI to be included as part of the Java Web Services Developer Pack (JWSDP). It should however be noted that the Jakarta Apache Taglibs Standard 1.0 project provides an implementation of the JSTL 1.0 specification.

In the future it's possible that most servlet and JSP containers will come preconfigured with an implementation of the JSTL (possibly with the container vendor's own optimized version!) but for now you must download an implementation and install it into Tomcat manually. The JSTL 1.0 reference implementation can be obtained at the following URL:

http://java.sun.com/webservices/downloads/webservicespack.html

At the time of writing, the latest version of the JWSDP is version 1.2, but it's possible that there will be a more recent release by the time you're reading this.

Sun made some changes from version 1.1 to 1.2 so if you're using a version later than 1.2, then we can't guarantee that these instructions will work. Read the supporting documentation if this problem occurs.

Once you've downloaded and installed the JWSDP, you'll have access to all of the contents of the JWSDP, which includes the following:

- JavaServer Faces (JSF) version 1.0 EA4
- XML and Web Services Security (xws-security) version 1.0 EA
- Java Architecture for XML Binding (JAXB) version 1.0.1
- Java API for XML Processing (JAXP) version 1.2.3
- Java API for XML Registries (JAXR) version 1.0.4
- Java API for XML-based RPC (JAX-RPC) version 1.1 EA
- SOAP with Attachments API for Java (SAAJ) version 1.2 EA
- JavaServer Pages Standard Tag Library (JSTL) version 1.1 EA
- Java WSDP Registry Server version 1.0_05
- Ant Build Tool 1.5.1
- Apache Tomcat version 5 development container

As you can see the JWSDP contains a whole host of very useful tools. Unfortunately most of them are of no interest to us other than the JSTL 1.1 implementation, which can be found in the following directory structure:

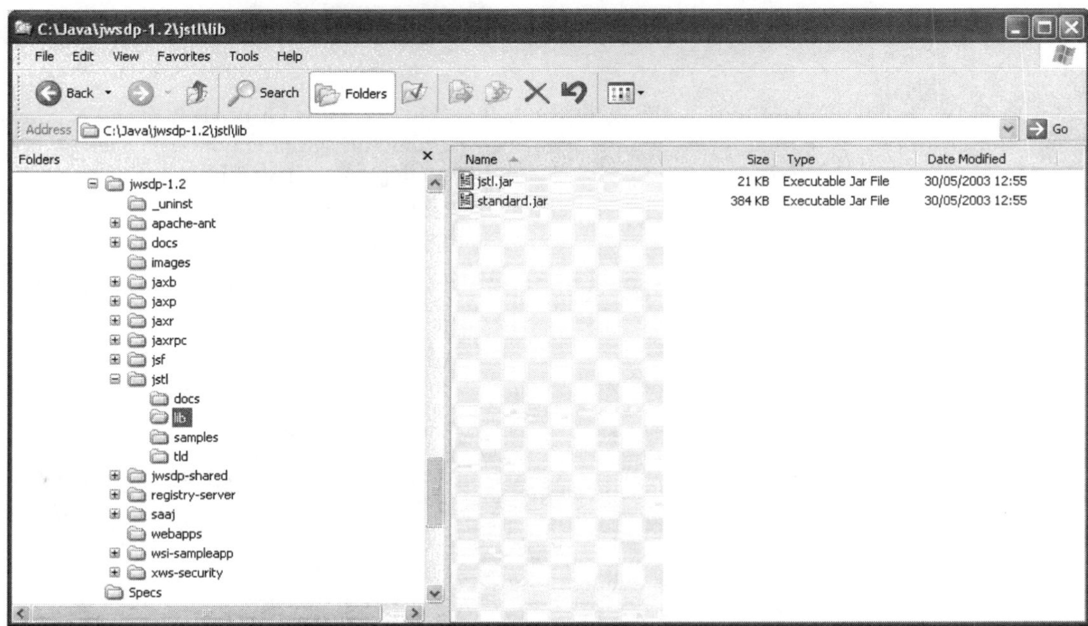

There are two JAR files that you'll need shortly:

- `jstl.jar`
- `standard.jar`

In order to install the JSTL and ensure it's working correctly, let's create a very small web application. Underneath the directory where you installed Tomcat (which from now on will be referred to as `%TOMCAT_HOME%`) you'll find a folder called `webapps`. As the name suggests this is the directory where you place your web applications in either a compressed Web ARchive file (WAR) format or in simple exploded directory format that represents the standard web application structure. For now create a directory inside the `webapps` directory called `jstltest` with the following structure:

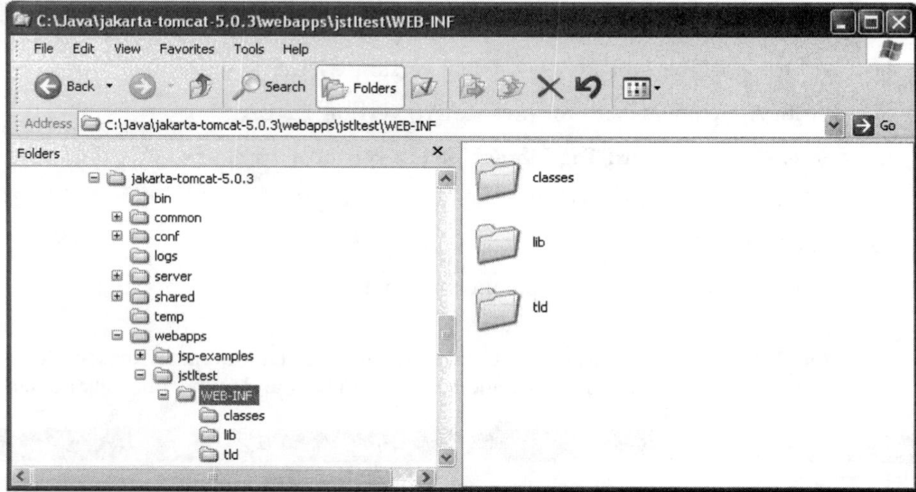

This structure is the standard web application structure that exists inside all WAR files and is known as the exploded directory format. There are perhaps two new directories that you haven't seen before in this structure. The `lib` directory is where you can place any dependent JAR files that the web application requires, while the `tld` directory holds the tag library descriptor (TLD) files for the tag libraries. You'll learn more about TLD files in the next few chapters.

Copy and paste this deployment descriptor into a file called `web.xml` and save it beneath the `WEB-INF` directory:

```
<?xml version="1.0"?>

<web-app xmlns="http://java.sun.com/xml/ns/j2ee"
         xmlns:xsi="http://www.w3.org/2001/XMLSchema-instance"
         xsi:schemaLocation="http://java.sun.com/xml/ns/j2ee/web-app_2_4.xsd"
         version="2.4">

  <taglib>
      <taglib-uri>http://java.sun.com/jstl/core</taglib-uri>
      <taglib-location>/WEB-INF/tlds/c.tld</taglib-location>
  </taglib>
```

```
    <taglib>
        <taglib-uri>http://java.sun.com/jstl/fmt</taglib-uri>
        <taglib-location>/WEB-INF/tlds/fmt.tld</taglib-location>
    </taglib>

    <taglib>
        <taglib-uri>http://java.sun.com/jstl/xml</taglib-uri>
        <taglib-location>/WEB-INF/tlds/x.tld</taglib-location>
    </taglib>

    <taglib>
        <taglib-uri>http://java.sun.com/jstl/sql</taglib-uri>
        <taglib-location>/WEB-INF/tlds/sql.tld</taglib-location>
    </taglib>

</web-app>
```

Now that you have a deployment descriptor for the web application you can install the required JSTL libraries that you downloaded earlier. In the newly created web application structure, create a directory in the `jstltest\WEB-INF` directory called `lib`. As the name suggests, this directory is used by web applications to store external library files (such as JAR files) that the web application has dependencies on. Any library files found in this directory are automatically loaded by the servlet container and made available to the web application.

Copy the two JSTL JAR files mentioned earlier into the `WEB-INF/lib` directory and you should then have the JSTL installed in the following structure:

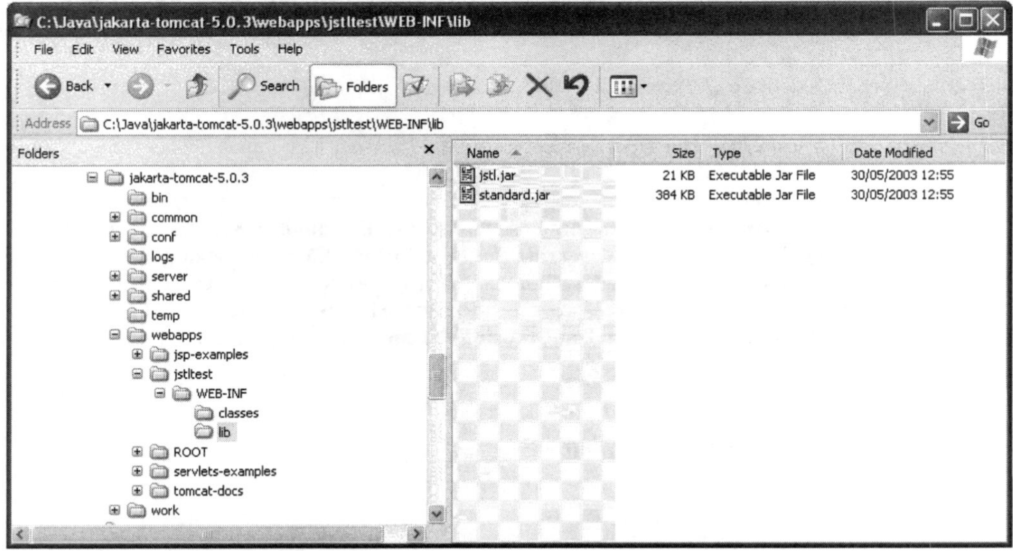

Now you need to place the TLD files referenced in the deployment descriptor into the `WEB-INF/tld` directory. These TLD files are located in the `META-INF` directory of the `standard.jar` file you just copied. Using a tool such as WinZip, open the JAR file and extract the `c.tld`, `fmt.tld`, `sql.tld`, and `x.tld` files:

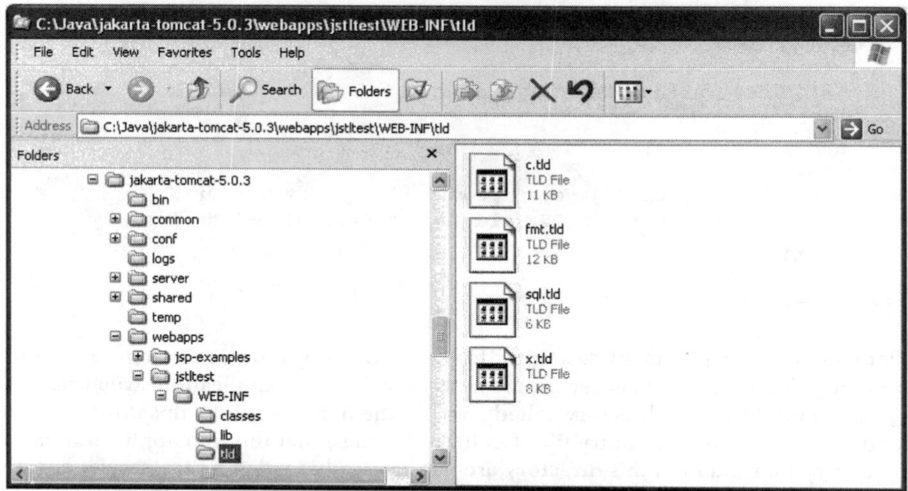

At this point you've successfully created the test web application and installed the JSTL libraries. All you need now is a JSP page to test one of the tags provided by the JSTL to see if the installation has succeeded. Copy and paste the following JSP code into a file called `isJSTLworking.jsp` and save it beneath the `jstltest` directory at the same level as the `WEB-INF` directory. Don't worry too much for now about understanding the content of the JSP; it will all be explained in further detail later:

```
<%@ taglib uri="http://java.sun.com/jstl/core" prefix="c" %>

<c:out value="Congratulations, JSTL is working!"/>
```

> **Version 1.2 of JWSDP requires either the use of the Java Developer's Kit (JDK) 1.4.1 or above, or alternatively you need to override the Java API for XML Processing (JAXP) endorsed classes from earlier JDK 1.4 versions. An easy way to do this with Tomcat is set the system variable** `JAVA_OPTS=-Djava.endorsed.dirs=%JWSDP_HOME%/jaxp/lib/endorsed`**, then start Tomcat using the command** `catalina run` **or** `catalina start`**.**

You're now ready to test the JSTL installation!

Start Tomcat and wait a few seconds for the Tomcat server to start. Once the server has started open a browser and go to the following URL:

http://localhost:8080/jstltest/isJSTLworking.jsp

You should refer to the application by requesting its context followed by the requested resource, `isJSTLworking.jsp`. As mentioned earlier, if you altered the port number or installed Tomcat onto a remote machine, make the appropriate changes to the URL. If all is well and JSTL is successfully installed then you should see the following response in your browser:

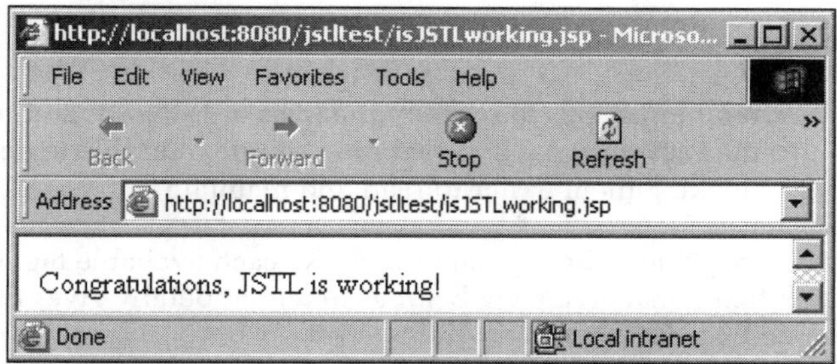

You may be wondering if it's possible to install the JSTL implementation libraries into a single location so that they're available to all web applications hosted by the container. While this is possible by placing the JSTL JAR files into the class path of the container, it's discouraged because different web applications may require different versions or even implementations of the JSTL that could cause complications.

Note that if you don't feel like downloading the JWSDP itself (it's around 30 MB) then a quicker alternative would be to use the Apache Taglibs JSTL implementation instead, which is available separately from the following URL:

http://jakarta.apache.org/taglibs/doc/standard-doc/intro.html

The installation is much the same as before. Extract the JSTL JAR files used earlier from the Apache download and place them in the `<WEB-INF>\lib` directory of your web application.

> **Note that throughout this chapter you'll see many examples of the JSTL in action. Should you wish to test or experiment with any of these examples then feel free to build upon the basic web application you've just created. Simply copy and paste any of the examples that you'll see into the `jstltest` directory and change the URL accordingly!**

The JavaServer Pages Standard Tag Libraries

The JSTL is often referred to as a single tag library when in fact it's actually a collection of four tag libraries. Each tag library provides useful actions (or tags) based around the following functional areas:

- Core
- Internationalization (I18N) and formatting
- Relational database access
- XML processing

One of the primary goals of the JSTL is to simplify the lives of JSP page authors. Providing a collection of tag libraries further reinforces this goal by separating simple, reusable logic further away from the page's presentation, thus making them easier to read and maintain.

Having four tag libraries provides a handy namespace for each available tag, which ultimately makes it easier to identify which functional area a tag belongs to and hopefully gives the JSP page author some indication of the intended use for the tag.

Before diving head first into an explanation of the tags provided by each of the four libraries, let's take a step back for a moment and understand the general functionality provided by each.

The Core Library

As its name suggests, this library contains a whole host of core, general-purpose actions that provide simple but effective solutions to everyday problems experienced in almost every JSP-based web application in existence. Simple tasks such as displaying content based on runtime conditions, or iterating over a collection of items as well as a host of URL manipulation features can all be achieved via the actions provided by the core library. Gone are the days of repeatedly embedding lots of ugly scriptlet code in your JSP pages!

The Internationalization and Formatting Tag Library

The huge popularity of the Internet has led to more and more organizations employing web-based technology to enable their applications to reach a wider client base. This trend has brought about a very important need to interact with clients from around the world using their own language and formatting conventions.

The process of constructing an application so that it's able to adapt to various languages and regions without any additional engineering effort is known as internationalization, or I18N for short. The Internationalization and Formatting tag library provides a series of actions to aid the use of the three key components associated with internationalization: locales, resource bundles, and base names.

The SQL Tag Library

The vast majority of enterprise web applications rely on a relational database to store their enterprise information. While it's generally preferred to make use of Model-View-Controller (MVC) architecture to separate the business logic and database access away from the presentation tier, there are sometimes situations such as rapid prototyping or small-scale application development in which database access from JSPs is a requirement.

To facilitate this requirement, the JSTL provides an assortment of actions via the SQL tag library to facilitate the basic interaction with a relational database such as `select`, `insert`, `update`, and `delete`.

The XML Processing Library

The use of XML to represent and exchange enterprise data is rapidly becoming the industry standard. XML is therefore becoming more and more important to the JSP page author and it should be of little or no surprise to find that the JSTL provides a separate tag library to deal with XML processing. The XML actions provided cater for the basic XML needs a page author is likely to require as well as more complex actions for XML flow control and XML transformations.

Twin Tag Libraries

Now that you're comfortable with the fact that the JSTL is actually comprised of four separate tag libraries, it's time to explain another interesting fact about the JSTL. There are actually two versions of each of the four tag libraries!

If you've worked with custom actions (also known as custom tags) before, or have used any third-party tag library, you'll be aware that before any actions may be used inside a JSP, it's necessary to inform the JSP container of your intention to do so. The `taglib` directive tells the container that the page makes use of a tag library and associates a tag prefix that will distinguish usage of the actions in the library:

```
<%@ taglib uri="tagLibraryURI" prefix="tagPrefix" %>
```

The following tables describe the functional areas covered by the individual JSTL tag libraries along with URIs used to reference each library and the recommended prefix. As mentioned previously, there are actually two versions of the JSTL tag libraries available in JSTL 1.0 to cater for the new EL.

Due to the fact that JSTL 1.0 was released prior to JSP 2.0, there was a requirement to ensure that the JSTL was fully supported by JSP 1.2-compliant containers. To be able to support both the scripting (`rtexprvalues`) and the EL (`elexprvalues`) worlds, it was decided to create a set of twin tag libraries, one to support the new EL and the second to support request-time expressions. Notice how similar the URI and recommended prefixes are for the two libraries; essentially they are the same but the runtime library has "`_rt`" appended to both its URI and prefix.

Expression Language-based Tag Libraries

Functional Area	URI	Prefix
Core	`http://java.sun.com/jstl/core`	`c`
XML processing	`http://java.sun.com/jstl/xml`	`x`
I18N and formatting	`http://java.sun.com/jstl/fmt`	`fmt`
Relational database access	`http://java.sun.com/jstl/sql`	`sql`

Runtime Expression-based Tag Libraries

Functional Area	URI	Prefix
Core	`http://java.sun.com/jstl/core_rt`	`c_rt`
XML processing	`http://java.sun.com/jstl/xml_rt`	`x_rt`
I18N and formatting	`http://java.sun.com/jstl/fmt_rt`	`fmt_rt`
Relational database access	`http://java.sun.com/jstl/sql_rt`	`sql_rt`

While it's anticipated that most people will prefer to use the new EL-based tag libraries, it's possible that some JSP page authors will prefer to use scripting with the JSTL with `rtexprvalues` for reasons of type safety and performance via the runtime-based tag libraries.

Note that it's possible to mix the use of the runtime and EL actions, as you can see in the following code snippet. For the time being don't worry too much if you can't figure out what the example actually does, just spot the use of tags from both the runtime and EL libraries:

```
<%@ taglib uri="http://java.sun.com/jstl/fmt" prefix="fmt" %>
<%@ taglib uri="http://java.sun.com/jstl/fmt_rt" prefix="fmt_rt" %>

<fmt:message key="stockPrice">
    <fmt:param value="${closePrice}">
    <fmt_rt:param value="<%=quoteBean.getOpenPrice()%>"/>
</fmt:message>
```

For the remainder of this chapter you'll focus on the use of the EL-based tag libraries and the examples will use the EL in order to be consistent with the JSTL specification. Rest assured though, if your preference is to stick with runtime expressions, use the "`_rt`" libraries instead and substitute any `elexprvalues` with their scripting equivalent.

> **It's anticipated that when JSP 2.0 is finalized there will be a maintenance release of JSTL to ensure that the EL support is consistent with the one specified with JSP 2.0, although no API change is expected.**

Hopefully by now you have a good feel for the JSTL–its composition and intended uses–so let's take a look at each of the tag libraries individually and the actions they provide.

The Core Tag Library

As mentioned previously, the core tag library is designed to provide JSP page authors with a set of reusable actions to cater for the simple "core" requirements that almost every JSP application has in some shape or form, such as object manipulation, looping, and so on.

Up until now, such common functionality has been implemented via two alternative methods: Java scriptlets and custom actions. As we've discussed, scriptlets are the least favorable approach, because they not only require the JSP page author to understand Java syntax but add clutter to JSPs thus reducing readability. A better alternative has been to encapsulate such functionality into a custom action, but of course it's up to the JSP page author to code such a component, which they may or not have the skills to do. While a custom action has up until now been the best solution because it enables a high level of reuse, why should every JSP page author be forced to write her own library of such simple core functionality?

Thankfully, the JSTL provides such a library, thus making it easier for JSP page authors to concentrate on what they do best–building attractive, functional presentation layers–without the burden of having to worry about the intricacies of the Java programming language. The JSTL core library can be split further to expose its main functional areas:

- Scoped variable manipulation
- Conditionals
- Looping and iteration
- URL manipulation

Let's take a closer look at each of the actions:

Scoped Variable Manipulation

This first group of actions provides the means to work with scoped variables (JSP-scoped attributes) as well as cope with errors.

The <c:out> Action

As the name suggests, the `out` action simply evaluates an expression and outputs it to the current `JspWriter`. It's equivalent to the JSP syntax `<%= expression %>`.

Let's look at an example of this very simple but useful action:

```
<%@ taglib uri="http://java.sun.com/jstl/core" prefix="c" %>

<c:out value="Good Afternoon!" />
<c:out value="${book.author.name}" default="Unknown"/>
```

The expression to be evaluated is supplied via the `value` attribute and the result is converted into a `String` before being returned as part of the response. Notice that an optional default value can be supplied that is returned if the expression evaluates to `null`. Should a Null expression be evaluated and no default value is supplied then an empty string is returned instead.

The <c:out> action also has a second form that enables the default attribute to be specified as part of the action's body content, which the JSP container will evaluate and trim on your behalf should the default value be required. Therefore you can rewrite the example as follows:

```
<%@ taglib uri="http://java.sun.com/jstl/core" prefix="c" %>

<c:out value="${book.author.name}">
  Unknown
</c:out>
```

The <c:set> Action

You can use the <c:set> action to set a variable in a particular web application scope (page, request, session, or application) and it's often used in conjunction with the <c:out> action.

Let's have a look at an example:

```
<%@ taglib uri="http://java.sun.com/jstl/core" prefix="c" %>

<c:set var="browser" value="${header['User-Agent']}" scope="session" />
Your Browser User Agent is : <c:out value="${browser}"/>
```

The var attribute sets the name by which the variable may be referenced in the given scope. In a similar manner to the <c:out> action the value of the variable can be specified in two possible ways. First, by simply using the value attribute or second, by supplying the tag with some body content that is automatically evaluated and trimmed by the JSP container.

In this case the <c:set> action is being used to store a session-scoped variable called browser, which stores the value of the User-Agent header that indicates the type of browser that initiated the request. The <c:out> action is then simply used to output the value stored inside the attribute.

On my machine the result is as follows:

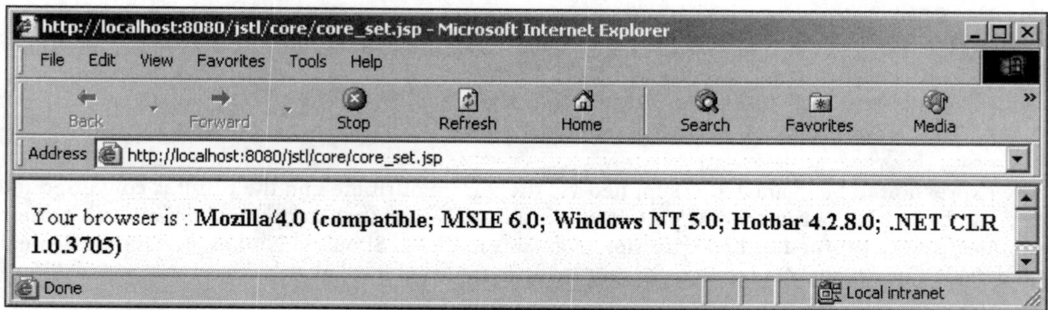

Note that should a null value be specified for the value attribute, then, if a scope is supplied, the behavior is determined by the action of PageContext.removeAttribute(var, scope) or PageContext.removeAttribute(var) because these methods provide the internal implementation. Otherwise, if a target attribute is specified then an accompanying property must also be specified.

The <c:remove> Action

To compliment the <c:set> action you probably won't be surprised to learn that the <c:remove> action removes a variable from a specific application scope.

If you were to add the following <c:remove> action to the previous example then the browser variable containing the user's browser type would be removed:

```
<%@ taglib uri="http://java.sun.com/jstl/core" prefix="c" %>

<c:set var="browser" value="${header['User-Agent']}" scope="session" />
<c:remove var="browser" scope="session">
Your Browser User Agent is : <c:out value="${browser}"/>
```

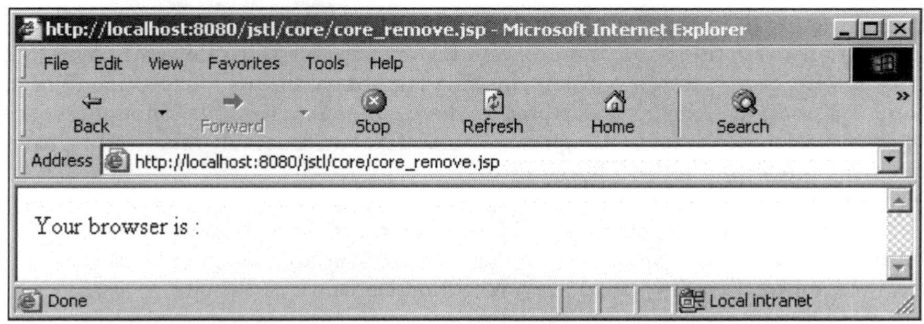

As you can see, this is one of the most simple actions provided by the JSTL because it simply accepts a var attribute that indicates the named attribute to remove as well as an optional scope attribute, which indicates the scope from which to remove the attribute.

Again, if an attribute scope is specified then the behavior is specified by the PageContext.removeAttribute(var, scope) method because this is the underlying method that is called, otherwise thePageContext.removeAttribute(var) method is used instead.

The <c:catch> Action

The <c:catch> action provides a simple mechanism for catching any java.lang.Throwable exceptions that are thrown by any nested actions.

This simple action has a single var attribute that holds a reference to any java.lang.Throwable exceptions that occur during execution of any of the nested actions that form the body content of the action. The JSP container processes each nested action in the normal way and any output is returned to the current JspWriter.

This action provides JSP developers with granular error handling, thereby allowing errors from multiple actions to be handled in a uniform way in a single place, which hopefully makes your applications more robust. It should be noted, however, that this action should not be used to provide error handling to actions that are of central importance to the page. Instead, exceptions from such actions should propagate to predefined error pages in the normal manner. Actions of secondary importance, however, may be enclosed inside the `<c:catch>` action:

```
<%@ taglib uri="http://java.sun.com/jstl/core" prefix="c" %>
<%@ taglib uri="http://java.sun.com/jstl/fmt" prefix="fmt" %>

<c:catch var="exception">
    fmt:parseDate var="dob" value="${param.birthDate}"
                  pattern="yyyy-MM-dd" />
</c:catch>

<c:if test="${exception != null}">
    <jsp:useBean id="dob" class="java.util.Date" />
</c:if>
```

You can see from the this example how the `<c:catch>` action can come in very handy for dealing with errors that don't warrant informing the user and forwarding to a separate error page. In this example the `<fmt:parseDate>` action from the formatting tag library throws a exception if an invalid date is entered and if it does, the exception is stored in the `exception` variable. Should an exception be thrown during execution, it can be caught and tested for, and a default value will be used instead without informing the user of the internal error.

Note that the scope of the `var` attribute will always be `page`, and should a `java.lang.Throwable` exception not be thrown by a nested action then the `var` variable won't exist. If a value for the `var` variable isn't supplied then the `java.lang.Throwable` won't be stored.

Conditionals

The content delivered by dynamic JSP-based web applications is very often dynamic in nature due to the fact that its generated content is dependent on the values of ever-changing application data. Up until the release of the JSTL, JSP page authors have been forced to provide such functionality via Java scriptlets containing `if` statements,which isn't just ugly, but prone to errors as well. The conditional tags provided by the JSTL core tag library are far better suited for this purpose.

The <c:if> Action

The first and most simple of the conditional actions is `<c:if>`, which simply decides to evaluate its body content depending on the value of an evaluated Boolean attribute. If the result of the attribute expression evaluates to `true` then the action's body content will be processed in the normal way by the JSP container and any output will be returned to the current `JspWriter`.

Let's use a really simple example to produce some dynamic content based on the current hour of the day:

```
<%@ taglib uri="http://java.sun.com/jstl/core" prefix="c" %>
<%@ page import="com.apress.projsp20.ch04.CalendarBean"%>


<jsp:useBean id="cal" class="com.apress.projsp20.ch04.CalendarBean"/>
```

```
The time is currently : <BR><BR>
<c:out value="${cal.time}"/>,

<c:set var="hour" value="${cal.hour}" scope="request" />

<b>
<c:if test="${hour >= 0 && hour <=11}">
    Good Morning!
</c:if>
<c:if test="${hour >= 12 && hour <=17}">
    Good Afternoon!
</c:if>
<c:if test="${hour >= 18 && hour <=23}">
    Good Evening!
</c:if>
</b>
```

As you can see, this JSP uses an instance of a simple JavaBean component called `CalendarBean` (a simple wrapper around the `java.util.Calendar` class) to set a variable called `hour` using the `<c:set>` action introduced earlier. After informing the user of the current time, you then dynamically provide the user with a greeting depending on if it's during the morning, afternoon, or evening. Notice how it takes three separate `<c:if>` actions to accomplish this task.

Note that the reason for using the `CalendarBean` class as a wrapper is that the standard `java.util.Calendar` class isn't a standard JavaBean component and hence cannot be instantiated by the `<jsp:useBean>` action or manipulated by the EL. An alternative would be to use scriptlet code to provide access to a `Calendar` object, but as mentioned elsewhere this makes your JSPs cluttered and harder to maintain.

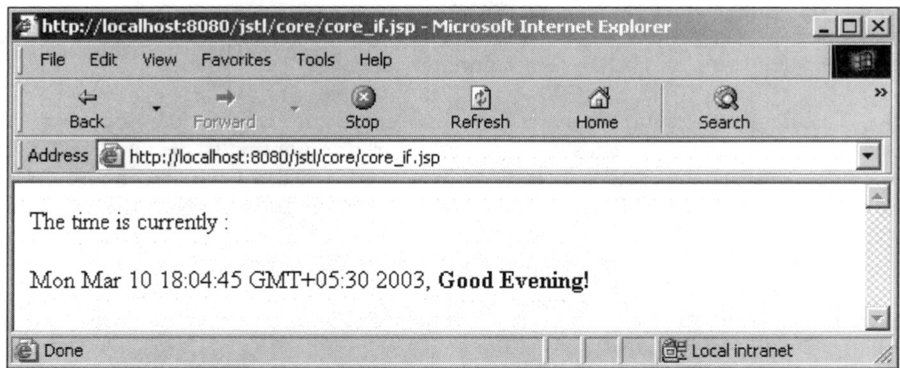

Additionally, the `<c:if>` action accepts an optional `var` attribute that represents a scoped variable that can be used to store the result of evaluating the Boolean `test` expression. The optional variable can either be set to a specific scope or the default page scope. You may be surprised to learn that there is no explicit `<c:else>` action, but you'll soon see why with the introduction of the `<c:choose>`, `<c:when>`, and `<c:otherwise>` actions.

The <c:choose>, <c:when>, and <c:otherwise> Actions

You've now seen how the `<c:if>` action can be used to provide content based on a specific condition. The `<c:choose>` action takes this step a little further and provides you with the ability to provide handling for a set of mutually exclusive conditions, instead of just one.

The syntax for the `<c:choose>` action is as follows:

```
<c:choose>
    body content (<c:when> and <c:otherwise> subtags)
</c:choose>
```

As you can see, the `<c:choose>` actions has two possible nested actions that form its body content, `<c:when>` and `<c:otherwise>`. The syntax for each is as follows:

```
<c:when test="testCondition">
    body content
</c:when>

<c:otherwise>
    conditional block
</c:otherwise>
```

The `<c:when>` action simply exists to provide handling for a specific condition, tested for via its `test` attribute. Unlimited `<c:when>` actions may exist within a `<c:choose>` action to provide handling for a wide range of conditions. The `<c:otherwise>` action may only appear once because it covers all remaining alternatives and must therefore appear after all `<c:when>` actions. Because it represents the last possible option, there's no need for it to evaluate a Boolean expression.

Combined together, the `<c:choose>`, `<c:when>`, and `<c:otherwise>` actions provide efficient handling for a range of alternative conditions in a similar manner to `if`, `else if`, `else` blocks or `case/switch` statements in modern programming languages.

When the JSP container first encounters a `<c:choose>` tag, it evaluates the body of the first `<c:when>` action whose test condition evaluates to `true` and returns any output to the current `JspWriter` without evaluating or processing any further `<c:when>` or `<c:otherwise>` actions. Should the `test` condition of every `<c:when>` evaluate to `false`, then and only then does the body of the `<c:otherwise>` action get processed. If no `<c:when>` condition evaluates to `true` and there's no `<c:otherwise>` action specified then the `<c:choose>` action will simply do nothing!

Let's revisit the example JSP that you created for the `<c:if>` action example, which prints an appropriate welcome based on the time of the day:

```
<c:if test="${hour >= 0 && hour <=11}">
    Good Morning!
</c:if>
<c:if test="${hour >= 12 && hour <=17}">
    Good Afternoon!
</c:if>
<c:if test="${hour >= 18 && hour <=23}">
    Good Evening!
</c:if>
```

As you can see there are three possible conditions that determine the welcome message returned to the user. This logic would be far better implemented using a <c:choose> action instead. Let's make the appropriate changes:

```
<c:choose>
    <c:when test="${hour >= 0 && hour <=11}">
        Good Morning!
    </c:when>
    <c:when test="${hour >= 12 && hour <=17}">
        Good Afternoon!
    </c:when>
    <c:otherwise>
        Good Evening!
    </c:otherwise>
</c:choose>
```

The new implementation of the welcome message logic is superior to the logic from the <c:if> example for a number of reasons. First, the code is more self-describing and readable to a nonprogrammer. Second, the code is more efficient. As soon as the JSP engine has found the first nested action whose test condition evaluates to `true`, it doesn't need to continue checking the test conditions of any other actions. Compare this to the <c:if> example where every action was tested regardless. Lastly, because the nested actions of the <c:choose> action are mutually exclusive, it's impossible to execute the body of more than one of the conditions. A simple bug in the logic of the <c:if> example could easily cause the body of more than one <c:if> action to be processed, thereby causing a very strange welcome message!

Looping and Iteration

Another facility often required by JSP page authors is the ability to be able to generate large amounts of presentation code (usually HTML tables or lists) by looping or iterating around the same JSP code. This functionality has up until now usually been implemented via scriptlets that contain either `while` or `for` Java statements. Embedding such blocks of code into JSP pages makes it very difficult for JSP developers who are not familiar with Java to do their job effectively, and scriptlets have a nasty habit of introducing silly, hard-to-detect bugs as well as reducing the readability of JSPs. The best JSPs will contain little, if any scriptlet code at all!

Thankfully, JSTL offers two useful actions for such purposes: <c:forEach> for general data and <c:forTokens> for string tokenizing.

The <c:forEach> Action

The <c:forEach> action is probably one of the most useful actions provided by the JSTL that enables its body content to be processed a number of times. The <c:forEach> action repeatedly processes its body content over a collection of objects or until a set number of iterations has been achieved.

The syntax for the <c:forEach> action is as follows:

Syntax 1: Iterate over a collection of objects

```
<c:forEach[var="varName"] items="collection" [varStatus="varStatusName"]
[begin="begin"] [end="end"] [step="step"]>
    body content
</c:forEach>
```

Syntax 2: Iterate a fixed number of times

```
<c:forEach [var="varName"] [varStatus="varStatusName"]
begin="begin" end="end" [step="step"]>
    body content
</c:forEach>
```

As mentioned earlier, the `<c:forEach>` action can either iterate over a collection of objects, or iterate a fixed number of times.

If iterating over a collection (Syntax 1), then the only required parameter is the collection itself, specified via the `items` attribute. The object referenced by the items variable can be any one of the following data types:

- An array
- An implementation of `java.util.Collection`
- An implementation of `java.util.Iterator`
- An implementation of `java.util.Enumeration`
- An implementation of `java.util.Map`
- A string of comma-separated values

Whichever data type `items` references, the type of the exposed `var` variable will be that of the object in the underlying collection. The only exceptions to this are arrays of primitives and `java.util.Maps` that are represented by the object wrapper class of the primitive type and `Map.Entry`, respectively.

Syntax 2 can be used when a fixed number of iterations are required. Using this particular syntax, the type of the exposed `var` variable will be `Integer` and will be incremented by 1 or `step` at the end of each iteration. The body content will be processed repeatedly until the `var` variable is greater than or equal to the `end` variable. This option is usually used when iterating over a finite (and known) collection.

Due to the flexibility provided by the `<c:forEach>` action it's inevitable it will be slightly more complex than some of the actions seen so far. For this reason the complete attribute list for the `action` is as follows:

Attribute	Required	Default	Description
items	No	None	Collection of items to iterate over. If null then no iteration takes place
begin	No	0	If specified, must be >=0 *If* items *specified:* Iteration begins at the item located at the specified value *If* items *not specified:* Iteration stats from specified value
end	No	Last object in the collection	If specified must be >=begin *If* items *specified:* Iteration stops at the item at the specified index (inclusive) *If* items *not specified:* Iteration stops when index reaches specified value
step	No	1 (process all objects)	If specified must be >= 1 Iteration processes every step item in the collection
var	No	None	Name of the scoped variable that represents the current item of the iteration
varStatus	No	None	Name of the scoped variable that represents the status of the iteration Object is of type javax.servlet.jsp.jstl.core.LoopStatus

As an example, imagine that as part of serving a client request, a controlling servlet has caused some business logic to query a database and retrieve a result set. The data retrieved is then used to populate a collection of objects, let's say Book objects, which are placed into the user's session before control is forwarded to a JSP in the presentation tier to display the results.

The <c:forEach> action is extremely useful for this purpose and is commonly used to retrieve the collection from the user's session and iterate over its contents to build an HTML table. Let's see an example of some code to do just that:

```
<c:forEach var="book" items="${sessionScope.books}">
  <tr>
    <td align="right" bgcolor="#ffffff">
    <c:out value="${book.title}"/>
    </td>
  </tr>
</c:forEach>
```

As you can see, the collection of books (which presumably was stored in the session scope by the name of books) is retrieved from the session and the action iterates over the collection of Book objects. The action then creates the data for a single row of an HTML table, populated by the title of each book.

The <c:forTokens> Action

The second iterating action provided by the JSTL is <c:forTokens>, which iterates over a string of tokens separated by a set of delimiters, much in the same way as the functionality provided by the java.util.StringTokenizer class that you may be familiar with.

The syntax for the action is as follows:

```
<c:forTokens items="stringOfTokens" delims="delimiters"
                       [var="varName"] [varStatus="varStatusName"]
                       [begin="begin"] [end="end"] [step="step"]>
    body content
</c:forEach>
```

As you can see, the attribute list is somewhat similar to the <c:forEach> action:

Attribute	Required	Default	Description
items	Yes	None	The string to tokenize
delims	Yes	None	The delimiter characters that separate the tokens of the string
begin	No	0	If specified, must be >=0 The token to start with
end	No	Last token in the string to be tokenized	If specified must be >=begin The token to end with
step	No	1 (process all objects)	If specified must be >= 1 Iteration processes every step item in the collection
var	No	None	Name of the scoped variable that represents the current item of the iteration
varStatus	No	None	Name of the scoped variable that represents the status of the iteration. Object is of type javax.servlet.jsp.jstl.core.LoopStatus

Instead of iterating over a collection of objects or between set values like the <c:forEach> tag, the <c:forTokens> tag works with a string of characters separated by designated delimiter characters. Data is often structured in this way, with probably the most common example being the Comma Separated Value (CSV) file often used with spreadsheet and database applications. As the name suggests, a CSV file contains "rows" of data with each "column" or piece of data separated by a comma. Let's take a look at a simple example of the <c:forToken> tag in action!

Imagine that you have some comma-separated data, perhaps the contents of a customer marketing CSV spreadsheet that has the following structure:

```
FirstName,LastName,Sex,Occupation,London
```

As you can see, the previous data is concerned with customer data. You want to present this information in a more readable format such as an HTML table. Because the data is structured with a consistent delimiter character separating the "tokens" of data, this task is very easy with the <c:forTokens> tag as you can see here:

```
<%@ taglib uri="http://java.sun.com/jstl/core" prefix="c" %>

<c:set var="queryResult" value="Dan,Jepp,Male,26,Java Developer,London"
       scope="request" />

<html>
<body>
<table border="1">
  <tr>
    <th>First Name</th>
    <th>Last Name</th>
    <th>Sex</th>
    <th>Age</th>
    <th>Occupation</th>
    <th>Location</th>
  </tr>
  <tr>
  <c:forTokens items="${queryResult}" delims="," var="token">
    <td><c:out value="${token}"/></td>
  </c:forTokens>
  </tr>
</table>
</body>
</html>
```

This very simple example has only a single string of data from which it has to build an HTML table with a single row of data. The main structure of our HTML table is constructed and each individual column of data (encompassed within <td></td>) is easily accessible via the <c:forTokens> tag, which iterates along the string of data declared in the queryResult attribute, thereby extracting each token separated via the comma delimiter (as noted by the delims parameter). Notice how each token is accessed from inside the body of the tag via the token variable, which is declared as an attribute of the <c:forToken> tag itself.

The output of the following JSP is as follows:

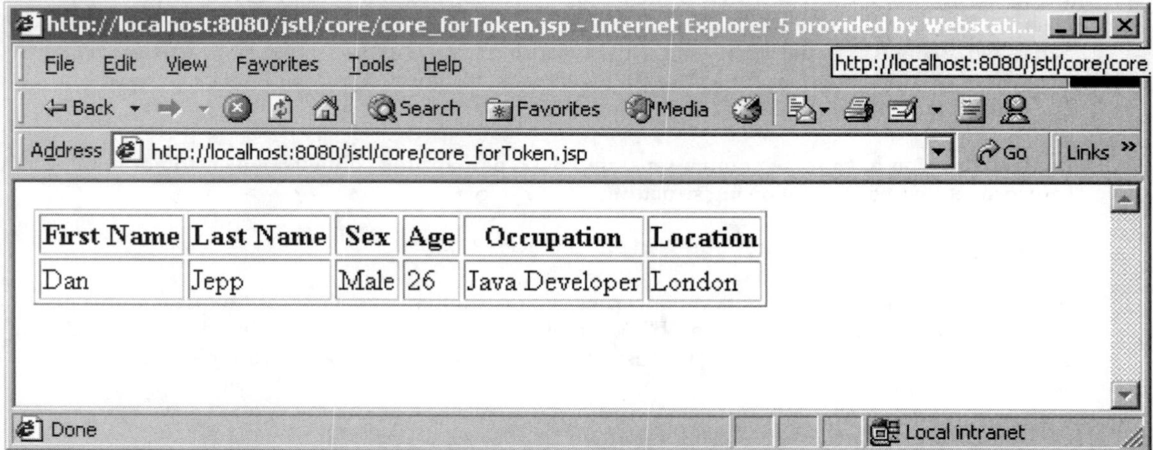

Without the `<c:forTokens>` tag this simple problem wouldn't have been as easy to overcome and may well have involved some ugly JSP scriptlet code and an instance of a `java.util.StringTokenizer` class. You can see that this is a far more readable and maintainable solution!

A slightly more realistic example may combine the use of the `<c:forEach>` tag to store multiple strings of delimited data, which is perhaps the result of a database search for files. As the `<c:forEach>` tag iterates through each delimited string, the `<c:forTokens>` tag can produce the necessary HTML table row.

URL-Related Actions

Obviously the ability to import, link, and redirect is fundamental in any JSP-based web application. The JSTL provides several useful URL-related actions to simplify these requirements.

The <c:import> Action

This action imports the content of a URL-based resource and provides a simple, generic way to access URL-based resources that can either be included or processed within the JSP page.

You can see a good example of the `<c:import>` action at work as it works with some of the actions from the XML library, which, of course, require an XML document to work with. The `<c:import>` action is the simplest way to retrieve a file containing XML or XSLT, which is then used by subsequent XML actions for processing. For example:

```
<%@ taglib uri="http://java.sun.com/jstl/core" prefix="c" %>
<%@ taglib uri="http://java.sun.com/jstl/xml" prefix="x" %>

<c:import url="http://mybokstore.com/book.xml" var="url" />
<x:parse xml="${url}" var="book" scope="session" />
```

Here you can see how the <c:import> action is used to retrieve a file called book.xml from a remote location, which is then utilized by the <x:parse> action from the XML tag library. Note that in this case, because of the presence of the var parameter, the actual contents of the file aren't written to the current JspWriter but are instead stored in the named parameter.

The <c:import> action can also be used to specify absolute, relative, foreign, context-relative, and FTP URL resources to provide a lot more functionality than the standard <jsp:include> action you're so used to having.

The <c:url> Action

The <c:url> action provides a handy way of constructing correctly formatted URLs that have the correct URL rewriting rules applied.

As you're no doubt aware, without session tracking or the ability to recognize a number of requests from the same user, the majority of complex web-based applications wouldn't be functionally possible due to the statelessness of the HTTP protocol. Generally, browsers provide the session-tracking mechanism by storing cookies (small text files stored on the client machine), which are sent back with each request the client makes during a "session." Because most modern browsers enable the user to disable cookies (usually for security reasons), it's very important to ensure that any URLs that your web applications use are URL-rewritten to ensure that their session-tracking capabilities are maintained if cookies are disabled.

A rewritten URL looks something like this:

http://www.myserver.com/shop/checkout.jsp;jsessionid=42eab543dc2

As you can see, the actual rewriting of a URL simply involves appending a special value to the end of the query string, which is used to track requests that originate from the same user. These requests are therefore part of the same session.

Previously, JSP scriptlets were typically used to ensure that all URLs were rewritten by calling the encodeURL() method provided by the HttpServletResponse interface.

The <c:url> action takes care of all the URL rewriting on your behalf without the need for any scriptlet code! For example, to encode the URL, all that's required is the following:

```
<c:url value="http://www.myserver.com/shop/checkout.jsp" />
```

The <c:redirect> Action

As the name suggests, the <c:redirect> action simply sends an HTTP redirect to a client.

For example, to redirect a user to perhaps an updated site or a moved application, the action is used as follows:

```
<c:redirect url="http://www.myNewUrl.com" />
```

It's as simple as that! The action does also support the use of another optional attribute called `context`, which can be used to identify the name of a context when redirecting to a relative URL that belongs to a foreign context. In more simple terms this means that you can actually forward the request to another web application hosted inside the same container!

The <c:param> Action

The `<c:import>`, `<c:url>`, and `<c:redirect>` actions all deal with URLs and as you're probably aware it's pretty common to pass request parameters as part of URLs by appending them to the query string.

The `<c:param>` action is designed solely for this purpose and may be used as a nested tag in the body content of either the `<c:import>`, `<c:url>`, or `<c:redirect>` actions. The `<c:param>` action takes two very simple attributes, `name` and `value`, which simply represent the name of the request parameter along with its value, respectively. Note also that the value of the `name` and `value` attributes are URL encoded by default.

For example:

```
<c:url value="http://www.myBookshop.com/books/catalogue.jsp" >
  <c:param name="isbn" value="123456" />
</c:url>
```

Like many of the JSTL actions, the `<c:param>` action can be used in two forms, first as shown previously, and second, whereby the value for the parameter is given inside the body content of the action itself. Let's take a look at the previous example using the alternative format:

```
<c:url value="http://www.myBookshop.com/books/catalogue.jsp" >
  <c:param name="isbn">123456</c:param>
</c:url>
```

The Internationalization and Formatting Tag Library

Preparing an application so it's ready for the global marketplace is known as internationalization (or I18n for short). A related term, localization (or l10n), refers to the process of customizing an application for a particular language or region.

The popularity of the Internet has enabled organizations to vastly increase their exposure and client base by exposing their services via dynamic web applications. Ensuring that clients from around the world can interact with such applications using their native language and conventions has never been more important.

The Internationalization and Formatting tag library provided by the JSTL provides a set of simple actions to aid this process and make use of the three key components associated with internationalization: locales, resource bundles, and base names.

Setting the Locale

The Internationalization and Formatting tag library provides a number of actions that allow you to control the locale settings for your JSP pages.

The <fmt:setLocale> Action

As the name suggests, this action can be used to override the client-specified locale for the processing of a JSP page. Any I18n formatting actions such as `<fmt:message>` that are found on the page will use this specified locale instead of the one sent by the client browser.

The chosen locale is stored in a variable called `javax.servlet.jsp.jstl.fmt.locale` and can be stored in any chosen scope.

This JSP code first sets the default locale for the page followed by the session:

```
<fmt:setLocale value ="en_US" />
<fmt:setLocale value ="fr_FR" scope="session" />
```

The `value` attribute accepts either a string representing the locale (a two letter, lowercase language code followed a two letter, uppercase country code), or a reference to a `java.util.Locale` object.

Note that it's also possible to set a default locale for use via the JSTL using the following configuration setting in the web applications deployment descriptor (`web.xml`):

```
<context-param>
  <param-name>javax.servlet.jsp.jstl.fmt.locale</param-name>
  <param-value>en</param-value>
</context-param>
```

As you can see, this configuration establishes English as the default locale for the application.

> **An important point to note is that the `<fmt:setLocale>` action overrides the browser-based locale setting. Therefore, if you use this action, make sure it's placed at the beginning of a JSP page before any I18n formatting actions.**

Messaging Actions

Once the locale has been defined for a client request, either by the client's browser settings or use of the `<fmt:setLocale>` action, the JSTL messaging actions can be used to display content to the client in its own language as identified by its locale.

To take advantage of localized messages, it's necessary as a developer to provide a collection of resources (usually strings) for each locale that you intend to support. Each collection of resources is known collectively as a `resource bundle` and is implemented via a standard `key=value` properties file. For more information, take a look at the Java 2 Platform, Standard Edition (J2SE) Javadocs for the `java.util.ResourceBundle` class.

The <fmt:bundle> and <fmt:setBundle> Actions

To enable the use of localized messages it's necessary to specify the required resource bundle that provides the localized messages.

Either the `<fmt:bundle>` or `<fmt:setBundle>` actions can be used to specify a resource bundle, and they're identified by the `basename` to be used in the JSP page. Once successfully declared, the resource bundle can then be used to provide localized messages via the `<fmt:message>` action, which you'll see shortly.

Although similar, the `<fmt:bundle>` and `<fmt:setBundle>` actions are used in different ways to produce localized messages in JSP pages.

The `<fmt:bundle>` action is used to declare an I18n localization context for use by I18n-aware tags within its body content:

```
<fmt:bundle basename="Labels">
    <fmt:message key="labels.firstName"/>
    <fmt:message key="labels.lastName"/>
</fmt:bundle>
```

Here, a resource bundle with the name `Labels` is declared to provide the localized resources for any nested `<fmt:message>` actions.

Due to the fact that the `<fmt:bundle>` action is designed to work so closely with nested `<fmt:message>` actions, a handy optional attribute can also be used as follows:

```
<fmt:bundle basename="Labels" prefix="labels">
    <fmt:message key="firstName"/>
    <fmt:message key="lastName"/>
</fmt:bundle>
```

As you can see, the optional `prefix` attribute enables the setting of a predefined prefix that is prepended to the key attribute of any nested `<fmt:message>` actions, which makes their use so much simpler.

The `<fmt:setBundle>` action also provides similar functionality to those you just saw, but with a subtle difference. Instead of having to nest any `<fmt:message>` actions as body content, the `<fmt:setBundle>` action enables a resource bundle to be stored in the configuration variable `javax.servlet.jsp.jstl.fmt.localizationContext`, so any `<fmt:message>` actions that appear elsewhere in the JSP page can access the bundle without having to continually declare it as follows:

```
<fmt:setBundle basename="Labels" />
<fmt:message prefix="labels.firstName" />
```

The `<fmt:setBundle>` action also enables you to declare the exported variable that stores the bundle along with its scope. This flexibility makes it simple to use multiple bundles within the same JSP interchangeably.

Note that the JSTL does provide a mechanism to set a default resource bundle for a web application via the following configuration setting in the applications deployment descriptor (`web.xml`):

```
<context-param>
  <param-name>
    javax.servlet.jsp.jstl.fmt.localizationContext
  </param-name>
  <param-value>messages.MyMessages</param-value>
</context-param>
```

The <fmt:message> Action

As mentioned earlier, localized messages are retrieved from a resource bundle using the `<fmt:message>` action, which uses a key parameter to extract the message from the resource bundle and print it to the current `JspWriter`.

You've also seen that the `<fmt:message>` action can be used by itself on a page or as body content to the `<fmt:bundle>` action. Should you wish to use the action by itself you can specify via the optional bundle attribute the resource bundle to use. This can be the default configured bundle or a localization content that has been configured and stored in a separate variable by the `<fmt:setBundle>` action.

Another optional parameter, `var`, enables the localized message to be stored in a parameter instead of being printed to the `JspWriter`. As with most of the JSTL tags, the scope of this variable can be set using the `scope` attribute.

Let's build a simple working example to demonstrate the `<fmt:setLocale>`, `<fmt:setBundle>`, and `<fmt:message>` tags working together to create a localized JSP page.

Your first task is to set up the locale-specific resources, and in this case you're simply going to localize some simple strings by utilizing a resource bundle. There are several ways in which a resource bundle can be created, but the most simple involves building a list of name-value pairs representing the locale-specific resources that you wish to externalize from the application code. Let's localize some simple strings and provide implementations in both English and Spanish.

```
nameQuestion=What is your name?
ageQuestion=How old are you?
locationQuestion=Where do you live?
submit=Send
```

Here you'll localize four strings whose name-value pairs are stored on the class path (under the `WEB-INF/classes` directory, for example) in a file called `labels_en.properties`. This file will be the English resource bundle for the localization-aware JSP. Next let's provide another resource bundle, this time in Spanish:

```
nameQuestion=¿Como te llamas?
ageQuestion=¿Quantos anios tienes?
locationQuestion=¿Donde vives?
submit=Mande
```

As you can see, the names stay the same but this time the values are in Spanish! This bundle must be placed in a file called `labels_es.properties`.

Now that you have the resource bundles in place you can code the localized JSP:

```
<%@ taglib uri="http://java.sun.com/jstl/core" prefix="c"%>
<%@ taglib uri="http://java.sun.com/jstl/fmt" prefix="fmt" %>

<fmt:setLocale value="en_GB" scope="request"/>
<fmt:setBundle basename="labels"/>

<h2>Survey</h2>
<form action="">
<table>
  <tr>
    <td><fmt:message key="nameQuestion"/></td>
    <td><input type="text" size="16"></td>
  </tr>
  <tr>
    <td><fmt:message key="ageQuestion"/></td>
    <td><input type="text" size="16"></td>
  </tr>
  <tr>
    <td><fmt:message key="locationQuestion"/></td>
    <td><input type="text" size="16"></td>
  </tr>
  <tr>
    <td><input type="submit" value='<fmt:message key="submit"/>'></td>
  </tr>
</table>
</form>
```

This JSP simply sets the locale to be `en_GB` and configures the resource bundle using the `<fmt:setBundle>` action along with the bundle `basename` called `labels`. The rest of the JSP simply builds a small HTML form that asks the user to input some information about herself. Notice how you have localized the labels for the form input fields using the `<fmt:message>` action.

Not surprisingly, when you run this code, the locale is set to `en_GB` and the appropriate resource bundle is loaded. With the help of the `<fmt:message>` actions, the following page is built:

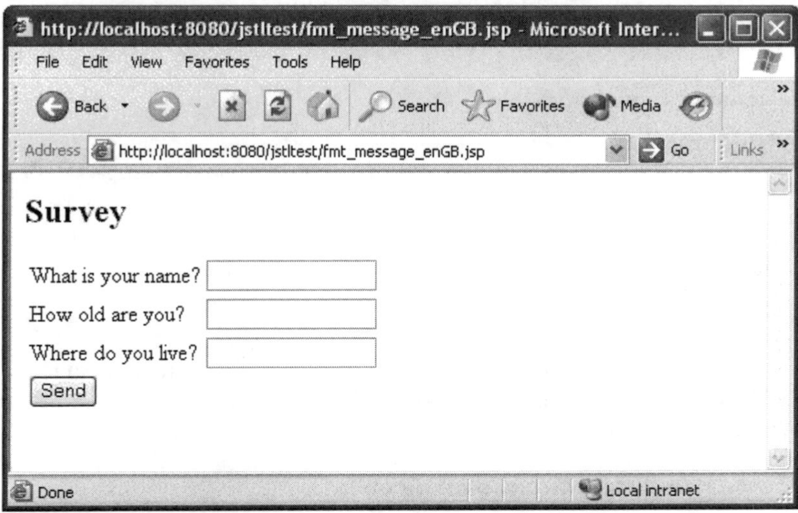

To demonstrate that the page is supported in both English-speaking countries as well as Spanish-speaking countries, you simply have to change the following line of code:

```
<fmt:setLocale value="es_ES" scope="request"/>
```

Of course in the real world, the locale is usually retrieved from a special header that is sent by the client's browser during the initial request. The only reason we explicitly set the locale here is to demonstrate how the JSP would work in a Spanish-speaking country. The output is as follows:

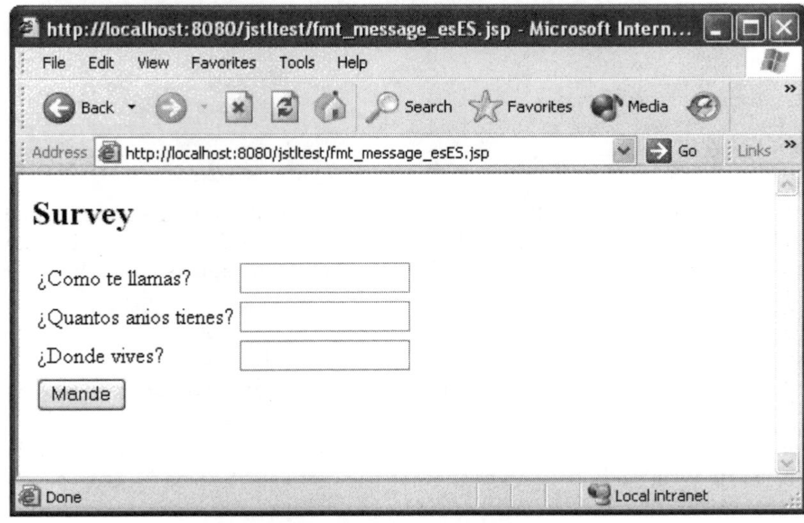

Formatting Actions

Ensuring that your clients view your JSP pages in their own language is just the tip of the iceberg with regard to building a fully internationalized and localized application. In addition to language, users from different locales have different standards regarding the following:

- Date and time formats
- Number formats
- Currency formats
- Colors
- Page layouts
- Address standards (zip code)

Luckily, to make your job easier, the formatting tag library provided by the JSTL enables various data elements in a JSP page, such as numbers, dates, and times, to be formatted and parsed in a locale-sensitive or customized manner.

The <fmt:timeZone> and <fmt:setTimeZone> Actions

Date-and-time information on a JSP page can be displayed in a manner consistent with the preferred time zone of a client. This is enormously useful if your server that hosts the page and the client reside in different time zones. The JSTL provides two actions to enable any I18n-aware date-and-time actions to format or parse their date-and-time information in an appropriate manner.

The `<fmt:timeZone>` and `<fmt:setTimeZone>` actions complement each other in a similar fashion as the `<fmt:bundle>` and `<fmt:setBundle>` actions introduced earlier. The `<fmt:timeZone>` action is used to specify a `TimeZone` for any nested I18n-aware actions that appear inside its body content whereas the `<fmt:setTimezone>` can be used to store a reference to a `TimeZone` in an exportable variable for use anywhere on a JSP page.

The `<fmt:timeZone>` action is simply used as follows:

```
<fmt:timeZone value="GMT">
    //…date/time actions go here
</fmt:timeZone>
```

As you can see, a single attribute called `value` is used to specify the time zone, which can either be a `java.util.TimeZone` object or a string that represents one of the time zone IDs supported by the Java platform (such as "America/Los Angeles" or a custom time zone such as "GMT-8").

The `<fmt:setTimeZone>` action is used as follows:

```
<fmt:setTimeZone value="GMT" var="myTimeZone" scope="request" />
```

This action enables a `java.util.TimeZone` object to be stored in a scoped variable that can be utilized by any I18n-aware actions such as the `<fmt:formatDate>` and `<fmt:parseDate>` actions, which you'll see shortly.

The <fmt:formatDate> and <fmt:parseDate> Actions

The two I18n-aware date actions provided by the JSTL are `<fmt:formatDate>` and `<fmt:parseDate>`. Both actions may be used in conjunction with the time-zone actions mentioned earlier.

The `<fmt:formatDate>` action provides flexible, time zone-aware formatting of `java.util.Date` objects so that the date and time may be displayed correctly depending on the client's time zone. In its most simplest form, the `<fmt:formatDate>` action applies the default formats of the current time zone and outputs them to the current `JspWriter` as follows:

```
<jsp:useBean id="now"  class="java.util.Date /">
<fmt:formatDate value="${now}"/>
```

As mentioned, the `<fmt:formatDate>` action is highly flexible and provides the ability to display dates and times in predefined or custom formats using the conventions as set out by the `java.text.DateFormat` class. The ability to store the formatted date in a scoped string variable is also provided.

The following example shows just some of the formatting options provided by the `<fmt:formatDate>` action. Notice how the standard `<jsp:useBean>` action is used here to create an instance of the `java.util.Date` class, which is used by the JSTL actions:

```
<%@ taglib uri="http://java.sun.com/jstl/fmt" prefix="fmt"%>

<jsp:useBean id="now" class="java.util.Date" />

<h1>Examples of Date & Time Formatting</h1>
<hr>
<h2>Default Time Zone</H2>
Default format : <fmt:formatDate value="${now}"/><br>
A Date only in a Custom dd/MM/yyyy format :
 <fmt:formatDate value="${now}" type="DATE" pattern="dd/MM/yyyy"/><br>
A Time only in MEDIUM format :
 <fmt:formatDate value="${now}" type="TIME" dateStyle="MEDIUM"/><br>
A Date and Time in FULL format :
 <fmt:formatDate value="${now}" type="BOTH" dateStyle="FULL"
                 timeStyle="FULL"/><br>
<hr>

<h2>America/Los_Angeles Time Zone</h2>

<fmt:timeZone value="America/Los_Angeles">
Default format : <fmt:formatDate value="${now}"/><br>
A Date only in a Custom MM-dd-yyyy format :
  <fmt:formatDate value="${now}" type="DATE" pattern="MM-dd-yyyy"/><br>
A Time only in MEDIUM format :
  <fmt:formatDate value="${now}" type="TIME" dateStyle="MEDIUM"/><br>
A Date and Time in FULL format :
  <fmt:formatDate value="${now}" type="BOTH" dateStyle="FULL"
                  timeStyle="FULL"/><br>
</fmt:timeZone>
```

Notice that in the first set of examples a time zone isn't specified, so the default time zone is used instead (GMT in this case). There are several examples that demonstrate the predefined date-and-time formats as well as a custom date format of dd/MM/yyyy.

The second set of examples explicitly set the time zone to America/Los_Angeles by using the <fmt:timeZone> action. Notice how the times have been automatically altered to their new time zone, clever eh! Also notice that you're using a different custom format of MM-dd-yyyy instead this time:

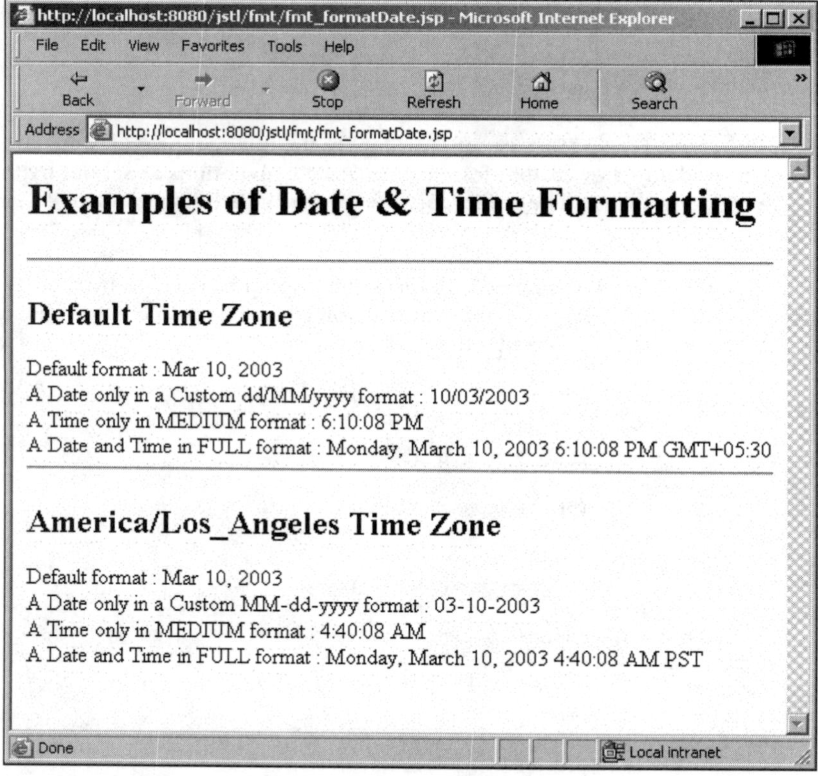

The <fmt:parseDate> action provides complimentary functionality to the <fmt:formatDate> action by parsing and converting the string representation of dates and times that were formatted in a locale-sensitive or customized manner into java.util.Date objects. This action is particularly useful if you need to enable clients from around the world to enter date-and-time information in their own local format and have it correctly parsed into the correct object at the server.

```
<fmt:parseDate type="date" pattern="dd/MM/yyyy" var="parsedDate">
    22/12/2002
</fmt:parseDate>
```

Note that the string representing the date to be parsed can either be passed in via the value attribute or in the actions body content as seen earlier. Here a custom date format is used to parse the string "22/12/2002" into a java.util.Date object and store a reference to it in the variable called parsedDate.

The <fmt:formatNumber> and <fmt:parseNumber> Actions

As mentioned earlier, there are many different forms of data that are represented differently based on the time zone or locale. You've seen the JSTL actions to support date-and-time localization so it should come as no real surprise that support is also provided for the formatting and parsing of numbers.

The <fmt:formatNumber> action is also flexible and capable of formatting a numeric value in a locale-sensitive or custom format as a number, currency, or percentage. For example, the following action ensures that the given number has at least three numbers of decimal places:

```
<fmt:formatNumber value="123.4" type="NUMBER" minFractionDigits="3" />
```

The result of this action will be to format the number 123.4 into the value 123.400. To demonstrate the I18n capabilities of the <fmt:formatNumber> action you can also automatically extract the correct currency symbol from the locale when working with monetary values:

```
<c:set var="salary" value="125000" />

<fmt:setLocale value="en_GB"/>
<fmt:formatNumber type="CURRENCY" value="${salary}" />

<fmt:setLocale value="it_IT"/>
<fmt:formatNumber type="CURRENCY" value="${salary}" />
```

As you can see, the previous example formats a currency (notice the type="CURRENCY" attribute) with the value of 125000 in both the English and Italian locales. The results of the following actions are as follows:

English Locale = £125,000.00
Italian Locale = ? 125.000,00

Notice how the change in locale radically affects the way the value is interpreted. The ? should of course be representing a Euro symbol (€).

As with the <fmt:parseDate> action, the <fmt:parseNumber> action is the reverse formatting tag, used to convert a formatted string representing either a number, currency, or percentage into an appropriate java.lang.Number.

The SQL Tag Library

The use of SQL or any form of direct-data access from inside the presentation tier is highly discouraged in production or large-scale applications in favor of a three-tier architecture. The benefits of such an architecture are that it encourages the presentation of your data (your JSP pages) to be cleanly separated from your business logic and data access thereby making your application far more adaptable and maintainable. Embedding SQL into your presentation tier is also a bad idea because of the implications it has on security.

However, as mentioned earlier, the JSTL specification was developed as part of the Java Community Process (JCP), and due to the fact that enough developers requested a library of actions to access relational databases, their wish was granted and they form part of the JSTL specification.

Love them or loathe them, the SQL access actions exist and their intended use is recommended for RAD prototyping or very small-scale applications only. Let's take a brief look at the functionality provided by the SQL tag library.

The <sql:setDataSource> Action

All of the actions provided in the SQL tag library operate on a data source defined by the `java.sql.DataSource` class. The primary job of the `<sql:setDataSource>` action is therefore to configure a data source that represents an underlying physical data store and expose it as either a scoped variable or the data source configuration object `javax.servlet.jsp.jstl.sql.DataSource`.

The configured data source is used by the remaining actions in the SQL library to source database connections so they may perform queries and updates, and so on.

A data source can be configured as follows:

```
<sql:setDataSource var="dataSource" driver="org.acme.sql.driver"
                   url="jdbc:msql://localhost/tempDB" user="Dan" password="pwd"/>
```

Note that that it's also possible to supply a relative path to a Java Naming and Directory Interface (JNDI) resource via the optional `dataSource` attribute.

The <sql:query> Action

Simple database query functionality is provided by the `<sql:query>` action:

```
<sql:query var="users" dataSource="${dataSource}" >
  SELECT * FROM User WHERE UserName='Dan'
</sql:query>
```

As you can see the `dataSource` attribute is used to reference a `DataSource` that was configured using the `<sql:setDataSource>` action. The mandatory `var` parameter is used to store the result of the query and is of type `javax.servlet.jsp.jstl.sql.Result`. It's possible to pass the string of SQL as either body content or using the `sql` attribute.

It's most familiar to see the <sql:query> and <c:forEach> actions working together to display the results of the query in an HTML table as follows:

```
<sql:query var="users" dataSource="myDataSource" >
  SELECT * FROM User WHERE UserName='Dan'
</sql:query>

<table>
<c:forEach var="row" items="${users.row}">
  <tr>
   <td><c:out value="${row.firstName}" /></td>
   <td><c:out value="${row.lastName}" /></td>
   <td><c:out value="${row.phoneNumber}" /></td>
  </tr>
</c:forEach>
</table>
```

> **Note that if the dataSource attribute is present then the <sql:query> action must not be nested inside a <sql:transaction> action.**

The <sql:update> Action

To compliment the <sql:query> action, the <sql:update> action enables SQL INSERT, UPDATE, and DELETE statements to be executed as well as a SQL DDL statement, which returns nothing (such as a table creation or alteration).

The syntax of this action is similar to that of the <sql:query> action. Again, a var attribute is available to store the result of the update statement except this time it's not mandatory. The type of the var parameter is java.lang.Integer.

```
<sql:update var="count" dataSource="myDataSource">
  DELETE FROM Users WHERE UserName <> 'Dan'
</sql:update>
```

The <sql:param> and <sql:dateParam> Actions

Both the <sql:query> and <sql:update> actions provide support for nested <sql:param> and <sql:date:param> actions that are used to pass parameters into a parameterized string of SQL.

Both actions are incredibly simple and only exist to hold a simple object via its value attribute.

```
<sql:param value="${userName}"/>
```

To see how these tags could be used as part of a parameterized SQL statement, let's revisit the example you saw in the <sql:update> example:

```
<sql:update var="count" dataSource="myDataSource">
  DELETE FROM Users WHERE UserName <> ? AND Status = ?
  <sql:param value="${userName}"/>
  <sql:param value="${status}"/>
</sql:update>
```

As you can see, the values held by each nested `<sql:param>` action are substituted for each parameter marker ("?") in the SQL. The order in which the `<sql:param>` actions occur determines which parameter is substituted.

The <sql:transaction> Action

The final action provided by the SQL tag library is the `<sql:transaction>` action, which enables a series of SQL actions to be grouped together to provide transactional behavior. Transactions enable a series of database actions (such as queries, inserts, deletes, and so on) to be treated as a single atomic action. The transaction is only committed permanently to the database when all the database actions within it complete successfully, otherwise the transaction is rolled back and any actions are reversed.

Any `<sql:query>` or `<sql:update>` actions that wish to be included as part of the transaction are simply nested inside of the `<sql:transaction>` action itself. For example, let's add the previous examples to demonstrate the `<sql:query>` and `<sql:update>` actions inside a transaction:

```
<sql:transaction dataSource="myDataSource" isolation="read_committed">
  <sql:query var="users">
    SELECT * FROM User WHERE UserName='Dan'
  </sql:query>
  <sql:update var="count">
    DELETE FROM Users WHERE UserName <> ? AND Status = ?
    <sql:param value="${userName}"/>
    <sql:param value="${status}"/>
  </sql:update>
</sql:transaction>
```

As you can see, it's simplicity itself! If both the `<sql:query>` and `<sql:update>` actions complete successfully then the transaction will automatically be committed!

The only points to be aware of are that any nested SQL tags must not supply their own `dataSource` attributes because this is declared by the `<sql:transaction>` action itself. An optional `isolation` attribute can also be supplied to set the isolation level of the transaction. This attribute must be one of the following values:

- `read_committed`
- `read_uncommitted`
- `repeatable_read`
- `serializable`

If not supplied, the isolation level is taken from the data source configuration itself.

The XML Processing Tag Library

XML has become the de facto standard for representing and exchanging data between enterprise applications. Data represented by XML isn't only "self-describing" and easy to validate, but it's also text based, which has further increased its popularity especially with the recent rise of web services technologies.

Increasingly XML is also being used by web applications internally to represent data retrieved from the business or database layer, which is then rendered into an appropriate format (HTML, WML, and so on) by the presentation layer. Therefore, more and more JSP page authors have to deal directly with the manipulation of XML in order to generate some content. Until now, dealing with data represented by XML has been a nontrivial task, often requiring specific programming skills of the page author. To address this problem the JSTL provides an XML processing tag library that is designed to solve many of the common tasks met by page authors dealing with XML data.

The XML processing tag library can be split into the following functional areas concerned with dealing with XML data.

- XML core actions
- XML flow control actions
- XML transformation actions

The first two functional areas are very similar in nature to the core and flow control actions provided by the core tag library, with the exception that they are designed to work with XML data. The XML transformation actions enable XML data to be transformed into other content using XSL Transformations (XSLT) stylesheets.

Naturally, one of the key requirements when dealing with XML documents is to be able to easily manipulate their content. The actions from the XML processing tag library are no different and are all based around XPath (a W3C recommendation since 1999) to select and specify individual parts of an XML document by a simple XPath expression.

The actions provided by the XML processing tag library only support the use of XPath expressions, which are evaluated by an appropriate XPath engine, via the `select` attribute. All other expressions are evaluated in the normal manner by the global EL in use.

In addition to the standard XPath syntax, the XPath engine provided by the JSTL also supports the following "scopes," which may be used in XPath expressions to access data stored in the various web applications scopes.

```
$param:
$header:
$cookie:
$initParam:
$pageScope:
$requestScope:
$sessionScope:
$applicationScope:
```

Hopefully you'll be familiar with these scopes as they are defined in the same manner as those used in the JSTL EL. Consider the following XPath expression:

```
$sessionScope:user
```

This expression could be used in a similar manner to the standard JSTL EL to reference an attribute called `user` stored inside the session scope.

XML Core Actions

As the name suggests, the XML core actions provide fundamental tasks required to interact with an XML document such as parsing and accessing the XML content.

The <x:parse>, <x:out>, and <x:set> Actions

The `<x:parse>` action simply parses a named XML document and saves it inside a scoped variable for use by other tags from the XML tag library. For example, let's imagine you're working with the following XML file that simply describes a book:

```
<book>
    <title>Professional JSP</title>
    <author>Brown et. al</author>
    <isbn>1-59059-225-5</isbn>
    <published>September 2003</published>
    <publisher>Apress</publisher>
    <url>www.apress.com/book/bookDisplay.html?bID=200</url>
</book>
```

Assuming this file is stored in a file called `book.xml`, you can parse this file and store the resulting object as follows:

```
<%@ taglib uri="http://java.sun.com/jstl/core" prefix="c" %>
<%@ taglib uri="http://java.sun.com/jstl/xml" prefix="x" %>

<c:import url="book.xml" var="url" />
<x:parse xml="${url}" var="book" scope="session" />
```

Hopefully you'll be comfortable with the `<c:import>` action from the core library, which is simply used to generate the appropriate URL to the `book.xml` file (which is stored in the same directory as the JSP page). The `<x:parse>` action parses the XML file and stores it in the session-scoped variable `book`. In the earlier example the `var` parameter was used to indicate the name of a scoped variable to hold the object created as a result of the parse. The JSTL specification doesn't define the type for this object and leaves it up to the container to specify the most appropriate type. However, if the parameter `varDom` were used instead then the JSTL specification would insist that the type of the resulting object must be `org.w3c.dom.Document`.

If you're familiar with the JSTL core tag library introduced earlier then you should be able to guess what the `<x:out>` and `<x:set>` actions do because they're like similarly named tags from the core tag library. These similarities aren't by chance; the `<x:out>` and `<x:set>` actions from the XML tag library are functionally identical to the `<c:out>` and `<c:set>` actions from the core tag library with the exception that they're designed to work with XML documents.

The `<x:out>` action simply evaluates an XPath expression (reference to somewhere in the XML document) and outputs the result of the evaluation to the current `JspWriter`. Let's build on the earlier example to demonstrate the use of the `<x:out>` action:

```
<%@ taglib uri="http://java.sun.com/jstl/core" prefix="c" %>
<%@ taglib uri="http://java.sun.com/jstl/xml" prefix="x" %>
<c:import url="book.xml" var="url" />
<x:parse xml="${url}" var="book" scope="session" />
<b><x:out select="$book/book/title"/></b><br>
<x:out select="$book/book/author"/><br>
<x:out select="$book/book/url"/><br>
```

You still parse the XML file in the same way but this time some `<x:out>` actions have been added that can be used to extract the values of the `title`, `author`, and `url` nodes from beneath the parent `book` node (take a look at the earlier `book.xml` listing if you're confused). The document is simply parsed and interrogated by the `<x:out>` actions that use XPath expressions to retrieve the required data. The output of the previous JSP is as follows:

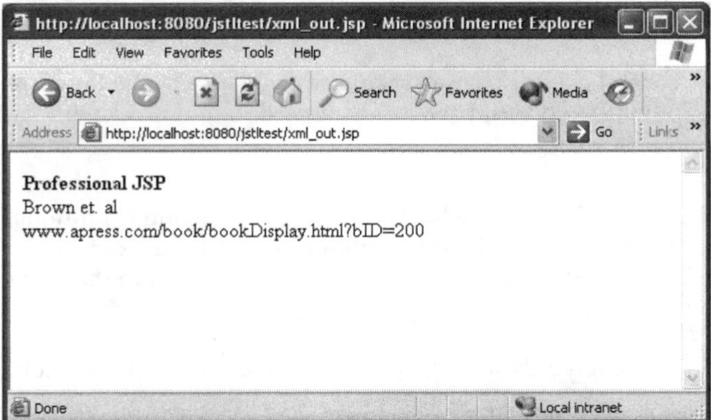

As mentioned earlier, the `<x:set>` action is also very close to the `<c:set>` action from the core tag library. Instead of evaluating an XPath expression and returning it to the current `JspWriter`, the `<x:set>` actions simply store the values inside scoped variables.

Just to demonstrate all three tags working together let's see how the <x:set> action can be used in the previous example:

```
<%@ taglib uri="http://java.sun.com/jstl/core" prefix="c" %>
<%@ taglib uri="http://java.sun.com/jstl/xml" prefix="x" %>

<c:import url="book.xml" var="url" />
<x:parse xml="${url}" var="book" scope="session" />

<x:set select="$book/book/title" var="title" scope="session"/>
<x:set select="$book/book/author" var="author" scope="session"/>
<x:set select="$book/book/url" var="bookUrl" scope="session"/>

<b><x:out select="$title" /></b><br>
<x:out select="$author" /><br>
<x:out select="$bookUrl" /><br>
```

As you can see, instead of using the <x:out> action to retrieve the values from the XML directly, you use the <x:set> action to store the values to scoped variables first and then output them via the <x:out> action.

XML Flow Control Actions

Now that you've seen how you can parse, store, and retrieve XML data, you can take a look at the XML flow control actions that conditionally process JSP code based on the result of an XPath expression and iterate over elements inside an XML document.

Again, the XML flow control actions bear a striking resemblance to the flow control actions from the core tag library. The only difference is, yes you've guessed it, they work with XML documents!

The <x:if> Action

Like the <c:if> action from the core tag library, the <x:if> action conditionally processes some JSP code based on a Boolean expression. The only difference is that the <x:if> action uses an XPath expression that is evaluated and converted into a Boolean according to the semantics of the XPath `boolean()` function:

- A number is true if and only if it's neither positive or negative zero nor NaN
- A nodeset is true if and only if it's nonempty
- A string is true if and only if its length is nonzero

The <x:if> action only processes its body content if the Boolean condition evaluates to true.

Let's use the book.xml example again to work on the marketing tactics for new Apress titles!

```
<%@ taglib uri="http://java.sun.com/jstl/core" prefix="c" %>
<%@ taglib uri="http://java.sun.com/jstl/xml" prefix="x" %>

<c:import url="book.xml" var="url" />
<x:parse xml="${url}" var="book" scope="session" />

<x:if select="$book/book/publisher='Apress'">
  Another great title from Apress!
  <p>
  <b><x:out select="$book/book/title"/></b><br>
  <x:out select="$book/book/author"/><br>
  <x:out select="$book/book/url"/><br>
</x:if>
```

You can see that the <x:if> action enables you to control whether to output any information based on the content of the XML. In this case if the value of the books Publisher attribute is 'APress' then you'll happily publicize the book and generate some content. If the Boolean condition is false and a different publisher has been used then you won't generate any information about the book…sneaky eh!

According to the book.xml you used earlier, the book has indeed been published by Apress and so the body of the previous <x:if> action may be processed. The result is as follows:

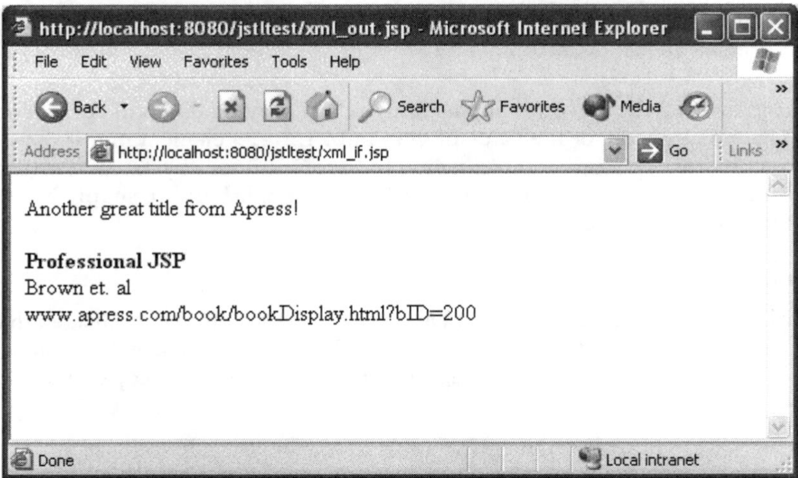

The <x:choose>, <x:when>, and <x:otherwise> Actions

To compliment the <x:if> action mentioned earlier there are also a set of actions to provide mutually exclusive, XML-dependant conditional behavior in exactly the same way as the actions in the core tag library.

The following JSP builds on the earlier example and provides you with the ability to market books from different publishers with different content:

```
<%@ taglib uri="http://java.sun.com/jstl/core" prefix="c" %>
<%@ taglib uri="http://java.sun.com/jstl/xml" prefix="x" %>

<c:import url="book.xml" var="url" />
<x:parse xml="${url}" var="book" scope="session" />

<x:choose>
  <x:when select="$book/book/publisher='Apress'">
    Another great title from Apress!
  </x:when>

  <x:when select="$book/book/publisher='Bloggs Publisher'">
    A reasonable title from Bloggs Publisher!
  </x:when>

  <x:otherwise>
    A title from an unknown publisher
  </x:otherwise>
</x:choose>

<p>
<b><x:out select="$book/book/title"/></b><br>
<x:out select="$book/book/author"/><br>
<x:out select="$book/book/url"/><br>
```

As you can see, by using the `<x:choose>` action you can provide different content depending on the value of an XPath expression, or the value of the `<Publisher>` element in this case. If the value is `'APress'` you provide the flagship introduction but provide books by `'Bloggs Plublisher'` with a separate but toned-down introduction. Any titles by other publishers are simply handled by the `<x:otherwise>` action to give a low-key introduction.

The <x:forEach> Action

Of course XML documents in the real world are likely to be far more complicated than the simple `book.xml` example you've been using. For one, the file only contains the description of a single book. Let's complicate matters slightly by changing the format of the XML to cope with multiple books as follows:

```
<books>
  <book>
    <title>Professional JSP</title>
    <author>Brown et. al</author>
    <isbn>1-59059-225-5</isbn>
    <published>September 2003</published>
    <publisher>Apress</publisher>
    <url>www.apress.com/book/bookDisplay.html?bID=200</url>
  </book>
  <book>
    <title>Macbeth</title>
    <author>William Shakespeare</author>
```

```
        <isbn>1123456789</isbn>
        <published>A long time ago</published>
        <publisher>Bloggs Publishers</publisher>
        <url>http://booksrus.co.uk/titles/1123456789.html</url>
    </book>
    <book>
        <title>Fly Fishing</title>
        <author>JR Hartley</author>
        <isbn>987654321</isbn>
        <published>May 1947</published>
        <publisher>ABC Printers Press</publisher>
        <url>http://books.com/books.jsp?id=987654321</url>
    </book>
</books>
```

It should be quite obvious that the existing solution for marketing the books as described by the XML won't work with multiple titles. You've also changed the XML structure as well so that the <books> element now contains several <book> elements. You need another solution.

Thankfully the JSTL XML library provides an iterating action <x:forEach> that is especially designed for such a purpose and works in a very similar way to the <c:forEach> action from the core tag library.

In order to iterate over the <book> elements the <x:forEach> action accepts an XPath expression that points to the <book> element and stores it in a scoped variable as follows:

```
<x:forEach select="$book/Books/book" var="currentBook">
  ...
</x:forEach>
```

As you can see, the first <book> element will be stored in the variable `currentBook` and may be accessed by XML actions such as <x:out>, <x:set>, and so on, inside the body of the action. All you need to do really is wrap the existing code from the previous example inside of an <x:forEach> action and the iteration will be handled automatically, then hopefully all of the books in `books.xml` will be publicized!

The following code listing demonstrates this simple functionality. Note that the only other changes that have occurred are some minor HTML changes to make the generated page look a little more professional. For now just concentrate on spotting how the <x:forEach> action encapsulates all the previous example code you've seen so far:

```
<%@ taglib uri="http://java.sun.com/jstl/core" prefix="c" %>
<%@ taglib uri="http://java.sun.com/jstl/xml" prefix="x" %>

<c:import url="books.xml" var="url" />
<x:parse xml="${url}" var="book" scope="session" />

<x:forEach select="$book/books/book" var="currentBook">
  <x:choose>
    <x:when select="$currentBook/publisher='Apress'">
      <font color="red">
```

```
          <h1>Another great title from Apress!</h1>
        </font>
      </x:when>

      <x:when select="$currentBook/publisher='Bloggs Publishers'">
        <font color="red">
          <h2>A reasonable title from Bloggs Publisher!</h2>
        </font>
      </x:when>

      <x:otherwise>
        <font color="red">
          <h3>A title from an unknown publisher</h3>
        </font>
      </x:otherwise>
    </x:choose>

    <table border="0">
      <tr>
        <td colspan="2"><b><x:out select="$currentBook/title"/><b></td>
      </tr>
      <tr>
        <td><i>Author :</i></td>
        <td><x:out select="$currentBook/author"/></td>
      </tr>
      <tr>
        <td><i>ISBN :</i></td>
        <td><x:out select="$currentBook/isbn"/></td>
      </tr>
      <tr>
        <td><i>Published :</i></td>
        <td><x:out select="$currentBook/published"/></td>
      </tr>
      <tr>
        <td><i>URL :</i></td>
        <td><a href='<x:out select="$currentBook/url"/>'>
                    <x:out select="$currentBook/title"/></a></td>
      </tr>
    </table>
    <hr>

  </x:forEach>
```

To give you an idea of what the finished article looks like take a look at the following screen shot. You'll agree that before the JSTL loading, parsing, and building such a page would have been a nontrivial task, but now it's really simple!

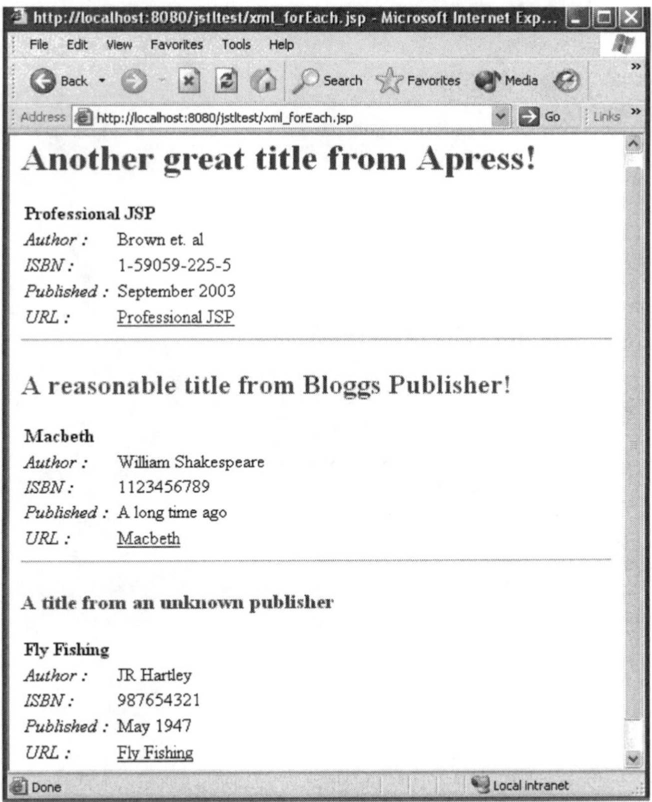

XML Transformation Actions

The <x:transform> Action

Quite simply, the XML transformation actions provided by the JSTL are designed to apply an XSLT stylesheet to an XML document. Usually, the result of the XSLT transformation is returned as output, but it's also possible to store the result inside a scoped variable instead so that it may be accessed by some of the other XML actions that you've already seen.

In order to demonstrate the capabilities of the `<x:transform>` actions let's transform the `books.xml` file that you saw earlier into a simple HTML table by applying an XSLT transformation. The first step is to create the XSLT stylesheet; let's call it `books.xsl`:

```
<?xml version="1.0"?>
<xsl:stylesheet version="1.0" xmlns:xsl="http://www.w3.org/1999/XSL/Transform">
<xsl:template match="/">
```

```
<html>
<body>
<h2>Our Current Book List</h2>
<table border="2">
  <tr>
    <!-- the header -->
    <td>title</td>
    <td>author</td>
    <td>isbn</td>
    <td>published</td>
    <td>publisher</td>
    <td>url</td>
  </tr>

  <xsl:for-each select="books/book">
    <tr>
      <td><b><xsl:value-of select="title"/></b></td>
      <td><xsl:value-of select="author"/></td>
      <td><xsl:value-of select="isbn"/></td>
      <td><xsl:value-of select="published"/></td>
      <td><i><xsl:value-of select="publisher"/></i></td>
      <td><xsl:value-of select="url"/></td>
    </tr>
  </xsl:for-each>
</table>

</body>
</html>
</xsl:template>
</xsl:stylesheet>
```

While this chapter isn't intended to be a guide to XSLT transformations, hopefully you can follow this code. In a nutshell, the `<xsl:for-each select="Books/Book">` expression is a simple way of iterating over a series of elements as defined by the XPath expression `books/book` (all of the `<book>` elements beneath the root `<books>` element). The code inside the `<xsl:for-each>` expression simply creates the data for a single row of the HTML table by extracting the required elements (that is, `<xsl:value-of select="title"/>` extracts the value of the `<title>` element).

In order to apply this stylesheet (`books.xsl`) to the XML file (`books.xml`), you can import the XML and XSL files and use the `<x:transform>` action as follows:

```
<%@ taglib uri="http://java.sun.com/jstl/core" prefix="c" %>
<%@ taglib uri="http://java.sun.com/jstl/xml" prefix="x" %>

<c:import url="books.xml" var="books" />
<c:import url="books.xsl" var="xslt" />

<x:transform xml="${books}" xslt="${xslt}"/>
```

You must agree that this is a very simple page, but thanks to the JSTL actions you now have a very powerful mechanism for producing content from XML files. JSP page authors need not have any Java skills whatsoever in order to produce rich content. Just consider how much more difficult (and cluttered, less maintainable, ugly, and so on) this would have been with a scriptlet-based approach. Thankfully, those days are behind you!

Let's take a look at the outcome of the JSTL-based XSLT transformation.

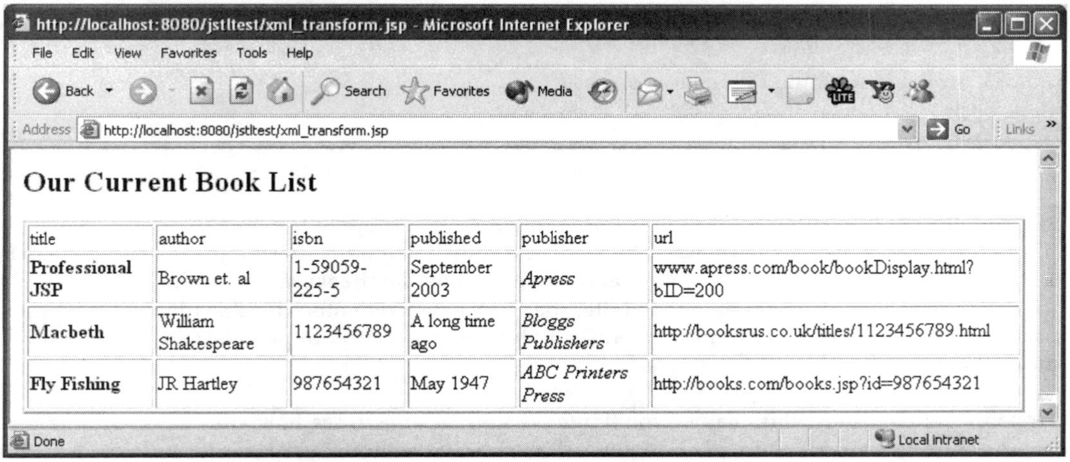
http://localhost:8080/jstltest/xml_transform.jsp - Microsoft Internet Explorer
File Edit View Favorites Tools Help
Back Search Favorites Media
Address http://localhost:8080/jstltest/xml_transform.jsp
Go Links
Our Current Book List
title | author | isbn | published | publisher | url
Professional JSP | Brown et. al | 1-59059-225-5 | September 2003 | Apress | www.apress.com/book/bookDisplay.html?bID=200
Macbeth | William Shakespeare | 1123456789 | A long time ago | Bloggs Publishers | http://booksrus.co.uk/titles/1123456789.html
Fly Fishing | JR Hartley | 987654321 | May 1947 | ABC Printers Press | http://books.com/books.jsp?id=987654321
Done
Local intranet

The <x:param> Action

It's also possible to pass parameters into XSL transformations by nesting `<x:param>` actions inside the `<x:transform>` action. This facility is very similar to the `<sql:param>` and `<sql:dataParam>` actions from the SQL tag library, which are used to pass SQL parameters to the various actions in the SQL library.

The `<x:param>` action is very simple and only has two attributes:

```
<x:transform xml="${books}" xslt="${xslt}">
  <x:param name="myParam" value="myValue"/>
</x:transform>
```

As with the SQL parameters, the value of the `<x:param>` action can either be passed as an attribute or as the body content of the action itself as follows:

```
<x:transform xml="${books}" xslt="${xslt}">
  <x:param name="myParam">MyValue</x:param>
</x:transform>
```

Summary

During this chapter you've learned the reasons for the creation of the JSTL, its dependencies on the Java Servlet 2.3 and JSP 1.2 specifications and taken an in-depth look at the actions provided by the individual tag libraries that collectively form the JSTL.

Let's take a quick recap of the topics covered:

- The Servlet 2.3/JSP 1.2 dependencies
- How to install the JSTL into Tomcat 5.0
- The JSP 2.0 EL support
- Introductions to the four tag libraries that encompass the JSTL

After reading this chapter you should be able to appreciate some of the drawbacks that developers have come across before the release of the JSP 2.0 specification. Cluttering JSP pages with too much scriptlet code makes them hard to read and less maintainable. Because one of the primary goals of JSP 2.0 is to make JSP pages easier to write, the JSTL perfectly embodies this ideology and can be used to provide reusable, easy-to-maintain functionality for many simple everyday tasks that JSP page authors are faced with.

Hopefully after reading this chapter you'll immediately be able to see how you can install and make use of the actions provided by the JSTL in your web applications, thereby making them a lot cleaner, easier to read, and ultimately, of a higher quality.

5

Tag Files and Simple Tags

Up until now you've seen how to write JSP pages that allow dynamic content to be created using several mechanisms.

First, you looked at scriptlets in the page, which provide an easy way to get started with JSP, particularly since they allow existing Java code to be easily migrated into a JSP-based environment. We also saw how JavaBeans could be integrated with JSP, making it easier to maintain and manipulate information residing within these reusable components.

Chapter 4 looked at the JSP Standard Tag Library (JSTL), which contains a number of useful, prebuilt tags that achieve tasks such as iterating over collections. In addition to helping you solve these common tasks easily, the tags contained within JSTL are extremely valuable for improving the readability and maintainability of the page. To enable your own functionality to be reusable in the same way, you can build your own **custom tags**.

This chapter takes a look at some of the methods that you can use to start encapsulating your own functionality by illustrating how to build custom tags. Specifically you'll be looking at

- What custom tags are and why they are useful
- Tag concepts
- The changes from JSP 1.2
- Tag files
- Simple tags

Subsequent chapters will take a look at classic tags and some of the more advanced topics.

JSP Tag Extensions

JSP tag extensions, or custom tags as they are usually known, are a way of encapsulating reusable functionality on JSP pages. One of the major drawbacks of scripting environments such as JSP is that it's easy to quickly put together an application without thinking about how it will be maintained and grow in the future. For example, the ability to generate dynamic content using Java code embedded in the page is a very powerful feature of the JSP specification. Custom tags allow such functionality to be encapsulated into reusable components. As you've already seen with the JSTL, custom tags provide a great way for the logic behind common and recurring tasks to be wrapped up in an easy-to-use package. However, one question still remains. Why should you go to all the trouble and effort of building custom tags when you can simply write code inside the JSP pages?

The Need for Custom Tags

Among the best practices that have been established around JSP, one of the most important suggests that there should be as little Java code embedded inside a JSP as possible. Experience has shown us that there are three key factors that benefit from this practice:

- Reusability
- Readability
- Maintainability

To recap on what you've already seen with JSTL, let's look at each of these in turn.

Reusability

A common goal associated with using any programming language is that of reuse, which is something that applies equally to building Java-based web applications with JSP. Because you can embed Java code inside JSP pages, you may be tempted to reuse code on a source-code level between JSP pages. While reuse is easier, it brings with it a dramatic decrease in maintainability as changes and bugs slowly creep in and around the system. Ideally, you're looking for reusability at the class or component level.

The way that JSP allows you to reuse code is through custom tags and tag libraries. A **tag library** (commonly known as a **taglib**) is simply a collection of one or more custom tags that are related in some way. Once the tags are bundled up into a tag library, that tag library can be reused in the following:

- A single page
- The pages of a web application
- Different web applications

The ability to reuse custom tags over more than a single page illustrates the true potential of using tag libraries when building web applications. This is something that you'll return to when you look at the best ways to design and build custom tags.

Readability

Another benefit to using custom tags is readability–something that is easy to compromise with a combination of HTML and Java code wrapped up as Java scriptlets. Wrapping up reusable functionality as custom tags removes this code from the page, therefore making it cleaner, shorter, and more readable. Choosing appropriate names for your custom tags can also make a page easier for page designers to read. This, as you'll see when we talk about some of the best practices associated with custom tags, is very important and often overlooked.

Maintainability

Having a system that promotes reusability and readability is great, but what does that mean in the real world? The maintainability of an application is how well the system can be modified and fixed further on during its lifetime, which for a given application is typically hard to measure. However, in looking at any system, there are several signs that help us to identify whether or not that system will be easy or difficult to maintain. In reality, this is dictated by reuse and ensuring that the code is as readable as possible. These are the two goals that custom tags can help us achieve.

Tag Terminology and Concepts

Now that you know why custom tags are a good idea, let's quickly look at some of key tag concepts and the principles behind how tags work.

Tags and Tag Libraries

A tag library (or `taglib`) is a collection of individual custom tags that are typically related to each other. For example, the JSTL core tag library contains all of those tags that help you solve some of the common problems that you encounter when building JSP pages, such as iterating over collections and performing simple conditional logic on the page. Another example, again from JSTL, is the format tag library that contains tags related to the formatting of information on the page. As you'll see throughout this chapter, and as you've already seen in preceding chapters, there are several ways in which tags can be built and deployed.

Importing and Using Tags

A defined and deployed tag library must be made available to a JSP page if it's to be used. As you'll see, this is done by importing the tag library through the JSP `taglib` directive, and by giving that tag library a namespace (or **prefix**) on the page to differentiate it from other tag libraries in the same way that you place classes inside packages. Once the tag library has been imported, the tags within that library can be used with XML syntax. For example, if the tag library contained a tag called `myTag`, you simply use the tag as follows:

```
<prefix:myTag></prefix:myTag>
```

Here, you simply use the tag as an XML tag on the page, with the start and end tags being explicitly stated. In this example there is no content between the start and end tags, although this is possible, too, and is written as follows:

```
<prefix:myTag>Here is some content</prefix:myTag>
```

Alternatively, if an XML tag has nothing between its start and end tags, that tag can be used in its shortened format as follows:

```
<prefix:myTag/>
```

Semantically, this shortened usage is identical to using the tag in its longer, more verbose syntax.

Body Content

Body content is defined as being anything that falls between the start and end tags. With the JSP 2.0 specification, there are now more options for tag-body content. As you'll see later in this chapter, these options provide you with a way to define the type of content that you'll permit within your tags. Let's look at each of these in turn.

Empty

As you've seen, a tag has empty body content when there is nothing between the start and end tags, although an `empty` body content type is strictly defined as nothing that can be returned to the client. In other words, content between the start and end tags cannot include things like HTML, text, and so on. As you'll see in the chapters on custom tags, a body content type of `empty` is quite common because it provides an easy way to use custom tags on the page, particularly in their shortened form.

JSP

The next type of body content is that of JSP, which is defined as anything that can usually appear within JSP pages. For example, this includes content such as HTML, Java scriptlets, other custom tags, and so on:

```
<prefix:myTag>Here is some <b>HTML content</b></prefix:myTag>
```

Scriptless

A new addition for the JSP 2.0 specification, scriptless body content is effectively the same as JSP body content with the restriction that it cannot contain any Java code wrapped up as scriptlets. As you've seen, moving Java code off the page and into reusable components is one of the best practices associated with JSP development, and using a body content of `scriptless` provides a way to enforce this. At translation time, the JSP container looks at the body content and will throw a fatal translation error if scriptlets are found. For new developments, a body content type of `scriptless` is recommended over `JSP`.

Tag Dependent

With tag-dependent body content, the custom tag has complete control over how its body content is included or evaluated in the page. Essentially, it means that the body content is treated as plain text, meaning that JSP constructs and expressions simply aren't evaluated. Although seemingly useless at first glance, there are a few good uses of this type of body content, including, for example, a tag that interprets its body content as another language. A custom tag could be written and used as a container for another language such as ColdFusion or another scripting language. The tag could then take its body content and pass it on to a parser that would execute the code.

Attributes

The final key concept related to how custom tags are used on the page is that of attributes. As you'll see later in the chapter, custom tags can be customized through the use of attributes in the same way that methods can be customized through the use of parameters. Attributes are written as `name=value` pairs within the actual tag itself, as shown here:

```
<prefix:myTag attributeName="attribute value"/>
```

In this example, the tag has a single attribute called `attributeName`, with a value of `attribute value`. A tag may have one or more attributes, and as you'll see later, you have full control over some of the attribute characteristics such as the type and whether it's required.

JavaBeans vs. Custom Tags

Now that you understand the purpose of custom tags and how they are used on the page, you need to know when to use tags and when to use JavaBeans for wrapping up reusable functionality for use on JSP pages. After all, JavaBeans are reusable components and the JSP specification provides a built-in mechanism with which to integrate and utilize the features provided by JavaBeans.

Although both technologies can be used to achieve the same goal, custom tags are aware of the environment in which they are running. For example, custom tags have access to the same implicit objects such as the ones available when developing JSP pages: `pageContext`, `request`, `response`, `session`, and so on. JavaBeans, however, are components that can be reused within any Java environment, hence they don't know about such JSP specifics. For this reason, custom tags are a much better choice for encapsulating reusable functionality that will be used on JSP pages. You'll look more closely at this in the discussion of the best practices around custom tags, but for the moment, keep in mind the following rules:

- Use JavaBeans for representing and storing information and state. An example here includes building JavaBeans that represent the business objects in your application.
- Use custom tags to represent and implement actions that occur on those JavaBeans, as well as logic related to the presentation of information. An example here from JSTL would be iterating over a collection of objects or conditional logic.

Now you'll look at the major changes from the previous version (1.2) of the JSP specification before moving on to build your first custom tag.

Changes from JSP 1.2

From a tag developer's perspective, there are several important changes from the previous version of the JSP specification. In the past, there was only a single mechanism for building custom tags. These are now called **classic tags**; building them involves writing the functionality provided by the custom tag as a Java class that implements the `javax.servlet.jsp.tagext.Tag` interface. This class containing the functionality provided by the tag is called the **tag handler**.

One of the biggest problems with building tags in this way is that the `Tag` interface, the tag life cycle, and the semantics of its usage in the container are rather complex. Through feedback and the Java Community Process (JCP)–the expert group responsible for defining the JSP 2.0 specification (available for download from http://jcp.org/en/jsr/detail?id=152)–two new ways for building custom tags have been introduced: **tag files** and **simple tags**. Both are the subject of this chapter and as you'll see shortly, tag files and simple tags allow the functionality of custom tags to be implemented using JSP fragments and Java code, respectively. Although they use different paradigms, they both greatly simplify the way in which custom tags can be built and will subsequently change the way that JSP-based web applications are built in the future.

Other changes relevant to tag developers include the ability of a custom tag to take any number of undefined (dynamic) attributes, and the ability to use the JSP expression language (EL) in conjunction with custom tags. You'll be seeing examples of this shortly.

Tag Files

Tag files are a new addition to the JSP 2.0 specification that provide a very simple way in which content and functionality can be abstracted away from JSP pages and into reusable components. So, what is a tag file?

In short, a tag file is simply a JSP fragment that contains some content or JSP code that you would like to reuse over and over again. In the past, you've typically achieved the same thing by taking JSP code out of a JSP page, placing it in a separate JSP file, and including it wherever necessary. So why do you need tag files? Let's answer this question with an example showing how you can reuse content between JSP pages.

Reusing Content

On many websites, small pieces of content are abstracted away from the main pages into smaller JSP pages that are included wherever necessary. Typical examples include header pages that contain references to cascading stylesheets (CSS) and common JavaScript functions, or alternatively, footer pages that may include a brief copyright and usage notice about the website. Let's recap how this is done, and then you'll look at how tag files can help.

Reusing Content with Included JSP Files

If you take an example where footer information is abstracted away from the main page, the following sample could be placed into a separate JSP/HTML file:

```
Copyright 2003, Apress
```

As you can see, there isn't a great deal of content within this JSP file, although the reason that this is so often done is because it increases the maintainability of the web application. If you need to add to or change the copyright notice, moving it out into a separate file means that you only have to change the content in a single place.

There are a couple of ways in which such pages can be included, although with static content the include directive is generally used:

```
<%@ include file="copyright.jsp" %>
```

At translation time, the text contained within the referenced file simply gets inlined into the resulting JSP page. This is a tried and tested technique for including static content, so why do you need tag files and how can you reuse content with them?

Reusing Content with Tag Files

One of the real problems with including files is that with many includes on the page, it can sometimes be cryptic with regards to the content of each file included. In addition to this, there is no standard method for distributing included files for reuse in other web applications. Tag files can help us address both of these drawbacks.

Defining Content in a Tag File

Building a tag file is almost the same as building the included JSP file–you simply copy out the content that you would like to reuse and place it in a file ending with a `.tag` extension:

```
Copyright 2003, Apress
```

As this example shows, there is, in fact, no difference between the content of this tag file and the included JSP page. The key difference is in how tag files are deployed and used.

In order to promote the use of custom tags to page authors and people that might not understand the Java programming side of JSP, the expert group behind JSP 2.0 has provided a very simple approach to defining tag files. Through a convention defined in the JSP 2.0 specification, tag files should be saved with a `.tag` file extension in a directory called `tags` (or a subdirectory of this) underneath the `WEB-INF` directory of your web application.

Using the Tag File

Tag files are used from within a JSP page as a custom tag in the same way that you've seen the custom tags in the JSTL used. Before using tag files on the page, you have to indicate that the tag file is a tag and import the tag library containing that tag.

For the purposes of this example, let's say that the tag file that we just defined is saved in our web application as `WEB-INF/tags/copyright.tag` along with any other tag files that may be defined in that directory. Since the individual tags are being placed within the `tags` directory, it could be said that the `tags` directory represents a collection of tags, or a tag library. For this reason, and to use the tags, you can import the tag library that corresponds to this directory with the following `taglib` directive:

```
<%@ taglib prefix="tags" tagdir="/WEB-INF/tags" %>
```

Behind the scenes, the container looks for all files that have a `.tag` extension in the directory specified by the `tagdir` attribute and makes them available to the page as custom tags with the specified prefix. The mechanics behind how each tag file is made available as a custom tag is up to the container, but the convention is that the name of the file is used as the name of the tag. For example, the `copyright.tag` file will become known as a custom tag called `copyright`. The process of importing the tag library with the `taglib` directive makes the tags within that tag available to use on the page, meaning that the copyright tag can be used as follows:

```
<tags:copyright/>
```

As this example shows, the `copyright` tag is used in the same way as any other tag–by specifying the prefix and the name of the tag. In comparison to the original included JSP, the actual usage of this tag isn't all that different. What is important here is that we now have a standard way to reuse this content. In addition, as you'll see in Chapter 7, using tag files provides a standard way to deploy and distribute the tag file to other project members, project teams, and organizations.

This, of course, is just a simple example to introduce the concept of tag files. To really appreciate the power and flexibility that they can provide page authors, let's look at a more complicated example that makes use of templating–again, it's something that often crops up in real-world projects.

Customizing Templates with Attributes

Many e-commerce websites have blocks on their home pages that stand out and inform potential customers of new products that have recently become available, or of special offers that are currently running:

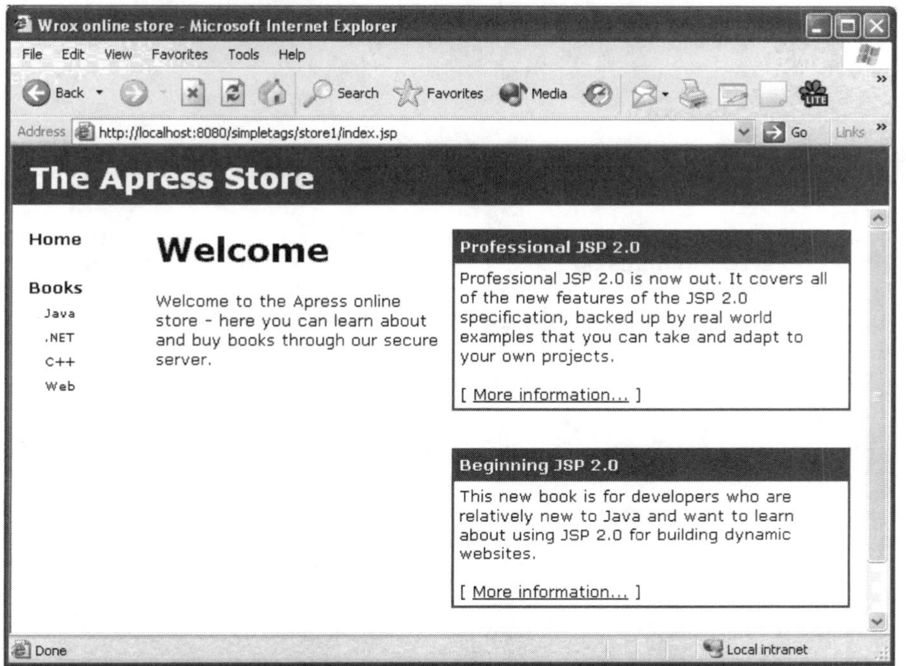

As this screen shot illustrates, often there will be more than one of these blocks, each of which may have the same look and feel with only the content changing between them. One way to implement this is to write the HTML code for the first block and simply copy it, modifying the content as necessary. For static websites this is very common. However, when building such a page using JSP, there are several other options available, all of which increase the reusability of common code, and therefore the readability, quality, and maintainability.

Templating with Included JSP Files

One option open to us is to take the common code (in this case HTML code) and place it in its own JSP file. As we want to parameterize each usage of the template, this rules out using the static include directive that you saw in the previous example. Instead, you have to use the `<jsp:include>` tag so that you can dynamically include this JSP file at runtime, substituting the content as appropriate.

Defining a Template

With the previous screen shot in mind, here's how you could write a JSP page to represent the template to be dynamically included:

```
<table width="320" bordercolor="${param.color}" border="1" cellpadding="4"
      cellspacing="0">
  <tr bgcolor="${param.color}" color="#ffffff">
    <td class="boxHeader" nowrap>
      ${param.title}
    </td>
```

```
    </tr>
    <tr>
      <td valign="top" class="boxText">
        ${param.body}
      </td>
    </tr>
  </table>
```

The example here contains three factors that we would like page authors to customize: the title of the box, the content displayed within the box, and the color of the box. For this reason, we have provided the ability for these to be specified at runtime using parameters, the values of which are simply inserted into the appropriate place in the template using JSP EL expressions. For the purposes of this example, let's say that this is saved as `box.jsp`.

Using a Template

With this in place, the template can be used with the `<jsp:include>` tag as follows:

```
<jsp:include page="box.jsp">
  <jsp:param name="color" value="#314289"/>
  <jsp:param name="title" value="Professional JSP 2.0"/>
  <jsp:param name="body" value=" Professional JSP 2.0 is now out. It covers all
    of the new features of the JSP 2.0 specification, backed up by real world
    examples that you can take and adapt to your own projects.
    <br><br>
    [
      <a href=\"projsp20.html\">More information...</a>
    ]"/>
</jsp:include>
```

As this sample shows, templating is a great way to separate content and the presentation of that content. However, from a page author's perspective, using a fairly low-level construct can look a little raw. Another point to note is that as you're passing the customized content as parameters to the included JSP, you have to ensure that you properly escape any special characters such as double quotes. Although this has worked in the past and will continue to work in the future, there is now a better way to achieve the same outcome.

Attributes

As earlier examples of the JSTL tags have demonstrated, it's possible to customize the use of the custom tag by using **attributes**. Without this ability, you would have to build a separate JSP file, or a separate tag for every different piece of content that you wanted to put in the template.

Attribute Syntax

Previous versions of the JSP specification provided only a single way in which attributes could be specified: inside the opening tag. JSP 2.0, however, introduces an additional method.

Specifying Attributes Within the Tag

This is the traditional way of specifying attributes with custom tags, and as you've seen in the JSTL examples, it means that those attributes are written in the same way that attributes for other XML tags are written, for example:

```
<prefix:myTag title="My Title"/>
```

Here, an attribute called `title` has been provided for the tag as a name and value pair and is written inside the actual tag itself. As with XML attributes in general, the value of an attribute must be wrapped up inside quote characters. This example uses double quotes, but there's nothing stopping you from using single quotes, too. This flexibility is particularly useful if the value of the attribute contains characters that need to be escaped, such as double quote characters.

Specifying Attributes Within the Body

The other mechanism for specifying attributes is new to JSP 2.0 and involves the use of the `<jsp:attribute>` tag. Taking the same example, this can now be written in one of the following ways:

```
<prefix:myTag>
  <jsp:attribute name="title" value="My Title"/>
</prefix:myTag>
```

```
<prefix:myTag>
  <jsp:attribute name="title">My Title</jsp:attribute>
</prefix:myTag>
```

One of the biggest problems with passing attributes to XML tags is that often attributes with large values make the tag awkward to read. For this reason, the new syntax can be used instead. Both syntaxes are equivalent, and while the traditional syntax is certainly the most concise, the newer syntax improves the readability with particularly long attribute values.

Required or Optional

The core elements of any attribute are its name and its value. However, with custom tags, there are various characteristics that can be configured. The first of these is to define whether an attribute is required or optional. In other words, this allows us to state whether an attribute and its value must be specified for any given custom tag. This is very useful in many situations because it forces us to specify values for attributes.

Looking at the template example, you may decide that all boxes should have a title. This isn't something that you can achieve easily with dynamically included JSP files, but with custom tags it's trivial. When an attribute is marked as required and is omitted, a fatal translation error will occur, indicating that the attribute hasn't been specified. In this example and by using custom tags, you can force users to specify a title.

Static or Dynamic (Request-Time Expressions)

Another characteristic that is commonly defined for attributes is whether their values can be the result of a request-time expression. In the JSTL examples, the value of many of the attributes was simply a static string passed to the tag. For example, looking at the JSTL `forEach` tag that provides iteration over a collection, you can see that the name of the variable with which you'll access each item in the collection (`myVar`) is supplied to the tag as a static string through the `var` attribute:

```
<c:forEach var="myVar" items="${myItems}">
  <c:out value="${myVar.name}"/>
</c:forEach>
```

This is known as a static attribute because its value is statically defined in the JSP page. A dynamic attribute, or a request-time expression as it's formally known, is written using one of the following methods:

- The JSP 2.0 EL, such as `${myItems}`
- Java code such as `<%= pageContext.findAttribute("myItems") %>`

In either case, if an attribute is marked as supporting request-time expressions, it means that expressions can be used to specify the value of the attribute. With the previous JSTL example, the actual collection over which the tag should iterate is being passed to the tag at request-time (runtime) using an EL expression.

Now let's look at how you can build a tag file equivalent to the dynamically included JSP file you saw earlier.

Templating with Tag Files

As you've seen, tag files are small snippets of content that have been abstracted out of the main page and wrapped up for reuse. In addition to this, tag files can be customized by attributes at runtime.

Defining a Customizable Template

Using the included JSP file as a basis, the following block of code shows how to implement a tag file to represent the same template:

```
<%@ attribute name="color" required="true" rtexprvalue="false" %>
<%@ attribute name="title" required="true" rtexprvalue="false" %>

<table width="320" bordercolor="${color}" border="1" cellpadding="4"
      cellspacing="0">
  <tr bgcolor="${color}" color="#ffffff">
    <td class="boxHeader" nowrap>
      ${title}
    </td>
  </tr>
  <tr>
    <td valign="top" class="boxText">
      <jsp:doBody/>
    </td>
  </tr>
</table>
```

Although the actual content and intent of the tag file (which you'll call `box.tag`) is the same as the included JSP page, there are three subtle differences. The first is the way in which attributes are defined. Rather than obtaining values through the normal `request.getParameter()` mechanism, the attributes for a tag file are declared at the top of the file using the `attribute` directive–a new feature of the JSP 2.0 specification and a directive that is only valid in tag files. Using this directive on a tag file indicates to the JSP container that the custom tag used to access the tag file can accept an attribute with the specified name:

```
<%@ attribute name="color" required="true" rtexprvalue="false" %>
<%@ attribute name="title" required="true" rtexprvalue="false" %>
```

The JSP 2.0 specification also introduces some other new directives that are only valid within tag files. Like the JSP page directive, these directives just allow aspects of the tag file to be configured. For more information about these directives, see Chapter 1.

In this example, you've declared two required attributes–one so that the color of the box can be specified, and one for the title. Because you want to specify the values of the attributes when writing the page, you should opt to not allow the use of request-time expressions by setting the value of `rtexprvalue` to `false`. What this means is that the values for the `color` and `title` attributes can only be static strings, such as `"#000000"` and `"My title"` respectively, rather than JSP expressions.

The second difference is in the way that the attributes are used. With a tag file, all that is needed is a simple EL expression in the same way that objects are used on regular JSP pages, with the result being that the value of the `color` attribute is substituted at runtime. Notice here that you don't need to look up the value as a parameter with the `${param.color}` syntax:

```
<tr bgcolor="${color}" color="#ffffff">
```

The final difference is that you no longer have to declare an attribute for actual content that is to be displayed in the box. Instead, you'll use the body content of the custom tag to single out this content, which is specified between the start and end tags. To access the content, you use the new `<jsp:doBody>` tag that is again only valid in tag files. An additional benefit here is that you can write the body content as is, without having to escape characters as you saw in the previous implementation of this example:

```
<td valign="top" class="boxText">
  <jsp:doBody/>
</td>
```

All that this tag does is ask the JSP container to invoke (or evaluate) the body content that was passed to the tag and in this case write it out to the page.

Using a Customizable Template

With the template defined, you can now use the tag file in the same way that you saw previously. That is, you import the tag library corresponding to the directory in which you saved the tag file. For the purposes of this example, let's say that the tag file that you just defined is saved as `box.tag` and is placed in the `WEB-INF/tags` directory. Knowing this, you can then import the tag library that corresponds to this directory with the following `taglib` directive:

```
<%@ taglib prefix="tags" tagdir="/WEB-INF/tags" %>
```

As previously discussed, the container looks for all files that have a `.tag` extension in the specified `tagdir` directory and makes them available to the page as custom tags with the specified prefix. Once imported through the `taglib` directive, the tag can be used as follows:

```
<tags:box>
  <jsp:attribute name="color">#314289</jsp:attribute>
  <jsp:attribute name="title">Professional JSP 2.0</jsp:attribute>
  <jsp:body>
    Professional JSP 2.0 is now out. It covers all of the new features of the JSP
    2.0 specification, backed up by real world examples that you can take and
    adapt to your own projects.
    <br><br>
    [
      <a href="projsp20.html">More information...</a>
    ]
  </jsp:body>
</tags:box>
```

As this example shows, the box tag is used in the same way as any other tag–by specifying the prefix and the name of the tag. In a similar way to how the parameters were passed to the included JSP page, the attributes for this tag are passed using the `<jsp:attribute>` tags, nested within the start and end box tags. As for the content that is being displayed within the box, it's passed as a section of JSP code and wrapped up inside the `<jsp:body>` tags, which are again nested between the start and end `box` tags. At runtime, these attributes and the body content is passed to the tag and substituted into the template, as you would expect.

In comparison to the original included JSP, the actual usage of this tag isn't all that different. After all, you have the same structure, with attributes being passed in a rather verbose way. However, this is just one way in which this tag can be used in the JSP 2.0 specification. Another way of using the tag is as follows:

```
<tags:box color="#314289" title="Professional JSP 2.0">
  Professional JSP 2.0 is now out. It covers all of the new features of the JSP
  2.0 specification, backed up by real world examples that you can take and adapt
  to your own projects.
  <br><br>
  [
    <a href="projsp20.html">More information...</a>
  ]
</tags:box>
```

In this example, the attributes are passed through as true attributes of the XML tag rather than as nested elements. This makes for a much cleaner and concise usage, which makes it easier to understand what is happening on the page. Also, since the attributes are being passed in this way, the content to be displayed no longer needs to be wrapped up inside a `<jsp:body>` tag; the content is now truly the body of the tag.

Both methods of passing attributes are permitted by the JSP specification, although there are some rules around the syntax of how this is done. If the attributes are passed using the `<jsp:attribute>` tag, then any body content must be wrapped up inside a `<jsp:body>` tag. The reason behind this is that with the extra `<jsp:attribute>` tags, the JSP container can't guess what you actually want the body content of the tag to be, and therefore you have to explicitly demarcate it. If, on the other hand, you specify all attributes as attributes of the XML tag, then the body content of the tag is implicitly taken to be anything that falls between the start and end tags.

Why Use Tag Files?

As these examples have demonstrated, it's possible to wrap up content and reuse it elsewhere. As this has always been possible with included JSP files, you might be asking why tag files have been introduced into the JSP specification and what their benefits are.

First of all, there are the technical aspects. Tag files provide a much cleaner way to build and subsequently use templates on JSP pages. However, there are some other, softer, benefits that arise from using tag files over JSP includes. Essentially, using custom tags gives you the ability to provide a natural interface to the content and functionality that you would like people to use and reuse. Having a custom tag called `box`, with the appropriate attributes, is much more understandable than having a generic JSP `include`. Also, naming custom tags appropriately provides page authors and developers maintaining the page with a much better idea of a tag's intent, which in turn makes it easier to use, read, understand, and maintain.

Using tag files to build templates is a great way to separate the content from the presentation of that content, and this makes it a natural progression from simply mixing the two together in JSP pages. However, there will be times when you want to encapsulate more than just pure presentation into a custom tag. Perhaps you have some Java code that you would like to wrap up and make reusable. Generally, any code that can appear in a JSP page can appear in a tag file. However, the best practices about keeping Java code out of JSP pages are also applicable to tag files, too. To wrap up logic that contains more code than content, simple tags are the answer.

Simple Tags

Previous versions of the JSP specification have supported the notion of building custom tags with Java code for sometime, and now the JSP 2.0 specification simplifies this process greatly by introducing **simple tags**. With tag files, the content and logic that you would like to reuse is defined using normal JSP syntax, thereby providing an easy way to wrap up reusable functionality and make the process of building tags available to those people who may not necessarily know how to program in Java. However, with simple tags, the reusable functionality is encapsulated within a Java class that implements a specific interface. This class is called the **tag handler**.

The characteristics of the tag such as its name and a list of any attributes that it takes are then defined in a **tag library descriptor** (**TLD**) file. When the tag is finally used on the page, an instance of the tag handler class is created and its methods are called to execute the reusable functionality.

Ultimately, this method of writing tags is more complex than building tag files, but it does provide a much greater level of flexibility and control over the functionality that a tag file can provide. Before you look at how to build a simple tag, let's take a look at the interface that a simple tag handler must implement.

The SimpleTag Interface

The `SimpleTag` interface, introduced as a part of the JSP 2.0 specification, defines the basic contract between simple tags and the JSP page on which they are used. The interface itself serves two purposes:

- It provides the simple tag with information about its execution environment.
- It provides a method with which to execute the functionality encapsulated by the simple tag handler.

Here is the `SimpleTag` interface:

```
package javax.servlet.jsp.tagext;

public interface SimpleTag extends JspTag {

  public void doTag() throws JspException, IOException;

  public JspTag getParent();

  public void setJspBody(JspFragment jspBody);

  public void setJspContext(JspContext jspContext);

  public void setParent(JspTag parent);

}
```

The Basic Tag Life Cycle

Although the `SimpleTag` interface supplies the contract that a simple tag must provide, interfaces in Java cannot specify the order in which operations are called. This information is instead specified within the JSP specification, as shown in the following diagram:

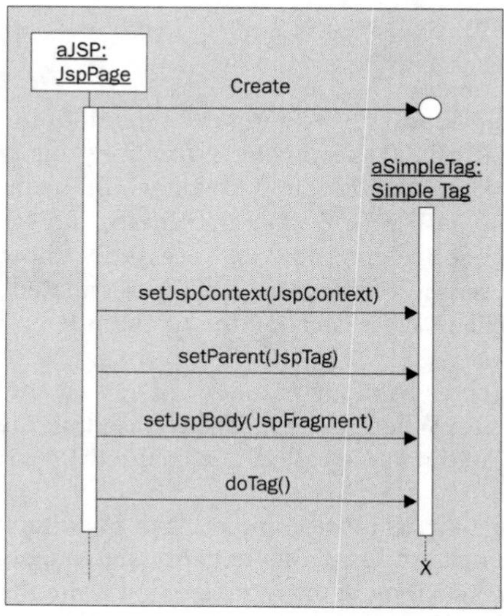

With classic tags, one of the most complex pieces of the tag life cycle is how tag handler instances can be pooled by the container and reused. Although this tends to increase performance and reduce the number of object instantiations that occur, the semantics for reusing tag handlers often causes confusion, hence side effects from misunderstanding the tag life cycle. For this reason, simple tags are used once and only once before the tag handler reference is discarded. In other words, each simple tag invocation causes the creation of a new tag handler instance, therefore greatly simplifying the programming model.

Creating a Tag Handler Instance

When a custom tag is used on a JSP page, the first thing that the JSP container must do is create a new instance of the tag handler class. Later on you'll see just how the JSP container locates the correct tag handler class for any given custom tag, but for now you should assume that this has been found and an instance is created.

Setting the Context

Next, the tag handler instance is made aware of the environment in which it's running through the `setJspContext()` method. This just involves passing a reference to the current `JspContext` into the tag handler.

One of the useful classes available to JSP developers is `PageContext` from the `javax.servlet.jsp` package. This is available from a JSP page as an implicit object called `pageContext`. It's effectively provided as a convenient way in which to access various objects that are used during JSP development. For example, the `PageContext` class provides an easy way to access attributes that are bound to any of the available scopes (`request`, `page`, `session`, and `application`). It can also get a reference to the current output `JspWriter` and programmatically include and forward requests. Although these features are available in JSP 2.0 through the standard JSP actions or the JSP EL, the power behind the `PageContext` class is that it can be used within custom tags.

One of the changes to the JSP API in JSP 2.0 is that some of the functionality previously provided by the `PageContext` class has been abstracted away into a new class called `JspContext`. This new base class provides all of the functionality that is not directly related to the Java Servlet API, including the methods that allow you to retrieve and set scoped attributes and obtain a reference to the current `JspWriter`. From a tag developer perspective, having access to this sort of information and the execution environment means that you can write tags that utilize values from the request, page, session, or application and write output from the tags directly back to the JSP page. You'll see some examples of how to use the `JspContext` and `PageContext` classes throughout this and the following chapters.

Setting the Parent

During our discussion of body content types, you saw that it's possible for custom tags to contain regular JSP syntax between the start and end tags. This includes custom tags and therefore means that it's possible for custom tags to be nested. The following block of code shows an example of nesting custom tags with JSTL. Here, the outer `forEach` tag iterates over each item in the specified collection, while the inner `out` tag outputs the name of each item:

```
<c:forEach var="myVar" items="${myItems}">
  <c:out value="${myVar.name}"/>
</c:forEach>
```

As you'll see in Chapter 7, it's possible for custom tag handlers to cooperate and communicate with one another. For this reason, part of the information about a tag's execution environment includes a reference to the closest enclosing tag handler, which is set by calling the `setParent()` method. That reference is of type `JspTag` (the superinterface for all tag handlers), but can be `null` if the tag isn't nested within another tag.

Setting the Body Content

Once the context has been set, an object representing the body content of the tag is passed to it. At runtime, the JSP container wraps up the body content between the start and end tags, creates a `JspFragment` object to represent it, and passes this `JspFragment` instance to the tag by calling the `setJspBody()` method. If there is no body content between the start and end tags, a `null` reference is passed to this method instead.

As you'll see later in this chapter, having a reference to the body content opens up a whole new way in which custom tags can be implemented.

Executing the Functionality

Finally, with the context and body content set, the only thing left to do is execute the functionality that the tag handler embodies. This is achieved by calling the `doTag()` method, and it's this method that contains the Java code responsible for the actions performed by the tag.

The SimpleTagSupport Class

Although implementing the `SimpleTag` interface is not a complex task, for convenience, the JSP specification provides the `javax.servlet.jsp.tagext.SimpleTagSupport` class, which provides default implementations for all of the methods previously described. This class can be used as a starting point for building your own simple tags if you extend it and override the `doTag()` method. This, as you'll see throughout this chapter, is the most common way to build simple tags.

Now that you understand the mechanics behind simple tags, you are now in a position to write one.

A Simple Example

As an example of the type of functionality that might be encapsulated within a custom tag, let's display the current date and time on the page. You could use Java code written inside a scriptlet or an EL function. Instead, you'll use a custom tag because it provides flexibility when you later need to add functionality.

Writing the Tag Handler

Now that you've decided that you're going to build a custom tag, the first step is to write the tag handler, which is the Java class that will embody the functionality that the custom tag will provide. Using the `SimpleTagSupport` class as a starting point, the code for the tag handler is as follows:

```
package com.apress.projsp20.ch05.tagext;

import java.io.IOException;
import java.text.DateFormat;
```

```
import java.util.Date;

import javax.servlet.jsp.JspException;
import javax.servlet.jsp.tagext.SimpleTagSupport;

public class DateTimeTag extends SimpleTagSupport {

  public void doTag() throws JspException, IOException {

    DateFormat df = DateFormat.getDateTimeInstance(
        DateFormat.MEDIUM, DateFormat.MEDIUM);

    // now write out the formatted date to the page
    getJspContext().getOut().write(df.format(new Date()));
  }
}
```

As you can see, the actual code for the tag handler is pretty straightforward. The `SimpleTag` interface provides the `doTag()` method, and as defined by the simple tag life cycle, this method is called to execute the functionality encapsulated within the tag. In this example, a `DateFormat` object is created and used to format the current date. This string is then output back to the page by using the `JspContext` object. The `getOut()` method on the `JspContext` object returns a reference to the `JspWriter` instance that is being used to render the JSP page. This is one of the reasons why a tag needs to know about the environment in which it's running. If it didn't, the tag would never be able to output content directly back to the page.

Compiling the Tag Handler

Compiling tag handlers is a straightforward task and requires that two JAR files are present in your CLASSPATH. The first of these is the `jsp-api.jar` file, which contains classes that make up the core JSP and tag APIs, including classes and interfaces such as `SimpleTag`, `SimpleTagSupport`, and `JspContext`. The second JAR file is called `servlet-api.jar`. This contains the classes that make up the core servlet API. With Tomcat 5.0, both of these JAR files can be found in the `TOMCAT_HOME/common/lib` directory.

> *With previous versions of Tomcat, the classes that made up the JSP and servlet APIs were bundled into a single JAR file called* `servlet.jar`*, which is again located within the* `TOMCAT_HOME/common/lib` *directory. If you are building tag libraries against an earlier version of Tomcat, be sure to put this file in your class path instead.*

Writing the Tag Library Descriptor File

With the tag handler written and compiled, the next step is to write the TLD file, which is an XML file that describes the tag, how it will be used on the page, the type of body content, whether the tag accepts any attributes, and so on. For this simple example, the TLD file is as follows:

```
<?xml version="1.0" encoding="UTF-8" ?>

<taglib xmlns="http://java.sun.com/xml/ns/j2ee"
  xmlns:xsi="http://www.w3.org/2001/XMLSchema-instance"
  xsi:schemaLocation="http://java.sun.com/xml/ns/j2ee/web-jsptaglibrary_2_0.xsd"
  version="2.0">
```

```
  <description>
    Tag library for Professional JSP 2.0, Chapter 5.
  </description>
  <jsp-version>2.0</jsp-version>
  <tlib-version>1.0</tlib-version>
  <short-name>ch05</short-name>
  <uri>http://www.apress.com/projsp20/ch05</uri>

  <tag>
    <name>datetime</name>
    <tag-class>com.apress.projsp20.ch05.tagext.DateTimeTag</tag-class>
    <body-content>empty</body-content>
    <description>
      Outputs the current date and time to the page.
    </description>
  </tag>

</taglib>
```

At first glance this file looks fairly complicated but in fact only a small portion of it is applicable to the custom tag that you're building. The first thing you notice is the standard XML header that indicates which version of XML you're using:

```
<?xml version="1.0" encoding="UTF-8" ?>
```

Next up is the root element along with the details of the XML schema to which this document must conform:

```
<taglib xmlns="http://java.sun.com/xml/ns/j2ee"
  xmlns:xsi="http://www.w3.org/2001/XMLSchema-instance"
  xsi:schemaLocation="http://java.sun.com/xml/ns/j2ee/web-jsptaglibrary_2_0.xsd"
  version="2.0">

  ... body of XML document ...

</taglib>
```

Previous versions of the JSP specification have used XML Document Type Definitions (DTDs) to define the structure of the TLD file. With XML schemas being much more powerful in defining allowable content and their increase in popularity, JSP 2.0 too has migrated to using XML schemas.

For backwards compatibility, JSP containers must still support the DTD-based TLDs that were a part of the earlier JSP 1.1 and JSP 1.2 specifications. This means that TLDs can still be defined using these older mechanisms. This is particularly useful for tag library developers who are targeting older versions of the specification, or for those developers who want to reach the widest audience.

The next set of elements within the TLD file, nested between the start and end `taglib` elements, are elements that describe the tag library. Rather than bundle custom tags up individually, all tags must be part of a tag library. From an implementation perspective, this just involves grouping the tags and defining them within the same TLD file. From a usage perspective, using those tags involves importing the tag library with the `taglib` directive. For this example, you'll bundle up all of the tags that you've built in this chapter into their own tag library, the definition of which is as follows:

```
<description>
  Tag library for Professional JSP 2.0, Chapter 5.
</description>
<jsp-version>2.0</jsp-version>
<tlib-version>1.0</tlib-version>
<short-name>ch05</short-name>
<uri>http://www.apress.com/projsp20/ch05</uri>
```

First is a short textual description of the tag library, followed by the `jsp-version` and `tlib-version` elements, which allow you to define the required JSP version and the version of the tag library.

Next is a short name for the tag library, used for identification purposes in JSP authoring or web-application management tools. For example, it could be used in a menu that lists the tag libraries that are available to the user.

Finally, you have the `uri` element. This causes the most confusion when writing tag libraries. Although the value of this element should be a valid URI, this simply represents a unique identifier for the tag library. The example uses the absolute URI `http://www.apress.com/projsp20/ch05`, even though there's nothing to stop a relative URI such as `/ch05` or even `/myTaglibs/chapter05` from being used instead. What is important here is that the URI is unique among the tag libraries that you'll be using. The URI doesn't have to exist in the real world; if you go to `http://www.apress.com/projsp20/ch05` you'll find nothing there–it's simply a unique, symbolic identifier.

The final part of the TLD file has the **tag description** itself:

```
<tag>
  <name>datetime</name>
  <tag-class>com.apress.projsp20.ch05.tagext.DateTimeTag</tag-class>
  <body-content>empty</body-content>
  <description>
    Outputs the current date and time to the page.
  </description>
</tag>
```

A definition of a custom tag falls between the start and end `tag` tags and in this example has four characteristics that are being defined. First of all is the name of the tag. This doesn't have to reflect the actual class name of the tag handler, but rather it's the name with which you would like to use the tag on the page. Following this is the *fully qualified class name* of the tag handler.

One of the common pitfalls encountered when building custom tags is that the tag handler classes are often placed in the default package—that is, the `package` statement is omitted from the source code. Due to the way in which JSP pages are translated into Java servlets, attempting to use unpackaged tag handler classes almost always results in exceptions, such as `ClassNotFoundException`, when the tag is used on the page. To ensure that this doesn't happen, you should always place your tag handler classes within a package.

Next, you have a definition of the type of body content for the tag. Earlier in this chapter, you looked at the various types of body content that a custom tag can have, and it's here in which this is defined for a custom tag. For the `datetime` tag, the body content is stated to be `empty`, meaning that no content is required or permitted between the start and end tags. Since the `datetime` tag simply outputs the current date and time to the page, it's not necessary for this tag to have any body content.

The `body-content` element is optional when writing TLD files, and if omitted, its value defaults to `scriptless`. As good practice, it's always a good idea to explicitly specify this so that anybody reading the TLD is certain about how the tag works.

Finally, there's a short description about the tag itself. Again, this is optional but it's useful for anybody reading the TLD file, whether it be somebody in your own team using the tag on your project, or somebody on the other side of the world who is reusing your tag library on their own project.

With the tag handler class and TLD file written, the next step is to deploy the tag. There are a couple of ways that tag libraries can be deployed and used–one in which the tag library is unpackaged and one in which it's packaged up and ready to be reused easily. The former method is typically how many developers deploy their tag libraries in a development environment, so let's take a look at that one and leave the other until Chapter 7 where you'll examine deployment in more depth.

Deploying the Tag Library

The first step is to ensure that the class files for the tag handlers in the tag library have been compiled and are available within the class path of your web application. In other words, you should ensure that your class files reside in either the `WEB-INF/classes` directory of your web application, or within a JAR file that has been copied into the `WEB-INF/lib` directory of your web application. If your tag handlers reference any other classes that you or a third party has written, don't forget that these must also be made available in one of these two ways.

With the classes residing within the web-application directory structure, the next step is to place the TLD file within the web-application directory structure, too. By convention, the JSP specification suggests that all TLD files be placed within the `WEB-INF/tlds` directory. Although this isn't mandatory, placing all TLD files here provides a central place for people to find them at a later date. For the purposes of this example, you call the TLD `ch05.tld` and place it in the `WEB-INF/tlds` directory. With these steps complete, you can now use the tag library.

As you saw with the JSTL examples in Chapter 4 and the tag file example in this chapter, using a tag library requires that the tag library be imported via the `taglib` directive. This allows you to specify the prefix with which to reference the tags within that tag library. With the TLD file for our example located at `WEB-INF/tlds/ch05.tld`, you can directly import this on a JSP page with the following directive:

```
<%@ taglib uri="/WEB-INF/tlds/ch05.tld" prefix="ch05" %>
```

Here, you're using the `uri` attribute of the `taglib` directive to explicitly specify the location of the TLD that represents the tag library that you would like to use. As before, the prefix attribute allows you to specify the prefix of the tags in the tag library, meaning that the `datetime` tag can be used on the page as follows:

```
The current date and time is <ch05:datetime/>
```

As expected, the output from the tag is illustrated by the following screen shot:

Of the many ways in which it's possible to deploy and use custom tags, this method is one of the most common. This is primarily because it allows you to save the TLD file straight into the web-application directory structure (that is, underneath the `WEB-INF` directory) and to explicitly specify the tag library that you would like to import. This, therefore, makes it very easy to quickly create and deploy a tag library in a development environment where the build and deploy and test cycles generally tend to be shorter than usual.

However, although it works, this method doesn't really take into account the ability that tag libraries have to be reusable. After all, tag libraries have the potential to be reused over the pages in a single project to the pages of multiple projects, within multiple organizations. Adopting this method for all of those projects means copying the tag handler classes and the TLD files into each and every web application. For this reason, the JSP specification provides an alternative mechanism for packaging up and then using and reusing tag libraries (see Chapter 7).

As this example illustrates, simple tags provide you with the ability to wrap up reusable functionality that is typically written using Java code. This is different from the template examples that you saw earlier in the chapter because where they were about parameterizing and reusing content, these are about reusing functionality. Of course, reusing the same functionality again and again is only useful up to a certain point. Fortunately, functionality–like content–can be parameterized and customized through the use of attributes.

Customizing Functionality with Attributes

Now that you understand the basics behind developing simple tags such as the tag handler class and the TLD file, you are now in a position to look at some of the more advanced features. Like tag files, simple tags can also be customized with attributes in the same way. What is different here is the way in which the use of attributes is implemented. With simple tags, attributes are implemented on the tag handler class.

As you saw with the tag file examples, attributes are defined within the tag file with the `attribute` directive, and it's here where you can specify the name and whether or not the attribute is required. With simple tags, this information is defined within the TLD file.

The Tag Life Cycle with Attributes

Introducing attributes into a custom tag does change the tag life cycle slightly because before the functionality of the tag can be executed (the doTag() method in the case of simple tags), the attributes must be passed to the tag handler so that they can be used by the tag.

The way in which the JSP specification allows this is through **setter methods** on the tag handler class. Just like a JavaBean, a tag handler must have one setter method for each and every attribute that it supports.

> *This is in fact a requirement of previous versions of the JSP specification, but with the introduction of **dynamic attributes**, this is strictly not true anymore. You'll look at dynamic attributes in the next chapter.*

These setter methods must conform to the standard JavaBeans naming convention, meaning that to support an attribute called name, the tag handler must declare a setter method with the following signature:

```
public void setName(String s)
```

With this example, at request-time, the value of the name attribute will be passed to the setName() method. With this in mind, you can now see how supporting attributes alters the tag life cycle. As an example, consider the following custom tag usage:

```
<prefix:myTag attribute1="abc" attributeN="def"/>
```

Here, the tag has two attributes that are being specified. By looking at the tag life cycle once again, you can see what happens behind the scenes:

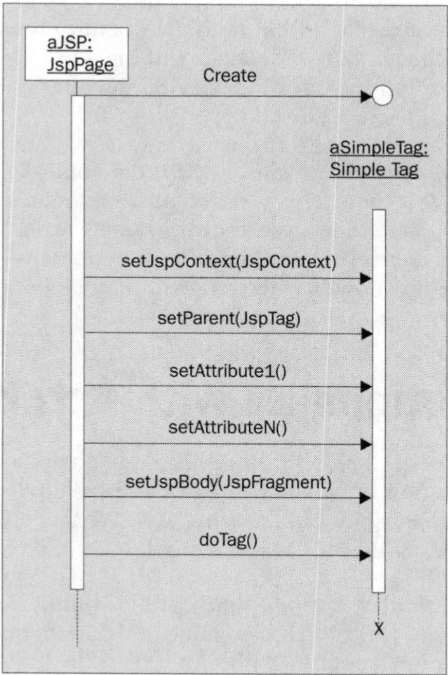

As this diagram shows, the setter methods for the attributes are called before the `doTag()` method is executed, and in the same order in which the attributes appear within the usage of the tag, from left to right. When it comes to implementing attributes in tag handler classes, attribute setter methods typically store a copy of the attribute away in an instance variable, ready for the `doTag()` method to use.

Attribute Types

Although the examples you've seen so far have used static strings that represent the values of attributes, they can in fact be Boolean values, numbers, and characters through an automatic conversion mechanism provided by the JSP container that will convert a string value into a specific type. In fact, even objects can be the values of tag attributes. Let's look at each of these in turn before referring to an example of how to use attributes with simple tags.

String Attributes

We've already said that string attributes are supported and implemented by having a setter method on the tag handler class as follows, where `X` is the name of the attribute:

```
public void setX(String s)
```

This is the most common attribute type, and probably the one that you'll find yourself coming back to time and time again.

Character Attributes

In addition to string values, the attribute setter methods can be written to accept a character as follows:

```
public void setX(char c)
public void setX(Character c)
```

Here, the automatic conversion performed by the JSP container simply takes the first character in the supplied string. For example, a value of `"hello"` will result in the character `'h'` being passed to the tag handler.

Boolean Attributes

Another common attribute type is Boolean. Supporting a Boolean attribute is simply a matter of providing one of the appropriate setter methods on the tag handler class as follows:

```
public void setX(boolean b)
public void setX(Boolean b)
```

The value for the Boolean attribute is specified in the page in the same way as you've seen before, and at request time, the JSP container will automatically convert this textual value to true or false according to the rules of the `java.lang.Boolean.valueOf(String)` method. To summarize this method, it returns a Boolean value of `true` from a textual value of "true" (ignoring case), otherwise it returns `false`. As an example, a Boolean value of `true` would be passed to the tag handler with the following tag usage:

```
<prefix:myTag x="true"/>
```

Although you could write the code to convert a string value into a Boolean inside the tag handler, letting the container do it for you saves time and is more convenient.

Numeric Attributes

Number-based attributes can also be automatically converted by the JSP container for the following primitive and wrapper types:

- `byte` and `java.lang.Byte`
- `short` and `java.lang.Short`
- `int` and `java.lang.Integer`
- `long` and `java.lang.Long`
- `float` and `java.lang.Float`
- `double` and `java.lang.Double`

As with the Boolean attributes, providing support is just a matter of implementing the desired setter method. For example, to support automatic conversion to a primitive integer, write the attribute setter method as follows:

```
public void setX(int i)
```

With the container providing the automatic conversion, it means that page authors can write the value as a string as with any other attribute, and the tag handler gets passed the value as a primitive `int`, as illustrated in the following example:

```
<prefix:myTag x="123"/>
```

> **A `NumberFormatException` will be thrown if anything other than a number in the appropriate range is supplied as the value for a numeric attribute.**

Again, you could convert the string value, but it's more convenient to let the conversion be done automatically. Of course, one benefit of writing the code to convert the value of the attribute within the tag handler class is that you have much more control over the conversion process, particularly over how errors like a `NumberFormatException` are handled.

Object Attributes

Up until this point we've said that the JSP container can automatically convert the string values supplied to attributes into a specific type such as a primitive `int`. However, as the JSP page is written (behind the scenes) as a Java class, and the tag handlers are also Java classes, there is nothing to stop objects from being passed as the values of attributes.

To achieve this, a reference to an object needs to be specified as the value of the attribute, and this is typically done using a request-time expression or an EL expression as follows:

```
<prefix:myTag x="${myObject}"/>
<prefix:myTag x="<%= myObject %>"/>
```

In the tag handler, the setter method for the attribute can be defined to take any class, regardless of whether it's a part of the Java APIs or one that you have written. You'll see examples of this in the next chapter.

JspFragment Attributes

One type of object that gets special support in JSP 2.0 is `JspFragment`. A `JspFragment` is essentially a class that wraps up a particular section (or fragment) of JSP code. At runtime, `JspFragment` objects can be invoked, meaning that the JSP code that they wrap up is translated and executed as if it were included in a regular JSP page.

If an attribute is defined as taking a `JspFragment`, this means that scriptless content can be passed as a JSP fragment into the tag handler. The only caveat here is in the way that the value of such an attribute can be specified in that it can only be passed using the body content of the `<jsp:attribute>` tag:

```
<prefix:myTag>
  <jsp:attribute name="x">Hello ${name}</jsp:attribute>
</prefix:myTag>
```

At runtime, the JSP container wraps up the value of the attribute and passes it as a `JspFragment` instance to the tag handler. During the execution of that tag, the tag handler can invoke and evaluate the fragment to have the results included whenever necessary.

Now you'll see an example of how to use attributes.

Displaying Thumbnails with a Tag

Imagine that you've been asked to write a JSP page that presents a list of thumbnail images to the user. There are several ways to do this. First of all, you could statically code the page, writing the appropriate HTML tags to present a thumbnail of all images in a particular directory. The downside to this approach is that when the images change, your page will also have to change. Therefore, instead of taking this approach you'll perform this dynamically, and rather than write a whole load of Java code into the JSP, you'll build a custom tag that you could reuse elsewhere.

The functionality provided by the custom tag will, given a directory name, look in that directory and generate the appropriate HTML to display the thumbnails. An example of how the finished page might look is as follows:

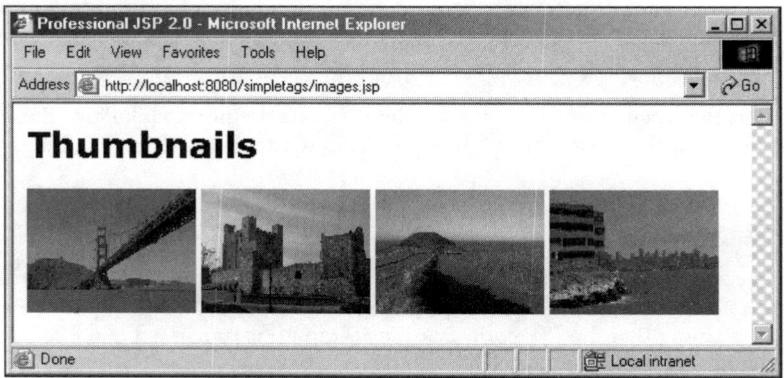

In terms of the custom tag that you would like to use to help generate this page, rather than hard-coding the directory in which it should look, you'll pass this as an attribute. In doing so, the ability to customize this tag opens it up for reuse elsewhere. In addition to this, you want to be able to specify the types of files that are displayed and do it by filtering only those files with a specific file extension. For example, you might only want to display `.jpg` files.

Building the Thumbnail Tag Handler

From an implementation perspective, the code for the tag is fairly straightforward, as you can once again use the `SimpleTagSupport` class as a starting point:

```
package com.apress.projsp20.ch05.tagext;

import java.io.IOException;
import java.util.*;

import javax.servlet.jsp.JspException;
import javax.servlet.jsp.PageContext;
import javax.servlet.jsp.tagext.SimpleTagSupport;

public class ThumbnailTag extends SimpleTagSupport {
```

Next, you have two instance variables to store the values of your two attributes, and the setter methods for those attributes:

```
  private String path;
  private String suffix;

  public void setPath(String s) {
    this.path = s;
  }

  public void setSuffix(String s) {
    this.suffix = s;
  }
```

Finally, you have the `doTag()` method, which contains the functionality that your tag provides. For simplicity, a private helper method has been created to locate the files in a specific directory, while the `doTag()` method is responsible for outputting the information:

```
  public void doTag() throws JspException, IOException {
    // first of all, find the names of the files
    Collection files = findFiles();

    if (files != null && !files.isEmpty()) {
      String filename;

      // now that the names have been found, iterate over each of them
      // and generate the appropriate HTML
      Iterator it = files.iterator();
      while (it.hasNext()) {
        filename = (String)it.next();

        getJspContext().getOut().write("<img src=\".");
        getJspContext().getOut().write(filename);
        getJspContext().getOut().write("\" width=\"128\" height=\"96\"> ");
      }
    }
  }

  private Collection findFiles() {
    PageContext pageContext = (PageContext)getJspContext();
    Collection resources =
      pageContext.getServletContext().getResourcePaths(path);

    List filteredResources = new ArrayList();

    if (resources == null || resources.isEmpty()) {
      return filteredResources;
    }

    Iterator it = resources.iterator();
    String uri;

    String testSuffix;
    if (this.suffix != null) {
      testSuffix = this.suffix;
    } else {
      testSuffix = ".jpg";
    }

    // now filter out those files that don't end in the suffix
    while (it.hasNext()) {
       uri = (String)it.next();

       if (uri.endsWith(testSuffix)) {
         filteredResources.add(uri);
```

```
        }
      }
      return filteredResources;
    }
  }
```

Although there's a fair amount of code, all this tag does is look for all of the files within a specified directory, and then filter these to include only those that end with the specified suffix or file extension. With this list, the `doTag()` method then iterates over each in turn and generates an HTML `img` tag to display the image on the page.

> *One of the aims in keeping simple tags simple to use is that they, unlike classic tags, don't rely directly on features provided by the servlet API. A benefit of this is that simple tags have the potential to be used within other technologies in the future. The price of this, however, is that you must now explicitly cast the `JspContext` to `PageContext` in order to access any of the servlet specific features such as the current servlet context.*

Describing the Thumbnail Tag

With the tag handler class written, the next step is to write the TLD file that describes the tag and its characteristics. For the sake of this example, you'll use the same TLD file as before. For brevity, the descriptions of the tag library and the `datetime` tag have been omitted:

```
<?xml version="1.0" encoding="UTF-8" ?>

<taglib xmlns="http://java.sun.com/xml/ns/j2ee"
    xmlns:xsi="http://www.w3.org/2001/XMLSchema-instance"
    xsi:schemaLocation="http://java.sun.com/xml/ns/j2ee/web-jsptaglibrary_2_0.xsd"
    version="2.0">

  ... the description of the tag library ...
  ... the description of the datetime tag ...

  <tag>
    <name>thumbnail</name>
    <tag-class>com.apress.projsp20.ch05.tagext.ThumbnailTag</tag-class>
    <body-content>empty</body-content>
    <description>
      Given a path, this tag generates HTML to display thumbnail images.
    </description>

    <attribute>
      <name>path</name>
      <required>true</required>
      <rtexprvalue>true</rtexprvalue>
    </attribute>

    <attribute>
      <name>suffix</name>
      <required>false</required>
```

```
        <rtexprvalue>false</rtexprvalue>
      </attribute>
    </tag>

</taglib>
```

As before, the content between the tag elements describes the `thumbnail` tag, with the `name`, `tag-class`, `body-content`, and `description` elements you've seen before. What's new here is that the TLD file defines the attributes that this tag supports. Attributes are defined within the body of the `tag` element, and the characteristics of each attribute are defined between the `attribute` tags.

In this example, you have two attributes–one named `path` that is marked as required and one called `suffix` that is optional (not required). To make it easier for page authors to use the tag, you shouldn't force them to have to specify the `suffix` attribute; this is why it's marked as optional. For this to work properly, you should always ensure that tag handlers work correctly regardless of whether a value is specified for optional attributes or not. For this reason, the code inside the tag handler checks whether the suffix has been specified and defaults to `.jpg` if it hasn't.

As in all programming situations where supplying a value is optional, you should always have a sensible default value to fall back on if an optional attribute is not supplied. In doing so, you not only make your tag easier to use, but you make it usable regardless of whether the value has been specified or not.

Finally, the `path` attribute allows request-time expressions and you'll see how this can be put to good use shortly.

Using the Thumbnail Tag

Once the tag handler has been written, compiled, and deployed, you're ready to start using the tag. Because you're using the same tag library from the previous examples, you can use the same import statement:

```
<%@ taglib uri="/WEB-INF/tlds/ch05.tld" prefix="ch05" %>
```

You can now use the tag in either of the following ways since the `suffix` attribute is optional:

```
    <ch05:thumbnail path="/ch05/photos"/>
    <ch05:thumbnail path="/ch05/photos" suffix=".jpg"/>
```

In these examples, both usages will look in the `/ch05/photos` directory for any `.jpg` files and generate the HTML that displays them as thumbnails.

Alternatively, you could use request-time expressions written using the EL to specify the path. For example, if you specified the path as a parameter to the JSP page on which the tag is being used (by appending `?path=/ch05/photos` to the URL), you could pass this information to the tag with a short EL expression:

```
<ch05:thumbnail path="${param.path}"/>
```

In this instance, the expression is evaluated automatically by the JSP container and the result is passed in as the value of the attribute.

> *Earlier versions of the JSP specification only supported request-time expressions using Java code. For example, the equivalent of `${param.path}` would be `<%= request.getParameter("path") %>`. While this is still supported, JSP 2.0 promotes the use of the new EL. Not only is the EL more concise, but it removes Java code from the page—something that helps improve the readability of JSP pages.*

This example shows how easy it is to parameterize the functionality encapsulated within a custom tag. By allowing attributes to be used to specify the location and types of files, you've built a fairly generic custom tag that can be used in many other places. However, in this example you have hard-coded the presentation within the tag handler class. The HTML might be dynamically generated, but the actual presentation of the list of files is locked away and wrapped up inside Java code. From a reusability perspective this is poor since it somewhat restricts how the tag can be used by other people. Also, maintaining the content means modifying the class file, recompiling it, and redeploying the tag library. To wrap up this chapter on building simple tags, let's take a look at how you can combine templating and customization to build a truly reusable component: a tag that evaluates its own body content.

Evaluating Body Content

During the previous sections on tags, we defined some templated content within a tag file. Essentially this is just regular JSP code that has been abstracted out of the page so it can easily be reused.

With the `thumbnail` tag, the functionality of finding the list of files was wrapped up alongside the presentation of that list. Although we've made the presentation as simple as possible, we can imagine the scenario where every usage of the tag requires a slightly different HTML to be generated. Perhaps the list of thumbnails should be a bulleted list, or perhaps it should be enclosed within an HTML table. To achieve this goal, ideally you need to break out the content (the files) from the presentation (generating the HTML). This is something that is easy to implement with the use of JSP fragments, or tag body content.

Essentially, the objective here is to leave the content on the page where it belongs and have the custom tag look up and locate the files. Once the tag has this list, in a similar way to the JSTL `forEach` tag, it should then evaluate its body content repeatedly for each and every file that is found. Consider the following JSP code:

```
<ch05:list path="/ch05/photos" suffix=".jpg">
  <img src="../${filename}" width="128" height="96">
</ch05:list>
```

```
<ch05:list path="/photos" suffix=".jpg">
  <td align="center">
    <img src=".${filename}" alt="${filename}" width="128" height="96">
  </td>
</ch05:list>
```

By splitting out the content (what is being displayed) from the presentation (how it's being displayed), you're introducing a separation between the list of files and its presentation in HTML. In addition to enabling this tag to be reused more often, this separation promotes easy maintenance and modification of the presentation. In other words, should you need to modify the way in which the list of files is presented, you can do this by editing the JSP rather than the tag handler code.

Separating Content from Presentation

With the previous example in mind, let's build a tag that is capable of generating a list of any type of file. In other words, the tag won't generate a list of HTML `img` tags, but rather it will implement a generic mechanism with which you'll be able to generate whatever HTML you like.

Building the Directory List Tag

To start with, you'll again use the `SimpleTagSupport` class as a basis for this new tag:

```
package com.apress.projsp20.ch05.tagext;

import java.io.IOException;
import java.util.*;

import javax.servlet.jsp.JspException;
import javax.servlet.jsp.PageContext;
import javax.servlet.jsp.tagext.SimpleTagSupport;

public class DirectoryListTag extends SimpleTagSupport {
```

Next, and in the same way as before, you have a couple of instance variables and setter methods to support the attributes for the tag:

```
  private String path;
  private String suffix;

  public void setPath(String s) {
    this.path = s;
  }

  public void setSuffix(String s) {
    this.suffix = s;
  }
```

Also, you have exactly the same `findFiles()` helper method as before:

```
  private Collection findFiles() {
    PageContext pageContext = (PageContext)getJspContext();
    Collection resources =
        pageContext.getServletContext().getResourcePaths(path);
```

```
    List filteredResources = new ArrayList();

    if (resources == null || resources.isEmpty()) {
      return filteredResources;
    }

    Iterator it = resources.iterator();
    String uri;

    String testSuffix;
    if (this.suffix != null) {
      testSuffix = this.suffix;
    } else {
      testSuffix = ".jpg";
    }

    // now filter out those files that don't end in the suffix
    while (it.hasNext()) {
      uri = (String)it.next();

      if (uri.endsWith(testSuffix)) {
        filteredResources.add(uri);
      }
    }

    return filteredResources;
  }
```

The key difference between this and the previous `thumbnail` tag is in the way that the `doTag()` method behaves. Where the `thumbnail` tag generated HTML that was output back to the page, this time you just want to invoke (or evaluate) the body content of the custom tag for each file in the resulting list:

```
  public void doTag() throws JspException, IOException  {
    // first of all, find the names of the files
    Collection files = findFiles();

    if (files != null && !files.isEmpty()) {
      String filename;

      // now that the names have been found, iterate over each of them
      // and invoke the body content (JspFragment)
      Iterator it = files.iterator();
      while (it.hasNext()) {
        filename = (String)it.next();

        if (jspBody != null) {
          getJspContext().setAttribute("filename", filename);
          jspBody.invoke(getJspContext().getOut());
        }
      }
    }
  }
}
```

If you think back to the tag life cycle, part of the tag creation and initialization process involves a reference to a `JspFragment` object representing the body content of the tag being passed to the tag via the `setJspBody()` method. The `JspFragment` has one method that is of interest here: `invoke()`. Calling this method effectively asks the JSP container to evaluate and process the body content and send it back to the page. This seemingly simple process provides a great deal of flexibility in building custom tags.

For example, it allows you to programmatically evaluate and include the body content, perhaps only including the body content if a certain condition is met. In this example, you're only invoking the body content object if there are files that were found, and for each file found, you invoke the body content and therefore generate some more content.

In addition to programmatically evaluating the body content, you can also evaluate the body content multiple times. Again, in this example, if files are found then you're invoking the body content of the tag once for each of them.

Describing the Directory List Tag

Again, you'll use the same TLD as before and omit the previous tags for brevity:

```
<?xml version="1.0" encoding="UTF-8" ?>

<taglib xmlns="http://java.sun.com/xml/ns/j2ee"
    xmlns:xsi="http://www.w3.org/2001/XMLSchema-instance"
    xsi:schemaLocation="http://java.sun.com/xml/ns/j2ee/web-jsptaglibrary_2_0.xsd"
    version="2.0">

  ... the description of the tag library ...
  ... the description of the datetime tag ...
  ... the description of the thumbnail tag ...

    <tag>
      <name>list</name>
      <tag-class>com.apress.projsp20.ch05.tagext.DirectoryListTag</tag-class>
      <body-content>scriptless</body-content>
      <description>
        Given a path, this tag provides a list of the files in that path.
      </description>

        <attribute>
            <name>path</name>
            <required>true</required>
            <rtexprvalue>true</rtexprvalue>
        </attribute>

        <attribute>
            <name>suffix</name>
            <required>false</required>
            <rtexprvalue>false</rtexprvalue>
        </attribute>
    </tag>

</taglib>
```

Describing this tag is pretty much the same as before, with the `list` tag having a required `path` attribute and an optional `suffix` attribute. Once again, the `path` attribute can accept an expression.

Using the Directory List Tag

As before, you first import the tag library and then use it in the way that we outlined previously–with the body content of the tag representing the presentation and formatting:

```
<%@ taglib uri="/WEB-INF/tlds/ch05.tld" prefix="ch05" %>

<table width="100%">
  <tr>
    <ch05:list path="/ch05/photos" suffix=".jpg">
      <td align="center">
        <img src="../${filename}" alt="${filename}" width="128" height="96">
      </td>
    </ch05:list>
  </tr>
</table>
```

As this example shows, it's possible to fuse the concepts of templating and wrapping up reusable functionality together to form a custom tag that is not only flexible, but reusable, too. With the previous implementation, the tag generated the HTML code and the information was presented in a limited way. However, with this tag you can locate a list of files in a specific directory and then, by customizing the body content, display a list of names, a list of hyperlinks, a set of thumbnails, and so on. The possibilities are vast.

Summary

This chapter has introduced the concepts of encapsulating your own content and functionality as reusable software components known as JSP tag extensions or, informally, as custom tags. These are a great way to promote several of the factors associated with JSP development, including the reusability, readability, and maintainability of JSP pages. Removing common Java code, content, and presentation from the page provides a way to clean up JSP pages, by speeding up development, increasing quality, and permitting a quicker time to market through reuse.

Traditionally, common content such as that found in headers and footers has been abstracted away from JSP pages and included wherever necessary. While this promotes maintainability and reuse, using the raw JSP constructs can often seem awkward to those that are not familiar with the technology and are more focused on the look and feel of a web application rather than the mechanics of how it works. Tag files, a new addition to the JSP 2.0 specification, help solve these problems by providing an easy-to-use mechanism for wrapping up and reusing common content. Next, you also learned how such content can be templated with tag files and parameterized with attributes. In addition to solving some technical problems, tag files also provide a more natural interface for anybody using the tags.

Simple tags are another new addition in the JSP 2.0 specification. Previous versions of JSP technology featured a way to wrap up common and recurring functionality as reusable custom tags, although the life cycle and semantics behind these techniques were often seen as too complicated by many developers. To address this, the `SimpleTag` interface was introduced to provide an effortless way to wrap up common functionality that is generally implemented in Java code as opposed to JSP code. As a convenience, the `SimpleTagSupport` class is also provided by the JSP specification to serve as a starting point for your tags.

While looking at this interface, you saw the development of a fairly trivial tag, followed by a look at how attributes can be used to customize the functionality. This led to a further discussion on how custom tags can best be used, which culminated in the assertion that content and presentation should ideally be separated if the best degree of reuse is to be achieved. Backing this up was a modified example of the `thumbnail` tag that allowed page authors to be flexible in the way that they used the tag as well as the content that they subsequently generated.

Tag files and the `SimpleTag` interface are great ways to wrap up reusable content and functionality for use by page authors in the pages of one or more web applications. For backwards compatibility, JSP 2.0-compliant containers still need to support the classic method for building custom tags. This is particularly useful when reaching a wide audience is desired, or when you are looking for more control of the functionality that tags provide. For this reason, you'll look at classic tags in the next chapter.

6

Classic Tags

In the previous chapter you looked at tag files and simple tags, both of which are new mechanisms for writing custom tags introduced as a part of the JSP 2.0 specification. As the examples in Chapter 5 demonstrated, these new mechanisms remove some of the complexity that was typically associated with building custom tags in the past. Rather than abandon the existing method of writing custom tags, JSP 2.0 supports full backwards compatibility with it.

This chapter takes a look at the facilities provided by former versions of the JSP specification for writing custom tags. As you'll see throughout the chapter, these previous methods, now called **classic tags**, provide more flexibility than current methods, and for this reason they're still useful in some scenarios. You'll also see how classic tags can take advantage of some of the new features that are now a part of the JSP 2.0 specification, including how custom tags can now support dynamic attributes.

Classic Tags Overview

There are now essentially three different mechanisms for building custom tags outlined in the JSP 2.0 specification: tag files, simple tags, and classic tags. As you saw in the previous chapter, tag files provide a natural progression for abstracting content away from JSP pages and into reusable components. Because tag files allow this content to be written using regular JSP constructs, it makes wrapping up content fairly straightforward and usable for JSP developers who might not necessarily know the Java programming language.

The next step up, in terms of complexity, is simple tags. These tags allow reusable functionality to be defined with Java code and used on the page as a custom tag. Although this process does require familiarity with the Java programming language, it allows complex behavior to be wrapped up and used by page authors in a straightforward way. As you saw in the previous chapter, simple tags offer a great deal of flexibility in the way that the functionality is encapsulated and, through body content and JSP fragments, they allow separation between content and content presentation. So, what are classic tags and why do you need them?

Classic tags are the original tag development methodology introduced in version 1.1 of the JSP specification. JSP 1.2 then added new functionality and simplified the programming model slightly, but essentially the model was the same, and it remains the same in the JSP 2.0 specification. As with simple tags, classic tags use the concept of a tag handler class that is written using Java code. This is then described with a tag library descriptor file in the same way it is with simple tags, and the resulting custom tags are again used in the same way. So, what differentiates classic tags from simple tags?

The Differences Between Simple and Classic Tags

There are several key differences between simple and classic tags. Let's take a quick look at each in turn and evaluate what it means to you as a tag developer.

The Tag Handler Interface

The fundamental difference between simple and classic tags is the way in which the tag handler class is implemented. With simple tags, any tag handlers you build must implement the `javax.servlet.jsp.tagext.SimpleTag` interface. With classic tags, however, the tag handlers must implement the `javax.servlet.jsp.tagext.Tag` interface or, as you'll see in this chapter, one of its subinterfaces.

For you as a developer, this means you need to learn a slightly different programming model. For example, with simple tags all of the functionality to be encapsulated within the tag is defined within the `doTag()` method. With classic tags, there are two methods you must implement: `doStartTag()` and `doEndTag()`.

Feedback from tag developers over the past couple of years has been mixed, and many people find the concepts employed by classic tag handlers confusing. For this reason, the interface has been simplified and simple tags are the result of this process.

The Tag Life Cycle

Another key, though often neglected difference relates to the tag life cycle. With simple tags, an instance of the tag handler class is created when needed and that instance is only used to serve a single invocation of a custom tag. In other words, a unique tag handler instance is created for each usage of a simple tag on a page. With classic tags, this may or may not be the case because the JSP specification provides the ability for container vendors to optionally improve classic tag performance by pooling and reusing tag handler instances. This means that, for example, a single tag handler instance could be created and reused to service all invocations of that custom tag per page.

The rules around reuse are fairly complicated, and to make matters worse, JSP container vendors don't always choose to implement this optional piece of the specification. Therefore, if you're not aware of the implications that this has, your tags may not function correctly on all vendors' JSP containers.

The problems that arise between different JSP contains is another reason simple tags were introduced and it's another area in which the complexity associated with developing them has been reduced. The downside is that there may be times when you'd like tag instances pooled and reused. For example, your tag might acquire some expensive resource when it is created. In this example, it makes sense to take advantage of any performance benefits that the container may provide. In many scenarios, however, this just isn't an issue and simple tags are more than adequate.

With our brief look at the differences between simple and classic tags over, let's take a look at the interface that classic tag handlers must implement.

The Tag Interface

The `Tag` interface, like the `SimpleTag` interface, provides the basic contract that must be upheld between the JSP page and the tag. The following code snippet shows the interface:

```
package javax.servlet.jsp.tagext;

import javax.servlet.jsp.JspException;

public interface Tag {

  public final static int SKIP_BODY = 0;
  public final static int EVAL_BODY_INCLUDE = 1;
  public final static int SKIP_PAGE = 5;
  public final static int EVAL_PAGE = 6;

  void setPageContext(PageContext pc);

  void setParent(Tag t);

  int doStartTag() throws JspException;

  int doEndTag() throws JspException;

  void release();
}
```

The Tag Life Cycle

As you learned in the last chapter, the life cycle of simple tags consists of the tag handler being created, contextual and environmental information being passed to it, and finally, the `doTag()` method being executed. As the following diagram shows, classic tags are not too different in this respect:

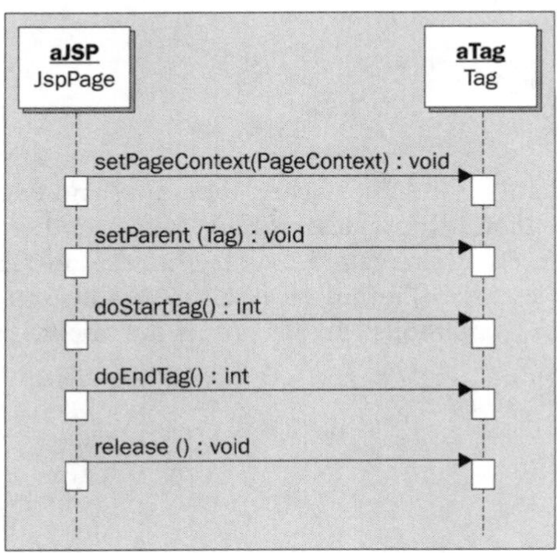

Creating a Tag Handler Instance

As with simple tags, when a custom tag is used on a JSP page, the first thing that the JSP container must do is create a new instance of the tag handler class. Again, this is performed by invoking the default, no arguments constructor.

Setting the Context

The next step in the tag life cycle is to make the tag handler instance aware of the environment in which it is running. This involves passing the tag handler a reference to the current `PageContext` through the `setPageContext()` method. Like `JspContext`, this method provides an easy way to access other objects such as the current output writer and scoped attributes. Notice here that it's a `PageContext` instance that gets passed to the tag and not a `JspContext` instance, as happens with simple tags. This moves simple tags away from being dependent on services and features provided by the Java Servlet API; `PageContext` uses such features, whereas `JspContext` doesn't. However, for consistency and backwards compatibility with earlier versions of the JSP specification, `PageContext` actually extends `JspContext`.

Setting the Parent

Like simple tags, classic tags can be nested, and as you'll see in Chapter 7, it's possible for custom tag handlers to cooperate and communicate with one another. As an example, a child (nested) tag may ask for information from its parent tag. For this reason, the `setParent()` method is called and passes a reference to the closest enclosing tag handler or `null` if the tag isn't nested.

With simple tags, this reference is of type `JspTag` (the superinterface for all tag handlers), but again for backwards compatibility with classic tags this reference is of type `Tag` (a subinterface of `JspTag`).

Executing the Functionality

With the context set, the next thing to do is execute the functionality provided by the tag. With simple tags, this involves calling the `doTag()` method. With classic tags, this means calling the `doStartTag()` and `doEndTag()` methods.

When you looked at how custom tags can be used on the page, you saw that they can be written in a long or shortened form as follows:

```
<prefix:myTag></prefix:myTag>
<prefix:myTag/>
```

With the long format you explicitly write the starting (opening) and ending (closing) tags, and with the shortened format you combine them. Regardless of how you write them, both the `doStartTag()` method and the `doEndTag()` method are called on a tag handler instance. The following diagram shows the tag life cycle from a slightly different viewpoint and illustrates the way in which the `doStartTag()` and `doEndTag()` methods can also affect the tag life cycle by the values that are returned by them:

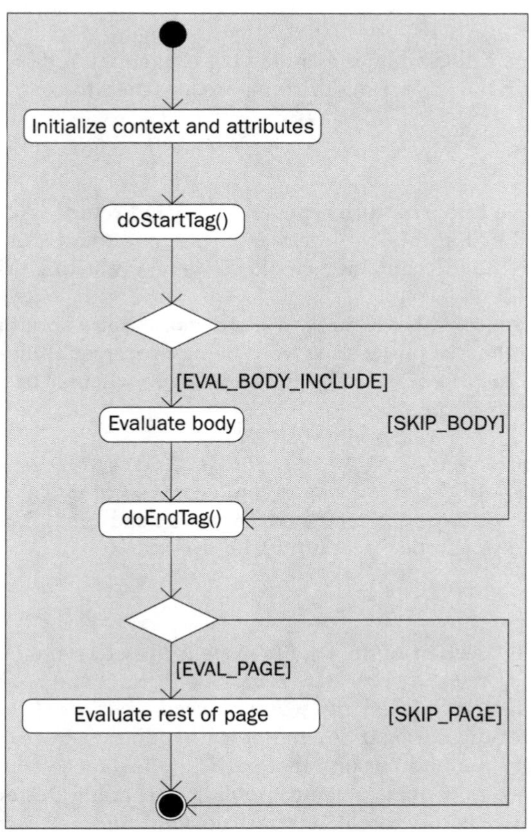

The Start Tag

The `doStartTag()` method is called when the starting tag is encountered on the page:

```
int doStartTag() throws JspException;
```

The method signature from the `Tag` interface states that a primitive `int` value is to be returned. This signals to the JSP page what do to next. Two values can be returned from tags implementing this interface, `SKIP_BODY` and `EVAL_BODY_INCLUDE`, which are defined as constants within the `Tag` interface.

Returning `SKIP_BODY` signals to the JSP page that after the `doStartTag()` method has been called, any body content for the tag should be ignored. For example, any body content such as JSP code, Java code, or content that would normally be output to the page is simply dropped. Following this, processing proceeds to the `doEndTag()` method.

On the other hand, returning `EVAL_BODY_INCLUDE` from the `doStartTag()` method signals that any body content should be evaluated and output to the page.

The End Tag

The doEndTag() method is called when the ending tag is encountered on the page, again, regardless of whether the tag is written on the page using the long or shortened format:

```
int doEndTag() throws JspException;
```

This method also specifies an integer return type, and the valid return types for this method are the other two constants defined within the Tag interface, SKIP_PAGE and EVAL_PAGE. Here, these return values signal whether or not the JSP container should continue evaluating the rest of the JSP page.

In reality, the SKIP_PAGE return value is rarely used, because there aren't many circumstances in which you'll want to actually stop the rest of the page from being processed. One such example might be a security tag that appears at the top of the JSP page and checks whether or not the current user is authorized to see the contents of the page.

The behavior produced by returning SKIP_PAGE from the doEndTag() method can also be achieved using simple tags. Here, instead of returning an integer value, an instance of SkipPageException should be thrown. SkipPageException is a subclass of JspException and therefore doesn't need to be added to the throws signature of the doTag() method.

Releasing State

The final method to be called as part of the tag life cycle is the release() method. This method is called to ask the tag handler to release any state it may be storing, and it's only called on the tag handler when that tag handler instance is finished and won't be used anymore. In other words, with JSP containers that don't support the optional pooling of tag handler instances, the release() method is called after the doEndTag() method because that particular instance will never be used again. On the other hand, with containers that provide instance pooling, this method is only called when the container has finished using the instance and before it gets garbage collected.

It's a common misconception that release() is always called directly after the doEndTag() method and hence used to clear the values of instance variables. This is not the case, and relying on this behavior means that your tags might not work as expected in all vendors' JSP containers. The next chapter looks at some of the best practices for using and taking advantage of the tag life cycle.

The TagSupport Class

Although the Tag interface contains more methods than the SimpleTag interface, providing an implementation is trivial. However, for convenience and in the same way that the SimpleTagSupport class provides a default implementation of the SimpleTag interface, the JSP specification provides the TagSupport class that you can use as a starting point for your own tag handlers. Here, the default implementations of the doStartTag() and doEndTag() methods return SKIP_BODY and EVAL_PAGE, respectively. We use this in many of this chapter's examples.

A Simple Example

You're now ready to build a small classic tag. To help provide a direct comparison with simple tags, you'll rebuild the `datetime` tag example from the previous chapter.

Building the DateTime Tag Handler

The first step is, of course, to build the tag handler class. You'll use the `TagSupport` class as a starting point:

```
package com.apress.projsp20.ch06.tagext;

import java.io.IOException;
import java.text.DateFormat;
import java.util.Date;

import javax.servlet.jsp.JspException;
import javax.servlet.jsp.JspTagException;
import javax.servlet.jsp.tagext.TagSupport;

public class DateTimeTag extends TagSupport {
```

Next is the functionality provided by the tag, which you've implemented within the `doStartTag()` method:

> **In situations in which it doesn't matter whether a custom tag will be used in the long or shortened form on the page, the functionality associated with the tag can be implemented within either the `doStartTag()` or the `doEndTag()` method.**

```
  public int doStartTag() throws JspException {
    DateFormat df = DateFormat.getDateTimeInstance(
                                 DateFormat.MEDIUM, DateFormat.MEDIUM);

    try {
      pageContext.getOut().write(df.format(new Date()));
    } catch (IOException ioe) {
      throw new JspTagException(ioe.getMessage());
    }

    return SKIP_BODY;
  }
}
```

As you can see, the code that provides the functionality of the tag is pretty much the same as that you used with the simple tag example in the previous chapter. The only real difference is in the way that this code is packaged within the tag handler. One point to note here is that unlike the `doTag()` method on the `SimpleTag` interface, the `doStartTag()` and `doEndTag()` methods don't declare that they throw `IOException`, therefore you must catch and handle this exception.

In this example, you're throwing a `JspTagException` (a subclass of `JspException`) to tell the JSP page that something went wrong. Throwing a `JspTagException` instead of a more generic `JspException` is a useful way to specify that the problem may be related to a custom tag rather than the page itself, during development and debugging.

Finally, as you're not interested in the body content of this tag, you return `SKIP_BODY` from the `doStartTag()` method.

Describing the DateTime Tag

With the tag handler written, the next step is to describe the tag. As with simple tags, you do this using the tag library descriptor (TLD) file:

```
<?xml version="1.0" encoding="UTF-8" ?>

<taglib xmlns="http://java.sun.com/xml/ns/j2ee"
  xmlns:xsi="http://www.w3.org/2001/XMLSchema-instance"
  xsi:schemaLocation="http://java.sun.com/xml/ns/j2ee/web-jsptaglibrary_2_0.xsd"
  version="2.0">

  <description>
    Tag library for Professional JSP 2.0, Chapter 6.
  </description>
  <jsp-version>2.0</jsp-version>
  <tlib-version>1.0</tlib-version>
  <short-name>ch06</short-name>
  <uri>http://www.apress.com/projsp20/ch06</uri>

  <tag>
    <name>datetime</name>
    <tag-class>com.apress.projsp20.ch06.tagext.DateTimeTag</tag-class>
    <body-content>empty</body-content>
    <description>
      Outputs the current date and time to the page.
    </description>
  </tag>

</taglib>
```

As this code illustrates, describing a tag with a TLD file is the same regardless of whether that tag is a simple tag or a classic tag.

The way in which custom tags are used on the page provides a nice abstraction for those tags and the way they're built. It's perfectly acceptable to mix simple and classic tags together in the same TLD file, and page authors will never know how the tags are actually implemented. In fact, as you'll see in the next chapter, it's also possible to describe tag files in the TLD, which makes it possible to wrap up any type of tag for easy reuse.

Using the DateTime Tag

If you assume that the TLD file has been saved at the location /WEB-INF/tlds/ch06.tld, then importing and using the tag library is the same as before:

```
<%@ taglib uri="/WEB-INF/tlds/ch06.tld" prefix="ch06" %>

The current date and time is <ch06:datetime/>
```

Not surprisingly, the results of using the tag are also the same as before. As this example shows, building trivial classic tags isn't that much different from building the simple tags you saw in the previous chapter, and essentially it's just a matter of using the Tag interface and implementing your functionality within the doStartTag() or doEndTag() method. Let's now continue our tour of classic tags by seeing how they, like other custom tags, can be customized with attributes.

Customizing Functionality with Attributes

In the previous chapter you learned how you can customize tag files and simple tags with attributes. With tag files this meant that you could parameterize content as templates, and with simple tags it meant that you could parameterize functionality. Classic tags are just another way to wrap up functionality, and therefore the same principles apply. You can use attributes to configure that functionality. In fact, the way in which attributes are implemented with classic tags is exactly the same as with simple tags. Let's see an example of this.

Building Lists in HTML Forms

A common feature of many web sites and HTML forms is a drop-down control that allows users to select an item from a list. An example here is a user registration form in which users select the country they live in from a list, as shown here:

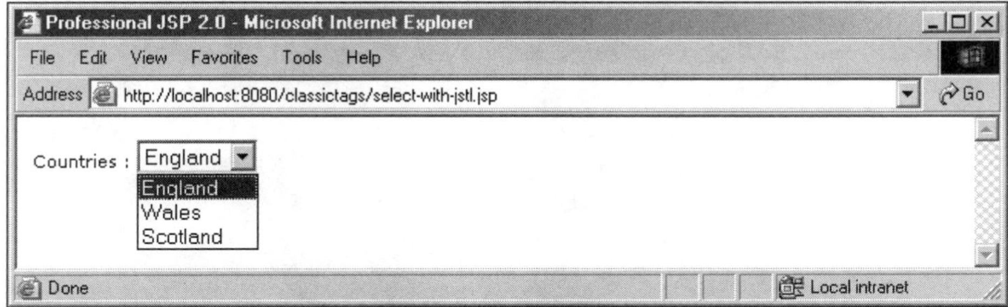

If the items in the list were available as a collection of JavaBeans (for example, a java.util.List containing Country beans), it would be possible to dynamically generate such a list with features provided by the JSP expression language and JSTL. One option is to use the JSTL forEach tag to iterate over the collection and generate the appropriate HTML for each item in the collection.

To hold the information for each country consisting of an ID and a name, a simple Country JavaBean might look like this:

```
package com.apress.projsp20.ch06.domain;

public class Country {

  private int id;
  private String name;

  public Country() {
  }

  public Country(int id, String name) {
    this.id = id;
    this.name = name;
  }

  public int getId() {
    return this.id;
  }

  public void setId(int i) {
    this.id = i;
  }

  public String getName() {
    return this.name;
  }

  public void setName(String s) {
    this.name = s;
  }
}
```

With a collection of `Country` objects available as a page-scoped attribute (for example), the following JSP code snippet shows how JSTL can be used to help build the list:

```
<%@ taglib uri="http://java.sun.com/jstl/core_rt" prefix="c" %>

  Countries :
  <select name="country">
    <c:forEach var="country" items="${countries}">
      <option value="${country.id}">${country.name}</option>
    </c:forEach>
  </select>
```

Here, you're using JSTL to iterate over the collection with short JSP EL expressions to extract the ID and name from the `Country` JavaBeans within that collection. Although this works, the logic related to building the list is embedded within the JSP page, meaning that it's not easily reusable. Also, the code itself is a little raw and unreadable, particularly because the HTML for the select control is mixed in with JSTL and EL expressions. A better way to implement this is to use a custom tag that generates the content for you.

Identifying the Attributes

Before building the tag handler, let's look at what you might want to allow users to customize when they use the tag. Looking at the previous example, there are essentially four things that you can customize:

- The `name` property of the HTML select control
- The value that is being displayed in the list (the label)
- The value behind the scenes that acts as a key for each item (the value)
- The collection of items to be displayed

Looking at what can be customized is an important step in figuring out what attributes a custom tag might need. It also allows the custom tag itself to be as generic as possible. After all, if you can specify all of the preceding information with attributes, it means that you can build a generic HTML `select` tag rather than one that displays just country names.

Building the Select Tag Handler

Keeping in mind the attributes you can customize, let's look at how to implement the tag handler. As before, you'll use the `TagSupport` class as a starting point:

```
package com.apress.projsp20.ch06.tagext;

import java.beans.PropertyDescriptor;
import java.util.Collection;
import java.util.Iterator;

import javax.servlet.jsp.*;
import javax.servlet.jsp.tagext.TagSupport;

public class SelectTag extends TagSupport {
```

Next, you have the code that provides support for the various attributes for the tag. These are implemented in exactly the same way as with simple tags, by having an instance variable and **setter method** for each attribute:

```
  private String name;
  private String label;
  private String value;
  private Collection items;

  public void setName(String s) {
    this.name = s;
  }

  public void setLabel(String s) {
    this.label = s;
  }

  public void setValue(String s) {
    this.value = s;
  }
```

```
public void setItems(Collection coll) {
  this.items = coll;
}
```

As in this book's previous examples, three of the four attributes here are simple string values. First, you have the name of the select control on the page. Then you have `label` and `value`, both of which are strings representing the name of the JavaBean property containing the information you'd like to extract from each bean. For example, with the `Country` JavaBean, these attributes would be set to `name` and `id`, respectively.

The fourth and final instance variable is of type `java.util.Collection`. When we covered attributes in the previous chapter, we mentioned that they can be more than just simple strings–they can be Boolean values, numeric values, and even objects. For this example, and in the same way as the `items` attribute in the JSTL `forEach` tag, you want to pass your tag handler a reference to a fully populated `java.util.Collection` instance containing the items that are to be displayed in the list. For this reason, the instance variable and setter method are defined to take `Collection` rather than `String`, and at request time the setter method will be called with a `Collection` of `Country` objects.

The only other part of the tag handler that you must define is the functionality provided by the tag. As in the previous example, this is implemented within the `doStartTag()` method, although the `doEndTag()` method can also be used.

> **Remember, don't implement the same functionality in the `doStartTag()` and `doEndTag()` methods, as they both get called.**

First, set up an `Iterator` instance that will operate over the collection:

```
public int doStartTag() throws JspException {
  Iterator iterator = items.iterator();
```

Next, generate and write the opening `<select>` tag back to the page:

```
  try {
    JspWriter out = pageContext.getOut();

    out.print("<select name=\"");
    out.print(name);
    out.print("\">");
```

Then, for each item in the collection, generate the appropriate HTML. To do this, you use a feature of the Java reflection mechanism to extract the values of the specified bean properties:

Using `PropertyDescriptor` objects provides an easy way to find the getter and setter methods associated with a bean property and saves you from writing the code to determine the method names.

```
    while (iterator.hasNext()) {
      // get the next JavaBean from the collection
      Object o = iterator.next();
```

```
            // and use it to create a description of the property used
            // to represent the displayable label
            PropertyDescriptor labelPD =
              new PropertyDescriptor(label, o.getClass());

            // and the property used to represent the hidden value
            PropertyDescriptor valuePD =
              new PropertyDescriptor(value, o.getClass());

            // and now generate the HTML
            out.print("<option value=\"");

            // call the accessor method for the value property
            // (this is the same as calling get<PropertyName>() on
            // the JavaBean instance)
            out.print(
              valuePD.getReadMethod().invoke(o, new Object[] {}).toString());
            out.print("\">");

            // and do the same for the label property
            out.print(
              labelPD.getReadMethod().invoke(o, new Object[] {}).toString());
            out.print("</option>");
          }
```

Finally, with the HTML generated for each and every item in the collection, you generate and output the closing `</select>` tag and return `SKIP_BODY`, as you're again not interested in the body content of this custom tag:

```
        out.print("</select>");

      } catch (Exception e) {
        throw new JspTagException(e.getMessage());
      }

      // and skip the body
      return SKIP_BODY;
    }
  }
```

Describing the Select Tag

Once again, you must next describe the custom tag with the TLD file. Some of the information in the TLD file is omitted for brevity:

```
<?xml version="1.0" encoding="UTF-8" ?>

<taglib xmlns="http://java.sun.com/xml/ns/j2ee"
    xmlns:xsi="http://www.w3.org/2001/XMLSchema-instance"
    xsi:schemaLocation="http://java.sun.com/xml/ns/j2ee/web-jsptaglibrary_2_0.xsd"
    version="2.0">
```

```
... the description of the tag library ...
... the description of the datetime tag ...

  <tag>
    <name>select</name>
    <tag-class>com.apress.projsp20.ch06.tagext.SelectTag</tag-class>
    <body-content>empty</body-content>
    <description>
      Creates an HTML select control based upon a collection of objects.
    </description>

    <attribute>
      <name>name</name>
      <required>true</required>
      <rtexprvalue>false</rtexprvalue>
    </attribute>

    <attribute>
      <name>label</name>
      <required>true</required>
      <rtexprvalue>false</rtexprvalue>
    </attribute>

    <attribute>
      <name>value</name>
      <required>true</required>
      <rtexprvalue>false</rtexprvalue>
    </attribute>

    <attribute>
      <name>items</name>
      <required>true</required>
      <rtexprvalue>true</rtexprvalue>
    </attribute>
  </tag>

</taglib>
```

There's nothing really new in concept here except that in addition to having three required attributes (`name`, `label`, and `value`), you have the `items` attribute that is required and allows request-time expressions. The only way to pass object attributes into tag handlers is to ensure that they support request-time expressions. This is made possible by setting the value of the `rtexprvalue` element to `true` in the TLD file for the attribute.

Using the Select Tag

To use the tag, you just import the tag library the same way you did before. Assuming that a collection of `Country` JavaBeans is accessible with the EL expression `${countries}`, you can use the tag in the following way:

```
<%@ taglib uri="/WEB-INF/tlds/ch06.tld" prefix="ch06" %>

Countries :
```

```
<ch06:select name="country" label="name" value="id"
            items="${countries}"/>
```

Of course, you can also use the traditional request-time expressions in the page as follows:

```
<ch06:select name="country" label="name" value="id"
      items="<%= (java.util.Collection)pageContext.findAttribute("countries") %>"
/>
```

In doing this, you introduce a lot of Java code into the page, and this is where things start to become unreadable–something that the JSP EL aims to fix, which is a very good reason to adopt the EL. However, even using the tag in this manner is better than writing the code to generate the HTML select control within the JSP page, because you've now encapsulated the logic to generate the appropriate HTML and made it reusable. By looking at the source code for the page, you can see that the generated HTML is as follows:

```
Countries : <select name="country"><option value="1">England</option><option
value="2">Wales</option><option value="3">Scotland</option></select>
```

Admittedly, the generated HTML isn't as neat, tidy, and well laid out as if you had written it yourself, but the important point is that you have a component that you can reuse to generate HTML select lists on other pages and within other web applications. There is, however, an inherent problem with the tag.

One of the most common uses for custom tags since their inception was to write custom tag versions of the standard HTML form controls such as text fields, lists, and buttons. This has always been a contentious use of custom tags, as it provides advantages at the cost of introducing limitations.

On the plus side, custom tags provide a great way to automate the creation of HTML form controls. For example, you can automatically set default values for text fields, automatically set the current selection in a list, and so on. A great way to implement this is through Jakarta Struts. Struts provide a complete framework with which to handle requests and link up JavaBean instances with HTML form controls so that the information contained within the bean is automatically populated into the form.

For further information about Struts, please see Chapters 13 and 14.

On the negative side, building a set of tags to mimic the standard HTML form controls means that page authors are no longer using standard HTML tags and are therefore limited in the tools that they can use to help build the page. Many page authors use visual editors such as Macromedia Dreamweaver to help them lay out and configure the HTML tags, but generally these types of editors have no knowledge of custom tags.

Probably the most important issue, though, is that unless HTML tags are properly implemented, the ability to customize the generated HTML is reduced. Each and every HTML form control tag has many, many attributes that can be used to customize how it looks and behaves on the page. For example, there are attributes that can be used to specify the CSS style to be used, and others that can be used to specify JavaScript event handlers that fire when actions occur to the controls. There are literally tens of such attributes for each HTML control, and providing the ability to customize them all through a mimicked tag would mean having the tag handler support all of the possible attributes. Struts achieves this, but it's no small task.

So, coming back to the select tag that you've just built, the inherent problem is that you've effectively stopped people from customizing the HTML that's being generated. What would happen if you wanted to change the drop-down list to display a single item into a regular list displaying ten items? Well, if you were writing the HTML, it would be as simple as specifying an attribute called size when you used the HTML select tag. Previously for your custom tag implementation, this would have meant going back to the tag handler, adding a new instance variable and setter method, amending the TLD file, and then redeploying the tag. Fortunately, JSP 2.0 provides a great new feature to help you solve just this problem.

Dynamic Attributes

All the attributes that you've seen up to this point have been static. In other words, a tag's attributes have all been defined up front within the TLD file, and support for those attributes has been specifically implemented within the tag handler class. The JSP 2.0 specification introduces the concept of **dynamic attributes**, in which the attributes for any tag don't have to be determined and defined in the TLD file. The benefit of dynamic attributes is increased flexibility, particularly when the full set of attributes is either very large or unknown at the time of development. Let's see how your own tag handlers can take advantage of this functionality.

The DynamicAttributes Interface

JSP 2.0 provides the ability to support dynamic attributes through an interface called DynamicAttributes within the javax.servlet.jsp.tagext package. The interface itself is fairly straightforward and provides a single method through which a dynamic attribute can be set:

```
package javax.servlet.jsp.tagext;

import javax.servlet.jsp.JspException;

public interface DynamicAttributes {

  public void setDynamicAttribute(
    String uri, String localName, Object value) throws JspException

}
```

It's possible to have a mixture of static and dynamic attributes for any specific tag, and when that tag is used on the page the JSP container looks at the attributes that have been (statically) defined in the TLD file. If an attribute is statically defined, the regular setter method is called in the same way that you've seen before. However, if the attribute isn't defined, then the setDynamicAttribute() method on the tag handler is called instead. The parameters of this method provide information about the namespace, name, and value of the attribute. The name and value of an attribute are self-explanatory, and the namespace simply provides a way to prevent attributes with the same name from clashing. For example, it might be the case that the dynamic attributes are used to customize some underlying content that's generated by the tag, or perhaps passed through to another JavaBean or component in order to configure it. In this situation, it's possible that the same attribute name is used more than once. To prevent attributes from clashing, a namespace can be applied to the attribute. The final point to note about this method is that it can throw a JspException, and this can be used to indicate to the JSP container that the tag doesn't support the specified attribute. If this is the case, no more methods on the tag handler will be called, effectively stopping invocation of the tag. To illustrate how dynamic attributes work in practice, let's look at an example.

Although you didn't see this in the previous chapter, providing support for dynamic attributes in simple tag handlers is achieved in exactly the same way as in classic tags, and the concepts that you'll see in the next example are all applicable to simple tags, too.

Further Customization with Dynamic Attributes

Taking the `select` tag as a basis, let's modify it to support dynamic attributes. This way, you'll be able to customize the generated HTML without resorting to explicitly supporting all of the attributes that the true HTML `select` tag can support.

Building the Select Tag Handler

As before, you'll use `TagSupport` as a starting point, although the tag will also implement the `DynamicAttributes` interface:

```
package com.apress.projsp20.ch06.tagext;

import java.beans.PropertyDescriptor;
import java.util.*;

import javax.servlet.jsp.*;
import javax.servlet.jsp.tagext.DynamicAttributes;
import javax.servlet.jsp.tagext.TagSupport;

public class SelectTagWithDynamicAttributes
          extends TagSupport implements DynamicAttributes {
```

Next up are the instance variables and setter methods for the original four attributes. One of the limitations of using dynamic attributes is that you can't specify which of them, if any, are required. By keeping the core attributes of your custom tags as statically defined, you have the best of both worlds: flexibility through dynamic attributes and the ability to ensure that people use your tag in the correct manner.

```
  private String name;
  private String label;
  private String value;
  private Collection items;

  public void setName(String s) {
    this.name = s;
  }

  public void setLabel(String s) {
    this.label = s;
  }

  public void setValue(String s) {
    this.value = s;
  }
```

```
public void setItems(Collection coll) {
  this.items = coll;
}
```

Having instance variables to remember the values of supplied attributes is necessary so they can be retrieved and used during the actual processing of the tag. For this reason, and because you don't know the names of the dynamic attributes, you can use a `HashMap` to store the values:

```
private Map dynamicAttributes = new HashMap();
```

Following this is your implementation of the `DynamicAttributes` interface's `setDynamicAttribute` method:

```
public void setDynamicAttribute(String uri, String name, Object value)
    throws JspException {
  dynamicAttributes.put(name, value);
}
```

This is fairly straightforward and involves inserting the dynamic attributes as `key=value` pairs into the map. Because you're not worried about the names of attributes clashing, ignore the namespace URI that's a part of the method signature.

Finally, here's the implementation of the `doStartTag()` method. The core functionality provided by this method hasn't changed too much, although the HTML select control is being generated to include any dynamic attributes that have been specified:

```
public int doStartTag() throws JspException {
  Iterator iterator = items.iterator();

  try {
    JspWriter out = pageContext.getOut();

    // write the starting tag of the select control
    out.print("<select name=\"");
    out.print(name);
    out.print("\"");

    // insert the dynamic attributes
    Iterator it = dynamicAttributes.keySet().iterator();
    while (it.hasNext()) {
      String key = (String)it.next();
      out.print(" ");
      out.print(key);
      out.print("=\"");
      out.print(dynamicAttributes.get(key));
      out.print("\" ");
    }

    out.print(">");
```

```
        while (iterator.hasNext()) {
          // get the next JavaBean from the collection
          Object o = iterator.next();

          // and use it to create a description of the property used
          // to represent the displayable label
          PropertyDescriptor labelPD =
            new PropertyDescriptor(label, o.getClass());

          // and the property used to represent the hidden value
          PropertyDescriptor valuePD =
            new PropertyDescriptor(value, o.getClass());

          // and now generate the HTML
          out.print("<option value=\"");

          // call the accessor method for the value property
          // (this is the same as calling get<PropertyName>() on
          // the JavaBean instance)
          out.print(
            valuePD.getReadMethod().invoke(o, new Object[] {}).toString());
          out.print("\">");

          // and do the same for the label property
          out.print(
            labelPD.getReadMethod().invoke(o, new Object[] {}).toString());
          out.print("</option>");
        }

        // write the ending tag of the select control
        out.print("</select>");

      } catch (Exception e) {
        throw new JspTagException(e.getMessage());
      }

      // and skip the body
      return SKIP_BODY;
    }

  }
```

Describing the Select Tag

Although the tag handler implements the DynamicAttributes interface, in the TLD file you also have to define that the tag supports dynamic attributes. Using the dynamic-attributes element as follows does this:

```
<?xml version="1.0" encoding="UTF-8" ?>

<taglib xmlns="http://java.sun.com/xml/ns/j2ee"
    xmlns:xsi="http://www.w3.org/2001/XMLSchema-instance"
    xsi:schemaLocation="http://java.sun.com/xml/ns/j2ee/web-jsptaglibrary_2_0.xsd"
    version="2.0">
```

```
... the description of the tag library ...
... the description of the datetime tag ...

  <tag>
    <name>selectWithDynamicAttributes</name>
    <tag-class>
      com.apress.projsp20.ch06.tagext.SelectTagWithDynamicAttributes
    </tag-class>
    <body-content>empty</body-content>
    <description>
      Creates an HTML select control based upon a collection of objects.
    </description>

    <attribute>
      <name>name</name>
      <required>true</required>
      <rtexprvalue>false</rtexprvalue>
    </attribute>

    <attribute>
      <name>label</name>
      <required>true</required>
      <rtexprvalue>false</rtexprvalue>
    </attribute>

    <attribute>
      <name>value</name>
      <required>true</required>
      <rtexprvalue>false</rtexprvalue>
    </attribute>

    <attribute>
      <name>items</name>
      <required>true</required>
      <rtexprvalue>true</rtexprvalue>
    </attribute>

    <dynamic-attributes>true</dynamic-attributes>
  </tag>

</taglib>
```

Essentially, this is all that's required to indicate to the JSP container that a tag supports dynamic attributes. If this element isn't specified, the default value is assumed to be `false`.

> **Neglecting to implement the `DynamicAttributes` interface and indicate a tag's ability to support dynamic attributes in the TLD file will result in your tag not working as expected.**

Using the Select Tag

Using the new version of the tag is the same as before, but remember that you can now specify more than just four attributes:

```
<%@ taglib uri="/WEB-INF/tlds/ch06.tld" prefix="ch06" %>

Countries :
<ch06:selectWithDynamicAttributes name="country" label="name" value="id"
                                  items="${countries}" size="3"/>
```

In this example, you're also specifying a `size` attribute to effectively transform the original drop-down control into an HTML list control:

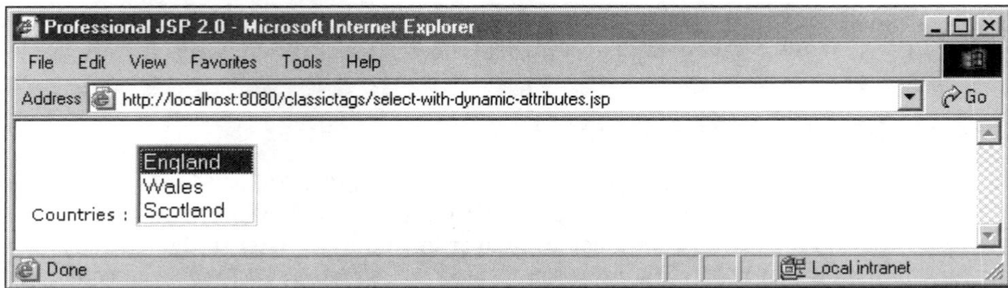

Again, the generated HTML shows you what really happens and how the additional `size` attribute has been used:

```
Countries :
<select name="country" size="3">
  <option value="1">England</option>
  <option value="2">Wales</option>
  <option value="3">Scotland</option>
</select>
```

As this example demonstrates, using dynamic attributes is a great way to increase the flexibility of custom tags, allowing page authors to further customize content and/or functionality. As you saw in the previous chapter, mixing too much content and presentation logic eventually leads to limitations in the way that the content can be presented. For this reason, it's best to use dynamic attributes only where fairly fine-grained customizations are required, such as this example that allows additional, optional attributes for underlying HTML controls. For more advanced customization, taking the approach outlined in the previous chapter (in which content was templated within the body content of the custom tag) is a much better option and is made possible by returning `EVAL_BODY_INCLUDE` from the `doStartTag()` method to signal to the JSP container that it should include/evaluate the body content.

Iteration Tags

Now that you're familiar with the Tag life cycle, you're in a good position to compare its functionality to that offered by the newer SimpleTag interface. For instance, both allow you to wrap up reusable functionality, generate content, and customize the tag through the use of static and dynamic attributes. Also, you can write a classic custom tag that evaluates or ignores its body content, achieving the same result as simple tags invoking or not invoking their body content via the supplied JspFragment reference that represents the tag's body content.

One difference between a classic tag and a simple tag is that a simple tag can invoke its body content multiple times by repeatedly calling the invoke() method of the JspFragment. With the Tag interface, this isn't possible, as the return value from the doStartTag() method determines whether the body content should be evaluated once or not evaluated at all. In terms of evaluating body content more than once, to implement similar functionality to that provided by the simple tag, we must use another classic tag interface called IterationTag.

The IterationTag Interface

The IterationTag interface was introduced as a part of the JSP 1.2 specification in an attempt to simplify the procedure for evaluating and reevaluating body content multiple times. This was previously possible with the JSP 1.1 BodyTag interface (we cover this interface later in the chapter), although the implementation details were complex. Let's see what the IterationTag interface consists of:

```
package javax.servlet.jsp.tagext;

import javax.servlet.jsp.JspException;

public interface IterationTag extends Tag {

  public final static int EVAL_BODY_AGAIN = 2;

  int doAfterBody() throws JspException;

}
```

The interface itself is fairly small, and this is due to the fact that it extends the Tag interface. Effectively, a single method has been added to the tag life cycle called doAfterBody(), and it's this method that provides you with the ability to ask that a tag's body content is evaluated more than once. Let's see how this affects the tag life cycle.

The Iteration Tag Life Cycle

This diagram of the iteration tag life cycle shows where the new `doAfterBody()` method fits in:

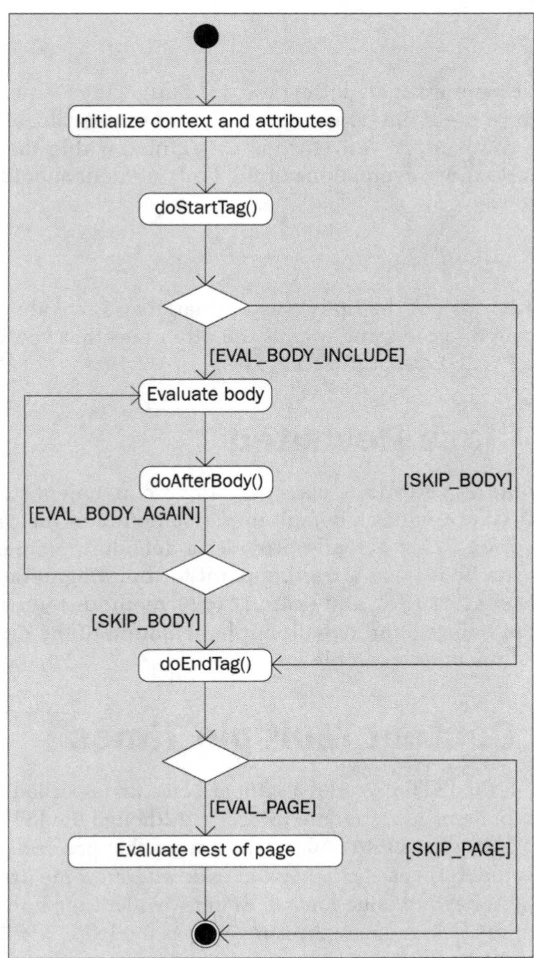

Setting the Context

As before, the first thing that happens is that the contextual information (the `PageContext` and parent `Tag`) is passed to the tag handler instance.

The Start Tag

Once the context has been set, the `doStartTag()` method is called and one of two things can now happen. First, the `doStartTag()` method can return `SKIP_BODY`, meaning that the body content is ignored and processing proceeds to the `doEndTag()` method as before.

Alternatively, a value of EVAL_BODY_INCLUDE can be returned from the doStartTag() method, signaling to the JSP container that the body content should be evaluated and included in the page. Again, this is the same as with the Tag interface, although it's after the body content has been evaluated that things start to change.

After the Body

After the body content has been evaluated, the new doAfterBody() method is called, the primary purpose of which is to determine if the body content should be reevaluated. If this is the case, the method should return the EVAL_BODY_AGAIN constant defined within the IterationTag interface. On the other hand, and when no more evaluations of the body content should happen, the SKIP_BODY value should be returned.

The End Tag

Finally, regardless of whether or not the body was evaluated and reevaluated multiple times, the doEndTag() method is called in the same way as the other tags that you've seen in this chapter. Again, possible return values are EVAL_PAGE and SKIP_PAGE.

The TagSupport Class Revisited

You've already seen how the TagSupport class provides a convenient starting place for you to build classic tags, and we said that it provides a default implementation of the Tag interface. This is only half of the truth, as the TagSupport class actually provides a default implementation of the IterationTag interface, meaning that it can be used as a starting point for building iteration tags too. The default implementations of the doStartTag() and doEndTag() methods return SKIP_BODY and EVAL_PAGE, respectively (as you've seen before), and default implementation of the doAfterBody() method returns SKIP_BODY. Let's look at an example.

Evaluating Body Content Multiple Times

As you learned in Chapter 4, the JSTL provides a standard custom tag called forEach that enables you to perform iteration over a set of items using simple JSP code. Although the JSTL is a standard, you still might encounter situations in which you'll want to build your own tag that performs iteration. For example, perhaps you have a graph of objects that can't easily be iterated over without some preprocessing, or perhaps you're unable to use JSTL for reasons beyond your control. Either way, let's see how you can build a tag that evaluates its body content more than once, in the same way as the JSTL forEach tag and the list tag that you saw in the previous chapter.

Building the Iteration Tag Handler

As before, the first step is to extend the TagSupport class:

```
package com.apress.projsp20.ch06.tagext;

import java.util.Collection;
import java.util.Iterator;

import javax.servlet.jsp.JspException;
import javax.servlet.jsp.tagext.TagSupport;
```

```
public class IteratorTag extends TagSupport {
```

Following this, you have the usual instance variables and setter methods to support any attributes that the tag will take. Here you have two–one for the name of the attribute that will represent each item in the iteration (`var`) and one for the collection to be specified (`items`):

```
  private String var;
  private Collection items;

  public void setVar(String s) {
    this.var = s;
  }

  public void setItems(Collection coll) {
    this.items = coll;
  }
```

Next, you have a `java.util.Iterator` instance. As you'll be iterating over the collection, you need some way to keep track of where you are in that collection. When you looked at the simple `list` tag example in the previous chapter, the iteration over the entire collection of items was performed within the `doTag()` method. However, here you must perform the iteration over several methods, hence you use an instance variable to maintain your position:

```
  private Iterator iterator;
```

Now you get to the functionality provided by the tag. The first thing to do is check that there are items to be iterated over and, if so, you can get a reference to the first one in the collection. With this reference obtained, you can set a page-scoped attribute under the name specified by `var` to point to this first item. You can then ask the JSP container to evaluate the body content of the tag, inside which you can, of course, access the page-scoped attribute with an EL expression.

Alternatively, if there are no items, then you simply ignore any body content and proceed straight to the `doEndTag()` method, a default version of which is implemented by the `TagSupport` class:

```
  public int doStartTag() throws JspException {
    // set up the iterator to be used
    iterator = items.iterator();

    if (iterator.hasNext()) {
      // if there are elements, put the first one into page
      // scope under the name provided by the "var" attribute
      pageContext.setAttribute(var, iterator.next());

      // and include the body
      return EVAL_BODY_INCLUDE;
    } else {
      // there are no elements so skip the body
      return SKIP_BODY;
    }
  }
```

As you may recall from the iteration tag life cycle, after the body content has been evaluated, the next thing that happens is that the doAfterBody() method is called on the tag handler. The purpose of the doStartTag() method is to find the first item in the collection, put it into the page scope, and evaluate the body content. Essentially, if there are more items in the collection, then you want to repeat the action again:

```
    public int doAfterBody() throws JspException {
      if (iterator.hasNext()) {
        // if there are more elements, put the next one into page
        // scope under the name provided by the "var" attribute
        pageContext.setAttribute(var, iterator.next());

        // and instruct the JSP engine to reevaluate the body of this tag
        return EVAL_BODY_AGAIN;
      } else {
        // there are no more elements so skip the body
        return SKIP_BODY;
      }
    }
  }
```

Here, doAfterBody() checks for more items, and if it finds them, it gets the next one, puts it into page scope, and asks the JSP container to evaluate the body content again. After the body content has again been evaluated, the doAfterBody() method is called. This cycle of calling doAfterBody() and evaluating the body content continues until there are no more items in the collection. At this time, the method returns SKIP_BODY, indicating that no more body content evaluations are required.

Don't forget to eventually return SKIP_BODY from the doAfterBody() method; otherwise, you'll run into an infinite loop by continuously evaluating the body content.

Describing the Iteration Tag

Once the tag handler is built, you must, of course, describe the iteration tag with the TLD file:

```
<?xml version="1.0" encoding="UTF-8" ?>

<taglib xmlns="http://java.sun.com/xml/ns/j2ee"
    xmlns:xsi="http://www.w3.org/2001/XMLSchema-instance"
    xsi:schemaLocation="http://java.sun.com/xml/ns/j2ee/web-jsptaglibrary_2_0.xsd"
    version="2.0">

  ... the description of the tag library ...
  ... the description of the datetime tag ...
  ... the description of the select tag ...

  <tag>
    <name>iterate</name>
    <tag-class>com.apress.projsp20.ch06.tagext.IteratorTag</tag-class>
    <body-content>scriptless</body-content>
    <description>
```

```
        Iterates over a specified java.util.Collection instance.
      </description>

      <attribute>
        <name>var</name>
        <required>true</required>
        <rtexprvalue>false</rtexprvalue>
      </attribute>

      <attribute>
        <name>items</name>
        <required>true</required>
        <rtexprvalue>true</rtexprvalue>
      </attribute>
    </tag>

</taglib>
```

Once again, the concepts here are the same as you've seen before, with the `iterate` tag having two required attributes: `var` and `items`.

Using the Iteration Tag

Using the iteration tag is also straightforward, with the same usage pattern as the JSTL `forEach` tag:

```
<%@ taglib uri="/WEB-INF/tlds/ch06.tld" prefix="ch06" %>

Countries :
<ul>
<ch06:iterate var="country" collection="${countries}">
  <li>${country.name}
</ch06:iterate>
</ul>
```

As the tag places each object in the collection into page scope (under the name supplied by the `var` attribute), all it takes is a simple EL expression to use that object on the page.

Before the introduction of JSTL, this was the only way in which iteration functionality could be implemented without resorting to Java code on the page. Consequently, fewer and fewer developers will need to use the functionality provided by the `IterationTag` interface, although for completeness we've included it here. After all, there may be times when you need the additional flexibility that building your own tag can provide. With this in mind, don't forget that it's easier to achieve the same functionality with the `SimpleTag` interface. You saw an example of this with the `list` tag in the previous chapter, in which the `doTag()` method repeatedly invoked the body content in the same way as you've just seen with the `iterate` tag. Additionally, this technique is useful if, for some reason, you can't work with a JSP 2.0 container.

The final topic that we look at in this chapter is body tags, a concept that takes iteration tags one step further by allowing precise control over what actually gets written back to the page.

Body Tags

So far, you've seen that classic tags can evaluate their body content zero, or one or more times, and this is particularly useful in those scenarios in which the content to be evaluated is trivial or, in other words, in which no transformation or manipulation of the content is required before it's output to the page. If such transformation is required prior to the content being written to the page, you must turn to the BodyTag interface.

The BodyTag Interface

The BodyTag interface further extends the IterationTag interface to add even more flexibility and capability:

```
package javax.servlet.jsp.tagext;

import javax.servlet.jsp.JspException;

public interface BodyTag extends IterationTag {

  public final static int EVAL_BODY_BUFFERED = 2;

  void setBodyContent(BodyContent b);

  void doInitBody() throws JspException;

}
```

Once again, this interface adds another new constant and two methods that are related to the body content of the tag in question. As you might expect, this means a slightly different life cycle for body tags.

The Body Tag Life Cycle

The following diagram summarizes the tag life cycle:

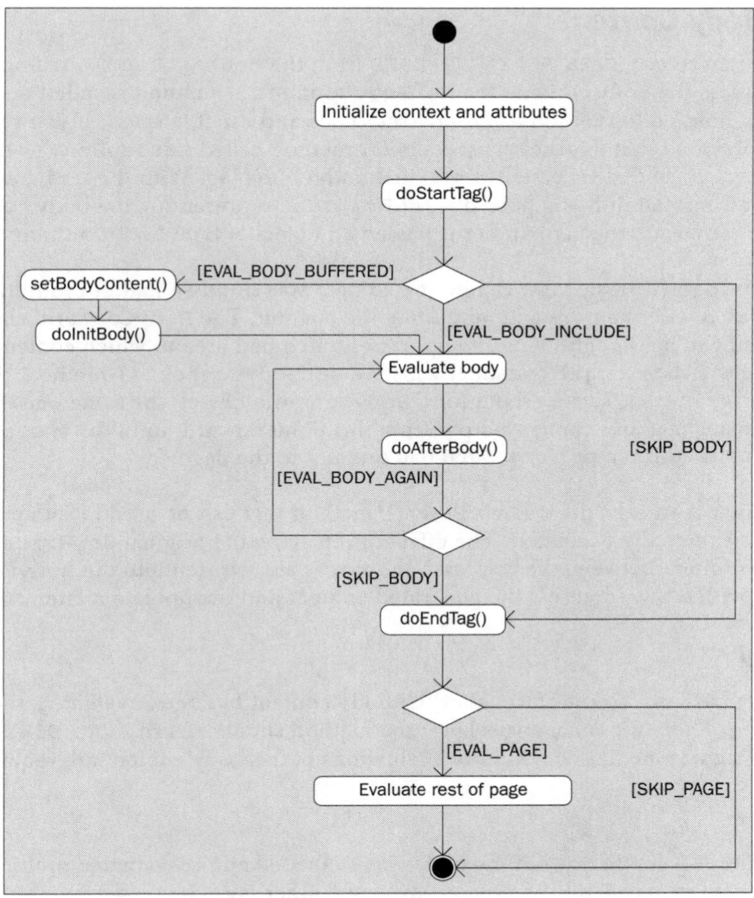

Setting the Context

As with all of the other classic tags, the first thing that happens is that the contextual information (the `PageContext` and parent `Tag`) is passed to the tag handler instance.

The Start Tag

Once the context has been set, the `doStartTag()` method is called, and with the `BodyTag` interface there are three different return values.

As before, the `doStartTag()` method can return `SKIP_BODY`, meaning that the body content is ignored and processing proceeds to the `doEndTag()` method, or it can return `EVAL_BODY_INCLUDE`, signaling that the body content should be evaluated and included in the page.

The difference is that the `doStartTag()` method can now return the `EVAL_BODY_BUFFERED` constant defined in the `BodyTag` interface. Returning this value indicates to the JSP container that you want to make use of the features provided by the `BodyTag` interface–specifically, that you would potentially like to manipulate the body content.

Setting the Body Content

Assuming that you return EVAL_BODY_BUFFERED from the doStartTag() method to indicate that you want to manipulate the body content, the setBodyContent() method is called on the tag handler so that the tag can hold on to the BodyContent reference and use it later on. If you remember the simple tags from the previous chapter, they have a similar method called setJspBody() that passes a JspFragment instance that represents the actual body of the tag. With the BodyTag interface, this is slightly different. Instead of being passed a JspFragment representing the body content that can subsequently be invoked, the tag handler is passed an object of type BodyContent.

Throughout our look at classic tags, generating content was simply a matter of finding the JspWriter instance associated with the page and outputting the content. The BodyContent class is a subclass of JspWriter and can be thought of as a temporary scratch-pad area to which content can be written. Behind the scenes, when the JSP container calls the setBodyContent() method, the regular output stream (the JspWriter) is swapped out for a BodyContent object–the same one that gets passed to the tag. This means that any content output from this point onward (until the end tag is reached) is actually written into this temporary scratch pad and not to the page.

The JSP container then calls the doInitBody() method that can be used to set up any state before the body content is eventually evaluated. The effect of replacing the original JspWriter is that when evaluated, any content between the start and end tags is also written into the BodyContent object, providing you with a way to access the generated content and manipulate it later on.

After the Body

As with the IterationTag interface, after the body content has been evaluated, the doAfterBody() method is called. There are no changes here; the method should return EVAL_BODY_AGAIN or SKIP_BODY to signal whether or not more evaluations of the body content are required.

The End Tag

Finally, regardless of whether or not the body was evaluated and reevaluated multiple times, the doEndTag() method is called in the same way as the other tags you've seen in this chapter. Again, possible return values are EVAL_PAGE and SKIP_PAGE.

At this point in the life cycle, all of the body content has been evaluated and output into the BodyContent object (the temporary scratch pad). With this in mind, you can now take this content and manipulate/transform it. When you're done, you can then write the final result to the original JspWriter instance.

The BodyTagSupport Class

Because the functionality associated with the BodyTag interface is slightly different from that provided by the other classic tag interfaces, another convenient base class, BodyTagSupport, has been provided for you to use as a starting point when building body tags. Talking about the BodyTag interface makes it sound fairly complex, so let's see it in action.

Filtering Content

Imagine that you're building a web-based mailing list or forum, a great example of which can be found at `http://saloon.javaranch.com`. One of the features that many of these types of forums offer is the ability to hide e-mail addresses from users so that potential spammers can't obtain this information. This facility, a piece of presentation logic, is undoubtedly useful for not only this project, but also perhaps other web applications that you may build in the future. For this reason, let's wrap it up as a custom tag.

Building the Filter Tag Handler

You'll start by extending the `BodyTagSupport` class:

```
package com.apress.projsp20.ch06.tagext;

import java.io.IOException;
import java.util.regex.Matcher;
import java.util.regex.Pattern;

import javax.servlet.jsp.JspException;
import javax.servlet.jsp.JspTagException;
import javax.servlet.jsp.tagext.BodyTagSupport;

public class EmailAddressFilterTag extends BodyTagSupport {
```

As you want to filter the body content of the tag, it makes sense to wait until that body content has been evaluated before you look at it. For this reason, you'll leave the processing until the `doEndTag()` method is called. This way, the JSP container will have already evaluated the tag's body content:

```
  public int doEndTag() throws JspException {
```

Now check that the body content object isn't `null`. This is an important step because using this tag with an empty body content will cause the container to skip the call to `setBodyContent()`:

```
    if (bodyContent != null) {
```

Next, use the `BodyContent` object to get a copy of its contents as a string. After you obtain the body content as a string, you can then call a private helper method to filter out all of the e-mail addresses:

```
      try {
        String content = bodyContent.getString();
        content = filter(content);
```

With the content filtered, you can delete (clear) the original body content and put your filtered copy in its place:

```
        // now clear the original body content and write back
        // the filtered content
        bodyContent.clearBody();
        bodyContent.print(content);
```

To ensure that the filtered copy actually gets output to the page, you mustn't forget to write out the contents of the `BodyContent` object (the temporary scratch-pad area) back to the page. This is possible because when the `BodyContent` instance is created, it's provided with a reference to the original (enclosing) `JspWriter`.

> **Neglecting to write the contents of the `BodyContent` object back to the enclosing writer will result in it being lost as soon as the object goes out of scope.**

```
        // finally, write the contents of the BodyContent object back to the
        // original JspWriter (out) instance
        bodyContent.writeOut(getPreviousOut());
      } catch (IOException ioe) {
        throw new JspTagException(ioe.getMessage());
      }
    }

    return EVAL_PAGE;
  }
```

The `getPreviousOut()` method is just a convenience method supplied by the `BodyTagSupport` class for `getBodyContent().getEnclosingWriter()`.

As far as the `filter()` method is concerned, you're just using the new regular expressions functionality that is a part of version 1.4 of the JDK:

```
  private String filter(String s) {
    Pattern p = Pattern.compile("@[A-Za-z0-9_.]+\\.[A-Za-z]{2,}");
    Matcher m = p.matcher(s);
    return m.replaceAll("@...");
  }
}
```

The `Pattern` class is used to represent a compiled regular expression, and the `Matcher` class is used to perform searches and replacements for that pattern on a particular string.

Describing the Filter Tag

Once again, although you've learned some new tag handler concepts from this example, the actual description of the tag is pretty much same as before. In fact, because this tag has no attributes, its definition is fairly short:

```
<?xml version="1.0" encoding="UTF-8" ?>

<taglib xmlns="http://java.sun.com/xml/ns/j2ee"
    xmlns:xsi="http://www.w3.org/2001/XMLSchema-instance"
    xsi:schemaLocation="http://java.sun.com/xml/ns/j2ee/web-jsptaglibrary_2_0.xsd"
    version="2.0">

  ... the description of the tag library ...
```

```
... the description of the datetime tag ...
... the description of the select tag ...
... the description of the iterate tag ...

<tag>
  <name>emailAddressFilter</name>
  <tag-class>
    com.apress.projsp20.ch06.tagext.EmailAddressFilterTag
  </tag-class>
  <body-content>scriptless</body-content>
  <description>
    Filters out the domain from e-mail addresses.
  </description>
</tag>

</taglib>
```

Using the Filter Tag

Using the tag is straightforward, and because the body content of the tag is defined to be `scriptless`, it provides a great deal of flexibility in the way that it can be used. For example, you can include EL expressions to generate content, which in turn are filtered by the tag. A good, real-world use of such a filter tag is in an online forum or mailing list to hide users' real e-mail addresses and help prevent spammers from obtaining such information:

```
<%@ taglib uri="/WEB-INF/tlds/ch06.tld" prefix="ch06" %>

<table>
<ch06:emailAddressFilter>
  <tr>
    <td><h1>${subject}</h1></td>
  </tr>
  <tr>
    <td><b>From : </b>${name} (${emailAddress})</td>
  </tr>
  <tr>
    <td>${message}</td>
  </tr>
  <tr>
    <td><br><br><input type="submit" value="Reply"></td>
  </tr>
</ch06:emailAddressFilter>
<table>
```

Assuming that the relevant information is accessible through the preceding EL expressions, the result of requesting the page would be as follows:

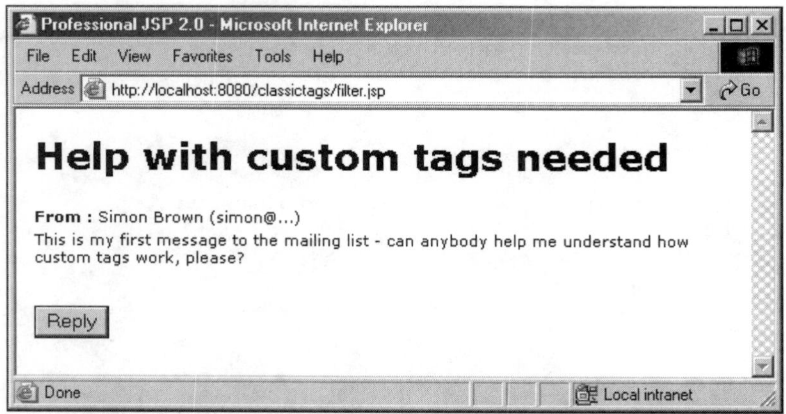

As you can see from the HTML code, the e-mail address has been completely filtered by the tag:

```
<table>
  <tr>
    <td><h1>Help with custom tags needed</h1></td>
  </tr>
  <tr>
    <td><b>From : </b>Simon Brown (simon@...)</td>
  </tr>
  <tr>
    <td>
      This is my first message to the mailing list - can anybody
      help me understand how custom tags work, please?
    </td>
  </tr>
  <tr>
    <td><br><br><input type="submit" value="Reply"></td>
  </tr>
<table>
```

The `BodyTag` interface provides a powerful way to transform and manipulate body content before it is finally sent to the JSP page and ultimately the user. In this example you specified a body content of `scriptless` for the tag, meaning that the content was evaluated in the normal way by the container.

Tag-Dependent Body Content

The other body content type supported by the JSP 2.0 specification is called `tagdependent`. Here, any content between the start and end tags is completely ignored (that is, it isn't processed) by the JSP container, and it's up to the custom tag to do something with it. For example, changing the body content of your `emailAddressFilter` tag to `tagdependent` yields the following result:

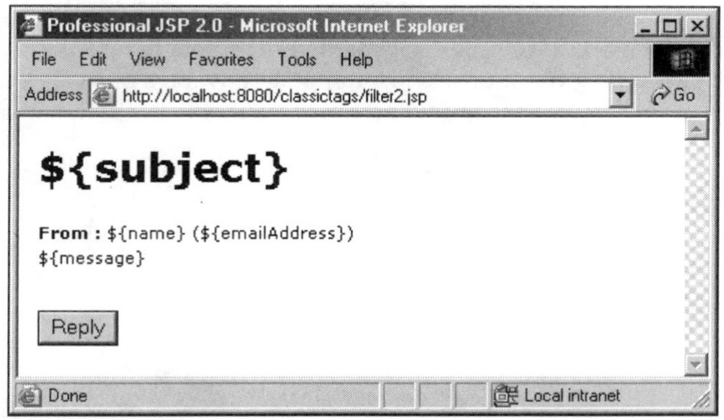

The JSP container simply doesn't process any expressions, custom tags, or Java code, leaving the body content exactly as is. So why is `tagdependent` body content useful?

Well, with the power of body tags, an example here might be tags that provide a way to emulate another programming language. Using `tagdependent` body content, you would be able to write code in this other programming language between the start and end tags, and then use the `BodyTag` interface to extract it and execute it in some way. When the code has been run (perhaps through an external interpreter), the body content could be cleared of the code and the results inserted instead. This is, in fact, what happens with the SQL tags that are a part of the JSTL. The SQL is taken from the body content, executed, and removed, and the results are then processed in some way.

Summary

After covering the simple tags in the previous chapter, we moved on to discuss the traditional methods for building custom tags, now called classic tags, in this chapter. The key differences between classic and simple tags are the interface that tag handlers must implement and the life cycle requirements around tag handler pooling and reuse. The complexity associated with these two differences is the primary reason simple tags were introduced into the JSP 2.0 specification.

We started our tour of classic tags by examining the `Tag` interface and the associated tag life cycle, and we presented a simple example to provide a direct comparison between a classic tag and a simple tag. Next, we covered how to customize classic tags with attributes by implementing a `select` tag that generated an HTML select control from a list of items. Then we looked at the inherent problems in building such tags and introduced the `DynamicAttributes` interface as a way to help solve such problems. In essence, the `DynamicAttributes` interface allows fine-grained customizations to be made to tags in which the set of attributes is not fully known at development time.

The next topic was the `IterationTag` interface, which provides a way to evaluate and reevaluate body content repeatedly. This functionality is easily achievable with simple tags, although there may be times when slightly more flexibility is required–for example, when iterating over a tree-like structure.

Finally, we discussed one of the most powerful features of custom tags: the `BodyTag` interface. This interface allows the body content of a tag to be evaluated and then subsequently modified, transformed, and manipulated. You put these concepts into practice in the `emailAddressFilter` tag example, which illustrated how you can achieve postprocessing of body content.

The past two chapters have provided a fairly comprehensive look at the facilities provided by the JSP 2.0 specification for building custom tags, and you should now be able to build many of the tags that you might need for your own web applications. To wrap up our coverage of custom tags, the next chapter takes a look at some of the more advanced features and best practices that will help make your tags even more powerful.

7

Custom Tag Advanced Features and Best Practices

Now that you understand the basics of building custom tags, it's time to wrap up your understanding by looking at more advanced features and best practices.

As some of the examples in the previous chapters have shown, it's possible for custom tags to place objects into the various scopes so that those objects can be used elsewhere in the page with an EL expression. Before the introduction of the EL, such functionality was achieved by tags introducing JSP scripting variables into the page, and this is the first topic that we cover in this chapter. Although developers no longer see introducing JSP scripting variables into the page as the best way, this method is still possible–and often useful–if you need to use Java code on the page, perhaps to integrate with some existing components or for maintenance reasons.

We then move on to look at how both simple and classic tags can cooperate on the page. This is an important use of custom tags and one that allows tags to be more flexible in the way that they're used on the page. As you'll see, this use of tags can increase page readability.

Next up, we examine validation, specifically how to implement the logic to validate that a tag's attributes are being used correctly. This is an often-overlooked topic, but it's important for anybody who is building tags that will be reused on many other web applications.

After this, we take a look at how exceptions can be handled with custom tags. Again, this is a topic that is often overlooked but provides a way to build much more reliable and resilient tags.

Having covered how to build tags, we then turn our focus to deployment and how tag libraries can be packaged for reuse. In particular, we show how to package a tag library and all of its constituent components as a single JAR file that can be easily distributed and reused by others. Then we discuss why it's important to test custom tags, and we cover the new tools available to help automate this process.

To wrap up our custom tag coverage, we take a look at some of the softer aspects around building custom tags. We examine what makes a good tag, some guidelines on naming tags, and some common usage patterns.

Introducing Scripting Variables into the Page

In the previous examples, you've seen that it's possible for custom tags to place objects into one of the various scopes (`request`, `page`, `session`, or `application`) so that those objects can subsequently be used elsewhere in the page or within the tag's body content. For example, in the `list` tag from Chapter 5, we placed the name of each file into the page scope so that it could be used with an EL expression within the body content of the tag:

```
jspContext.setAttribute("filename", filename);
```

The `PageContext` class has always been available to custom tags, so this mechanism of placing information into one of the available scopes was available in previous versions of the JSP specification. However, before the introduction of the JSP 2.0 EL, one of the biggest problems associated with making use of these objects was that you had to access them with Java code on the page. Taking the same example again, instead of an EL expression such as `${filename}`, the name of the file would have traditionally been accessed with a request-time expression such as `<%= pageContext.findAttribute("filename") %>`.

To provide a simpler way of accessing information from within a JSP page, it's possible for custom tags to introduce scripting variables back into the page, meaning that the variable can be accessed directly rather than through the `PageContext`. For example, if the `list` tag introduced a scripting variable into the page to represent the file name, that value could be accessed by using a simple expression such as `<%= filename %>`. Invoking the custom tag would lead to the creation of a Java scripting variable on the page.

This is a tried and tested method for allowing custom tags to introduce information (in this case, Java objects) into the JSP page, but it brings with it some consequences. The first consequence is that the information is most easily accessible on the page by using Java scriptlets and expressions, and a downside to this is that it can make the page very difficult to read, particularly because of the verbose syntax. In addition, having Java scripting variables ready to use on the page tends to encourage people to use more and more Java code on their JSP pages. As we've mentioned before, this is now seen as a bad practice because it not only reduces the maintainability of the page, but also tends to encourage copy-and-paste–style reuse.

To support backwards compatibility with older versions of the JSP specification, this method of introducing scripting variables into the page is still possible. Therefore, for completeness, let's take a quick look at how to do this. Also, this technique is useful if you find yourself working on previous versions of the JSP specification or if you need to integrate with other pages/components that require Java variables to be available on the page.

There are two methods in which scripting variables can be placed into the JSP page. The first is to provide the definitions of those variables within the TLD file (declaratively). The second is achieved using a `TagExtraInfo` class (programmatically).

Defining Variables in the TLD File

Behind the scenes, the process of introducing scripting variables into the JSP page is fairly straightforward. All you need to do is place an object in one of the available scopes (`request`, `page`, `session`, or `application`) and then indicate to the JSP container that you'd like to be able to access this as a scripting variable. Then, when the tag is invoked, the JSP container finds your object and automatically declares a scripting variable for you.

So how do you indicate to the JSP container that it should create a variable? Well, the easiest way is to place this information in the TLD file. Let's look at an example.

Building the Cookie Tag Handler

In this section, you'll build a custom tag that looks up a named cookie and makes it available as a scripting variable. Let's look first at the tag handler. In this case, you'll use the classic `TagSupport` class because this makes it easier to gain access to some of the HTTP-specific classes that you need to access cookies.

> *Remember, the `Tag` interface relies on features provided by the Java Servlets API, unlike the new `SimpleTag` interface.*

```
package com.apress.projsp20.ch07.tagext;

import javax.servlet.http.Cookie;
import javax.servlet.http.HttpServletRequest;
import javax.servlet.jsp.JspException;
import javax.servlet.jsp.tagext.TagSupport;

public class CookieTag extends TagSupport {
```

This tag will have two attributes: `id` and `name`. You use the `id` attribute to specify the name of the scripting variable on the page, and you use the `name` attribute to specify the name of the cookie that you'd like to look up. Another benefit of using the `TagSupport` class in this example rather than the `SimpleTagSupport` class is that the instance variable and setter method for the `id` attribute are already provided.

> *Traditionally, the `id` attribute has been used to specify the name of scripting variables on the page and, as it used to be such a common requirement, the `id` attribute has been implemented for us in the `TagSupport` class.*

```
  private String name;

  public void setName(String s) {
    this.name = s;
  }
```

Next, you have the processing associated with this tag. Essentially, all this does is look up the named cookie with a private helper method. If the cookie is found, the `Cookie` object is placed into page scope under the name supplied by the `id` attribute. The body content of the tag is then evaluated. If the cookie isn't found, the body content is simply skipped. This is yet another example of how tags can programmatically evaluate their body content:

```
  public int doStartTag() throws JspException {

    // find the current cookies
    HttpServletRequest request;
    request = (HttpServletRequest)pageContext.getRequest();
    Cookie cookies[] = request.getCookies();

    // now try to find the named cookie
    Cookie cookie = getCookie(cookies, name);

    if (cookie != null) {
      // the cookie was found so evaluate the body content
      pageContext.setAttribute(id, cookie);
      return EVAL_BODY_INCLUDE;
    } else {
      // the cookie wasn't found so skip the body content
      return SKIP_BODY;
    }
  }

  private Cookie getCookie(Cookie cookies[], String name) {
    if (cookies != null) {
      for (int i = 0; i < cookies.length; i++) {
        if (cookies[i].getName().equals(name)) {
          return cookies[i];
        }
      }
    }

    // we got this far so the specified cookie wasn't found
    return null;
  }

}
```

Note that you don't mention anything about scripting variables–the object that you'd like to access as a scripting variable is just placed into page scope.

Describing the Cookie Tag

Now you must describe the tag in the TLD file. Here you indicate to the JSP container that you'd like a scripting variable with which to access your object:

```
<?xml version="1.0" encoding="UTF-8" ?>

<taglib xmlns="http://java.sun.com/xml/ns/j2ee"
    xmlns:xsi="http://www.w3.org/2001/XMLSchema-instance"
```

```
    xsi:schemaLocation="http://java.sun.com/xml/ns/j2ee/web-jsptaglibrary_2_0.xsd"
    version="2.0">

  <description>
    Tag library for Professional JSP 2.0, chapter 7.
  </description>
  <jsp-version>2.0</jsp-version>
  <tlib-version>1.0</tlib-version>
  <short-name>ch07</short-name>
  <uri>http://www.apress.com/projsp20/ch07</uri>

  <tag>
    <name>cookie</name>
    <tag-class>com.apress.projsp20.ch07.tagext.CookieTag</tag-class>
    <body-content>JSP</body-content>
    <description>
      Looks up a named cookie and makes it available as a scripting variable.
    </description>

    <variable>
      <name-from-attribute>id</name-from-attribute>
      <variable-class>javax.servlet.http.Cookie</variable-class>
      <declare>true</declare>
      <scope>NESTED</scope>
    </variable>

    <attribute>
      <name>id</name>
      <required>true</required>
      <rtexprvalue>false</rtexprvalue>
    </attribute>

    <attribute>
      <name>name</name>
      <required>true</required>
      <rtexprvalue>false</rtexprvalue>
    </attribute>
  </tag>

</taglib>
```

There are two points to note about this otherwise normal tag description. First, the body content of the tag has been set to `JSP`. This means that any JSP content (tags, scriptlets, and so on) can appear within the body content of the tag. If `scriptless` were used instead, a page translation error would occur if you attempted to use Java scriptlets or expressions.

The second difference is that you've added a new `variable` element to the tag description, and this is where the scripting variable is defined. In a similar way to defining attributes, this section allows you to define the name and type of the variable, along with some other information.

When you're defining the name of a scripting variable in a TLD file, you can use two tags. The first of these is `<name-given>`, which allows you to statically define the name of the scripting variable. The result of this is that the scripting variable will be accessible through the same name on every page on which that tag is used. The drawback to this approach is that the name you statically define may clash with existing variables on the page, causing a page translation error to occur. The other option you have is to use the `<name-from-attribute>` tag, as shown in this example. Instead of statically defining the name of the variable, you tell the JSP container to use the value of the named attribute. In this example, you're telling the JSP container that the scripting variable should be given the name provided by the `id` attribute.

Next is the `<variable-class>` element. This is just the fully qualified class name of the scripting variable. Because you're introducing a cookie into the page, the class name is `javax.servlet.http.Cookie`–a class from the Servlet API.

Finally, you have two elements that are related to how the variable is used on the page. You can decide whether or not a new variable should be declared on the page with the `<declare>` element. If you specify `true` (the default value), a new variable is automatically created. If you choose `false`, then the JSP container assumes that a variable has already been declared for it to use. Subsequently, if that variable hasn't been previously declared on the page, a compilation error will occur when the JSP is translated into a Java servlet.

Following this is the `<scope>` element, which can have one of the following values:

- `AT_BEGIN`
- `NESTED` (the default value)
- `AT_END`

The `<scope>` element allows you to define where on the page the scripting variable will be accessible. The three possible values mean from the start tag until the end of the page, between the start and end tags, and anywhere from the end tag until the end of the page, respectively. For this example, you want the variable accessible only between the start and end tags, so you choose `NESTED`.

Using the Cookie Tag

As with the other examples, using the tag is then just a matter of importing the tag library and using the tag with the correct prefix:

```
<%@ taglib uri="/WEB-INF/tlds/ch07.tld" prefix="ch07" %>

<ch07:cookie id="myCookie" name="lastVisited">
  You last visited this website on <%= myCookie.getValue() %>
</ch07:cookie>
```

At request time, this JSP snippet looks for a cookie called `lastVisited`. If it finds `lastVisited`, the `Cookie` object is made available as a scripting variable called `myCookie` within the body content of the tag, and the body content is then evaluated. If the cookie can't be found, the body content is skipped. As this example demonstrates, this type of functionality is useful for providing customized pages to the users of your web application, and it's another way in which custom tags can help you build JSP-based web applications.

Defining Variables in a TagExtraInfo Class

The other method for declaring scripting variables in the page is programmatically, by using a `TagExtraInfo` class. This was the original JSP 1.1 method by which variables were introduced into the page, and it allows for an additional level of flexibility in the way that variables are defined. Although the `<variable>` element in the TLD file allows you to be flexible in the name you give to the scripting variable, it doesn't provide a way to specify the type of that variable to be defined at page creation time; instead, it only allows you to statically define the type within the TLD file.

If you remember back to the `iterate` tag example from the previous chapter, it could be the case that you'd like a scripting variable available to access each element of the collection over which you're iterating, as shown in the following JSP snippet:

```
<%@ taglib uri="/WEB-INF/tlds/ch07.tld" prefix="ch07" %>

Countries :
<ul>
<ch07:iterate id="country" type="com.apress.projsp20.ch07.domain.Country"
  items="${countries}">
  <li><%= country.getName() %>
</ch07:iterate>
</ul>
```

There are several differences between this code and the code for the `iterate` tag that you built in the previous chapter and the way in which that tag was used on the page. First, you now have an `id` attribute through which to specify the name of the scripting variable. Second, you have a new attribute called `type` that is used to specify the fully qualified class name of the objects within the collection. Within the body content, you can then access each item in the collection through Java code, perhaps with an expression or inside a scriptlet. So, how do you implement this type of functionality where the type of the variable is declared on the page instead of within the TLD file?

Building the Iterate Tag

As before, you have the tag handler class. In fact, this is almost identical to the version you saw in the previous chapter, except that you have `id` and `type` attributes:

```
package com.apress.projsp20.ch07.tagext;

import java.util.Collection;
import java.util.Iterator;

import javax.servlet.jsp.JspException;
import javax.servlet.jsp.tagext.TagSupport;

public class IteratorTag extends TagSupport {

  private String type;
  private Collection items;

  private Iterator iterator;
```

```
    public void setType(String s) {
      this.type = s;
    }

    public void setItems(Collection coll) {
      this.items = coll;
    }

    public int doStartTag() throws JspException {
      // set up the iterator to be used
      iterator = items.iterator();

      if (iterator.hasNext()) {
        // if there are elements, put the first one into page
        // scope under the name provided by the "id" attribute
        pageContext.setAttribute(id, iterator.next());

        // and include the body
        return EVAL_BODY_INCLUDE;
      } else {
        // there are no elements so skip the body
        return SKIP_BODY;
      }
    }

    public int doAfterBody() throws JspException {
      if (iterator.hasNext()) {
        // if there are more elements, put the next one into page
        // scope under the name provided by the "id" attribute
        pageContext.setAttribute(id, iterator.next());

        // and instruct the JSP engine to reevaluate the body of this tag
        return EVAL_BODY_AGAIN;
      } else {
        // there are no more elements so skip the body
        return SKIP_BODY;
      }
    }

  }
```

Building the Iterate TagExtraInfo Class

This is where things are slightly different from the `iterate` tag in the previous chapter. You need to additionally write a class that extends the `TagExtraInfo` class for the tag:

```
package com.apress.projsp20.ch07.tagext;

import javax.servlet.jsp.tagext.TagData;
import javax.servlet.jsp.tagext.TagExtraInfo;
import javax.servlet.jsp.tagext.VariableInfo;

public class IteratorTagExtraInfo extends TagExtraInfo {
```

```
    public VariableInfo[] getVariableInfo(TagData data) {
      return new VariableInfo[] {
        new VariableInfo(
          data.getId(),
          data.getAttributeString("type"),
          true,
          VariableInfo.NESTED)
      };
    }

  }
```

Here you're implementing a single method called `getVariableInfo()`, which is called by the JSP container to obtain information about the variables that your tag wishes to make accessible. A `TagData` object is passed to this method, and this is just a translation-time view of the tag's usage on the page, specifically including information about its attributes.

To signal to the JSP container that you'd like a scripting variable accessible on the page, you return an array of `VariableInfo` objects containing one `VariableInfo` object for each scripting variable that you'd like. The API provided by the `TagData` class provides you with a method to look up the values of a tag's attributes and, using this method, you can easily find out the name and type of the scripting variable that you want to introduce into the page.

The `VariableInfo` class constructor takes four parameters. These parameters map to the subelements of the `<variable>` element within the TLD file: name (`name-given` or `name-from-attribute`), `variable-class`, `declare`, and `scope`. In this example, the name is being set as the value of the `id` attribute (available through the convenient `getId()` method on the `TagData` class), the variable class is being set as the value of the `type` attribute, and the other properties are being statically defined as before.

Describing the Tag

Whereas in the previous example you defined the variables within the TLD file, all you need to do here is tell the JSP container that you wish to use a `TagExtraInfo` (TEI) class. This is specified in a similar way to the tag handler class:

```
  <?xml version="1.0" encoding="UTF-8" ?>

  <taglib xmlns="http://java.sun.com/xml/ns/j2ee"
      xmlns:xsi="http://www.w3.org/2001/XMLSchema-instance"
      xsi:schemaLocation="http://java.sun.com/xml/ns/j2ee/web-jsptaglibrary_2_0.xsd"
      version="2.0">

      ... the description of the tag library ...
      ... the description of the cookie tag ...

      <tag>
        <name>iterate</name>
        <tag-class>com.apress.projsp20.ch07.tagext.IteratorTag</tag-class>
        <tei-class>
          com.apress.projsp20.ch07.tagext.IteratorTagExtraInfo
        </tei-class>
```

```
    <body-content>JSP</body-content>
    <description>
      Iterates over a specified java.util.Collection instance.
    </description>

    <attribute>
      <name>id</name>
      <required>true</required>
      <rtexprvalue>false</rtexprvalue>
    </attribute>

    <attribute>
      <name>type</name>
      <required>true</required>
      <rtexprvalue>false</rtexprvalue>
    </attribute>

    <attribute>
      <name>items</name>
      <required>true</required>
      <rtexprvalue>true</rtexprvalue>
    </attribute>
  </tag>

</taglib>
```

Using the Iterate Tag

As you've seen already, using the tag is then a matter of setting the values for the id and type attributes before you can use the new scripting variable within the body content of the tag:

```
<%@ taglib uri="/WEB-INF/tlds/ch07.tld" prefix="ch07" %>

Countries :
<ul>
<ch07:iterate id="country" type="com.apress.projsp20.ch07.domain.Country"
  items="${countries}">
  <li><%= country.getName() %>
</ch07:iterate>
</ul>
```

Both implementation techniques shown here for introducing scripting variables into the page are useful for previous versions of the JSP specification and for when you really do need to have a scripting variable declared in the page. However, as you've seen in previous chapters, it's much better to use a simple EL expression and not introduce scripting variables into the page. After all, allowing people to use Java code in one page tends to encourage them to use it elsewhere, and before you know it you have a mass of unmaintainable Java code sitting inside your JSP pages.

We recommend you make use of the JSP EL when you can or, failing that, the JSTL with its expression language.

Cooperating Tags

Up until now, the examples we've presented have all been tags that work on their own to achieve a specific goal. However, custom tags don't have to work in isolation–they can cooperate with one another, either by sharing information or by directly accessing methods/fields on other tag handlers that are being used on the page. These are useful techniques and, as you'll see, they allow you to make your tags more generic and therefore more reusable.

Cooperating by Sharing Information

The most common way in which custom tags cooperate is by sharing information, which is typically implemented by using one of the available scopes (`request`, `page`, `session`, or `application`) as a shared resource in which information can be placed and retrieved later on. There are generally two ways in which this can happen.

In the first method, a tag places an object in one of the available scopes, and then the name of that object is passed to another tag as an attribute. A good example of this in practice is the `<jsp:useBean>` tags that you saw in Chapter 1. To demonstrate this, you'll use a simple JavaBean called `Forum` that has `id` and `name` properties:

```
<jsp:useBean id="forum"
  class="com.apress.projsp20.ch07.domain.Forum" scope="page">
  <jsp:setProperty name="forum" property="id" value="1"/>
  <jsp:setProperty name="forum" property="name" value="Servlets"/>
</jsp:useBean>
```

Here, the `<jsp:useBean>` tag is setting up a page-scoped variable called `forum`, and the name of this object is being passed to the `<jsp:setProperty>` tags so that they can find the object for themselves. To achieve this type of functionality within your own tags, you need to use the `setAttribute()` and `getAttribute()` methods on the `JspContext` and `PageContext` classes for simple tags and classic tags, respectively. Essentially, information is being shared in a specific scope, under a name that is well known to both tags.

With the introduction of the JSP EL, the second way in which tags commonly share information is through EL expressions. Let's again look at an example, this time from the JSTL:

```
<c:forEach var="forum" items="${forums}">
  <c:out value="${forum.name}"/>
</c:forEach>
```

Here, assuming that a collection of `Forum` JavaBeans is accessible with the EL expression `${forums}`, this small snippet provides iteration over that collection and displays the name of each forum. You're using the `<c:out>` tag to actually write out the information, and this information is being specified by another EL expression. Although behind the scenes a `Forum` bean is being placed into page scope upon each iteration, instead of simply passing the name of the object, you're now using an EL expression to pass the actual information that the tag needs to perform its processing. In this case, the processing is to output the specified information.

Although these two techniques differ slightly, they're very useful and commonly used in sharing information between custom tags, therefore allowing them to cooperate to achieve a common goal. However, sometimes a little more flexibility is required in that the child (nested) tags should pass information on to their parents. In this situation, you can use a tag's ability to directly access its parent tag or tags.

Cooperating by Accessing Other Tag Handlers

Something that happens early on in the tag life cycle is that a tag is passed a reference to its closest enclosing parent via the `setParent()` method on the tag handler class. Using this reference to a `JspTag` or a `Tag` on a simple or classic tag, respectively, you can directly access the parent tag handler instance and directly call methods on it. So, why is this useful?

In the previous example of how tags can cooperate on the page, you saw that it's very easy for a parent tag to pass an object to its child tags, effectively using one of the available scopes as a shared area. However, a side effect of this technique is that unless the information is removed from the scope when it's finished, that information is readily available to other tags on the page. Although this generally isn't a problem, having all this information lying around could interfere with other parts of the page–or worse, the application–making debugging more difficult.

Another situation in which sharing information isn't appropriate is when you'd like to use nested tags to configure the characteristics of the enclosing parent tag. If you look back to the `select` tag example from the previous chapter, you can see that you were able to configure it through the use of dynamic attributes, meaning you could customize the HTML select control that was eventually generated. One of the ways in which you can choose to customize the select control might be to add a JavaScript event handler that forwards the user to another page when an item in the list is selected–this is something that is done on web sites, such as JavaRanch, that allow users to easily navigate between the many forums. Because these event handlers are implemented as attributes on the generated HTML tag, forwarding the user to another page is fairly easy to achieve with the dynamic attributes version of the select from the previous chapter:

```
<ch06:selectWithDynamicAttributes
  name="forum" label="name" value="id" items="${forums}">
  <jsp:attribute name="onChange">
    window.location=('view-forum.jsp&forumId='
                    + this.options[this.selectedIndex].value)
  </jsp:attribute>
</ch06:selectWithDynamicAttributes>
```

Remembering that attributes can be specified using the `<jsp:attribute>` tag, in essence all you're doing is specifying an attribute called `onChange`, the value of which is the JavaScript code that you'd like executed when an item in the list is selected. Although this works, imagine that you'd like to build a custom tag to explicitly specify this information instead, the usage of which would be as follows:

```
<ch07:select name="forum" label="name" value="id" items="${forums}">
  <ch07:eventHandler name="onChange">
    window.location=('view-forum.jsp&forumId='
                    + this.options[this.selectedIndex].value)
  </ch07:eventHandler>
</ch07:select>
```

The benefit in adopting this sort of approach is twofold. First, it provides a standard and natural way to add event handlers to the generated HTML tag. Having a specific `eventHandler` tag is more readable than having a generic `<jsp:attribute>` tag. Second, it provides a way to ensure that the JavaScript code doesn't get interpreted in any way by the JSP compiler; you can specify the body content of the `eventHandler` tag as `tagdependent`. For this to work, the `eventHandler` tag will take the body content (the JavaScript code) and pass it directly to the enclosing `select` tag. The `select` tag can then use this information when generating the underlying HTML.

Building the Tag Handlers

The first step is to build the tag handlers, and you'll start with the `select` tag. This time you'll implement the `select` tag as a simple tag and the `eventHandler` tag as a classic tag. The reason for this is so that you can see how to perform cooperation between a simple and a classic tag.

Starting with the `select` tag, the implementation is pretty much the same as before in that you have four instance variables and their setter methods to support the four attributes you need:

```
package com.apress.projsp20.ch07.tagext;

import java.beans.PropertyDescriptor;
import java.io.IOException;
import java.util.*;

import javax.servlet.jsp.*;
import javax.servlet.jsp.tagext.SimpleTagSupport;

public class SelectTag extends SimpleTagSupport {

  private String name;
  private String label;
  private String value;
  private Collection items;

  public void setName(String s) {
    this.name = s;
  }

  public void setLabel(String s) {
    this.label = s;
  }

  public void setValue(String s) {
    this.value = s;
  }

  public void setItems(Collection coll) {
    this.items= coll;
  }
```

Next, you have a HashMap in which to contain the event handlers for the generated tag, initialized within the public no arguments constructor, which is called when the tag handler instance is created. As event handlers on HTML controls are just name=value pairs, you can store the event handler information easily in a map:

```
private HashMap eventHandlers;

public SelectTag() {
  this.eventHandlers = new HashMap();
}
```

Following this, you have the processing associated with the tag. All that additionally happens in this version is that before any processing happens, the body content of the tag is invoked. This is necessary because it allows the child tags to be processed, and these child tags provide the invoked tag with the information on any event handlers that should be included in the generated HTML:

```
public void doTag() throws JspException, IOException {

  try {
    // first of all we must evaluate the body content
    if (getJspBody() != null) {
      getJspBody().invoke(jspContext.getOut());
    }
```

Once this has been done, you can generate the HTML as before. Don't forget to include the list of event handlers:

```
    JspWriter out = getJspContext().getOut();

    // write the starting tag of the select control
    out.print("<select name=\"");
    out.print(name);
    out.print("\"");

    // and now write out any event handlers
    Iterator it = eventHandlers.keySet().iterator();
    String eventHandlerName;
    while (it.hasNext()) {
      eventHandlerName = (String)it.next();
      out.print(" ");
      out.print(eventHandlerName);
      out.print("=\"");
      out.print(eventHandlers.get(eventHandlerName));
      out.print("\"");
    }

    out.print(">");

    it = items.iterator();
    while (it.hasNext()) {
      // get the next JavaBean from the collection
      Object o = it.next();
```

```
        // and use it to create a description of the property used
        // to represent the displayable label
        PropertyDescriptor labelPD =
          new PropertyDescriptor(label, o.getClass());

        // and the property used to represent the hidden value
        PropertyDescriptor valuePD =
          new PropertyDescriptor(value, o.getClass());

        // and now generate the HTML
        out.print("<option value=\"");

        // call the accessor method for the value property
        // (this is the same as calling get<PropertyName>() on
        // the JavaBean instance)
        out.print(
          valuePD.getReadMethod().invoke(o, new Object[] {}).toString());
        out.print("\">");

        // and do the same for the label property
        out.print(
          labelPD.getReadMethod().invoke(o, new Object[] {}).toString());
        out.print("</option>");
      }

      // write the ending tag of the select control
      out.print("</select>");
    } catch (Exception e) {
      e.printStackTrace();
      throw new JspTagException(e.getMessage());
    }
  }
```

So, how do child tags actually pass information about event handlers to this tag? You provide them with a public method that they can call, which places the information into the `HashMap` the tag handler maintains:

```
  public void addEventHandler(String name, String code) {
    eventHandlers.put(name, code);
  }

}
```

With the code for the `select` tag written, it's time to turn to the `eventHandler` tag. As you'd like the body content for this tag to be `tagdependent`, you'll use the `BodyTagSupport` class as a starting point.

> *Having* `tagdependent` *body content is possible with simple tags, although actually getting hold of the content is easier to achieve with body tags.*

```
package com.apress.projsp20.ch07.tagext;

import javax.servlet.jsp.JspException;
import javax.servlet.jsp.tagext.BodyTagSupport;
import javax.servlet.jsp.tagext.TagAdapter;

public class EventHandlerTag extends BodyTagSupport {
```

With this tag you have a single attribute called `name`, and this attribute is used to represent the name of the event handler:

```
  private String name;

  public void setName(String s) {
    this.name = s;
  }
```

As with the other body tags that you've seen, the processing associated with this tag takes place in the `doEndTag()` method, as this allows you to gain access to the body content. Here, with the body content representing the JavaScript code for the event handler, all that you need to do is get that body content, find the parent tag, and pass the information using the public method that you defined in the `SelectTag` class:

```
  public int doEndTag() throws JspException {
    if (bodyContent != null) {
      // get the body content (the JavaScript code)
      String content = bodyContent.getString();

      // now find the parent tag
      SelectTag tag = (SelectTag)((TagAdapter)getParent()).getAdaptee();

      // and add the event handler to the select tag
      if (tag != null) {
        tag.addEventHandler(name, content);
      }
    }

    return EVAL_PAGE;
  }
}
```

One of the reasons for choosing to show cooperation between simple and classic tags is that it's not as straightforward as cooperation between tags of the same type. If you're solely using simple tags, the `getParent()` method will return an object of type `JspTag`–the super class of all tag interfaces. However, with classic tags, historically the `getParent()` method returns an object of type `Tag`, and this has been maintained for backwards compatibility. In this example, the outer tag is a simple tag (of type `SimpleTag`), and the inner tag is a classic tag (of type `BodyTag`).

An object implementing the `SimpleTag` interface can't be cast to the `Tag` interface, and for this reason the JSP container provides an adapter class called `TagAdapter` that wraps up a `SimpleTag` and makes it look like a `Tag`. Behind the scenes, it's actually this object that's passed to the `setParent()` method on your `EventHandlerTag`, which is why you need to do some additional processing to extract a reference to the enclosing tag handler instance. Basically, it all comes down to providing backwards compatibility for existing classic tags while making them fully interoperable with the newer simple tags.

As an alternative, another way to find a specific parent tag is with the `findAncestorWithClass()` method provided by the `SimpleTagSupport` and `TagSupport` classes. This method provides a way to automatically search through all of the parent tag handler instances until it finds an instance that implements a specific interface. For example, you could use the following line of code to locate the parent `SelectTag` class:

```
SelectTag tag = (SelectTag)findAncestorWithClass(this, SelectTag.class);
```

This line says, "Starting from `this` tag handler, look at each parent in the tree in turn until you find one that is of type `SelectTag`." This will even work if you're mixing tag types and the actual tag handler is wrapped up inside the `TagAdapter` class behind the scenes.

Another benefit is that you can search for parent tags that implement a specific Java interface, making it possible to allow the implementation of cooperating tags to be substituted, provided that they implement the same interface. A good example here is that the `SelectTag` class could implement an interface that allows event handlers to be added. The `eventHandler` tag can then look for a parent implementing this interface, which gives you the flexibility to use the `eventHandler` tag nested inside other event handler-capable tags and to substitute the implementation of the `select` tag if necessary.

Describing the Tags

Next, you must describe both tags in a TLD file. The `select` tag is the same as before–it has `scriptless` body content and the four required attributes:

```
<?xml version="1.0" encoding="UTF-8" ?>

<taglib xmlns="http://java.sun.com/xml/ns/j2ee"
    xmlns:xsi="http://www.w3.org/2001/XMLSchema-instance"
    xsi:schemaLocation="http://java.sun.com/xml/ns/j2ee/web-jsptaglibrary_2_0.xsd"
    version="2.0">

  ... the description of the tag library ...
  ... the description of the cookie tag ...
  ... the description of the iterate tag ...

    <tag>
      <name>select</name>
      <tag-class>com.apress.projsp20.ch07.tagext.SelectTag</tag-class>
      <body-content>scriptless</body-content>
      <description>
        Creates an HTML select control based upon a collection of objects.
      </description>
```

```
    <attribute>
      <name>name</name>
      <required>true</required>
      <rtexprvalue>false</rtexprvalue>
    </attribute>

    <attribute>
      <name>label</name>
      <required>true</required>
      <rtexprvalue>false</rtexprvalue>
    </attribute>

    <attribute>
      <name>value</name>
      <required>true</required>
      <rtexprvalue>false</rtexprvalue>
    </attribute>

    <attribute>
      <name>items</name>
      <required>true</required>
      <rtexprvalue>true</rtexprvalue>
    </attribute>
  </tag>
```

The `eventHandler` tag, on the other hand, has `tagdependent` body content and a single, required attribute called `name`:

```
  <tag>
    <name>eventHandler</name>
    <tag-class>com.apress.projsp20.ch07.tagext.EventHandlerTag</tag-class>
    <body-content>tagdependent</body-content>
    <description>
      Used to represent a JavaScript event handler.
    </description>

    <attribute>
      <name>name</name>
      <required>true</required>
      <rtexprvalue>false</rtexprvalue>
    </attribute>
  </tag>

</taglib>
```

Using the Tags

As you've already seen, using the tags is simply a matter of nesting one inside the other:

```
<%@ taglib uri="/WEB-INF/tlds/ch07.tld" prefix="ch07" %>

Forums :
<ch07:select name="forum" label="name" value="id" items="${forums}">
```

```
    <ch07:eventHandler name="onChange">
      window.location=('view-forum.jsp&forumId='
                          + this.options[this.selectedIndex].value)
    </ch07:eventHandler>
  </ch07:select>
```

If you then look at the generated HTML, you can see how the event handler has been implemented on the control:

```
<select name="forum" onChange="window.location=('view-
forum.jsp&forumId='+this.options[this.selectedIndex].value)"><option
value="1">Servlets</option><option value="2">JSP</option><option
value="3">EJB</option><option value="4">JMS</option></select>
```

As we mentioned at the start of this example, having a dedicated tag with which to specify event handlers can help make the JSP page more readable and provide you with a way to ensure that the JavaScript code doesn't get mistaken for JSP code. However, you might be wondering whether the additional development overhead of this example provides any substantial, tangible benefit over using the dynamic attributes version that you built in the previous chapter. To answer this question, let's look at how you can put some validation around the use of tag attributes.

Tag Validation

Having built custom tags, you're now probably aware that the JSP container does, in fact, perform some rudimentary validation on the way in which custom tags are used on the page. For example, it checks that you've specified the start and end tags correctly, that the body content matches up with that defined in the TLD file, and that you've specified any required attributes for your tags. The failure of any of these checks results in a page translation error.

This is very useful in ensuring that, at a basic level, the tags are used properly on the page, but it would be nice if you could go a step further and check the actual values of attributes. This way, you could detect problems up front if attributes are being misused, perhaps because a value is out of your desired range. Thankfully, the JSP specification provides two mechanisms to perform validation: the `TagLibraryValidator` and `TagExtraInfo` classes.

Validation with a TagLibraryValidator Class

The `TagLibraryValidator` (TLV) class was introduced in version 1.2 of the JSP specification. It provides an extremely flexible method to perform validation. Behind the scenes, when a JSP page is being translated into a servlet, an intermediate version of the page is generated that is represented as a pure XML document. This document is useful because it provides a standard way for JSP containers to parse, process, and validate the JSP page. In essence, in the XML view of the page, all of the elements of the JSP page (content, directives, actions, scriptlets, and so on) are converted and represented as XML tags. With the TLV class, it's possible to get a reference to this document and validate anything on the page. This could include anything from checking that the values of tag attributes are acceptable to looking at the structure of the page and determining whether your tags have been used correctly (perhaps checking that they've been nested in the right way).

Unfortunately, this flexibility comes at a price in that TLV classes are fairly complicated to build because they require a fair amount of XML knowledge. For this reason, they aren't often used, and the `TagExtraInfo` class is favored.

Validation with a TagExtraInfo Class

`TagExtraInfo` classes are inherently much simpler to use than TLV classes, but of course they don't offer anywhere near as much flexibility, with the main function of TEI classes being to validate tag attributes. However, for those developers who need to implement such validation logic, a TEI class is usually sufficient.

Implementing a TEI class is fairly straightforward, although the process has changed slightly from previous versions of the JSP specification. Before JSP 2.0, the validation logic would be implemented within a method called `isValid()`, returning `true` if valid and `false` otherwise. Although this was very simple to implement, it couldn't provide anybody with information should a particular tag not be valid. Of course, a `System.out.println()` statement can be used to output error details to the console, but this is hardly a desirable solution.

For this reason, JSP 2.0 offers similar functionality to that provided by the much more complex `TagLibraryValidator` class with a method called `validate()`. Instead of returning `true` or `false`, JSP 2.0 allows an array of `ValidationMessage` instances to be returned to the JSP container that details exactly what the problem is. Let's put this into practice with an example.

Building the TagExtraInfo Class

For this example, imagine that you'd like to add some validation to the `eventHandler` tag to check that the value of the `name` attribute (the name of the JavaScript event handler) is valid. To do this, you can define a list of the permitted names and compare the value of the `name` attribute to this list.

First, you'll set up the list:

```
package com.apress.projsp20.ch07.tagext;

import java.util.HashSet;
import java.util.Set;

import javax.servlet.jsp.tagext.*;

public class EventHandlerTagExtraInfo extends TagExtraInfo {

  private static List EVENT_HANDLERS = new ArrayList();

  static {
    // here is a list of the valid event handlers for the select tag
    EVENT_HANDLERS.add("onblur");
    EVENT_HANDLERS.add("onchange");
    EVENT_HANDLERS.add("onclick");
    EVENT_HANDLERS.add("ondblclick");
    EVENT_HANDLERS.add("onfocus");
    EVENT_HANDLERS.add("onkeydown");
    EVENT_HANDLERS.add("onkeypress");
```

```
        EVENT_HANDLERS.add("onkeyup");
        EVENT_HANDLERS.add("onmousedDown");
        EVENT_HANDLERS.add("onmousemove");
        EVENT_HANDLERS.add("onmouseout");
        EVENT_HANDLERS.add("onmouseover");
        EVENT_HANDLERS.add("onmouseup");
    }
```

Now all the `validate()` method has to do is find the value of the `name` attribute through the API provided by the `TagData` class and compare it with the list of valid values. The `TagData` class itself is just a translation-time view onto the way the tag has been used on the page that allows the values of a tag's attributes to be obtained.

> *Because* `TagData` *is a view of the tag's attributes at page translation time, it isn't possible to get the values of those attributes that are request-time expressions because the page hasn't yet been requested–it's still in the process of being translated into a Java servlet.*

```
    public ValidationMessage[] validate(TagData data) {
        String name = data.getAttributeString("name");

        // validate that the name is valid
        if (!EVENT_HANDLERS.contains(name.toLowerCase())) {
            return new ValidationMessage[]{
                new ValidationMessage(null, "Event handler called " + name + " not valid")
            };
        } else {
            return null;
        }
    }

}
```

The result of executing this method is that if the value of the `name` attribute is in the list of permitted values, a `null` value is returned, indicating that the attributes are valid. An array containing a `ValidationMessage` instance is returned to indicate that something is wrong.

Describing the Tag

Now that you've built the TEI class, you must tell the JSP container that you want to use it. To do this, you define the TEI class within the description of the tag in the TLD file:

```
<?xml version="1.0" encoding="UTF-8" ?>

<taglib xmlns="http://java.sun.com/xml/ns/j2ee"
    xmlns:xsi="http://www.w3.org/2001/XMLSchema-instance"
    xsi:schemaLocation="http://java.sun.com/xml/ns/j2ee/web-jsptaglibrary_2_0.xsd"
    version="2.0">

  ... the description of the tag library ...
  ... the description of the cookie tag ...
  ... the description of the iterate tag ...
  ... the description of the select tag ...
```

```
    <tag>
      <name>eventHandler</name>
      <tag-class>com.apress.projsp20.ch07.tagext.EventHandlerTag</tag-class>
      <tei-class>
        com.apress.projsp20.ch07.tagext.EventHandlerTagExtraInfo
      </tei-class>
      <body-content>tagdependent</body-content>
      <description>
        Used to represent a JavaScript event handler.
      </description>

      <attribute>
        <name>name</name>
        <required>true</required>
        <rtexprvalue>false</rtexprvalue>
      </attribute>
    </tag>

  </taglib>
```

As with the name of the tag handler class, the name of the TEI class must be a fully qualified class name.

Using the Tags

With the TEI class in place, you can use the tags in the same way as before. At page translation time, the information about a tag's attributes is passed to the TEI class so that the validation can happen. The way in which JSP containers present error messages varies among vendors, but with Tomcat 5, the following error is shown if you try to set the value of the name attribute of the eventHandler tag to onDoubleClick:

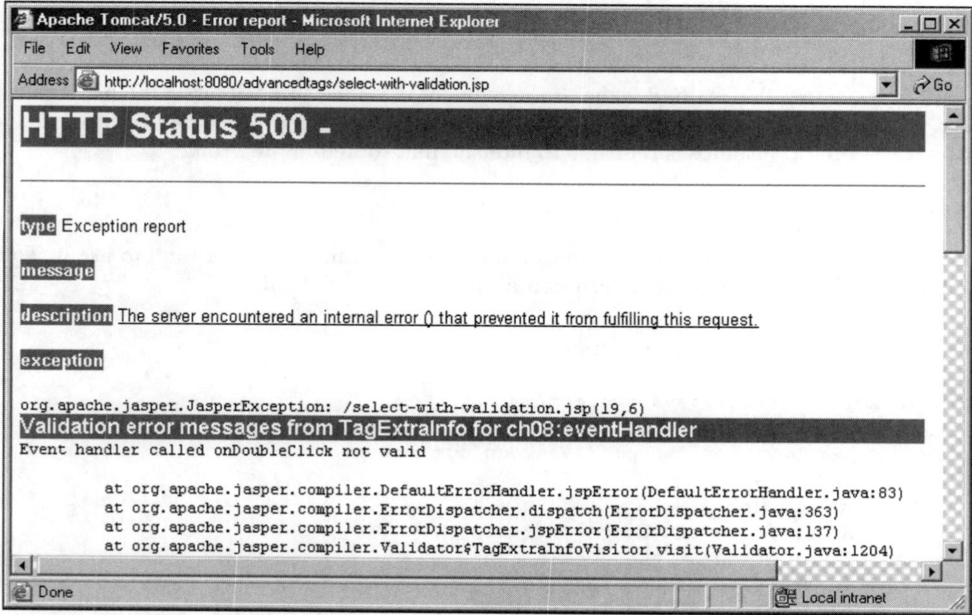

As this example shows, validating the values of attributes is a useful way to ensure that your tags are used correctly. More important, validating the values helps guarantee that the generated HTML is error-free. After all, picking up these sorts of errors is easier to do up front during the JSP translation process at deployment rather than at request time, when users start to complain that the pages of your application don't seem to work correctly.

With the usage of the tags now more resilient, let's see how you can make the tags themselves more robust in the way that they handle exceptions.

Handling Exceptions

Because custom tags have full access to the rich set of APIs provided by Java and J2EE, it's possible that something could go wrong. For example, a network connection might be unexpectedly terminated, or perhaps a file read could fail. Typically, you'd just wrap functionality that may potentially fail inside a `try-catch` block, and with simple tags this isn't much of a problem because all of the processing associated with the tag is wrapped up within the `doTag()` method. However, with classic tags, this logic can potentially be split across the `doStartTag()` method, the tag's body content, and the `doEndTag()` method. Therefore, it's not possible to place a `try-catch` block around all of this logic. The JSP specification addresses this issue through the `TryCatchFinally` interface that classic tag handlers can implement.

The TryCatchFinally Interface

The `TryCatchFinally` interface was introduced in the JSP 1.2 specification. This interface provides a way to gracefully handle exceptions that may occur during the processing of classic tags, regardless of whether the tag implements the `Tag`, `IterationTag`, or `BodyTag` interface:

```
package javax.servlet.jsp.tagext;

import javax.servlet.jsp.*;

public interface TryCatchFinally {

  void doCatch(Throwable t) throws Throwable;

  void doFinally();

}
```

The `TryCatchFinally` interface has two methods, `doCatch()` and `doFinally()`, in which you can place functionality that might typically be written into `catch` and `finally` blocks. For example, in the `doCatch()` method, you might choose to roll back a transaction, and in the `doFinally()` method, you might choose to close a file or a connection to a remote resource. In essence, tags should implement this interface if you want them to have more control over exception handling.

Let's revisit the tag life cycle to see how this interface affects it. Later on, we cover each of the methods in turn:

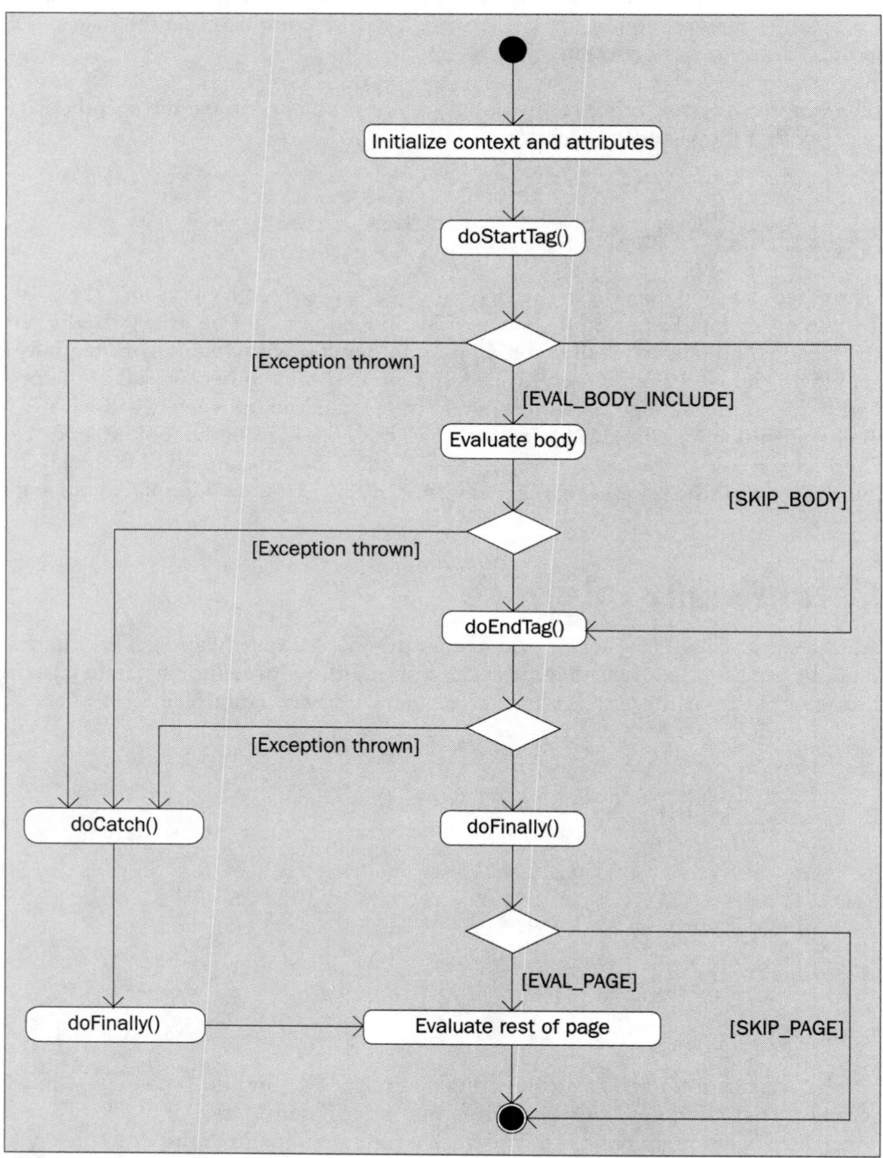

The doCatch() Method

The JSP specification guarantees that the `doCatch()` method will be called if an exception is thrown in the `doStartTag()` method, the tag's body content, or the `doEndTag()` method. Additionally, if the tag handler implements the `IterationTag` or `BodyTag` interface, the `doCatch()` method will be executed if an exception is thrown within the `doAfterBody()` and `doInitBody()` methods, respectively.

Something to notice is that the `doCatch()` method won't be called if an exception is thrown before the execution of the `doStartTag()` method–perhaps when the context or attributes are being set. For this reason, it's best not to put any logic into attribute setter methods that may cause an exception to be thrown.

If the exception should be propagated further up the calling stack, perhaps by a JSP error page, the `doCatch()` method can handle the exception as required and then subsequently rethrow the same or a new exception. This is useful because there's no way to tell the tag handler class to catch only specific subclasses of `Exception` in the same way you would when writing `try-catch` blocks in your code. Instead, the `doCatch()` method handles all exceptions, and it's up to us as tag developers to decide which to handle and which to rethrow.

The doFinally() Method

When you write `try-catch-finally` blocks in regular Java code, the `finally` block always gets called, regardless of whether or not an exception was thrown. Similarly, the `doFinally()` method on the tag handler will always get called.

Although tag handlers are generally small components, there is still much that can go wrong, especially when you're dealing with databases and remote objects such as Enterprise JavaBeans. Implementing the `TryCatchFinally` interface is a way to build tags that are better equipped to deal with such problems; it will make your tag libraries more robust and resilient to failure. With this in mind, let's now take a look at how you can deploy these resilient tags and make them available for use in the easiest possible way.

Tag Library Deployment

Tag libraries can be deployed and used within web applications in several ways. The examples that you've seen up until this point have all made use of one of these methods that focuses on deploying tag libraries within a development environment. There is, however, a much better way of deploying tag libraries that allows you to package all of your tag resources into a single JAR file. Before we cover how to do this packaging, we briefly recap the former method of deployment.

Deploying a Tag Library for Development

Assuming that the tag handler classes have been written and compiled, the first step is to ensure that the class files for the tag handlers in the tag library are in the class path of your web application. In other words, the class files should reside in the `WEB-INF/classes` directory of your web application or, if you've placed your class files within a JAR file, this JAR file has been copied into the `WEB-INF/lib` directory of your web application. If your tag handlers reference any other classes that you or a third party has written, don't forget that these classes must also be present in one of these two places.

As you've seen in the previous examples, the next step is to place the TLD file within the web application directory structure. By convention, the JSP specification suggests that all TLD files be placed within the `WEB-INF/tlds` directory, and although this isn't mandatory, placing all TLD files there provides a central place for people to find them at a later date.

Importing the tag library is then simply a matter of using the `taglib` directive. This allows you to specify the tag library that you want to import and the prefix with which to reference the tags within that tag library. As an example, you used the following directive in Chapter 5 to import the tags within the tag library that you built:

```
<%@ taglib uri="/WEB-INF/tlds/ch05.tld" prefix="ch05" %>
```

The `uri` attribute of the `taglib` directive explicitly specifies the location of the TLD representing the tag library that you'd like to use, and the prefix dictates how that tag library will be used and identified on the page.

As we've said before, this method of deploying tag libraries is mainly used when deploying custom tags within a development environment. It allows you save the TLD file straight into the web application directory structure underneath the `WEB-INF` directory and explicitly specify the tag library from within the JSP page. With an agile development environment, the build-deploy-test cycles are generally very short, and this is one reason this mechanism for deploying tags is often adopted–it's very quick and lightweight.

However, a drawback to this method is that it makes tag libraries harder to reuse. In essence, you have to copy all of the tag handler and dependent classes along with the TLD file into a new web application structure and place them in the correct directories. Although this procedure isn't complicated, individual files could easily get lost. What happens when new versions of the tags are available? Also, you haven't considered reusing tag files that simply reside underneath the `WEB-INF/tags` directory.

Thankfully, the JSP specification addresses these issues by providing an alternative mechanism for packaging and deploying tag libraries containing all types of tags.

Deploying a Tag Library for Reuse

The key to achieving reuse with tag libraries, as with many other Java technologies, is the JAR file. Essentially, packaging a tag library for reuse involves creating a JAR file that contains the following items:

- The (compiled) tag handler classes, along with any dependent classes you've created
- The TLD file that describes the tag library

As with other JAR files, the classes must be stored within the JAR file with the directory structure mirroring the package structure maintained. As for the TLD file, this must reside inside the JAR file in a directory called `META-INF`. The only requirement here is that the TLD file must have a file extension of `.tld` so the JSP container can find it.

A requirement of previous versions of the JSP specification was that the TLD file would have to be called `taglib.tld`, although this requirement has since been lifted. In fact, it's possible to place more than one TLD file in the `META-INF` directory for distributing more than one tag library in the same JAR file.

Creating the JAR File

Creating the JAR file is a fairly simple process that can be achieved with the regular `jar` command line tool or via a build tool such as Jakarta Ant. To learn how you might create such a JAR file to contain a tag library, you'll take the examples from Chapter 5 and package them.

First, create an empty directory. In this directory, place the class files that are required for the tag library, and don't forget to maintain the directory structure representing the packages to which these classes belong. Next, create a `META-INF` directory and place the TLD file inside it:

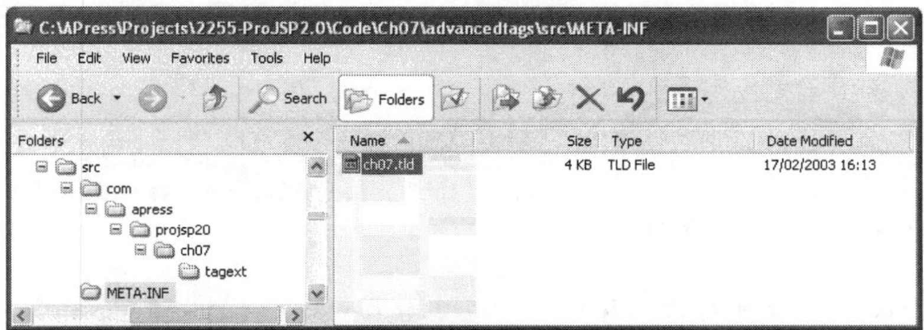

With a command prompt, change to the directory that you created to contain the classes and TLD file and run the `jar` command as follows:

```
jar cvf ch07.jar .
```

Using the current location as a starting point, this creates a JAR file that includes everything in the appropriate structure. To check that this was successful, run the following command to list the contents of the JAR file:

```
jar tf ch07.jar
```

This should show that the tag handler class files are located within the appropriate directory structure and that the TLD file resides in the `META-INF` directory:

```
C:\WINDOWS\System32\cmd.exe

C:\APress\Projects\2255-ProJSP2.0\Code\Ch07\advancedtags\src>jar tf ch07.jar
META-INF/
META-INF/MANIFEST.MF
com/
com/apress/
com/apress/projsp20/
com/apress/projsp20/ch07/
com/apress/projsp20/ch07/tagext/
com/apress/projsp20/ch07/tagext/DateTimeTag.java
com/apress/projsp20/ch07/tagext/DirectoryListTag.java
com/apress/projsp20/ch07/tagext/ThumbnailTag.java
META-INF/ch07.tld
```

Deploying the Tag Library

With the JAR file built, the final step in deploying the tag library contained within is to copy the JAR file into the WEB-INF/lib directory of your web application.

Using the Tag Library

Use of the tag library is made possible with the taglib directive. However, rather than explicitly specifying the location of the TLD file representing the tag library, specify the URI (the unique identifier for the tag library) that you defined in the TLD. In this example, the tag library can be used on the page with the following taglib directive:

```
<%@ taglib uri="http://www.apress.com/projsp20/ch05" prefix="ch05" %>
```

Notice here that the URI you're using is the same as the one you defined for the tag library in the TLD file. From a usage perspective, as you've specified the same prefix, the tags within the imported tag library can be used in the same way as before.

> **Remember, the URI is just a unique identifier for the tag library—it doesn't have to represent a valid resource on the Internet.**

Packaging Tag Files

This method works because the custom tags in the tag library are described using a tag library descriptor file, something that you don't have to do for tag files. However, the packaging mechanism does allow for tag files to be deployed alongside simple and classic tags by providing a way for them to be described in the TLD too.

To do this, the first step is to ensure that the tag files will be included in the correct place within the JAR file structure. The JSP specification states that tag files must reside underneath the META-INF directory, in a subdirectory called tags. In Chapter 5, you built two tag files: one to generate a copyright statement and another to generate a template for an HTML box that can be used to highlight areas of importance on the page. Therefore, your new JAR file structure will be as follows:

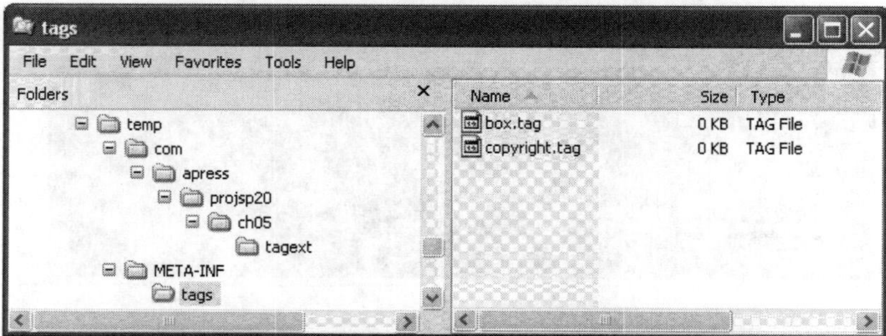

Next, you must define the tag files within the TLD file. This is made possible by using the new tag-file element:

```
<?xml version="1.0" encoding="UTF-8" ?>

<taglib xmlns="http://java.sun.com/xml/ns/j2ee"
    xmlns:xsi="http://www.w3.org/2001/XMLSchema-instance"
    xsi:schemaLocation="http://java.sun.com/xml/ns/j2ee/web-jsptaglibrary_2_0.xsd"
    version="2.0">

  ... the description of the tag library ...
  ... the description of the datetime tag ...
  ... the description of the thumbnail tag ...
  ... the description of the list tag ...

  <tag-file>
    <name>box</name>
    <path>/META-INF/tags/box.tag</path>
  </tag-file>

  <tag-file>
    <name>copyright</name>
    <path>/META-INF/tags/copyright.tag</path>
  </tag-file>

</taglib>
```

Two subelements to the `tag-file` element, `name` and `path`, represent the name of the tag as it will be used on the page and the path to the corresponding tag file in the JAR file, respectively. Once the JAR file has been generated and deployed, the tag library can be used in the same way as before–just import the tag library and use the tags within it.

There are many benefits to adopting this approach to deploying tag libraries, but the primary benefit is that it makes deployment and reuse of tag libraries easy. Another benefit relates to technology independence. With the ability to define a mixture of tag files, simple tags, and classic tags within a tag library, the end users of that tag library will never know how those tags are actually implemented. This means that should you need to reimplement a tag using a different technology in the future, this is no problem. Essentially, custom tags provide a nice abstraction to reusable Java components.

Best Practices

To wrap up this chapter's look at custom tags, we briefly cover some of the best practices that have emerged over the past few years.

Common Usage Patterns and Granularity

Custom tags have access to the full range of APIs that are provided by the J2SE and J2EE platforms. This means that they can pretty much wrap and provide any functionality for use on JSP pages, from generating content and providing iteration to reading files and accessing remote data sources. However, just because you can provide this type of functionality doesn't necessarily mean that you should. One of the key things to remember when you design custom tags is your audience. Who will be using the tags? Generally, there are two user extremes, although most people tend to fit somewhere in between.

At one extreme are web designers (or page authors). These people are responsible for the look and feel of a web application. As part of their role, they're much more concerned with the creative aspects of the JSP pages than the mechanics behind how the pages work. At the other extreme are developers, who are more focused on providing functionality than on how the web application looks. This split of responsibility may not be as clear-cut on many of your own projects, but the principles are worth bearing in mind.

Typically, the skill sets of these two types of people will be dramatically different. One has expert knowledge in web design and markup, and the other has expert knowledge of how a web application works from a technical perspective. In essence, this is why it's important to consider your audience when you design custom tags and to work in conjunction with that audience to ensure that your custom tags meet the audience's needs.

When programming, we as developers are typically used to building up high-level functionality from a series of low-level constructs. For example, to iterate over a collection we might choose to use a `for` loop. Within the `for` loop, we might use the `counter` variable to find a specific item in the collection. Although this may seem basic to us, it won't to web designers, therefore they won't want to see such logic on JSP pages. The point here is that custom tags should be fairly granular in nature. In other words, to achieve a specific goal you shouldn't have to use many custom tags in cooperation with one another. A good example here is providing iteration over an array. Before the introduction of JSTL, many people would build two custom tags to implement iteration functionality–one tag to loop and one tag to get the next item in the collection, as follows:

```
<prefix:for from="0" to="10">
  <prefix:getBean id="myBean" array="${myBeans}"/>
  ... content to be displayed on each iteration ...
</prefix:for>
```

From a developer's perspective this makes sense, but from a page author's perspective it doesn't. In summary, keep the tags as simple as possible and don't try to simply replicate programming constructs.

Naming

On a related note, the name you give to a tag or its attributes can also affect how that tag is perceived by others. Using overly technical language for naming these items can cause confusion. For example, the tag that provides iteration in JSTL is called `forEach`, and the list of items that it iterates over is called `items` instead of collection, list, or array. Once again, keep your audience in mind when describing your tags–if you're wrapping up technology-focused functionality such as accessing databases or using XML, then generally these tags are going to be used only by technologists anyway. Giving tags simple, appropriate names is a great way to make JSP pages readable and maintainable.

Another point related to naming is giving cooperating tags an appropriate name that reflects their intent. For example, you built a specific `eventHandler` tag with which to specify event handlers for the `select` tag. Although passing this information to the `select` tag is possible with dynamic attributes, a side effect is that the readability of the page suffers. In essence, the key is to make tags and using those tags seem natural, and you can help by providing good names for tags and making them easy to use together, in cooperation.

What Makes a Good Tag Library?

Finally, let's address the question of what makes a good tag library. A useful comparison to make is between tags and other development disciplines such as object orientation (OO) and component-based development (CBD). A common goal in these disciplines is reuse. With OO, you aim to get reuse at the class level, and with CBD, you aim to get reuse at the component level. Mapping this back to custom tags, you can see that you'd like to get reuse at the tag level. With OO and CBD, a good class or component is one that has high cohesion and low coupling. In other words, the class contains highly related functionality and doesn't depend too much on other classes/components.

You can go one step further and look for reuse at the package level or, with custom tags, at the tag library level. Ideally, you'd like to be able to take a tag library and reuse it as-is on other web applications in the future.

So, coming back to the question of what makes a good tag library, essentially it's the same aspects of achieving reuse at the package level with OO and CBD. The tags within a tag library should form a highly cohesive collection of functionality that's loosely coupled to other tag libraries. You'd like to take a tag library and reuse it elsewhere without having dependencies on other libraries. In this way, your initial goals to increase the readability, reusability, and maintainability of JSP development are all achieved.

Summary

In this final chapter on custom tags, we looked at some of the more advanced custom tag features. First, we discussed how custom tags can introduce scripting variables into the page. This is something that has always been possible in previous versions of the JSP specification, and in essence nothing has changed. However, with the introduction of the JSP EL, you should see scripting variables being used within JSP pages less and less, meaning that these techniques should also be used less frequently by people writing new tags. After all, the JSP EL provides a much better, cleaner way to access information from within a JSP page.

Next, we examined how tags can cooperate with one another on the page. You learned that this is possible through a couple of methods: one in which information is shared between the tags and one in which child (nested) tags look up their parent and directly access the corresponding tag handler instance. Both methods are widely implemented and allow custom tags to be more flexible in the way that they're used on the page. Also, these methods provide a way for more generic tags to be created that can be used in cooperation with different tags to achieve different goals.

Then we looked at how more resilient tags can be built using techniques that allow a tag's attributes to be validated. This is an often-overlooked part of tag development, although it provides a very easy way to ensure that your tags are used in the way that is expected and therefore work in the way that is expected. After this, we took a brief look at the `TryCatchFinally` interface, which allows you to make your tags more resilient to failure. This is particularly important if you're dealing with files and network connections, for example.

With our look at developing tags over, we then focused on how tag libraries can be deployed in both development environments and specifically for reuse. We described how it's possible to mix tag files, simple tags, and classic tags into a single tag library that is distributable and deployable as a single JAR file. Also, we covered the importance of testing custom tags and the options available to automate this process.

Finally, we discussed some of the important best practices relating to developing custom tags, particularly with respect to how tags are used on the page and how the audience can make a difference in how your tags are perceived. To wrap up, we looked at what makes a good tag library and how this can help you achieve the original goals we outlined when we started looking at custom tags as a technology–that is, increased readability, reusability, and maintainability.

8

Data Access Options for Web Applications

Now that you have a full understanding of web applications, JSP, and servlets, it's time to start discussing how these technologies fit together in a JSP application. No matter what type of JSP application you're writing, you'll need to either store the data that is created by your application, or use data from an external source in your application. You need **data access**. There are many different options for data access from a JSP application including file storage, object-oriented databases, XML databases, and relational databases. In almost all cases, a relational database is the best choice.

For simple applications intended for small-scale use on a single-instance application server, you might choose to store your data in files. However, if you want to scale your application up to meet the needs of a large number of users, then you'll need to distribute application processing across multiple servers. All J2EE application servers make this easy and transparent to you, the application programmer, but you need to store your data in a location that is accessible to all of your servers. Unfortunately, file system storage isn't the best way to do this.

For more complex larger-scale applications you should use a database, but what type of database should you choose? While object-oriented and XML databases might be appealing to some developers, most IT managers prefer to use tried-and-true relational database technology. Relational database technology is preferred because it's ubiquitous, well understood, standardized, and supported by a tremendous number of tools and applications.

In this chapter we'll discuss four different Java database access options, several JSP database access architectures, and an example of a JSP database application. By the end of this chapter you should have enough knowledge to evaluate and select a database access technology, design database access architecture, and implement database access for your JSP application.

This chapter assumes that you have knowledge of Java, JavaBeans, JSP, Java Database Connectivity (JDBC), SQL, and relational database technology.

Data Access Technologies

Database access has been part of Java since Sun added the Java Database Connectivity (JDBC) API as an add-on to Java 1.0. Since then, Sun has also added Enterprise JavaBeans (EJB) and most recently Java Database Objects (JDO) to Java. That isn't all; Sun is only one of the many organizations supporting database access from Java. Numerous vendors have sprung up over the years to provide JDBC implementations and Object-Relational Mapping (O/R) frameworks for Java.

The good news is that there are a lot of choices for data access. That's also the bad news. In this section we'll sort out the choices by dividing them up into four categories starting with the simplest and ending with the most sophisticated. The five data access technologies, from simplest to most sophisticated are

- JSP tags for SQL
- JDBC
- O/R frameworks
- JDO
- EJB Entity Beans

When you choose a data access technology, you should consider both the nature of the web application that you're developing and the skills of your development and support teams. Generally speaking, if you have simple requirements and a less experienced team, then you should favor the simple end of the spectrum. If you have more complex requirements and a more experienced team you should favor the sophisticated side. Here are some questions to consider:

- Does your application have fairly simple database access requirements? Perhaps you need only to display a couple of reports based on information in a database. For simple applications, you might want to avoid the learning curve, complexity, and overhead of a more sophisticated data access technology.
- Will your application have a complex Java object model that must be persisted to a database? If so, you might find that you really cannot do without the sophisticated automated object-relational mapping capabilities of an O/R framework or of EJB Container Managed Persistence (CMP).
- Is your application one that is highly transactional, requires high availability, and is likely to support a very large number of concurrent users? If so, you might find that you need the declarative transaction support, fault tolerance, and load balancing provided by EJB servers.
- Which Java data access technologies do your developers know? What level of database knowledge do your developers have? Will you need training? If your team has previous experience with database access, that might influence your selection of a database access technology.

With these types of questions in mind, let's discuss the pros and cons of each of the four data access options, starting with the most simple.

JavaServer Pages Tags for SQL

The JSP Standard Tag Library or JSTL, which is covered in Chapter 4, includes a set of JSP tags that allow you to access a database via SQL directly from your JSP pages.

The obvious advantage of the JSP tags for SQL is simplicity. It's very easy to query the database and to throw the results up on a web page. This is great for simple applications that need only to display database data on a web page and make simple database table updates–JSP tags for SQL work well. You can execute database queries. The `<sql:query>` tag executes an SQL query and returns a result set object which you can iterate over and display with other JSTL tags. You can also do database table updates. The `<sql:update>` tag executes an SQL update.

For larger projects, there are a couple of disadvantages to keep in mind. One disadvantage is that you must embed SQL queries with table and field names into your JSP pages. If database table and field names change, then you'll have to make the corresponding changes in your JSP files. For a small project, this might not be a big problem, but larger projects should consider other data access options. Other data access options, such as O/R frameworks and EJB, can provide some level of indirection so that changes to the database schema do not have as much of an effect on your application code.

Another disadvantage is updates. The JSP tags for SQL allow you to do updates on a database, but you have to build the SQL update string yourself. Again, for small projects with simple update needs, this might not be a problem, but larger projects should consider other data access options. Other data access options can provide infrastructure to make updates much easier to program.

If you would like to learn more about the JSTL tags, refer to Chapter 4. The Sun Web Services tutorial also covers JSTL and includes a section on the JSTL SQL tags: http://java.sun.com/webservices/docs/1.0/tutorial/index.html

JavaServer Pages Tags for SQL Example

The following is an example of JSP tags for SQL. This example illustrates how to execute a query, iterate through the results, and display the results in an HTML table:

```
<%@ page language="java" %>
<%@ taglib uri="/WEB-INF/c.tld" prefix="c"%>
<%@ taglib uri="/WEB-INF/sql.tld" prefix="sql"%>

<!DOCTYPE HTML PUBLIC "-//w3c//dtd html 4.0 transitional//en">
<html><head><title>jstl-example</title></head>
<body bgcolor="#ffffff">

<sql:query var="items"
  dataSource="jdbc:hsqldb:hsql://localhost,org.hsqldb.jdbcDriver,sa">
  SELECT TITLE,TIME FROM ITEM ORDER BY TIME
</sql:query>

<h1>News Items</h1>

<table border="1">
  <th>Title</th><th>Time</th>
```

```
    <c:forEach var="row" items="${items.rows}">
      <tr>
        <td><c:out value="${row.TITLE}"/></td>
        <td><c:out value="${row.TIME}"/></td>
      </tr>
    </c:forEach>
  </table>

  </body>
  </html>
```

The following is a screen shot of the page:

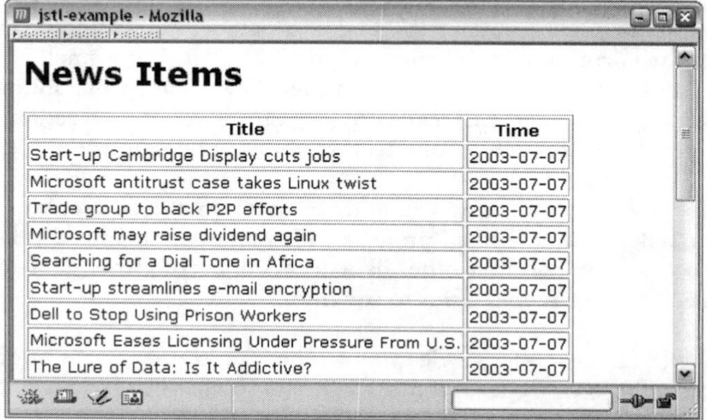

Let's examine the code more closely. At the top of the page, you see the two `taglib` directives:

```
<%@ taglib uri="/WEB-INF/c.tld" prefix="c"%>
<%@ taglib uri="/WEB-INF/sql.tld" prefix="sql"%>
```

The first directive declares that this example uses JSTL Core tags and the second directive declares use of the JSTL SQL tags. The corresponding TLD files, `c.tld` and `sql.tld`, must be in the example web application's `WEB-INF` directory.

The next interesting block of code is the actual query itself, shown here, and expressed using the JSTL `<sql:query>` tag:

```
<sql:query var="items"
  dataSource="jdbc:hsqldb:hsql://localhost,org.hsqldb.jdbcDriver,sa">
  SELECT TITLE,TIME FROM ITEM ORDER BY TIME
</sql:query>
```

The tag has two attributes: `var` and `dataSource`. The `var` attribute specifies the name of an object (of type `javax.servlet.jsp.jstl.sql.Result`) that will be created by the query to hold the results of the query.

The `dataSource` attribute specifies the database connection string. This is a comma-separated string with the format connection URL, the JDBC driver class name, the username, and password. In the example, the password is an empty string and can be omitted from the connection string. The `<sql:query>` tag will use these parameters to obtain a connection from the JDBC driver manager. Within the body of the `<sql:query>` tag is the SQL query string to be executed: "`SELECT TITLE,TIME FROM ITEM ORDER BY TIME`".

Once the query has been executed and the results are available in the `items` object, you display the HTML table by using the JSTL `<c:forEach>` tag to iterate through the rows that are contained in the `items` object:

```
<table border="1">
  <th>Title</th><th>Time</th>
  <c:forEach var="row" items="${items.rows}">
    <tr>
      <td><c:out value="${row.TITLE}"/></td>
      <td><c:out value="${row.TIME}"/></td>
    </tr>
  </c:forEach>
</table>
```

For each row of data, you use the `<c:out>` tag to display each column of data.

Java Database Connectivity

JDBC is a standard part of Java and provides a uniform API that can be used to access any relational database. The low-level JDBC API is the foundation for the other database access technologies discussed in this chapter, but many programmers use the JDBC API directly. If your application has fairly limited database access needs, JDBC might be all you need.

The advantages of JDBC are simplicity and flexibility. There are only about 25 classes and interfaces in JDBC, and for the most part, to use them you need only to know the basics of SQL. It's simple. You execute queries and updates written in standard SQL and each query returns a `ResultSet` object containing the resulting rows and columns of data. The JDBC API is simple, but it still provides the flexibility to do just about anything you'll need to do with a database.

The simplicity of JDBC is also a disadvantage. If you have a lot of queries and updates to do, using JDBC can be a lot of work. You'll find yourself writing a lot of repetitive boilerplate code to build up query and update strings, iterate through the `ResultSet` objects returned by your queries, and map Java object fields to and from database table fields. In the next section we'll discuss how using an O/R persistence framework can eliminate the repetitive boilerplate coding required by JDBC.

JDBC gives you cross-database portability, which is wonderful, but that portability isn't perfect. You still have to watch for SQL incompatibilities, data-type differences, and other problems. You still have to write a database creation script for each of the different types of databases you intend to support.

JDBC is a relatively small and easy-to-use API, but complete coverage of JDBC is really beyond the scope of this book. For more information on JDBC, please refer to Sun's JDBC home page and the Sun JDBC tutorial:

- JDBC home page: http://java.sun.com/products/jdbc/
- JDBC tutorial: http://java.sun.com/docs/books/tutorial/jdbc/basics

Obtaining a JDBC Connection in a Web Application

All of the database access technologies that are discussed in this chapter are built on the foundation laid by JDBC. So, before you can use any of them you need to understand how to configure a JDBC database connection. Let's discuss the two database connection mechanisms provided by JDBC, the `java.sql.DriverManager` and the `javax.sql.DataSource`.

Using the java.sql.DriverManager

The `java.sql.DriverManager` is a standard part of JDBC and a standard part of Java available to stand-alone Java programs, JSP applications, and application server-hosted J2EE applications in general.

If you're going to use the `DriverManager` to obtain a database connection or if you're configuring a software package that does, you'll need to provide the following database connection parameters:

- The location of the JDBC driver JAR file for your database
- The name of the JDBC driver class to be used
- The JDBC connection URL for your database
- Your database username-password combination

Using the `DriverManager` to obtain a database connection is a two-step process. First you must load your JDBC driver class by name, which causes it to become registered with the `DriverManager`. Second, you call the static `DriverManager.getConnection()` method, passing in your database connection parameters, and receiving in return a `Connection` ready for use. For example, the following code shows how to obtain a connection to MySQL using the JDBC driver class `org.gjt.mm.mysql.Driver`:

```
Class.forName("org.gjt.mm.mysql.Driver");
Connection con = DriverManager.getConnection(
   "jdbc:mysql://localhost/ag","username","password");
```

Those connection parameters are a problem. If you use the `DriverManager` then you'll have to manage those connection parameters. You know you cannot hard-code them in your Java classes or JSP pages and you cannot store them in the database, so you'll probably end up storing them in a property file. When your application is installed, somebody will have to edit that property file.

Using a javax.sql.DataSource

The `javax.sql.DataSource` interface was introduced as part of the JDBC 2.0 Standard Extension to provide Java applications with a standard way to tap into the database connection management and connection-pooling functionality provided by Java application servers.

If you use the `javax.sql.DataSource` approach, you no longer have to manage database connection parameters in your code. Instead, you declare the names of the data sources required by your application and you expect the administrator who installs your application to set up those data sources for you in the deployment environment.

For example, in your example application you need one data source and you declare this need by adding a resource reference to the application's `web.xml` file, as shown here:

```
<resource-ref>
  <res-ref-name>jdbc/agdb</res-ref-name>
  <res-type>javax.sql.DataSource</res-type>
  <res-auth>Container</res-auth>
</resource-ref>
```

Once you've done that you can assume that the name `jdbc/agdb` is bound to a data source. You can use the following code to look up this data source via JNDI and to obtain a database connection:

```
  javax.naming.InitialContext ctx = new javax.naming.InitialContext();
  javax.sql.DataSource ds =
          (javax.sql.DataSource) ctx.lookup("java:comp/env/jdbc/agdb");
  Connection con = ds.getConnection();
```

Setting Up a javax.sql.DataSource

So, how do you set up one of these data sources? That depends on your application server and every application server is a little different. Some application servers include a web interface that allows you to set up new data sources and to administer the connection pools associated with those data sources. Other application servers require you to edit configuration files.

For example, on the Tomcat servlet container, you must configure your application's data source within the Tomcat `server.xml` configuration file (located in `%TOMCAT_HOME%/conf/`). If your application doesn't have a `<Context>` entry in `server.xml`, you'll have to add one. The following is the context entry for this chapter's example application:

```
<Context path="/ch08" docBase="ch08" debug="0">
  <Resource name="jdbc/agdb" auth="Container" type="javax.sql.DataSource" />
  <ResourceParams name="jdbc/agdb">
    <parameter>
      <name>factory</name>
      <value>org.apache.commons.dbcp.BasicDataSourceFactory</value>
    </parameter>
    <parameter><name>username</name><value>sa</value></parameter>
    <parameter><name>password</name><value></value></parameter>
    <parameter>
      <name>driverClassName</name>
```

```
        <value>org.hsqldb.jdbcDriver</value>
      </parameter>
      <parameter>
        <name>url</name>
        <value>jdbc:hsqldb:hsql://localhost</value>
      </parameter>
    </ResourceParams>
  </Context>
```

Within the Context element, you declare the data source as a resource named jdbc/agdb, and then you declare the parameters for the data source. As you can see, you specify the same parameters that you had hard-coded before into the JSP code. These include the JDBC driver class name, the database connection URL, the database username, and the corresponding password. If you need to change any of these values, you no longer have to modify the code of your application as you would when using the JDBC driver manager.

Please note that before you can use JDBC, you need to ensure that your JDBC driver JAR file is in the right class path. If you're using the JDBC driver manager to obtain your connections, then you can put your JDBC driver JAR in your application's WEB-INF/lib directory. However, if you're using a JDBC data source, then you'll need to ensure that your JDBC driver jar is in your server's class path. On Tomcat, this means putting your JDBC driver jar into the %TOMCAT_HOME%/common/lib directory.

You can also find information on configuring data sources in Tomcat at the Apache Jakarta Tomcat website:

- Apache Jakarta Tomcat website–http://jakarta.apache.org/tomcat
- Apache Jakarta Tomcat 4.1 JNDI DataSource HOW-TO: http://jakarta.apache.org/tomcat/tomcat-4.1-doc/jndi-datasource-examples-howto.html

Object/Relational Persistence Frameworks

O/R persistence frameworks make it easy to store and retrieve Java objects in a relational database. O/R frameworks come in a variety of shapes and sizes, but generally speaking, an O/R framework is a class library and a small set of development tools that support the storage and retrieval of Java objects in a relational database. The main advantages of using an O/R framework over JDBC are

- **Easier to program:** With an O/R framework, you can easily store and retrieve your Java objects without writing a lot of repetitive boilerplate code to map fields to and from SQL queries.
- **Better cross-database support:** O/R frameworks make it easier for you to support different vendors' databases because the framework handles query creation, data-type mapping, and some frameworks will even generate database creation (DDL) scripts for different databases.
- **Better performance:** O/R frameworks often include database connection pooling, object caching, and other performance enhancing features.

There are a number of ways to use an O/R framework. The authors of the open source Hibernate O/R framework wrote about four different approaches to O/R persistence. Most of the O/R frameworks support these four approaches so let's take a look at each one:

Name	Description
Top-down	Starting with an existing set of Java objects, you develop a mapping specification file that describes your objects and their relationships, use tools provided by the O/R framework to generate a DDL script to create database tables to store your objects, and use the O/R frameworks API to store and retrieve your objects in the database.
Bottom-up	Starting with an existing database schema, you develop a mapping-specification file that describes your tables and their relationships, use tools provided by the O/R framework to generate your Java objects, and use the O/R frameworks API to store and retrieve your objects in the database.
Middle-out	In this approach you start by writing a mapping specification that describes your objects and their relationships, use tools provided by the O/R framework to generate both your Java objects and your DDL script, and use the O/R frameworks API to store and retrieve your objects in the database.
Meet-in-the-middle	Take this approach if you already have an existing set of Java objects and an existing database schema. All you have to do is write a mapping specification that maps your Java objects to your database tables, and then you're ready to use the O/R frameworks API to store and retrieve your objects in the database.

O/R persistence frameworks are popular among Java web application developers and there are many choices, both commercial and open source. Popular commercial O/R frameworks include TopLink, now owned by Oracle, and CocoBase, developed by Thought, Inc. The open source O/R frameworks include Popular Castor, Hibernate, and Jakarta OJB.

Later in this chapter, you'll use the open source Hibernate framework because it's well supported and well documented. Hopefully, this chapter will give you enough knowledge to evaluate the strengths and weaknesses of the various other O/R frameworks for yourself.

The following are links to the websites of the O/R frameworks previously mentioned:

- Castor (open source): http://castor.exolab.org
- CocoBase (Thought, Inc.): http://www.thoughtinc.com
- Hibernate (open source): http://hibernate.bluemars.net/
- Jakarta OJB (open source): http://jakarta.apache.org/ojb/
- Toplink (Oracle): http://otn.oracle.com/products/ias/toplink

Java Data Objects

Each of the O/R frameworks previously mentioned has its own unique API and its own unique way to specify the mapping of Java objects to database tables. This is a problem because it means that Java programmers may have to learn multiple persistence APIs and mapping techniques as they move through their careers, and because the Java programs written by those programmers will each be locked into one persistence API. Wouldn't it be better if there were only one standard persistence API? Sun thinks so and that is why Sun worked closely with the Java community to create the Java Database Objects (JDO) API specification.

JDO is a relatively new Java API specification that is designed to provide a standard API to enable the persistent storage of Java data in relational databases, object databases, and other enterprise information systems. The JDO specification was finalized in March 2002; since then a number of commercial and open source implementations have been released. Commercial JDO implementations include small name vendors such as PrismTech, Signsoft, and SolarMetric. Open-source implementations include Jakarta OJB and TriActive JDO (TJDO).

The advantages of using JDO are that it provides the same benefits as using an O/R frameworks and that it does so through a standardized API and mapping technique. As a Java standard, JDO is likely to be very well supported and very well known among Java developers. The disadvantage of using JDO is that it's new and, some would say, untested. The big-name Java vendors, IBM, BEA Systems, and Oracle, haven't committed to JDO and the open-source JDO implementations aren't yet ready for production use.

It's important to note that JDO is very different from Microsoft's ActiveX Data Objects (ADO) API, despite the similar names. ADO is a lower-level API, similar to JDBC, that allows you to execute SQL queries and retrieve data as `RecordSet` objects of tabular data. JDO, on the other hand, allows you to save and retrieve any arbitrary Java object to and from a database. JDO includes an object query language (OQL) and when you execute an OQL query, you receive a collection of objects instead of tabular data as you would with ADO or JDBC.

Like JDBC, JDO is a fairly small API, but complete coverage is well beyond the scope of this book. For more information please refer to Sun's JDO home page, the JDO central website, and the various vendors that are supporting JDO. The following are links to these resources:

- Sun's JDO home page: http://java.sun.com/products/jdo
- JDO central: http://www.jdocentral.com
- Open Fusion JDO: http://www.prismtechnologies.com/English/Products/JDO
- IntelliBO JDO: http://signsoft.verio-de.com/en/intellibo
- Kodo JDO: http://www.solarmetric.com/Software/Kodo_JDO
- Jakarta OJB (open source): http://jakarta.apache.org/ojb/
- TJDO (open source): http://tjdo.sourceforge.net/

EJB Entity Beans

EJB is a Java API specification that provides a component architecture for the development and deployment of distributed business objects, but many Java programmers use EJB only for its database access and Java object-persistence capabilities. If your application is highly transactional, requires high availability, and is likely to have a very large number of concurrent users then you might want to consider using EJB.

EJB is a standard part of the J2EE and is therefore supported by all J2EE-compliant application servers. Application servers that support EJB do so by providing an EJB container that hosts EJB components just as a servlet container hosts servlets and JSPs. Just as servlet containers may be clustered to provide load balancing and fault tolerance for servlets, EJB containers can be clustered to provide the same functionality for distributed business objects.

An EJB container can support three types of components: entity beans, session beans, and message beans. We won't discuss session and message beans because they aren't persistent. We'll focus on entity beans, which can be persisted to a data store using one of the following two mechanisms:

- **Container-managed persistence (CMP):** You provide a mapping that specifies how to map fields from your entity bean objects to fields in a database and the EJB container manages the persistence of your entity beans in the database.
- **Bean-managed persistence (BMP):** You implement the persistence of your objects by using JDBC, an O/R framework, JDO, or some other technology. The EJB container will notify your code when it's time to store or retrieve an object to or from the database.

The benefits provided by using EJB for persistence are many; here are some of the most significant:

- **Built-in O/R framework**: If you use EJB CMP, you get all of the benefits of using an O/R framework plus the added benefits of EJB. However, the O/R mapping capabilities of CMP don't address some of the harder tasks in O/R mapping such as optimistic locking, batch updates, and so on.
- **Scalability and high availability:** EJB containers can be clustered to allow your application to scale up to meet the needs of more and more users. If an EJB container fails, the objects that were running in that container will automatically and transparently failover to continue execution in another EJB container.
- **Declarative transaction support**: EJB allows you to declare the transactional characteristics of your business objects. Instead of writing the code to begin and end transactions, you simply declare the transactional requirements of each of your object's methods and let the EJB container do the rest. If you have a complex and highly transactional system, this is an important benefit.
- **Declarative method-level security**: EJB allows you to declare the security characteristics of your business objects. Instead of writing code to ensure that only certain users working in certain roles can use your objects, you simply declare the security constraints of each of your object's methods and let the EJB container handle the security.
- **Distributed object support**: EJB is designed to support the development and deployment of distributed business objects that are callable via Java Remote Method Invocation (RMI) or CORBA IIOP.

One disadvantage of EJB is complexity. The technology is complex and the learning curve is steep. To learn EJB development, you need to learn the EJB philosophy, the EJB API, recommended EJB patterns, EJB development tools, and the EJB deployment descriptors. To learn EJB deployment, you need to learn how to use the administration and deployment tools provided by the various J2EE application servers that you intend to support, each of which can vary quite significantly.

Another disadvantage of EJB is development overhead. To write even a single EJB you need to create at least three (often four) files, and while there are tools that can help with generating them, there is a lot of complexity in developing even simple beans. There is also considerable runtime overhead associated with using entity beans as the container interposes a variety of services for your beans.

EJB does a lot for you, but with increased complexity and significant development overhead. Make sure that you really need the benefits provided by EJB before you commit to using it in your application.

Comparing the Choices

Now that you've learned about the five data access options, JSTL, JDBC, O/R, JDO, and entity beans, let's review the pros and cons of each.

Option	Pros	Cons
JSTL	Simple and easy to use with JSP	Only useful for displaying query results and performing simple updates
JDBC	Simple and easy to use Also very flexible and powerful	Can require repetitive, tedious, and error-prone boilerplate coding
O/R	Makes it easy to persist objects to DB Eliminates much repetitive boilerplate coding Good tool support Better support for portability Many open- and closed-source implementations	Each O/R framework has its own nonstandard API and query language
JDO	The official standard Java persistence API with building momentum among developers Easy to persist objects to DB Easy to use API and OQL Most of the same benefits as O/R frameworks	Currently, supported only by small vendors Currently, open-source versions not ready

Option	Pros	Cons
EJB	Widely supported, well-known, well-documented, and standard Java API EJB CMP provides a built-in O/R framework Scalability and high-availability features Declarative transactions and security Distributed object support	Complex solution, lots to learn High development overhead Poor performance if used improperly

Data Access Architectures

We have discussed a number of different data access technologies and now we'll discuss how data access fits into the architecture of a web application. Of course, there isn't *one true* web application architecture. Every application is different, and different applications often need different architectures.

According to UML gurus Booch, Rumbaugh, and Jacobson in *The UML User Guide,* architecture is a "set of significant decisions about the organization of a software system."[1] When you come up with a new architecture, you're deciding how to divide up your software into different parts and you're deciding how these parts will work together. These decisions will affect your application's performance, maintainability, reusability, ease of development, and resilience to change.

Architectural decisions often involve trade-offs and can only be made by somebody who knows the unique requirements of the software being developed. In this section, we'll discuss architectures at three increasing levels of complexity. You'll learn the advantages and disadvantages of each type of architecture, so that you can decide for yourself which architecture is best for each of your web applications.

Example: RSS Newsreader

Before we discuss the three types of architectures, we should introduce the example application that we'll use to illustrate these architectures. This chapter's example is a JSP-based Rich Site Summary (RSS) Newsreader.

RSS is a simple XML-based format for representing the current news stories available on a website. A website that supports RSS may provide several RSS news feeds, each covering one topic and each available at a different URL. An RSS news feed is represented by an RSS file, which is dynamically generated and updated on a regular schedule. An RSS file contains a `<channel>` element that describes the contents of the file, and that channel element contains a series of `<item>` elements with each representing one news story. Each news item has a title, description, publication time, and link that points to the full story on the website that is associated with the news feed.

[1] Booch, Grady et al., *The Unified Modeling Language User Guide* (Boston: Addison Wesley, 1998).

An RSS Newsreader allows a user to subscribe to one or more RSS news feeds, and then to view the news stories from those news feeds within a single interface such as a desktop application or a web page. RSS Newsreaders are often referred to as aggregators because they typically read news stories from multiple sites and aggregate them together for display.

In this chapter, you'll develop a simple JSP-based RSS Newsreader. If you would like to see a more full-featured web-based RSS Newsreader, then take a look at O'Reilly's Meerkat, which can aggregate and filter news stories from numerous professional sources. An alternative is Atlassian's JavaBlogs.com, which aggregates numerous Java-oriented weblogs.

Now that you know a little bit about RSS and RSS Newsreaders, you're equipped to understand the examples that follow. Now, let's move on to the architectures.

One-Layer Architecture

In the simplest JSP data access architecture, an application accesses data directly from the presentation layer. You might be tempted to use this type of architecture because it seems like the easy route. After all, you don't have to design and implement a business layer or a data layer. The following figure illustrates the single-layer architecture. As you can see, the presentation layer not only depends on the Servlet API, but also has a direct dependence on the data access technology, which might be JDBC, JDO, or some other persistence framework:

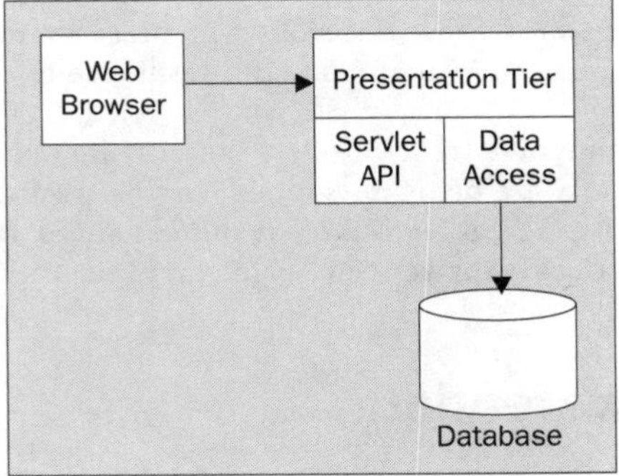

With single-layer architecture, you're sacrificing maintainability, reusability, and resilience to change in order to make development a little easier. This might be acceptable for a smaller application, but for a larger application this type of architecture will make your code:

- **Difficult to maintain**, because presentation, business, and persistence logic are all mixed together and cannot be considered or changed separately.
- **Difficult to reuse**, because the business logic cannot easily be separated from the presentation logic. If you need to create a new application or a web service that uses your business logic, you're out of luck because your business logic is mixed in with your JSP and servlet-based presentation code.
- **Not resilient to change**. If you need to switch to a new data access technology, you'll have to make sweeping changes in your code. You cannot change the persistence logic without putting the business logic and presentation logic at risk.

Two-Layer Architecture

Splitting your application up into a presentation layer and a business layer can solve the one-layer problems previously mentioned. This is a more difficult task because it involves designing business objects to model the business concepts and entities in your application. It also involves creating an interface or a set of interfaces through which your presentation layer can invoke business operations and access business objects.

The following figure illustrates the two-layer architecture. As you can see, the presentation layer depends on the Servlet API but it calls upon the business layer to perform business operations and data access. The business layer depends on data access technology, which again can be JDBC, JDO, or some other persistence framework. Looking at the following figure, you can see that the business layer is now an independent and reusable software entity. You could take that business layer and place it in a desktop application or you could take it and build a SOAP-accessible web service around it.

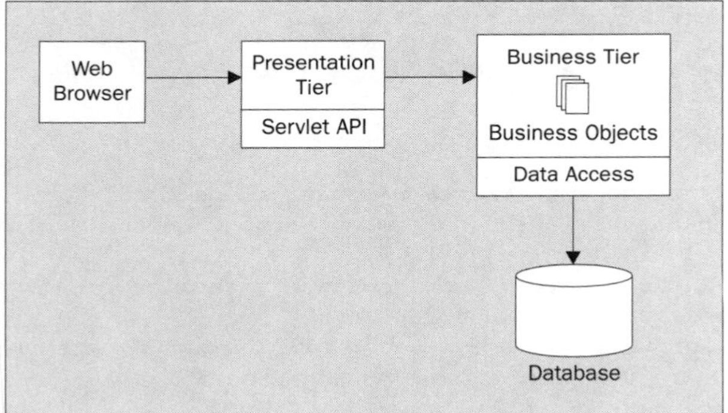

You're probably wondering what is going on inside the business layer box in the previous figure. The best way to understand the concepts of business interfaces and business objects is by example. So, let's take a look at the business objects and business interface of the RSS Newsreader that was mentioned earlier.

An RSS Newsreader allows a user to subscribe to a number of news feeds and then to read the news items retrieved from those news feeds. By looking at the nouns in that sentence, you can see what objects are going to be involved in this application. You'll need objects to model users, subscriptions, news feeds, and news items. The following diagram shows these objects, their attributes, and their relationships:

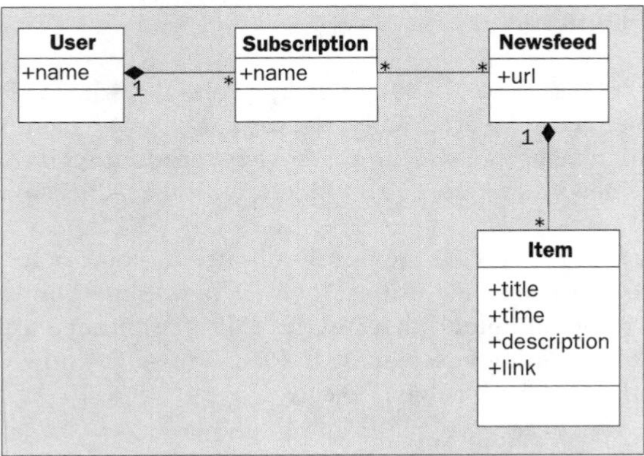

The diagram, which uses UML notation, shows that the Users have a one-to-many relationship with Subscriptions, Subscriptions have a many-to-many relationship with Newsfeeds, and Newsfeeds have a one-to-many relationship with Items. In this example, you'll have a one-to-one correspondence between classes and database tables. So you'll have `User`, `Subscription`, `Newsfeed`, and `Item` objects as well as corresponding User, Subscription, Newsfeed, and Item tables.

Now that you've designed the objects needed for your application, you'll need to design the business-layer interface. This interface will be used by the presentation layer to invoke Newsreader operations and to access the Newsreader objects that were discussed earlier.

To implement the presentation layer you need to be able to add subscriptions, remove subscriptions, access users, and run the news feed aggregation operation. The following interface fulfills all of these requirements:

```
package com.apress.projsp20.ch08;
/**
  * Business interface for Newsfeed aggregation.
  */
public interface Aggregator {

  /** Gets user by name, create new user if necessary. */
  public User getUser(String userName) throws Exception;

  /** Add new subscription and associate with a newsfeed. */
  public Subscription addSubscription(
      User user, String name, String url) throws Exception;

  /** Remove subscription by id. */
  public void removeSubscription(String id) throws Exception;

  /** Run the aggregator and fetch items from all Newsfeeds. */
  public void aggregate() throws Exception;
}
```

The `Aggregator` interface distills the interface between the presentation layer and the business layer down to only four methods. The interface is so simple because the `getUser()` method does a lot of work. It returns a `User` object that has a collection of `Subscription` objects. Each Subscription has a `Newsfeed` object and each `Newsfeed` has a collection of `Items`, the most recent news stories retrieved from the `Newsfeed`'s website.

The `addSubscription()` and `removeSubscription()` methods allow you to do subscription management in the presentation layer. Finally, the `aggregate()` method allows you to launch the aggregate operation, which visits each of the news feeds represented by subscriptions in the database, parses the RSS from the news feed into `Item` objects, and stores those objects in the database.

With the simple `Aggregator` interface previously discussed, you can totally separate the presentation layer of the RSS Newsreader from the business layer. The presentation layer doesn't need to know anything about what is going on behind that interface. It doesn't need to know what type of RSS parser is being used to parse the incoming news feeds. It doesn't need to know what type of data access technology is being used to persist business objects.

A two-layer architecture is usually sufficient, but in some cases you may wish to take the architecture one step further and use a three-layer architecture.

Three-Layer Architecture

The two-layer architecture works well. It allows you to separate presentation logic from business logic and that is good. Why would anybody want to introduce yet another layer into an application? After all, each additional layer adds another layer of complexity, and all these layers cannot be good for performance. You have to think carefully before you decide to add another layer to your application, but there are some reasons you may want to do so.

With the two-layer architecture, you separated business logic from presentation logic. However, you didn't separate the business logic from the data access logic. Business logic and data access logic seem to go together. Business rules are often built right into database schemas in the form of database constraints and business logic is often coded into databases in stored procedures and triggers. What is the point of separating the business logic from the data access logic?

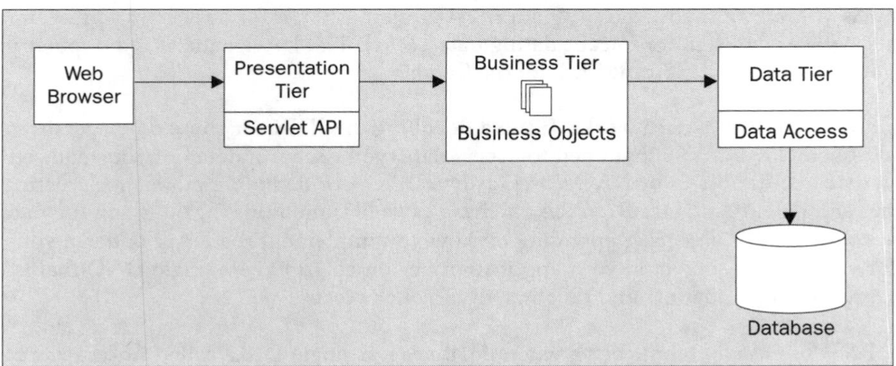

There are at least two reasons that you might want to separate your business logic and data access logic out and into separate business and data layers, as shown in the previous figure. These reasons come right off the list of trade-offs that we discussed when we introduced the topic of architecture. The following are reasons to consider separate business and data layers:

- **Reusability:** Someday you may want to take your business layer and turn it into a stand-alone desktop application that doesn't require a database. If your data access logic is mixed in with your business logic then this is going to be a difficult and error-prone task.
- **Resilience to change:** Changes in the persistence logic will be less likely to affect the business logic and changes in the business logic will be less likely to affect the persistence logic. For example: Someday you might find that the O/R persistence framework you chose has some fatal flaw or is no longer going to be supported. You might need to replace your chosen O/R framework with something else, and separation of business logic and data access logic will make this task easier.

Reusability and resilience to change are forms of flexibility, and most developers consider flexibility to be a good thing. However, it's important to realize that flexibility comes at the price of added complexity and complexity makes software more difficult to develop and to maintain. You don't want to do a lot of extra work now for some event that may possibly occur at some point in the future, especially if that extra work is going to make your application more difficult to maintain. The following are a couple of other reasons not to use separate business and data layers:

- Developing an abstract interface to data access isn't an easy task and it requires some knowledge of each of the various data access technologies that you may wish to use behind that interface.
- Hiding your data access technology behind an abstract interface may make it difficult to use some of the advanced features of your chosen data access technology.

The Data Access Object Pattern

If you decide that you *do* want to implement a three-layer architecture and you *do* want to separate out your data access logic into a data layer, then you should consider using the **Data Access Object (DAO) pattern**. As you may already know, a pattern is a general design for a recurring problem. The DAO pattern is a general design for encapsulating data access. The DAO pattern is a popular pattern and is documented as part of the Sun J2EE Patterns Catalog.

Here is how the DAO pattern works. Instead of calling the JDBC or some other persistence API directly from all of your Java classes that need to access data, you encapsulate all of your data access code in one or more data access objects or DAOs. Typically a DAO will include methods for creating, retrieving, updating, and deleting objects from the database as well as methods for querying the database to retrieve collections of objects. Depending on how you implement the DAO pattern, you could have a DAO for each class of object in your application or you could have a single DAO that is responsible for creating, retrieving, updating, and deleting all of your objects.

In your RSS Newsreader application example, there is a single DAO called `AggregatorDAO`, which is shown in the code excerpt that follows. The `AggregatorDAO` contains methods for creating, retrieving, updating, and deleting all of the different types of objects that are part of the application. These objects are `User`, `Subscription`, `Newsfeed`, and `Item`.

```
package com.apress.projsp20.ch08.persist;

import java.util.List;

/** Aggregator Data Access Object (DAO) interface. */
public interface AggregatorDAO {

  /** Gets user by name, create new user if necessary. */
  public User getUser(String userName) throws DAOException;

  /** Add new subscription and associate with a newsfeed */
  public Subscription addSubscription(
    User user, String name, String url) throws DAOException;
```

```
    /** Retrieve subscription by ID */
    public Subscription retrieveSubscription(String id) throws DAOException;
    /** Remove subscription but not associated Newsfeed. */
    public void removeSubscription(Subscription sub) throws DAOException;

    /** Get all newsfeeds. */
    public List getAllNewsfeeds() throws DAOException;

    /** Remove newsfeed and associated subscriptions. */
    public void removeNewsfeed(Newsfeed feed) throws DAOException;

    /** Store newsfeed. */
    public void storeNewsfeed(Newsfeed feed) throws DAOException;

    /** Add item to newsfeed. */
    public void addItem(Newsfeed feed, Item item) throws DAOException;

    /** Add a newsfeed (for testing only). */
    public Newsfeed addNewsfeed(String url) throws DAOException;

    /** Get all items (for testing only). */
    public List getAllItems() throws DAOException;

}
```

`AggregatorDAO` is an interface that you could implement using just about any data access technology. For example, you could write a `JdbcAggregatorDAO` class that implements data access with JDBC or you could write an `XmlAggregatorDAO` that stores `User`, `Subscription`, `Newsfeed`, and `Item` objects in an XML file. In the next section, you'll learn the steps involved in implementing the `AggregatorDAO` interface using the Hibernate O/R persistence framework.

Implementing the RSS Newsreader Example

The RSS Newsreader example that we have been discussing in this chapter is developed using a three-layer architecture as described in the previous section. The application includes a presentation layer, a business layer, and a data layer. In this section we'll first discuss the package organization of the RSS Newsreader and then we'll cover each of the steps that were taken in the development of the application.

Package Organization

Before talking about the steps involved in building this application, let's talk a little more about how the pieces fit together. The following figure shows the three layers of the application, the Java packages that exist within each layer, and the dependencies that exist between these packages indicated by arrows.

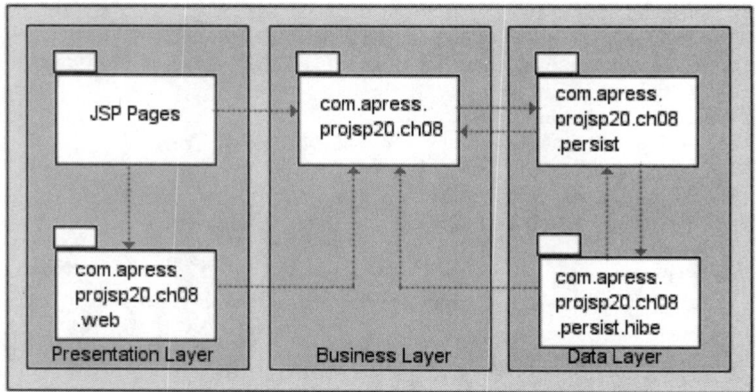

The business layer is made up of the business objects and the `AggregatorImpl` class, which implements the `Aggregator` business interface that was discussed earlier in the section on two-layer architectures. The business layer depends only on the data layer and the sole interface to the data layer is the `AggregatorDAO` interface.

The presentation layer is implemented with JSP pages, JSTL tags, and Java classes in the package `com.apress.projsp20.ch08.web`, which are responsible for parsing request parameters and calling the business layer. The presentation layer depends only on the business layer. The sole interface to the business layer is the `Aggregator` business interface.

The data layer exists under the `com.apress.projsp20.ch08.persist` package and is made up of the `AggregatorDAO` interface, the `DAOException` class, and the DAO implementation class `HibeAggregatorDAO`. The DAO implementation uses the Hibernate O/R persistence framework.

Step 1: Implementing the Object Model

You've already learned first steps in the RSS Newsreader development process. These steps were the design of the object model, the design of the business interface, and the design of the DAO interface that will encapsulate data access.

The next step in the process is to implement the object model. This is easy because there are only four business objects and these business objects are simple JavaBeans with each having only a small number of properties. The following is an example of one of the business objects, the `Item` class:

```
package com.apress.projsp20.ch08;

import java.util.Date;
import java.util.Set;

/**
```

```
   * Represents a single news item retrieved from a newsfeed.
   */

public class Item {
   private String mId;
   private String mLink;
   private String mDescription;
   private String mContent;
   private String mTitle;
   private Date mTime;
   private Newsfeed mNewsfeed;
   private Item mItem;

   /**
   * Construct Item using all field values.
   * @param title  Title of this news item.
   * @param time  Time of publication.
   * @param link  Link article on originating website.
   * @param desc  Description of article (or full text of article).
   * @param content (Optional) full text of article.
   */

   public Item( String title, Date time, String link,
     String description, String content ) {
     mTitle = title;
     mTime = time;
     mLink = link;
     mDescription = description;
     mContent = content;
   }

   /** Default constructor */
   public Item() {
   }

   public String getId() {
     return mId;
   }

   public void setId(String id) {
     mId = id;
   }

   public Newsfeed getNewsfeed() {
     return mNewsfeed;
   }

   public void setNewsfeed(Newsfeed newsfeed) {
     mNewsfeed = newsfeed;
   }

   public String getTitle() {
     return mTitle;
   }
```

```
    public void setTitle(String title) {
      mTitle = title;
    }

    public String getContent() {
      return mContent;
    }

    public void setContent(String content) {
      mContent = content;
    }

    public String getDescription() {
      return mDescription;
    }

    public void setDescription(String description) {
      mDescription = description;
    }

    public String getLink() {
      return mLink;
    }

    public void setLink(String link) {
      mLink = link;
    }

    public Date getTime() {
      return mTime;
    }

    public void setTime(Date time) {
      mTime = time;
    }
  }
```

Similar JavaBeans exist for `User`, `Subscription`, and `Newsfeed`.

Step 2: Creating an Object-Relational Mapping

The next step in the development of the RSS Newsreader is the development of the data layer to store and retrieve the business objects developed in step 1.

This step is a little more difficult because you must learn the ins and outs of your persistence choice–in our case the Hibernate O/R persistence framework. Luckily, the Hibernate documentation is very good and Hibernate is fairly easy to use.

Before you can use Hibernate to store Java objects in a relational database, you have to create an object-relational mapping for each object to be stored. A mapping specification is an XML file that describes how to map one or more Java class to tables in a database. For example, the mapping for the `com.apress.projsp20.ch08.Newsfeed` class, from the file `Newsfeed.hbm.xml` is as follows:

```
<?xml version="1.0"?>
<!DOCTYPE hibernate-mapping PUBLIC
   "-//Hibernate/Hibernate Mapping DTD 2.0//EN"
   "http://hibernate.sourceforge.net/hibernate-mapping-2.0.dtd">

<hibernate-mapping>

   <!-- ag.Newsfeed root -->
   <class name="com.apress.projsp20.ch08.Newsfeed" table="newsfeed">

      <id column="id" name="id" >
         <generator class="uuid.hex"/>
      </id>

      <property name="url" column="url" type="string"
                not-null="true" unique="true" />

      <set name="items" table="item" cascade="delete" >
         <key column="newsfeed_id" />
         <one-to-many class="com.apress.projsp20.ch08.Item" />
      </set>

      <set name="subscriptions" table="subscription" cascade="delete">
         <key column="newsfeed_id" />
         <one-to-many class="com.apress.projsp20.ch08.Subscription" />
      </set>

   </class>

</hibernate-mapping>
```

Let's analyze the contents of the Hibernate mapping.

After the standard XML declaration and the DOCTYPE tags, you find the root element of a Hibernate mapping file, the <hibernate-mapping> element. Within the root element, you'll find one or more <class> tags. The <class> tag maps one class to a database table, so the tag has two attributes. The name attribute specifies the name of the Java class and the table attribute specifies the name of the table that the Java class is to be mapped to:

```
<hibernate-mapping>
  <class name="com.apress.projsp20.ch08.Newsfeed" table="newsfeed">
```

The first element within the class mapping is the <id> element. This element specifies which JavaBean property and which database table column are to be used as a primary key for the class. Within the <id> tag is the <generator> tag, which specifies which method should be used to generate primary keys for new objects:

```
<id column="id" name="id" >
   <generator class="uuid.hex" />
</id>
```

Hibernate supports ten different primary key generation methods. The `class="uuid.hex"` method results in a 32-character key that is generated using the IP address of the machine upon which Hibernate is running. It's also possible to tell Hibernate to allow the database to generate the key by using `class="sequence"` or to allow the application to assign the key by using `class="assigned"`.

The `<property>` tag maps a simple `java.lang.String` property named `url` to a database column called `url`. The property isn't allowed to be Null and is required to be unique.

```
<property name="url" column="url" type="string"
          not-null="true" unique="true" />
```

The next two elements are interesting. The `<set>` tag indicates that you're mapping a `java.util.Set` collection to the database. Each `Newsfeed` is associated with a collection of Items and a collection of Subscriptions. This is a classic one-to-many relationship. `com.apress.projsp20.ch08.Newsfeed` objects are stored in the `newsfeed` table, `com.apress.projsp20.ch08.Item` objects are stored in the `item` table, and the two tables are related by a `newsfeed_id` column in the `item` table:

```
<set role="items" table="item" cascade="delete">
  <key column="newsfeed_id" />
  <one-to-many class="com.apress.projsp20.ch08.Item" />
</set>

<set role="subscriptions" table="subscription" cascade="delete">
  <key column="newsfeed_id" />
  <one-to-many class="com.apress.projsp20.ch08.Subscription" />
</set>
```

If you're having a hard time visualizing these relationships, refer back to the UML diagram in the "Two-Layer Architecture" section, which shows the relationships between `User`, `Subscription`, `Newsfeed`, and `Item` objects.

It's possible to map more than one class within a single `<hibernate-mapping>` element, but it's a recommended practice to map only one class per mapping file. At runtime, the `Newsfeed.hbm.xml` file should be placed in the same package as the `Newsfeed.class` so that Hibernate can find it.

The Hibernate mapping file may look complicated, but it's complicated for a reason. The mapping is designed to accommodate all of the different data and relationship types that one might use in a Java application and in a relational database schema. If you have problems coming up with the right mappings then consult your friendly database administrator. Ask for help on the Hibernate mailing list.

Step 3: Creating the Database Tables

Creating the object-relational mappings for the RSS Newsreader classes is relatively difficult, but once you have those mappings Hibernate starts to earn its keep.

Hibernate includes a command-line tool that reads mapping files and can then either generate a database creation script or connect to your database and create the tables for you. This tool is called

SchemaExport and it can handle twelve different database dialects including Oracle, Sybase, Microsoft SQL Server, MySQL, and PostgreSQL among others.

SchemaExport is just a command-line Java program, so it may be easily run from an Ant build script. For example, the following Ant build script excerpt is used to run the SchemaExport and create the tables for the RSS Newsreader example:

```
<target name="create-tables">

   <java classname="net.sf.hibernate.tool.hbm2ddl.SchemaExport"
      fork="true" dir="./build/projsp20-ch08/WEB-INF/classes">
      <arg value="--quiet"/>
      <arg value="--output=../ag.ddl"/>
      <arg value="--properties=hibernate.properties"/>
      <arg value="./com/apress/projsp20/ch08/Subscription.hbm.xml"/>
      <arg value="./com/apress/projsp20/ch08/Newsfeed.hbm.xml"/>
      <arg value="./com/apress/projsp20/ch08/Item.hbm.xml"/>
      <arg value="./com/apress/projsp20/ch08/User.hbm.xml"/>
      <classpath>
         <path refid="jdbcdriver.path"/>
         <path refid="hibernate.path"/>
         <pathelement
         path="./build/projsp20-ch08/WEBINF/classes/com/apress/projsp20/ch08"/>
      </classpath>
   </java>

</target>
```

The `<java>` element runs the class `cirrus.hibernate.tools.SchemaExport` within the build directory so that it can find the mapping files. The `-output` argument tells the SchemaExport to generate a database creation script named `rss.ddl`. The `-properties` argument tells SchemaExport where to find the Hibernate properties file, which contains the database connection parameters needed to connect to the target database. The rest of the arguments indicate which mappings are to be processed.

The `create-tables` target in the previous example code comes from the Chapter 8 example build script `build.xml`. This Ant build script compiles the example Java classes, builds the example WAR file, and creates the example's database tables using the `create-tables` target. For more information on the Chapter 8 example build script, please refer to the `readme.txt` file in the Chapter 8 examples directory.

Step 4: Implementing the AggregatorDAO

The next step in RSS Newsreader development is to write the Hibernate implementation of the `AggregatorDAO` interface. This implementation is in the package `com.apress.projsp20.ch08.persist.hibe` and is named `HibeAggregatorDAO`.

This task requires some knowledge of the Hibernate API, but the excellent *Hibernate Reference Document* (available at http://hibernate.bluemars.net/hib_docs/reference/html) and Javadocs really shortened the learning curve. Obviously, we don't want to discuss every line of code in the implementation. Looking at the code for the constructor and the logic for persisting one object should give you a good understanding of the implementation.

The constructor for the HibeAggregatorDAO class is shown in the following code excerpt. The constructor creates a Hibernate Datastore, loads the mappings for the classes that will be persisted, and creates a SessionFactory for use during the rest of the lifetime of the DAO object. The SessionFactory represents a database connection pool and is responsible for creating Session objects. The Session interface is the main Hibernate interface used by a Java program; a Session object holds a database connection:

```
package com.apress.projsp20.ch08.persist.hibe;

import com.apress.projsp20.ch08.*;
import com.apress.projsp20.ch08.persist.*;
import net.sf.hibernate.*;
import net.sf.hibernate.cfg.*;
import java.util.List;

/** Hibernate implementation of Ag DAO. */
public class HibeAggregatorDAO implements AggregatorDAO {

    private static SessionFactory sessionFactory;

    public HibeAggregatorDAO() throws DAOException {
        try {
            Configuration config = new Configuration();
            config.addClass(Newsfeed.class);
            config.addClass(Subscription.class);
            config.addClass(User.class);
            config.addClass(Item.class);
            sessionFactory = config.buildSessionFactory();
        }
        catch (MappingException e) {
            throw new DAOException(e);
        }
        catch (HibernateException e) {
            throw new DAOException(e);
        }
    }
```

The storeNewsfeed() and storeObject() methods, as shown here, illustrate the code necessary to add a new object into the data store. The first step in the method is to open a session, which begins a database transaction. Next, you'll save the object database. To finalize the operation, you commit the transaction. If an exception occurs, roll back the transaction and throw a DAOException so that the business layer can handle the error condition. The finally block ensures that, no matter what happens, the session is closed and therefore the database connection that was used by the connection is released back to the database connection pool.

```
    public void storeNewsfeed(Newsfeed feed) throws DAOException {
      storeObject(feed);
    }

    private void storeObject(Object obj) throws DAOException {
      Session ses = null;
      try {
```

```
        ses = sessionFactory.openSession();
        ses.saveOrUpdate(obj);
        ses.flush();
        ses.connection().commit();

      } catch (Exception e) {
        try { ses.connection().rollback(); }
        catch (Exception ex) { e.printStackTrace(); };
        throw new DAOException(e);


      } finally {
        try { ses.close(); }
        catch (Exception ex) { ex.printStackTrace(); };
      }
    }
```

The `retrieveNewsfeed()` method and `retrieveObject()` methods in the following code excerpt, show the code necessary to retrieve and object from the database using the object's primary key. The steps are simple. You open a session, load the object, close the session, and return the object:

```
    public Newsfeed retrieveNewsfeed(String id) throws DAOException {
      return (Newsfeed)retrieveObject(Newsfeed.class, id);
    }

    private Object retrieveObject(Class clazz, String id) throws DAOException {
      Object obj = null;
      Session ses = null;
      try {
        ses = sessionFactory.openSession();
        obj = ses.load( clazz, id );

      } catch (Exception e) {
        throw new DAOException(e);

      } finally {
        try { ses.close(); }
        catch (Exception ex) { ex.printStackTrace(); };
      }
      return obj;
    }
```

The `getAllNewsfeeds()` method, shown in the following excerpt, illustrates the code necessary to fetch a collection of objects from the database using a query. This is also a simple operation. You open a session and run a query to get all Newsfeeds using the `ses.find()` method. The query is expressed using Hibernate's own OQL, which is similar to, but not quite the same as SQL:

```
    public List getAllNewsfeeds() throws DAOException {
      List feeds = null;
      Session ses = null;
      try {
```

```
        ses = sessionFactory.openSession();
        feeds = ses.find("from newsfeed in class " +
                         "com.apress.projsp20.ch08.Newsfeed");

      } catch (Exception e) {
        throw new DAOException(e);

      } finally {
        try { ses.close(); }
        catch (Exception ex) { ex.printStackTrace(); };
      }
      return feeds;
    }
```

The `removeNewsfeed()` and `removeObject()` methods show the code necessary to remove an object from the database. The steps here are very similar to the steps involved in the `storeNewsfeed()` method, except that we call `ses.delete()` to delete the object. Note that, because you specified the `cascade="true"` attribute in the mapping for the associated `Item` and `Subscription` collections, any Items and Subscriptions associated with the `Newsfeed` object will also be removed from the database.

You might be wondering why you have to call `ses.load()` on the object before you can delete it. That call is necessary because objects have associations and associations will not be handled properly at delete-time if the object and its associations aren't created within the same session as the `ses.delete()` call:

```
    public void removeNewsfeed(Newsfeed feed) throws DAOException {
      removeObject(Newsfeed.class, feed.getId(), feed);
    }

    private void removeObject(Class clazz, String id, Object obj)
        throws DAOException {
      Session ses = null;
      try {
        ses = sessionFactory.openSession();
        obj = ses.load(clazz,id);
        ses.delete(obj);
        ses.flush();
        ses.connection().commit();

      } catch (Exception e) {
        try { ses.connection().rollback(); }
        catch (Exception ex) { e.printStackTrace(); };
        throw new DAOException(e);

      } finally {
        try { ses.close(); }
        catch (Exception ex) { ex.printStackTrace(); };
      }
    }
```

Step 5: Implementing the Business Layer Interface

The next step after implementing the AggregatorDAO interface is to implement the business-layer interface. The business-layer interface is the Java interface Aggregator and the implementation is the Java class AggregatorImpl.

The Aggregator interface is a very small interface and most of its methods correspond directly to methods in the AggregatorDAO interface, so they are very easy to implement.

The only real application logic that exists in this sample application is the Aggregator.aggregate() method. This method is responsible for walking the list of news feeds in the database, fetching the RSS data for each news feed, parsing the RSS data, and saving the news items found in each news feed to the database.

The code for the aggregator() method is shown here. The method uses an RSS parsing API from an open-source product known as Flock.

First, you create a FlockFeedFactory to help you to parse the RSS XML. Next, you get an iterator so that you may iterate over all of the news feeds in the database. You call upon Flock to parse each news feed into articles. Each article is then stored into the database using the AggregatorDAO.addItem() method:

```
package com.apress.projsp20.ch08;

import net.sourceforge.flock.FlockArticleI;
import net.sourceforge.flock.FlockFeedI;
import net.sourceforge.flock.parser.FlockFeedFactory;

import java.net.URL;
import java.util.Iterator;

import com.apress.projsp20.ch08.persist.*;

public class AggregatorImpl implements Aggregator {
  private AggregatorDAO dao;

  public AggregatorImpl(AggregatorDAO dao) {
    this.dao = dao;
  }

  /** Run aggregation, collection items, store them in database */
  public void aggregate() throws Exception {
    FlockFeedFactory factory = new FlockFeedFactory();

    Iterator feedIter = dao.getAllNewsfeeds().iterator();
    while ( feedIter.hasNext() ) {
      Newsfeed feed = (Newsfeed)feedIter.next();
      String url = feed.getUrl();
```

```
      try {
        FlockFeedI flockFeed = factory.createFeed(new URL(url));
        Iterator articleIter = flockFeed.getArticles().iterator();

        while ( articleIter.hasNext() ) {
          FlockArticleI article = (FlockArticleI)articleIter.next();
          Item item = new Item(
             article.getTitle(),
             article.getCreationTime(),
             article.getLink().toString(),
             article.getDescription(),
             "");
          dao.addItem(feed,item);
        }
      } catch (Exception e) {
        e.printStackTrace();
      }
    }
  }

  /** Gets user by name, create new user if necessary. */
  public User getUser( String userName ) throws Exception {
    return dao.getUser(userName);
  }

  /**
   * Add new subscription and associate with a newsfeed, creating
   * a new newsfeed only if necessary.
   */
  public Subscription addSubscription(
    User user, String name, String url) throws Exception {
    return dao.addSubscription(user,name,url);
  }

  /**
   * Remove subscription but not associated Newsfeed.
   */
  public void removeSubscription(String id) throws Exception {
    Subscription sub = dao.retrieveSubscription(id);
    dao.removeSubscription(sub);
  }

}
```

For more information on the Flock RSS news aggregator and parser, please refer to the Flock website: http://flock.sourceforge.net/.

Step 6: Implementing the Web User Interface

The final step in the development of the RSS Newsreader is the creation of the presentation layer. The presentation layer is made up of a simple controller servlet, three action classes, and three JSP pages that correspond to those three action classes. The controller servlet and the action classes constitute a very simple Struts-like Model View Controller (MVC) framework. All requests are handled initially by the controller servlet, `com.apress.projsp20.ch08.web.Controller`. The controller determines which action to call and does so. All of the action classes implement the `com.apress.projsp20.ch08.web.Action` interface. Each action class follows the same pattern:

1. Perform an action.
2. Load some objects (the model) into scope.
3. Forward the request to a JSP page (this is the view).

The following table summarizes the three web pages and lists the JSP page and action class for each page:

Name	Action class	JSP page	Description
Login or Change User	`com.apress.projsp20.ch08.web.LoginAction`	`login.jsp`	Allows user to log in by entering a username. If username doesn't exist in database, new user will be created.
Manage Subscriptions	`com.apress.projsp20.ch08.web.SubscriptionAction`	`subs.jsp`	Allows user to add new subscriptions and to remove existing subscriptions.
Read News	`com.apress.projsp20.ch08.web.AggregationAction`	`news.jsp`	Allows user to view news items that have been previously aggregated and to request aggregation of new news items.

The SubscriptionAction Class

Before you dive into Java code, let's take a look at how the Manage Subscriptions page looks in a web browser. The following screen shot below shows what the page looks like just after a new subscription was added:

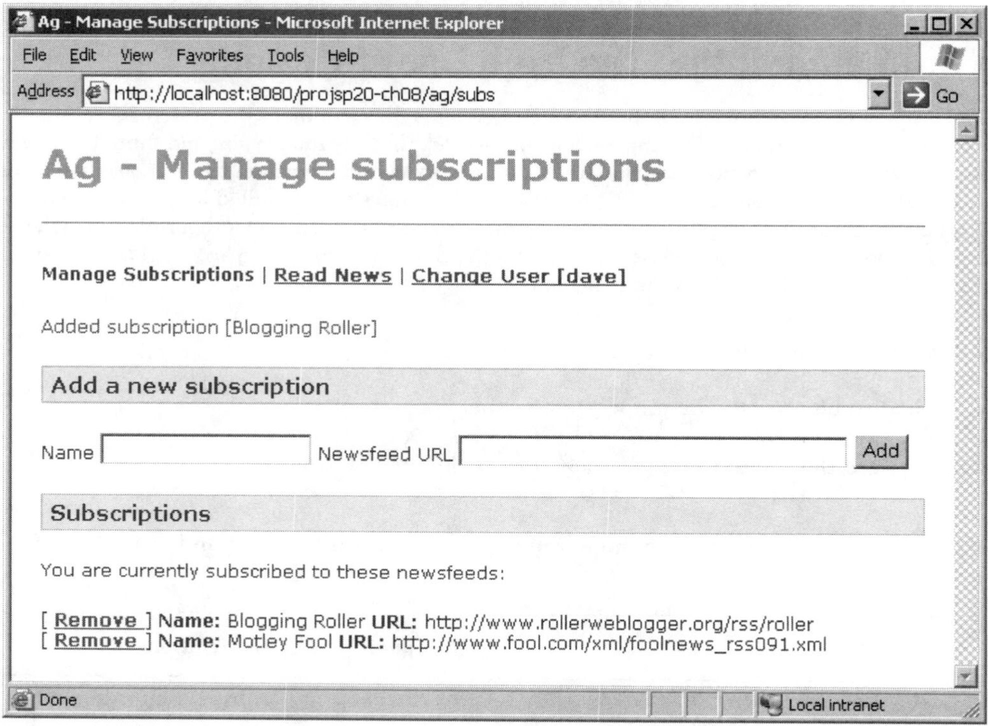

The page starts out with a title Manage subscriptions and a menu that allows the user to access the Read News page and the Change User page. After that there is a status message area and one status message that indicates the result of the last action performed. In this case, the last action performed was the addition of a new subscription named Roller. Under the status message is the Add a new subscription form. The form includes a subscription name field, a subscription URL field, and a button to submit the form. Finally, under the Subscriptions heading, there is a list of the user's current subscriptions.

How does the page work? Let's start from the beginning, the URL. As you can see in the screen shot, the URL is http://localhost:8080/projsp20-ch08/ag/subs. The `/ag` part of the URL maps the incoming request to the controller servlet. The controller servlet uses the path-info part of the URL (in this case `subs` is the path-info) to determine which action is to be called. Then it calls the action object's `doGet(request, response)` method to process the request. In this example, the path-info `subs` maps to an action object of class `com.apress.projsp20.ch08.web.SubscriptionAction`.

`SubscriptionAction` is responsible for responding for posts from the Add a new subscription form, for removing subscriptions, for adding to scope the objects required for displaying the Manage Subscriptions page, and, finally, for forwarding the request to the `subs.jsp` page for display. Let's take a closer look at `SubscriptionAction.java`.

The code is shown in full here and is interspersed with comments:

```
package com.apress.projsp20.ch08.web;

import com.apress.projsp20.ch08.User;
import java.util.Collection;
import javax.servlet.ServletContext;
import javax.servlet.http.HttpServletRequest;
import javax.servlet.http.HttpServletResponse;

/** Action for subscription management. */
public class SubscriptionAction extends BaseAction {

  public SubscriptionAction(ServletContext mContext) throws Exception {
    super(mContext);
  }
```

The previous code shows the class declaration and the constructor. The class implements the `Action` interface, but like the other action classes, it does so by extending the `BaseAction` class.

```
  /** Process subscription action. */
  public void doGet(HttpServletRequest req, HttpServletResponse res) {
    try {
      String verb = req.getParameter("verb");
      String name = req.getParameter("name");
      String url = req.getParameter("url");
      String remove = req.getParameter("remove");

      // Perform action specified by request attribute 'verb'
      if ((verb != null) && verb.equals("Add")) {
        User user = (User) req.getSession().getAttribute("ag.user");
        mAggregator.addSubscription(user, name, url);
        req.setAttribute("processMessage", "Added subscription [" + name + "]");

      } else if ((remove != null) && verb != null && verb.equals("Remove")) {
        mAggregator.removeSubscription(remove);
        req.setAttribute("processMessage", "Removed subscription ["
                         + remove + "]");
      }
```

The first half of the `doGet()` method looks for a request parameter called `verb`. If that parameter equals "add" then the action attempts to add a subscription. If it equals "`remove`" then the action attempts to remove a subscription. If either of these actions succeeds, then a status message is put into the request as a request attribute using the name `processMessage`. If there is an exception, then an error message is put into the request using the name `processError`.

```
      // Load model into context for page
      User user = (User) req.getSession().getAttribute("ag.user");
      user = mAggregator.getUser(user.getName());
      req.setAttribute("user", user);

      Collection subs = user.getSubscriptions();
```

```
        req.setAttribute("subs", subs);

        // Forward to view
        req.getRequestDispatcher("subs.jsp").forward(req, res);

      } catch (Exception e) {
        String msg = "ERROR Processing form action [" +
                     e.getCause().getMessage() + "]";
        req.setAttribute("processError", msg);
        mContext.log(msg, e);
      }
    }
  }
```

The second half of the doGet() method places the objects required by the Manage Subscriptions page into the appropriate scope, in this case the appropriate scope is request scope. Finally, it uses the request dispatcher to forward the request to the subs.jsp page for display.

The subs.jsp Page

Now let's take a close look at the subs.jsp code. The code is shown here in its entirety, interspersed with comments:

```
<%@ page language="java" %>
<%@ taglib uri="/WEB-INF/c.tld" prefix="c"%>
```

You start the page by including the Core JSTL taglib from the file /WEB-INF/c.tld. After the familiar <html> and <body> tags, you emit a menu consisting of links to the other actions in the application news and login:

```
<!DOCTYPE HTML PUBLIC "-//w3c//dtd html 4.0 transitional//en">
<html>
<head>
   <style type="text/css"><jsp:include page="/ag.jsp" /></style>
   <title>Ag - Manage Subscriptions</title>
</head>
<body bgcolor="#FFFFFF">

<h1>Ag - Manage subscriptions</h1><hr />

<p>
   <b>Manage Subscriptions</b> |
   <a href="news">Read News</a> |
   <a href="login">Change User <c:out value="[${user.name}]" /></a>
</p>
```

To display status information, you start using some of the objects that were put into the request by the action object. The user object is a business layer object of type com.apress.projsp20.ch08.User. The processMessage and processError objects are strings that, if they exist, contain status or error information:

```
<c:if test="${ processMessage != '' }">
  <p><font color="green"><c:out value="${processMessage}" /></font></p>
</c:if>

<c:if test="${ processError != '' }">
  <p><font color="red"><c:out value="${processError}" /></font></p>
</c:if>
```

Next, you have the Add a new subscription form. This form has two fields called name and url. As you can see, this form posts to the subs action:

```
<h2>Add a new subscription</h2>

<form action="subs" method="POST">
      Name <input type="text" name="name" />
      Newsfeed URL <input type="text" name="url" size="40"/>
      <input type="submit" name="verb" value="Add"/>
</form>
```

Finally, there is the Subscriptions list. Here, you use a JSTL <c:forEach> tag to loop through the subs collection that was placed into the request by the SubscriptionAction object. For each com.apress.projsp20.ch08.Subscription object in the collection, you use the JSTL <c:url> tag to construct a remove link. The remove link is just a link back to the subs action, but with a request parameter named remove whose value is the ID of the subscription to be removed:

```
<h2>Subscriptions</h2>

<p>You are currently subscribed to these newsfeeds:</p>

<c:forEach var="sub" items="${subs}">

    [<c:url value="subs" var="url">
         <c:param name="verb" value="Remove"/>
         <c:param name="remove" value="${sub.id}"/>
     </c:url>
    <a href="<c:out value='${url}'/>">  Remove </a> ]

    <b>Name:</b> <c:out value="${sub.name}"/>
    <b>URL:</b> <c:out value="${sub.newsfeed.url}"/> <br/>

</c:forEach>

</body>
</html>
```

Castor: An Alternative to Hibernate

Castor is an open-source persistence framework like Hibernate. Although Castor has been around longer than Hibernate and may be more widely accepted, Hibernate has better documentation and that is why Hibernate was chosen for this chapter. However, the RSS Newsreader example program can be configured to use either Hibernate or Castor.

If you take a look at the example source code you'll find a class in the package `ag.persist.castor` named `CastorAggregatorDAO`. This class is an implementation of the `AggregregatorDAO` interface that uses Castor instead of Hibernate. If you would like to compare the Castor and Hibernate APIs, then compare the methods in `HibeAggregatorDAO` class to the methods in the `CastorAggregatorDAO` class. You'll find that, in some cases, the APIs are very similar. If you would like to configure the RSS Newsreader example to use Castor instead of Hibernate, then refer to the example `readme.txt` file for instructions on how to make the switch.

Summary

In this chapter you've learned the basics of using JDBC in a simple JSP application, the advantages of using an object-relational persistence framework, and how to design a sophisticated data access architecture.

With your new knowledge of basic JDBC concepts you should be able to add data access to simple JSP applications by using code on page or by using the JSTL SQL tags. You should be able to access any sort of database as long as it has a JDBC driver. In addition to that, you should also be able to configure a JDBC driver using either the old data manager approach or the newer JNDI Data Source technique.

With your new knowledge of the concepts behind O/R persistence frameworks, you should be able to work with any of the frameworks available from commercial software vendors and from open-source projects. Your knowledge of one-, two-, and three-layer architectures as well as your understanding of the flexibility-complexity trade-off will help you to choose the appropriate architecture for your next JSP application.

You've also taken a close look at a complete example JSP application, the RSS Newsreader, which illustrates how to use an O/R persistence framework within a modular three-layer architecture. You can use the RSS Newsreader example as a starting point for your own projects. The example relies only on open-source components that are free of charge and free for you to distribute with your own applications.

You should now have enough knowledge to evaluate database access technologies and to design and implement database access within your JSP applications.

9

Introduction to Filtering

Filtering is a standard feature of all Servlet 2.4-compliant containers. Since its introduction in the Servlet 2.3 specification, filters have found widespread use among J2EE developers. Some popular uses for filters include authentication, auditing, compression, encryption, and on-the-fly format transformation, to name but a few. For the very first time, an application-level programmer can tap into the request-processing pipeline of the container–in a portable, nonserver-specific manner. Servlet 2.4 further enhances container support of filters by providing filtering for dispatched requests–a feature that you'll be looking at in detail over this chapter and the next.

The unique positioning of filters in the processing pipeline, the relative ease with which they can be written and designed, and the versatile way these filters can be configured make them ideal design choices for a wide range of web application features that were formerly impossible, difficult, or awkward to implement.

In this chapter you'll learn the following:

- What a filter is, what it can do and why it's needed.
- How filters fit in with the rest of the servlets and JSP machinery.
- The container-managed life cycle of filters.
- The power of filter mapping.
- The importance of filter chaining.
- How `RequestDispatcher` interacts with the action of filters and filter chains.
- You'll gain hands-on experience working through the development procedure and the requirements for filters in the three complete code samples of filters.
- Finally, you'll conclude with some words of wisdom on filter design and coding, and you'll contrast filters with two common filter-like mechanisms–interceptors and valves–that often get confused with Servlet 2.4 filters.

The material covered in this chapter will provide a basic understanding of what Servlet 2.4 filtering is all about. You'll dive into the important concepts, and illustrate them with easy-to-understand code wherever necessary. We have purposely deferred advanced concepts in filtering, together with detailed design issues for more complex filters, to the next chapter.

This chapter is concept-heavy and code-light, while the next one will be both concept and code heavy as we provide insight into the design and coding of many typical filters. It will focus on the techniques in programming filters and will serve as a "cookbook" for the practicing JSP programmer, letting you incorporate filters into your favorite application recipes.

Common Filter Applications

Before you take a technical look at what a filter really is, let's start with a quick look at some applications of filters in the real world. Here is a short list of common filter applications, together with a description of the specific feature that makes filter appropriate for the application:

- Filters can **intercept request header information before it reaches the resource** in the processing pipeline and can therefore be used to create customized authentication schemes. For example, a filter can be written to authenticate a user against an external legacy system before allowing access to a resource. Having "wide open" exposure to all the request headers, filters can be written to perform sophisticated logging and auditing. Combining the use of filters with URL pattern-based filter mapping, you can have fine-grained control on the set of resources to protect or audit.

- Filters are also useful in **data transformation**. For example, you can use filters to present an XML document as HTML via an XSLT transform filter on the fly. Another form of data transformation filter might perform encryption or compression. For example, a filter can first detect if a user agent (browser) supports compressed data streams. If the browser can handle it, the filter can then compress the response from a resource on the fly.

- Filters can **preempt the serving of a particular resource** altogether, and generate their own response. One example could be a time-sensitive filter that blocks access to certain resources (such as an Internet proxy server) outside certain set hours. Yet another interesting application in this category is customized caching. A filter can maintain a cache of most frequently requested (static) resources based on prespecified criteria, and serve a cached copy instead of accessing the real resource whenever possible.

By strategically combining the request dispatcher and filters, web-application frameworks designers can create specialized filters that perform a service: such as form validation, data pre-fetch, and other functions. In these cases, filters can become fully fledged, bona fide resource processors in the request-processing pipeline.

The Big Picture of Filtering

The middle tier component of the J2EE architecture consists of an application server often fronted by a web server. These servers serve up web content and execute servlets and JSP pages in response to incoming client requests. Here we illustrate how client requests flow through a stand-alone application server such as Tomcat:

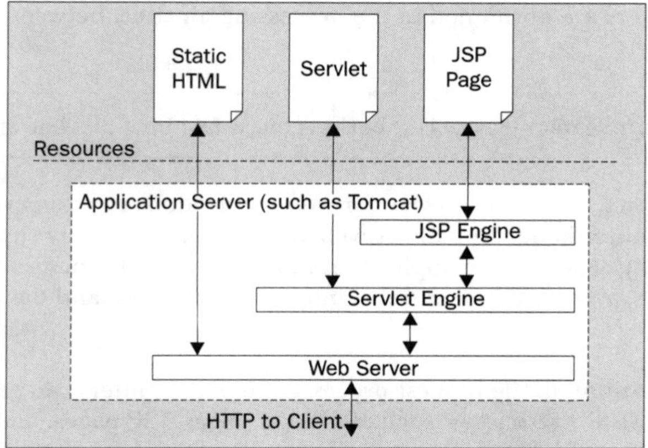

One way of looking at this diagram is to view it as a server for resource requests. In this view, you don't differentiate between static and dynamically generated resources. Therefore, the middle tier server becomes a server that serves one of three different types of resources based on incoming requests:

- Static content (HTML, images, and so on)
- A servlet
- A JSP (which may be considered a specialized case of a servlet)

> **This chapter and the next continually refer to this resource-based view of request processing. This is the way a filter designer looks at the container. Note that servlets and JSP pages are sometimes called "processing resources" since they can actively perform processing on a request.**

We can illustrate this simplified view of the middle-tier server, emphasizing the request and response flow and showing where filters fit into the picture:

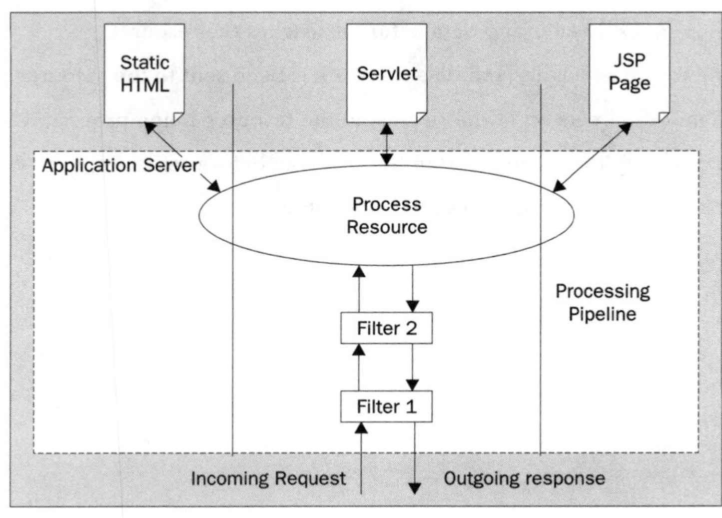

You can see that the filters are positioned in the **processing pipeline**, between the application server and the client.

> **A filter provides application-level access in the request-handling pipeline of the container.**

Before the advent of filters, there was no way for web applications to participate in the processing being performed along the request-handling path. A web application could only supply and define the resources that were being served. If an application required access to the processing pipeline, you had to resort to nonportable server-level extensions (interceptors, valves, and the like which you'll look at later).

Due to their strategic position in the request-processing pipeline, filters can easily handle the pre- and postprocessing of requests for resources (such as HTML pages, JSP pages, and servlets). The specialized construction of filters, as you'll discover later, will actually allow them to participate in the processing of the request or response throughout the processing path.

You also have the option of chaining several filters together dynamically to process each incoming request. This allows the filter deployer to combine the action of two or more filters together at deployment time. At runtime, the container uses filter mappings to determine the filter or filters that each request and response will pass through.

Filtering the Pipeline

Filters enable a developer to tap into the pipeline of request and response processing. A filter can do its work just before the resource is fetched (or executed in the case of dynamic output), and immediately after the resource is fetched and executed. It's even possible to inject custom behavior **while** the request is being processed by the resource.

More specifically, when you apply this notion to the HTTP-based request and response that is serviced by the middle-tier servers, filters can be used to do the following:

- Inspect the request header and data **before** it reaches the resource
- Inspect the response header and data **after** it has been sent to the resource
- Provide a modified version of the request to the resource being processed by the container
- Access and modify the response from the resource before returning it
- Stop a request from reaching a resource altogether

This behavior is depicted here:

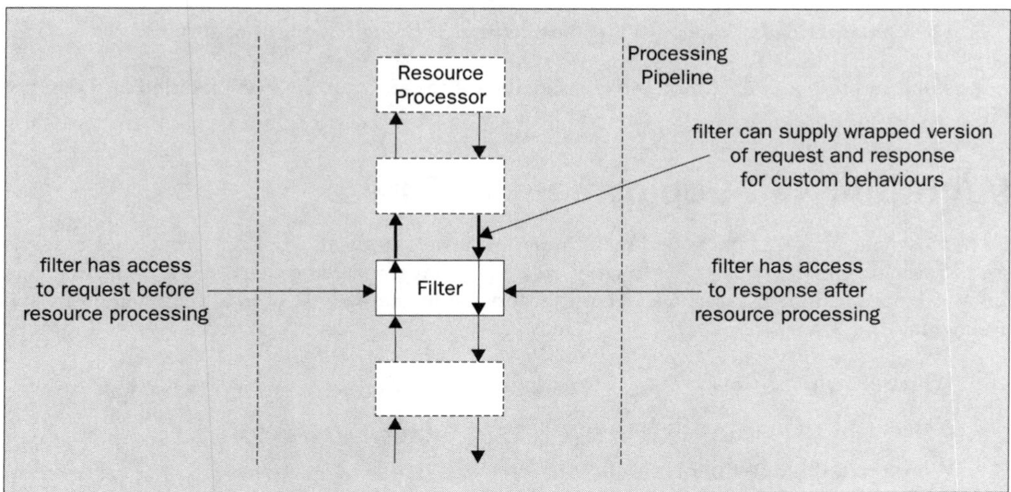

You'll examine filter implementations that perform each of these actions in this chapter and the next. You should note that code implemented in filters can have the same power, if not more, as the code implemented in the resources (in other words servlets and JSP pages) when it comes to request processing. In some ways, one can view the servlet engine and the JSP engine simply as end-point filters in this processing pipeline.

Filters in Depth

You'll now take a more concrete, technical look at what filters really are. First, you'll become intimately acquainted with the single interface that defines a filter: the `Filter` interface.

The Filter Interface

A filter is simply a class that implements the `javax.servlet.Filter` interface. Similar to the `javax.servlet.Servlet` interface, there are three life-cycle methods that a filter must implement:

```
public void init(FilterConfig config)throws ServletException
```

The container is responsible for setting the `FilterConfig` object before the `doFilter()` method (described next) is called for the first time. The `FilterConfig` object provides the initialization parameters for the filter and also allows access to the associated `ServletContext`.

```
public void doFilter(ServletRequest req, ServletResponse res, FilterChain chain)
        throws IOException, ServletException
```

The `doFilter()` method contains the logic of the filter. It's where almost all of the work of a filter is done. The container will call this method each time an applicable request is being handled. You'll see how to associate filters with types of requests in the next section.

```
public void destroy()
```

The container calls `destroy()` when the filter is being taken out of service.

Any class that implements this interface is officially a filter and can then be included as a component of a web application.

Configuration and Deployment of Filters

In the deployment phase, filters are an integral part of a web application, at the same level as servlets, JSP pages, or static resources. Filters are typically created by developers and delivered as bytecode classes within a web application. Typically, a web application's filters are configured at deployment by specifying the following:

- Which filter(s) to use
- Any initialization parameters to the filter
- Where to apply the filter
- The order in which multiple filters are chained together (if applicable)

All of the previous items are specified within the "standard" J2EE web application deployment descriptor (`web.xml`).

In this way, filters are configured and deployed in a similar fashion as servlets in a web application. The servlet container supporting filters will parse the following two types of filter-related declarations present within this file:

- **Filter definition:** Tells the container the textual name associated with the filter
- **Filter mapping:** Tells the container which resources the filter will be applied to

You'll cover these in more detail shortly when you examine filter definition and configuration.

Now that you know what a filter is, you need to take a look at the interactions that occur between a container and the filter and specifically the life cycle of a filter.

The Life Cycle of a Filter

Just like servlets and JSP pages, the container manages the life cycle of a filter. You'll learn the following in this section:

- When the container instantiates a filter
- How initialization parameters are passed into a filter
- How the container determines how many instances of the filter to create
- When the `doFilter()` method is called
- How filters can clean up on application shutdown

We can illustrate the life cycle of a filter using a block diagram to represent states that the filter can be in. In fact, there are only two explicit states:

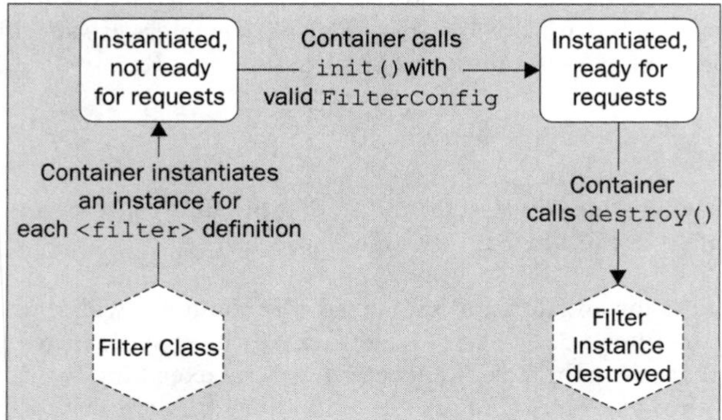

For each filter definition in the web application (as specified in web.xml), the container will create and initialize a filter instance. That single filter instance, with its initial parameters, will service all requests that correspond to its filter mapping specified within the deployment descriptor. The only exception to this occurs when the engine consists of multiple Java Virtual Machine (VM) servicing requests. In this case, the container mechanism will create one instance in each VM, thereby allowing all participating VMs to service filtered resources equally. The container will call destroy() when the web application is shut down.

The initialization must occur before the first request is mapped through the filter instance. During initialization, the container passes a FilterConfig object via the init() method of the javax.servlet.Filter interface.

The FilterConfig can be used by the filter to obtain initialization parameters of the filter, the textual name of the filter, or the ServletContext that the application is running under.

The FilterConfig Interface

The FilterConfig interface declares four methods:

```
public String getFilterName()
```

You can use the previous method to obtain the textual name of the filter, as defined in the web.xml deployment descriptor.

```
public String getInitParameter(String paramName)
```

The getInitParameter() method obtains the string value of a specific initialization parameter by name. Returns null if not found.

`public Enumeration getInitParameterNames()`

This method obtains a `java.util.Enumeration` consisting of all the names of the initialization parameters for this instance. These parameters are specified in the `web.xml` deployment descriptor within the `<filter>` definitions. Returns `null` if no parameter is set.

`public ServletContext getServletContext()`

This method obtains the `ServletContext` that the filter is executing within. This context is typically specified in the `server.xml` file of the server.

In all cases, once a filter is instantiated and initialized, the container will send all requests that the filter maps to through the filter's `doFilter()` method. For most static pages, JSP pages, and servlet resources, this means that many threads of execution may be executing the `doFilter()` method at the same time. Because of this, one must take care to write filters that are thread-safe.

The filter instance will be kept alive to process a request until the container (or a VM in the container) shuts down or the associated web application is undeployed. Before this happens, the container calls `destroy()` to give the filter a chance to perform any cleanup work that may be necessary.

Filter Definitions

Filters are defined for each web application. Their definition appears in the `web.xml` deployment descriptor inside the `<filter>` element. Each `<filter>` element must have a `<filter-name>` child element, a `<filter-class>` child element, and optionally one or more `<init-param>` child elements. Here is a brief description of each:

- `<filter-name>`
  Textual name to associate with the filter. Used in filter mapping. This is a mandatory element.
- `<filter-class>`
  The actual class that implements a filter. Should be a fully qualified class name with a package prefix. This is a mandatory element.
- `<init-param>`
  Specifies the initial parameters to supply to this instance of the filter. Contains `<param-name>` and `<param-value>` subelements, specifying the name and value of the parameter, respectively. Note that `<init-param>` is an optional child element of `<filter>`, which can also appear multiple times–once for each initialization parameter for the filter.

As an example, consider an audit filter that logs all access to certain specified resources. The `AuditFilter` class would be set up in the application's `web.xml` file as

```
<filter>
  <filter-name>Audit Filter</filter-name>
  <filter-class>filters.AuditFilter</filter-class>
</filter>
```

The previous segment associates the name `Audit Filter` with the filter implementation in `AuditFilter.class`.

You'll examine the details of the initial parameters of filters after you've looked at how filters are mapped to resources.

Filter Mapping

You've seen how to define a filter in the `web.xml` deployment descriptor file. Now let's move on to look at how to map a filter. Filter mapping allows you to specify resources that the filter will be applied to within our application on a by-request basis. Applying a filter to a resource literally means adding the filter to the processing pipeline when accessing that resource.

Filter mappings are XML-based entries, specified per web application within the `web.xml` file. The "mapping" that is performed is between the filter's textual name and one or more resources that the filter will be applied to. Since the filter mapping uses the filter's textual name, the corresponding `<filter>` element must precede a `<filter-mapping>` element within the `web.xml` file.

This is what the filter mapping for our audit filter might look like:

```
<filter-mapping>
  <filter-name>Visual Audit Filter</filter-name>
  <servlet-name>mylocate</servlet-name>
</filter-mapping>
```

Here, the mapping specifies that the filter declared as `Visual Audit Filter` (in a previous `<filter>` declaration) will be applied only when a request is received for the servlet resource called `mylocate`. It's assumed, of course, that the servlet name is defined within the same `web.xml` file, like this:

```
<servlet>
  <servlet-name>mylocate</servlet-name>
  <servlet-class>FindProd</servlet-class>
</servlet>
```

To map a filter to more than one resource, you need to either create multiple mapping entries or create a filter mapping that uses a URL pattern. Now let's take a look at how to make use of URL patterns.

Matching URL Patterns

The real power of filter mapping becomes evident when you use URL pattern matching. URL patterns allow users to apply a filter to a group of resources with some commonality in its URL. You can also use wildcard characters (such as `*`) within the URL to match multiple URLs. This is similar to the handling of the `<servlet-mapping>` element.

Depending on how the URL pattern is specified, you can apply a filter to a set of homogeneous resources (for instance, just servlets) or a set of heterogeneous resources (a mix of static HTML files, servlets, and JSP pages). Here are some samples of URL patterns:

URL Pattern	Matches
`/*`	Everything that is served by this web app, including static pages, servlets, and JSP pages
`/servlet/*`	All servlets (assuming all servlets are mapped under the `/servlet` path)
`/jsp/*.jsp`	All JSP pages located on the `/jsp` path
`/dept/accounting/*`	All resources in the accounting department branch of the web

The following is an example of filter mapping that uses a URL pattern:

```
<filter-mapping>
  <filter-name>Audit Filter</filter-name>
  <url-pattern>/*</url-pattern>
</filter-mapping>
```

This declaration applies the `Audit Filter` filter to all resources served by the application. Here's another example:

```
<filter-mapping>
  <filter-name>Stop Games Filter</filter-name>
  <url-pattern>/servlet/*</url-pattern>
</filter-mapping>
```

Assuming that servlets in this web application are mapped under the `/servlet` path, this filter mapping would apply the `Stop Games Filter` to all servlets in the application.

Inserting Filters into the Request Flow

Prior to Servlet 2.4, filters could only operate on requests as they originated from the client. However, many modern web applications and frameworks make extensive use of the ability to dispatch requests from one processing resource to another (servlet to servlet, servlet to JSP, JSP to servlet, JSP to JSP, and so on). The inability of filters to work in the processing pipeline between dispatch points handicapped earlier versions of servlet containers. This has changed with the Servlet 2.4 specification and Servlet 2.4-compliant containers, such as Tomcat 5, have full flexibility to insert filters into the request flow–even in-between programmatically dispatched points.

Filters and the Request Dispatcher

To better understand how the request dispatcher interacts with filters, you'll examine a series of figures depicting the request flow in a servlet container. First, you'll examine the action of Servlet 2.3-compliant containers. These containers support filters, but don't support interactions with the request dispatcher.

Servlet 2.3-Compliant Container Filtering

Given a filter mapping similar to the following:

```
<filter-mapping>
  <filter-name>F1</filter-name>
  <url-pattern>/*</url-pattern>
</filter-mapping>

<filter-mapping>
  <filter-name>F2</filter-name>
  <url-pattern>/*</url-pattern>
</filter-mapping>

<filter-mapping>
  <filter-name>F3</filter-name>
  <url-pattern>/*</url-pattern>
</filter-mapping>
```

The following illustrates the filtering that will be performed:

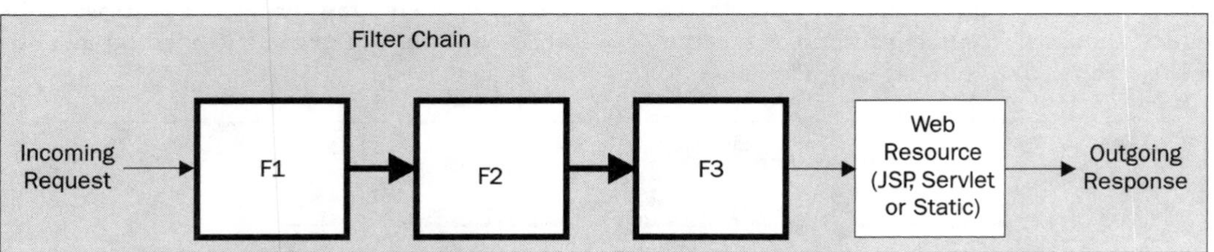

The previous figure is the conventional request flow. The incoming request is optionally passed through a mapped filter chain before being sent to the final processing resource–typically a servlet or JSP page. This is the typical filtered request data flow for older Servlet 2.3-compliant containers.

The next case you'll look at reveals what happens when you use the same filter mapping with two resources that are included by the main web resource (via `RequestDispatcher.include()` in a servlet or `include` directive in JSP) when using Servlet 2.3-compliant containers:

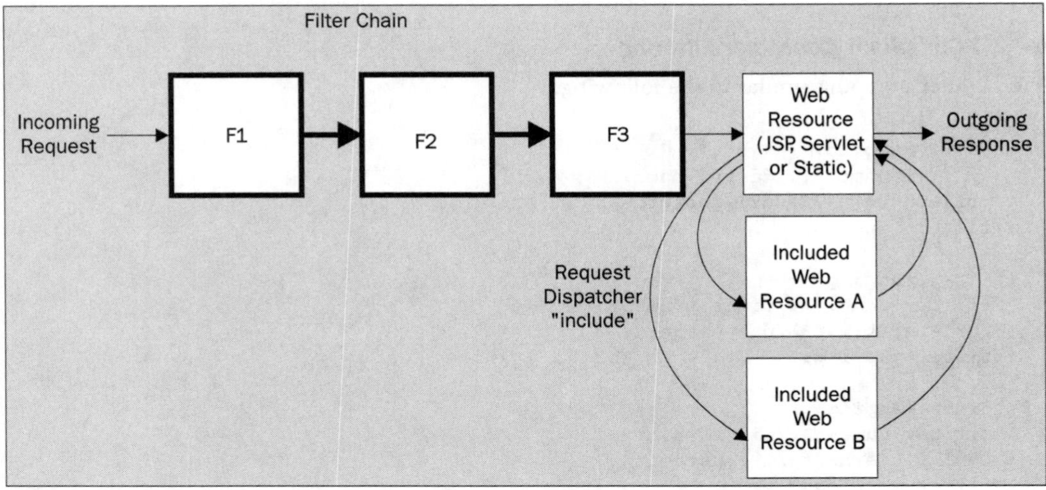

In other words, under Servlet 2.3-compliant container control, when the primary web resource uses the request dispatcher to include other processing resources, the included processing resource cannot be filtered. The same thing happens when the web resource uses the request dispatcher to forward the request to other processing resources (via the `RequestDispatcher.forward()` method in a servlet or the `<jsp:forward>` tag in JSP):

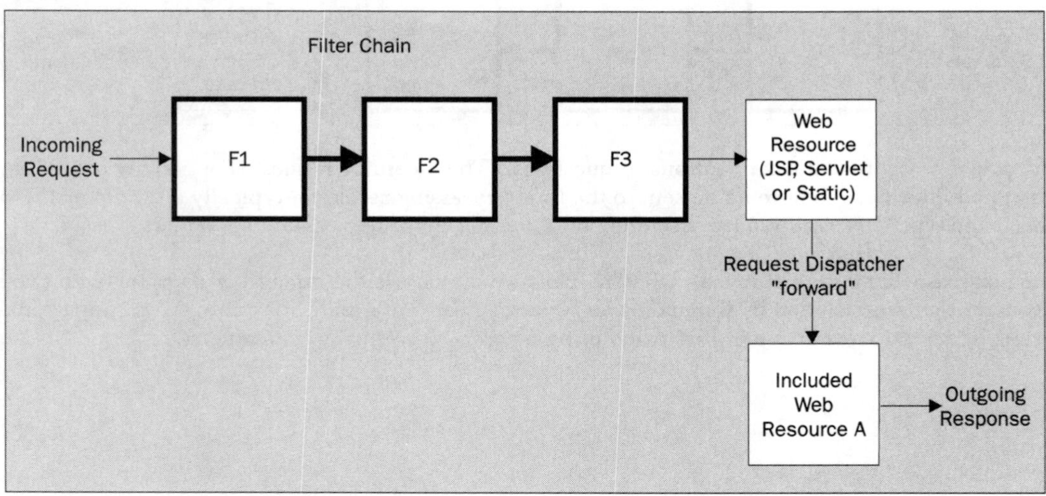

In Servlet 2.3 containers, the request *cannot* be filtered during the forward.

Servlet 2.4-Compliant Container Filtering

A Servlet 2.4-compliant container, such as Tomcat 5, allows filtering to occur with both the include and forward action of the request dispatcher. Consider the following Servlet 2.4 filter mapping:

```
<filter-mapping>
  <filter-name>F1</filter-name>
  <url-pattern>/*</url-pattern>
  <dispatcher>REQUEST</dispatcer>
  <dispatcher>INCLUDE</dispatcher>
</filter-mapping>

<filter-mapping>
  <filter-name>F2</filter-name>
  <url-pattern>/*</url-pattern>
  <dispatcher>REQUEST</dispatcer>
  <dispatcher>INCLUDE</dispatcher>
</filter-mapping>

<filter-mapping>
  <filter-name>F3</filter-name>
  <url-pattern>/*</url-pattern>
  <dispatcher>REQUEST</dispatcer>
  <dispatcher>INCLUDE</dispatcher>
</filter-mapping>
```

The new Servlet 2.4 `<dispatcher>` subelement of a filter mapping has allowed you to specify that filtering is to be performed during regular request dispatch as well as when the request dispatcher is called to include additional web resources. The following diagram illustrates the action of this filtering mapping on two included web resources (A and B):

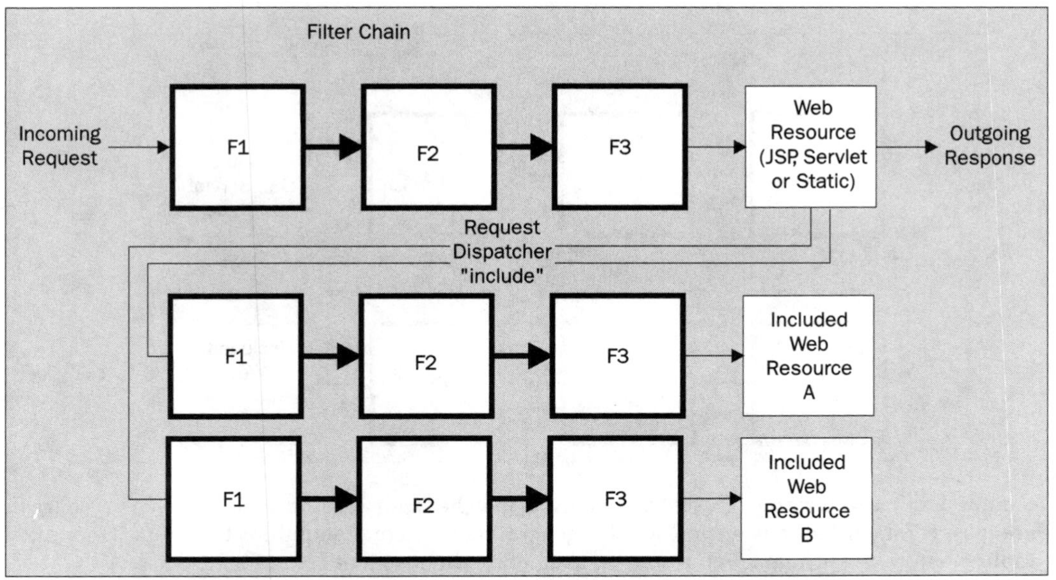

Now filters can be applied in-between the first processing resource and any included resources. For example, if the first JSP page included the output from multiple JSP pages or servlets, filters could be applied to each included resource.

Next, you'll look at the case when the request dispatcher forwards processing to a web resource. Consider the following filter mapping:

```
<filter-mapping>
  <filter-name>F1</filter-name>
  <url-pattern>/*</url-pattern>
  <dispatcher>REQUEST</dispatcher>
  <dispatcher>FORWARD</dispatcher>
</filter-mapping>

<filter-mapping>
  <filter-name>F2</filter-name>
  <url-pattern>/*</url-pattern>
  <dispatcher>REQUEST</dispatcher>
  <dispatcher>FORWARD</dispatcher>
</filter-mapping>

<filter-mapping>
  <filter-name>F3</filter-name>
  <url-pattern>/*</url-pattern>
  <dispatcher>REQUEST</dispatcher>
  <dispatcher>FORWARD</dispatcher>
</filter-mapping>
```

In this case, the filter chain will operate on both the standard request processing and the forwarded web resource processing:

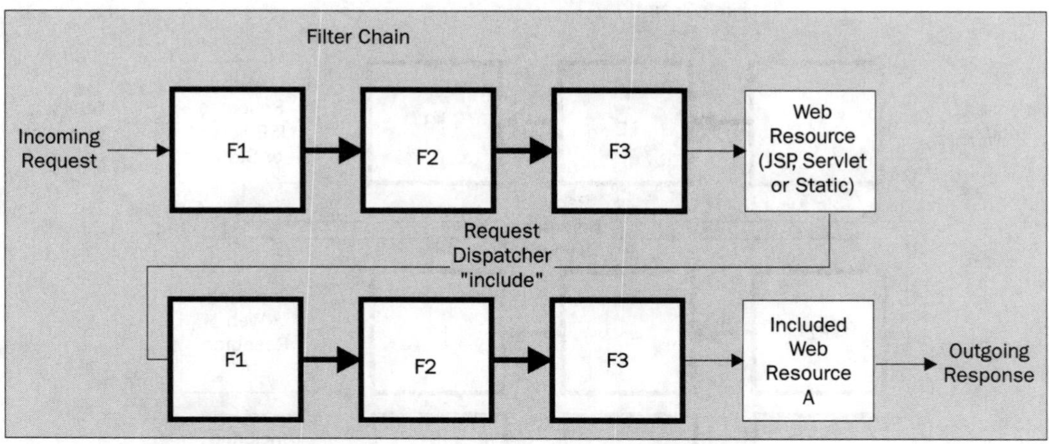

This time the first web resource uses the request dispatcher's forwarding capability. The resource that the request is forwarded to is responsible for generating the actual output for the client. Here, the filter is applied before the primary web resource, *and* before the resource being forwarded to.

Filter interactions with the dispatcher are controlled by the `<dispatcher>` subelement of `<filter-mapping>`, as you saw earlier. Let's take a more detailed look at this new subelement.

The <dispatcher> Element

The `<dispatcher>` subelement in `<filter-mapping>` is optional. If omitted, then the `<filter-mapping>` declaration is backwards compatible with Servlet 2.3 containers. In this case, the mapped filter will only work on the request level, and not when the request is dispatched via a request dispatcher. This compatibility mode is entirely equivalent to specifying the following Servlet 2.4 `<filter-mapping>` segment:

```
<filter-mapping>
  .
  .
  .
  <dispatcher>
    REQUEST
  </dispatcher>
</filter-mapping>
```

REQUEST, FORWARD, INCLUDE, or ERROR <dispatcher> Values

The allowed values inside a `<dispatcher>` element are tabulated as follows:

Value	Description
REQUEST	Enables filter mapping for incoming requests
FORWARD	Enables filter mapping for forwarded requests using the request dispatcher
INCLUDE	Enables filter mapping when the request dispatcher is used to include the output of multiple processing resources
ERROR	Enables filter mapping when the request is forwarded to an error-handling resource

For any single filter mapping, you can specify one or more of these values, thereby allowing fine-grained control over filter action. It enables you to apply some filters under all circumstances and selectively apply others using the `<filter-mapping>` elements.

Error Filters

In Servlet 2.4, the error-handling action is equivalent to a request dispatcher "forward" action to the error-handling resource. This enables specific filters to be configured to work in conjunction with the error-handling resource–they will be applied before the request reaches the actual error-handling resource.

Filter Chaining

Chaining is the action of passing a request through multiple filters in sequence before accessing the resource requested. For example, you may want an authentication filter on an XML-based resource that is also processed by an XSLT transformation filter. The good news is that all filters are inherently chainable. Unlike most other chaining mechanisms, however, filter chaining also means passing the response from the resource back through the chains of filters in the reverse order. This is a very important concept and is an essential component in the versatility of Servlet 2.4 filters.

The FilterChain Interface

The container and the filter implementation work together to ensure that every filter is chainable. This is done through a filter chain object that implements the `javax.servlet.FilterChain` interface. This filter chain object is passed into the core `doFilter()` method of a filter by the container. This object allows the filter to directly call the next filter in the chain after its own processing. The interface contains this `doFilter` method:

```
public void doFilter(ServletRequest req, ServletResponse res)
       throws IOException, ServletException
```

Calling this method invokes the `doFilter()` method of the next filter in the chain. If the filter is the very last filter in the chain, the actual resource processing will occur. This method doesn't return until all downstream filters have returned from their `doFilter()` calls.

All Filters Are Chainable

Compatibility with filter chaining is an integral requirement of every filter. Filter chaining is provided by a series of interactions between the container and the filter:

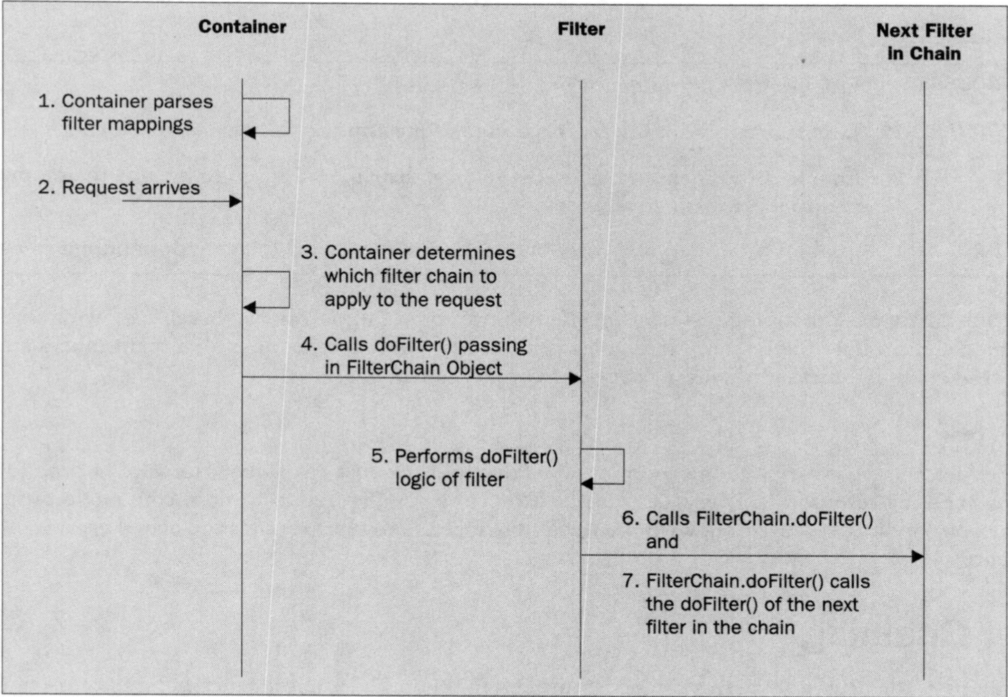

Here is an examination of what happens:

1. The container parses the filter mappings defined in the `web.xml` file of the application.
2. A request arrives, accessing a resource in the application.

3. The container determines the filter chain that will be applied to this request.

4. The container invokes the `doFilter()` method of the first filter in the chain, passing in the request, a response (holder), and a `FilterChain` object reference. The container loads the filter chain information into the `FilterChain` object that is passed in.

5. The filter performs its `doFilter()` logic.

6. The filter completes its filter logic and calls the `doFilter()` method of the `FilterChain` object reference, passing in the request and response. All filters are required to do this, since all filters are intrinsically chainable.

7. Logic in the `doFilter()` method of the `FilterChain` object calls the `doFilter()` method of the next filter chain to be called. Repeat from step 4 until the last filter in the chain has completed its work. The `FilterChain.doFilter()` call on the last filter in the chain will actually cause the access of the resource to occur.

Note that the mechanism of chaining is inherently different from most other conventional filtering or server extension mechanism (such as Apache modules and Microsoft's Internet Information Server and ISAPI).

Unique Properties of Filter Chaining

Note the following interesting properties regarding this approach to extending server functionality:

- Each of the `FilterChain.doFilter()` method calls are stacked upon one another, so program flow is blocked in a nested fashion across all the filters involved.
- After the actual resource access, the `FilterChain.doFilter()` method on the last filter on the chain returns. At this point, the response object is filled with header and content from the actual resource access. This last filter now has the freedom to examine and modify the response header and body contents at will. When it finishes, it will return from `doFilter()`. The next filter up the chain then gets a chance to process the response, and so on.
- The logic in a filter's `doFilter()` method has full access to the request in its incoming flow, prior to the `FilterChain.doFilter()` call. The logic in a filter's `doFilter()` method has full access to the response in its outgoing flow, after the `FilterChain.doFilter()` call.
- The local variables declared within the `doFilter()` method are consistent and available to both the incoming flow-processing logic and the outgoing flow-processing logic since the same thread will be executing both pieces of the logic.

These properties of the chaining mechanism are perhaps the hardest concepts to understand with respect to filters.

> **In essence, filter chaining is not a "call and forget" mechanism provided by container intervention, but rather a "nested call" mechanism assisted by the container.**

Of course, you must realize that even though filter chaining is built into every single filter, the processing logic within the filter is not obliged to chain to the next filter. In fact, this is one major application area for filters–blocking access to the actual resource. For example, an authorization filter can determine that the client isn't allowed to access a resource and generate a refusal response all on its own without further chaining.

A Fly in the Filtering Ointment

The avid reader (and indeed experienced JSP and servlet programmer) will realize that not all containers buffer their resource response in the response object after the resource completes processing. JSP pages and servlets may write and flush their output stream as the response is generated. This places dubious value on the processing window that each filter gets during a response's return trip through the filter chain. Although this processing window is perfect for resources and containers that *do* encapsulate the entire output in the response object, you must also deal with the reality of those that don't.

The way that filters deal with processing resources that generate output on the fly is via a customized wrapped-response object. That is, the filter will pass a specialized version of the response object to the `FilterChain.doFilter()` method instead of the one that it received as its invocation parameter.

This wrapped-response object can then provide its own version of `OutputStream` and `PrintWriter` for downstream filters or resources to work on. You'll delve into these "wrapped response" and "wrapped request" mechanisms in the next chapter.

When working with dispatched requests, note that wrapped-response and wrapped-request objects will be passed down the processing chain–except in the case of an error dispatch. In this case it's the original container-generated request and response that will be passed to the error-processing resource (and any filters that may be associated with it). This is necessary because of the asynchronous nature of the error-handling mechanism.

> **Custom wrapped-response and wrapped-request classes can be used to provide downstream processors with enhanced functionality (through special extended APIs) not available with the default response or request classes. In these cases, the filter and processing resources must cooperate with one another.**

Mapping Requests Through a Filter Chain

The order of `<filter-mapping>` elements in the `web.xml` file is significant. This is the order in which the container will build filter chains. Therefore, filter declarations within `web.xml` must be in the order that you want them to be applied to a resource–whenever filter chaining is used.

When the order of chaining for the same set of filters is changed, the final result can be completely different. This typically happens when a downstream filter depends on the result of an upstream filter for proper operations. For example, imagine a filter that transforms XML data from a resource to HTML using XSL Transformations (XSLT), and another filter that translates the HTML document via cascading stylesheets, level 1 (CSS1) (another stylesheet language, typically for HTML). If you place the XSLT filter first in the chain, the XML resource will be translated to HTML and subsequently formatted by the CSS1 filter. If you place the CSS1 filter first, however, it won't work on the XML data. As a result, only the XSLT transformation will be applied in this chain:

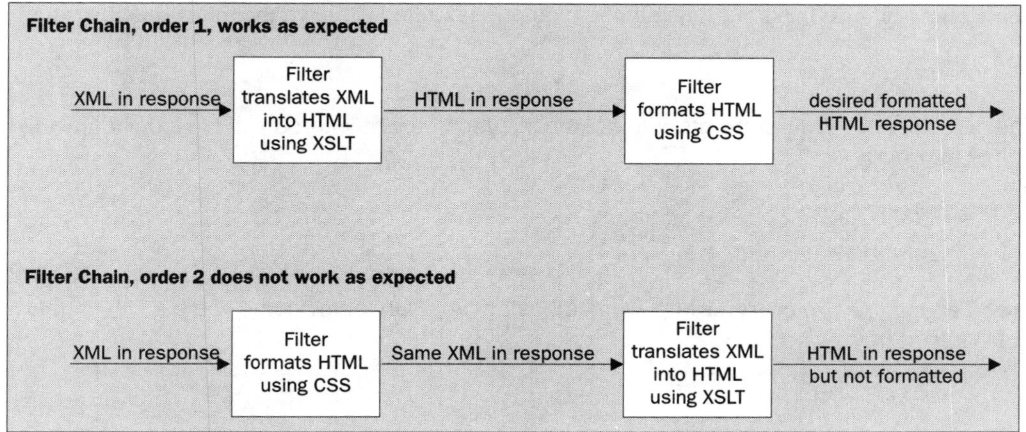

The filter application order has been determined by the order that the `<filter-mapping>` elements occur in the `web.xml` file. For example, consider the following set of filter mappings:

```
<filter-mapping>
  <filter-name>Audit Filter</filter-name>
  <url-pattern>/*</url-pattern>
</filter-mapping>

<filter-mapping>
  <filter-name>Authentication Filter</filter-name>
  <url-pattern>/*</url-pattern>
</filter-mapping>
```

In this case, both `Audit Filter` and `Authentication Filter` are mapped to all resources served by this server–both filters will be applied to all resources. The order of application will be `Audit Filter` followed by `Authentication Filter`. Remember that the order of chained filter execution on the incoming request is **down** the filter stack, while the order of chained filter execution on the outgoing path is **up** the filter stack.

Given an incoming request, the container will go through the list of filter mappings to determine which filter to apply on a per-request basis. For example, if you have the following filters mapping defined in order:

```
<filter-mapping>
  <filter-name>Audit Filter</filter-name>
  <url-pattern>/*</url-pattern>
</filter-mapping>

<filter-mapping>
  <filter-name>Authentication Filter</filter-name>
  <url-pattern>/servlet/*</url-pattern>
</filter-mapping>

<filter-mapping>
  <filter-name>Visual Audit Filter</filter-name>
  <servlet-name>mylocate</servlet-name>
</filter-mapping>
```

An incoming request for http://tomcathost/myapp/index.html will have the following filter applied:

- Audit Filter

While an incoming request for http://tomcathost/myapp/servlet/listprod will have the following filters applied in order:

- Audit Filter
- Authentication Filter

Finally, an incoming request for http://tomcathost/myapp/servlet/mylocate will have the following filters applied in order:

- Audit Filter
- Authentication Filter
- Visual Audit Filter

Initial Parameters for Filters

You can specify `<init-param>` as a child element of `<filter>` to provide initial parameters for the filter instance, as in the following snippet. This `web.xml` file segment controls the hours that a "games playing blocking" filter may operate:

```
<filter>
  <filter-name>Stop Games Filter</filter-name>
  <filter-class>filters.StopGamesFilter</filter-class>
  <init-param>
    <param-name>starthour</param-name>
    <param-value>10</param-value>
  </init-param>
  <init-param>
    <param-name>stophour</param-name>
    <param-value>11</param-value>
  </init-param>
</filter>
```

The container will associate the textual name `Stop Games Filter`, with the `StopGamesFilter` filter class. The parameters are accessed within the filter and instruct the filter to restrict gaming activities between 10 and 11 am by default. The `starthour` and `stophour` will be accessible within the filter via a call to the `FilterConfig` object:

```
String startHour = filterConfig.getInitParameter("starthour");
String stopHour = filterConfig.getInitParameter("stophour");
```

Initialization for Multiple Instances of Same Filter

Note that a container will create an instance of a filter for each `<filter>` definition encountered within the application. You can therefore define two instances of the same filter within the same web application–each with different initialization parameters. Of course, the two instances should have different textual names. For example, you may want to set up an instance of a `StopGamesFilter` to block access from 8 am to 10 pm for the Administration department, and another instance to block access from 8 am to 9 am to the Engineering department, because you don't want to discourage them from having breakfast:

```
<filter>
  <filter-name>Stop Games Filter For Administration Department</filter-name>
  <filter-class>filters.StopGamesFilter</filter-class>
  <init-param>
    <param-name>starthour</param-name>
    <param-value>8</param-value>
  </init-param>
  <init-param>
    <param-name>stophour</param-name>
    <param-value>22</param-value>
  </init-param>
</filter>

<filter>
  <filter-name>Stop Games Filter For Engineering Department</filter-name>
  <filter-class>filters.StopGamesFilter</filter-class>
  <init-param>
    <param-name>starthour</param-name>
    <param-value>8</param-value>
  </init-param>
  <init-param>
    <param-name>stophour</param-name>
    <param-value>9</param-value>
  </init-param>
</filter>
```

Interaction with the Filter Life Cycle

When working with filter initial parameters it's important to bear in mind that these parameters are only set once per filter instance: when the filter instance is first instantiated and before the arrival of the first filtered request. Subsequently, all new requests will be processed through the same filter instance–potentially simultaneously via multithreading. In containers that use multiple Java VMs, there will be one instance of a declared filter per container Java VM. You can use `filterConfig.getInitParameter()` to obtain the initial parameters' value from inside `doFilter()` when you need them. The handling of these initial parameters is very similar to servlets parameter handling. If a filter instance is removed from service by the container (say, due to server system load), the container is responsible for ensuring that a new instance is created and initialized to process any future requests. Such removals and reinstantiations should be completely transparent to the filter creator.

This concludes the initial conceptual coverage of filters, and it's time to get your hands on some code and implement your very own filter.

Hands-On Filter Development

In this section, you'll discover how to set up a development and testing environment for filters. You'll also code, configure, and test some simple filters in this environment.

The very first version of Tomcat to support the Servlet 2.4 specification is Tomcat 5. While the 4.x series of Tomcat supports filters, the new Servlet 2.4 functionality (namely support for filtering the request dispatcher pipeline) will only be available in the 5.x versions.

Our First Filter—SimpleFilter

Before coding your first filter, let's take a quick look at one additional interface that you'll be using within the filters sample.

The ServletContext Interface

Using the `getServletContext()` method on the `javax.servlet.FilterConfig` object, the filter can obtain a reference to the current `ServletContext` that it's executing under. There is a `ServletContext` for each running web application. Because of this single instance nature, the `ServletContext` is frequently used for sharing information globally.

Using this reference, the filter can utilize the context's logger service. It can also use this interface to attach arbitrary attributes to the context during runtime. An attribute can be an arbitrary object associated with a `String` name. Attaching attributes to `ServletContext` is a popular way to pass information between processing agents during runtime. For example, state information can be passed between filter instances using these attributes. Here are several of the most frequently used methods by filter writers, and you'll see them used in the sample filters later:

`Object getAttribute(String name)`

Obtains the value of a named attribute.

`void setAttribute(String name, Object object)`

Attaches a named attribute to the `ServletContext`.

`void removeAttribute(String name)`

Removes a previously attached attribute.

`Enumeration getAttributeNames()`

Returns a `java.util.Enumeration` consisting of the names of all the currently attached attributes.

You'll need to write to the log file in your filters, using the following methods of the `ServletContext` object:

```
void log(string msg)
```

Writes a string to the currently active logging facility associated with the context.

```
void log(String msg, Throwable throw)
```

Writes a string and a stack trace to the log.

Coding the Filter

Your first filter is called `SimpleFilter`. Place the source code to `SimpleFilter` in the `webapps/filters1/WEB-INF/classes/com/apress/projsp20/ch09/filters` directory. This simple filter won't do anything useful for now. It will simply make a log entry before calling `FilterChain.doFilter()` and another one right after it. Here is the source code:

```
package com.apress.projsp20.ch09.filters;
import java.io.*;
import javax.servlet.*;
import javax.servlet.http.*;
```

As mentioned before, all filters must implement the `javax.servlet.Filter` interface, and your `SimpleFilter` is no exception:

```
public final class SimpleFilter implements Filter {
  private FilterConfig filterConfig = null;
```

Here's the essential `doFilter()` method. Note the parameters: a `request`, `response`, and a `FilterChain` object:

```
  public void doFilter(ServletRequest request, ServletResponse response,
                       FilterChain chain)
         throws IOException, ServletException {
```

The container will set `filterConfig` to `null` before shutting itself down. `doFilter()` should never be called before `filterConfig` is set by the container via the `init()` call:

```
    if (filterConfig == null)
      throw new ServletException("FilterConfig not set before first request");
```

To write to the log, you access the `ServletContext` from `filterConfig` as provided by the container. The `log()` method will write a line using the logger set up earlier for this context:

```
    filterConfig.getServletContext().log("in SimpleFilter");
    chain.doFilter(request, response);
    filterConfig.getServletContext().log("Getting out of SimpleFilter");
  }
```

The rest of the methods are standard trivial implementations required for the Filter interface:

```
  public void init(FilterConfig filterConfig) {
    this.filterConfig = filterConfig;
  }

  public void destroy() {}

}
```

Declaring the Filter and Configuring Filter Mapping

Now, you need to add a <filter> element to the web.xml file, the deployment descriptor for your web application. Create the web.xml file and save it to webapps/filters1/WEB-INF. It starts with some required Servlet 2.4 XML preamble together with your filter definition:

```
<?xml version="1.0" encoding="UTF-8"?>
<web-app xmlns="http://java.sun.com/xml/ns/j2ee"
         xmlns:xsi="http://www.w3.org/2001/XMLSchema-instance"
         xsi:schemaLocation="http://java.sun.com/xml/ns/j2ee
         http://java.sun.com/xml/ns/j2ee/web-app_2_4.xsd"
         version="2.4">
  <display-name>ProJSP Example Filters</display-name>
  <distributable />

  <filter>
    <filter-name>Simple Filter</filter-name>
    <filter-class>com.apress.projsp20.ch09.filters.SimpleFilter</filter-class>
  </filter>
```

Add the following <filter-mapping> element immediately after the <filter> element so the filter is applied to every resource within this web application:

```
  <filter-mapping>
    <filter-name>Simple Filter</filter-name>
    <url-pattern>/*</url-pattern>
  </filter-mapping>

</web-app>
```

If you're working with the source-code distribution downloaded from the book's web site, these filter definitions and mappings are included but commented out. You should uncomment each set as appropriate as you progress through the example.

All that's left to do now is to create a resource to access. You'll create a static `index.html` page and place it in the `webapps/filters1` directory:

```
<html>
  <head></head>
  <body>
    <h1>Welcome to Filtering Demo Application!</h1>
  </body>
</html>
```

Testing the Filter

You're now ready to test the filter. Assuming that Tomcat isn't currently running, perform the following steps:

- Go to Tomcat's `logs` subdirectory and delete all files.
- Start Tomcat 5 using the `startup` script in the Tomcat `bin` directory.
- Start a browser and navigate to http://localhost:8080/filters1/.
- After the web page has loaded in the browser, shut down Tomcat using the `shutdown` script in the `bin` directory.

Your browser will display the following HTML resource page being served:

Now to check that the filter has actually worked for this simple static page, let's read the application log file found lurking in the Tomcat `logs` directory. The log file will be named after the current date, something like `localhost_log.2003-12-04.txt`.

Inside, you find the two log entries written by the filter, one in the processing window **before** the web page is accessed and the other one **after**:

```
.
.
.

2003-12-04 09:55:25 ContextListener: contextInitialized()
2003-12-04 09:55:25 SessionListener: contextInitialized()
2003-12-04 09:55:45 in SimpleFilter
2003-12-04 09:55:45 Getting out of SimpleFilter
```

Experimentation with Filter Chaining

Now you'll create a second filter called `SimpleFilter2`. Like `SimpleFilter`, it just logs each request in the log file. By chaining these filters together, it will give us some insight into the action of filter chaining under Tomcat 5. The name of the filter and class have changed from the original `SimpleFilter`:

```
import javax.servlet.*;
import javax.servlet.http.*;

public final class SimpleFilter2 implements Filter {
  private FilterConfig filterConfig = null;
```

Other than that, all you've done is change the output to the log to reflect the new filter name:

```
  .
  .
  .
  filterConfig.getServletContext().log("in SimpleFilter2");
  chain.doFilter(request, response);
  filterConfig.getServletContext().log("leaving SimpleFilter2");
  .
  .
  .
```

Additions to web.xml

You can now add the `SimpleFilter2` to the chain. Add the following entries to `web.xml`, making sure the ordering of `<filter-mapping>` entries is followed exactly:

```
  .
  .
  .

  <filter>
    <filter-name>Simple Filter</filter-name>
    <filter-class>com.apress.projsp20.ch09.filters.SimpleFilter</filter-class>
  </filter>
```

```
<filter>
  <filter-name>Simple Filter 2</filter-name>
  <filter-class>com.apress.projsp20.ch09.filters.SimpleFilter2</filter-class>
</filter>
<filter-mapping>
  <filter-name>Simple Filter</filter-name>
  <url-pattern>/*</url-pattern>
</filter-mapping>
<filter-mapping>
  <filter-name>Simple Filter 2</filter-name>
  <url-pattern>/*</url-pattern>
</filter-mapping>

.
.
.
```

This mapping now maps both `Simple Filter` and `Simple Filter 2` to all resources being accessed. This effectively chains them for all resources.

Clear the log files, start Tomcat, access the URL http://localhost:8080/filters1/ again, then shut down Tomcat.

Now, open the log file again and you should see something similar to the following:

```
.
.
.

2003-12-04 10:01:52 ContextListener: contextInitialized()
2003-12-04 10:01:52 SessionListener: contextInitialized()
2003-12-04 10:02:01 in SimpleFilter
2003-12-04 10:02:01 in SimpleFilter2
2003-12-04 10:02:01 Getting out of SimpleFilter2
2003-12-04 10:02:01 Getting out of SimpleFilter
```

Notice the nesting of the log entries, which clearly show that the filter-chaining mechanism consists of a series of nested `doFilter()` calls on the two participating filters. The chaining order is the order of `<filter-mapping>` declaration within the `web.xml` file, as expected.

Creating an AuditFilter

Both `SimpleFilter` and `SimpleFilter2` just write to the log, so now let's create the first filter that delivers a little extra. It will audit resource access by logging the time of access, the IP address of the client, the resource being accessed, and the time spent fulfilling the request.

For brevity, you'll only show the code for the `doFilter()` method from the `AuditFilter` class here; the rest of the code is no different from the previous filters. This filter takes advantage of the request object to obtain the required information. It also times the access to the resource by storing the system time before the `FilterChain.doFilter()` call. After the resource processing, it creates the log entry containing all the information:

```
public void doFilter(ServletRequest request, ServletResponse response,
                    FilterChain chain)
      throws IOException, ServletException {

  if (filterConfig == null)
    return;

  long startTime = System.currentTimeMillis();
  String remoteAddress = request.getRemoteAddr();
  String remoteHost = request.getRemoteHost();
  HttpServletRequest myReq = (HttpServletRequest) request;
  String reqURI = myReq.getRequestURI();
  chain.doFilter(request, response);
  filterConfig.getServletContext().log("User at IP " + remoteAddress + "("
                    + remoteHost + ") accessed resource " + reqURI
                    + " and used " + (System.currentTimeMillis() - startTime)
                    + " ms");
}
```

Note the ease with which this summary information is maintained and written, using local variables in the `doFilter()` method itself. Thanks to the nested call nature of filters, maintaining states across the two processing windows before and after resource access is simple.

Edit the `web.xml` file, removing the `<filter>` and `<filter-mapping>` entries for `SimpleFilter` and `SimpleFilter2` from our last example. Instead, add the following declarations to the file:

```
<filter>
  <filter-name>Audit Filter</filter-name>
  <filter-class>com.apress.projsp20.ch09.filters.AuditFilter</filter-class>
</filter>

<filter-mapping>
  <filter-name>Audit Filter</filter-name>
  <url-pattern>/*</url-pattern>
</filter-mapping>
```

To make things more interesting, you'll add a JSP resource and a servlet resource to do this test. They are located at `webapps/filters1/jsp/FindProd.jsp` and at `webapps/filters1/WEB-INF/classes/FindProd.class`, respectively.

The FindProd.jsp

This JSP page is very straightforward. It reads the `DEPT` request parameter using the expression language and displays it on screen:

```
<html>
<head></head>
<body>
```

```
    <h1>You have submitted as ${param.DEPT} department!</h1>
  </body>
  </html>
```

The FindProd Class

The servlet performs exactly the same function as the previous JSP:

```
import javax.servlet.*;
import javax.servlet.http.*;
import java.io.*;

public class FindProd extends HttpServlet {

  public void doGet(HttpServletRequest req, HttpServletResponse res)
         throws java.io.IOException {

    res.setContentType("text/html");
    PrintWriter out = res.getWriter();

    out.println("<html><head></head>");
    out.println("<body><h1>You have called from the " +
                req.getParameter("DEPT"));
    out.println(" department!</h1></body></html>");

    out.close();
  }
}
```

Additions to web.xml

Add the following servlet declaration to the `web.xml` file as well:

```
  <servlet>
    <servlet-name>mylocate</servlet-name>
    <servlet-class>FindProd</servlet-class>
  </servlet>

  <servlet-mapping>
    <servlet-name>mylocate</servlet-name>
   <url-pattern>/servlet/mylocate</url-pattern>
  </servlet-mapping>
```

Now we're ready to test. Follow these steps:

1. Clear out the Tomcat `logs` directory.

2. Start Tomcat.

3. Navigate to http://localhost:8080/filters1/FindProd.jsp?DEPT=Engineering.

4. Next, go to http://localhost:8080/filters1/ FindProd.jsp?DEPT=Accounting.

5. Open http://localhost:8080/filters1/.

6. Here, let's try a servlet resource instead of a JSP page, so navigate to http://localhost:8080/filters1/servlet/mylocate?DEPT=Engineering.

7. Access the URL http://localhost:8080/filters1/servlet/mylocate?DEPT=Accounting.

8. Shut down Tomcat.

Now, if you examine the log file, you'll see the audit trail left by AuditFilter:

```
2003-12-04 10:10:23 ContextListener: contextInitialized()
2003-12-04 10:11:30 SessionListener: contextInitialized()
2003-12-04 10:11:30 User at IP 127.0.0.1(127.0.0.1) accessed resource
/filters1/FindProd.jsp and used 255 ms
2003-12-04 10:11:55 User at IP 127.0.0.1(127.0.0.1) accessed resource
/filters1/FindProd.jsp and used 10 ms
2003-12-04 10:12:06 User at IP 127.0.0.1(127.0.0.1) accessed resource /filters1/
and used 10 ms
2003-12-04 10:12:30 mylocate: init
2003-12-04 10:12:30 User at IP 127.0.0.1(127.0.0.1) accessed resource
/filters1/servlet/mylocate and used 20 ms
2003-12-04 10:12:41 User at IP 127.0.0.1(127.0.0.1) accessed resource
/filters1/servlet/mylocate and used 0 ms
```

You can glean some very interesting data from this. The initial compile and load of the JSP page took 255 milliseconds to complete, while subsequent access required negligible time. You can also see that the initial servlet access took about 20 milliseconds, while subsequent access to the same instance again required negligible time.

If you want to experiment with URL patterns, repeat the experiment with the following <filter-mapping> element in the web.xml file instead:

```
<filter-mapping>
  <filter-name>Audit Filter</filter-name>
  <url-pattern>/servlet/*</url-pattern>
</filter-mapping>
```

Try the experiment again, and you'll see that now only access to the servlet resource will be logged.

Writing this potentially useful auditing filter has been quite painless. You'll find in general that, once you're familiar with the model of operation of the Servlet 2.4 filter, writing highly functional filters can be quite a straightforward task.

Other Filterlike Technologies

Prior to Servlet 2.4 filters, there had been many server extension mechanisms based on similar concepts to filtering. In fact, **interceptors** form a key server-extension mechanism that is used quite heavily in many Tomcat 3.x-based containers. However, there are fundamental differences between filters and these mechanisms: **They aren't the same**. The following section will briefly describe the essential differences between the technologies.

Filters Aren't Tomcat 3.x Interceptors

Interceptors are a server-level extension mechanism for servers that support them. It's not an application-level technology. Being a server-extension technology, it's specific to Tomcat. Furthermore, effects of interceptors are typically global to the server–filter effects are local to the web application that the filters belong to.

The general architecture of interceptors and filters are completely different. Interceptors are "hooked in" modules that are called at specified points in the processing pipeline by the container. There are different types of interceptors for different access points. Filters, however, rely on nested chain calling (and custom wrapping of the request or response) to get their work done. There is only one "type" of filter. All filters implement the same `javax.servlet.Filter` interface.

Filters Aren't Valves

Valves are a system-level mechanism used extensively within the design of Tomcat 4.x and 5.x. On an architectural level, they're almost identical to filters. But that's where the similarity ends.

Valves are Tomcat-specific and typically aren't portable to other Servlet 2.4-compatible servers. On the other hand, filters are portable. Valves are also internal to the Tomcat server and have privileged access to many structures and resources that application-level filters cannot access.

Filter Design Best Practices

There are a few rules of thumb that you should consider when designing and writing filters. Some of these may give you novel ideas on how you can use filters in your own applications, while others may save you significant debugging time during the development cycle. In the next section, we present an encapsulation of five such guidelines. You'll see several more in the next chapter when you explore the design and coding of more involved filters.

Make Code Thread-Safe

This cannot be stressed enough. Remember that there is typically only one instance of a filter per Java VM (unless the same filter is declared multiple times with different names or initial parameters). This makes it inevitable that that the `doFilter()` method will be entered by many threads simultaneously, so your filter code must be thread-safe. This means the following:

- Local variables in `doFilter()` may be used freely (except for complex objects that may hold references to instance variables, in which case the next bullet applies).

- Instance variables in the filter class scope should be read-only, or the scope's access must be synchronized.
- Beware of calling methods that may modify instance variables indirectly or outside of synchronization.

The following figure provides a spatial representation of this approach:

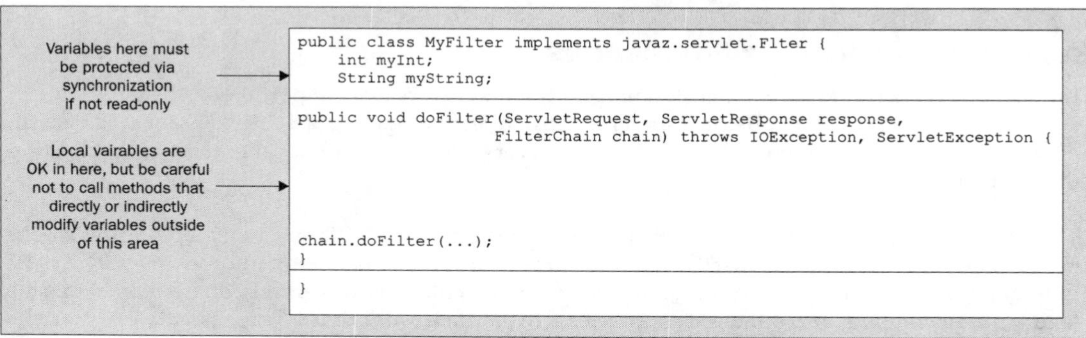

Handle State Carefully

State information can be readily maintained via local variables in `doFilter()`. The prerequest and postresponse processing window within the `doFilter()` method has full access to this state information. To pass state information between filters on the same chain, you can associate attributes with the `ServletContext`, returned by the `FilterConfig.getServletContext()` method. The reason why `ServletContext` attributes can be used rather than request attributes will be clear when you examine request and response wrapping in the next chapter.

You should note that, in general, filters should not maintain state across multiple requests since the very same instance of a filter can service a very large number of requests in a given period. Logic requiring this degree of state maintenance is best served by servlets or JSP pages.

Think of Filters as In-Series Resource Processors

When designing web applications that follow the well-documented Model-View-Controller (MVC) design pattern or model 2 JSP architecture, consider the use of filters as in-series resource processors in conjunction with the request dispatcher.

For example, in a push-model web application, a filter may perform part of the controller's responsibility by fetching data from the model and attaching it to the request in the form of attributes for the view component to display.

Another interesting example is form processing. When a form is submitted and before the controller component is called, a filter can be used to perform data validation on the incoming form data.

Filter Reuse via Chaining

Break up your filter-processing work into reusable, independent, chainable filters whenever possible. This will enhance the reuse potential of the filters and also allow users to use your filters in new and innovative ways.

Avoid Duplicating System Features

Many problems addressed by filters can be solved instead via configuration of standard server features. This is especially true with Tomcat 5, where logging, authentication, authorization, and fine-grained access control support is built-in. Encrypted sessions via transport-level security (TLS), more commonly known as secured sockets (HTTPs), are also supported natively.

You should avoid duplicating system features in your filter design: Investigate all the server features first, looking to see if your filter application can be accomplished by simple server configuration. Write your filter only after you have determined that it's the only appropriate solution, given project requirements and constraints.

Summary

In this chapter, you've been introduced to the filtering feature of Servlet 2.4 containers (such as Tomcat 5). You've discovered the following:

- Filters enable web application programmers to tap into the request processing pipeline of the container.
- Filters are packaged code components in a web application, at the same level as servlets and JSP pages.
- Filters are deployed in the same way as servlets and JSP pages, through the deployment descriptor for the application.
- The filter has access to incoming requests before they reach the final resource and to the outgoing response immediately after the resource processing.
- Filters can also substitute their own version of the request and response (typically wrapped) for consumption of the resource.
- Symbiotic, well-defined interactions between the request dispatcher and filters enable one to create filters that act as in-series processors for request-switching web applications and application frameworks such as Apache's Struts and Turbine.

You've explored the life cycle of a filter, as managed by the container. You've seen how to define filters in deployment descriptors, how to supply initialization data to a filter instance, how to specify its interaction with the request dispatcher, and how to define filter mappings. You've noted how Servlet 2.3 is unable to filter dispatched requests and learned how Servlet 2.4 has remedied the situation.

Next, we discussed the very important concept of filter chaining. You learned that Servlet 2.4 filter chaining actually makes use of a nested call mechanism, unlike most other filtering schemes. One major advantage of this approach is the preservation of thread state throughout the filter invocation.

Working with actual code, you've created two simple filters and practiced deploying them. You've also experimented with filter chaining and observed its effect using log files. You've also created a useful audit filter and learned how easily it can be constructed.

Finally, you provided some guidelines to follow when programming filters and contrasted two other filterlike mechanisms (valves and interceptors)–noting the differences in approach and level of abstraction to that of filters.

This chapter has hopefully provided a sound foundation to proceed on to the next chapter, where you'll get code-intensive and explore a variety of filter design. Along the way, you'll create wrapped requests and responses to offer customized dynamic behavior throughout the request-processing pipeline.

10

Advanced Filtering Techniques

In the previous chapter we discussed what Servlet 2.4 filtering involves. Filtering offers the ability to intercept and process requests and responses before and after processing by the underlying resource (servlet, JSP, or whatever). Filters can add great value to many J2EE web applications by transforming the behavior of existing servlets, JSP pages, or even static pages.

Chaining multiple filters together combines their transformations, offering the application developer or deployer great flexibility when configuring the final behavior of a web application. Now that you've built and configured some simple filters in the last chapter to experiment with the basic concepts, you'll turn your attention to the more advanced techniques involved in applied filter programming.

This chapter is a cookbook for the application of filters. Our goal is to deliver sample code that covers a broad spectrum of the most frequently applied areas for filters. We've designed each sample to illustrate several subtleties or important points to consider when you program each type of filter.

Filters for Five Problem Domains

You'll build, test, and deploy a total of five filters in this chapter:

Application Domain	Filter Sample
Auditing	A visual auditing filter that includes audit information inline with every resource that it services
Authorization	A filter that disallows access to the server during certain hours of the day
Adapter (legacy)	An adapter filter that allows newly formatted queries to work with a legacy set of resources

Table continued on following page

Application Domain	Filter Sample
Authentication	An ad hoc authentication filter that can add simple login protection to any (group of) resources
Pipeline processing	A data processing filter that takes advantage of the request flow along the processing pipeline

First we present the functionality and design considerations for each filter. Then we provide the actual code, annotated with detailed comments highlighting the design issues addressed. Finally, we give detailed deployment, configuration, and testing information for each filter.

Most filter applications fall into one or more of the five problem domains, so the code we present serves as a base for your own filter development. Furthermore, during the development of several of this chapter's filters, we pause to cover the main techniques used in filter programming. These are the very same "filter application patterns" that you'll see again and again when designing filters–they're an encapsulation of the type of work that a filter can perform, on a conceptual level. An understanding of these patterns can prove helpful in your own experimentation and application of Servlet 2.4 filters.

The techniques we cover and the filter examples that they appear in are listed here:

Technique Illustrated	Filter
Transforming incoming request headers	Adapter filter
Stopping downstream request flow	Authorization filter Authentication filter
Generating response	Authorization filter Authentication filter
Transforming outgoing response content	Auditing filter
Dynamically adapting filter behavior based on incoming requests	Authentication filter
Wrapping request objects	Adapter filter
Wrapping response objects	Auditing filter
Adding to or modifying the attributes of a request in a processing pipeline	Pipeline processing filters Authentication filter
Interacting with the request dispatcher's `include()` and `forward()` actions	Pipeline processing filters

Be warned that this chapter is extremely code intensive. By the end of the chapter, you'll be fluent in Servlet 2.4 filter concepts, design, and programming. To boot, you'll have an extensive code framework and library to start your filter projects immediately.

Setting Up the Development Environment

Most of the code for the filters in this chapter is in a package called `com.apress.projsp20.ch10`. The classes are located as usual under the `webapps\filters2\WEB-INF\classes` directory.

Now, in the `filters2` application's `web.xml` file, add this servlet definition:

```
<?xml version="1.0" encoding="UTF-8"?>
<web-app xmlns="http://java.sun.com/xml/ns/j2ee"
         xmlns:xsi="http://www.w3.org/2001/XMLSchema-instance"
         xsi:schemaLocation="http://java.sun.com/xml/ns/j2ee/web-app_2_4.xsd"
         version="2.4">

  <display-name>Pro JSP Example Filters 2</display-name>
  <distributable />

  <servlet>
    <servlet-name>findprod</servlet-name>
    <servlet-class>FindProd</servlet-class>
  </servlet>

  <servlet-mapping>
    <servlet-name>findprod</servlet-name>
    <url-pattern>/servlet/findprod</url-pattern>
  </servlet-mapping>
</web-app>
```

The FindProd Servlet

Here you create a simple `FindProd` servlet, which you may have already seen in the previous chapter. This servlet emulates the legacy resource being accessed by a user. It's hard-coded to display the `DEPT` parameter (department information). Later on, you'll create a filter that automatically provides this parameter even though the client system accessing the legacy resource doesn't know how to supply it. Save this code in the `filters2`'s `classes` directory (under `WEB-INF`):

```
import javax.servlet.*;
import javax.servlet.http.*;
import java.io.*;

public class FindProd extends HttpServlet {
  public void doGet(HttpServletRequest req, HttpServletResponse res)
      throws java.io.IOException {
    res.setContentType("text/html");
    PrintWriter out = res.getWriter();

    out.println("<html><head></head>");
    out.println("<body><h1>You have called from the "
           + req.getParameter("DEPT"));
    out.println(" department!</h1></body></html>");

    out.close();
  }
}
```

The FindProd JSP Page

You can find a similar JSP page in `webapps\filters2\jsp\FindProd.jsp` (again, you may have seen this file in the previous chapter). This trivial JSP page is used to test the handling of JSP resources:

```
<html>
  <head></head>
  <body>
    <h1>You have submitted as the ${param.DEPT} department!</h1>
  </body>
</html>
```

Like the `FindProd` servlet, this JSP page prints out a message containing the department name using EL and expects the client to supply the `DEPT` parameter. This completes your preparation for filter testing.

A Brief Word on Terminology

Before you go any further, take a look at this figure:

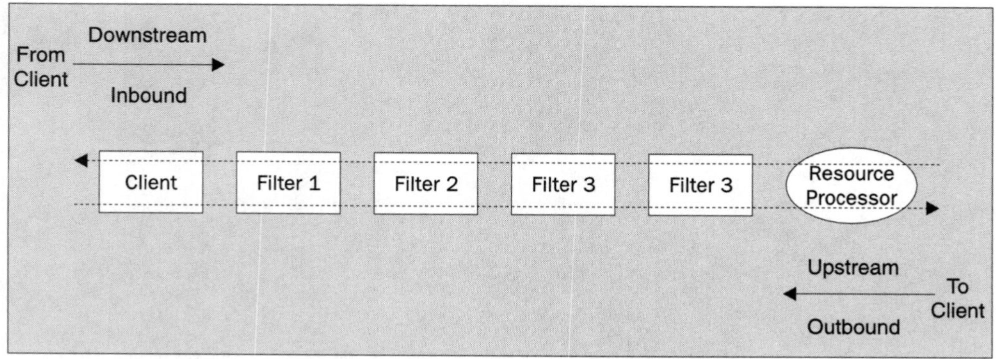

We clarify some of the terminology that is used in this diagram throughout this chapter. The request originates from the client and goes through a **chain of filters** before reaching the final **resource processor** in this figure. First, the request travels from the client, through the first filter, through the second filter, and so on. We call this the **downstream**, or **inbound**, trip. The downstream trip is always toward the final goal: the resource processor. Once the resource processor has finished with the request, a response then will travel **upstream**, or **outbound**, back through all the filters and onward to the client. Upstream trips are always away from the resource processor and toward the client.

New to Servlet 2.4 and JSP 2.0 is the ability of filters to participate in the forward and include redirection requests of the request dispatcher. This is a very important advance architecturally. We discuss this new feature in depth in the last section of this chapter.

Filter 1: A Visual Auditing Filter

The first filter that you'll tackle is similar to the `AuditFilter` that you developed toward the end of the previous chapter. Like the `AuditFilter`, it will be deployed using the following `web.xml` fragment:

```
<filter>
  <filter-name>VisAudit Filter</filter-name>
  <filter-class>com.apress.projsp20.ch10.VisAuditFilter</filter-class>
</filter>

<filter-mapping>
  <filter-name>VisAudit Filter</filter-name>
  <url-pattern>/*</url-pattern>
</filter-mapping>
```

Unlike the previous `AuditFilter`, instead of quietly writing the audit information to the log, this filter will include the auditing information in the output of the resource. The screen shot in the section "Filter Configuration and Testing" shows an example of this filter being applied to a web page. Note the audit information at the bottom of the page–this information is inserted by the filter, and it changes with every access to the page.

Wrapping the Response Object for Content Modification

The crucial concept to understand from this example is **custom response wrapping**. This is also one of the most difficult techniques to grasp for novice Servlet 2.4 programmers. In custom response wrapping, you provide your own implementation of a custom response object to downstream filters and resources, with the response object that was passed to you wrapped inside. This means that you can modify the response content (inside your custom response wrapper object) after the resource has completed processing the request. The following figure illustrates the interception:

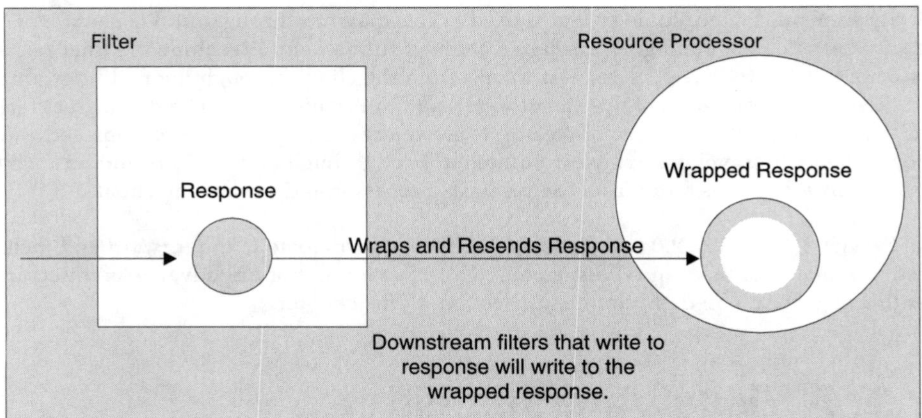

In the `VisAuditFilter` example, you'll use your own custom `OutputStream` class (`VisAuditOutputStream`) and a wrapped response class (`VisAuditResponseWrapper`). The classes you'll use and their relationships are shown in the following class diagram:

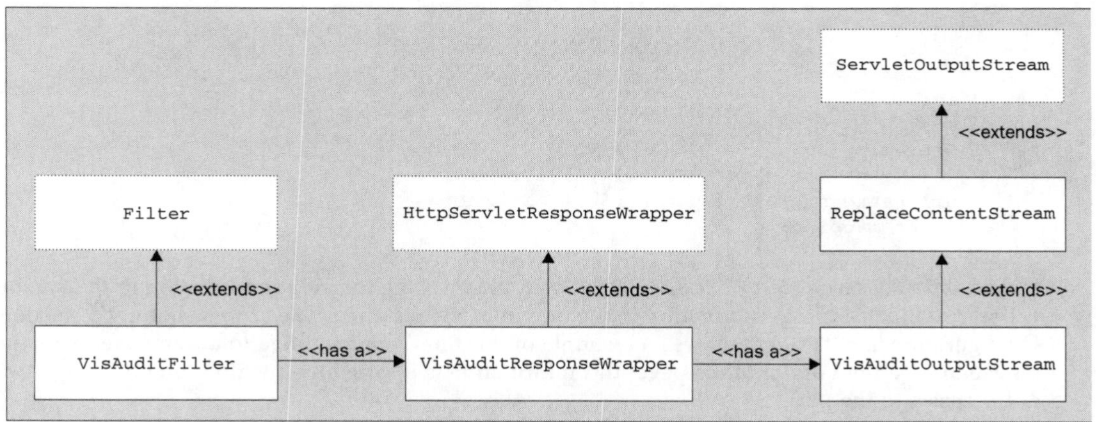

Together, these classes will intercept the output of the web resource added to the auditing information footer. The following interaction diagram shows how this interception is carried out:

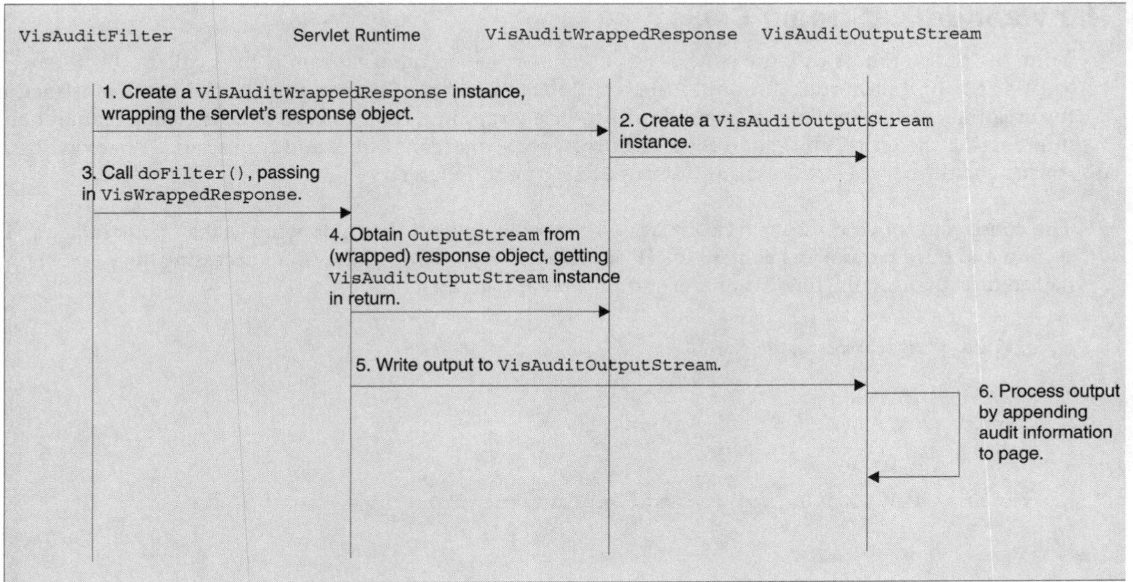

Note that you must wrap the response with your own custom version during the request's inbound trip, before you call `Chain.doFilter()`. In fact, the following happens:

1. The filter supplies a custom wrapped version of the response to downstream filters when it calls the `Chain.doFilter()` method.

2. This custom wrapped response object hands down a custom `OutputStream` or `PrintWriter` object that is actually a byte array managed in your own code.

3. When downstream filters, or the resource processor, write to your custom `OutputStream` or `PrintWriter`, you're buffering all the output.

4. When downstream filters, or the resource processor, flush or close your custom `OutputStream` or `PrintWriter`, you examine the buffered output for the closing `</body>` tag and insert your auditing information just before it (if found).

Any downstream filters on the inbound trip (including the actual resource processor) are actually writing their data into your custom stream. Of course, it's possible that some other downstream filters may perform further wrapping of your custom response with one of their own. The filter chaining mechanism supports this successive nested wrapping of response (and requests) as a means of multiple layers of content interception. In this case, your custom response wrapper object will add the "Big Brother is watching you" visual audit message to all resources that are accessed through this filter. End users will see this auditing message at the bottom of every resource that they access and won't be able to tell that the output originates from a filter.

Now let's examine the source code for this filter.

The VisAuditOutStream Class

Your custom stream is called `VisAuditOutStream`, which inherits from a class called `ReplaceContentOutputStream`. `ReplaceContentOutputStream` is a utility library (abstract) class for creating custom streams to be used in response wrapping. It takes care of buffer management and intercepting the write, close, and flush calls by the downstream filters and processors. We examine the source code for `ReplaceContentOutputStream` a little later.

The constructor of your `VisAuditOutStream` takes the output stream to wrap as the first parameter. The second and third parameters contain the IP address and host name of the client accessing the page, and are passed directly from the filter when the custom stream is created:

```
package com.apress.projsp20.ch10;

import java.io.*;
import javax.servlet.*;
import javax.servlet.http.*;

class VisAuditOutStream extends ReplaceContentOutputStream {
  String Addr;
  String Host;

  public VisAuditOutStream(OutputStream outStream, String inAddr,
                           String inHost) {
    super(outStream);
    Addr = inAddr;
    Host = inHost;
  }
```

The single method that a child class must override, because the method is declared abstract in `ReplaceContentOutputStream`, is the `replaceContent()` method. This method takes a byte array as input–this is the content that is written into the buffer by the downstream filters and processors. The return value is another byte array, which is the content that you wish to write to the client. In this case, you look for the </body> closing tag:

```
  public byte [] replaceContent(byte [] inBytes) {
    String retVal = "";
    String firstPart = "";

    String tpString = new String(inBytes);
    String srchString = (new String(inBytes)).toLowerCase();

    int endBody = srchString.indexOf("</body>");
```

Once you've found the </body> tag, you can insert your auditing information just before the end of the document:

```
    if (endBody != -1) {
      firstPart = tpString.substring(0, endBody);
      retVal = firstPart + "<br><small><i>Big Brother is watching you. " +
               "You have accessed our page from " + Addr +
```

```
                  " and on a machine called " + Host + "</i></small></br>" +
                  tpString.substring(endBody);

      } else {
        retVal = tpString;
      }

      return retVal.getBytes();
    }
  }
```

The Customized Response Wrapper Class

The next class you'll define is the response wrapper called `VisAuditResponseWrapper`. It conveniently inherits from `javax.servlet.http.HttpServletResponseWrapper`. This wrapper class allows you to readily wrap any `HttpServletResponse` object and override only the methods that you want to customize. The `HttpServletResponseWrapper` class has provided trivial implementations of all the methods of the `HttpServletResponse` interface–they all call the corresponding method of the class being wrapped:

```
  class VisAuditResponseWrapper extends HttpServletResponseWrapper {
    private PrintWriter tpWriter;
    private VisAuditOutStream tpStream;
```

The constructor passes the IP address and host name of client, in addition to the response that will be wrapped. Note that you create your customized stream in the constructor, and pass the IP address and host name right through. You also create a `PrintWriter` object based on the stream:

```
    public VisAuditResponseWrapper(ServletResponse inResp, String inAddr,
                                   String inHost)
           throws java.io.IOException {

      super((HttpServletResponse) inResp);
      tpStream = new VisAuditOutStream(inResp.getOutputStream(), inAddr,
                                       inHost);
      tpWriter = new PrintWriter(tpStream);
    }
```

The two other methods that you override are `getOutputStream()` and `getWriter()`. These methods hand out your customized stream instead of the response's actual stream:

```
    public ServletOutputStream getOutputStream() throws java.io.IOException {
      return tpStream;
    }

    public PrintWriter getWriter() throws java.io.IOException {
      return tpWriter;
    }
  }
```

The Filter Logic

Finally, you get to the actual filter class, `VisAuditFilter`. You'll recognize the general organization from the last chapter's examples. Focus your attention on the `doFilter()` method:

```
public final class VisAuditFilter implements Filter {
  private FilterConfig filterConfig = null;

  public void doFilter(ServletRequest request, ServletResponse response,
                       FilterChain chain)
        throws IOException, ServletException {

    if (filterConfig == null)
      return;
```

This code is executed on the inbound request. You find out the client's IP address and the host name. This information will be passed down to the custom stream:

```
    String clientAddr = request.getRemoteAddr();
    String clientHost = request.getRemoteHost();
    filterConfig.getServletContext().log("in VisAuditFilter");
```

Here you create a new customized wrapped response, passing in the actual response as well as the IP and host name:

```
    VisAuditResponseWrapper myWrappedResp = new VisAuditResponseWrapper(response,
                                                  clientAddr, clientHost);
```

Then you pass the wrapped response downstream to other filters and the resource processor:

```
    chain.doFilter(request, myWrappedResp);
```

Some resource processor and downstream filter combinations don't close the output stream properly, so here you force a close. You'll see shortly that the implementation of the `ReplaceContentOutputStream` class is guarded against multiple closes, so this is safe even if the stream was closed previously:

```
    myWrappedResp.getOutputStream().close();
    filterConfig.getServletContext().log("Getting out of VisAuditFilter");
  }
```

The rest of these methods implement the filter interface and are standard implementations that you saw within the samples of the previous chapter. For brevity's sake, we don't repeat them after this example, unless we change them significantly:

```
  public void init(FilterConfig filterConfig) {
    this.filterConfig = filterConfig;
  }

  public void destroy() {}
```

```
    public String toString() {

      if (filterConfig == null) return ("VisAuditFilter()");

      StringBuffer sb = new StringBuffer("VisAuditFilter(");
      sb.append(filterConfig);
      sb.append(")");

      return (sb.toString());
    }

  }
```

The ReplaceContentOutputStream Class

The custom stream, `VisAuditOutStream`, depends on the `ReplaceContentOutputStream` class to do a lot of its magic. This class wraps an `OutputStream` and does the following:

- Supplies its own byte array–based stream for the `write()` method, called by downstream filters and the resource processor
- Handles the `close()` or `flush()` method by calling a child's `ReplaceContent()` method to transform the byte array stream
- Takes the transformed content and writes it to the `OutputStream`

This class can be used for any filter that transforms or replaces the response content:

```
package com.apress.projsp20.ch10;

import java.io.*;
import javax.servlet.*;
```

This abstract class extends another abstract class, called `ServletOutputStream`, which is the base class of the `OutputStream` returned by `getOutputStream` on a response. `ServletOutputStream` requires the `write(int)` method to be implemented by its subclass. It implements all the other `write()` variants based on this method. Your own `ReplaceContentOutputStream` requires the `ReplaceContent()` method to be implemented by all its subclasses:

```
public abstract class ReplaceContentOutputStream
       extends ServletOutputStream {

  private OutputStream intStream;
  private ByteArrayOutputStream baStream;
  private boolean closed = false;
  private boolean transformOnCloseOnly = false;
```

Note the use of the following two flag variables:

- `closed`: Initially `false`, this variable is used to ensure that the wrapped stream is closed only once, regardless of how many times the `close()` method may be called.

- transformOnCloseOnly: This variable controls when the ReplaceContent() method will be called. The default is false, meaning that ReplaceContent() will be called on every flush() as well as the close() method call. Setting this variable to true will ensure that stream transformation is only performed once, when the close() method is called for the first time.

The constructor simply hides a reference to the stream being wrapped and creates the memory-based ByteArrayOutputStream() for the downstream processors:

```
public ReplaceContentOutputStream(OutputStream outStream) {
  intStream = outStream;
  baStream = new ByteArrayOutputStream();
}
```

Next, you implement the required write(int) method, which writes to your in-memory stream called baStream. This ensures that all writes on this stream write to baStream (essentially a buffer):

```
public void write(int i) throws java.io.IOException {
  baStream.write(i);
}
```

When close() is called for the first time, you transform the output in the in-memory stream. After the transformation, you write the results to the actual wrapped stream. Multiple calls to close() don't cause a problem in this case:

```
public void close() throws java.io.IOException {
  if (!closed) {
    processStream();
    intStream.close();
    closed = true;
  }
}
```

When flush() is called, the action that occurs depends on the transformOnCloseOnly flag. If this flag is set to true, the method does nothing. If this flag is set to false, the default, a stream transformation and write, will occur to the underlying wrapped stream. A new ByteArrayStream is then created to catch any additional output after the flush() and before close() or the next flush():

```
public void flush() throws java.io.IOException {
  if (baStream.size() != 0) {
    if (!transformOnCloseOnly) {
      processStream();
      baStream = new ByteArrayOutputStream();
    }
  }
}
```

Here's the definition of the replaceContent() abstract method. It transforms the inBytes byte array and returns the transformed byte array as the return value:

```
    public abstract byte [] replaceContent(byte [] inBytes)
          throws java.io.IOException;
```

The processStream() method calls the replaceContent() method to transform the in-memory stream and write the transformed output to the wrapped output stream:

```
    public void processStream() throws java.io.IOException {
      intStream.write(replaceContent(baStream.toByteArray()));
      intStream.flush();
    }
```

The setTransformOnCloseOnly() method is used by the subclass to control the close() and flush() behavior as described previously:

```
    public void setTransformOnCloseOnly() {
      transformOnCloseOnly = true;
    }
  }
```

This is the end of the code analysis for the ReplaceContentOutputStream abstract class. You'll rely on this class for two subsequent filters that transform their outgoing response's content.

Filter Configuration and Testing

To deploy the filter, add this filter definition and filter mapping to the web.xml file:

```
<filter>
  <filter-name>VisAudit Filter</filter-name>
  <filter-class>com.apress.projsp20.ch10.VisAuditFilter</filter-class>
</filter>

<filter-mapping>
  <filter-name>VisAudit Filter</filter-name>
  <url-pattern>/*</url-pattern>
</filter-mapping>
```

This mapping will apply the filter to every resource served by the application. Next, you'll try a servlet resource instead. Open http://localhost:8080/filters2/servlet/findprod (note the casing). The output is once again intercepted and the auditing information is appended:

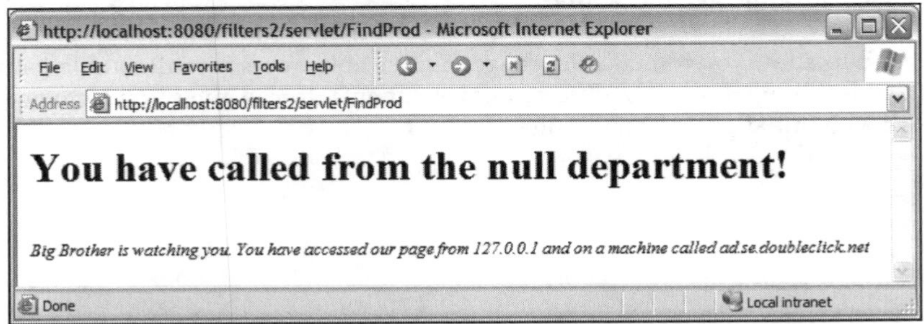

If you're creating filters that must work across many types of resources, you *must* test against each type of resource. This is necessary because each type of resource is passed through a different resource processor, each of which potentially has different assumptions and behavior from the others (servlets are passed to Catalina, JSP pages are passed to Jasper first, and so on).

Filter 2: An Authorization Filter

A filter can generate its own output and deprive the downstream filters and resource processor of a chance to see the request altogether. Obviously, there's very little application for a filter that does this all the time, but a filter that does this based on some dynamic criterion can be useful. One example is a filter that blocks resource access based on the time of day. You'll create such a filter in this section.

Generating Your Own Response

The filter you're going to create falls into the authorization filter application domain. More specifically, it allows or disallows an incoming request to reach its destined resource processor depending on the time of day. The application is intended to stop users from accessing game-playing resources during certain hours. Here's an illustration of the filter action:

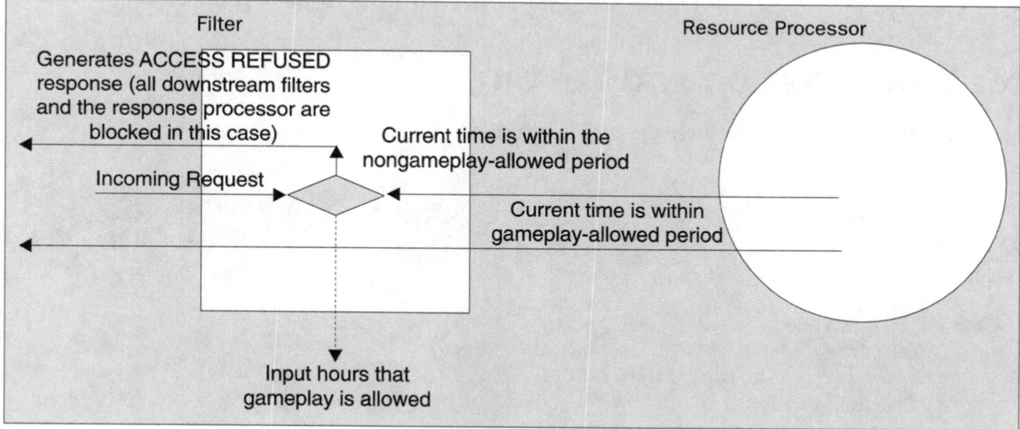

If a request arrives during the allotted time window, the user is allowed through to the resource processor to play games. If a request arrives outside of the allotted time window, the filter generates a response of its own, depriving the downstream resource processor of a chance to see the request. This effectively blocks the use of the game resources.

The filter is designed to allow you to make the range of allowable hours a configurable parameter, to make the filter flexible enough for use in different environments. It also gives you a chance to see how to access and work with initial parameters in filters.

The StopGamesFilter Class

Here's a brief analysis of this filter code:

```
package com.apress.projsp20.ch10;

import java.io.*;
import javax.servlet.*;
import javax.servlet.http.*;
import java.util.Calendar;

public final class StopGamesFilter implements Filter {
```

There are no wrapper or customized stream classes because you won't transform the response or modify requests:

```
  private FilterConfig filterConfig = null;
```

First, you set up the default hours of operation, which allows game playing all the time. These parameters are used if the filter is configured without initial parameters, or if the access to the initial parameters failed. It's always a good idea to set some usable default value for the filter. Note the instance scope of these private variables:

```
  private int starthour = 0;
  private int stophour = 24;  // default is to allow all the time

  public void doFilter(ServletRequest request, ServletResponse response,
                       FilterChain chain)
        throws IOException, ServletException {

    if (filterConfig == null) return;
```

You obtain the current hour, which depends on a 24-hour clock to make things simple. You also assume that the start and stop hours don't cross the 12 am boundary to keep the logic simple:

```
    Calendar myCal = Calendar.getInstance();
    int curhour = myCal.get(Calendar.HOUR_OF_DAY);
```

Next, you make a log entry to show the various values, which is useful for auditing or debugging purposes:

```
    filterConfig.getServletContext().log("in StopGamesFilter cur:" + curhour
                             + ", start: " + starthour + ", end: " + stophour
);
```

If the incoming request arrives outside of the allowed time range, you simply generate the content of the response. The generated content lets the user know that access to the game resource page is disallowed. The content generation is simple and uses the same call as most servlets:

```
    if (( curhour >= stophour) || (curhour <= starthour)) {
      PrintWriter out = response.getWriter();

      out.println("<html><head></head><body>");
      out.println
              ("<h1>Sorry, game playing is not allowed at this time!</h1>");
      out.println("</body></html>");

      out.flush();
      filterConfig.getServletContext().log("Access to game page denied");
      return;
    }
```

Finally, you let the request through to access the game resource and log an entry to indicate this:

```
    filterConfig.getServletContext().log("Access to game page granted");

    chain.doFilter(request, response);
    filterConfig.getServletContext().log("Getting out of StopGamesFilter");

  }
}
```

Thread-Safety Considerations

One question that the alert reader may have is, "Where do I access the initialization parameters?" The answer is, generally **not** in the `doFilter()` method. This goes back to our discussion in the previous chapter about thread-safe programming. The `starthour` and `stophour` variables are instance-scoped variables. Modifying the value of instance-scoped variables in `doFilter()` requires careful synchronization, because `doFilter()` **will** be accessed in multiple threads at the same time. Following the filter life cycle, however, there's a natural place to set the value of your initialization parameters.

Taking Advantage of the Filter Life Cycle

After an instance of a filter has been created, and before the very first `doFilter()` is called, the container calls the `init()` method to set the `FilterConfig` object for the filter. This is a natural point at which to perform any initialization required, and it's conceptually equivalent to the `init()` method of a servlet.

In this case, you'll take advantage of it by setting your instance variables with values from the filter definition. The container always calls `init()` in a single thread when it sets up the filter instance. In the following `init()` method, the `filterConfig.getInitParameter()` method reads the `web.xml` file for initialization parameters:

```
  public void init(FilterConfig filterConfig) {
    String tpString;

    if ((tpString = filterConfig.getInitParameter("starthour")) != null)
      starthour = Integer.parseInt(tpString, 10);

    if ((tpString = filterConfig.getInitParameter("stophour")) != null)
      stophour = Integer.parseInt(tpString, 10);
    this.filterConfig = filterConfig;
  }

  public String toString() {
    .
    .
    .
  }
}
```

Installing and Configuring the StopGamesFilter

To install and configure the filter, first make sure all other `<filter>` and `<filter-mapping>` elements are removed or commented out of the `web.xml` file. Then add the following entries:

```
<filter>
  <filter-name>Stop Games Filter</filter-name>
  <filter-class>com.apress.projsp20.ch10.StopGamesFilter</filter-class>
  <init-param>
    <param-name>starthour</param-name>
    <param-value>8</param-value>
  </init-param>
  <init-param>
    <param-name>stophour</param-name>
    <param-value>9</param-value>
  </init-param>
</filter>

<filter-mapping>
  <filter-name>Stop Games Filter</filter-name>
  <url-pattern>/games/*</url-pattern>
</filter-mapping>
```

Make sure that you've configured the `starthour` and `stophour` variables to make the current time outside of the allowable range, and create a `games` directory off the `filters2` web application directory that contains an appropriate `index.html` file. Start Tomcat and try to access the following URL through a browser: http://localhost:8080/filters2/games/index.html.

You should see an "access denied" message:

This is the custom-generated response straight from the filter. Now, shut down Tomcat and modify the `<filter>` element in `web.xml` to include the current time within the range. Restart Tomcat and try to access the same URL. You should now see the game-playing page:

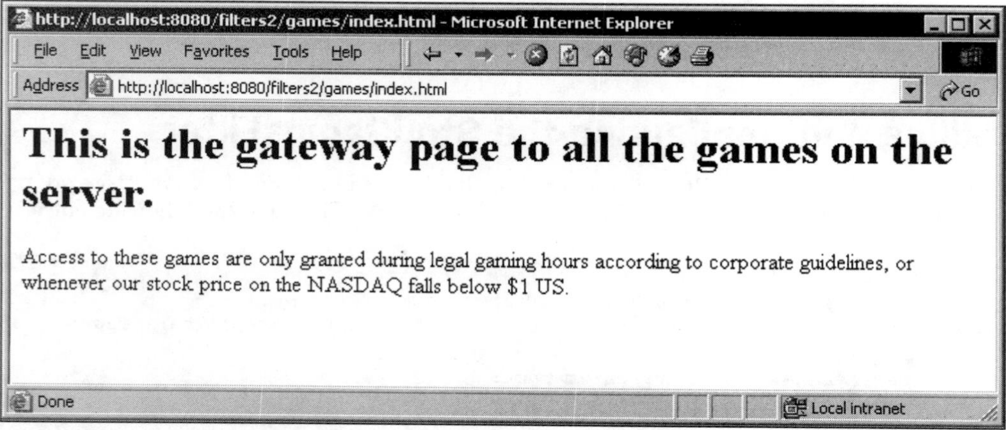

Filter 3: A Filter for Adapting to Legacy Resources

The next filter we examine addresses a very common problem in the real world when two independent systems refer to each other through hyperlinks. Over time, the requirement and access has changed because of independent evolution. Due to the size of the independent projects, or due to political situations, you can't change the links to either one of the systems. To keep them working, you'll create a filter that adapts one system to another, without modifying a single line of code in either system. The following figure shows the action of just such an "adapter" filter within a typical system:

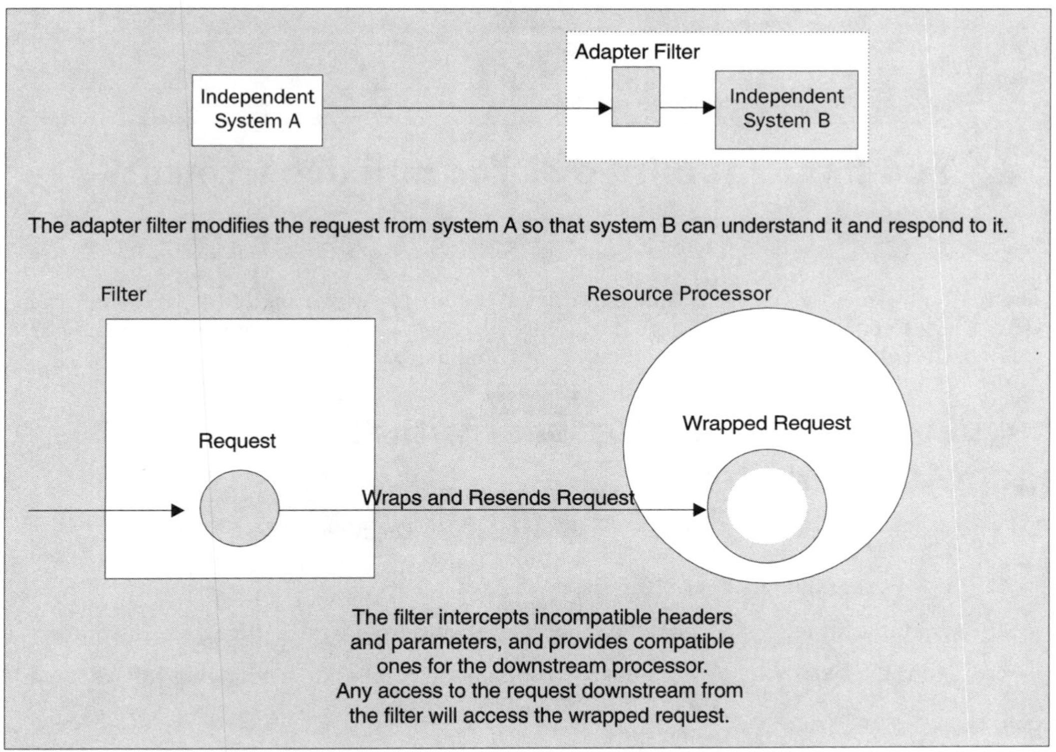
Adapter Filter
Independent System A
Independent System B
The adapter filter modifies the request from system A so that system B can understand it and respond to it.
Filter
Resource Processor
Request
Wrapped Request
Wraps and Resends Request
The filter intercepts incompatible headers and parameters, and provides compatible ones for the downstream processor.
Any access to the request downstream from the filter will access the wrapped request.

In this example, a JSP page represents the legacy resource. A centralized administrative server that is accessed by multiple departments in a company services this JSP page. This legacy system requires the originating department information supplied in the form of a `DEPT` parameter in order to work properly. Unfortunately, due to political situations in this hypothetical company, the links coming into this server don't and won't contain the originating department information (the `DEPT` parameter). Therefore, you'll design a filter to adapt the two systems.

This filter intercepts the request, examines where it's from, and generates the required `DEPT` parameter for the JSP resource so that it can function properly. It determines the department of the incoming client by examining its subnet portion of the IP address corresponding to the client (assume you have the subnet IP to department mapping information). Therefore, this adapter translates an incoming IP address to a required `DEPT` parameter and allows two incompatible systems to work together.

You can easily imagine many more involved examples from the real world that may require significantly more adaptation code; however, the general structure and technique for creating such adapter filters remains the same.

For this example, you'll revisit `FindProd.jsp`:

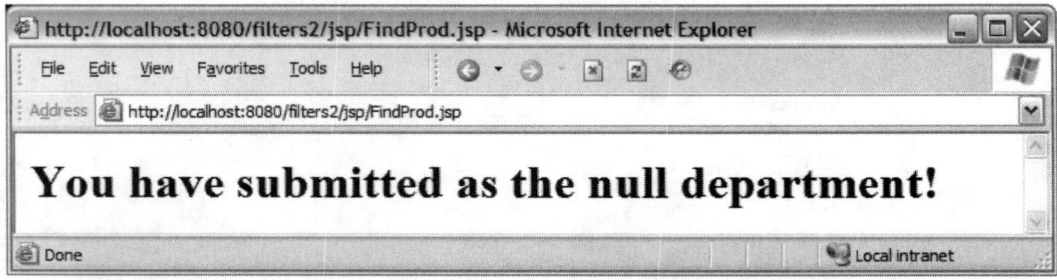

The reason the message contains "null department" is due to the missing DEPT parameter when the URL is accessed. You'll fix this by creating a filter that will adapt any incoming requests by detecting the department information and providing the missing parameter.

Wrapping an Incoming Request with the LegacyAdapterFilter

Let's now analyze the code of the LegacyAdapter filter. The filter

- Determines the incoming IP address
- Finds out which department the request originates from by examining the IP address
- Adds the DEPT parameter to the request before it reaches the underlying JSP resource

Let's review key parts of the source code:

```
package com.apress.projsp20.ch10;

import java.io.*;
import javax.servlet.*;
import javax.servlet.http.*;
import java.util.*;
```

In this example, you must wrap the incoming request. Unlike with the VisAudit filter in which you wrapped the outgoing response, you'll actually be modifying header information associated with the incoming request.

The wrapper class here, called LegacyAdapterRequestWrapper, extends the useful HttpServletRequestWrapper class. HttpServletRequestWrapper will take as an argument for its constructor the actual HttpServletRequest to wrap. It implements all of its methods by calling the methods of the wrapped request. By inheriting from this class, you can choose to override only the methods that you're interested in:

```
class LegacyAdapterRequestWrapper extends HttpServletRequestWrapper {
  String myDept = null;
```

Note that you take the department as an argument for the constructor of your custom wrapper class:

```
public LegacyAdapterRequestWrapper(HttpServletRequest inReq,
                                   String deptString) {
  super(inReq);
  myDept = deptString;
}
```

The methods that you provide custom implementation for are `getParameterMap()`, `getParameterValues()`, and `getParameter()`. This ensures that you can work with most of the resources that may access parameters. In fact, for your specific JSP case, you had to override only the `getParameter()` method because this is the only method it uses. In each of the following overrides, you can see how the `DEPT` parameter is added. The downstream filter or processor accessing the headers will have no way of knowing that the `DEPT` parameter was added by your filter and not from the original request. This demonstrates the beauty of filter chaining:

```
  public Map getParameterMap() {

    Map tmpMap = super.getParameterMap();
    tmpMap.put("DEPT", myDept);
    return tmpMap;
  }

  public String [] getParameterValues(String paramName) {

    if (paramName.equalsIgnoreCase("DEPT")) {
      String [] tpAry = new String[1];

      tpAry[0] = myDept;
      return tpAry;

    } else {
      return super.getParameterValues(paramName);
    }
  }

  public String getParameter(String paramName) {

    if (paramName.equalsIgnoreCase("DEPT")) {
      return myDept;
    } else {
      return super.getParameter(paramName);
    }
  }
}
```

The filter class starts here:

```
public final class LegacyAdapterFilter implements Filter {

  private FilterConfig filterConfig = null;
```

```
    public void doFilter(ServletRequest request, ServletResponse response,
                    FilterChain chain)
          throws IOException, ServletException {

      LegacyAdapterRequestWrapper aCustomReq;

      if (filterConfig == null) return;
```

The code first determines the department that the request is coming from. It does so by mapping the subnet of the IP address to a department. In this case, it examines the subnet–if it's zero, `DEPT=Accounting` is used; otherwise `DEPT=Engineering` is used:

```
      String clientAddr = request.getRemoteAddr();
      System.out.println("the addr is " + clientAddr);

      int idx = clientAddr.indexOf(".");
      clientAddr = clientAddr.substring(idx + 1);

      idx = clientAddr.indexOf(".");
      clientAddr = clientAddr.substring(idx + 1);

      idx = clientAddr.indexOf(".");
      clientAddr = clientAddr.substring(0, idx);

      System.out.println("the subnet is " + clientAddr);

      String dept = null;
      if (clientAddr.equals("0")) {
        dept = "Engineering";
      } else {
        dept = "Accounting";
      }
```

Next, it creates a wrapper request, passing in the department and calling downstream filters/processor via filter chaining:

```
      aCustomReq = new LegacyAdapterRequestWrapper ((HttpServletRequest) request,
                                                    dept);

      filterConfig.getServletContext().log("in LegacyAdapterFilter");

      chain.doFilter(aCustomReq, response);

      filterConfig.getServletContext().log("leaving LegacyAdapterFilter");

    }

    public void init(FilterConfig filterConfig) {
      .
      .
      .
    }
```

```
    public FilterConfig destroy() {}

    public String toString() {
      .
      .
      .
    }
  }
```

Installing and Configuring the LegacyAdapterFilter

To install and configure the filter, first make sure all other `<filter>` and `<filter-mapping>` definitions are removed or commented out (you want to reduce the side effect of chaining other sample filters). Then add the following entries to the `web.xml` file:

```
<filter>
  <filter-name>Legacy Adapter Filter</filter-name>
  <filter-class>com.apress.projsp20.ch10.LegacyAdapterFilter </filter-class>
</filter>

<filter-mapping>
  <filter-name>Legacy Adapter Filter</filter-name>
  <url-pattern>/jsp/FindProd.jsp</url-pattern>
</filter-mapping>
```

This will specifically apply the filter to the `FindProd.jsp` resource. Start Tomcat and open http://localhost:8080/filters2/jsp/FindProd.jsp.

You should see a page similar to this:

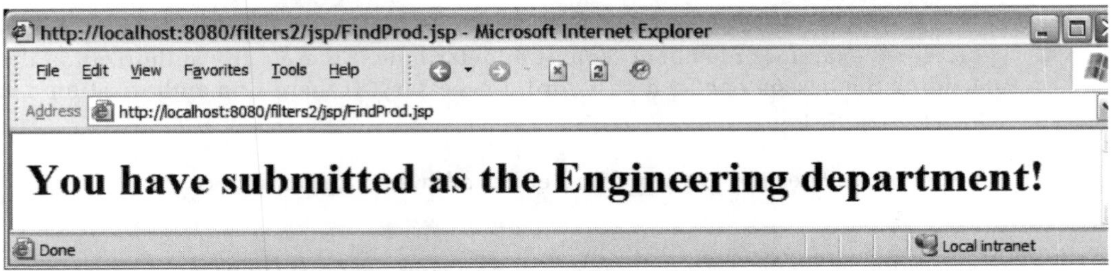

Note that the message no longer indicates "null department" as it did when you accessed the page in the `VisAudit` filter example. The JSP page is picking up the `DEPT` parameter from your wrapped request. If you can do so, you may want to access the JSP page from another subnet to see the automatic department detection at work.

Filter 4: An Ad Hoc Authentication Filter

Tomcat 5 and almost all Servlet 2.4–compliant containers come with extensive authentication and authorization support, so in theory there should be little need to implement your own authentication filter. In practice, however, there's almost always room to apply an ad hoc authentication filter on a selected resource without affecting the rest of the application or involving the overhead of setting up, say, JDBC realms.

You should always analyze the problem at hand to see if it would be better solved by the native authentication support of the server. In those cases in which you need simple, temporary protection of selected resources, the `AdHocAuthenticate` filter can be the best choice.

The action of this filter is straightforward. It triggers basic authentication on the client browser. Almost all known browsers, including even the earliest versions, support basic authentication. It works like this:

1. A client attempts to access a protected resource.
2. The server examines the client's request to determine if there's any authorization data in the "Authorization" header.
3. If authorization data isn't found, the server sends back HTTP status code 401 (unauthorized access) and a header with `WWW-authenticate: BASIC realm=<realm>`, where `realm` is a text string that will be displayed to the client.
4. The client pops up a login screen in which the user should enter a username and password.
5. The client encodes the username and password using simple base64 encoding and sends both to the server.
6. The server examines the client request to determine if there's any authorization data, decoding the base64-encoded password if necessary. If there's no authorization data, it goes back to step 3.
7. The server verifies the password and either allows or rejects access.

Basic authentication isn't very secure, because base64 encoding can easily be deciphered. However, for applications that just need to protect resources from casual access, it's usually sufficient. For more details on different kinds of authentication, see Chapter 11.

The `AdHocAuthenticate` filter recognizes two passwords: one for "regular" users and one for privileged, "gold member" users. Both passwords are configured as initial parameters for the filter. If a user logs on using the "gold member" password, a Boolean attribute is created and attached to the request. You'll learn later (in the pipeline processing filters section) how this attribute is used. For now, let's focus on the authentication action of this filter.

The AdHocAuthenticateFilter Class

Here's a brief analysis of the source code for this class:

```
package com.apress.projsp20.ch10;

import java.io.*;
import javax.servlet.*;
import javax.servlet.http.*;
import java.util.Map;
import sun.misc.*;
```

There's no need to wrap the response or request in this filter. Note the instance variable that will be used to hold the two read-only passwords: `adhocPassword` and `adhocGoldPassword`. These variables are initialized by the container from the `web.xml` values via the `init()` method:

```
public final class AdHocAuthenticateFilter implements Filter {

  private FilterConfig filterCofig = null;
  private String adhocPassword = null;
  private String adhocGoldPassword = null;

  public void doFilter(ServletRequest request, ServletResponse response,
                       FilterChain chain)
         throws IOException, ServletException {

    if (filterConfig == null) return;
```

You cast the request and response to their HTTP servlet versions to access and manipulate the headers associated with them:

```
    HttpServletRequest myReq = (HttpServletRequest) request;
    HttpServletResponse myResp = (HttpServletResponse) response;
```

Here you perform the basic authentication request if you don't find authorization data:

```
    String authString = myReq.getHeader("Authorization");

    if (authString == null) {

      myResp.addHeader("WWW-Authenticate", "BASIC realm=\"PJSP2\"");
      myResp.setStatus(HttpServletResponse.SC_UNAUTHORIZED);

      return;
    } else { // authenticate
```

If you find authorization data, you decode the username and password. The following `substring(6)` skips over the constant string `Basic` of the authorization header, getting to the beginning of the base64-encoded username and password:

```
        BASE64Decoder decoder = new BASE64Decoder();

        String enString = authString.substring(6);
        String decString = new String(decoder.decodeBuffer(enString));

        int idx = decString.indexOf(":");

        String uid = decString.substring(0, idx);
        String pwd = decString.substring(idx + 1);
```

You call the methods `externalGoldAuthenticate()` and `externalAuthenticate()` to perform the actual authentication for "gold member" users and "regular" users, respectively. In production, authentication via an external server could be implemented here. Successful authentication allows access to the protected resource. In addition, "gold member" authentication will result in the, ahem, `goldmember` Boolean attribute being attached to the request. Failed authentication will cause the login dialog box to pop up again on the client's browser:

```
        if (externalGoldAuthenticate(uid,pwd)) {
          request.setAttribute("goldmember", new Boolean(true));
        } else {

          if (!externalAuthenticate(uid,pwd)) {

            myResp.addHeader("WWW-Authenticate", "BASIC realm=\"PJSP2\"");
            myResp.setStatus(HttpServletResponse.SC_UNAUTHORIZED);

            return;

          } // of if
        } // of else
      } // of outer else
```

If you reach this point, everything has been authenticated properly, and access to the resource can begin:

```
      filterConfig.getServletContext().log("in AdHocAuthenticateFilter");
      chain.doFilter(request, response);
      filterConfig.getServletContext().log("Getting out of " +
                                           "AdHocAuthenticateFilter");
    }
```

The `externalAuthenticate()` and `externalGoldAuthenticate()` methods encapsulate the authentication mechanism. In this case, each authenticates against a single password from the initial parameters. You can modify each to perform any type of authentication you desire, including authentication against some physically external servers:

```
    private boolean externalAuthenticate(String user, String password) {

      if (adhocPassword == null) return false;
```

```
      return adhocPassword.equals(password);
    }

    private boolean externalGoldAuthenticate(String user, String password) {

      if (adhocGoldPassword == null) return false;

      return adhocGoldPassword.equals(password);
    }

    public void destroy() {}
```

Again, it's in the `init()` method that the initial parameters are read and set in the filter:

```
    public void init(FilterConfig filterConfig) {

      if (adhocPassword == null)
        adhocPassword = filterConfig.getInitParameter("adhocpassword");

      if (adhocGoldPassword == null)
        adhocGoldPassword = filterConfig.getInitParameter("goldpassword");

        this.filterConfig = filterConfig;
    }

    public String toString() {
      .
      .
      .
    }
  }
```

Installing and Configuring the AdHocAuthenticateFilter

To install and configure the filter, first make sure all other `<filter>` and `<filter-mapping>` elements are removed or commented out of the `web.xml` file. Then, add the following entries:

```
  <filter>
    <filter-name>AdHoc Authentication Filter</filter-name>
    <filter-class>com.apress.projsp20.ch10.AdHocAuthenticateFilter</filter-class>
    <init-param>
      <param-name>adhocpassword</param-name>
```

```
        <param-value>bestofbreed</param-value>
      </init-param>
       <init-param>
          <param-name>goldpassword</param-name>
          <param-value>viponly</param-value>
        </init-param>
   </filter>

   <filter-mapping>
     <filter-name>AdHoc Authentication Filter</filter-name>
     <url-pattern>/jsp/*</url-pattern>
   </filter-mapping>
```

Note that you've chained with the legacy adapter filter to supply the missing originating department information for the JSP page. This protects all JSP access with the passwords `bestofbreed` and `viponly`. Now, start Tomcat and go to http://localhost:8080/filters2/jsp/FindProd.jsp.

You should be prompted with a login dialog box.

Enter the username (any username will do) and an invalid password. You'll see that you're barred from accessing the protected resource until you enter one of the correct passwords.

Filter 5: A Filter in the Request Processing Pipeline

Thus far, this chapter's focus has been on filters that either control the flow of a request (stopping it or letting it through) or generate the response to a request. Vast as their fields of application may be, these filter design styles only partially cover the potential spectrum of applications for filters. The fact that these filters are directly responsible for some portion of the final appearance of the response HTML page often makes them difficult to compose (chain in a value-added component fashion). This is because, by definition, they're specific to the page output that they directly generate.

The pipeline data-processing model provides a new style of filter that our fifth and final filter exemplifies. The first enabler for this model is the new `<dispatcher>` child element of the servlet `<filter-mapping>` definition. The new element enables filters to participate in every stage of the pipeline request-processing model. In this model, filters are themselves bona fide processors for a request traveling through a pipeline.

Understanding the Pipeline Model

There are many different names given to the pipelined data-processing model. It's often identified as the enabling element of **Model-View-Controller** (**MVC**) web application design, and sometimes it's referred to as the **push model** of application design, in contrast with the more conventional **pull model**.

The idea is simple, but you have to think beyond the conventional web application wisdom to get the bigger picture. Consider this illustration of the model:

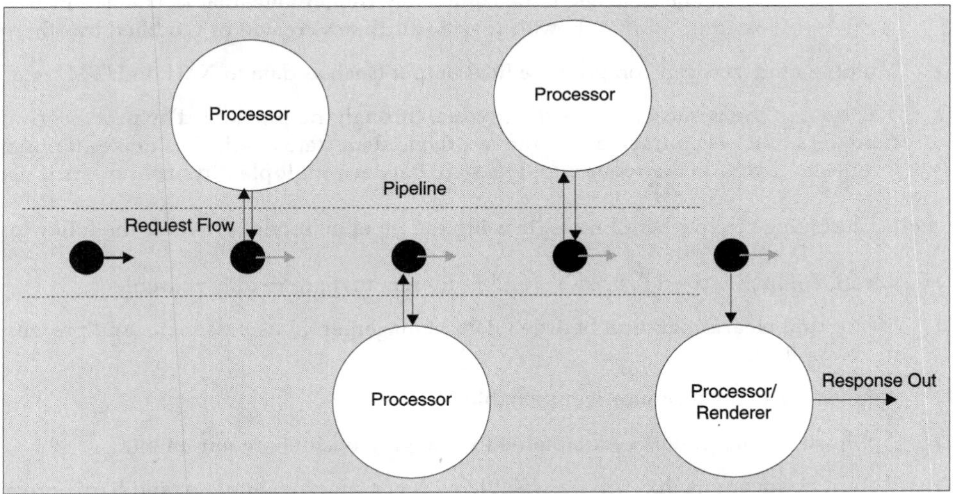

A request enters the system and is shuttled along a pipeline. As it traverses the pipeline, a sequence of processors has access to the content of the request. Each processor performs some task on the request, and then it either attaches some new attribute or modifies an existing attribute as the result of that work. The request remains intact until it hits the final stage of the pipeline, in which special processors called renderers examine all the work being done to the request and produce the final response (renderers are also called the **view component** in the MVC paradigm because they alone are responsible for the final presentation to the user). You can see why this is often called the "push" model; data attributes are fetched by processors, pushed along the pipeline with the request, and rendered only at the final stage.

Another common analogy for the pipeline model is a conveyer belt or assembly line, where each processor mirrors the workers (or robots) along the belt or line.

Some of the highly desirable properties of a pipeline model are as follows:

- The request stays intact as it traverse the pipeline, with work being carried out only on the attached attributes (sometimes called **decorators**).
- Data management, business logic, and presentation logic can be cleanly separated into different processors and renderers.
- The processors can be designed to be completely **composable** (that is, chained in any order) or highly specialized (to work only with specific attributes created or modified by other processors).
- Multiple renderers can compose the final output (such as data to XML to HTML via XSLT).
- The state of the request *travels with the request* through the pipeline. The processors and renderers don't keep track of the request-dependent state at all. This makes it possible to duplicate or shuttle the request and its state between multiple physical servers if necessary.

In general, designing request-handling logic using the pipeline model provides the following:

- Clean, componentized processors and renderers that are readily reusable
- Strong and clear separation between data management, business logic, and presentation logic in an application
- Applications that are more maintainable
- Applications that are more adaptable to changing business requirements
- Robust applications that will be scalable with container technology and hardware advances
- Web applications whose performance is highly optimizable

The last point may not be immediately obvious, but any processors in the pipeline that don't depend on others' outcomes can in principle be executed concurrently (perhaps on two physical processors, for instance) and any grouping of processors that has an outcome independent of others can also execute concurrently.

In the past, limitations in container implementation have prevented the use of a clean pipeline design model. JSP 2.0 and Servlet 2.4 have new features that bring the dream of creating a pipelined application closer to reality.

Inserting Filters into the Pipeline

The `<dispatcher>` subelement enables you to insert filters into the request processing pipeline. Recall that the `<dispatcher>` element now allows filters to intercept the request dispatcher's `forward()` and `include()` calls. These are additional locations in the processing pipeline previously unavailable with Servlet 2.3 containers, where filters can go to work for you. You've learned how this mechanism works in the last chapter, so let's see it in action here.

First, you'll revisit the `SimpleFilter` class that you saw in the last chapter. All it did was write a couple of lines to the log, letting you know that it had been invoked. Now you'll change it to process the request traveling through the pipeline.

Instead of directly generating log output, it will now simply change attached attributes. The modification looks to see if an attribute named `MsgOut` exists in the request. If it does exist, then the code will append `" : SimpleFilter"`; otherwise, `MsgOut` will be set to `"SimpleFilter"` (without the leading colon). The first time the filter (processor) operates on a request, the attached `MsgOut` attribute will be set to `"SimpleFilter"`. After the second time, it will contain `"SimpleFilter : SimpleFilter"`, and after the third time, `"SimpleFilter :SimpleFilter :SimpleFilter"`.

Eventually, the `MsgOut` attribute will be displayed on an HTML page, so you can see the number of times that this filter has operated on the specific request as it traveled through the pipeline. You'll find the code in the `com.apress.projsp20.ch10.SimpleFilter` class:

```
package com.apress.projsp20.ch10;

import java.io.*;
import javax.servlet.*;
import javax.servlet.http.*;

public final class SimpleFilter implements Filter {
  private FilterConfig filterConfig = null;

  public void doFilter(ServletRequest request, ServletResponse response,
                       FilterChain chain)
         throws IOException, ServletException {

    if (filterConfig == null) return;

    filterConfig.getServletContext().log("in SimpleFilter");
    Object curVal = request.getAttribute("MsgOut");

    if (curVal == null) {
      request.setAttribute("MsgOut", new String("SimpleFilter"));
    } else {
      request.setAttribute("MsgOut", (String) curVal + " :SimpleFilter");
    }

    chain.doFilter(request, response);
    filterConfig.getServletContext().log("leaving SimpleFilter");
  }
  .
  .
  .
```

You'll also revamp your `FindProd.jsp` file (the renderer processor in your pipeline) to display the new attribute. JSP 2.0's EL is great for creating renderers–that is, JSP pages that render HTML from attached attribute values. You'll name this modified file `Sub.jsp`:

```
<html>
  <head></head>
  <body>
```

```
      <h1>You have accessed this page from the ${param.DEPT} department!</h1>
      ${param.MsgForwarder}<br/>
      ${requestScope.MsgOut}
    </body>
  </html>
```

The MsgOut attribute, attached to the request, is displayed using EL here. Note that a parameter called MsgForwarder is also displayed. You'll see the use of this parameter later when you work with the forward() action of the request dispatcher.

Default REQUEST-Only Filtering: Servlet 2.3 Compatibility

To specify that filtering is to be performed only for requests that come directly from outside of the container, you can add the following <dispatcher> element inside the filter's <filter-mapping> element:

```
<dispatcher>REQUEST</dispatcher>
```

For example, you might have the following in web.xml:

```
<filter>
  <filter-name>Simple Push Filter</filter-name>
  <filter-class>com.apress.projsp20.ch10.SimpleFilter</filter-class>
</filter>

<filter-mapping>
  <filter-name>Simple Push Filter</filter-name>
  <url-pattern>/jsp/*</url-pattern>
  <dispatcher>REQUEST</dispatcher>
</filter-mapping>
```

Now, if you open the URL http://localhost:8080/filters2/jsp/Sub.jsp?DEPT=Accounting, you'll see a page like this:

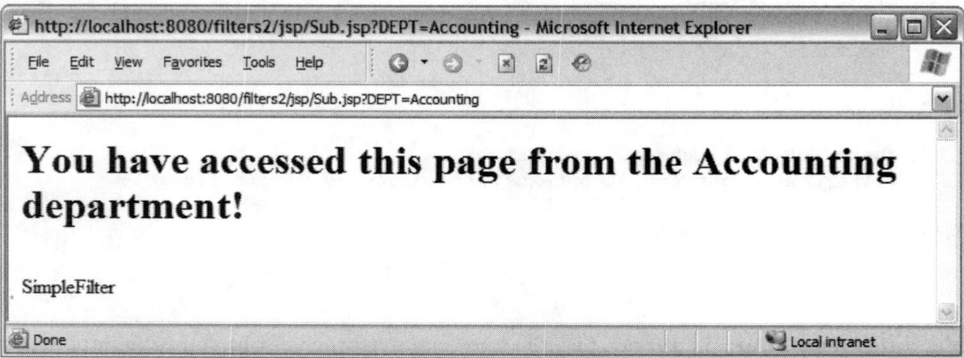

Note the EL rendering of the MsgOut attribute on the page–you know that the filter has been called once. This behavior is all that you have with filter support prior to the Servlet 2.4 standard. It's also the default behavior with Tomcat 5 if you don't specify any <dispatcher> subelement for compatibility reasons.

INCLUDE-Only Filtering

With Tomcat 5 and Servlet 2.4, you can specify that your filter only work on included requests. Try this out by changing `web.xml` to this:

```
<filter-mapping>
  <filter-name>Simple Push Filter</filter-name>
  <url-pattern>/jsp/*</url-pattern>
  <dispatcher>INCLUDE</dispatcher>
</filter-mapping>
```

Restart Tomcat and try accessing `Sub.jsp` directly via the following URL:

http://localhost:8080/filters2/jsp/Sub.jsp?DEPT=Accounting

Notice that the `MsgOut` attribute isn't present, indicating that the resulting page hasn't passed through `SimpleFilter`.

By specifying `INCLUDE` in the `<dispatcher>` subelement, you're saying that the filter should map only to included requests. To see this in action, take a look at the `jsp/Master.jsp` file:

```
<html>
  <head></head>
  <body>

    <h1>First Inclusion</h1>
    <jsp:include page="/jsp/Sub.jsp" flush="true">
      <jsp:param name="DEPT" value="Accounting"/>
    </jsp:include>
    <hr/>

    <h1>Second Inclusion</h1>
    <jsp:include page="/jsp/Sub.jsp" flush="true">
      <jsp:param name="DEPT" value="Engineering"/>
    </jsp:include>

  </body>
</html>
```

This JSP file makes two calls to the request dispatcher, each time to include the `/jsp/Sub.jsp` that you've been working with. The output from both of these `include()` actions is merged as the output response. Note that you're also supplying a different `DEPT` parameter with each inclusion.

Now navigate to http://localhost:8080/filters2/jsp/Master.jsp, and your resulting page should match the following:

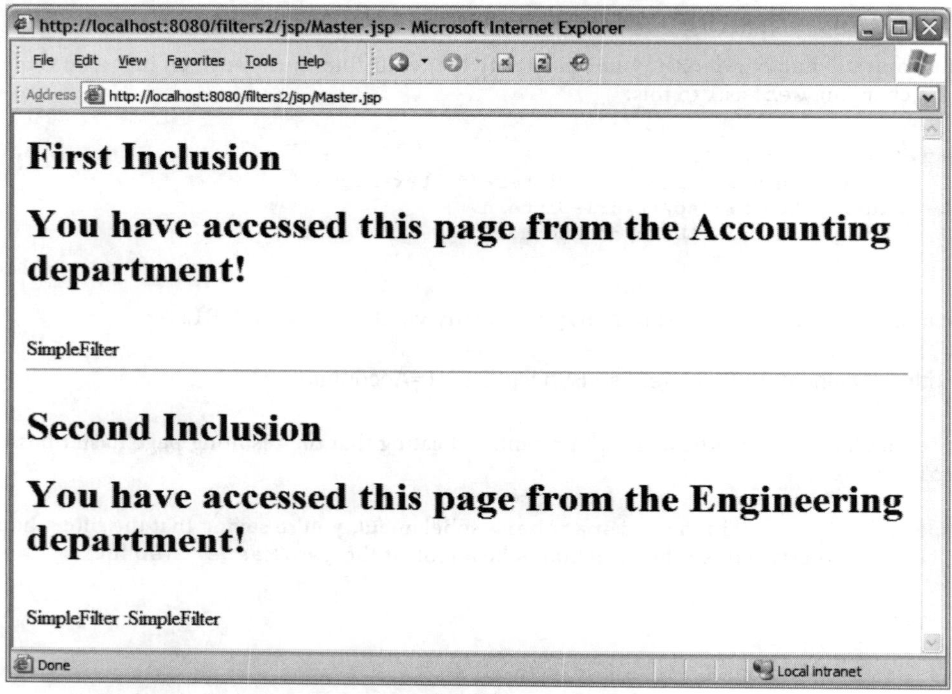

Note the MsgOut attribute value–it reflects the action of SimpleFilter. The attribute is "SimpleFilter" after the first inclusion of Sub.jsp and "SimpleFilter : SimpleFilter" after the second inclusion. The request has been operated on by SimpleFilter twice, once for each inclusion in Master.jsp.

FORWARD-Only Filtering

To make the filter operate only on forwarded requests, modify the web.xml file as follows:

```
<filter-mapping>
  <filter-name>Simple Push Filter</filter-name>
  <url-pattern>/jsp/*</url-pattern>
  <dispatcher>FORWARD</dispatcher>
</filter-mapping>
```

Because FORWARD is specified in the <disptacher> element, only forwarded requests will be passed to the filter. To see this in action, look at the jsp/Forwarder.jsp file:

```
<jsp:forward page="/jsp/Sub.jsp">
  <jsp:param name="DEPT" value="Accounting"/>
  <jsp:param name="MsgForwarder" value="Forwarded from forwarder.jsp"/>
</jsp:forward>
```

This JSP page simply forwards the request to Sub.jsp, and sets the DEPT and MsgForwarder parameters. Both parameters are displayed in Sub.jsp using EL.

Reload the application or restart Tomcat. Now try the following URLs in turn:

http://localhost:8080/filters2/jsp/Sub.jsp?DEPT=Accounting

http://localhost:8080/filters2/jsp/Master.jsp

http://localhost:8080/filters2/jsp/Forwarder.jsp

For the first two URLs, notice that direct request and included requests are no longer being filtered. The third URL should result in a page similar to this:

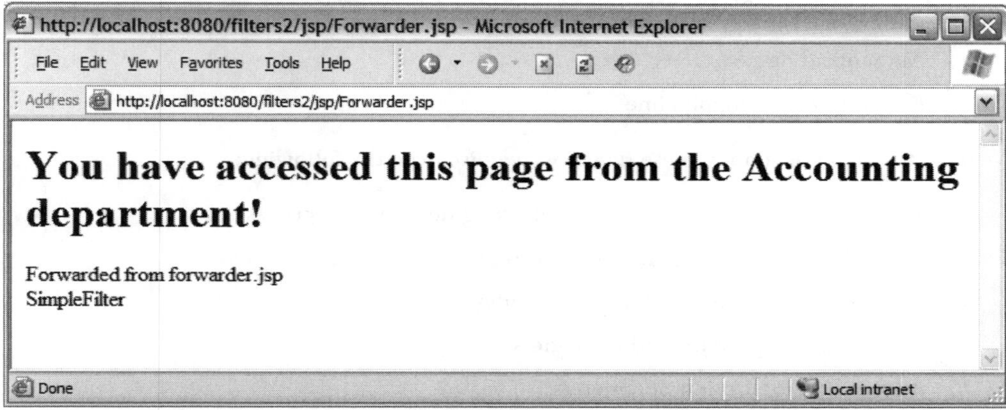

You can see from this experiment that only the forwarded request is filtered.

Combining Dispatcher Actions

Of course, you can use more than one `<dispatcher>` element to indicate multiple locations for the filter to apply to. For example:

```
<filter-mapping>
  <filter-name>Simple Push Filter</filter-name>
  <url-pattern>/jsp/*</url-pattern>
  <dispatcher>FORWARD</dispatcher>
  <dispatcher>INCLUDE</dispatcher>
  <dispatcher>REQUEST</dispatcher>
</filter-mapping>
```

Now, try the three previous URLs, and you'll observe the following:

URL 1: The filter is active on `Sub.jsp` when requested alone.

URL 2: The filter is active on `Master.jsp` PLUS each of the included `Sub.jsp`s.

URL 3: The filter is active on `Forwarder.jsp` PLUS the forwarded `Sub.jsp`.

Summary

In this chapter, we've worked through five complete filter examples covering these application domains:

- Auditing
- Authorization
- Adapting legacy resources
- Authentication
- Request processing pipeline

Working through the code to these filters, we've discussed the following:

- Generating our own response and blocking downstream processing
- Wrapping a response to transform or replace its content
- Wrapping a response to change its headers
- Wrapping a request to modify headers
- Accessing initialization parameters
- Dynamically altering filter behavior based on the incoming request
- Controlling the interaction of filters and the request dispatcher
- Applying filters in a processing pipeline configuration

You now have five examples that you can use as the basis for your own filter implementation. You also have one versatile class, `ReplaceContentOutputStream`, that you can use whenever you need to wrap a response to modify its content.

You should now be fluent in Servlet 2.4 filtering technology, and you should be able to apply filters to many challenges that the real world may throw at you.

11

Security in Web Applications

A web application lives a hazardous existence in the land of 1s and 0s. The Internet–the virtual environment we all know and love–can be a dark and dangerous place. It's filled with calm, collected programmer types like us, but there are also zealous hackers wandering through the dark alleys, scanning for open ports and passwords to steal. Is your web application safe? Have you protected your resources from the vulnerable, open, and sometimes dangerous information superhighway? In such a treacherous environment, most web applications will have security requirements, such as encrypting passwords or protecting certain pages from unauthorized viewing. Sun Microsystems has come to the rescue and made this easier for Java developers. In the Java Servlet specification, compliant containers are required to have built-in mechanisms to support your security requirements.

First, we should define **authentication** and **authorization**. Authentication is the process by which a web application verifies that *you are who you say you are.* For example, when a user logs into a web page with a username and password, the web application validates the entered credentials against its user data store (for example, file-, database-, or Lightweight Directory Access Protocol [LDAP]-based) and the login succeeds or fails. Authorization, on the other hand, is when the application checks to see if you're *allowed* to do something. For example, to delete a user from the database, you need to be an administrator.

Having security built into servlet containers isn't something new in the Servlet 2.4 specification–it's been around since Servlet 2.2 with the advent of the `web.xml` deployment descriptor. The security features that all servlet containers provide for you are as follows:

- **Authentication**: The process of proving your identity to an application
- **Access control for resources**: The means by which interactions with resources are limited to users and roles or programs for the purpose of enforcing integrity, confidentiality, or availability constraints
- **Data integrity**: The means for proving that a third party hasn't modified information while it was in transit
- **Confidentiality or data privacy**: The means used to ensure that information is made available only to users who are authorized to access it

So far, you've learned how to develop the different components in a web application, and now we'll show you how you can use the built-in mechanisms of the servlet and JSP APIs to configure authentication and authorization. It's really quite simple, given the proper instruction, and it helps even more if your application server is J2EE compliant. Container-managed authentication, where you configure or *declare* who can access your web application in your `web.xml` deployment descriptor file, is one of these mechanisms, and it takes only about 5 minutes to set up when you're using a J2EE-compliant server.

When we refer to an application in this chapter, we're speaking about a web application unless otherwise specified. When we refer to application servers or servlet containers, we're speaking about Java application servers that have a servlet container.

Remember that security is very important in all tiers of an application, from the presentation layer (JSP pages, HTML, JavaScript) to the underlying hardware and the network that the application uses. You must ask yourself if your database, network, and operating system are secure. If you leave any of these open to attack, there would be no point in securing the front-end of your application. In this chapter you'll concentrate on securing the front-end of your application.

For more information on securing your database, network, or operating system, please see http://www.owasp.org and http://online.securityfocus.com.

As a web developer, you shouldn't be tasked with the security in these areas, but it's something you should be aware of. You also need to prevent your application from a **denial of service (DoS)** attack, where your application or site is attacked by an enormous number of hits at the same time. Most good application servers have mechanisms to handle this, but it's a good idea to test for DoS if you're developing a highly visible site or application.

In this chapter we hope to show you that you can build a secure application, complete with user authentication and authorization, using the existing pieces of J2EE. Using these mechanisms will further translate into the other layers of your application, particularly if you're using Enterprise JavaBeans (EJBs).

We've worked on projects in the past in which we rolled our own security mechanism. Although it worked well (interfacing with LDAP), it was a real pain to maintain and very difficult for new developers to understand. By using container-managed security, your application will be much easier to maintain and comprehend. You can easily add new roles to your application by adding or altering a few lines in your application's deployment descriptors. It also makes it easy to switch from using a file-based user data store (or realm) to a database or LDAP-based realm. If you use what J2EE provides–and a new developer should be familiar with J2EE–then understanding your application's architecture will be a breeze.

In the Servlet 2.4 specification, there isn't much that's new regarding security. It still recommends that you use the deployment descriptor as your primary vehicle to implement security. This is so the application developer doesn't get bogged down with implementation details, and the application deployer has control over matters such as which roles to allow, which resources to protect, and so on. It's easy to roll your own security mechanism when you fulfill both the application developer and application deployer roles on your development team. However, if you work in a large team or you're developing a product for customers to install, an application with declared security will be much easier to maintain. Read on, and we'll show you how easy it is to develop and maintain container-managed security.

The Secure Example Application

In this chapter we focus on building a web application that allows for configurable authentication and access control. A more common name for this is **declarative security**, which basically involves changing an XML file (`web.xml`) to control who can log in and who can do what. This allows you to keep an application's security configuration separate from your servlet and JSP code. This can be very helpful in making your application more portable across application servers, as well as making it easier for a deployer (versus a developer) to change.

> *We use Tomcat in this chapter's examples, but we attempt to point out areas that might be problematic on other application servers.*

This chapter covers the aspects of security that we've encountered as web developers, particularly with JSP-based web applications:

- Secure Sockets Layer (SSL)
- Authentication mechanisms (form, basic, mutual)
- Security certificates
- Protecting secure resources
- Hiding resources under `WEB-INF`
- Java Authentication and Authorization Service (JAAS)

We provide examples that are available as a downloadable and ready-to-install WAR file from the Downloads section of the Apress website (http://www.apress.com). This application contains features that you might think unworkable with container-managed security, such as the following:

- Password encryption (declarative and programmatic)
- SSL switching
- Login from an error page
- A filter for retrieving a user's information

Authentication

One of the most popular JSP/servlet sample applications produced today is the "how to log in" application. This application usually consists of a couple of JSP pages, some Java Database Connectivity (JDBC) code to access a database, and possibly a tag library that rejects or allows users on the basis of their logged-in status. Although these elements make for easy-to-understand applications, they promote an overly difficult method of performing authentication.

Container-managed authentication has existed since the Servlet 2.2 specification, but unfortunately many application server vendors didn't implement it correctly. Tomcat has an awesome implementation of container-managed authentication. With a J2EE-compliant application server, all that is needed is some deployment descriptor manipulation and your resources are protected. The beauty of it is that the level of security is up to the developer or the deployer.

First, we'll define a couple of terms that we use throughout this section. A **realm** is a "database" of usernames and passwords that identify valid users of a web application (or a set of web applications), plus an enumeration of the list of **roles** associated with each valid user. You can think of roles as similar to *groups* in operating systems, because access to specific web application resources is granted to all users possessing a particular role (rather than enumerating the list of associated usernames). A particular user can have any number of roles associated with his username.

> *You can also find these definitions in Tomcat 5.0's documentation at http://jakarta.apache.org/tomcat/tomcat-5.0-doc/realm-howto.html.*

All configuration settings (servlet or filter mappings, URL patterns, and so on) in the `web.xml` file relate to the root directory of your web application. They don't include your application's context path. To prove how easy it is to use container-managed authentication, you can add the following lines to your `web.xml` file to protect your entire application. The following `<security-constraint>` and `<login-config>` elements should be entered toward the bottom of your `web.xml` file:

```
<security-constraint>
  <web-resource-collection>
    <web-resource-name>My Application</web-resource-name>
    <url-pattern>/*</url-pattern>
  </web-resource-collection>
  <auth-constraint>
    <role-name>*</role-name>
  </auth-constraint>
</security-constraint>

<login-config>
  <auth-method>BASIC</auth-method>
</login-config>
```

Most of these 12 lines of code are the XML syntax! The elements you care about (`<url-pattern>`, `<role-name>`, and `<auth-method>`) are short and sweet:

- The `<url-pattern>` element defines the characters to look for in a client's request. This value can be a path-based pattern (such as `/admin/*`) or an extension-based pattern (such as `/admin/*.jsp`), and it doesn't include the context path.
- The `<role-name>` element indicates the roles allowed to view the secured resource(s). There can be one or more role-names defined, and an asterisk (*) indicates all roles defined in the realm.
- The `<auth-method>` defines the type of authentication mechanism to use, such as `BASIC` (a simple dialog box with the username/password) or `FORM` (a redirect to an HTML-based login page).

If you have Tomcat installed, we encourage you to try typing the preceding XML into the `ROOT` application's `web.xml` file (which you can find at `%TOMCAT_HOME%/webapps/ROOT/WEB-INF/web.xml`). Alternatively, you can use the sample application for this chapter.

This chapter's sample application uses a role of `tomcat` to protect its resources. There should already be a `tomcat` user in `%TOMCAT_HOME%/conf/tomcat-users.xml` with a role `tomcat` and password `tomcat`. The `tomcat-users.xml` file has the following entries by default:

```
<tomcat-users>
  <user name="tomcat" password="tomcat" roles="tomcat" />
  <user name="role1"  password="tomcat" roles="role1"  />
  <user name="both"   password="tomcat" roles="tomcat,role1" />
</tomcat-users>
```

Here, `name` represents the username used for logging in and `roles` is a comma-delimited list of roles. A role in this list should match the `security-role` in your `web.xml` file. To add a new user to this file (aka realm), simply create a new line:

```
<tomcat-users>
  <user name="tomcat" password="tomcat" roles="tomcat" />
  <user name="role1"  password="tomcat" roles="role1"  />
  <user name="both"   password="tomcat" roles="tomcat,role1" />
  <user name="new"    password="test"   roles="tomcat" />
</tomcat-users>
```

You will need to restart Tomcat for this change to take effect.

Keep in mind this is a simple example of how to protect your entire application and how to allow all roles in your realm. If you do add roles by name, you'll need to add the following `<security-role>` element after `<login-config>`:

```
<security-role>
    <role-name>YOUR ROLE NAME</role-name>
</security-role>
```

Also, if you want to name your realm so the user sees a friendly name in the login dialog box, you can add a <realm-name> element to <login-config>:

```
<login-config>
    <auth-method>BASIC</auth-method>
    <realm-name>My Test Application</realm-name>
</login-config>
```

This will result in the following login dialog box:

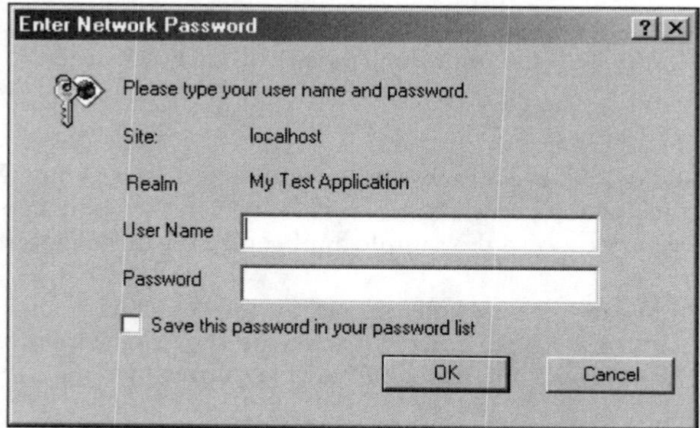

If you don't define a realm-name, the realm's value will be *server:port*, such as localhost:8080. This simple example of BASIC authentication in an application brings us to the authentication options.

Authentication Options

Using a deployment descriptor, a web client can authenticate to a web server by using one of the following mechanisms:

Mechanism	Configuration
HTTP basic authentication	<auth-method>BASIC</auth-method>
HTTP digest authentication	<auth-method>DIGEST</auth-method>
HTTPS client authentication	<auth-method>CLIENT-CERT</auth-method>
Form-based authentication	<auth-method>FORM</auth-method>

When using HTTP basic authentication, the server will authenticate a user by using a username and password from the client. In a web environment, this is basically a pop-up dialog box (see the previous screen shot). It's based on a username and password, and the password is sent using simple base64 encoding, but it isn't encrypted:

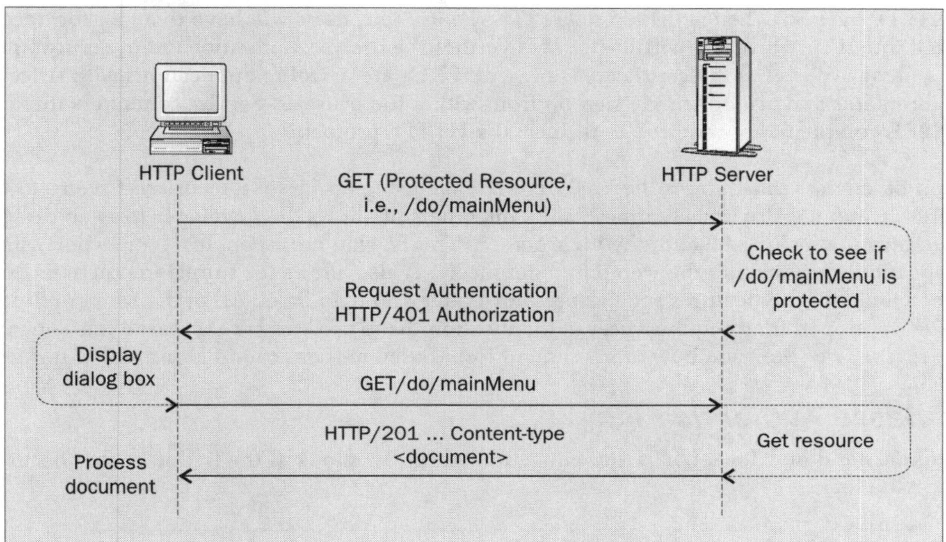

The target server isn't authenticated; therefore, this isn't a secure mechanism. The client has no proof that the server is who it says it is. For a server to prove its identity, it needs to obtain an SSL certificate from a certificate authority (such as VeriSign). If you need greater security but still wish to use basic authentication, you can combine it with SSL or a virtual private network (VPN).

HTTP digest authentication also authenticates a user on the basis of a username and password. However, the client transmits the password in an encrypted form, such as SHA or MD5. In the web arena, HTTP 1.1–enabled browsers will support this. According to the Servlet 2.4 specification, HTTP digest authentication isn't currently in widespread use, therefore servlet containers are encouraged but not required to support it. Tomcat, JBoss, and Resin support this authentication method. When you use HTTP digest authentication, the user is prompted with a username/password dialog box that looks similar to the basic authentication dialog box. However, the digest authentication dialog box indicates that the user is accessing a secure site:

HTTPS client authentication requires the user to possess a **Public Key Certificate (PKC)** and is based on HTTP over SSL, hence the name HTTPS. To use this, users will have to apply for, receive, and then install into their browser a certificate. This verifies the browser's identity and often prompts the user for a password even if the certificate is present. PKCs are useful in applications with strict security requirements and also for single sign-on from within the browser. Servlet containers that you want to be J2EE compliant are required to support the HTTPS protocol.

Form-based authentication is the final option when using declarative security. It seems to be the most desirable and it's also our favorite. Unlike the others, it allows the developer (or web designer) to customize the look and feel of the login screen. This is what most people expect when using a web application, so it fits into the web paradigm nicely. It also allows for simple instructions on the login screen and usability features such as password hints and help links. All of the web applications that we've developed (that required user authentication) have used an HTML-based implementation. For this reason, we show you how to implement form-based authentication along with a few tricks.

Form-Based Authentication

To understand how form-based authentication works, let's look at the five steps that occur in a successful login:

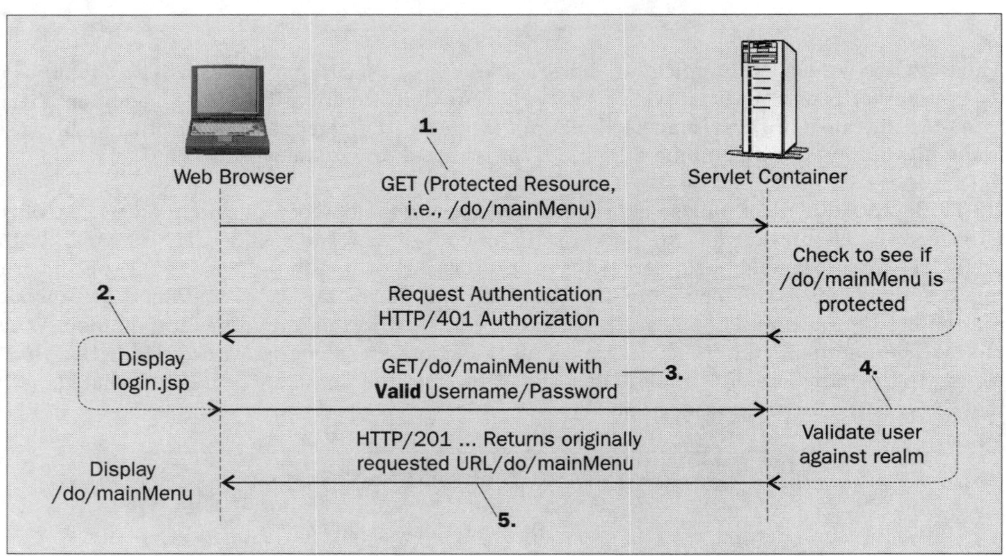

1. A user requests a protected resource (defined as protected in `web.xml`) by clicking a link, selecting a bookmark, or typing in a URL.

2. The login form associated with this protected resource is sent to the client, and the container stores the URL that the client tried to access. This is to say that the container remembers the fact that the client originally requested "/do/mainMenu".

The current servlet API doesn't allow you to get the URL the user originally tried to access. However, some servlet containers will store this value as a hidden field in the form. View the servlet container documentation to see if yours does.

3. The user populates the form with her username and password and submits it.

4. The container attempts to authenticate the user with the form's information.

5. If authentication succeeds, the client is redirected to the resource using the stored URL path.

Unfortunately, this authentication mechanism was designed to resemble HTTP basic authentication, meaning that when you enter an incorrect username or password, it returns an HTTP status code of 401. HTTP status code 401 means "This resource requires HTTP authentication." Therefore, your deployment descriptor contains entries for a login form and an error page; the error page is served up when a 401 error is encountered. This process involves the same steps as those described previously, except that last step changes to the following.

6. If authentication fails, the error page is returned and the status code of the response is set to 401.

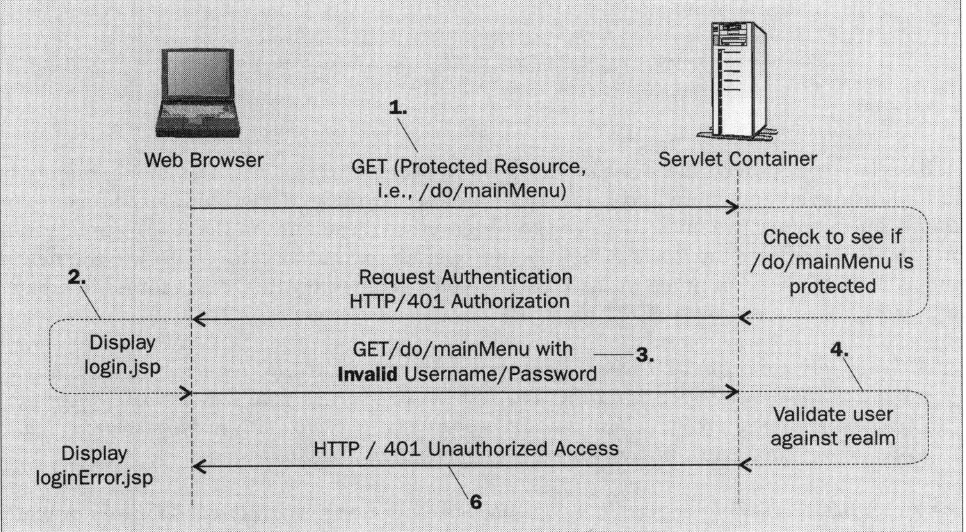

To implement form-based authentication, the first thing you need is a page with a form. The only requirements by the specification are that your form's action is `j_security_check`, and your username and password fields are named `j_username` and `j_password`, respectively. Here's an example of how this might be coded in an HTML or JSP page:

```
<form id="loginForm" method="post" action="j_security_check">
  <p>
    Username: <input type="text" name="j_username" id="j_username" />
    <br/>
    Password: <input type="password" name="j_password" id="j_password" />
    <br/>
    <button type="submit">login</button>
  </p>
</form>
```

The form error page can contain anything, but most likely it's a page explaining that the user entered an invalid username or password.

To configure form-based authentication in the deployment descriptor, let's build upon the earlier example. We've highlighted the additions:

```
<security-constraint>
    <web-resource-collection>
        <url-pattern>/*</url-pattern>
    </web-resource-collection>
    <auth-constraint>
        <role-name>*</role-name>
    </auth-constraint>
</security-constraint>
<login-config>
    <auth-method>FORM</auth-method>
    <form-login-config>
        <form-login-page>/login.jsp</form-login-page>
        <form-error-page>/loginError.jsp</form-error-page>
    </form-login-config>
</login-config>
```

You'll notice we removed the `<realm-name>` from the `<login-config>` block, mainly because it won't be displayed anywhere and is therefore useless. If you've never configured form-based authentication before, we encourage you to try entering these lines in the `ROOT` application's `web.xml` (you can also duplicate the `ROOT` directory and operate on that directory–just use the new directory name as your application name in the URL). If you decide to try this, don't forget to create `login.jsp` and `loginError.jsp` in the `ROOT` directory.

> *Although this works fine on Tomcat, it may not work on some application servers. This is because you're actually protecting* `login.jsp` *and* `loginError.jsp` *with your* `/*` `url-pattern`*. Therefore, you might need to adjust your* `url-pattern` *to protect only certain resources, your* `*.do` *actions (in Struts), rather than* all *your application's resources.*

Once a user has successfully logged in, an instance of `HttpSession` is created for him or matched up with an existing session he created. This session is active for the duration that the `<session-timeout>` value specifies in the deployment descriptor (`web.xml`). This value determines how long the server retains a user's session between interactions. Thus, if the user clicks a link or somehow sends a request to your application, the server will recalculate how long it will wait to expire the session. Once the session expires or is killed by a reboot of the application server, the user will be required to log in again. If a `session-timeout` value isn't specified, a default of 30 minutes is used. Some application servers have the ability to persist sessions to the file system (or a database), so a session can live through a reboot (provided it hasn't timed out).

It's important to note that it isn't currently possible to configure logout declaratively. This is usually done using a JSP or servlet that calls `session.invalidate()` or `session.logout()`. When you use `session.invalidate()`, all objects bound to the session are removed. If the user tries to access a protected resource again, he'll be prompted for a username/password again. In most instances, logging out is accomplished by placing a link on a page that calls `logout.jsp` or a `Logout.java` servlet. Other ways that a user can log out are by closing the browser or by exceeding the minutes of inactivity specified by the `session-timeout` parameter.

The `HttpSession.logout()` method is new in the Servlet 2.4 specification. This method logs the client out of the web server and invalidates all sessions associated with this client. The scope of the logout is the same as the scope of the authentication. For example, if the servlet container implements single sign-on, the logout logs the client out of all web applications on the servlet container and invalidates all sessions associated with the same client.

Tomcat Realms

In this section we illustrate how to set up different realms in Tomcat. As mentioned previously, a realm is a "database" of usernames, passwords, and user roles. We show you how to set up a `MemoryRealm`, a `JDBCRealm`, a `JNDIRealm`, and a `JAASRealm`.

MemoryRealm

If you have a fresh Tomcat installation that you've been using to run these examples, you should be able to log in using `tomcat/tomcat` for the username/password. These values are specified in `%TOMCAT_HOME%/conf/tomcat-users.xml`. This file is considered a `MemoryRealm`, which stores basic user information. This is the default realm for Tomcat, as specified in its `server.xml` file (located in the same directory). The following examples are from Tomcat 4.0.*x* and 4.1.*x*/5.0.*x*:

Tomcat 4.0.*x*:

```
<Realm className="org.apache.catalina.realm.MemoryRealm"/>
```

Tomcat 4.1.*x*/5.0.*x*:

```
<Resource name="UserDatabase" auth="Container"
   type="org.apache.catalina.UserDatabase"
   description="User database that can be updated and saved">
</Resource>
<ResourceParams name="UserDatabase">
     <parameter>
          <name>factory</name>
          <value>org.apache.catalina.users.MemoryUserDatabaseFactory</value>
     </parameter>
     <parameter>
          <name>pathname</name>
          <value>conf/tomcat-users.xml</value>
     </parameter>
</ResourceParams>
          ...
<Realm className="org.apache.catalina.realm.UserDatabaseRealm"
     debug="0" resourceName="UserDatabase"/>
```

In the Tomcat 4.0.*x* example, the path to the tomcat-user.xml file appears to be configured into the code base, whereas it's now configurable in the latest versions of Tomcat. Other application servers will likely support a similar file-based mechanism for storing user information, but we doubt you'd ever see this on a production system. One of the main problems with using a file-based mechanism is that most servers require a shutdown and restart to pick up any changes. It's great to use for prototyping, but if you decide to add more user information, you'll likely want to use a database or directory service. Although it's possible to use a file-based realm for usernames and passwords, and a database for the rest of the users' information, it's easier to maintain if everything is kept in the database. For that, Tomcat provides you with the JDBCRealm.

JDBCRealm

The JDBCRealm allows you to configure *declaratively* the location for storing your users' information. When we say "declaratively," we mean that the location is typed in an XML file, rather than programmed and compiled into a Java class. Tomcat also supports a JNDIRealm for looking up and authenticating users in an LDAP directory server. When using either of these methods, you'll have to create a Context for your application, so you can override the default MemoryRealm. The following is an example using the security context and a JDBCRealm to authenticate with a MySQL database named security:

```
<Context path="/security" docBase="security" debug="0">
   <Realm className="org.apache.catalina.realm.JDBCRealm" debug="99"
          driverName="com.mysql.jdbc.Driver"
          connectionURL="jdbc:mysql://localhost:3306/security?autoReconnect=true"
          connectionName="test"
          connectionPassword="test"
          userTable="users"
          userNameCol="username"
          userCredCol="password"
          userRoleTable="user_roles"
          roleNameCol="role_name" />
</Context>
```

In the preceding example, you must have a users table that contains one row for every valid user that this realm should recognize. The users table must contain at least two columns, a username (userNameCol), and a password (userCredCol). You must also have a user_roles table that contains one row for every valid role that is assigned to a particular user. A user can have zero, one, or many roles. This table must contain at least two columns, a username, and a role name (roleNameCol). The username from both the users table and the user_roles table should match the value a person enters as a username. The role name value will match up to roles specified in your application's web.xml file.

We recommend using the username as the primary key and requiring an e-mail address in this field. This will make it much easier to perform logic on a user in your application because all you need to get the user's name is request.getRemoteUser(). It will also make it easier to migrate your authentication to use an LDAP server as your user base grows or if you need to integrate with an existing system.

The following example SQL script creates the needed tables. This script has been tested only on MySQL:

```
create database if not exists security;
grant all privileges on security.* to test@localhost identified by "test";
grant all privileges on security.* to test@"%" identified by "test";
use security;

create table users (
  username          varchar(50) not null primary key,
  password          varchar(25) not null
);

create table user_roles (
  username          varchar(50) not null,
  role_name         varchar(20) not null,
  primary key (username, role_name)
);
```

Now you need to add a user to both the `users` and `user_roles` tables. You can do this with the following SQL:

```
insert into users (username, password) values ('tomcat', 'tomcat');
insert into user_roles (username, role_name) values ('tomcat', 'developer');
```

A script to create the `security` *database and a default user is located in this application's download at* `lib/metadata/sql/mysql-create.sql`.

The next step is to place a copy of the JDBC driver you'll be using inside the `%TOMCAT_HOME%/common/lib` directory. In the example application (`security-example`) for this chapter, you can find a MySQL JDBC driver JAR file at `lib/mysql-connector-java-2.0.14/mysql-connector-java-2.0.14-bin.jar`.

To demonstrate that this works, perform the following steps:

1. Put the preceding context into a file named `security.xml` and place it in `%TOMCAT_HOME%/webapps`.

2. Create a `security` directory in the webapps directory, and create an `index.jsp` file in this directory. Type in something like "Congratulations, you've authenticated successfully!"

3. Create a WEB-INF directory in the security directory, and create a web.xml file in this directory. Put the following XML in this file. Note that you're allowing all roles to log into this application:

```
<?xml version="1.0" encoding="ISO-8859-1"?>

<web-app xmlns="http://java.sun.com/xml/ns/j2ee"
         xmlns:xsi="http://www.w3.org/2001/XMLSchema-instance"
         xsi:schemaLocation="http://java.sun.com/xml/ns/j2ee/web-app_2_4.xsd"
         version="2.4">

    <display-name>Security Example</display-name>
    <description>Web Application Security Example</description>
    <security-constraint>
        <web-resource-collection>
            <web-resource-name>My Application</web-resource-name>
            <url-pattern>/*</url-pattern>
        </web-resource-collection>
        <auth-constraint>
            <role-name>*</role-name>
        </auth-constraint>
    </security-constraint>
    <login-config>
        <auth-method>BASIC</auth-method>
        <realm-name>My Test Application</realm-name>
    </login-config>
</web-app>
```

4. Start Tomcat and navigate to http://localhost:8080/security. You should be prompted with a dialog box that looks like the following:

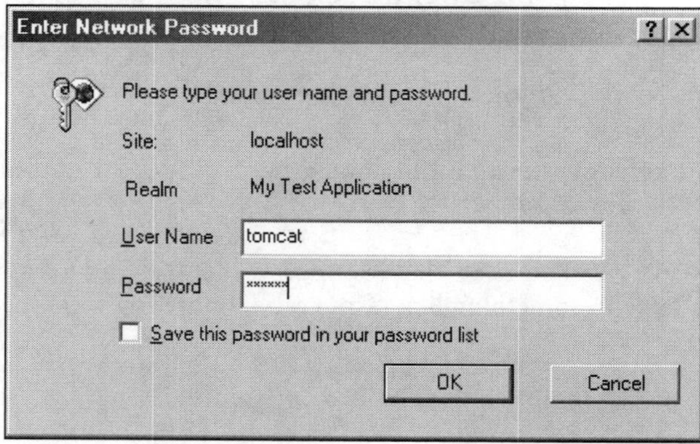

5. After you enter a username of "tomcat" and a password of "tomcat", you should see the following in your browser:

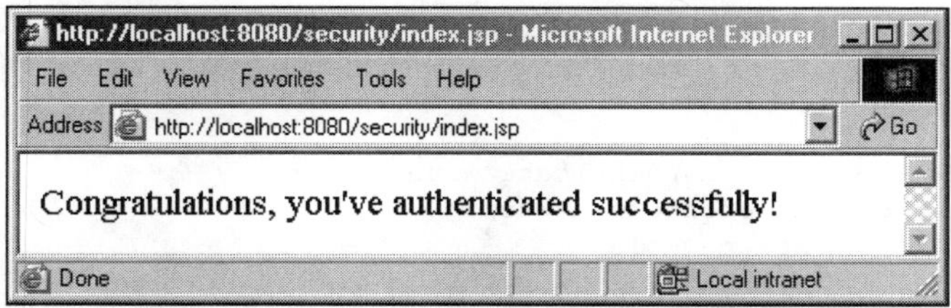

If you'd rather authenticate with an LDAP server, you can also configure a `JNDIRealm` in Tomcat. On most large projects we've worked on, an LDAP server was involved for storing user information.

JNDIRealm

The `JNDIRealm`'s configuration is similar to the `JDBCRealm`'s because it is configured using XML; however, the realms' attributes are slightly different. For this example, we installed OpenLDAP version 2.1.12 on a RedHat 8.0 machine. This machine's host name is drevil.

We installed the OpenLDAP server according to the quick start guide at http://www.openldap.org/doc/admin/quickstart.html. Then we edited the `slapd.conf` file. At the top of the file, we had to include two additional schema entries:

```
include         /usr/local/etc/openldap/schema/core.schema
include         /usr/local/etc/openldap/schema/cosine.schema
include         /usr/local/etc/openldap/schema/inetorgperson.schema
```

By default, only `core.schema` was included. In the same file, at the bottom, we defined the settings as follows:

```
database bdb
suffix "dc=raibledesigns,dc=com"
rootdn "cn=Manager,dc=raibledesigns,dc=com"
rootpw secret
directory /usr/local/var/openldap-data
```

Then we created an **LDAP Data Interchange Format (LDIF)** file to create our top-level organization entry, the organization units for groups and people and, finally, the `tomcat` user and the `developer` role:

```
# Define top-level entry
dn: dc=raibledesigns,dc=com
objectClass: dcObject
objectClass: organization
o: Raible Designs, Inc.
dc: raibledesigns

# Define Manager Role to authenticate with
dn: cn=Manager,dc=raibledesigns,dc=com
objectclass: organizationalRole
cn: Manager
description: Directory Manager

# Define an entry to contain people
# searches for users are based on this entry
dn: ou=people,dc=raibledesigns,dc=com
objectClass: organizationalUnit
ou: people

# Define a user entry for Tomcat User
dn: uid=tomcat,ou=people,dc=raibledesigns,dc=com
objectClass: inetOrgPerson
uid: tomcat
sn: user
cn: tomcat user
mail: tomcat@raibledesigns.com
userPassword: tomcat

# Define an entry to contain LDAP groups
# searches for roles are based on this entry
dn: ou=groups,dc=raibledesigns,dc=com
objectClass: organizationalUnit
ou: groups

# Define an entry for the "developer" role
dn: cn=developer,ou=groups,dc=raibledesigns,dc=com
objectClass: groupOfUniqueNames
cn: developer
uniqueMember: uid=tomcat,ou=people,dc=raibledesigns,dc=com
```

We named this file `entries.ldif`, placed it in the root user's home directory, and imported it using the `ldapadd` command:

```
ldapadd -x -D "cn=Manager,dc=raibledesigns,dc=com" -W -f ~/entries.ldif
```

Following this procedure should result in a number of "adding new entry" lines displayed in your console window:

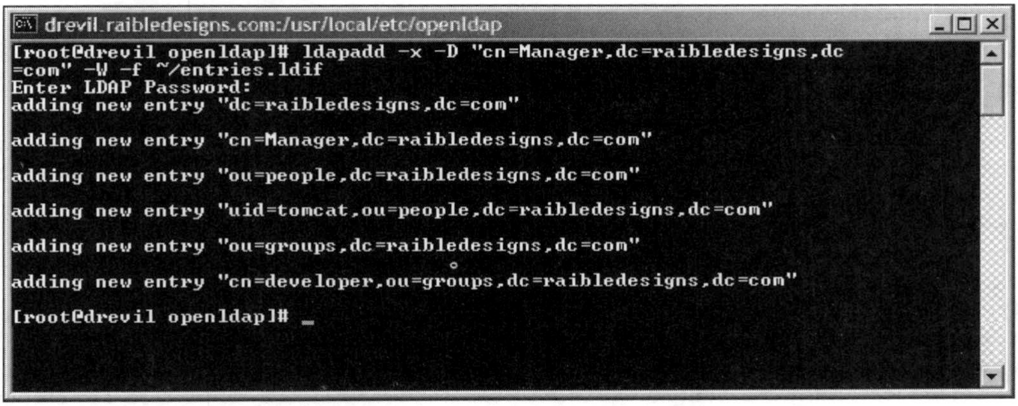

```
drevil.raibledesigns.com:/usr/local/etc/openldap
[root@drevil openldap]# ldapadd -x -D "cn=Manager,dc=raibledesigns,dc
=com" -W -f ~/entries.ldif
Enter LDAP Password:
adding new entry "dc=raibledesigns,dc=com"

adding new entry "cn=Manager,dc=raibledesigns,dc=com"

adding new entry "ou=people,dc=raibledesigns,dc=com"

adding new entry "uid=tomcat,ou=people,dc=raibledesigns,dc=com"

adding new entry "ou=groups,dc=raibledesigns,dc=com"

adding new entry "cn=developer,ou=groups,dc=raibledesigns,dc=com"

[root@drevil openldap]# _
```

If you get any errors, we found that it was easy to start over by stopping LDAP (using the `kill` command), and removing the contents of the `/usr/local/var/openldap-data/` directory.

The `slapd.conf` and `entries.ldif` files used for this example are located in the example application in `metadata/ldif/`. To enable use of the `JNDIRealm` (instead of the `JDBCRealm`), replace the previous realm configuration with the following:

```
<Realm className="org.apache.catalina.realm.JNDIRealm" debug="99"
       connectionName="cn=Developer,dc=raibledesigns,dc=com"
       connectionPassword="secret"
       connectionURL="ldap://drevil:389"
       userPassword="userPassword"
       userPattern="uid={0},ou=people,dc=raibledesigns,dc=com"
       roleBase="ou=groups,dc=raibledesigns,dc=com"
       roleName="cn"
       roleSearch="(uniqueMember={0})"
/>
```

You'll need the JNDI drivers for LDAP in your class path for this to work. You can download the latest LDAP Service Provider (version 1.2.4) from http://java.sun.com/products/jndi/index.html#download. After you've downloaded it, extract `ldap.jar` into `%TOMCAT_HOME%/common/lib`.

Optionally, you can set the default realm for your entire server to be a JDBC or JNDI realm. To do this, edit Tomcat's `server.xml` file (in `%TOMCAT_HOME%/common/lib`), and replace the default realm (shown next) with your desired realm's information.

```
<Realm className="org.apache.catalina.realm.UserDatabaseRealm"
    debug="0" resourceName="UserDatabase"
/>
```

JAASRealm

Tomcat has support for a `JAASRealm` as well, but it's not included in the Tomcat documentation, so information is a little scarce. We show you how to configure a `JAASRealm` in the "Java Authentication and Authorization Service" section later in this chapter.

For the purposes of this chapter and its associated example application, we use a JDBCRealm.

Using Secure Sockets Layer

So far, we've discussed setting up a form-based login and configuring it to talk to a realm. One problem with the example so far is that the communication between the browser and server isn't secure. If someone were listening with a password sniffer, your security would be compromised. Furthermore, these sniffers are easy to come by–try searching Google for "password sniffer".

According to "The Guide to Building Secure Web Applications, Version 1.1.1" from the Open Web Application Security Project (http://www.owasp.org), "The most common method of securing the HTTP protocol is to use **SSL**. The **Secure Socket Layer** protocol, or SSL, was designed by Netscape and was introduced in the Netscape Communicator browser in 1994. It's most likely the widest spoken security protocol in the world, and is built into all commercial web browsers and web servers. The current version is Version 2. Since the original version of SSL is technically a proprietary protocol, the **Internet Engineering Task Force (IETF)** took over responsibilities for upgrading SSL, and have now renamed it **Transport Layer Security (TLS)**. The first version of TLS is version 3.1, and has only minor changes from the original specification."

SSL is a technology that allows web browsers and web servers to communicate over a secure channel. In SSL, data is encrypted at the browser (before transmission) and then decrypted at the server before reading the data. This same process takes place when the server returns data to the client. This process is known as the *SSL handshake*. There currently are three different levels of encryption supported by this protocol: 40-bit, 56-bit, and 128-bit. The more security you need, the more bits you should use. For more on the SSL handshake, visit http://medialab.di.unipi.it/doc/JNetSec/jns_ch11.htm.

The best way to gain a good understanding of SSL is to implement it. The first step to setting up SSL on your web server (in this case, Tomcat) is to generate a certificate. Keep in mind that if you are proxying your JSP/servlet requests through a traditional web server (such as Apache or IIS), you'll need to set up SSL on those servers. The documentation for setting up Tomcat's SSL support is excellent, but we go over it here so it's familiar to you.

Secure Sockets Layer on Tomcat

If you're using JDK 1.3.*x*, you'll need to download the **Java Secure Socket Extension (JSSE)** from http://java.sun.com/products/jsse/ and install the associated JARs (jcert.jar, jnet.jar, and jsse.jar) into $JAVA_HOME/ jre/lib/ext/. If you're using JDK 1.4.*x*, JSSE has been integrated into its core, so no additional download is needed.

Create a certificate keystore by executing the following command:

```
$JAVA_HOME/bin/keytool -genkey -alias tomcat -keyalg RSA
```

Specify a password value of changeit. This process should resemble the following session:

```
C:\WINDOWS\System32\cmd.exe
C:\>keytool -genkey -alias tomcat -keyalg RSA
Enter keystore password:  changeit
What is your first and last name?
  [Unknown]:  localhost
What is the name of your organizational unit?
  [Unknown]:  Java
What is the name of your organization?
  [Unknown]:  Apress
What is the name of your City or Locality?
  [Unknown]:  Berkeley
What is the name of your State or Province?
  [Unknown]:  CA
What is the two-letter country code for this unit?
  [Unknown]:  US
Is CN=localhost, OU=Java, O=Apress, L=Berkeley, ST=CA, C=US correct?
  [no]:  yes

Enter key password for <tomcat>
        (RETURN if same as keystore password):

C:\>_
```

We've used **localhost** as the **first and last name** values, because this is the value matched by your browser when verifying authenticity of the certificate. It actually shows up as the *certification path* in the resulting certificate. This is still not a valid certificate because you're generating it yourself. To get a valid certificate, you must purchase one from a **certificate authority (CA)** such as VeriSign. In this example, using localhost will result in one less warning in the user's browser.

Now, edit `%TOMCAT_HOME%/conf/server.xml` and remove the comments around the `SSL HTTP/1.1 Connector` entry. Once you've set this up, you should be able to access Tomcat using https://localhost:8443. Don't forget the s after http. The port has to be specified because it isn't the default port for HTTPS (port 443). If you don't want to specify your port numbers on your URLs when using Tomcat, you can easily change them in the `server.xml` file. When accessing Tomcat for the first time on its SSL port, you should be prompted with a security alert:

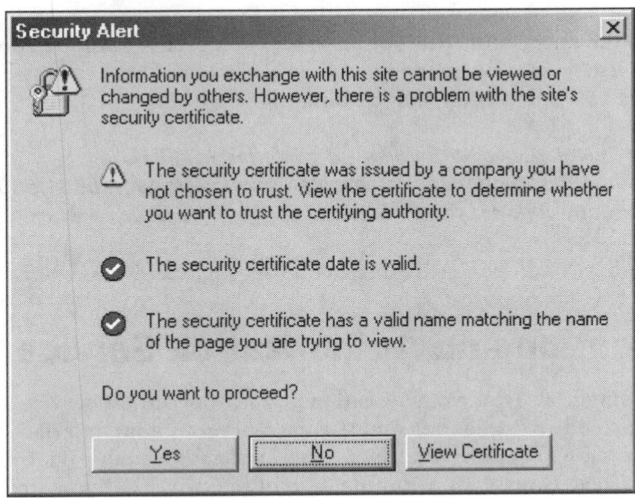

If you use your real name rather than localhost when generating this certificate, this security alert will warn you that the certificate's name doesn't match the name of the page you're trying to view:

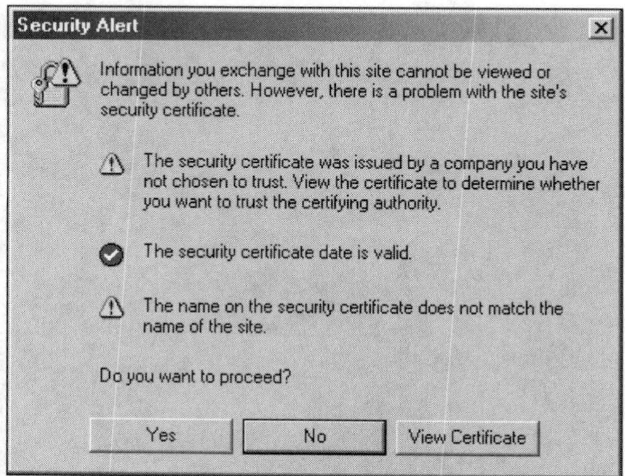

As a word of caution, we've encountered problems when running Tomcat on 80/443 and IIS on a Windows machine at the same time. Shutting down IIS allowed us to run Tomcat on 443. The strange part is that IIS was running on port 81 and we had no secure port running. When you see Tomcat start and then immediately shut down, a port conflict is often the cause of the problem.

One thing you'll probably notice after setting this up is that your browser warns you about the certificate. This is because the issuer of the certificate is unknown (you) and the browser doesn't recognize you as a CA. CAs, such as VeriSign (http://www.verisign.com), Thawte (http://thawte.com), and TC TrustCenter (http://www.trustcenter.de/set_en.htm), are trusted organizations that verify and certify that a server is who it says it is. Also, you can obtain client certificates if you want to set up both client and server certificates. This may be necessary in highly secure, top-secret, *X Files*–flavored applications, but it's not necessary for most web applications.

One drawback to using SSL in your web application is that it tends to slow things down significantly. This is mainly due to the encryption/decryption process on each end of the connection. Therefore, we recommend that you use it only for the parts of your application that really need it, for instance, when a user logs in or when a user submits a credit card number.

> *You can find more information on performance degradation with SSL at http://www.computerworld.com/securitytopics/security/story/0,10801,58978,00.html. This article also contains links to other articles and options for SSL acceleration.*

Next, we'll show you how to do SSL switching upon user login and also before the user logs in.

Java Authentication and Authorization Service

You might be wondering how **Java Authentication and Authorization Service (JAAS)** fits into all of this. JAAS is designed to provide a framework and standard programming interface for authenticating users and for assigning privileges. Together with Java 2, an application can provide code-centric access control, user-centric access control, or a combination of the two. JAAS was invented to make login services independent of authentication technologies and allow **Pluggable Authentication Modules (PAM)**. Most modern application servers use JAAS under the covers to configure container-managed security–you're using it without even knowing that you are!

JAAS can be helpful when you need to use complex authentication schemas or when you grant resource-specific privileges to users (for example, inserting a row in the database or assigning write permissions to a file). At its core, JAAS is essentially a security mechanism (now integrated into J2SE 1.4) that allows you to specify authentication and authorization via policy files. When you run your application server with a security manager, a policy file is checked, and then the user is allowed to run your application or is prompted for credentials. As we mentioned, JAAS does allow for complex login schemas, such as a Windows NT domain or smart cards (SecurID).

> *You can find more information on the login schemas supported at* http://java.sun.com/j2se/1.4/docs/guide/security/jaas/JAASRefGuide.html#AppendixB.

To set up your application server to use JAAS specifically for your application, rather than its own authentication mechanism, you usually have to select a JAAS custom realm and then perform a few additional steps. The following steps set up a `JAASRealm` on Tomcat *4.x-5.x* (on a Windows machine) to authenticate with an NT domain.

The easiest way to do this is to download Andy Armstrong's JAAS login modules from http://free.tagish.net/jaas/. These modules were written specifically for authenticating with a Windows NT domain and are similar to the helper classes that make the `JDBCRealm` work behind the scenes. Once you've downloaded the ZIP file, extract the contents of the downloaded file to a `jaas-modules` directory. At the time of this writing, version 1.0.3 was the latest available download.

Once you've downloaded the login modules, add the path to the `NTSystem.dll` file to your `$PATH` environment variable. In the `Samples config` folder, you'll find a `tagish.login` file and a `java.security.sample` file. Copy the last few lines from `java.security.sample` and put it at the end of the `java.security` file (located in `$JAVA_HOME/jre/lib/security`). This line looks as follows:

```
# Login configs
login.config.url.1=file:${java.home}/lib/security/tagish.login
```

Then move the `tagish.login` file into the same directory (`$JAVA_HOME/jre/lib/security`). If your users always log into the same domain (which is what we've configured here), just set the `defaultDomain` property in `tagish.login` as follows:

```
NTLogin
{
    com.tagish.auth.win32.NTSystemLogin required returnNames=true
        returnSIDs=false defaultDomain=raibledesigns;
};
```

> *Make sure to change the* `defaultDomain` *value from* `raibledesigns` *to the domain you want to communicate with.*

Once you've completed these setup steps, you need to change your context to have the following realm configuration:

```
<Realm className="org.apache.catalina.realm.JAASRealm" debug="99"
    appName="NTLogin"
    userClassNames="com.tagish.auth.win32.NTPrincipal"
    roleClassNames="com.tagish.auth.win32.NTPrincipal" />
```

We tested this setup and configuration on a Windows XP machine, and everything worked smoothly. We were able to log in using the same username/password combination we used for logging onto Windows. Also, we didn't have a domain, just a workgroup, and everything worked flawlessly there as well.

If you don't want to use Andy Armstrong's JAAS login modules, you can create your own file-based JAAS `LoginModule` by performing the following steps.

First, create a `LoginModule` class that implements `javax.security.auth.login.LoginContext`:

```
package com.apress.projsp20.ch11.jaas;

import java.util.Map;
import java.security.Principal;
import javax.security.auth.login.LoginContext;
import javax.security.auth.Subject;
import javax.security.auth.callback.*;
import javax.security.auth.login.*;
import javax.security.auth.spi.LoginModule;
import java.io.IOException;

public class MyLoginModule implements LoginModule {
    protected CallbackHandler callbackHandler = null;
    protected boolean committed = false;
    protected boolean debug = false;
    protected Map options = null;
    protected Principal principal = null;
    protected Map sharedState = null;
    protected Subject subject = null;
    protected void log(String message) {
        System.out.print("MyLoginModule: ");
        System.out.println(message);
    }

    public boolean abort() throws LoginException {
        log("abort");
        return (true);
    }

    public boolean commit() throws LoginException {
        log("commit phase");
        // If authentication was not successful, just return false
        if (principal == null){
            log("no principal commit fails");
            return (false);
        }
        if (!subject.getPrincipals().contains(principal))
            subject.getPrincipals().add(principal);
        // add role principals
        subject.getPrincipals().add(new MyRolePrincipal("admin"));
        committed = true;
        log("commit successful");
        return (true);
    }

    public void initialize(Subject subject,
                           CallbackHandler callbackHandler,
                           Map sharedState, Map options) {
```

```
        // Save configuration values
        this.subject = subject;
        this.callbackHandler = callbackHandler;
        this.sharedState = sharedState;
        this.options = options;
    }

  public boolean login() throws LoginException {
        log("login phase");
        // Set up our CallbackHandler requests
        if (callbackHandler == null)
            throw new LoginException("No CallbackHandler specified");
        Callback callbacks[] = new Callback[2];
        callbacks[0] = new NameCallback("Username: ");
        callbacks[1] = new PasswordCallback("Password: ", false);

        // Interact with the user to retrieve the username and password
        String username = null;
        String password = null;
        try {
            callbackHandler.handle(callbacks);
            username = ((NameCallback) callbacks[0]).getName();
            password =
                new String(((PasswordCallback) callbacks[1]).getPassword());
        } catch (IOException e) {
            throw new LoginException(e.toString());
        } catch (UnsupportedCallbackException e) {
            throw new LoginException(e.toString());
        }
        if (!authenticate(username,password))
            return false;
        principal = new MyPrincipal(username);
        return true;
    }

    public boolean logout() throws LoginException {

        subject.getPrincipals().remove(principal);
        committed = false;
        principal = null;
        return (true);
    }

    boolean authenticate(String s,String p){
       return (s.compareTo("jaas") == 0) && (p.compareTo("jaas") == 0);
    }

    static public void main(String args[]) throws Exception{
        LoginContext ctx = new LoginContext("TomCatAdminApplication");
        ctx.login();

    }
}
```

Create a `MyPrinciple` class that implements `java.security.Principle`, and a role class (this can extend your existing `MyPrinciple` class):

```
package com.apress.projsp20.ch11.jaas;

public class MyPrincipal implements java.security.Principal {
    String m_Name = new String("");
    public MyPrincipal(String name) {
        m_Name = name;
    }

    public boolean equals(Object another) {
        try {
            MyPrincipal pm = (MyPrincipal)another;
            return pm.m_Name.equalsIgnoreCase(m_Name);
        } catch(Exception e){
            return false;
        }
    }

    public String getName() {
        return m_Name;
    }

    public int hashCode() {
        return m_Name.hashCode();
    }
    public String toString() {
        return  m_Name;
    }
}
```

```
package com.apress.projsp20.ch11.jaas;

public class MyRolePrincipal extends MyPrincipal {
    /** Creates a new instance of MyRolePrincipal */
    public MyRolePrincipal(String s) {
        super(s);
    }
}
```

Now you'll need to configure your application's context to use these newly created (and compiled, of course) classes:

```
<Realm className="org.apache.catalina.realm.JAASRealm" debug="99"
    appName="MyApp"
    userClassNames="com.apress.projsp20.ch11.jaas.MyPrinciple"
    roleClassNames="com.apress.projsp20.ch11.jaas.MyRolePrinciple" />
```

Configure the location of your JAAS configuration file in `jre/lib/security/java.security`:

```
login.config.url=file://${path/to/auth.conf}
```

Finally, configure JAAS for your application in the auth.conf file:

```
MyApp {
    com.apress.projsp20.ch11.jaas.MyLoginModule required;
};
```

Form-Based Authentication Tips and Tricks

Now that we've discussed how to use form-based authentication with your server's realms, we'd like to share some tips and tricks. Many of these have been client requests or usability enhancements, and we think they'll make developing your secure application easier.

The Welcome File

It's important in a web application to configure the opening page that users will see. Adding the following <welcome-file-list> element to your web.xml file can do this:

```
<welcome-file-list>
    <welcome-file>index.jsp</welcome-file>
</welcome-file-list>
```

In some application servers, this is already configured to be index.html and index.jsp by default, but it doesn't hurt to specify this and increase your application's portability. After you've configured your welcome file, it's easy to add a few simple lines to forward the user to a protected resource:

```
<% response.sendRedirect("/welcome.do"); %>
```

One nice addition to the Servlet 2.4 specification is that you can actually set your welcome file to use a servlet; you were unable to do this in earlier versions. This is to say that the following will work when using a Servlet 2.4–compliant container:

```
<welcome-file>/welcome.do</welcome-file>
```

When you use form-based authentication and you forward to a protected resource, you're presented with the page specified in your web.xml file–in this chapter's example application, it's login.jsp. To make this page friendlier than just a login form, we usually do one of the following:

- Include a welcome message on this page
- Include a welcome message from another JSP using <jsp:include>
- Use a templating mechanism such as Tiles or SiteMesh to combine the two pages and the appropriate URL in the redirect's value

You can find more information on Tiles and SiteMesh at http://jakarta.apache.org/struts/userGuide/dev_tiles.html *and* http://www.opensymphony.com/sitemesh/, *respectively.*

Allowing Login on an Error Page

With HTTP basic authentication, users may find it frustrating when their login fails. In some browsers (Internet Explorer for the Mac), if you enter invalid credentials an HTTP status code (401 – Unauthorized) is returned and an error message is displayed on the screen. Mozilla handles this better by prompting you again for valid credentials. This is the ideal situation and is what most usability experts recommend. The default behavior with form-based authentication is similar to the undesirable behavior previously described.

Don't worry, though—there are a couple of techniques that help solve this problem. The first involves using one JSP to serve up both the login page and the error page. The second involves using cookies to capture the requested URL and reuse it.

Using the same page as your `form-login-page` and `form-error-page` is as simple as configuring your `web.xml` to handle this:

```
<form-login-config>
    <form-login-page>/login.jsp</form-login-page>
    <form-error-page>/login.jsp</form-error-page>
</form-login-config>
```

One problem with this approach is that the user will see the same page again—with no error information—if the login fails. So let's add a little indicator to the `form-error-page` to indicate that the login has failed:

```
<form-error-page>/login.jsp?error=true</form-error-page>
```

Now it's possible to grab this parameter in your JSP and display an error message if authentication fails:

```
<c:if test="${param.error != null}">
    <div class="error">
        Invalid username and/or password, please try again.
    </div>
</c:if>
```

Though this seems easy enough, it has been known to fail on some containers. When this happens, the containers are still complying with the specification. However, you can work a little magic to attempt to log in again from the error page.

In working with iPlanet Application Server 6.*x*, which required two separate pages in `<login-config>`, we stumbled upon this solution when viewing the source of the `login.jsp` in the browser. The HTML source showed all kinds of good information, in particular the original URL requested as a hidden field. Using this hidden field, we were able to set this value as a cookie and reuse it in our form's action on the `login-error-page`.

You can find the details of this procedure at http://husted.com/struts/resources/fb-auth.htm.

Unfortunately, there's no portable mechanism to acquire the URL that was originally requested, and there's no guarantee that this is even possible. All you know is that the container has detected that a protected URL was requested and that there was no user currently authenticated. One solution might be to use a filter to track all recently requested URLs and get the last requested URL from it. You'll want to make sure your login form is a `*.jspf` (JSP fragment) file so you can include it in both the `form-login-page` and `form-error-page`.

We tried this on Tomcat with the `BreadCrumbFilter` *in this chapter's example application, and although we were able to get the requested URL with Internet Explorer, it didn't work in Mozilla. Because this chapter is designed to describe the Servlet specification, and Tomcat is the reference implementation, the sample application uses the first (same JSP) method.*

Using Secure Sockets Layer for Login Only

As mentioned earlier, using SSL can slow down the performance of your application, so it's wise to use it only when it's needed. A good use of SSL is when a user logs in. This means that a user who accesses the login page using the HTTP protocol (http://) will be switched over to HTTPS (https://) when the username and password are sent across the wire. In this example, you'll use a `Login` servlet to process the initial login request, switch to SSL, and then redirect to the container's authentication mechanism.

This is the first time the sample application comes into play, so we explain it a bit. This application, which we refer to as `security-example.war` for simplicity's sake, is designed to hold all the security mechanisms described in this chapter. Both source code and binary versions of this application are available for download. You can complete most of these exercises by using the binary version and tweaking the `security-example.xml` file and the application's `web.xml` file.

Using a Servlet

The first feature that this application offers is an SSL-based login. To do this, you create a servlet that will intercept login requests. This servlet is called `LoginServlet`, and it maps to a `url-pattern` of `/auth/*`. Then rather than using `j_security_check` for your login form's `action` attribute, you'll use `auth/`. Here's what the form looks like on the login page:

```
<form id="loginForm" method="post" action="auth/">
```

To turn secure login on, you need to edit the `web.xml` file that ships with this application, setting the `isSecure` `init-parameter` to `true`:

```
<servlet>
    <servlet-name>login</servlet-name>
    <display-name>Login Servlet</display-name>
    <servlet-class>org.appfuse.webapp.action.LoginServlet</servlet-class>
     <init-param>
        <param-name>authURL</param-name>
        <param-value>j_security_check</param-value>
     </init-param>
     <init-param>
        <param-name>isSecure</param-name>
        <param-value>true</param-value>
     </init-param>
     <init-param>
```

```
        <param-name>encrypt-password</param-name>
        <param-value>false</param-value>
    </init-param>
    <init-param>
        <param-name>algorithm</param-name>
        <param-value>SHA</param-value>
    </init-param>
    <load-on-startup>3</load-on-startup>
</servlet>
```

If you're building the security-example project from source, the parameters for the login servlet are specified at build time. The default settings are contained in the `app-settings.xml` file and can be overwritten from the command line by using `-Dname=<value>` (which would mean `-Dsecure.login=true` in this case). The `secure.login` is turned off by default, so you'll need to add `secure.login=true` to your `build.properties` file or pass it in on the command line.

Now let's dig into this servlet and see what makes it tick. First, we must confess that we did get some of the magic that makes this work from a *JavaWorld* article by Steve Ditlinger. We're using two classes from this article: `SslUtil` and `RequestUtil`.

> *You can find Steve Ditlinger's article, titled "Mix protocols transparently in Web applications," online at* http://www.javaworld.com/javaworld/jw-02-2002/jw-0215-ssl.html.

If your HTTP and HTTPS ports are different from the defaults, 80 and 443, you'll need to change the two context parameters in `web.xml` for the HTTP and HTTPS ports. In the source distribution, you can edit `web.xml` in the `web/WEB-INF` folder. Currently, these values are set as follows:

```
<context-param>
    <param-name>listenPort_http</param-name>
    <param-value>8080</param-value>
</context-param>

<context-param>
    <param-name>listenPort_https</param-name>
    <param-value>8443</param-value>
</context-param>
```

These values, along with the servlet's initialization parameters, are loaded when the servlet starts. We don't provide the code here, because we're guessing you already understand how to retrieve context and initialization parameters. Here's the `LoginServlet.init()` method, which retrieves these values from `web.xml`:

```
public void init() throws ServletException
{
    // Get the container authentication URL for FORM-based Authentication
    // J2EE specification says should be j_security_check
    authURL = getInitParameter(Constants.AUTH_URL);

    // Get the encryption algorithm to use for encrypting passwords before
    // storing in database
    algorithm = getInitParameter(Constants.ENC_ALGORITHM);

    /* This determines if the login uses SSL or not */
    secure = Boolean.valueOf(getInitParameter("isSecure"));

    /* This determines if the password should be encrypted programmatically */
    encrypt = Boolean.valueOf(getInitParameter("encrypt-password"));

    if (log.isDebugEnabled()) {
        log.debug("Authentication URL: " + authURL);
        log.debug("Use SSL for login? " + secure);
        log.debug("Programmatic encryption of password? " + encrypt);
        log.debug("Encryption algorithm: " + algorithm);
    }

    // ensure the authorization url parameter is present
    if (authURL == null) {
        throw new ServletException(
            "No 'authURL' Context Parameter supplied in web.xml");
    }

    initializeSchemePorts(getServletContext());
    getServletContext().setAttribute(Constants.HTTP_PORT, httpPort);
    getServletContext().setAttribute(Constants.HTTPS_PORT, httpsPort);
    getServletContext().setAttribute(Constants.SECURE_LOGIN, secure);
    getServletContext().setAttribute(Constants.ENC_ALGORITHM, algorithm);

    if (log.isDebugEnabled()) {
        log.debug("HTTP Port: " + httpPort);
        log.debug("HTTPS Port: " + httpsPort);
    }
}
```

In this servlet's `execute` method (which both `doGet` and `doPost` call), you have the following code to determine if the current protocol is correct and, if not, to switch protocols:

```
    String redirectString = SslUtil.getRedirectString(request,
        getServletContext(), secure.booleanValue());

    if (redirectString != null) {
        // Redirect the page to the desired URL
        response.sendRedirect(response.encodeRedirectURL(redirectString));
        if (log.isDebugEnabled()) {
            log.debug("switching protocols, redirecting user");
        }
    }
```

In the preceding code, `secure.booleanValue()` is the value set by the `isSecure` `<init-param>` of the servlet. Once you have the correct protocol (in this case, HTTPS), you execute the servlet again, and this time the `redirectString` will be null. Therefore, the rest of the code will execute:

```
/* URLEncoder.encode is called to convert any non-allowed characters to
 * their URL Safe equivalent - response.encodeURL only adds the session id
 * The URLEncoder.encode method has changed its signature between J2SE 1.3.1
 * and 1.4, and therefore we use the org.apache.struts.util.RequestUtils class
 * from Struts. This class uses reflection to determine the appropriate
 * encoding.
 */

    String req = authURL + "?j_username=" + RequestUtils.encodeURL(username)
                 + "&j_password=" + RequestUtils.encodeURL(encryptedPassword);

    if (redirectString == null) {
        // signifies already correct protocol

        if (log.isDebugEnabled()) {
            log.debug("Authenticating user '" + username + "'");
        }

        response.sendRedirect(response.encodeRedirectURL(req));
    }
```

Using a Tag Library

If you're running your application on the default HTTP (80) and HTTPS (443) ports, you can use a tag library to force the use of a protocol on that particular page. A nonstandard port for HTTPS causes problems in Internet Explorer and results in a Server Not Found error. The "Using a Servlet" section of this chapter describes a nice workaround for this problem.

In the example application, we have a `Secure.java` tag library (written by John Lipsky, http://blog.xesoft.com/jon.lipsky/blog/) that can be used to force SSL or non-SSL on a particular JSP. Its syntax is as follows:

```
<security-example:secure mode="secured"/>
```

Here, `mode` can be `secured`, `unsecured`, or `either`. Also, if you leave out the `mode` attribute, it will default to `secured` mode.

Building on the `Servlet` example, where the variable `secureLogin` is set in the application scope, you can retrieve it and use it on your `login.jsp` page to force SSL:

```
<c:if test="${applicationScope.secureLogin == 'true'}">
    <security-example:secure />
</c:if>
```

Secure Sockets Layer Summary

Hopefully, this section has given you an idea of how you can control SSL for a specific servlet in your application. If you need to guarantee SSL for your entire application, we recommend setting the `<transport-guarantee>` element in the `web.xml` file to `INTEGRAL` or `CONFIDENTIAL`. This value is used to specify the how data should be sent between the client and server. In the example application, this value is set as illustrated here:

```
<user-data-constraint>
    <description>
        Encryption is not required for the application in general.
    </description>
    <transport-guarantee>NONE</transport-guarantee>
</user-data-constraint>
```

The Servlet specification defines each of these values as follows:

Value	Description
NONE	The application doesn't require any transport guarantee. This is the same as not including the `<user-data-constraint>` element in `web.xml`.
INTEGRAL	The application requires that the data sent between the client and server be sent in such a way that it can't be changed in transit.
CONFIDENTIAL	The application requires that the data be transmitted in a fashion that prevents other entities from observing the contents of the transmission.

Most servlet containers will switch the client to SSL when this value is set to `INTEGRAL` or `CONFIDENTIAL`. Although this is great for applications that require it, you have to be careful when implementing it. On most servlet containers, if you set this value to either `INTEGRAL` or `CONFIDENTIAL`, your application will be available *only* on the SSL port. The slick thing is that the server will automatically redirect you to https://serverName:443 when you try to access your application. However, if you're running your secure server on a port other than 443, you'll get a Server Not Found error in Internet Explorer. This leads into our next trick: using a filter to inspect requests to your protected resources.

Using a Filter on Protected Resources

When you filter protected resources, it's possible to use the same SSL switch to make your entire application secure on any port and also to retrieve a user's information. After the user has authenticated with your application, you'll probably want to get more information about her. One limitation of container-managed security is that all you'll know about a user is her username and what roles she belongs to. To solve this, we suggest using a filter that checks for a `User` object in the session and populates it if it's null. To demonstrate this, you need to create a `User` object, database access code, and a database to talk to.

> *In the security project, you can create a populated MySQL database using a* `setup-db` *Ant task. The download has a* `security-example.sql` *file in it that you can use to create and populate the database as well.*

Now that you've populated the database, you can get information from it using your filter. We've created a filter named `ActionFilter.java` that is mapped to the same `<url-pattern>` (`*.do`) as our protected resources. This way, it will get called only after someone has authenticated successfully. We like to use a helper class for calling the persistence layer–this class is named `UserManager.java`, and it uses the **Business Delegate** pattern.

You can find more information about the Business Delegate pattern at http://java.sun.com/blueprints/corej2eepatterns/Patterns/BusinessDelegate.html.

It's important to hide the implementation details from your filter by using a Business Delegate so that you can switch to a new persistence layer (for example, EJBs) at any given time. We don't go into the details behind the `UserManager` and how it works, so you'll have to trust us when we say that the `UserManager.getUser()` method returns a populated JavaBean of user properties. Let's take a look at the deployment descriptor for this filter:

```
<filter>
  <filter-name>actionFilter</filter-name>
  <display-name>Action Filter</display-name>
  <filter-class>com.apress.projsp20.ch11.filter.ActionFilter</filter-class>
  <init-param>
     <!-- Change this value to true if you want
          to secure your entire application. -->
     <param-name>isSecure</param-name>
     <param-value>false</param-value>
  </init-param>
</filter>
...
<filter-mapping>
  <filter-name>actionFilter</filter-name>
  <url-pattern>*.do</url-pattern>
</filter-mapping>
```

In the `doFilter()` method, the following code executes before `chain.doFilter()` is called:

```
UserForm userForm = (UserForm) session.getAttribute(Constants.USER_KEY);
ServletContext ctx = filterConfig.getServletContext();
String username = request.getRemoteUser();

// user authenticated, empty user object
if (username != null && userForm == null) {
    try {
        ses = getSession(); // get persistence session

        UserManager mgr =
            new UserManagerImpl((String) ctx.getAttribute(Constants.DAO_TYPE));
        UserForm user = mgr.getUser(ses, username);
        session.setAttribute(Constants.USER_KEY, user);
    } catch (UserNotFoundException unf) {
        log.error("User not found in user realm!");
        throw new ServletException(unf);
    }
}
```

The UserManager retrieves the user's information and hides the dirty work from your client, which is the filter in this case. In this example, you're throwing a UserNotFoundException when the user isn't found, but this could just as well be a FinderException that is used for all "not found" errors. You're throwing a ServletException here because the user has already been authenticated successfully, probably a split second before, and if the user's information isn't there, something might be amiss. However, if you use a file-based realm authentication mechanism and then your application talks to a database, this might be expected behavior. In that case, you'd probably want to add the user to the database when a user isn't found. Another, cleaner option is to get a RequestDispatcher and forward to a JSP that explains the problem. For example:

```
request.getRequestDispatcher("userNotFound.jsp").forward(req,res);
return;
```

It's important to hide the implementation of retrieving the user's details so that you have the ability to switch to LDAP at a later date, or to another type of user database. To use LDAP, all you'd need to do is create a new class that implements UserManager and talks to LDAP, rather than to a database. To make it even better, you can add a context parameter in your web.xml to allow switching between a database and LDAP. The nice thing about using a directory server such as LDAP is that you get encrypted passwords as part of your data store. With file and database realms, you have to either encrypt passwords programmatically or configure your servlet container to do it for you.

Encrypting Passwords

In Tomcat, it's easy to encrypt passwords by adding the digest attribute to your realm definition. The value must be one of the digest algorithms supported by the java.security.MessageDigest class (SHA, MD2, or MD5). To expand on the earlier example, you'll add SHA encrypting to your file-based realm:

```
<Realm className="org.apache.catalina.realm.UserDatabaseRealm"
       debug="0" resourceName="UserDatabase" digest="SHA" />
```

To log into your application, you now need to encrypt the password you set in tomcat-users.xml to its encrypted form. You can do this by executing the following command:

```
java org.apache.catalina.realm.RealmBase -a SHA {cleartext-password}
```

where catalina.jar is in your class path. Now, copy and paste this new password into the %TOMCAT_HOME%/conf/tomcat-users.xml file to test it.

The problem with this method of password encryption is that it might not be portable. Let's take a look at programmatic encryption. The good news is that you've already created a LoginServlet, so you can use it to encrypt passwords. Because it's off by default, you'll need to add encrypt.password=true to your build.properties file, pass it in from the command line with ant -Dencrypt.password=true, or edit the default setting in app-settings.xml. If you're using the binary version (.war file) of this application, simply edit the following <init-param> of the LoginServlet (in the web.xml file):

```
<init-param>
  <param-name>encrypt-password</param-name>
  <param-value>true</param-value>
</init-param>
```

Next, you need to actually encrypt the password within your servlet. To do this, create an `encodePassword(String password, String algorithm)` method in a `StringUtil.java` class. This method uses the `MessageDigest` class from JSSE to encrypt a string:

```
import java.security.MessageDigest;

public static String encodePassword(String password, String algorithm) {
    byte[] unencodedPassword = password.getBytes();

    MessageDigest md = null;

    try {
        // first create an instance, given the provider
        md = MessageDigest.getInstance(algorithm);
    } catch (Exception e) {
        log.error("Exception: " + e);

        return password;
    }

    md.reset();

    // call the update method one or more times
    // (useful when you don't know the size of your data, e.g. stream)
    md.update(unencodedPassword);

    // now calculate the hash
    byte[] encodedPassword = md.digest();

    StringBuffer buf = new StringBuffer();

    for (int i = 0; i < encodedPassword.length; i++) {
        if (((int) encodedPassword[i] & 0xff) < 0x10) {
            buf.append("0");
        }

        buf.append(Long.toString((int) encodedPassword[i] & 0xff, 16));
    }

    return buf.toString();
}
```

This method encrypts a string based on the algorithm you pass in. This algorithm is defined in `LoginServlet` and configurable when building via the `${encrypt-algorithm}` variable. The default setting is `SHA`.

> *More information on these algorithms and how they work is available at http://theory.lcs.mit.edu/~rivest/crypto-security.html#Algorithms.*

If you're using password encryption and also have a `retrieve password` feature, you'll probably want to add a `password_hint` column in your user store. It's hard enough to remember all the passwords you keep, and it's annoying when you have to create a new password, so the "send me a hint" tactic is useful.

Servlet 2.4 Security Changes

The Servlet 2.4 specification has a whole chapter on security, but not much has changed. The JSP 2.0 specification doesn't contain any security-related information. It simply points out helpful information for programming security via the `HttpServletRequest` interface, giving you the following methods:

- `getRemoteUser()`
- `isUserInRole(String roleName)`
- `getUserPrinciple`

The `getRemoteUser()` method returns the authenticated user's login name or `null` if no authenticated user exists. The `isUserInRole()` method is helpful in determining a role's authorization to certain resources.

One important thing to remember with roles, if you're coding them into your servlets, is to create links using the `<security-role-ref>` element in `web.xml`. Here's an example:

```
<security-role-ref>
    <role-name>admin</role-name>
    <role-link>accounting</role-name>
</security-role-ref>
```

This way, you can code your servlets without worrying if the `admin` role changes from the accounting group to the IT department. All you have to do is configure/code with `admin` and know that your code will be safe from change. Of course, we recommend placing this value in a `Constants.java` file so you can change it easily if the need does ever arise.

The `HttpSession` interface has a new `logout()` method that may be handy for logging out users. Up until now, we've always used `session.invalidate()`, and it has worked fine for us. This new method is designed for implementation in your application when it's running in single sign-on containers. Currently when you call `session.invalidate()`, it invalidates the session and then unbinds any objects bound to it. On the other hand, `session.logout()` logs the client out of the entire server and invalidates all sessions associated with this client. Essentially, the `session.logout()` method calls `session.invalidate()` for all applications on the server.

Other Authentication Options and Considerations

There are alternative options to container-managed authentication if you aren't satisfied with its ease of development or you have stricter security requirements. The most common option is to build your own authentication mechanism. If you decide to go this route, we highly recommend you look into JAAS and try to use its APIs.

Security Filter

Security Filter (http://securityfilter.sf.net) is an open source project that mimics container-managed security. It looks exactly like container-managed security, and it supports the programmatic security methods of `HttpServletRequest`. Unfortunately, it doesn't automatically propagate a user's principle to EJB calls.

Secure Sockets Layer Extension for Struts

The SSL Extension for Struts (http://sslext.sf.net/) is good for HTTP/HTTPS switching. It is an open source project that allows you to configure HTTP/HTTPS switching using modified Struts tag libraries and configuration settings in the Struts configuration file. It was written by Steve Ditlinger, who also authored the previously mentioned SSL switching article.

Remembering Passwords

You've probably seen the remember my password feature on many portal sites such as Yahoo. Usually, this is done by storing the user's username and password combination in a cookie. If you have an application that requires a login, and you'd like to add this feature, it would be fairly simple to do, especially with Servlets 2.4. You could use a servlet as your welcome file and check for the cookie's existence. Of course, you could also use a JSP to mimic this same behavior, grab the username and password cookies, and redirect to the `LoginServlet` with these cookies as parameters. The nice thing about most modern browsers is that they offer to remember your passwords, and this is probably more secure than a cookie.

Remember Me Feature

As an example of how this functionality might be implemented, you'll add a Remember Me feature to this chapter's example application. You do this by making use of cookies to remember the username and password, and looking for these when the users first access the application. If they exist, you attempt to authenticate the user. There are three cookies involved in this process; the first two were mentioned previously. The third cookie is used to indicate that the user wants to use the Remember Me feature. You then use a filter to detect if these cookies are present and, if so, attempt to log the user in.

First, add a check box to the `login.jsp` page to allow the user to indicate that he wants the application to remember his password:

```
<input type="checkbox" name="rememberMe" id="rememberMe" /> Remember Me
```

If this box is selected, set a cookie to indicate the user wants to use this feature. Also, set a cookie to remember the user's username and password. Because you're using `LoginServlet` to forward the login request to `j_security_check`, you add the code to set these cookies in the `execute` method:

```
if (request.getParameter("rememberMe") != null) {
    response =
        RequestUtil.setCookie(response, "rememberMe", "true", false);
    response =
        RequestUtil.setCookie(response, "password",
                              StringUtil.encodeString(encryptedPassword),
                              false);
}
```

For the password cookie, you use an `encodeString()` method from the `StringUtil.java` class. This is a simple method that encrypts the password cookie's value using the `sun.misc.BASE64Encoder()`:

```
public static String encodeString(String str) throws IOException {
    sun.misc.BASE64Encoder encoder = new sun.misc.BASE64Encoder();
    String encodedStr = new String(encoder.encodeBuffer(str.getBytes()));

    return (encodedStr.trim());
}
```

The base64 encoding works well for this feature because it can be decoded (you'll need this for autologin) and it ensures client's passwords aren't stored in plain text.

If you're not using a `LoginServlet`, and you're simply using `j_security_check` as the action on your form, you can still use this feature. Just use a little JavaScript to set these cookies in the `onsubmit()` handler of your form. You'll lose the encrypted password functionality, but this feature will still work.

The real meat of this feature resides in the `BreadCrumbFilter.java` class. This class does the checking and autologin if the required cookies exist. In the `doFilter()` method for this class, the following code handles this logic:

```
// Get the relevant cookies for the "remember me" feature
Cookie rememberMe = RequestUtil.getCookie(request, "rememberMe");
Cookie passCookie = RequestUtil.getCookie(request, "password");
String password =
    (passCookie != null)
    ? URLDecoder.decode(passCookie.getValue(), "UTF-8") : null;

// Detect if authentication has failed - indicated by the error=true
// parameter from the <form-error-page> in web.xml
// StringUtils.equals is a convenience method from commons-lang that handles
// nulls gracefully.
boolean authFailed =
    StringUtils.equals(request.getParameter("error"), "true");

// Check to see if the user is logging out, if so, remove the
// rememberMe cookie and password cookie.
if ((authFailed ||
        (request.getRequestURL().indexOf("logout") != -1)) &&
        (rememberMe != null)) {
    if (log.isDebugEnabled()) {
        log.debug("deleting rememberMe-related cookies");
    }

    response =
        RequestUtil.deleteCookie(response,
                                 RequestUtil.getCookie(request,
                                                       "rememberMe"));
    response = RequestUtil.deleteCookie(response, passCookie);
}
```

```
// Check to see if the user is logging in. If so, check to see
// if he/she has enabled rememberMe functionality.
// Only attempt to authenticate when "login" is requested
if ((request.getRequestURL().indexOf("login") != -1)) {
    // Check to see if we should automatically login the user
    // container is routing user to login page, check for remember me cookie
    Cookie userCookie = RequestUtil.getCookie(request, "username");
    String username =
        (passCookie != null)
        ? URLDecoder.decode(userCookie.getValue(), "UTF-8") : null;

    if ((rememberMe != null) && (password != null)) {
        // authenticate user without displaying login page
        String route =
            request.getContextPath() +
            "/auth?j_username=" + username +
            "&j_password=" + StringUtil.decodeString(password);

        if (log.isDebugEnabled()) {
            log.debug("I remember you '" + username +
                      "', attempting authentication...");
        }

        response.sendRedirect(response.encodeRedirectURL(route));
        return;
    }
}
```

That's it! It even handles password changes in the realm by checking for the `error` parameter–a slick feature that I've added into most of the recent applications I've worked on.

Authorization

After a user has logged into the application, you might have requirements for what the user can do or see. This is made much simpler with container-managed security, as you'll have the user's role available to you. Using your own authentication architecture, you could probably get a similar result, but you might not be able to take advantage of the wealth of available plug-ins. By **plug-ins**, I am referring to tag libraries and other Java-related packages that allow for role configuration. For instance, the Struts Logic tag library has a `<logic:present>` tag that allows you to perform logic based on a user's role. The Tiles templating framework also allows you to configure showing/hiding sections of your template based on roles.

In the next section, we supply a few recommendations and tricks for controlling *who sees what* within a web application. Most of these techniques are much easier to implement if you're using container-managed authentication, but it's not required.

Protecting Pages and URLs

The first thing you'll want to consider is what choices a user should have after the user has logged in. Usually these choices are in the form of links, but they can be other menu-type systems, such as pick lists or DHTML drop-downs. One simple way to control what links a user might see is to show or hide links on the basis of a user's role. However, this is just hiding the link, and it might still be reachable by typing in the URL.

One recommended practice is to place your JSP files and fragments under the `WEB-INF` directory when deploying your application. By doing this, you'll prevent browsers from directly accessing JSP pages using a URL, and it also forces you (as a developer) to follow the MVC pattern. Your JSP pages will be protected, because all resources under `WEB-INF` are secluded and not accessible from a URL. The Servlet specification mandates that security be provided inside `WEB-INF`, and it also ensures good separation of controller and view by forcing each request to go through a servlet controller. However, we've seen some containers that don't support this–they either allow access to `WEB-INF` through the browser or don't allow you to render JSP pages that live under `WEB-INF`. If your servlet container is J2EE compliant, it should allow you to do this.

If you're working with a framework that allows configuration of your servlet-to-JSP mappings, this is fairly easy to do. We usually develop JSP pages in a directory alongside directories for stylesheets, JavaScript files, and images. Then when we deploy, we move the directory containing the JSP pages (`pages`) into a directory under `WEB-INF`.

By placing your JSP pages under `WEB-INF`, you ensure that the necessary application logic will be executed before displaying them. After all, users will have to navigate through this logic to get to your JSP.

After securing the locations of your pages, you'll need to secure access to them so that unauthorized users can't execute the logic to get to them. You can do this in a couple of different ways. The method built in with servlets is to use a different `security-constraint` for each servlet (or group of servlets) that you want to protect. To do this, you'll have to create servlet mappings for each servlet or group–your `web.xml` may become quite large if you have many servlets. An easier way is to proxy all requests through an initial servlet that checks permissions and forwards appropriately, or even better, use a filter. We've also seen another alternative in which you put a tag library at the top of every JSP file. This tag library does a check to see if the user has access to that page.

The problem with programmatically checking for user roles and dispatching accordingly, or displaying an error message in the case of the JSP, is that it can become a maintenance nightmare. We've been on projects where we used this type of architecture, and it's become much easier since we moved to container-managed authentication.

Summary

We hope we've convinced you that security is pretty easy to add to a web application. It offers many benefits once it's been added: customization based on role, an auditing log, and password encryption. In our experience, using container-managed security has made our development existence more enjoyable. We've done it programmatically by using LDAP and lots of application logic to show or hide links and to allow or deny access to pages. Even though it worked, and it worked well, it took much longer to program initially, and it was quite a nuisance to maintain. On the other hand, if you already have an authentication and authorization framework that offers you all the same benefits, you should, by all means, use it, and if it's portable and works well, share it!

Our biggest issues with container-managed security have been related to the servlet container's implementation of the Servlet specification. We recommend testing your application on Tomcat if you're experiencing problems with configuring security. If your application works on Tomcat, your container might have some problems, and it's time to do some research or write a workaround, or even to move to a different container (if that's an option). Developing on Tomcat can be a great time-saver!

12

Improving Web Application Performance and Scalability

The distributed and multiuser nature of web applications makes performance and scalability an important concern. Web applications are distributed systems. Users access web applications from remote clients distributed across a network, and web applications typically depend on remote systems such as databases, enterprise information systems, and web services. Network connection overhead, slow network connections, and slow remote systems can cause your web application to exhibit poor performance.

Web applications are often called upon to scale up to meet the needs of an increasing number of users. Once a web application is put into production, it seems very easy to add more users because there is no client-side software required for access, other than the ubiquitous web browser. Adding more users is easy, but ensuring that your application will perform well with these additional users takes some effort.

In this chapter you'll look at some of the steps that you can take and techniques you can employ to improve the performance and scalability of your web applications. Before you get started, we should clarify the terms we use in this chapter:

- **Performance:** Each application will have its own definition of performance. For a web application, a common performance metric is **response time**–the time taken for the application to complete any given request from the end user. So, you might demand of your application a maximum response time of 3 seconds. However, to be complete, any such metric must account for the number of users that are likely to be interacting with the application at any given time. So, a more complete performance statement might read: *The application must support 100 simultaneous users, with a maximum response time of 3 seconds.*

- **Scalability:** With reasonable coding skills and enough hardware, you may find it fairly easy to meet a performance target such as the one preceding. However, suppose that your application is a success and, as a result, is suddenly required to support 200 users. If you double your processing power, in the form of additional Java VMs on each server or additional server computers, will your application be able to support (roughly) double the number of users, while continuing to meet performance requirements? If the answer is yes, then your application is scalable.

So, how do you go about ensuring that your JSP applications meet their performance and scalability requirements? As a software developer, you're probably familiar with the following classic performance quote attributed to Donald Knuth:

> *"We should forget about small efficiencies, say about 97% of the time: premature optimization is the root of all evil."*

In this chapter we don't focus on small efficiencies and we avoid premature optimization; instead, we focus on the larger steps that you can take to ensure you meet your JSP application performance goals. We start by covering two specific techniques that can definitely enhance the performance and scalability characteristics of our JSP applications: **page caching** and **database connection pooling**. We move on to discuss more general performance tips and best practices, before finishing with a discussion of how you can actually go about testing the performance and scalability of your application to ensure that you're really meeting your requirements.

General Principles

The following items apply to the development of high-performance web applications in general and thus are guiding principles for your JSP application design:

- **Don't execute code unnecessarily.** One of the best ways to improve code performance is to simply avoid executing it. Don't execute code unless absolutely necessary. We discuss how page caching can help in this regard in this chapter.
- **Don't create objects unnecessarily.** Creating new objects is an expensive operation, both in terms of the processing time to create them and the memory required to store them. As you write your code, try to minimize the number of objects that you create. Where possible, reuse the objects that you do create. One of the most expensive objects in a JSP application is the database connection object. In this chapter we discuss how to use database connection pooling to avoid repeatedly creating database connection objects.
- **When you must create objects, create them in the right scope.** In a web application, there are three levels of scope: **request**, **session**, and **application**. To scale a web application to meet the needs of a large number of users, carefully consider what is to be stored in the session scopes. We discuss this and other ways to ensure that your application is ready to scale in this chapter.

Now that we've covered the general principles, we next discuss the details of how you can apply the concepts of page caching and database connection pooling to JSP applications.

Page Caching

In a typical JSP application, web pages are dynamically generated by Java code that pulls data from a database and formats that data for display. This processing takes time, causes the creation of Java objects, and uses network resources. If we could find a way to avoid regenerating a page for every incoming page request, we could not only speed up the page response time, but also improve the overall performance and scalability of our JSP application. What we would really like to do is save each dynamically generated page in cache memory. When a request comes in for a page that we've already generated, we just pull that page out of the cache and send it out to the browser. This technique is called **page caching** and it can dramatically improve the performance of a JSP application.

When Should You Use Page Caching?

You've probably used caching before, perhaps by writing your own simple cache. If you're using an MVC framework such as Struts, then you could use a simple cache for objects that you built from database data and have little need for page caching. When do you need page caching?

Page caching is useful when you can't put all of the data needed for a web page into context before the JSP page or servlet that's responsible for emitting the page is called. Also, page caching is useful when your JSP pages are composed of multiple JSP tags or other components that themselves are responsible for expensive operations such as fetching data or rendering complex HTML.

How Long Should You Cache Data?

To reduce the load on your servers, you'll want to cache pages for as long as possible. How long is that? The answer depends on the nature of your application. Of course, for highly interactive pages, you might not be able to use caching at all, or you may be able to cache only some small, fairly static portions of the pages. You might decide to cache some pages for a very long time but to a flush some portion or all of the cache every time your site's database is updated.

To get a better understanding of page caching technology, let's take a closer look at one of the most popular open source Java caching packages: OSCache.

OSCache

OSCache is an open source caching library that's available free of charge from the OpenSymphony organization (http://www.opensymphony.com/oscache). OSCache includes a set of JSP tags that make it very easy to implement page caching in your JSP application, along with a `ServletFilter`-based cache implementation so that you can cache content that's generated by any servlet, not just JSP pages.

OSCache applies the following general page caching concepts:

- **Cache entry:** An object that's stored into a page cache is known as a cache entry. In a JSP application, a cache entry is typically the output of a JSP page, a portion of a JSP page, or a servlet.
- **Cache key:** A page cache is like a hash table. When you save a cache entry in a page cache, you must provide a cache key to identify the entry. In a JSP application, you might combine several request parameters together to form a cache key, or you might use a page's request URI as its cache key.

- **Cache duration:** This is the period of time that a cache entry will remain in a page cache before it expires. When a cache entry expires, it's removed from the cache, and the application that placed it in the cache will be forced to regenerate it. For a JSP page that displays frequently updated data, you should set a short cache duration so that the cache is updated frequently and users aren't presented with stale information. For a JSP page that displays data that's infrequently updated, you can set a longer cache duration.
- **Cache scope:** This is the scope at which the cache is stored. In a JSP application, it make sense to store cache entries at either the application scope, so that cache entries are shared by all users, or at the session scope, so that cache entries are stored on a per-user basis.

OSCache JSP Tags

Using the OSCache tags is simple. All you need to do is place the `<os:cache>` tag around the sections of your JSP pages that you wish to have cached. The example JSP page that follows indicates how to do this. You can find this JSP code in the example application file `web/longop-cached.jsp`:

```
<%@ page language="java" %>
<%@ taglib uri="/WEB-INF/oscache.tld" prefix="os" %>
<!DOCTYPE HTML PUBLIC "-//w3c//dtd html 4.0 transitional//en">

<html>
  <head><title>Long operation - cached</title></head>
  <body>

    <h1>Long operation - cached</h1>

    <os:cache time="60">
      <% Thread.sleep(10000); %>
      <p>Woke up at: <%= new java.util.Date().toString() %></p>
    </os:cache>

    <p>
      The reason this JSP page took so long to load is because
      it contains a 10 second sleep.
    </p>

    <p>
      This page uses page cache with a 60 second timeout,
      so if you run this page again in the next 60 seconds
      it will take less than a second to run.
    </p>

  </body>
</html>
```

In the preceding example, you have a JSP page that sleeps for 10 seconds and then displays a wake-up time and some other text. As you can see, the call to the `sleep()` method and the wake-up time message are enclosed inside `<os:cache>` tags with a cache time of 60 seconds.

The first time that this page is executed it takes 10 seconds. However, it caches a copy of the output that was produced inside the `<os:cache>` tags. If you run the page again, within 60 seconds, it will take less than a second to run because it will return the output from the cache instead of executing the code inside the `<os:cache>` tags. If you wait 60 seconds and then run the page again, you'll have to wait for the 10-second sleep to complete because the cache entry will have timed out and the output will have to be regenerated.

In this example, you didn't specify a cache key so, by default, OSCache will use the request URI to key the cache entry. You also didn't specify a cache scope so, by default, application scope will be used.

OSCache Servlet Filter

You can also use OSCache to cache the output of servlets, using the OSCache servlet filter class, `com.opensymphony.module.oscache.web.filter.CacheFilter`. All you have to do is add this filter to the application's `web.xml` file and add filter mappings for all of the URL patterns that you wish to have cached.

For example, the code download for this chapter includes a servlet that takes 10 seconds to run. This `LongOpServlet` produces almost the same output as the `longop.jsp` page that we discussed in the previous section. To cache the output of the `LongOpServet` in the same way as you cached the JSP page, you need to add the following filter configuration to the example application's `web.xml` file:

```
<?xml version="1.0" encoding="UTF-8"?>

<web-app xmlns="http://java.sun.com/xml/ns/j2ee"
        xmlns:xsi="http://www.w3.org/2001/XMLSchema-instance"
        xsi:schemaLocation="http://java.sun.com/xml/ns/j2ee/web-app_2_4.xsd"
        version="2.4">

    <context-param>
        <param-name>debug</param-name>
        <param-value>true</param-value>
    </context-param>

    <filter>
        <filter-name>CacheFilter</filter-name>
        <filter-class>
            com.opensymphony.module.oscache.web.filter.CacheFilter
        </filter-class>
        <init-param>
            <param-name>time</param-name>
            <param-value>60</param-value>
        </init-param>
    </filter>

    <filter-mapping>
        <filter-name>CacheFilter</filter-name>
        <url-pattern>/servlets/*</url-pattern>
    </filter-mapping>
```

```
    <servlet>
      <servlet-name>LongOpServlet</servlet-name>
      <servlet-class>
        com.apress.projsp20.ch12.servlets.LongOpServlet
      </servlet-class>
    </servlet>

    <servlet-mapping>
      <servlet-name>LongOpServlet</servlet-name>
      <url-pattern>/servlets/longop</url-pattern>
    </servlet-mapping>

  </web-app>
```

As you can see, filter configuration elements should be included after the context parameters but before the servlet and listener configurations.

The `<filter>` element configures the `CacheFilter` itself. It specifies the class name for the filter and sets one parameter: the cache time. As with the `longop.jsp` example in the previous section, the cache time is set to 60 seconds. Other parameters, such as the cache key and cache scope, have been omitted, so default values will be used. The `<filter-mapping>` element configures the `CacheFilter` so that it will cache the response output for all request URLs that match the pattern `/servlets/*`. This works well for the `LongOpServlet`, because it's mapped to the URL `/servlets/longop`.

For more information on servlet filters, refer to Chapters 9 and 10. For more information on OSCache, visit the following URLs:

- http://www.opensymphony.com: OpenSymphony website
- http://www.opensymphony.com/oscache: OSCache website
- http://www.opensymphony.com:8668/space/OSCache: OSCache WIKI

Database Connection Pooling

Page caching can help to reduce the frequency of database access in a JSP application, but it can't eliminate database access entirely. Eventually, the application will have to open a database connection to query, create, update, and delete records in the database. Unfortunately, opening a database connection is an expensive operation that consumes processing time, memory, and network resources.

One of the most effective ways to boost JSP application performance is to use a technique called **database connection pooling**. With this technique, you keep a pool of database connections open at all times. When you need a connection, you take it from the pool, and when you're done with it, you return it to the pool.

Database connection pooling is a very well-known technique that's available in almost every J2EE application server. It's also built into many JDBC drivers and some persistence frameworks. For example, the Hibernate persistence framework discussed in Chapter 8 includes an easy-to-use database connection pool.

There are a lot of database connection pool alternatives, and we don't discuss them all here. Instead, we discuss the common database connection pool configuration parameters and then take a look at an example. Most database connection pools allow you to set the following configuration parameters:

- **Maximum active connections:** This is the maximum number of connections that are allowed to be open in the pool. If a request is made for a connection while all connections in the pool are in use, then the call to the `getConnection()` method will block until a connection is released by another thread or until a configurable maximum wait time is reached.
- **Maximum idle connections:** This is the maximum number of connections that are allowed to be open but not in use in the pool. If you set this parameter to zero, then no maximum limit will be set.
- **Maximum wait time:** This is the maximum length of time that a call to `getConnection()` will block while waiting for a connection to released. If the wait exceeds this time, then the `getConnection()` call will throw an exception, or you can use some other technique to indicate that a connection isn't available.
- **Abandoned connection timeout:** In some cases, an application may fail to properly release a database connection. This is called abandoning a connection and is a serious problem because until a connection is released it isn't returned to the pool for reuse. Some database connection pools monitor unreleased connections, and if one has been idle for longer than the abandoned connection timeout, it's considered to be abandoned and is automatically released and returned to the pool.

Jakarta Commons Database Connection Pool

It isn't possible for us to cover all of the different options for database connection pooling, so instead we take a close look at **Jakarta Commons Database Connection Pool (DBCP)**. DBCP is the database connection pooling technology built into the popular open source Tomcat servlet engine.

Normally, to deploy an application to the Tomcat servlet engine, you just copy the application's WAR file, or deployment directory, to the Tomcat `webapps` directory. However, in order to configure DBCP for your application, you need to do a bit more work: You need to add the application to the Tomcat server configuration file `conf/server.xml`.

To do this, you need to add a new `<Context>` entry to the Tomcat `server.xml` file. Open the `server.xml` file with your favorite editor and look for the `Tomcat Root Context`. You need to add the `<Context>` entry in the correct part of the `server.xml` file. For example, you can add it after the `ROOT` context and before the `examples` context, as shown here:

```
<!-- Tomcat Root Context -->
<!--
  <Context path="" docBase="ROOT" debug="0"/>
-->

<Context path="/myapp" docBase="roller" debug="0">
  <Resource name="jdbc/mydb" auth="Container" type="javax.sql.DataSource" />
  <ResourceParams name="jdbc/mydb">
    <parameter>
      <name>factory</name>
```

```
      <value>org.apache.commons.dbcp.BasicDataSourceFactory</value>
    </parameter>
    <parameter><name>maxActive</name><value>100</value></parameter>
    <parameter><name>maxWait</name><value>100</value></parameter>
    <parameter><name>username</name><value>scott</value></parameter>
    <parameter><name>password</name><value>tiger</value></parameter>
    <parameter>
      <name>driverClassName</name>
      <value>org.gjt.mm.mysql.Driver</value>
    </parameter>
    <parameter>
      <name>url</name>
      <value>jdbc:mysql://localhost:3306/mydb?autoReconnect=true</value>
    </parameter>
  </ResourceParams>
</Context>
```

```
<!-- Tomcat Examples Context -->
<Context path="/examples" docBase="examples" debug="0"
    reloadable="true" crossContext="true">
    <Logger className="org.apache.catalina.logger.FileLogger"
        prefix="localhost_examples_log." suffix=".txt" timestamp="true"/>
```

The preceding example shows how to configure DBCP for an application called `myapp`. The first entry inside the `<Context>` element is the `<Resource>` declaration. The `<Resource>` declaration declares a `javax.sql.DataSource` and binds it to the JNDI name `jdbc/mydb`. The `<ResourceParams>` element and the nested `<parameter>` elements within specify the DBCP parameters for the application's database connection pool. We've already discussed the `maxActive` and `maxWait` parameters. The `driverClassName` and `url` parameters are standard JDBC connection parameters.

The next code excerpt shows how to obtain a connection from the previous connection pool. First, you use JNDI to look up a `javax.sql.DataSource` interface, and then you ask that interface for a connection. When you've finished with the connection, you close it and return it to the pool for reuse. Closing the connection doesn't actually close the underlying physical connection; it just returns the connection to the pool.

```
javax.naming.InitialContext context = new InitialContext();

// Look up the data source
javax.sql.DataSource dataSource =
  (javax.sql.DataSource)context.lookup ("jdbc/mydb");

// Get a connection from the pool
java.sql.Connection conn = dataSource.getConnection();

// ...Use the connection...

// Close the connection to return it to the pool
conn.close();
```

For a working example that uses DBCP, see the section "Obtaining a JDBC Connection in a Web Application" in Chapter 8.

Designing for Scalability

Java application servers are designed to support scalability. By using your application server's administrative console or by editing configuration files, you can increase the amount of memory devoted to each server process, increase the number of request processing threads within each process, add additional server processes, and configure additional server machines to run server processes.

No matter how you design your application, you'll probably be able to make it run faster and serve more users by running on a more powerful computer. If your server is a multiprocessor machine, you can configure your application server to use more threads to process requests. If your server has lots of memory, you can configure your application server to devote more memory to each server process. Your application server documentation should provide some guidelines to help you decide how to configure these thread and memory settings.

There is a limit to what you can do with one server process running on one server machine. Your Java application server will allow you to scale up beyond a single process running on a single machine, but in order to take advantage of this, you need to follow some simple guidelines in the development of your JSP applications:

- **Minimize the data that's stored in each session.** In a typical JSP application, a session object of type `javax.servlet.HttpSession` is created for each user. As the amount of data stored per session increases, the number of users that can be supported by each server decreases. This is just simple arithmetic. For example, say the application server is running in a Java VM that's configured for a 100 MB heap. If the application server itself uses 10 MB of memory, and each user session consumes 1 MB of memory, then you can support a maximum of 90 simultaneous users per application server instance.
- **Where possible, avoid creating sessions**. Each session that's created uses some memory so, wherever possible, try to handle requests without creating sessions.
- **Store only serializable objects in the session object**. J2EE application servers support scalability by running JSP applications in parallel across multiple servers. When a session is created, it's assigned to one server. A technique called **load balancing** is used to ensure that sessions are distributed evenly across all participating servers. Some J2EE application servers, such as IBM WebSphere, support a special load-balancing technique called **session migration**. If session migration is enabled and one server becomes overloaded, then sessions from that server may be migrated to another, less busy server. Session migration is usually implemented by serialization, so in order for a JSP application to work with session migration you need to make sure that every object stored in the session implements the interface `java.io.Serializable`.
- **Don't write to the file system.** If a JSP application is running across multiple servers, then you can't use the file system for storage. Files that you write to one server may not be available on all of the other servers running the application. In this case, use a database rather than the file system for storage.

Other Performance Tips and Resources

A good source of information for best practices for performance and scalability is the IBM website. A search for "performance" on the WebSphere and Developer Works website (http://www.ibm.com/developerworks) reveals a series of white papers and best practices guides for WebSphere development. Most of the information on WebSphere also applies to other J2EE application servers and to JSP applications in general.

The white paper "WebSphere Application Server Development Best Practices for Performance and Scalability" (http://www.ibm.com/software/webservers/appserv/ws_bestpractices.pdf) is especially useful. Again, most of the best practices in this white paper apply to any J2EE application server. Many of the recommendations apply to EJB applications only, but a good number apply to JSP applications, for example:

- **Avoid thread synchronization and single-threading.** Synchronizing methods and blocks of code can make a JSP application behave as if it is single-threaded, and this results in lower throughput. It's important that JSP pages and servlets are thread-safe, so don't be tempted to use the `isThreadSafe=false` page directive. When you write a servlet, don't be tempted to implement the `javax.servlet.SingleThreadModel` interface.
- **Avoid use of `System.out.println()`.** The seemingly harmless `System.out.println()` method is actually pretty harmful. According to the IBM white paper, "Because `System.out.println()` statements and similar constructs synchronize processing for the duration of disk I/O, they can significantly slow throughput." Instead of using `System.out` and `System.err`, consider using a logging system such as log4J.
- **Avoid string concatenation.** This is widely known, but it bears repeating. Using the + and += operators to concatenate strings is slow and results in the creation of unnecessary temporary objects. Instead, use the `java.lang.StringBuffer` class to concatenate strings.

Measuring JSP Application Performance

In addition to implementing the best practice design advice that we've been discussing, you need to be able to prove that your application will actually meet the performance criteria set by your customers. You need to be able to profile your application and root out and fix any code that's taking up undue resources or memory, or is causing contention issues that will reduce scalability.

A wide variety of web application performance testing tools and products are available, and any of these can be applied to measuring JSP application performance. Typically, a performance test tool will support the following features:

- **Custom test plans** to build complex test plans that simulate what users are doing as they use a particular JSP application

- **Response time statistics** to measure and collect statistics on the minimum, maximum, and average response time of each page
- **Load testing** to simulate any number of users accessing a site
- **Error detection** to detect and log when errors occur on any page

One option for performance testing is the open source **Apache JMeter** product. JMeter allows you to develop test plans for testing HTTP, FTP, and JDBC-accessible database servers. JMeter can handle servlet authentication using cookies and URL rewriting, so it works well for testing JSP applications. The biggest advantage of JMeter is that it's free. You can download it, try it out, learn about performance testing, and if you like it you can keep it. If you find that it's unsatisfactory, you can evaluate one of the other performance testing tools. At the end of this section is a list of some of the popular performance testing products.

You can download JMeter from the Apache Jakarta website (http://jakarta.apache.org/jmeter).

Let's take a look at JMeter and use it to test one of the performance recommendations that we discussed earlier in this section. You'll use a very simple JSP page with a 3-second runtime, `threesec.jsp`:

```
<%@ page language="java" %>

<!DOCTYPE HTML PUBLIC "-//w3c//dtd html 4.0 transitional//en">

<html>
  <head><title>Three second operation</title></head>
  <body>

    <h1>Three second operation</h1>
    <p>
      The reason this page JSP took 3 seconds to load is because
      it contains a 3 second sleep.
    </p>

    <% Thread.sleep(3000); %>

  </body>
</html>
```

The page takes 3 seconds to run because it includes a 3-second sleep. To test this page in JMeter, you first create a thread group with five threads and a loop count of 100. This will simulate the effects of five browsers, each running through the test plan 100 times. You do this by right-clicking the Test Plan icon in the tree and then choosing the Add | Thread Group menu option to add a Thread Group. The following screen shot shows the new Thread Group created:

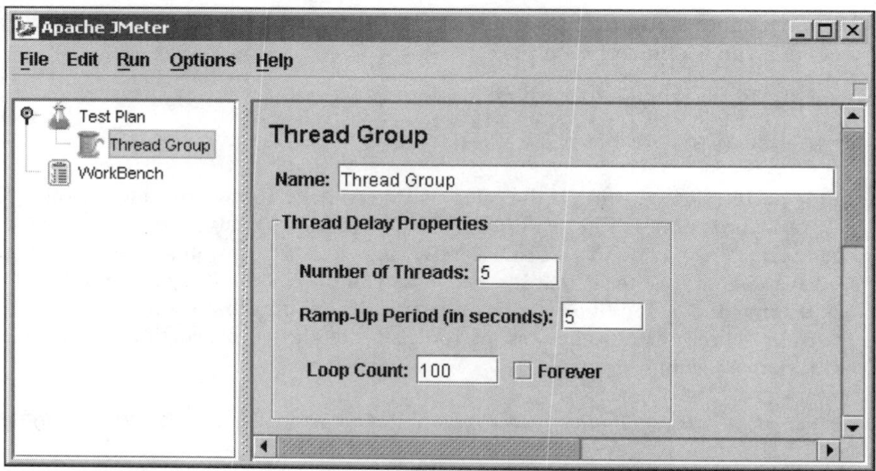

You're going to test only one page, so under the thread group you'll create one HTTP request and configure it to access your `threesec.jsp` page. Next, add an Aggregate Report so you can view the minimum, maximum, and average response times for running the test page. The following screen shot shows the test plan, with the HTTP request editor loaded into the right pane:

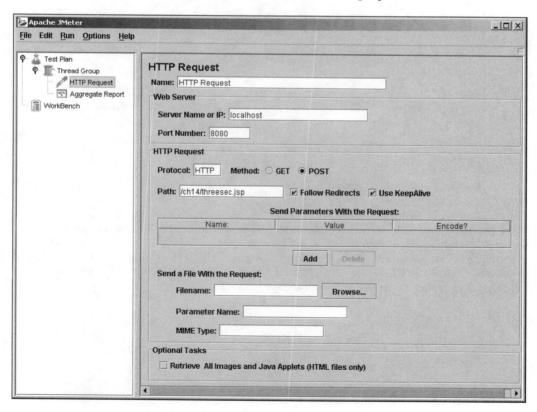

The next step is to run the test plan. Use the JMeter **Run | Start** menu item to do this. The test should take a couple of minutes to run. As the test runs, you can watch the results in the **Aggregate Report** window, and when the test completes that window should look like the one in the following screen shot. Your results will differ depending on your hardware, operating system, and servlet engine:

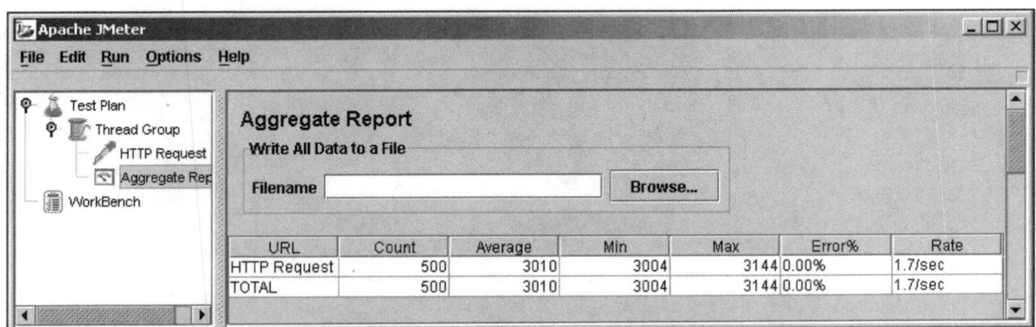

Looking at the **Aggregate Report** window results, you can see that 500 requests were processed with an average response time of 3,024 milliseconds. This makes sense because the page included a 3-second sleep and almost nothing else. You can see that no errors occurred and that you achieved a throughput rate of 1.7 requests per second, or 102 requests per minute.

One of our performance recommendations was to avoid single-threading. There may an occasion when you feel it's necessary to serialize access to a certain call in a JSP page. However, you should be aware that, if this call is made often, it could have drastic performance consequences. Let's see what happens when you run the same test, but with a single-threaded JSP page. To do this, you need to make a simple modification to your `threesec.jsp` page. You add a lock to the class so that all access to the `Thread.sleep()` call is synchronized. Here's the new `threesec-single.jsp` page:

```
<%@ page language="java" %>

<!DOCTYPE HTML PUBLIC "-//w3c//dtd html 4.0 transitional//en">

<html>
  <head><title>Three second operation: single-threaded</title></head>

  <body>
    <%! static String lock = new String(); %>

    <h1>Three second operation: single-threaded</h1>
    <p>
      The reason this page JSP took 3 seconds to load is because
      it contains a 3 second sleep.
    </p>

<% synchronized (lock)
  {
    Thread.Sleep(3000);
  }
%>
```

```
    </body>
  </html>
```

Now run the test again. This time, it takes about 20 minutes rather than 5 minutes. The results are as follows:

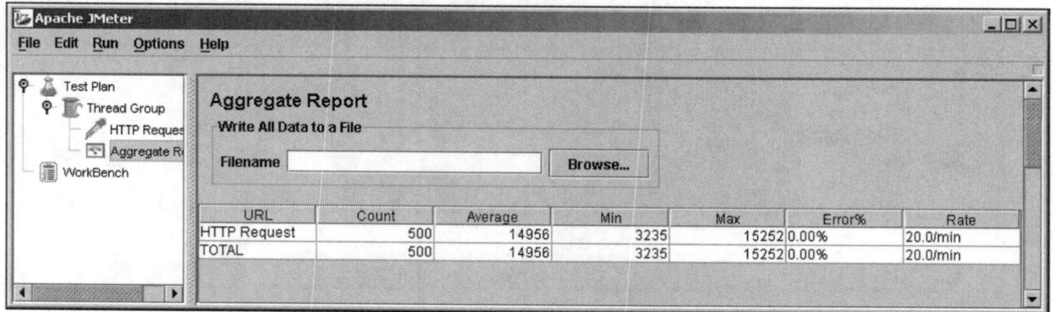

As expected, the performance of the single-threaded page is much worse than that of the multithreaded page. The throughput of the single-threaded page is 20.1 requests per minute compared to 102 requests per minute for the thread-safe JSP.

For more information on web application performance testing, visit the following product sites:

- Apache JMeter: http://jakarta.apache.org/jmeter/
- Mercury LoadRunner: http://www.mercuryinteractive.com/products/loadrunner/
- Web Performance, Inc.: http://www.webperformanceinc.com/

The Web Performance, Inc., site in particular is a good resource. It includes a glossary of performance testing terms, presentations on performance testing, and a report that compares the performance of J2EE servlet engines including Tomcat, WebSphere, Orion, Jetty, and Resin.

Testing the Performance Techniques

Now you'll put the techniques we covered in this chapter into practice by applying them to a realistic example program. You'll use an enhanced version of the data access example from Chapter 8 because it's a simple but fairly typical database-driven web application.

As you may remember, the Chapter 8 example is a web-based RSS newsreader program called Ag. Ag allows you to sign in by entering a user name, maintain a list of subscriptions to RSS newsfeeds, fetch the news items for your subscriptions, and view the headlines for each of your newsfeeds.

For the purposes of this case study, we've added a new front page to Ag. This new front page displays the most recent newsfeed items from all users and allows visitors to view the items in reverse-chronological order or by the number of hits that each item has received. With this new front page, Ag is a lot like the popular community newsfeed aggregation websites Java-Blogs (http://javablogs.com) and Weblogs at ASP.NET (http://weblogs.asp.net). Here's a screen shot of the new front page:

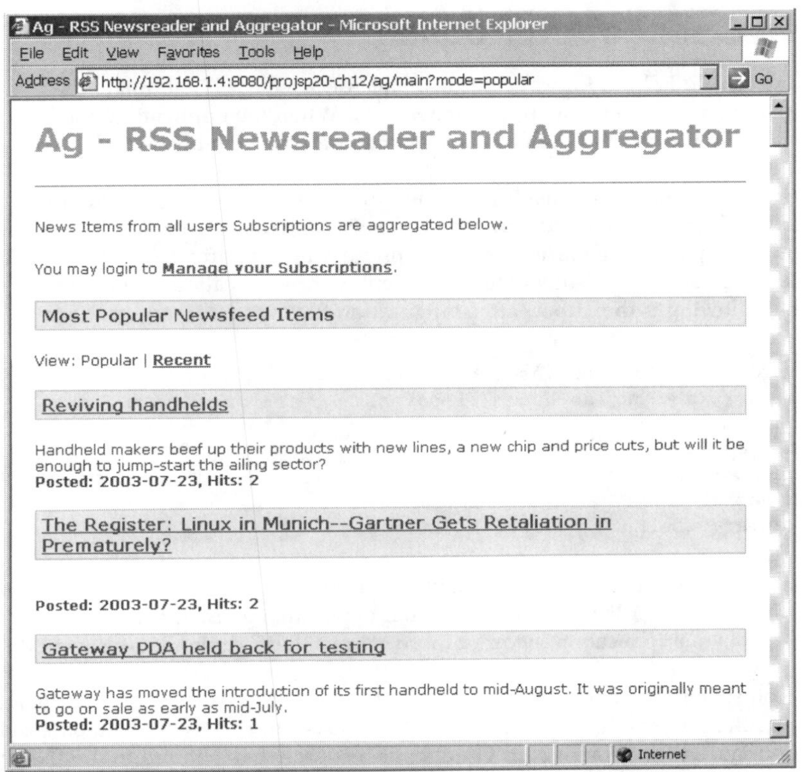

With a small number of users hitting the new Ag front page, performance seems to be fine. The page is displayed in a second or less. However, when you use JMeter to simulate a large number of users hitting the site, the performance drops to an unacceptable level. The page takes 5 to 10 seconds to display, and the load on the server rises to an unacceptable level. Running a 10-thread JMeter test plan with a total of 30 iterations, you get the following results:

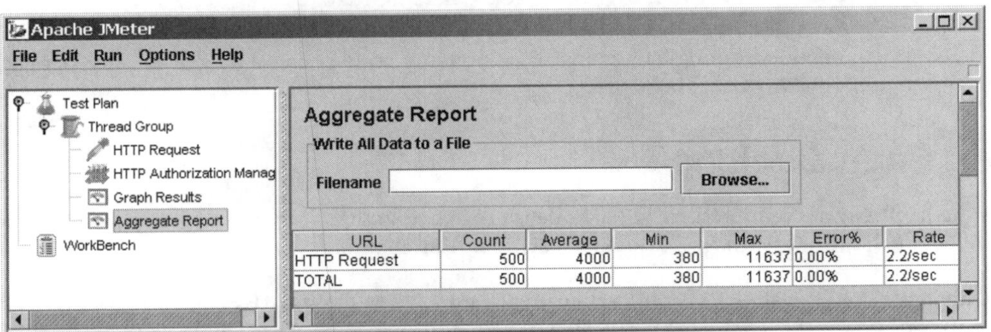

URL	Count	Average	Min	Max	Error%	Rate
HTTP Request	500	4000	380	11637	0.00%	2.2/sec
TOTAL	500	4000	380	11637	0.00%	2.2/sec

Each page is taking an average of 4 seconds to run. On top of this, during this test, the CPU meter is at 100%. Ag is dragging the whole server down. Why is Ag performing so poorly? For each incoming request, Ag must obtain a database connection, make a database query, and render the results as HTML. How can you reduce the amount of work per request? Let's start by applying database connection pooling.

Applying Database Connection Pooling

Database connection pooling should help to improve performance because it will eliminate the overhead that surrounds opening and closing database connections. When the application needs a database connection, it will obtain it from a pool of already opened database connections.

So, how do you go about applying database connection pooling to the Ag application? Well, it turns out that because Ag uses Hibernate for all database access, Ag is *already* using database connection pooling. Hibernate has built-in connection pooling. Hibernate connection pooling is configured in the Hibernate configuration file, `hibernate.properties`, in which you specify your application's database connection parameters. The following is the Hibernate configuration file for the Ag application:

```
hibernate.connection.driver_class=org.hsqldb.jdbcDriver
hibernate.connection.url=jdbc:hsqldb:hsql://localhost
hibernate.connection.username=sa
hibernate.connection.password=
hibernate.connection.pool_size=30
hibernate.statement_cache.size=6
hibernate.dialect=net.sf.hibernate.dialect.HSQLDialect
```

Hibernate's built-in connection pooling is convenient, no doubt, but it isn't always the right answer. Your application server administrator may prefer that you configure your application to use the database connection pooling capabilities of your application server or those of your JDBC driver. How do you do that?

If you're using Hibernate, you specify the name of the JNDI data source, provided by your application server administrator, in the Hibernate configuration file. You'll also have to specify the database dialect. The following example is configured for accessing an Oracle9 data source that's bound to the JNDI name `java:comp/env/jdbc/oracle1`. There's no need to specify a JDBC driver class, connection URL, or anything else because those were specified by your server administrator when he or she configured the data source. For more information on data source usage and configuration, see the section "Obtaining a JDBC Connection in a Web Application" in Chapter 8.

```
hibernate.connection.datasource=java:comp/env/jdbc/oracle1
hibernate.dialect=net.sf.hibernate.dialect.Oracle9Dialect
```

Adding database connection pooling isn't going to do you any good because you're already using it, so let's move on to applying page caching.

Applying Page Caching

The new Ag front page is rendered by the JSP file `main.jsp`, so that's where you'll add your caching. You'll use OSCache JSP tags that we discussed earlier in this chapter.

You already have the OSCache JAR file in your application's `WEB-INF/lib` directory and the `oscache.properties` file in the `WEB-INF`/classes, so all you need to do is add the OSCache JSP `Taglib` declaration to the top of `main.jsp` and the OSCache tags around the part of the page that you wish to cache. Here's the code for `main.jsp` with the new OSCache additions shown in bold:

```
<%@ page language="java" %>
<%@ taglib uri="/WEB-INF/c-rt.tld" prefix="c" %>
<%@ taglib uri="/WEB-INF/oscache.tld" prefix="os"%>

<!DOCTYPE HTML PUBLIC "-//w3c//dtd html 4.0 transitional//en"><html>
<head>
    <style type="text/css"><jsp:include page="/ag.jsp" /></style>
    <title>Ag - RSS Newsreader and Aggregator</title>
</head>
<body bgcolor="#FFFFFF">
<h1>Ag - RSS Newsreader and Aggregator</h1>
<hr />

<p>News Items from all users Subscriptions are aggregated below.</p>

<p>You may login to <a href="subs">Manage your Subscriptions</a>.</p>

<os:cache time="3600" key="${param.mode}">

<c:choose>
  <c:when test="${param.mode == 'popular'}" >

     <h2>Most Popular Newsfeed Items</h2>
     View: Popular | <a href="main?mode=recent">Recent</a>

     <c:set var="items" value="${ag.popularItems}" />
  </c:when>
  <c:otherwise>

     <h2>Recent Newsfeed Items</h2>
     View: <a href="main?mode=popular">Popular</a> | Recent

     <c:set var="items" value="${ag.recentItems}" />
  </c:otherwise>
</c:choose>

<c:forEach var="item" items="${items}">
   <c:url var="url" value="/ag/link">
     <c:param name="link" value="${item.link}"/>
   </c:url>

   <h3><a href="${url}">${item.title}</a></h3>
   ${item.description} <br />
   <b>Posted: ${item.time}, Hits: ${item.hits}</b>

</c:forEach>

</os:cache>

<hr />

</body>
</html>
```

The OSCache tags were added around the portion of the page that's responsible for fetching the items to be displayed and for displaying those items. Let's focus on the OSCache tags:

```
<os:cache time="3600" key="${mode.param}">

   . . .

</os:cache>
```

The cache time is set to 3,600 seconds, or 1 hour. This means that the main page will be refreshed with new data every hour. The cache key is set to use the request parameter "mode" because the page has two modes of operation. In "popular" mode, the page displays the items with the most hits first. In "recent" mode, the page displays the most recent items first. By using the parameter value as the cache key, you ensure that both versions of the page are cached.

Now that you've applied page caching to your page, you'll rerun the very same JMeter test. The results, shown in the following screen shot, indicate a dramatic improvement. The page now runs ten times faster. It runs, on average, in 0.391 seconds rather than 4 seconds. During the test, the server's CPU was running at about 5% instead of 100%

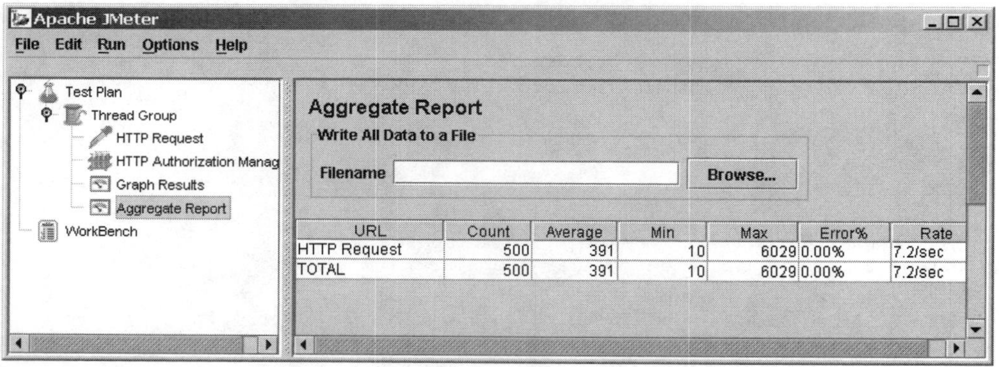

Summary

In this chapter we covered many techniques for improving the performance of JSP applications. We discussed how to use the OSCache page caching system to avoid regenerating a page for every incoming page request. Knowing that a database connection is an expensive operation that consumes processing time, memory, and network resources, we discussed the use of connection pooling to minimize the cost of this operation in JSP applications.

Performance and scalability are primary concerns for any JSP application. Once a JSP application is deployed on a corporate intranet or on the Internet, it may become more popular than initially envisaged. If you apply the design practices discussed in this chapter, you have a much better chance of meeting your customer's performance requirements and continuing to meet them as your user base expands. We looked at a specific performance testing tool, Apache JMeter, which you can use during development to prove that performance and scalability requirements are being met.

As you read about JSP application frameworks in the following chapters, keep in mind what you've learned about designing for performance and scalability.

13

Web Application Design and Best Practices

The previous chapters covered a great deal of the functionality that is provided by the JSP specification. You're now in a good position to take this knowledge and start using it to build Java-based web applications. So then, why should you read this chapter? Well, although knowing the classes and APIs is very important in getting the most out of JSP and servlets, there are some other key factors that will really help you to achieve success. This chapter brings together the techniques covered earlier in the book and shows you how to build maintainable, extensible Java-based web applications.

In this chapter we look at the importance of good design and how it can help you build high-quality web applications that are easy to maintain and extend in the future. To do this, we take a look at some of the standard architectures that have been proven to help achieve these goals. Continuing on the theme of good design, we then take a lower level look at how you can use design patterns to help implement these architectures. Specifically, we cover how some of the best practices around building Java-based web applications have been documented as patterns and explain how you can apply them to your own web applications.

Of course, having a good design is essential, but not if the actual task of implementing the web application is neglected. For this reason, we take a look at some of the best practices around development and testing. Here we cover topics ranging from the use of logging and debugging through to how to actually test web applications and design them to be testable. Finally, we discuss some general guidelines covering topics such as how to enhance the user's experience with your web application. By the end of the chapter, you'll be able to take the knowledge you already have and apply it in a much more structured way, which will help you to build better web applications.

The Importance of Design

When we talk about **design**, regardless of whether it's used within the context of software engineering, what we're essentially talking about is the thought process that goes into something before it's created. This up-front thinking helps us come up with the best possible way for achieving our end goal. For example, you normally wouldn't just go and build a new kitchen without giving consideration to the location of things such as water pipes, electricity outlets, windows, doors, and so on. Although you could just go ahead and build the kitchen, without some up-front thought you probably wouldn't come up with the best solution. This is equally applicable to software. We could just dive straight in, but some forethought is required on our part.

The software industry is often likened to many other forms of industry, although probably the best-known analogy is to the building industry. Although this comparison works on many levels, there are several key differences between making software and creating buildings. Buildings are designed for a specific purpose and they must be designed to withstand known tolerances caused by the environment. Software, on the other hand, is much more dynamic. After all, in general, building software isn't currently seen as being as precise as building houses. This isn't to say that it shouldn't be–it's just that it isn't there as an industry yet. When was the last time you saw bug-free software? The other point to pick up on here is that software typically changes throughout its lifetime. Sometimes these changes are simple bug fixes; more often than not, they're major functionality changes/additions. It's this characteristic of the software industry that really makes design important. To try and quantify the importance of design, let's look at some of the characteristics that it can directly affect.

Maintainability

Maintainability is the ability to maintain a piece of software. It works at several levels. At its most basic level, maintainability involves the work needed to keep that particular piece of software up and running (cleaning up logs, archiving old data, and so on). At another level, maintaining an application can involve fixing bugs as they're reported and making performance enhancements to cope with the increasing demands of the business. Maintainability isn't something that can easily be measured, although it is related to how well the software is designed and implemented. Well-designed software is easier for anybody maintaining the software to understand, and those people can make the small changes that they need to do their job with the knowledge that they aren't about to break unrelated features. This is something that can't be said for badly designed software.

Extensibility

The other aspect affected by the design of a system is **extensibility**, the ability to extend and enhance. Again, well-designed software will typically have a defined structure so that existing features can be changed and new features can be added easily, without causing side effects to the remainder of the system. Particularly for mission-critical business systems, extensibility is an important characteristic of software, as it allows the software to keep up with the business processes that it's realizing with a minimum of cost and overhead.

Web Application Design

Now that you understand that design–even just a little design–is important, let's take a look at some of the common and proven architectures for Java-based web applications.

Page-Centric (Also Known As Model 1)

The first common architecture for building web applications is **page-centric**, which is more commonly known within Java web application circles as the **model 1 architecture**. This is the easiest way in which a web application can be put together. It involves simply building the application as a set of JSP pages, as illustrated in the following diagram:

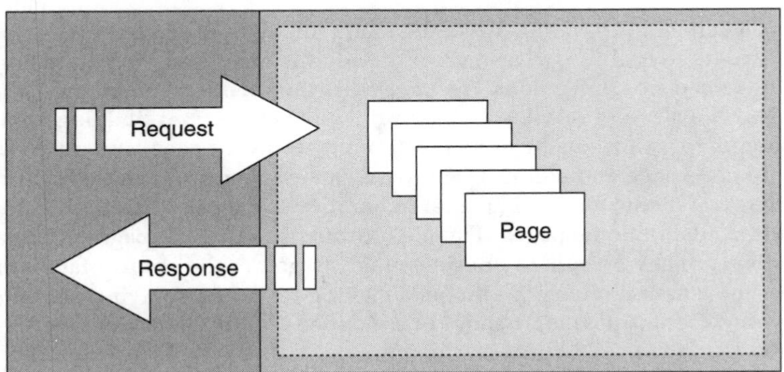

Of course, applications are generally built to share information (typically from some sort of database) with the users, and with page-centric applications, information is typically represented in a couple of ways. The first of these is that any information required by a page is accessed directly from the database using embedded SQL. Usually this SQL code is written straight into the page along with the code to make the database connections and retrieve the results. As a twist on this paradigm, the code to deal with the database connections is often pushed into reusable Java classes or custom tags such as those found in the JSTL. Of the various ways to build a web application, this is probably the least maintainable because all of the logic to access data is embedded right inside the JSP pages. Any change to the database schema means potentially opening up every page in the application to fix it.

The other mechanism for accessing data within page-centric applications is to use JavaBeans to represent the persistent entities within your system, as illustrated by the following diagram. For example, you might have a JavaBean called `Customer` to represent the customers within your system. By taking this approach, data access code is kept off of the individual pages and can be pushed back into reusable Java classes. By doing this, you instantly attain a greater level of code reuse throughout the application while at the same you increase the maintainability of the application. Here, changes to the database schema require changes to a select few Java classes:

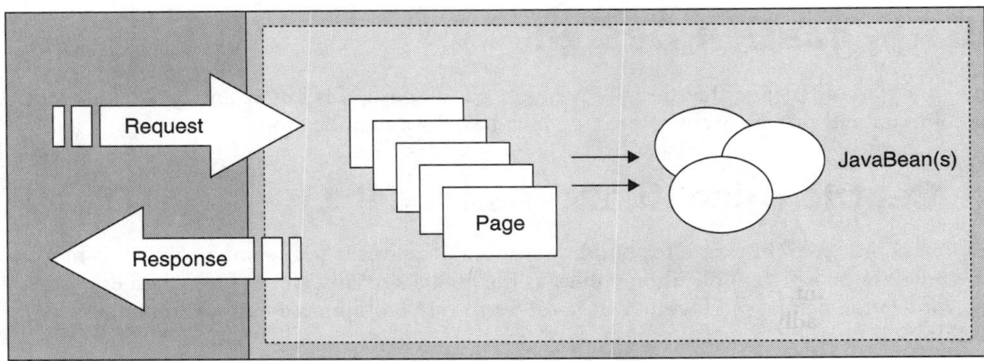

So, although you can take steps to increase the maintainability of page-centric applications, the real limitation lies within your ability to change or modify the end-to-end functionality provided by the system. With page-centric applications, the pages that the user sees are all implemented as stand-alone JSPs. In fact, you can also use servlets, but the principle is the same: Building applications this way has limitations. Should you want to add some functionality to every page (such as security or logging), you have to open up each page and edit it. Want to add a new flow of functionality through the application? Chances are that you'll have to open up a large number of pages to edit links and ensure that the required data is available to the pages. The main problem is that the pages of the application have too much responsibility. They contain the business logic to gather the appropriate information (and make changes to that information) alongside the presentation logic of displaying that information to the user. Ideally, changes to the business logic should be independent of the presentation logic and vice versa.

Model-View-Controller (Also Known As Model 2)

The other major architecture used to build web applications is based upon the classic **Model-View-Controller (MVC)** architecture and is commonly referred to as **model 2**. In page-centric web applications, a single request is generally serviced by a single page containing the business and presentation logic. Model-2, however, involves three major components in the servicing of a request, as summarized in the following diagram:

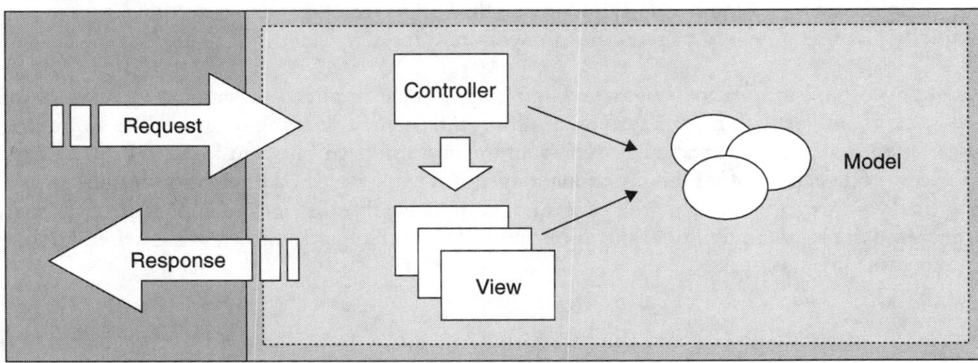

The first of these is the **controller,** the component through which all requests are routed to be serviced. It effectively acts as the gateway to the functionality provided by the web application and is typically implemented as a Java servlet. Having a single point of access for all requests in the system has a couple of benefits. First, it provides a common location for systemwide aspects such as security, logging, and so on. Second, it's the responsibility of the controller to find and execute the business logic that will be used to service the request. This could range from simply locating information that is to be displayed through to processing an update request and modifying some data residing in a database. The important point to note about the controller is that it doesn't have anything to do with the presentation of information back to the user.

The next component, or set of components, used by the model 2 architecture represent the **model**. There are a couple of broadly accepted definitions for the model components, but we like to think of them as the information that the controller uses to perform its processing. In other words, the controller contains the business logic and the model represents the business/domain objects upon which that logic operates. If you've done any Swing programming, think of the model as the Swing model components that just provide a representation of the data being manipulated and displayed. Like Swing, model components are generally implemented as JavaBeans.

The final type of components in the model 2 architecture is the **view** components. These are solely responsible for the presentation of information back to the user. Because all business logic is performed by the controller on the model, the view components only have to present the information provided by the model to the user. For this reason, view components are typically implemented with JSP pages because these are most aligned to allow easy presentation of information back to the user (for example, using a markup language such as HTML).

Although this separation of concerns does seem slightly more complicated than the design used by simple page-centric designs, it gives you the ability to modify each of the three components in isolation. You can modify the data schema, the business logic, or the presentation separately. Not only is the application more maintainable because there is a centralized place for locating each specific type of code, but also the system as a whole is now much more extensible. Need to add a new flow of functionality? Simply add the logic into the controller component and add a new view to display the relevant information back to the user. Of course, it's still possible to build unmaintainable model 2 web applications, and for this reason there are now a collection of proven patterns that can be used during design and development.

Design Patterns

A simple way to describe **design patterns** is that they're reusable solutions to common problems within a given context. In addition to this, and through the way that they're documented, patterns provide a common language with which to understand and make use of them. Patterns really came into the limelight with the release of the "Gang of Four"'s (Erich Gamma, Richard Helm, Ralph Johnson, and John Vlissides) book entitled *Design Patterns: Elements of Reusable Object-Oriented Software* (Addison-Wesley, 1995). This book details a large number of reusable solutions to common, language-independent design problems related to structural, behavioral, and creational contexts. From this, and using the original design patterns as a basis, many people have extended this work to document new patterns around the design and implementation of J2EE systems, including many that are relevant to building Java-based web applications.

Why Use Patterns?

At first sight, patterns can be seen to complicate the design of a system, and to a degree this is true. After all, why implement a feature with a handful of related classes when just a single class will do? Well, the benefits come at several levels. Using patterns and the common language that they use allows us, as software developers, to easily communicate about how a particular part of the application works. For example, if we have a class that's responsible for creating other types of classes on demand, using the common name for this pattern (in this case, "factory") provides a certain level of common understanding. This is useful, as it helps other members of the project team, or anybody looking at the code, to come to grips with it easily.

The ability to use patterns also helps to ensure that there's some consistency in the way that recurring problems are solved within the application. This practice subsequently promotes code reuse (and therefore quality) and maintainability, again because the design is easier to understand. Furthermore, because patterns have the ability to introduce a certain degree of structure to a design, the extensibility of that design is often greater than if the same functionality was built using a single class.

J2EE Patterns and Web Application Components

Probably the most well-known collection of J2EE patterns available to date is that cataloged by the Sun Java Center (http://developer.java.sun.com/developer/restricted/patterns/J2EEPatternsAtAGlance.html). The patterns contained within this catalog cover all tiers of the J2EE architecture, and if you're building multitier enterprise applications, they're well worth taking a look at. For the purpose of this chapter, you're only interested in those patterns that are relevant to building the web tier of J2EE applications. Let's take a look at some of these and see how they can help you build well-designed web applications.

Front Controller

As you learned in the discussion of the model 2 architecture, the controller component acts as the gateway into the web application and is the central place from which all requests are serviced. As it stands, the MVC architecture is programming language independent, and in translating this to the world of Java-based web applications, the Sun Java Center came up with the **front controller** pattern, a J2EE-specific version of the controller in MVC. The following code snippet shows a prototypical implementation of this pattern:

```
package com.apress.projsp20.ch13;

import java.io.IOException;

import javax.servlet.RequestDispatcher;
import javax.servlet.ServletException;
import javax.servlet.http.*;

public class FrontController extends HttpServlet {

  protected void processRequest(HttpServletRequest request,
                                HttpServletResponse response)
      throws ServletException, IOException {
```

```
    // Step 1 - perform business logic and manipulate the model
    // someObject.someBusinessLogic();

    // Step 2 - dispatch to the appropriate view component
    RequestDispatcher dispatcher =
      getServletContext().getRequestDispatcher("name of a view component");
    dispatcher.forward(request, response);
  }

  protected void doGet(HttpServletRequest req, HttpServletResponse res)
      throws ServletException, IOException {

    processRequest(req, res);
  }

  protected void doPost(HttpServletRequest req, HttpServletResponse res)
      throws ServletException, IOException {

    processRequest(req, res);
  }

}
```

As this example implementation shows, a front controller can be as simple as a servlet that responds to HTTP GET and POST requests. Although the code doesn't actually show any real business logic being called, it does show the steps involves in servicing the request. First, you process the request by executing some business logic, and then you redirect to, or dispatch to, the view component that will be presenting the user with information. The main problem with this implementation is that if all business logic for an application is wrapped up inside a single controller, that controller will quickly become bloated and have a vast set of responsibilities. To overcome this problem, you can use the command and controller strategy.

The Command and Controller Strategy

There are many ways in which the front controller pattern can be implemented, each of which is called a **strategy**. For example, in the previous example the front controller was implemented as a Java servlet, although there's nothing stopping that implementation from being a JSP page. To overcome the problem of the controller becoming bloated with all of the application logic for a particular system, the command and controller strategy combines the controller pattern with the **command** design pattern. Essentially, the command pattern says that the logic required to perform a specific task is wrapped up into a single class with a standard interface to execute that code. For example, you might wrap up the logic to locate a customer's details into a single class, inside a method called `execute()`. First, you might define a standard interface for all of the commands to be used by the front controller:

```
package com.apress.projsp20.ch13;

import javax.servlet.ServletException;
import javax.servlet.http.HttpServletRequest;
import javax.servlet.http.HttpServletResponse;
```

```
public interface Action {

  public String execute(HttpServletRequest request, HttpServletResponse response)
       throws ServletException;

}
```

This interface contains a single method with which to execute the logic that will be encapsulated within concrete implementations of this interface. Essentially, all you want to do is delegate the servicing of requests to an `Action` instance instead of putting that code inside the controller. For this reason, the method signature is defined to take references to the same request and response objects that are used when processing an HTTP request with a servlet. With this interface, you then can then supply an implementation that, given a customer ID, looks up that customer and places the corresponding domain object into the HTTP request to be displayed by the view component:

```
package com.apress.projsp20.ch13;

import javax.servlet.http.HttpServletRequest;
import javax.servlet.http.HttpServletResponse;
import javax.servlet.ServletException;

public class ViewCustomerAction implements Action {

  public String execute(HttpServletRequest request, HttpServletResponse response)
      throws ServletException {

    String id = request.getParameter("id");
    Customer customer = CustomerFactory.getInstance().getCustomer(id);
    request.setAttribute("customer", customer);

    return "/view-customer.jsp";
  }

}
```

Assuming that all of the necessary code to look up customers has been written, when a `Customer` instance is found, you can use the request object as an area in which to place any objects that are relevant for the lifetime of this request via the `setAttribute()` method. The final point to note about this implementation is that the value returned from the `execute()` method is the name of the JSP page representing the view component. In other words, this is the name of the JSP page that will be used to render, or present, the information back to the user.

With all of the business logic then wrapped up inside `Action` instances, the front controller itself becomes very small and hence much more cohesive:

```
package com.apress.projsp20.ch13;

import java.io.IOException;

import javax.servlet.http.*;
import javax.servlet.ServletException;
import javax.servlet.RequestDispatcher;
```

```
public class FrontController extends HttpServlet {

  private ActionFactory actionFactory = new ActionFactory();

  protected void processRequest(HttpServletRequest request,
                                HttpServletResponse response)
      throws ServletException, IOException {

    Action action;

    try {
      action = actionFactory.getAction(request);
    } catch (ActionNotFoundException anfe) {
      throw new ServletException(anfe);
    }

    // Now process action, finding out which view to show the user next
    String nextView = action.execute(request, response);

    // and finally redirect to appropriate view, remembering to prefix the path
    try {
      if (nextView != null) {
        RequestDispatcher dispatcher =
          getServletContext().getRequestDispatcher(nextView);
        dispatcher.forward(request, response);
      }
    } catch (Exception e) {
      e.printStackTrace();
      throw new ServletException(e);
    }
  }

  protected void doGet(HttpServletRequest req, HttpServletResponse res)
      throws ServletException, IOException {
    processRequest(req, res);
  }


  protected void doPost(HttpServletRequest req, HttpServletResponse res)
      throws ServletException, IOException {
    processRequest(req, res);
  }

}
```

In this version of the front controller, you're simply using a helper class to find which `Action` implementation should be used to service this particular request. How does the controller know which action to use? Well, there are various ways in which the name of the action can be communicated to the controller. These range from using a named parameter within the query string to encoding the name of the action inside specially mapped URLs. One such example might be as follows:

http://www.mycompany.com/controller/ViewCustomer?id=123456

The key benefit of combining the controller and command patterns is that it allows you to maintain a central place for accepting requests, while keeping the logic to actually service an individual request separate from that needed to service other types of requests.

View

With the controller responsible for the business logic related to servicing a request, you may be asking how to implement the view components. In the simplest case, the views are implemented as JSP pages that are forwarded to by the controller component. The job of the controller (or an action class if you're using that strategy) is to perform any processing and set up the environment for the view to present the information. In Chapter 8, you saw that it's quite possible for JSP pages to contain database code so that they can find the data they're supposed to display. However, the model 2 architecture turns this on its head because it's now the responsibility of the controller to find that data. As you saw in the previous sample action implementation, it's possible to use the `request` object to store information that's required for the lifetime of the current request:

```
request.setAttribute("customer", customer);
```

Here, you're just placing a `Customer` instance into the map of objects maintained by the request. When it comes to presenting the information from the view, you can use the new JSP 2.0 EL to locate that `Customer` instance and display it. For example, you can use the following expression to display the name of the customer (assuming that a method called `getName()` exists):

```
${customer.name}
```

This separation of business and presentation logic gives you the ability to easily change one or the other independently if necessary. Should you need to change the way in which the customer is presented to the user, this is no problem. You can just modify the JSP page without danger of breaking the existing business logic of locating that customer.

View Helper

Although the front controller is responsible (possibly through delegation to commands) for executing the business logic required to service a given request, there is still often logic that is related to only the presentation of that information. View components such as JSP pages are great at displaying information, but sometimes some more code is needed. Perhaps a list of objects needs to be sorted prior to being displayed, or perhaps the information needs to be formatted in some specific way. Although that code can simply be embedded into the view components, the **view helper** pattern describes a way to wrap up this code and make is reusable over multiple views.

You have already seen many examples of view helpers. If you look back to Chapter 6, one of the tags you saw filtered the domain of e-mail addresses, making it harder for spammers to obtain addresses. Although extremely useful, such logic isn't really classed as business logic. Instead, this is presentation logic–code that is used to help the view present information back to the users. Of course, such code could have been written and embedded into the JSP page, but this is considered bad practice for reasons of quality, maintainability, and so on. Instead, that code is wrapped inside a custom tag so that it can be used and reused throughout the pages of the web application. In effect, this custom tag is an implementation of the view helper pattern. In this case, the tag is a component that the view uses to help it perform its task.

Service to Worker

Each of the patterns that we've covered so far has tackled a different problem within the design of web applications. The front controller provides a single point of access for requests to centralize business logic, whereas views and view helpers separate the process of presenting information from the process of finding the information and manipulating it. To bring all of these patterns together, the J2EE patterns catalog defines a macro pattern called service to worker. By "macro pattern," we mean that this is really just a combination of other patterns–in this case, the front controller, views, and view helpers:

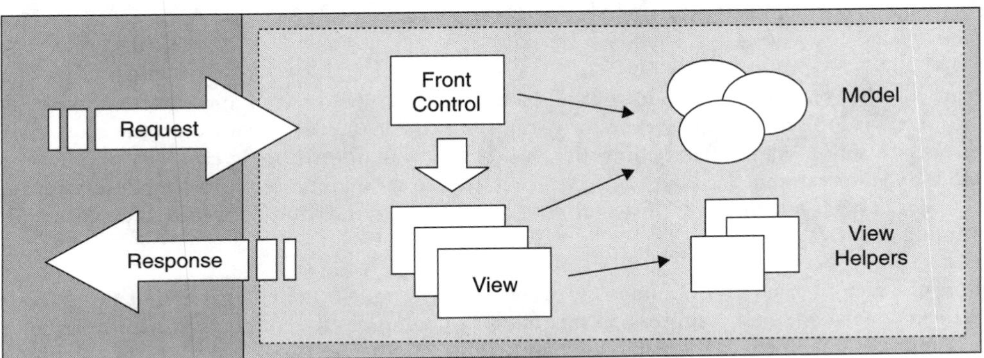

Bringing all of these patterns together is the basis for a model 2 architecture and provides a common ground on which web applications can be designed and easily understood. It also helps to emphasize the benefits of the individual patterns and demonstrates that they're much more useful if used in conjunction with one another. As you'll see shortly, the service to worker pattern, or model 2 architecture, forms the basis of many web application frameworks currently in use.

Filter

Another useful, although not widely used, pattern worth briefly talking about is called **filter**. The filter API that you saw in the previous chapters is an implementation of this pattern, so instead of how to implement a filter, let's take a look at how it can be used in the design of web applications and talk about some more typical uses.

Essentially, filters can play in important role in the design of web applications because they can have responsibilities unrelated to any particular JSP or servlet. Filters can be seen as channels through which all requests and responses can be passed through.

One of the uses that I've put filters to on web applications is as a way to interpret user-friendly URLs. To help me keep my website up to date, I built some weblogging software–a simple date-based content management system to which I post short entries a daily basis. The weblog (abbreviated to "blog") then displays the most recent of these entries in reverse date order on the front page. In addition, when readers want to locate older entries, they can simply jump directly to a page containing all of the entries for an individual day.

In the past, such websites have been built of static pages, organized in such a way that it made it easy to find the page for a specific day. For example, the blog entries for June 10, 2003, can be found at http://www.simongbrown.com/blog/2003/06/10.html.

With technologies such as JSP and servlets providing many benefits over writing static pages, I decided to write my weblog as a Java-based web application. All of the entries are stored separately on the filing system, and with the help of the front controller pattern, a couple of JSP pages are used to assemble the individual entries into a page that is presented back to the user. However, rather than show the user a URL such as http://www.simongbrown.com/blog/servlet/ViewDailyBlog?year=2003&month=6&day=10, I decided that I'd still like URLs such as the one shown previously to work. To implement this, I used a filter.

Because a filter can be set up to look at all incoming requests to a web application, all that the filter needs to do is look for a request matching `yyyy/mm/dd.html` and forward on the request to the appropriate action via the front controller. Essentially, the filter is being used to catch these requests for seemingly static content through user-friendly URLs into dynamic requests for content through the front controller. This is a simple yet powerful implementation of the filter pattern that performs filtering on incoming requests.

Filters can also be used on outgoing responses. One example often cited is a filter that, once a request has been processed, uses compression techniques to compress the outgoing stream in an attempt to make more efficient use of the available bandwidth. Another example is a filter that highlights the usage of search terms in the page. Through the interfaces provided by the servlet API, it's possible to find the complete URL of the website that the user came from to visit your site. For example, somebody might click a link in Google to get to your website. Using this information, you could write a filter to check for referrals from Google and highlight the occurrences of the search terms used before the response is subsequently sent back to the user. Again, this is another way in which you can use filters to enhance the user's experience of your web applications.

Other Web Application Patterns

In addition to the J2EE patterns that we've just covered, there are other patterns or best practices that can help you to build web applications. Also, JSP 2.0 provides a much better and often easier way to implement some of these patterns, as we describe in the following sections.

Including Standard Headers and Footers

Probably one of the most commonly used best practices when building JSP-based web applications is to separate out the common code used in headers and footers into JSP pages or fragments that are included wherever necessary. Such files might include all of the HTML tags to define well-formed HTML headers, the `<%@ taglib %>` directives to import common tag libraries, defining objects to be used in the page, and so on. Whatever it is you're trying to achieve, you'll typically implement this practice by statically including the header on every page with the JSP include directive:

```
<%@ include file="header.jspf" %>
```

On translation of the JSP into a servlet, the JSP compiler inlines the included file into the source code of the generated servlet class. This is a useful way to make some of the content reusable, although it does rely on the page author remembering to include the header wherever possible. Also, often different headers are needed for different parts of the web application. For example, you might have a separate include file for secure parts of the site.

To address this, the teams behind the new JSP and Servlet specifications have come up with the idea of **preludes** and **codas**–opening and closing includes. The basic idea is that given any set of one or more JSP pages, it's possible to define one or more preludes or codas that are included before and after the main body of those JSPs. So, instead of including a header and footer on every page, it's possible to achieve the same result with the following fragment within the `web.xml` deployment descriptor:

```
<jsp-property-group>
    <url-pattern>*.jsp</url-pattern>
    <include-prelude>/header.jspf</include-prelude>
    <include-coda>/footer.jspf</include-coda>
</jsp-property-group>
```

This is a great way to further increase the maintainability of your web applications and reduce the amount of duplicated content that they contain.

Templating

Templating is another common implementation technique in web applications. A **template** is essentially a predefined skeleton that you can customize at runtime with the use of parameters. If you look back to Chapter 5, one of the examples used to demonstrate tag files was a web page that contained a number of promotional notices on the homepage. Although the content contained within each tag was different, the actual structure and code to build them was the same. These are effectively templates that are being used and customized.

Before the introduction of tag files, templating was fairly hard to achieve with JSP because there was no easy way to express how templates should be customized. A couple of possible options included using short scriptlets or even custom tags to indicate where dynamic content should be inserted inside the body of the template. However, the problem with these is that all too often, using such methods introduced some Java code into the page. Perhaps objects needed to be set up or some presentation logic was needed. Once code is introduced, many people stop calling those pages templates. After all, instead of simply indicating where dynamic content should be inserted, you basically have complete control over how the template works.

Another option is to use a specific templating framework such as Velocity (discussed shortly).

With JSP 2.0 comes the introduction of the EL, which provides the ability to perform templating. Because the EL is an integral part of the JSP specification, templates are now much easier to build. Simply write the static content inside a JSP file and then insert EL expressions where the dynamic content is to be inserted. The expressions themselves can be fairly powerful, although they're still simple enough for people to understand, and they don't expose the inner workings of the template.

Frameworks for Building Web Applications

So far we've looked at some proven ways of building web applications and a lot of patterns for translating these ideas into working code. Do you really have to write all of this every time you build an application?

A Bespoke Framework

By combining the implementations of the J2EE patterns discussed previously, you basically have a bespoke framework on which to build a model 2–based web application. In fact, many of the web applications that I've worked on (open source and for clients) have used these simple implementations as a basis for a lightweight model 2 framework used to service all of the requests throughout the application. I subscribe to the "keep it simple" approach to software design, and using such a lightweight framework has several benefits. The framework is easy to learn, easy to maintain and, when necessary, easy to extend, one such example being to handle validation errors from HTML forms that users submit.

However, writing a bespoke framework isn't always the best option. The implementation of the front controller pattern presented here is fairly simple and straightforward, but there are many improvements that can be made. Examples include a standard way to build HTML forms and perform validation, more sophisticated components to display information from the model, and so on. Although such work isn't particularly complex, it's time consuming. For this reason, a number of third-party frameworks are available for developers to use as a starting point for their web applications.

Struts

Struts from the Jakarta Project (http://jakarta.apache.org) is an open source framework providing an implementation of not only a front controller, but also a complete implementation (or framework) of the model 2 architecture. The key components are similar to those presented here, including, for example, a controller servlet (called `ActionServlet`), `Action` classes in which to place functionality for processing a request, and `ActionBean` classes in which to encapsulate data coming in from a request. In addition, Struts contains a comprehensive collection of JSP tag libraries for the easy assembly of HTML-based forms and JSP pages in general.

One of the most important features of Struts is that pretty much everything about it is externally configured through the `struts-config.xml` file. This includes the mappings between action names and `Action` classes (called `ActionMappings`), and also a concept called `ActionForwards`. For the simple implementation presented before, the `Action` classes return a string representing the URI of the JSP page that should be displayed next. In Struts, however, the `Action` classes return a symbolic name (wrapped up in an `ActionForward` instance) representing which view component should be displayed next. As an example, consider a login form containing a username and password. On submission of the form, the login is either successful or unsuccessful. In this case, the `Action` class could return symbolic names such as success or failure. These symbolic names are then configured in the `struts-config.xml` file, and it's here that the physical URI to the appropriate JSP page is specified. The following snippet shows how two different flows through a login action might be handled:

```
<action path="/login" type="com.mycompany.myapp.LoginAction">
  <forward name="success" path="/index.jsp"/>
  <forward name="failure" path="/login-failed.jsp"/>
</action>
```

Here, we're saying that there are two possible outcomes for the login action. The first is that the login is successful, and if this is the case, the user is directed to the index page. Alternatively, a failed login takes the user to a page explaining that the user's login failed. Generally, this logic and the page names would have to be hard-coded into the actions. With Struts and its configuration file, the flows through an application can be easily changed, and it's another way in which the flow and structure of the web application can be taken out of the code to increase maintainability. After all, if the structure of the site changes, only the configuration file needs to change. We look at Struts in more detail in the next chapter.

WebWork

WebWork (http://www.opensymphony.com/webwork/) is another model 2 framework that is often compared to Struts. It too uses the concepts of classes that implement the command pattern, although one of the key differences between Struts and WebWork is that WebWork is built on top of another framework (XWork) that isn't actually tied to the Web and concepts such as HTTP requests and responses. Therefore, it's possible to share implementations between web applications and other Java implementations such as a Swing client. In essence, the action classes are just JavaBeans, and in a web environment, parameters are simply mapped on to bean properties.

WebWork provides similar features to Struts in terms of components to build user interface components/HTML forms, customizable validation, an expression language for accessing information from the model, and so on. However, what makes WebWork more than just a Struts copy is that it doesn't rely on just JSP for the presentation tier. The view components themselves *can* be JSP, but they can also be written using other technologies, including XML and Velocity (see the next section for more information on Velocity).

A unique feature of WebWork is that it supports interceptors that can be used to execute logic before and/or after an action invocation. In essence, it's similar to the way that filters can be used to intercept incoming requests and outgoing responses. Like aspect-oriented programming (AOP), WebWork interceptors give you a way to insert cross-cutting concerns throughout your code base without having to open every action class up and edit it. By "cross-cutting concerns," we mean logic that isn't specifically tied to the business function provided by the system, such as logging, security, caching, and so on. Typically, business logic can be seen as vertical in that in any application you have a collection of vertical slices providing business logic. With interceptors, you can build code that works across all of these vertical slices and, in WebWork, you can configure this declaratively.

In summary, WebWork is a simpler, although arguably more powerful, alternative to Struts that provides a quick way to build model 2–based web applications. Additionally, the simple interface provided by the action classes makes testing WebWork actions much easier than Struts, without the need for a testing framework such as Cactus. The only downside to using WebWork is that the user community is currently small and there isn't much information readily available. Hopefully, this will start to change.

Velocity

Velocity (http://jakarta.apache.org/velocity/) is a Java-based templating engine that provides an alternative way to build the view components of web applications. In fact, Velocity is capable of much more than this, as it can be used outside of the context of a web application, perhaps for helping to generate reports or XML. Velocity provides its own templating language (the Velocity Templating Language, or VTL) that provides a way to access pretty much anything that can be accessed through regular Java method calls. At the time that Velocity was created, JSP didn't include its own expression language, and Velocity was an attempt to fill this void and provide an easy way for developers to build true templates.

Although JSP 2.0 does include an EL, Velocity has a large following and has been deployed in many applications, particularly web applications. With frameworks such as WebWork providing easy integration with Velocity, it will still be a popular choice for web applications that are heavily based on dynamic content that can be easily templated.

JavaServer Faces

JavaServer Faces, or JSF (http://java.sun.com/j2ee/javaserverfaces/), is an interesting twist on the classic web application programming model in that it's a new framework and programming model for simplifying the development of web-based user interfaces. It does this by allowing users of the framework to build user interfaces by assembling prebuilt components such as text fields, lists, and so on. The programming model itself is based around MVC and provides a way for web-based applications to be built in a similar way to regular GUI applications by representing the UI component hierarchy on the server side.

When developers build web applications with JSP, they typically have to hardwire the information displayed by the presentation layer to the underlying model by explicitly accessing and manipulating the data stored within it. With JSF, the components are bound into the model in the same way that Swing UI components are bound to an underlying data model. In theory, this should allow web-based UIs to be built much quicker, potentially by nondevelopment staff, and provide a true separation between the behavior of the application and the presentation of information.

One of the major advantages of building regular GUI-based applications over web-based applications is the flexibility and richness of the UI. A good example here is that a GUI can respond and react to user interactions, such as unchecking a check box or selecting an item in a list. One of the goals of the JSF specification is to provide a similar level of richness, and to facilitate this, JSF also provides an event model allowing client-generated events to be tied into server-side event handlers. JSF provides APIs for performing server-side validation, defining page navigation, and internationalization (i18n).

Many existing frameworks such as Struts are centered on producing web applications for a specific presentation technology. One of the goals of the JSF specification is to provide a framework that's independent of the underlying presentation tier technology. In fact, JSF goes one step further than this in stating that the programming model and API is markup language independent, client independent, and protocol independent.

It achieves this independence by providing APIs for the various parts of the framework (the UI components, event handlers, and so on) and allows specific implementations to run on top of the framework. In addition, rendering kits provide the ability to render the UI components for multiple markup languages and client types. However, as a convenience JSF includes a JSP implementation so that developers can start building JSP-based web applications out of the box. This implementation provides an HTML 4.0 rendering kit along with custom tag libraries representing the various components that developers can assemble on their JSP pages.

JSF is still in development. It's an interesting project to keep an eye on, especially because Sun is targeting JSF as a replacement for building web applications with languages such as Visual Basic.

Now that you've looked at some of the design aspects of web applications, let's move on to examine how you can test those web applications and how you can design them *to* be tested.

Testing

Testing plays an important role in the software development life cycle, although when time scales are short and deadlines loom, testing often doesn't get the attention that it should. Fortunately, new development methods such as eXtreme Programming (XP) are doing a great job of promoting automated testing with tools such as JUnit, in which unit tests are actually written in Java. So then, how do these principles apply to testing web applications and what exactly can you test? Web applications are often complex by nature, and this can lead to confusion over exactly what can and should be tested. From an automated testing perspective, there are two types of testing that generally take place: unit testing and functional testing.

Unit Testing Web Applications

Unit testing is the process of testing software from the perspective that you know how it works. It's also called **white box testing** because you can see how the software works–you can see inside the box. The opposite of this is **black box testing**, which we look at shortly. The idea with unit testing is to ensure that all (or most) of the paths throughout the unit are sufficiently tested, including things such as boundary conditions on loops and method calls, correct and incorrect (for example, null) parameters into method calls, and so on. By doing this, you're making sure that the unit being tested is correct, does what it's supposed to do, and doesn't break when you throw inputs it just isn't expecting. So, how can you apply unit testing to web applications?

The simple answer to this question is that you just unit test all of the classes and components that make up the web application–everything from the JavaBeans representing business objects to the servlets servicing requests. Although this sounds good in theory, in practice it's difficult to achieve because of the plumbing required by many of the J2EE components that live inside a server. With stand-alone Java classes, it's very straightforward to write automated unit tests with the JUnit framework. Typically, such tests might create new instances of the class being tested, call methods on that instance, and subsequently perform assertions on the results to ensure that they were correct. However, with components such as servlets and JSP pages (which get compiled to servlets), this just isn't something that can be done in the same way. After all, these components need to be executed within the context of a server that supports the technologies. In essence, these components rely heavily on the plumbing, infrastructure, and services provided by such servers. Fortunately, people have realized this and have come up with some ways of making unit testing such components easier. However, there will generally a cutoff point at which unit testing becomes unfeasible and other testing methods must be used. With these thoughts in mind, let's now move on to look at what you can test and the tools you can use to do so.

JUnit

JUnit (http://www.junit.org), now the de facto standard for building automated tests within the Java language, is widely used on projects ranging from desktop applications to enterprise-scale distributed servers. JUnit provides a very lightweight framework with which to write tests. At a high level, you simply extend one of the provided classes and write one or more methods to test each aspect of the class or classes that you wish to test. Once you've compiled the test classes, you then run the tests through one of the JUnit test runners, and it's this that keeps a tally of the passes and fails, issuing a result at the end of the process.

The following code fragment illustrates how easy it is to write automated unit tests in JUnit by showing you how you might test a simple JavaBean representing a customer having two properties, `firstName` and `lastName`. In this example, the class has an additional method called `getFullName()` that simply joins the first and last names together with a space between them. With JUnit, you might want to test that the various get methods function as expected by setting the appropriate properties and performing assertions on the results of accessing those properties:

```
import junit.framework.TestCase;

public class CustomerTest extends TestCase {

  public void testFirstName() {
    Customer customer = new Customer();
    customer.setFirstName("Simon");
    assertEquals("Simon", customer.getFirstName());
  }

  public void testLastName() {
    Customer customer = new Customer();
    customer.setLastName("Brown");
    assertEquals("Brown", customer.getLastName());
  }

  public void testFullName() {
    Customer customer = new Customer();
    customer.setFirstName("Simon");
    customer.setLastName("Brown");
    assertEquals("Simon Brown", customer.getFullName());
  }

}
```

All that you're doing here is extending one of the classes provided by JUnit and implementing `testXXX()` methods for the various pieces of functionally that you'd like to test. In this case, you're testing the ability to set/get the first, last, and full names. Of course, this is a simple example and it doesn't cover exceptional cases such as null values. However, it does demonstrate how easy it is to write unit tests with JUnit and shows its potential.

Getting started with JUnit can sometimes be tricky, particularly with respect to finding the motivation to write the tests in the first place. However, once they've gotten over the learning curve and experienced the benefit of JUnit, most people become hooked or, to use a phrase coined by the JUnit team, "test infected."

> *Seeing JUnit for the first time is a little daunting, especially when you start to think about how much more Java code you have to write for each and every class that you're building. However, from our experience of using JUnit, we've found that after you use JUnit for a while there will come a day when you will suddenly start to appreciate the power of automated unit tests and the confidence that it can give you when refactoring or redesigning parts of a system. The feeling of confidence you get when you do a big design change and the tests still work is amazing!*

With JUnit, the types of classes that you can test include those representing the business domain, the business logic, model 2–style action classes, helper classes, and so on. Essentially, anything that stands alone can be tested using JUnit. In many web applications, this set of classes will cover the majority of the code being developed and should hopefully lead to a good level of confidence that the code works correctly. However, there may be times when you have stand-alone classes that still need to be run and therefore tested inside of a J2EE container environment. For these situations, JUnitEE is useful.

JUnitEE

JUnitEE (http://www.junitee.org) basically provides a way to run regular JUnit tests inside of a J2EE container. Why would you want to do this? Well, perhaps you have some classes that require the use of a database connection that is set up and made available to those classes through the container's JNDI tree. Or perhaps those classes need access to some other enterprise resource to function properly. With JUnitEE, you can bundle up all of your classes and their tests into a WAR file that you can then deploy onto a J2EE web container such as Tomcat. To execute those tests, you then point your web browser to the newly deployed web application and a servlet runs behind the scenes to execute the JUnit tests and presents the results back to you.

JUnitEE is effectively a lightweight test runner that allows you to execute tests within a server environment. However, it doesn't allow you to test components such as servlets and JSPs any easier than JUnit. For this you have to look at other options such as Cactus.

Cactus

Cactus (http://jakarta.apache.org/cactus/) is an extension to JUnit that provides a mechanism for running unit tests inside of a running J2EE container. With JUnitEE, although you're able to run regular JUnit tests within a server environment, you still don't have the complete infrastructure necessary to test those classes that depend on information delivered to them on a request-by-request basis. For example, to be able to truly test a servlet, you need to have a live request and response object available to you because the code inside the servlet might extract parameters from the request or push out information into the response. Cactus gives you the ability to test these types of components with the confidence that they're running within their real environment.

In Cactus, the testing functionality is broken into two halves. First is a client part. This looks just like a normal JUnit test and is used to initiate the test. The second part of Cactus lives on the server. Here, you can use Cactus-provided test classes to instantiate the components that you wish to test and invoke their methods. For example, you might choose to create a new instance of a servlet class and call the `doGet()` method. Of course, to actually call this method you need to have access to the HTTP request and response objects, so where do they come from?

The key here is a test redirector component that sits between the client and server test classes. When a test is initiated by the client, a request is made to the J2EE container and this is intercepted by a Cactus-provided servlet that must also be running on the server. This servlet (the test redirector) then determines which server-side test needs to be run and initiates the appropriate test class. As an actual HTTP request has been made to the J2EE container, Cactus simply wraps this up and passes it on to the server-side test class to use as necessary. The object representing the HTTP response is also wrapped up for use by the test class. With access to these, the server-side test class and the class being tested can extract parameters, write output to the response, and so on. Assertions can then be made that the class being tested works as expected, with the results of these assertions being passed back to the client for reporting.

As an example, consider the `ViewCustomerAction` class that we introduced during our discussion of MVC earlier in the chapter. Because this class relies on the server for a real request, it's a great candidate for testing with Cactus. The following code snippet shows how you might achieve this:

```
import javax.servlet.ServletException;

import junit.framework.Test;
import junit.framework.TestSuite;
import org.apache.cactus.ServletTestCase;
import org.apache.cactus.WebRequest;

public class ViewCustomerTest extends ServletTestCase {

  public ViewCustomerTest(String theName) {
    super(theName);
  }

  public static Test suite() {
    return new TestSuite(ViewCustomerTest.class);
  }

  public void beginExecute(WebRequest webRequest) {
    webRequest.addParameter("id", "123");
  }

  public void testExecute() {
    Customer customer = CustomerFactory.getInstance().getCustomer("123");
    ViewCustomerAction action = new ViewCustomerAction();
    try {
      action.execute(this.request, this.response);
      assertEquals(customer, request.getAttribute("customer"));
    } catch (ServletException e) {
      fail();
    }
  }
}
```

In many ways, this class is similar to the JUnit tests that you saw in the previous section, except this time you subclass a Cactus-specific class. Again, you write a `testXXX()` method to test the functionality, but Cactus allows you to write a corresponding `beginXXX()` method that gets called before your test method. It's here that you can initialize request parameters and so on. The class that you've subclassed (`ServletTestCase`) provides you with access to a real request/response, and it's because of this that testing the server-side action is so straightforward.

Cactus provides a very flexible way of testing those components that really do need to be tested inside a J2EE container, and it currently provides support for testing servlets, JSPs, custom tags, and filters. The biggest problem with Cactus is that it can seem very complicated to begin with, particularly with respect to setting up the framework. The great thing about Cactus is that it provides a way to actually test all of those components that would otherwise be untested if you used JUnit on its own. On the flip side, Cactus tests do require you to write some of the code that would normally be executed automatically by the container. If you create a servlet instance, you should ideally also call the container-management methods such as `init()` and `destroy()`. In general, this isn't too much of a problem because the life cycle of servlets and filters is straightforward. Custom tags, however, are a slightly different story.

TagUnit

One of the most complicated parts of custom tags (certainly before JSP 2.0 came along) was that the life cycle of tag handler instances seemed cryptic and hard to understand. JSP 2.0 has addressed these features with the new `SimpleTag` interface, but before this the JSP specification placed some very strict rules around the life cycle and pooling of tag handler instances that were never widely understood. Because the code to implement these life cycle requirements is generally the responsibility of the J2EE container (such as Tomcat), this generally isn't a problem. To test custom tags with Cactus, however, the developer must write this code to accurately mimic the way in which tags are used on the page. Unfortunately, this process can be error-prone, and for this reason the TagUnit testing framework was created.

TagUnit (http://www.tagunit.org) is a framework for testing custom tags. It differs from other testing tools in that it allows tags to be tested within the same environment that they'll eventually be used. In other words, the tests themselves are written as JSP pages with regular JSP syntax. To achieve this, TagUnit provides a tag library of its own that contains testing and assertion tags that mimic the `assertXXX()` methods found in JUnit. Therefore, testing custom tags becomes very easy. You just use your tags on the page and wrap them up within the TagUnit tags. Examples of assertions include comparing the generated content with some expected content, looking for the presence of scoped variables/attributes, and checking that exceptions are correctly handled. Here's an example that tests the content generated from the e-mail address filter tag you saw in Chapter 6, in which you tested that the custom tag does in fact filter out the domain part of the e-mail address:

```
<%@ taglib uri="http://www.tagunit.org/tagunit/core" prefix="tagunit" %>
<%@ taglib prefix="myTags" uri="/WEB-INF/tlds/myTags.tld" %>

<tagunit:assertEquals name="Simple filter test">
  <tagunit:actualResult>
    <x:emailAddressFilter>simon.brown@somedomain.com</x:emailAddressFilter>
  </tagunit:actualResult>
  <tagunit:expectedResult>simon.brown@...</tagunit:expectedResult>
</tagunit:assertEquals>
```

Unlike JUnit and Cactus, the tests for TagUnit are written as JSPs, with the assertions written using TagUnit-specific custom tags.

TagUnit tests are wrapped up as a WAR file and therefore can be deployed in any compatible J2EE container. As an additional benefit, this makes it easy to deploy the tests onto another server, which makes cross-vendor testing very easy, particularly when each test can implement aspects of the tag life cycle and pool in slightly different ways. Although Cactus provides a much richer framework for testing server-side components, TagUnit is ideally suited to building custom tags, especially custom tags that will be reused by other people.

Other Unit Testing Tools

The tools that we've mentioned in this chapter are just a sample of the wide variety of testing tools available. For more information on the tools available to unit test web applications, take a look at the JUnit web extensions page at http://www.junit.org/news/extension/web/index.htm.

Now that we've covered how to perform unit testing with respect to web applications, let's now switch gears and look at functional testing.

Functional/Acceptance Testing Web Applications

The other key method to test web applications is **functional testing**. In contrast to unit testing, functional testing treats the application as a black box (you can't see inside it) and tests that the outputs are correct given a set of inputs. For example, this might include the request to add an item to your shopping cart in an online store. Here you're not interested in how the request works–you just want to know that it does work and that the desired result is achieved.

Functional testing is often broken down into two categories, with the tests being written by two different types of people. The first of these are written by developers in addition to the unit tests that they might write for the classes and components that they're writing. Unit testing classes in isolation is undoubtedly very useful, but there are times when developers want to run some functional tests that span multiple classes and components. Typically, these tests are written with the internal flows of the application in mind and really help back up the unit tests in proving that the software works for a given set of inputs. On the other hand, functional tests are written by dedicated testing teams whose responsibilities vary from system testing in which the end-to-end flows throughout the system are exercised to writing tests that will be used to formally state that the functionality meets the requirements and will be accepted by the project sponsor or end users.

One of the problems associated with acceptance is that traditionally acceptance testing, sometimes called user acceptance testing (UAT), was performed by manually following a textual script. Although this works and it's widely used, these manual tests must be reexecuted whenever a new version of the software is released for whatever reason. Although tools do exist that allow testers to capture the process of manually testing an application for automatic playback, many of these tools can be expensive and cumbersome to use. On the other hand, many open source options are now available, although these tend to be oriented toward the developer community and require tests to be written with programming languages, scripting languages, or XML. This is an area of flux at the moment and it's worth bearing in mind your testing audience before you make a definitive tools selection. Let's see how functional level testing can be automated with another widely used open source framework: HttpUnit.

HttpUnit

HttpUnit (http://www.httpunit.org) is another extension to JUnit, but it's different from the others that we've looked at because it allows you to write tests at a slightly different level. Whereas you can use tools such as JUnit and Cactus to test that individual classes and components work correctly, HttpUnit is a framework that you can use to test the functionality provided by a web application. As you've seen, unit testing classes is easy, but how do you test the functionality of a web application from a programming language?

The answer lies in the tools that HttpUnit gives you. In essence, the framework provides a collection of classes that allows you to simulate the process of a user using a web browser to connect to and use a website. Under the covers, it does this by making HTTP requests to the website, passing information that the user would normally type in manually. As far as the functionality available to you through the framework, HttpUnit allows you to access individual web pages and perform assertions that the web page returned contain certain elements. For example, if you're testing an online store, you might want to test that all pages contain the current total of your shopping cart. In addition to these basic features, HttpUnit provides a way to look for HTML forms on a page and programmatically fill out those forms to be sent back to the server where the response can then be checked. Again, with an online store, you might want to test that a user can add an item to his cart and that the subsequent page shows the user the updated cart state.

HttpUnit provides a way to programmatically test the functionality provided by a website with Java code, and the real benefit of this is that these tests can be rerun to regression test the web application when new versions are available. In fact, because HttpUnit uses the HTTP protocol, it can be used to test any other sort of HTML-based web application, including those written with Active Server Pages (ASP), Perl, PHP, and so on.

Other Functional Testing Tools

To round off our look at functional testing tools, a couple of other frameworks are worth a quick mention. The first of these is jWebUnit (http://jwebunit.sourceforge.net), which is really an extension of HttpUnit. The team behind jWebUnit was using HttpUnit on a project and realized that many of the tests contained duplicate code to set up request objects and perform assertions. For this reason, the team built a collection of wrapper classes for HttpUnit that simplified the API for its purposes. This has been refined over time and released into the open source community. Some people like the control that HttpUnit gives them, whereas others prefer the simpler interface provided by jWebUnit. At the end of the day, it's all up to personal preference.

The other framework worth mentioning is called Jameleon (http://jameleon.sourceforge.net). This framework provides a way to functional test an application, but from the perspective of the features that it provides. It differs from HttpUnit and jWebUnit in that it breaks out testing of the features from the actual test cases. A feature can be something as fine-grained as logging in, and it might be something that has to happen before every test. With Jameleon, you write the feature tests separately and then script them together into a reusable test case. These test cases can then be made data-driven by associating them with a particular dataset at runtime, which provides an easy way of running specific tests on specific environments. Jameleon itself is not specifically designed to test web applications; instead, it has a plug-in architecture in which testing code can be plugged in and executed. At the time of this writing, Jameleon provides a plug-in for HttpUnit/jWebUnit; hence it can be used to functional test web applications. This is a great idea and is something that has typically only been found in commercial testing tools. As always, the open source testing space is worth keeping an eye on as new tools and enhancements are released on a regular basis. Again, the JUnit site has a page for web testing tools (http://www.junit.org/news/extension/web/index.htm) that's regularly updated.

Now that we've looked at the various ways in which web applications can be tested, let's look at how the design can influence the ability to test web applications.

Designing Web Applications for Testing

Although unit testing individual classes is straightforward, as we've hinted at, sometimes unit testing classes within web applications can be tricky. This is particularly true when the various flavors of business and presentation logic have all been mixed up with components such as servlets that need to be executed within a web server. To solve such problems, we must again turn to architecture and design.

Architectural Layering

Although we haven't explicitly talked about architectural layering, we have talked about the model 2 architecture and how it helps achieve a separation of concerns between the various components. For example, the controller is the overall component responsible for managing requests, the model represents the domain information being operated upon, and the views present information back to the user. Compare this with the model 1 architecture, in which all of these responsibilities were embedded in a single component, and you can start to see how separating these responsibilities can lead to easier testing.

We've already said that the hardest part of unit testing web applications is testing those components that are reliant on the context of a J2EE web server, and one of the things that you can do to aid testing is to try and make these components as small and lightweight as possible. By making these components lightweight wrappers for functionality that's encapsulated within Java classes, you give yourself a much better chance of being able to unit test the application. For example, cast your mind back to the model 2 architecture and, specifically, to the command and controller pattern in which the functionality to service incoming requests was split up among individual command objects. As each of these is just a stand-alone Java class, you can now use the same techniques for unit testing as you do with ordinary Java classes–you can use JUnit to create new instances and call methods on those instances.

One of the keys to being able to unit test web applications is to ensure that each of your classes has a well-defined role. With the model 2 architecture, this involves breaking classes into one of the main categories of components: controller/action, model, and presentation. Furthermore, and regardless of whether or not you adopt a model 2 architecture, certain types of classes are much easier to test than others. We've already alluded to this, but to recap, classes that can stand on their own are generally much easier to test. Within a J2EE web application, this usually means classes that represent business/domain objects and those classes that encapsulate some level of business logic and processing.

> *On the projects that I've worked on, testing web application components has always been one of the areas that has come up repeatedly as being difficult. At the end of the day, breaking components into distinct architectural layers really does improve your ability to test those components. In addition, it's often too much effort to try to achieve complete test coverage of all the components within your web application. If you've broken out the majority of the functionality into classes that can stand alone from the web server environment, testing these should provide a satisfactory level of confidence in the code that you're producing. The whole point of testing is to provide you with a certain level of confidence that the code will perform as expected rather than striving to achieve complete coverage.*

A Testing Strategy

When you're writing regular Java code (not J2EE related), a testing tool such as JUnit generally suits most of your needs. However, for J2EE applications, it isn't feasible to get by with just a single tool. For example, with JUnit and Cactus, it's only really possible to test stand-alone classes. With TagUnit, it's only possible to test custom tags. With HttpUnit, you can only test the end-to-end functionality provided by the application. Each of these different tools provides a different angle on testing the software, and it's for this reason that you can't get away with using only one tool. The purpose of testing is to provide confidence that the software works, and this is just not possible with a single tool.

Testing can be performed at many layers, and this is also true of web application testing. At the very bottom, you have the unit tests that can be performed with tools such as JUnit and Cactus. Moving up from this, you have slightly larger groups of classes interacting, or components. These can be again tested with JUnit and Cactus, although other tools such as TagUnit start to provide benefits. Moving further up, you start to test more functionality of the system, and this is where functional testing tools come into play. Testing one of these layers is great, but it doesn't guarantee that the system as a whole will work. After all, unit tests tend to be much more detailed and much more focused on robustness. Functional tests, on the other hand, tend to be more geared toward checking that the functionality works as expected. In essence, you should view all of these testing tools as complementary, and it's up to you to pick the ones you feel give you the confidence that your software works.

Compatibility Testing Web Applications

As an additional level of testing, many developers test their applications for compatibility between servers. By writing to the J2EE platform, you are (at least in theory) guaranteed that your application will work on any other compliant or compatible J2EE implementation. For many people, this just isn't an issue because they'll only run their applications on a single type of J2EE server. For others, particularly those building products (regardless of whether those products are commercial or open source), testing compatibility can be essential to the success of their web applications.

A few years ago, J2EE compatibility was still very much something that was being worked on by the server vendors and this is especially true when the specifications were still maturing. Fortunately, this situation has improved considerably and now most web applications will run as is on any J2EE-compatible server. However, if you're building products, then there's still some mileage in testing that your web application does function as expected on some of the various implementations available. For example, small bugs in one vendor's implementation may stop your application from working completely. Other times, you may have been unknowingly relying on a specific implementation feature or just the way that a specification point has been implemented. As an example, the Tomcat team has recently changed some of the default security settings related to the way that servlets could be called directly through the servlet dispatcher. When upgrading to a newer version of Tomcat, many developers found that their web applications no longer worked because they had used this method of calling servlets within their JSP pages.

> *I was involved on a project in which I was responsible for the web tier of an enterprise application for a large investment bank. The licenses for the application server my team was using, BEA WebLogic, hadn't yet arrived, so we started building the web tier with Tomcat. When the licenses finally did arrive, we literally had to port some of the code between the servers because of incompatibilities in how the JSP/Servlet specifications had been implemented between the vendors. Thankfully, the implementations have matured a great deal and most code can be run as is on different J2EE servers.*

The moral of the story is that it's beneficial to run your web applications on other J2EE-compatible servers, even if you perhaps aren't planning to use one from another vendor. For anybody building commercial products based upon J2EE, Sun has a verification program consisting of a compatibility-testing suite that can test to see if your application makes correct and standard use of the APIs provided by the J2EE specification. See http://java.sun.com/j2ee/verified/avk_enterprise.html for more details.

Security

Although we covered security in Chapter 11, there are some security best practices worth recapping within the context of this chapter about web application design and best practices.

Using the Standard Security Model

Try to use the standard security model if possible. Many web applications make use of their own, custom security model for authentication and authorization. Although this is sometimes necessary, perhaps because the standard model doesn't meet your requirements, many web applications don't even integrate with the servlet security model. Apart from making use of the available technology, there are many reasons for using the servlet security model.

The first of these reasons is related to how secure your web application is. Without the standard security model, every JSP page, servlet, and resource underneath your web application root is effectively public. With bespoke frameworks, generally developers must insert programmatic code into the top of their JSP pages of servlet classes that determines whether the request should be allowed or denied, perhaps by using the value of a session variable that indicates whether the user has logged in. But what happens if this code is omitted and users that aren't logged in are able to access those resources?

One of the projects that I provided some consultancy for implemented their own security model. Although the authorization of resources was complex, the actual authentication of users was nothing unusual. Rather than adopting the standard model, a bespoke solution was implemented for both authentication and authorization throughout the entire system. The system itself was mostly built around a model 2 architecture, although there were parts that were simply page centric. Therefore, and to ensure security, a custom tag was built to be inserted at the top of every page in order to determine whether or not the current user should be able to see the contents of the page. Although this works, and as I found by reviewing the application, there were pages where this custom tag hadn't been inserted and pages were left unsecured. Probably the worst of these was a page that allowed anybody to get a report of all the data within the system. Had the standard security model been used, every single JSP could have easily been restricted to only authenticated users.

Not only does using the standard security model simplify the design of web applications, but also it really does provide an additional level of confidence in the security of your web applications.

Securing View Components

Even if your web application doesn't require security in the sense of users logging in and authenticating themselves, there's still a need for ensuring that your application is secure and will only work as expected. For example, take a model 2–based web application. Typically, a request is serviced by the controller component, which in turn gets forwarded to a view component for presenting information back to the user. If the view components were simple JSP pages, what would happen if the user found out the name and location of that JSP and tried to access it directly? In many cases, they would probably get a page containing no information or a nasty stack trace. Perhaps your JSP pages contain code that has other side effects on the system. If you're authenticating users, perhaps they'll be able to see somebody else's information because their request hasn't gone through the controller.

To get around this potential problem, one solution is to ensure that the view components (the JSPs) are subjected to the standard servlet security model. For example, if all of the view components are placed within a directory called `view-components`, you can place the following line in the `web.xml` file to disallow all direct access:

```
<security-constraint>
    <web-resource-collection>
      <web-resource-name>No direct access</web-resource-name>
      <url-pattern>/view-components/*</url-pattern>
    </web-resource-collection>

    <auth-constraint>
      <role-name>some-nonexistent-role</role-name>
    </auth-constraint>
</security-constraint>
```

This specifies that anything under that directory can only be accessed by users in the specified role. Therefore, if you don't map that role to any users, nobody can directly access the pages from her browser. Of course, the controller component can still forward to the JSPs because it isn't subject to the same rules. Similarly, another option is to place all view components underneath the `WEB-INF` directory of your web application, which by definition doesn't have direct access. Either way, securing your view components can make your web application more secure and more resilient.

Troubleshooting

A number of common problems can occur in JSP- and servlet-based applications. In this section we review some of these problems and provide quick pointers to help you debug them.

The Servlet Engine Runs Out of Memory

If the servlet engine or application server stops responding to requests and you receive a series of `OutOfMemoryExceptions` in the log files, chances are that your application has consumed all available memory. This could be the result of a memory leak in the application code. Perhaps it's holding references to a large number of objects and thus preventing them from being garbage collected. If this is the case, then you'll need to resort to careful code reviews to understand where the problem is occurring. Some application servers provide a workaround for this problem: a feature called **server recycling**, whereby idle servlet engines are periodically restarted. Restarting a JVM is a sure way to clean up leaked objects.

Even if there isn't a memory leak in the code, it's still possible to run out of memory. Typically, a session object is created for each concurrent user of a JSP application. Session objects consume memory, and memory is a limited resource. Therefore, too many concurrent users can cause the servlet engine to run out of memory. Once the server starts issuing `OutOfMemoryExceptions`, it will need to be restarted. One way to address this problem is to configure the servlet engine for a shorter timeout period. Setting a shorter session timeout usually results in fewer concurrent sessions and lessens the chances of running out of memory. Other solutions to this problem are as follows:

- Add more memory so that each server can support more users.
- Add more application server instances to handle a larger total number of users.
- Keep the number and size of objects stored in the session to a minimum.

In addition to these solutions, if you have a completely stateless application, then you can tell the container not to use sessions with the following JSP page directive and save yourself a great deal of memory:

```
<%@ page session="false" %>
```

The memory debugging tools built into commercial performance tuning products such as Borland's Optimizeit (http://www.borland.com/optimizeit) and Quest Software's JProbe (http://java.quest.com/jprobe/jprobe.shtml) can be very helpful in tracking down memory leaks. These tools are moderately expensive, but they can be very useful when you're trying to pinpoint a memory leak. When you're running an application under one of these tools, you can pause execution and examine memory usage statistics for each class of object in memory, list methods responsible for largest number of object allocations, and determine where the objects currently in memory were allocated.

The Database Connections Are Exhausted

If an application starts behaving strangely, emitting database connections exhausted or cannot obtain database connection errors, then it has consumed all database connections. The cause may be a database connection leak, meaning that database connections aren't being properly released after use. If the application is using database connection pooling, then you may be able to turn on features of the connection pool so that you can locate the misbehaving code that's taking but not giving back connections. Failing this, careful code reviews and log files are probably the only options.

Even if an application isn't leaking database connections, it can still exhaust your connections. When using database connection pooling, you might be able to solve this problem by simply configuring the database connection pool to allow a larger number of maximum connections. If that doesn't work, then talk to a database administrator about increasing the number of database connections allowed on the database server.

The Servlet Engine Stops Responding

If the servlet engine or application server stops responding to HTTP requests and there are no instances of `OutOfMemoryException` in the log files, then there are two other possible causes of this problem:

- There's a **thread deadlock**. Deadlock occurs in a multithreaded JSP when two or more threads can't continue because each is waiting on a lock held by the other.
- There's an **infinite loop** in application code. An infinite loop condition occurs when a thread becomes trapped in an improperly programmed `for`, `while`, or `do` loop.

Locating the exact location of the cause of the problem can be very difficult. Usually, careful code reviews and examination of log files are the only options. This is one situation in which detailed debug logs can be very helpful.

You Get a ClassCastException

Servlet engines use special class loaders to isolate web applications from each other and from the classes used internally by the servlet engine itself. These class loaders can cause problems that often appear to be incomprehensible. For example, you might get a `ClassCastException` that complains that you have incompatible versions of the same class. Often, these types of problems are caused when JARs that conflict with the JARs provided by the servlet engine are placed into the application's `WEB-INF/lib` directory, although in theory the class-loading mechanism should take care of this for you. Alternatively, redeploying your applications can also make this problem occur. Behind the scenes, although the web application reloads all of the classes, if you have references to objects residing in the session (and use the same browser instance), when the JSP container tries to cast these existing objects with the old class definition into the new definition, it will fail, throwing a `ClassCastException`. Simply restarting the container will solve the majority of such problems.

The Page Runs Too Slowly

If a JSP page or a servlet is running too slowly, and the performance techniques described in this chapter haven't uncovered the cause of the problem, then try a **profiler**. A profiler will produce a report on the amount of time spent in each method of your application, allowing you to narrow down your search for the cause of the performance problem. The commercial performance tuning tools that we discussed earlier, Optimizeit and JProbe, include profilers. Also, under development at the time of this writing is a profiling plug-in called the Eclipse Profiler, for the Eclipse IDE. You can follow the progress of this project at http://eclipsecolorer.sourceforge.net.

Debugging

Debugging is often the most difficult and frustrating aspect of programming. JSP- and servlet-based applications are often rather complex and therefore especially difficult to debug. Why are JSP applications so complex? Here are a few reasons:

- **JSP applications are distributed:** When deployed in a production environment, a JSP application can involve multiple distributed systems, including load balancing routers, web servers, application servers, databases, and other back-end systems.
- **JSP applications include a mixture of different programming languages:** JSP applications can include HTML, JavaScript, Java code, SQL, XML, and other programming and markup languages. When you read a JSP page, it's often difficult to follow which parts of the page are executed on the server and which are executed on the client.
- **JSP applications run in a multithreaded environment:** JSP applications need to be thread-safe to achieve the best performance. Threading is a complex and confusing topic for many programmers, and threading problems can be difficult to debug.
- **JSP applications involve many components:** A JSP application's technology stack typically includes a servlet engine, a JSP compiler, an MVC framework, a persistence framework, a JDBC driver, a database, and other back-end systems.

Learning how to solve problems in complex, distributed, and multithreaded programs takes time and often involves a lot of deep thought, so be prepared to think. If a particularly difficult problem arises, get some sleep and then think some more. Explain the problem to another, more experienced programmer. If no one is available, then explain it to that plastic dinosaur sitting on top of your monitor. Often, simply explaining a problem in detail can spark the thought that leads to a solution.

If you can figure out how to explain your problem in simple terms, or you can isolate the problem in a simple code example, you might be able to get some help from a newsgroup, mailing list, or other online forum. Before you post a message to one of these forums, you should read the previous postings in the forum archive to see if your problem or question has been asked before. Using a search engine such as Google may also be helpful for some problems.

Logging

Logging is a best practice for any JSP application and is supported by the servlet API, application servers, and a wide variety of logging tools. There are many ways in which you can perform logging, from using simple `System.out.println()` statements to using a full-featured logging API.

Logging with the Servlet API

The servlet API includes logging methods in the `javax.servlet.ServletContext` interface. The `ServletContext` interface's `log()` methods make it easy to write log messages and exception stack traces to your application server's logging system. The advantages of using the servlet API's built-in logging methods are as follows:

- Log messages are automatically prefixed with a timestamp string and written to log files. This means that you can access them after they scroll off the console and after the server is shut down.
- The application server manages log files and ensures that they never grow too big and consume all of the disk space.
- Application servers generally provide an administration program so that you can easily view and search log files even if they're written to multiple remote servers.

All of this sounds good but, in fact, the servlet API provides only minimal support for logging. You can log a string message and you can log an exception. However, if you want to enable and disable logging, then you need to add configuration properties and implement the conditional logic by adding a parameter to the `web.xml` file, for example. However, implementing your own ad hoc logging as shown previously isn't the best approach. There are many advantages to be had from instead using a full-featured logging system such as log4j or the J2SE 1.4 logging API.

Full-Featured Logging Systems

A full-featured logging system, such as the open source log4j framework (http://jakarta.apache.org/log4j), offers a number of advantages over using `System.out.println()` calls or using the logging methods in the servlet API:

- **Control over logging levels:** You can log messages at different severity levels. For example, log4j supports log levels of `DEBUG`, `INFO`, `WARN`, `ERROR`, and `FATAL` (listed in order of increasing severity). When you set a log level, the system will output messages for that log level and for all log levels above that. So, for example, the `INFO`-level logging will include `INFO`, `WARN`, `ERROR`, and `FATAL` level messages. By simply changing a configuration parameter in the log4j properties file, you can enable `DEBUG`-level logging to help you debug a problem. When you've found and fixed the problem, you can set the log level back to `ERROR` so that only `ERROR` and `FATAL` log messages are recorded in the logs.
- **Multiple loggers:** You can use different logical loggers in different parts of your application. For example, you might use one logger named `com.mydomain.ui` in the presentation tier and another logger named `com.mydomain.db` in the data access tier. This allows you to control the log level in only the part of the application that's experiencing a bug.
- **Multiple log destinations:** You can configure logging systems to send log messages to files, operating system logs, databases, message queues, remote systems via TCP/IP, and other destinations. This can be very helpful in production in which an application may be running in a heterogeneous and distributed environment.

- **Better management of log files:** Log files can grow to large sizes very quickly, especially when DEBUG-level logging is enabled. You can configure a logging system to *roll over* or start a new log when the current log file grows too large. You can configure the logging system to delete or archive old log files so that your disk space isn't consumed.
- **Control over log formatting:** You can configure the format of the log messages produced by the logging system to suit specific needs.

J2SE 1.4 now includes its own logging API under the `java.util.logging` package. This new logging API is a welcome addition to Java and is similar to the log4j API in many ways, but it isn't as powerful and flexible as log4j. For example, log4j can direct log messages to UNIX system logs, the Microsoft Windows event log, JMS message queues, and e-mail. The Java 1.4 logging API can log only to the console, files, and sockets. Like many aspects of development, people become attached to their favorite logging framework and this is often a problem when deciding which one to use. Also, there some technical reasons for choosing one over another. Perhaps you need the functionality available in a specific API, or perhaps your J2EE server ships with log4j. Either way, to ensure that you retain the ability to be able to freely switch between the two, Jakarta Commons Logging provides a solution.

Jakarta Commons Logging

Jakarta Commons Logging (JCL, from http://Jakarta.apache.org/commons/logging/) is a thin wrapper around both log4j and J2SE 1.4 logging, with the sole purpose of providing a common interface between the two. With the Commons Logging JAR file in your class path, the framework will automatically locate either of the two logging frameworks and use whichever one it finds in your class path. It will first look for log4j and, if it doesn't find log4j, it will check to see J2SE 1.4 logging is available. This is a simple trick, but it really works well. If you need to use log4j in your application, just make sure it's in the class path.

Regardless of which logging framework you use, actually using JCL is easy, as demonstrated by the following code snippet:

```
Log log = LogFactory.getLog(MyClass.class);
```

Following this, and with the log initialized, you can write messages at the various levels with the following method calls:

```
log.fatal("Here is some useful information!");
log.error("Here is some useful information!");
log.warn("Here is some useful information!");
log.info("Here is some useful information!");
log.debug("Here is some useful information!");
log.trace("Here is some useful information!");
```

Like the framework that it ultimately delegates to, JCL has various levels of severity that map to those used by the underlying logging framework. If you need more control, then perhaps JCL isn't for you. For many people, the sacrifice in control can easily be negated by the simplicity that JCL provides.

Jakarta Commons Logging has worked really well on the projects I've used it on, and this is especially true for my open source work. After all, you can never tell which logging library your users might prefer, or perhaps their J2EE server ships with log4j or isn't supported on J2SE 1.4. JCL gives you that extra degree of flexibility.

General Guidelines

To wrap up this chapter, we take a look at some general guidelines for building web applications. Although these guidelines aren't specifically related to design, they can be just as important for building a successful website.

Error Reporting

One of the things that we as developers like to see when errors happen are stack traces. After all, they're very useful for tracking down the source and cause of a problem. Users, on the other hand, probably don't want to see them, and they certainly don't add anything to the user experience.

Seeing stack traces or other forms of technical error messages on websites tends to put me off from returning to that site. For example, one particular e-commerce site that I visit regularly presents me with messages about how some Visual Basic component can't connect to their database. Though I don't confess to know anything about Visual Basic, seeing such messages does make me think twice about ordering from that site.

Unfortunately, even with the most tested of websites, errors will happen and for this reason the JSP specification provides JSP error pages. You already saw these in Chapter 2 and, to recap, they're just pages that get forwarded to when an uncaught exception is encountered by the container. Setting your web application up to use these is a great way to ensure that you have a standard way to handle errors and that the user doesn't end up seeing a nasty stack trace in the process.

On a related note, another recommendation is to use a consistent exception handling strategy and make sure that you handle and log all exceptions. This will help you to understand what went wrong and where it went wrong when an error occurs. Use the exception handling facilities built into JSP where appropriate–they're there to help you. If you're using an MVC framework such as Struts, take advantage of its exception handling facilities as well.

i18n and l10n

Internationalization (i18n) and localization (l10n) are built into the Java platform, and there's nothing stopping you from using them within web applications, particularly if you intend to reach an international audience. Typically, and especially with public websites, a lot of effort is put into making the site both function correctly and look good. However, often little work is put into maximizing the appeal for international audiences. After all, the Internet is a global network and you can never tell exactly who will be using your site.

Putting in such features doesn't have to be a massive job, with tools such as JSTL supporting most of the functionality required to internationalize and localize a web application. For example, this can range from simply localizing dates and times to providing internationalized text and/or content. The overriding guideline here is to think about your audience.

Adopting New Technologies and Standards

The Web has changed a great deal over the past few years, and some web applications have kept up with the changes better than others. Although there's an argument for not always adopting the latest and greatest technologies, there's a fine line between adopting those features that make most sense and never adopting at all. With technologies changing on almost a monthly basis, this provides an opportunity to try out new technologies and standards on every new web application that you work on. Most web developers have now taken up standards such as cascading style sheets (CSS), but you won't find that many sites (relatively speaking) that make use of newer standards such as XHTML. This does have much to do with the fact that keeping existing sites up-to-date is expensive, but when you start a new web application, take a look around to see what's happening within the industry and use this to figure out if there's anything that can help you achieve your goals.

One of the projects that I worked on involved helping a team inside a client company build a web application for internal use. The system itself was replacing a "green screen" application, and this was the first time that the team had used Java, let alone built web applications. Although the first prototype of the system was functional, the user interface closely resembled that found on the original mainframe application. After just a day or so playing with the view components in conjunction with the team, we came up with something that matched the company's corporate image and was much closer to the sort of web applications that you find on the Internet. We showed them CSS and guided them through how some of the most popular websites on the Internet work. The result? Not only did the application look and feel much better, but also the business sponsors and users of the system suddenly became much more enthusiastic about the project. It's amazing what a little HTML and CSS can do!

To sum up, let your previous experiences of building web applications help you, but don't let them limit you.

Adopting Existing Components

The final guideline worth talking about is the use of third-party components, particularly those that are open source. In the past couple of years, the open source community has really moved on in terms of adoption and the sheer number of projects that are currently being undertaken. A quick look at websites such as The Jakarta Project (http://jakarta.apache.org), SourceForge (http://sourceforge.net), and java.net (http://java.net) confirms this. With project budgets and timescales decreasing, there's an opportunity here to take much of what has been built and use it in your own projects.

As I mentioned earlier in the chapter, I decided to build a blogging system and this was implemented as a Java-based web application. In building the application, I made use of several open source projects, including Jakarta Commons Logging and log4j for logging, Jakarta Commons FileUpload for uploading files to the website, Apache XML-RPC for accessing web services, and Lucene to provide a search facility for users. Had I implemented all of these features myself, it would have taken an incredibly long time. As it was, each of these open source tools took a maximum of a few hours to integrate, meaning that I could concentrate on the real purpose of the web application.

Let's take a quick look at some popular open source tools currently available.

Jakarta Commons

Jakarta Commons (http://jakarta.apache.org/commons/) is an umbrella project for all sorts of common functionality that developers are build over and over again. You've already seen one component (Jakarta Commons Logging), but others include a servlet-based file upload component, an object pool implementation, an expression language, JavaBean utilities, and much, much more. This is an incredibly useful project, and new components and features are being added to it all the time.

Lucene

Lucene (http://jakarta.apache.org/lucene/) is an open source implementation of a complete search engine. It's held in very high regard throughout the Java open source community because it's so robust, full-featured, and fast. The API is very easy to pick up, and in just a few lines of code you can create an index for your data. Similarly, just a few lines are required to actually search that index. If you're looking to integrate a search facility on your website, then look no further than Lucene.

Summary

This chapter covered several topics related to web application design and best practices, bringing together many of the topics we explored in the previous chapters. First, we looked at why design is important and we recapped the two major architectures for building web applications: model 1 and model 2. Then we looked at how design patterns can help design your application and described how some of the J2EE patterns can be used to build web applications based upon the model 2 architecture. These patterns included the following:

- Front controller
- View
- View helper
- Service to worker
- Filter

We then moved on to explore some third-party frameworks such as Struts, WebWork, and Velocity.

After this, we looked at how testing is an important part of web application development and introduced unit testing and functional (or acceptance) testing. Automated testing has now really taken off with regard to web applications, and to illustrate this we looked at some of the testing tools that are now available. We then related testing back to the design aspects we presented earlier in the chapter by showing how the design of a web application can affect the ability to test it.

Finally, we covered some implementation topics, including logging, troubleshooting, and some general guidelines for building web applications.

14

Using Struts, XDoclet, and Other Tools

You can see from the previous chapters that there are many options for building a web application. If you develop a web application from scratch, you'll be a stronger programmer for it, but it will (most likely) be a long and laborious process. In this chapter, we'll describe the tools to use for web development, and how to use them in developing this chapter's resume-building application. By sharing our experiences and knowledge, hopefully you won't have to endure the same painful memorize-learn-develop progression that we've been through. To prepare you for the vast array of subjects in this chapter, let's first take a look a the various open-source tools and technologies that we'll be covering:

- Ant: A Java-based build tool for rapid compiling, deploying , and testing Java-based applications.
- XDoclet: A code-generation engine for creating Java classes and deployment descriptors. It requires the user to add `@tags` to Javadoc statements and produces files via Ant.
- Struts: A web application framework using a servlet-based Model-View-Controller (MVC) architecture.
- Validator: A validation framework integrated with Struts. Supports both client (JavaScript) and server-side validation.
- Tiles: A JSP-based templating framework integrated with Struts.
- JUnit: A Java-based regression-testing framework.
- Cactus: A Java-based testing framework for testing web applications.
- StrutsTestCase: An extension of Cactus for testing Struts's `Action` classes.

You were introduced to Struts in the previous chapter and you might well have seen references to it scattered throughout the whole book. This is because since version 1.0 was released in June of 2001, it has gained wide acceptance and praise in the Java community.

The big advantage of using Struts to underpin your web applications is that it provides a set of ready-made services, and encourages you to structure your applications according to published standards and proven design patterns, which will make your applications highly extensible, flexible, and maintainable.

However, in this chapter we aren't going to teach you Struts from scratch: There are a lot of good books out there that teach you the basics of using Struts from scratch in far more depth than we could in one chapter! If you want a great Struts kickstart tutorial for free (and who doesn't want something great for free?!), try downloading Ted Husted's "Strut by Strut" article (from http://husted.com/struts/strutByStrut.html).

Instead, in this chapter, we're going to assume that you have a basic understanding of how to use Struts, and focus upon enhancing Struts-based development through the use of third-party tools (including Ant, XDoclet, Validator, Tiles, StrutsGen, Struts Menu, Struts Console, Easy Struts, Hibernate, and StrutsTestCase). The idea is to show you how to use these tools to create your Struts-based applications more quickly, easily, and cost-effectively. To do this, you'll use them to create an example application that can build and view resumes.

Through the course of the chapter, you'll learn how XDoclet can generate the `web.xml` deployment descriptor and the `struts-config.xml` file. We'll also discuss the IDE tools for Struts, exception handling, built-in actions, modules, DynaFormBeans and Struts Tags (including the JSTL and JSP 2.0). We'll be using JSP pages for a view layer, because that is what we're familiar with (and this book is about JSP after all!). We'll also touch on good practices using XHTML and cascading style sheets (CSS).

However, let's start with a lightning-quick refresher on the Struts architecture.

Struts Refresher

A **web framework** provides a set of services that can be used and reused across many different web applications. Struts is an open-source (therefore free to use!) web framework that is based upon the tried-and-trusted MVC design pattern. Its core is made up of Java servlets, JavaBeans, resource bundles, XML, and tag libraries.

Struts provides the following services:

- A controller servlet
- Ready-made tag libraries
- A framework for internationalizing messages
- A generic error and exception-handling mechanism
- XML parsing
- File upload and logging utilities

Craig McClanahan originally wrote the Struts framework, mostly while on his Memorial Day vacation in 2000! The framework was subsequently donated by Craig to the Apache Software Foundation. The fact that it was mostly written in one weekend should suggest to you that it's a very simple framework. In my experience, not only is it simple, but it's also easy to work with once you get to know it.

You should also note that anything that can be done with JSP pages and servlets can still be done with Struts. So you can still write regular servlets that extend `HttpServlet` in your application or have JSP pages with whatever embedded scriplet code you want.

On the other hand, Struts does try to encourage certain better practices for coding web applications, and it does make it easier to write and deploy them. For instance, when using Struts, you don't need to write a whole slew of `request.getParameter()` calls in your servlet to get all your form's values. Struts does this for you with an `ActionForm`, which handles the population and grabbing of an HTML form's values.

Struts Architecture

So how do these `ActionForms` fit into the overall Struts architecture? Here's a schematic of a simple Struts application in general:

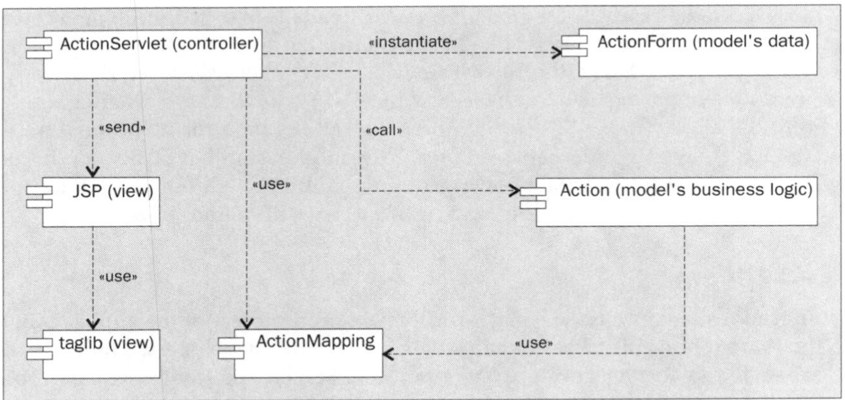

Let's quickly review the features of this diagram.

First, you can see that we've assumed that you're using JSP pages for the view, and that these are built using the Struts tag libraries. Each client request for the application to perform a particular **action** is passed to the controller servlet (known as the `ActionServlet`), which dispatches to an `Action` class.

The business logic needed to perform each action (process each type of request) is present in this corresponding `Action` class. The `Action` classes represent the controller logic for your application. They control which view elements are presented to the user. For instance, if an error occurs, the action is responsible for displaying errors on an input page.

There also may be a corresponding `ActionForm` JavaBean class for each action. Each `ActionForm` validates user data and can be used by the `Action` class to retrieve user data. The `ActionForm` classes represent the data of the model. The model is your data and the code you write to retrieve, save, or delete that data.

So, as you would expect from the controller, the ActionServlet provides the link between the view and the Action/ActionForm model components. To do this it needs to map the request data to the appropriate Action/ActionForm classes, depending upon the action requested by the client. The correct mapping of request actions to Action/ActionForm classes is defined in a configuration file, struts-config.xml. This file defines a set of ActionMapping objects that each represent a mapping of an action to the appropriate model classes. Therefore, the ActionServlet checks this struts-config.xml file to find which is the appropriate mapping for the current request.

Finally, if the Action class processes the request correctly, it indicates to the ActionServlet where the user should be forwarded to (usually a JSP page), by passing the ActionServlet an ActionForward object.

For more in-depth information about the architecture and implementation of the Struts framework, you can refer to the books and article referred to in the introduction to this chapter, or try pointing your browser to the following links:

- http://jakarta.apache.org/struts/–Struts homepage (you can download the latest version from here)
- http://jakarta.apache.org/struts/userGuide/index.html–Struts user guide

As you may have spotted already, a big benefit of using Struts is that you implement many proven J2EE design patterns without even knowing it. The Front Controller (ActionServlet and Action), View Helper (Action), Composite View (the Tiles framework that we'll discuss later), Service to Worker (ActionServlet to actions) and Dispatcher View (ActionForward) are all integrated into the Struts framework. From the book, *Core J2EE Patterns,*[1] these are all the patterns mentioned in the "Presentation Tier Patterns" chapter, save the Intercepting Filter. The only reason that Struts doesn't incorporate the Intercepting Filter pattern is to maintain backwards compatibility with the Servlet 2.2 specification (and for Struts 2.0, there is talk of replacing the ActionServlet with a filter).

Struts Tag Libraries

Most Struts applications seem to use JSP pages for the view component of the application. This is most likely due to the rich set of tag libraries that are available to Struts developers. These tags make several things much easier. If you've ever developed a pure JSP or servlet application, you'll probably remember using JavaBeans, the <useBean> tag, or perhaps even writing a lot of request.getParameter() calls. Struts basically eliminates this need and easily populates forms using its controller and tag library architecture. Of course, other architectures, such as Velocity and XML, can be used. But since I've never implemented them on a project to date, I don't feel it's fair to comment on their usefulness.

More information on using Velocity and XML or XSL for rendering your view can be found at http://jakarta.apache.org/struts/resources/views.html.

At the time of this writing, there were seven available tag libraries within the Struts framework. These libraries are listed in the following table, coupled with a high-level definition of their function.

[1] Alur, Deepak, John Crupi, and Dan Malks, *Core J2EE Patterns: Best Practices and Design Strategies.* (Upper Saddle River, NJ: Prentice Hall, 2001)

Library	Function
Bean tags	Tags to interact with beans in any given scope. Uses include creating and rendering an `ActionForm`'s properties. Also used for internationalization with the `<bean:message>` tag. Many of these tags can be replaced with JSTL tags.
HTML tags	Tags to render HTML elements on a form. Also contains helpful tags for rendering context-sensitive URLs. No replacement in the JSTL. Using regular HTML tags and JSP 2.0 syntax may be easier though.
Logic tags	Tags to perform logic such as checking for the presence of roles, iteration of bean lists, and forward or redirects. Many of these tags can be replaced with JSTL tags.
Nested tags	These tags extend the basic Struts tags mentioned earlier, but allow them to relate to each other in a nested nature. No equivalent in the JSTL.
Template tags	As of Struts 1.1, these tags have been deprecated in favor of Tiles, which offers the same functionality.
Tiles tags	Tags to perform JSP "templating" of your site. Very useful for creating applications from small, reusable components. We'll discuss this in more depth a little later.
Struts EL tags	A subproject that was recently created to use the expression language evaluation engine from the JSTL. Some of the Struts tags weren't ported, as their functionality already exists in JSTL.

The online API documentation for these tags is excellent (refer to the links available from the Struts User Guide page at http://jakarta.apache.org/struts/userGuide/index.html). Also, recent books (as mentioned earlier) have done a terrific job of documenting these tags thoroughly.

One recently added feature (end of November 2002) of the Struts HTML tags is the ability to render XHTML-compliant tags. This means that if you add `xhtml="true"` to the top of your JSP or Tiles layout definition, all HTML tags will be well formed XML (that is, closed with an end tag or trailing `/>`). To demonstrate, you can simply add the following tag to the top of a page, and then view the source in your browser:

```
<html:html xhtml="true"/>
```

If you're using JSP includes or Tiles, you'll likely have to use the `<html:xhtml />` tag at the top of your included pages to force rendering XHTML syntax. At the time of this writing, only XHTML 1.0 Transitional was supported as a DOCTYPE. This is because the `name` attribute is still rendered on a form. XHTML 1.0 Strict requires that only an `id` attribute be present.

You can give your Struts tags any prefix you want when importing them into your JSP pages. Let's take, for instance, the contents of this `taglibs.jsp` file:

```
<%@ taglib uri="http://jakarta.apache.org/struts/tags-bean" prefix="bean" %>
<%@ taglib uri="http://jakarta.apache.org/struts/tags-html" prefix="html" %>
<%@ taglib uri="http://jakarta.apache.org/struts/tags-logic" prefix="logic" %>
<%@ taglib uri="http://jakarta.apache.org/struts/tags-tiles" prefix="tiles" %>
<%@ taglib uri="http://java.sun.com/jstl/core" prefix="c" %>
```

You may well have already seen this de facto standard for Struts prefixes. There's really no reason to use these verbose prefixes though, and you may rather use single-letter prefixes like JSTL if you prefer, such as these:

```
<%@ taglib uri="http://jakarta.apache.org/struts/tags-bean" prefix="b" %>
<%@ taglib uri="http://jakarta.apache.org/struts/tags-html" prefix="h" %>
<%@ taglib uri="http://jakarta.apache.org/struts/tags-logic" prefix="l" %>
<%@ taglib uri="http://jakarta.apache.org/struts/tags-tiles" prefix="t" %>
```

We've come to know and love a couple of additional tag libraries that make developing web UIs a bit easier. The first is the **display tag library** (http://displaytag.sf.net) originally authored by Ed Hill, which facilitates column sorting and pagination of data and integrates nicely with Struts. All you need to do is create a `List` (or other collection) of `ActionForms` and pass those to the tag in the JSP. This tag library also supports exporting your table's data to Excel, CSV, and XML. However, we've had some issues (with version 0.8.5) when trying to use the export feature in conjunction with Tiles.

The second is the **Struts menu tag library**. This component is a Menu framework that can be used to declare your menu items in an XML file. It integrates with Struts as a plug-in, supports popular menu styles (for instance CoolMenus and standards-compliant DHTML menus), and allows for hiding and showing menus and items based on roles. Currently, it supports absolute and context-relative links, as well as Struts forwards.

Both of these tag libraries are implemented in this chapter's application.

To reference the Struts tag libraries, you simply drop the `struts.jar` file into `WEB-INF/lib` and match the URIs as specified in each library's tag descriptor (TLD) file. I've seen that some servlet containers require you to declare the location of your TLD in `web.xml`. This is also necessary if your TLD file doesn't declare a URI to map to. In our example `struts-resume` application, `struts-resume.tld`, and `struts-menu.tld` require entries in `web.xml` for this reason.

JSP 2.0 helps keep the code concise by allowing a JavaBean's properties to be accessed directly in a JSP page. Previously, you had to use `<c:out value="${beanName.propertyName}"/>`, while now, JSP 2.0 lets you simply use `${beanName.propertyName}`. We expect JSTL-type syntax to be around for a while, as will the Struts tags, if only for backwards compatibility.

Overview of the Example Struts-Résumé Application

The example `struts-resume` application you're going to use as an example throughout this chapter uses Ant (an open-source build tool) and XDoclet (an open-source code generation, too) as its core engines. They will generate a significant portion of the application for you as well as run any JUnit and Cactus tests you may have.

Screen flow and Requirements

Let's explore the project's initial requirements and screen flow. The nice thing about this application is that I'm my own customer, because I want to develop a better way to publish my résumé online. However, I'm not the only person that will use this application, and therefore I'm going to include administrator and user roles.

I'm looking for a web-based system that supports the traditional résumé sections: user contact information, summary, objective, skill categories, skills, education, training, and extracurricular activities. Although I haven't completed all of these sections at the time of this writing, this is what I want the application to grow into. I want to be able to render my résumé in XML and use XSL to produce HTML, text, Word's rich text format, and PDF files. To demonstrate roles and security, I'll make this a multiuser system in which there are administrators and users. Administrators can see and do everything, while users can only view or change their own résumé.

I envision the screen flow to be something like this:

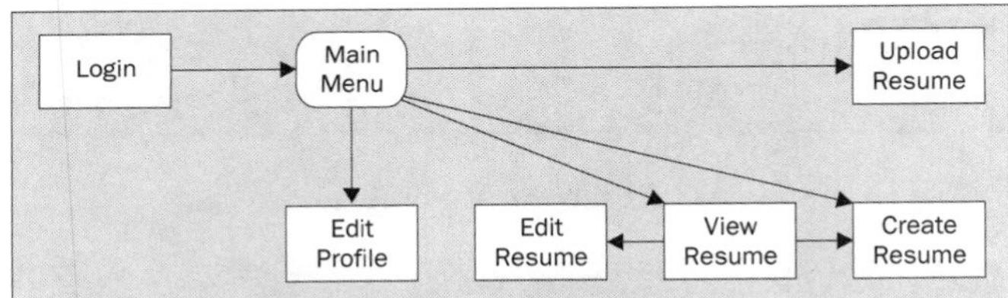

After users have signed in, they may choose to create, edit, view, and upload résumés. They can also edit their user details. Let's take a look at what each screen looks like by taking a quick walk through the application.

When you first access the application, you're presented with the Login page:

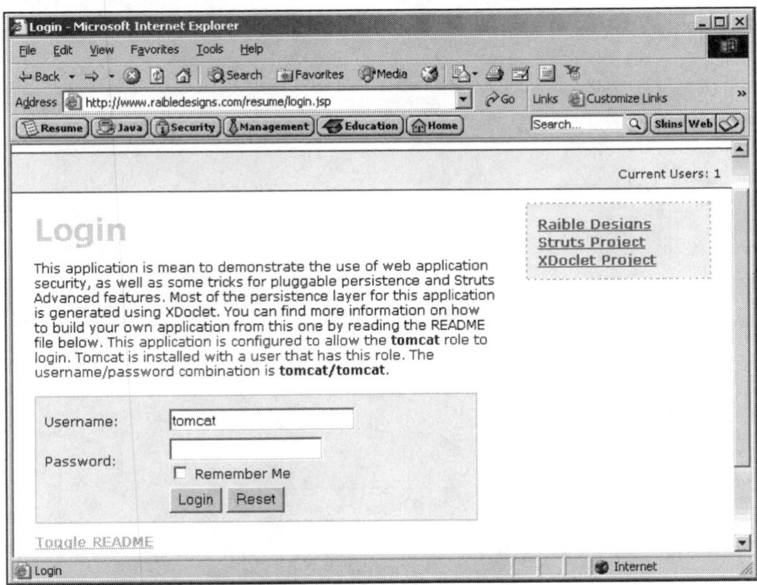

Filling in the appropriate username and password and clicking Login invokes the Main Menu page, the jumping-off point for the other pages:

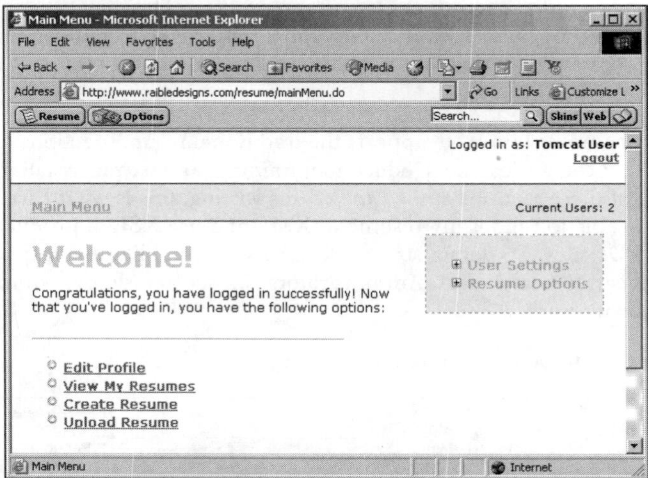

If you now click View My Resumes, you'll see the View Resumes page:

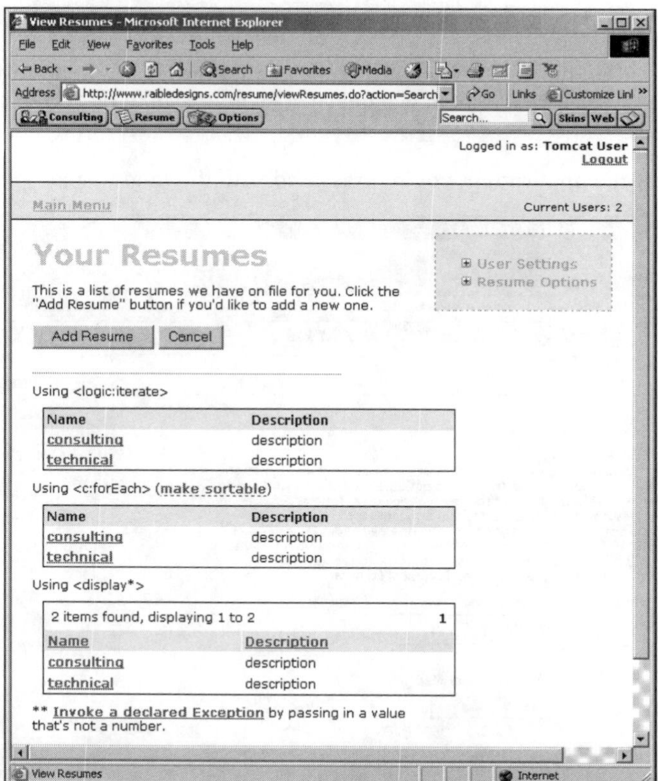

This page allows you to view existing résumés or add a new one. Try clicking on the name of one of the existing résumés, and you'll see the following:

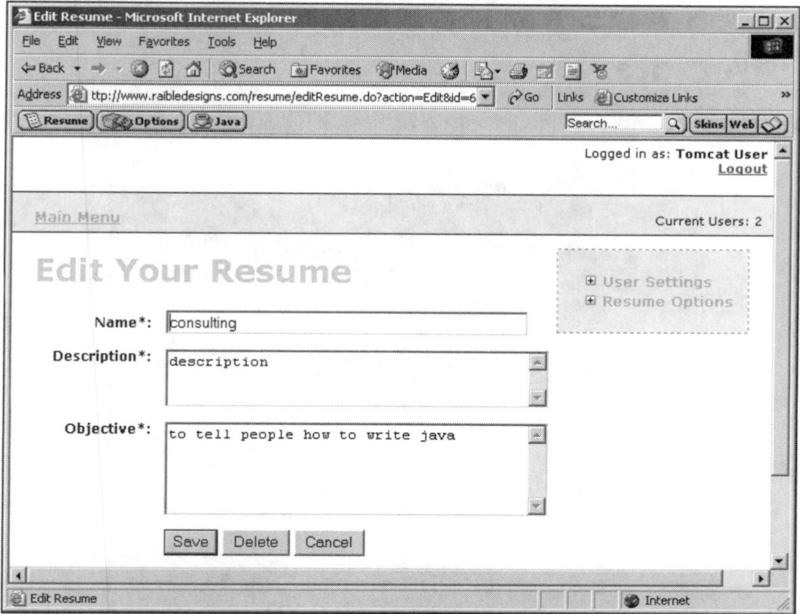

In other words, you have the ability to modify the contents of existing resumes. Now go back to the View Resumes page and select Add Resume. You'll see a blank canvas for you to add a new résumé:

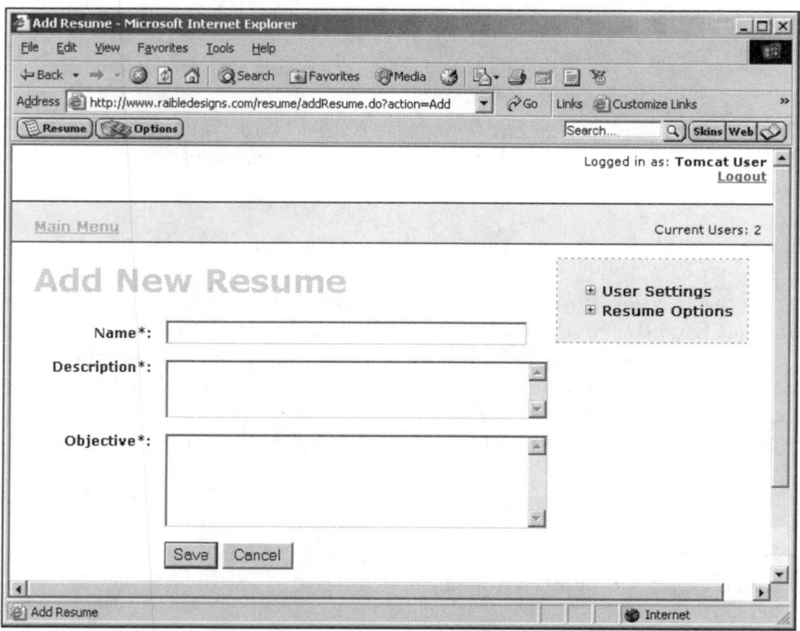

Finally, go back to the Main Menu page. You'll see that there are two other options: Edit Profile and Upload Resume. Edit Profile allows you to change your user profile, including your login name, password, and contact details. Upload Resume allows you to upload a file from your hard drive.

Directory Structure

To familiarize you with `struts-resume`'s architecture, we'll start with the directory structure:

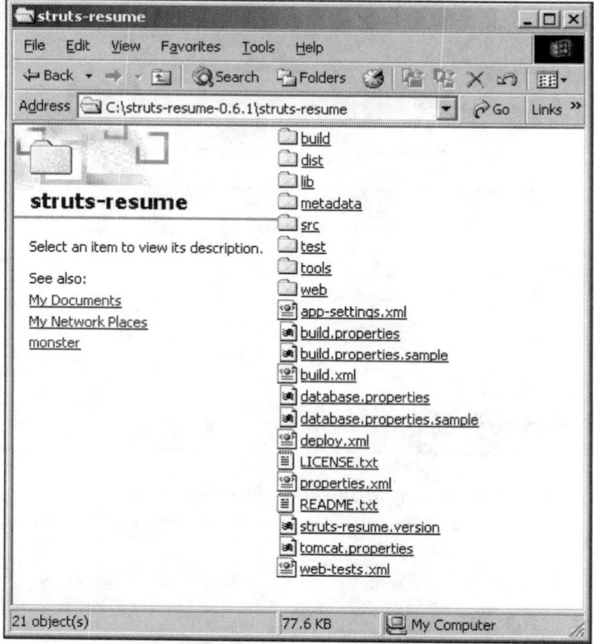

The code for `struts-resume` *can also be downloaded from* http://javawebapps.com/downloads. *A CVS version is available at* http://sf.net/projects/struts. *A* `README.txt` *file is provided with the code download that gives full application deployment instructions.*

Let's go over what each file in the root directory is used for and what's in each subdirectory.

The `app-settings.xml` file allows you to easily customize your application. The Ant tool allows you to set properties from the command line using the `"-DpropertyName=propertyValue"` syntax. We separated these properties out of the main build file for readability. The main Ant build script, `build.xml`, at execution time, includes this `app-settings.xml` file. The `build.properties` file contains application name settings and build directory settings. The `database.properties` file allows you to configure which database you want to talk to through Hibernate. Most databases are supported.

The `lib` directory contains all the third-party libraries (JARs) used by the project. We use several large third-party libraries, therefore this directory weighs in at approximately 11 MB. XDoclet, Cactus, Struts, and other libraries are contained in this directory. A `lib.properties` file within this directory will allow you to change version numbers for packages.

The `metadata` directory has a `web` subdirectory containing XML files that together make up `web.xml` and `struts-config.xml`. This is known as the **merge directory** in XDoclet terminology. If you were to add EJBs to this project, you could place any relevant XML fragments inside a new `metadata/ejb` directory.

The `properties.xml` file loads all `.properties` files and environment variables. It then uses these values to set class path properties, database properties, and Tomcat deployment properties.

The `src` directory is (obviously) where all Java source files are kept. There are three directories underneath it: `common`, `ejb`, and `web`. Also, it makes sense to have an `ejb` directory for the persistence layer, because this makes the directory layout extensible for the future. XDoclet is used to generate a `ValidatorForm`, and the Hibernate Mapping XML file from a plain old Java object (POJO). The `ValidatorForm` is further marked up with `@struts.validator` XDoclet tags and used to generate a `validation.xml` file. The reason I've done it this way is because it allows new columns to be added to my tables easily. On my last project, I used Validator Forms, Value Objects, and DAOs, and if I added a new column to a table, I had to add getters and setters in two places (on the form and the POJO) and also change the SQL in the DAO. Using XDoclet and Hibernate eliminates this headache–especially since Hibernate generates a schema and can build your database for you. I've written a `db-create` Ant task to perform this table creation for you automatically.

The `tools` directory contains the StrutsGen tool written by Erik Hatcher. This tool runs uses Ant and XDoclet to generate a skeleton JSP and an associated properties file from an `ActionForm`, greatly speeding up application development.

The `web` directory contains all web-related files: images, JavaScript files, CSS files, properties files, and XML configuration files. It contains separate directories for most of these and also a `WEB-INF/classes` directory. The JSP files in the `pages` directory are copied to `WEB-INF` at deployment time.

By the way, this application was created using AppFuse (http://raibledesigns.com/downloads) as a baseline, and I recommend that you use it too when you develop your own Struts-based applications. It already has a directory layout built, a build script for compiling, testing, and deploying, and XDoclet fragments for generating your XML files. After downloading, simply execute `"ant new -Dapp.name=yourAppName -Ddb.name=yourDBName"`*. Feel free to remove those files you don't find necessary.*

Struts Development Techniques and Tools

Now that we've reminded you of the architecture of a typical Struts application and provided an overview of an example `struts-resume` application, let's review some techniques, tools, and frameworks that you may not be aware of, which can enhance or speed up your Struts application development. We'll focus on Struts version 1.1 and mainly on its advanced features.

Struts has many great features, extensions, and plug-ins available for developers. Some of these plug-ins can seem intimidating at first, because they're very powerful and extremely configurable. When I first discovered some of them, I asked myself, "Who ordered the kitchen sink?" However, there's nothing wrong with just using just a small piece of them if that's all you need.

We'll start off by looking at two open-source tools we can use to build and generate code respectively: Ant and XDoclet. Then we'll work through a series of techniques or tools you can use as you write code.

Using Ant to Build Struts Applications

Apache Ant (available from http://jakarta.apache.org/ant) is a powerful Java-based build tool. Using Ant will make your compile, assemble, or deploy process much easier.

Ant is by far my favorite tool to use with Struts and Java as a whole. Yet I've met too many developers that either haven't heard of it or aren't using it. *JavaWorld's* readers voted it the "Most Useful Java Community-Developed Technology" of 2002 and in 2003, *JavaPro's* readers voted it the "Most Valuable Java Deployment Technology." I used to be trapped within the confines of an IDE to compile my code and now that I use Ant, I feel like I've been set free.

Ant is basically a technology that, at its very core, compiles your `.java` files into `.class` files using a build file (commonly named `build.xml`). Using Ant, it's much easier to configure your class path for compiling files, as illustrated by the following example:

```
<!-- Set a path reference that points to all Struts' JAR files -->
<path id="web.compile.classpath">
  <fileset dir="/lib/jakarta-struts-1.1" includes="*.jar"/>
</path>

<target name="compile" description="compiles .java files into .class files">
  <mkdir dir="${build.dir}/web/classes"/>
  <javac srcdir="src/web"
      destdir="${build.dir}/web/classes"
      debug="false"
      deprecation="true"
      optimize="true"
      classpathref="web.compile.classpath"
  />
</target>
```

For this chapter's example application, version 1.5.1 (or higher) of Ant is required. After downloading, you'll need to extract it to a location on your hard drive (`c:\Tools\jakarta-ant-1.5.1` on Windows or `/usr/local/jakarta-ant-1.5.1` on Linux and Unix). After extraction, you'll need to set `ANT_HOME` as an environment variable that points to this extracted location and also add `$ANT_HOME/bin` to your `$PATH` environment variable.

Ant Tasks

Executing `"ant -projecthelp"` will display the basic Ant tasks, but the following are ones you'll use most often:

- `ant deploy`: Generates and compiles everything, then deploys to Tomcat (if you have it installed).
- `ant compile-`*`module`*: Where *`module`* is `ejb`, `web`, or `common`.
- `ant ejbdoclet`: Generates `ValidatorForms` and Hibernate's XML-based mapping file.
- `ant webdoclet`: Generates `web.xml`, `struts-config.xml`, `validation.xml`, and the TLD.

- ant test-*module*: Where *module* may have the same values as for the compile option mentioned previously. This recursively runs all tests in the test/*module* directory. I recommend using ant test-*module* -Dtestcase=*ClassName*, where *ClassName* is the name of your test class.
- ant test-cactus -Dtestcase=*ClassName*: Starts Tomcat before tests are run and stops it once they're complete. Use ant test-web -Dtestcase=*ClassName* if Tomcat is already running.

Many third-party libraries in struts-resume require that you define a *task definition* for them to integrate with Ant. For instance, to use XDoclet to generate the Struts configuration file struts-config.xml, you must define the "webdoclet" task:

```
<taskdef name="webdoclet"
    classname="xdoclet.modules.web.WebDocletTask">
  <classpath>
    <path refid="xdoclet.classpath"/>
    <path refid="web.compile.classpath"/>
  </classpath>
</taskdef>
```

After defining this task, it can be used in your build.xml file, just like the <javac> task (see previous example) is used. The available attributes for this task can be viewed in the next section on XDoclet.

Using Ant in the Example Application

Within struts-resume, Ant performs all of the following tasks:

- Generates Java code and XML files (via XDoclet).
- Builds (compiles) the entire source tree (.java files).
- Assembles the components into JAR and Web ARchive (WAR) files.
- Deploys the WAR file to Tomcat.
- Runs unit tests and in-container testing (via Cactus).

Ant is one of those technologies that I love because it *just works.* I've modeled the build.xml file in the struts-resume application to fit with the Ant Best Practices recommended by Erik Hatcher in his book *Java Development with Ant.*[2] I've used much of his architecture from his book's sample application and exchanged quite a few e-mails with him about it. The flexibility granted by having a test source-code directory (test/src) separate from the regular source-code directory (src) makes it easy to exclude test classes from a production deployment.

Finally, to me Struts has been an extremely stable framework–even the nightly builds. When you look at the Ant build file for your example application, you'll see I've created it so that you can easily switch versions of any third-party library, including Struts. All you need to do is download and extract a new version into the lib directory and change the version number given in lib/lib.properties. This

[2] Hatcher, Erik and Steve Loughran, *Java Development with Ant* (Greenwich, CT: Manning Publications Co., 2002)

really makes it easy to test a new version of a library and see if your application still works. You can also override library directories from the command line using something like `ant -Dstruts-dir=/path/to/struts/jars`.

Using XDoclet to Generate Configuration Files

XDoclet is a code-generation engine. It enables **attribute-oriented programming** for Java. In short, this means that you can add more significance to your code by adding metadata (attributes) to your Java sources. This is done in special JavaDoc tags. XDoclet will parse your source files and generate many artifacts such as XML descriptors and/or source code from it. These files are generated from templates that use the information provided in the source code and its Javadocs tags. At the time of this writing, XDoclet can only be used as part of a build process utilizing Ant. Documentation and downloads for XDoclet are available from http://xdoclet.sourceforge.net/.

For the build process, you'll be using the power of Ant and XDoclet to generate the deployment descriptor (`web.xml`), the Struts configuration file `struts-config.xml`, and even the form validation configuration file (`validation.xml`). To speed up the development process, you'll also use XDoclet to generate the Java code for the `ValidatorForms` from POJOs. Also, you'll generate Hibernate's XML-based mapping files to map POJOs to database tables.

Wow, that sounds like we're doing a lot doesn't it?! The truth is that before I found XDoclet, I was doing all of those activities manually, and it *was* a lot of work. Using XDoclet (which depends on Ant) has made it *much* easier to create all of the required XML artifacts for a web application and is a huge timesaver.

I like using XDoclet because I don't need to worry about editing my XML files as much when developing an application. It's simply a case of adding some tags to a class (or method) Javadoc and these files are generated for you. For example, I have the following normal Javadoc code at the top of my `UserAction` class:

```
/**
 * Implementation of <strong>Action</strong> that interacts with the {@link
 * UserForm} to retrieve/persist values to the database.
 *
 * @author Matt Raible
 * @version $Revision: 1.5 $ $Date: 2003/06/26 13:48:46 $
 *
 */
public final class UserAction extends BaseAction {
```

By adding some XDoclet tags to this Javadoc header, you can generate the `<action-mappings>` definition for the `struts-config.xml` file:

```
/**
 * Implementation of <strong>Action</strong> that interacts with the {@link
 * UserForm} and retrieves values. It interacts with the {@link
 * BusinessManager} to retrieve/persist values to the database.
 *
 * @author Matt Raible
 * @version $Revision: 1.5 $ $Date: 2003/06/26 13:48:46$
 *
```

```
 * @struts.action name="userForm" path="/editUser" scope="session"
 *       validate="false" parameter="action" input="mainMenu"
 */
public final class UserAction extends BaseAction {
```

In your Ant build file's (`build.xml`) "`webdoclet`" task, you use the following XML to generate the `struts-config.xml` file.

```
<target name="webdoclet" description="Generate web and Struts descriptors">
  <taskdef name="webdoclet"
     classname="xdoclet.modules.web.WebDocletTask">
    <classpath>
      <path refid="xdoclet.classpath"/>
      <path refid="web.compile.classpath"/>
    </classpath>
  </taskdef>
  <webdoclet destdir="${webapp.target}/WEB-INF"
     force="${xdoclet.force}"
     mergedir="metadata/web"
     excludedtags="@version,@author"
     verbose="true">
    <fileset dir="src/web"/>
    <fileset dir="${build.dir}/web/gen"/>
    <configParam name="cactusOn" value="${enable.cactus}"/>
    <deploymentdescriptor validatexml="true"
       servletspec="2.3" sessiontimeout="30"
       destdir="${build.dir}/web/WEB-INF"
       distributable="false">
      <configParam name="security" value="${security.mode}"/>
    </deploymentdescriptor>
    <jsptaglib validatexml="true"
      description="Tag Libraries for Security and Labels"
      validateXML="true"
      shortName="struts-resume"
      filename="struts-resume.tld"
    />
    <strutsconfigxml validatexml="true" version="1.1"/>
    <strutsvalidationxml/>
  </webdoclet>
</target>
```

That's all it takes to generate the following mapping in the resulting `struts-config.xml` file (I've prettied the XML up a bit to save space, but no text has changed):

```
<action path="/editUser" type="org.appfuse.webapp.action.UserAction"
    name="userForm" scope="session" input="mainMenu"
    parameter="action" unknown="false" validate="false">
</action>
```

Of course, you can still code your configuration files by hand, adding your own custom data by producing specifically named files known as **merge points**. These files are included in the main file when the items are produced. In the `metadata/web` directory (also known as the merge directory) of struts-resume, a README.txt file lists available merge points for web.xml, struts-config.xml and validation.xml. For example, to specify global-forwards for your application, you can create a global-forwards.xml file that contains the following:

```
<global-forwards>
    <forward name="mainMenu" path="/mainMenu.do"/>
</global-forwards>
```

This file will then be included in the generated struts-config.xml file. XDoclet knows to look in this directory for these files by examining the mergedir attribute of the webdoclet task:

```
<webdoclet destdir="${webapp.target}/WEB-INF"
    force="${xdoclet.force}"
    mergedir="metadata/web"
    excludedtags="@version,@author"
    verbose="true">
```

XDoclet also works for producing form-bean entries in struts-config.xml as well as generating the validation.xml file for the Validator. For form beans, you can simply add the following in your class's Javadoc:

```
* @struts.form name="UserForm"
```

You can also use this tag to generate ActionForms from POJOs (or entity beans) by simply using @struts.form. However, if you want to include all the entity bean's fields, you'll need to add include-all="true". You can also add an optional extends attribute to specify that it extends ValidatorForm or your own base class. For instance, in struts-resume, the User.java file has the following in its Javadoc header:

```
/**
 * User class
 *
 * This class is used to generate the Struts Validator Form
 * as well as the Hibernate persistence later.
 *
 * @author Matt Raible
 * @version $Revision: 1.6 $ $Date: 2003/06/27 03:27:44$
 *
 * @struts.form include-all="true"
 *  extends="org.appfuse.webapp.form.BaseForm"
 *
 * @hibernate.class     table="app_user"
 */
public class User extends BaseObject {
```

Then you can add method-level tags to generate the validation.xml file. If you're adding XDoclet tags to an existing ValidatorForm, make sure to put these tags on your **setters** as nothing will be generated otherwise!

```
* @struts.validator type="required" msgkey="errors.required"
```

If you're generating `ValidatorForms` from POJOs or entity beans, you'll need to put the `@struts.validator` tags on the class's `get` methods. In `struts-resume`, we've set up a custom XDoclet template for generating Struts's forms (in `metadata/templates/struts_form.xdt`), which will generate a `ValidatorForm`, complete with `@struts.validator` tags on the setters. Since this wasn't core functionality of XDoclet at the time of this writing, I was inspired to create a custom template to get it.

I don't know if I'd recommend coding your action-forwards into your classes, I've done it both ways and both seem comfortable. Of course, I've being working on a lot of one-person development teams lately, so that might skew my view a little. If you want to externalize your global forwards, you can put them in a merge-point file named `global-forwards.xml`. If you want to do it locally to the class, you can use the following syntax at the beginning of the class:

```
 * @struts.action-forward name="list" path=".resumeList"
```

One great thing about XDoclet's integration with Ant is that you can specify Ant properties in your source code as well and these will be substituted at build time. Thus, you could configure all your values via Ant rather than hard-coding them. For example, in `LoginServlet`, I have the following XDoclet tags as part of the Javadoc header:

```
 * @web.servlet-init-param
 *      name="encrypt-password"
 *      value="${encrypt-password}"
```

This value is set by default in the `app-settings.xml` file:

```
<property name="secure-login" value="false"/>
```

However, it can easily be overwritten by executing Ant with this parameter specified:

```
ant -Dsecure-login=true
```

This results in the following being generated in the deployment descriptor (web.xml) for the `LoginServlet`:

```
<init-param>
  <param-name>encrypt-password</param-name>
  <param-value>true</param-value>
</init-param>
```

If you already have a database schema and want to develop a J2EE-based application, you could use Middlegen (http://boss.bekk.no/boss/middlegen/). Middlegen is a database-driven code-generation engine based on JDBC, Velocity, Ant, and XDoclet. It can generate code for container-managed persistence (CMP) Enterprise JavaBeans (EJBs), Java Database Objects (JDO), and JSP or Struts–straight from a database! This is a great tool for rapid prototyping. Currently however, it only supports code generation for Struts 1.0. Struts 1.1 compatibility is expected to be added soon, once the Struts plug-in has been reworked to support different databases.

The StrutsGen Tool

There is a small, yet nimble tool in the `struts-resume` application. Erik Hatcher originally wrote it for his sample application in *Java Development with Ant.* It uses Ant and XDoclet to generate a JSP page and a `ResourceBundle` by inspecting a form's property files. The template used for both of these files is simple and customizable. This tool can be found in the `tools/strutsgen` directory of the `struts-resume` application. To use it, you first need to run the command `"ant webdoclet"` to generate your forms in the `build/gen/web` directory. Then navigate to `tools/strutsgen` and run `ant "-Dform.name=MyForm"` where `MyForm` is the name of the form you would like to generate files for. If you run this command on the `UserForm` in `struts-resume`, you should see results similar to the following screen shot:

```
Cygwin
$cd tools/strutsgen/
$ant -Dform.name=UserForm
Buildfile: build.xml

clean:

init:
    [mkdir] Created dir: D:\source\struts-resume\tools\strutsgen\build


compile:
    [javac] Compiling 1 source file to D:\source\struts-resume\tools\s
trutsgen\build

gen:
  [xdoclet] Running <template/>
  [xdoclet] Generating output for 'org.appfuse.webapp.form.UserForm' u
sing template file 'file:/D:/source/struts-resume/tools/strutsgen/src/
FormKeys.xdt'.
  [xdoclet] Running <template/>
  [xdoclet] Generating output for 'org.appfuse.webapp.form.UserForm' u
sing template file 'file:/D:/source/struts-resume/tools/strutsgen/src/
StrutsForm_jsp.xdt'.

default:

BUILD SUCCESSFUL
Total time: 11 seconds
$
```

This will result in two files being generated in the `tool/strutsgen/build` directory, one named `UserForm.jsp` and the other named `UserForm.properties`. You can also run the tool without specifying a form name and it will generate these files for all your forms.

This tool uses a `TreeMap` for grabbing the properties from the form, so this means that the new files will contain the properties in alphabetical order. In most cases, you'll probably need to customize the order of your fields to make them user-friendly anyway, this tool just speeds things up a bit. It also only supports generating `<html:text>` fields at this time, but since you'll have to get into the JSP to rearrange the order of fields anyway, it's not a big deal. I found it to be very useful during development of this application.

Handling Persistence in Struts

In my opinion, Struts does a great job of giving you, the developer, great ways to implement your view and your controller, but it doesn't provide much for the model. `ActionForms` are great and `ValidatorForms` are even better, but if you want a database back end to your application, there isn't much in Struts that makes it easier to code it. Forms provide a nice interface to the back end, but Struts isn't in the business of providing data access, and therefore doesn't provide any classes for retrieving data. While there are many different ways to code your controller-to-database logic, I'll be telling you how I've done it and what's worked for me.

When I first started developing with Struts, our architecture had been predetermined and all I had to do was hook into it. We were using EJBs on the project and used RowSets for our list screens. It was fairly easy on my part, because all I had to do was call a particular session bean for each action and interact with it appropriately. I actually found it very easy to create accessors and mutators (getters and setters) for our data objects (or value objects or data transfer objects) on each form. I discovered later that this wasn't a recommended "design pattern"–my data objects should never make it to the presentation layer. However, it worked, and it worked great–and we were happy with it.

The topic of persistence options seems to grace the Struts user mailing list almost weekly. I believe this is because there are so many choices. In reality, you can use almost any Java-based persistence framework with Struts. It's all Java after all. It's tough to choose a framework when none has proved to be a dominant, well-used framework. This is an advantage of Struts in that it allows you to choose any framework–but I'm guessing this is a big headache for many developers as well.

However, choosing a persistence framework for a Struts application can be easy if you stick to the technologies you know. If you're going to choose an open-source implementation, make sure the documentation is good, the development mailing list is active, and there are example applications. It's much easier to copy an existing example than to develop from scratch. It's worth your time to investigate code-generation tools that exist for databases, because this will save you a lot of time in the long run. Above all, learn and use XDoclet (we'll discuss this a little later) to help with your persistence layer. I expect you'll be very happy with it.

Persistence Options

In Chapter 8, you spent a good bit of time evaluating the different persistence options available, so I won't bother to repeat that discussion here. Instead, I'll just let you know that I chose to use Hibernate on the example `struts-resume` project. I'm very happy with it so far. It seems to have great documentation and also has XDoclet support. XDoclet support was a big seller for me, because I want to generate most of the database access code.

The examples in `struts-resume` are modeled after Dave Johnson's examples (author of the Chapter 8) in his sample application as well as help I've received from the Hibernate development mailing list.

Enhancing Struts ActionForm Development

There are a few features of Struts that are often overlooked but may be useful when you come to develop your `ActionForms`. Let's take a look at them.

Using DynaActionForms

The `DynaActionForm` is a new feature of Struts 1.1. It basically allows you to declare your form's properties via XML, rather than writing a form using Java. The advantage for the developer is that you don't have to write and compile an `ActionForm`. However, if you're using XDoclet to generate an `ActionForm`, then you might not have a use for a `DynaActionForm`. They can be handy for providing simple forms that aren't persisted–for instance a `MessageForm` that is used to send e-mail. Let's use that as an example and look at its `struts-config.xml` settings:

```
<form-bean name="messageForm"
           type="org.apache.struts.action.DynaActionForm">
  <form-property name="name" type="java.lang.String"/>
  <form-property name="email" type="java.lang.String"/>
  <form-property name="subject" type="java.lang.String"/>
  <form-property name="content" type="java.lang.String"/>
</form-bean>
```

Just like an `ActionForm`, all your properties should be strings for interaction with the web tier. Only object types (`String`, `Integer`, or `Boolean`) can be used as the form-property's type–primitives aren't allowed. After specifying the form's properties, you can reference the form in an action mapping just like a regular `ActionForm` or `ValidatorForm`. A `DynaActionForm` can also utilize the Validator by using a type of `org.apache.struts.action.DynaValidatorActionForm`.

This form can then be retrieved in your `Action` class using the following code:

```
DynaActionForm msgForm = (DynaActionForm) form;
```

To retrieve values from the form, you must use the `form.get(propertyName)` syntax (similar to how values are retrieved from a `HashMap`):

```
String subject = (String) theForm.get("subject");
```

You can also create and initialize a `DynaActionForm` (or `DynaValidatorActionForm`) in an `Action` class:

```
DynaActionForm msgForm = (DynaActionForm) DynaActionFormClass
    .getDynaActionFormClass("messageForm").newInstance();
```

Then values can be set on the form using `form.set("propertyName", object)`. Just like a normal `ActionForm`, you'll need to place it into its assigned scope after you've populated it. If you plan on doing a lot of getting and setting of properties on a form, the `DynaActionForm` can be a bit of a pain, because of all the type casting you need to do, rather than the simple `form.getProperty()`. I suggest generating your `ActionForms` and `ValidatorForms` forms using XDoclet before using `DynaActionForms`. At the same time, there are good uses for it, as in the message form.

Using Indexed Properties with Forms in Struts

Indexed properties are a feature of Struts that has been available since the beginning. If you've used it, you probably really like it, because it allows you to get and set lists of objects (such as an `ArrayList` of child forms on a parent form). In the `struts-resume` application, this might be something like getting/setting an `ArrayList` of `SkillForms` on a `ResumeForm`. Basically, the syntax involves tags like `<logic:iterate>` and `<c:forEach>` and setting an index on the form element's name:

```
<logic:iterate id="skill" name="userSkills" indexId="index">
```

Then you need to add get and set accessors to your form to allow these values to be retrieved and altered based on an index. Here is an example of how you might implement this in `struts-resume` on a `SkillGroup` form, where a user is assigning multiple `SkillForms`:

```
/**
 * The skill attribute.
*/
private ArrayList skill;

/**
 * Getter for skill. For the sake of the iterator
 * tags and the indexing of objects.
 */
public SkillForm getSkill(int index) {
  return (SkillForm) skill.get(index);
}
/**
* Setter for the above getter.
*/
public void setSkill(int index, SkillForm skill) {
  this.skill.set(index, skill);
}

/**
 * Getter for ArrayList of skills
 */
public ArrayList getSkills() {
  return skill;
}

/**
 * Setter for ArrayList of skills
 */
public void setSkills(ArrayList skills) {
  this.skill = skills;
}
```

I haven't implemented indexed properties as yet, although I plan to, and may already have done so by the time you're reading this.

Form Validation

My favored method of performing form validation is to use Struts Validator. Validator was originally authored by David Winterfeldt to overcome the tediousness of writing validation logic in `ActionForms`. It can perform basic validations to check if a field is required, matches a regular expression, e-mail, credit card, and server-side type checking and date validation. You can use the Validator in any JSP and servlet application, but it was originally designed for Struts and is therefore easiest to use within Struts. Since Struts 1.1 Beta 2, the Validation framework has been integrated into the core Struts library (`struts.jar`).

For detailed online information about Validator, go to http://jakarta.apache.org/struts/userGuide/dev_validator.html.

Using Validator

The Validator framework relies on a `validator-rules.xml` file, which defines all of the pluggable validator definitions. These definitions are basically Java classes for server-side validation and JavaScript functions for client-side validation. Let's look at the "required" pluggable validator as an example:

```
<validator name="required"
           classname="org.apache.struts.validator.FieldChecks"
           method="validateRequired"
           methodParams="java.lang.Object,
                         org.apache.commons.validator.ValidatorAction,
                         org.apache.commons.validator.Field,
                         org.apache.struts.action.ActionErrors,
                         javax.servlet.http.HttpServletRequest"
           msg="errors.required">
  <javascript><![CDATA[
    ... insert JavaScript function here ...
  ]]>
  </javascript>
</validator>
```

I've left out the JavaScript function because it's 40 lines long and you're here to learn JSP, not JavaScript, right? In the previous definition, the `FieldChecks` is a class within the Validator framework, and it has a method named `validateRequired()` that takes the parameters listed. The `<javascript>` element defines the JavaScript function to do client-side validation. Having the definitions in this file makes the Validator framework easily configurable.

To enable the Validator in a Struts application, you first need to add the following XML into the `struts-config.xml` file. According to the Struts DTD, `<plug-in>` elements should appear towards the end of this file. If you're using XDoclet, you can put this XML into a `struts-plugins.xml` file in your `merge` directory:

```
<plug-in className="org.apache.struts.validator.ValidatorPlugIn">
  <set-property property="pathnames"
                value="/WEB-INF/validator-rules.xml,/WEB-INF/validation.xml"/>
</plug-in>
```

You can see from this example that there are two files that the Validator is loading. These can be renamed to whatever you like; you just have to make sure your `<plug-in>` configuration is set correctly. Since these file names are the de facto standards for the Validator, I'll use these in my examples. The Validator also allows for extensions such as the following for validating that two fields match:

```
public static boolean validateTwoFields(Object bean, ValidatorAction va,
    Field field, ActionErrors errors, HttpServletRequest request,
    ServletContext application) {

  String value = ValidatorUtil.getValueAsString(bean, field.getProperty());
  String sProperty2 = field.getVarValue("secondProperty");
  String value2 = ValidatorUtil.getValueAsString(bean, sProperty2);

  if (!GenericValidator.isBlankOrNull(value)) {
    try {
```

```
        if (!value.equals(value2)) {
          errors.add(field.getKey(), ValidatorUtil.getActionError(
                     application, request, va, field));
          return false;
        }
      } catch (Exception e) {
        errors.add(field.getKey(), ValidatorUtil.getActionError(
                   application, request, va, field));
        return false;
      }
    }

    return true;
  }
```

You can then add this class to the `validator-rules.xml` file by adding the following element:

```
<validator name="twofields"
           classname="com.mysite.StrutsValidator"
           method="validateTwoFields"
           msg="errors.twofields"/>
```

Then, in `validation.xml`, you can configure a field to use this validation rule:

```
<field property="password"
       depends="required,twofields">
  <arg0 key="typeForm.password.displayname"/>
  <var>
    <var-name>secondProperty</var-name>
    <var-value>password2</var-value>
  </var>
</field>
```

You could also easily add a JavaScript function to `validator-rules.xml` for client-side validation. This merely requires adding a `<javascript>` element inside the `<validator>` element.

Without the Validator, the easiest way to program validation logic into your application is to override the `validate()` method in your `ActionForm`. Its signature is as follows:

```
public ActionErrors validate(ActionMapping mapping, HttpServletRequest request);
```

This `ActionForm` method returns `null`, like the `ActionForm` `reset()` method, and similarly, overriding it isn't required if you don't want to.

```
public void reset(ActionMapping mapping, HttpServletRequest request);
```

The `reset()` method is designed to reset all your properties back to their default state. It is called before the bean is repopulated by the controller servlet and can be very helpful when using check boxes on your view forms. This is because neither the value nor the name of a check box is passed in the request when it's unchecked. This is the main reason the `reset()` method exists–to set the default state of check boxes so they behave like other form elements and are always passed along in the request as a name-value pair.

To be perfectly honest, I've only used the `validate()` method in any of my `ActionForms` when validating indexed properties, and I've only used `reset()` when I had check boxes on a form. I discovered the Validator framework about a month after I started working with Struts and haven't looked back since. The Validator is great for performing basic required field validation as well as more advanced functions such as regular expression matching, e-mail address syntax (not actual validation of addresses), credit card, and type checking (string, number, date). Furthermore, different validation rules can be defined for different locales. In order to make good use of the Validator, you do need to understand regular expression syntax fairly well however.

To configure an `Action` to call the `validate()` method on an `ActionForm` or to use the `ValidatorForm`'s declarative validation, you don't need to do anything because validation is **turned on** by default. Personally, I like to specify `validate="true"` or `validate="false"` in my `<action-mappings>` element to avoid confusion. Also, you'll need to specify an input attribute for your `<action-mappings>` or the Validator won't know where to return to for server-side validation. **This is very important**, especially when using the Tiles framework we'll discuss later–you'll get the blank screen of nothingness if you don't add the `input` attribute. Configuring this in XDoclet looks like the following example:

```
* @struts.action name="userForm" path="/saveUser" scope="session"
*   validate="true" parameter="action" input="editProfile"
```

This produces the following action-mapping:

```
<action path="/saveUser" type="org.appfuse.webapp.action.UserAction"
  name="userForm" scope="session" input="editProfile" parameter="action"
  unknown="false" validate="true">
</action>
```

We're using `inputForwards` in the `struts-resume` application, so the value `editProfile` actually refers to a global-forward.

I really like the Validator because it performs client-side (through JavaScript) as well as server-side validation. In my experience, most customers prefer client-side validation, as do developers. Why should the browser even attempt to submit the form if the required fields aren't populated? There are some larger organizations that discourage the use of JavaScript for the sake of compatibility, and it's a shame as it can help your web applications to behave more like traditional desktop applications. However, there are some HTML elements that require server-side validation. For instance, the `<input type="file" ... />` element. It doesn't allow JavaScript manipulation or access, and therefore, cannot be checked to see if a value has been entered. This is for security reasons, because you wouldn't want a script to grab files from your hard drive without your consent.

When developing rich web clients with JavaScript, the most important things to remember are accessibility standards. Currently, there are two. In the United States, there is the federal government's Section 508 Initiative.

> *Section 508 requires that federal agencies' electronic and information technology is accessible to people with disabilities. More information can be found at* http://www.section508.gov.

The second standard, which is more worldwide, is the W3C's Web Accessibility Initiative (WAI).

> *The World Wide Web Consortium's (W3C) commitment to lead the Web to its full potential includes promoting a high degree of usability for people with disabilities.*
>
> *WAI, in coordination with organizations around the world, pursues accessibility of the Web through five primary areas of work: technology, guidelines, tools, education and outreach, and research and development. More information can be found at* http://www.w3.org/WAI/.

These accessibility standards are built on top of other standards, such as XHTML and CSS. If you follow these standards when developing your web application, you'll find that making your application accessible will be much easier. I've found that accessibility standards discourage the use of JavaScript to change pages on a `<select>`'s `onchange` event, but pop-up JavaScript alerts, like those used by the Validator, are fine. Most screen readers can understand and read them–the major accessibility concerns related to client-side JavaScript are one, that the message is easy to understand and two, that messages are still given when JavaScript is turned off. Since the Validator provides both client and server-side validation, it satisfies many accessibility requirements.

Generating validation.xml Using XDoclet

In the `struts-resume` application, XDoclet generates the `validation.xml` file from the `ActionForms` and their subclasses, including the `ValidatorForm`. I created a `BaseForm` that extends `ValidatorForm` and implements `Serializable` (for clustered environments) then all my forms extend it. The process by which `UserForm` and `validation.xml` are generated is shown here, where the arrows represent names of the Ant targets or tasks:

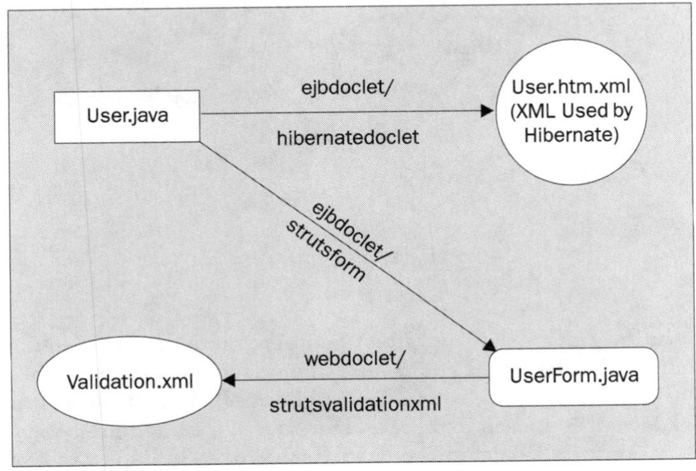

There are three method-level XDoclet tags you can use to generate values:

- `@struts.validator`
- `@struts-validator.args`
- `@struts.validator-var`

The simplest example of this is using the required validator to generate an entry. We'll use the username attribute that is generated on UserForm to illustrate. It starts, as illustrated in the previous diagram, at the User.java file, and these tags are transferred to the generated ActionForm. On the getter field for the username, you'll find the following tags:

```
/**
 * Returns the username.
 * @return String
 *
 * @struts.validator type="required" msgkey="errors.required"
 * @struts.validator type="email" msgkey="errors.email"
 * @hibernate.property
 *   column="username" type="string" not-null="true" unique="true"
 */
public String getUsername() {
  return username;
}
```

This code must be on the getter in order for the form generation to work correctly. At the time of writing, the strutsform task is a subtask of ejbdoclet, so I'm still running it as an ejbdoclet task. When the ejbdoclet task is run, the <strutsform> subtask within it will generate the following entry in validation.xml:

```
<formset>
  <form name="userForm">
    ...
    <field property="username"
           depends="required,email">
      <msg name="required"
           key="errors.required"/>
      <msg name="email"
           key="errors.email"/>
      <arg0 key="userForm.username"/>
    </field>
    ...
  </form>
</formset>
```

I should point out that the <msg> elements aren't required; therefore you don't need to specify the msgkey attribute in the XDoclet tag. If you choose to eliminate this element, the Validator's default message from the validation-rules.xml file will be applied. This value is represented in validation-rules.xml by the msg attribute. For example, the required Validator has msg="errors.required". XDoclet creates msg entries for us in validation.xml, providing greater flexibility in the long run.

Now that you know how to generate validation.xml, let's examine what the parts actually mean. There are four different elements in the previous extract: <form>, <field>, <msg>, and <arg>.

The <form>'s name attribute defines the name of your ActionForm, and this name should match the one defined in struts-config.xml. Since you're using XDoclet to generate the form and struts-config.xml file, you can be certain that these names will match.

The <field> element has two attributes, property and depends. The property attribute defines the name of the variable in UserForm.java to validate, while the depends attribute identifies which validation rules to apply.

There are two <msg> elements that signify which messages to use from the ApplicationResources.properties file or whatever the ResourceBundle is named in struts-config.xml. In struts-resume, these are defined as follows:

```
errors.required={0} is required.
errors.email={0} is an invalid e-mail address.
```

The last element, <arg0>, specifies the message key for the substitution value of {0} in each respective message. In struts-resume, this is defined as the following:

```
userForm.username=Username
```

If there is more than one argument you'd like to replace in your error message, you can add more arguments in ApplicationResources by incrementing the number, so {1} would signify the second argument. To add this argument's replacement value on your form, you could add another XDoclet tag to the original form:

```
@struts.validator-args arg1resource="username.lastName" arg1value="My Surname"
```

Of course, you would never use both of these attributes, because the first (arg1resource) is for looking up a resource key, and the second (arg2value) is for placing a literal string in your validation.xml. Running the previous code through the webdoclet task produces the following XML:

```
<arg0 key="username.lastName"/>
<arg0 key="My Last Name" resource="false"/>
```

Now that you've configured the form's validation, you should add some JavaScript to the JSP to enforce client-side validation. The first step is to use the <html:messages/> tag library to catch any server-side validation errors:

```
<logic:messagesPresent>
  <div class="error">
    <html:messages id="error">
      <bean:write name="error" filter="false"/><br/>
    </html:messages>
  </div>
</logic:messagesPresent>
```

In the struts-resume application, the previous code appears in a messages.jsp file. This file also contains code to catch regular messages (not error messages) and is located in the web/common folder. It's included in the Tiles template so I don't have to add it to every page that should use validation.

Secondly, you need to add an `onsubmit` event handler to your form:

```
<html:form action="/userSave" method="post" styleId="userForm"
    focus="password" onsubmit="return validateUserForm(this)">
```

While you're examining this form's syntax, I'd like to point out a couple of other things. By default, if you don't use a `method` attribute on your form, the `<html:form>` tag will render one for you. The problem with the one it renders is that it's not XHTML compliant. That is, it renders as `method="POST"`, where XHTML requires that predefined attribute values be in lowercase. I usually add a `styleId` attribute to all my forms and form elements (such as `<html:text>` or `<html:password>`), so that they can be accessed via the Document Object Model (DOM) with `document.getElementById(elementId)`. One thing you have to be aware of is that all `Id`s must be unique within a page. Lastly, to increase the usability of the application, you should try to use the `focus` attribute on your forms but use it cautiously: If you hide fields based on a user's role or other logic, this may result in a JavaScript error.

After configuring the form, you need to add an `onclick` handler to the form's Submit and Cancel buttons to talk to the Validator's `validateForm` JavaScript function. This is so clicking the Cancel button won't invoke any validation:

```
<html:cancel styleClass="button" onclick="bCancel=true">
  <bean:message key="button.cancel">
</html:cancel>

<html:submit styleClass="button" onclick="bCancel=false">
  <bean:message key="button.submit">
</html:submit>
```

In the previous example, I've added the `styleClass` attribute to signify a CSS rule for my buttons. Lastly, you add the following to include the JavaScript necessary to perform the actual validation:

```
<html:javascript formName="userForm" cdata="false"
                 dynamicJavascript="true" staticJavascript="false"/>
<script type="text/javascript"
        src="<html:rewrite page="/scripts/validator.jsp"/>">
</script>
```

I always try to use `<html:rewrite />` when referencing JavaScript or CSS files, because this will render a URL that includes the application's context. That is, it will create a URL that is relative to the web server's root (/) directory. `validation.jsp` contains the following code in order to render all the JavaScript functions from the `validation-rules.xml` file:

```
<%@ page language="java" contentType="javascript/x-javascript" %>
<%@ taglib uri="http://jakarta.apache.org/struts/tags-html"
    prefix="html" %>
<html:javascript dynamicJavascript="false" staticJavascript="true"/>
```

Testing the Validation

Now that you've configured everything, let's test it out! To do this, you'll need to log in to the `struts-resume` application and click on the **Edit Profile** link. This will bring up your user information. If you clear the username field, you'll get the following error:

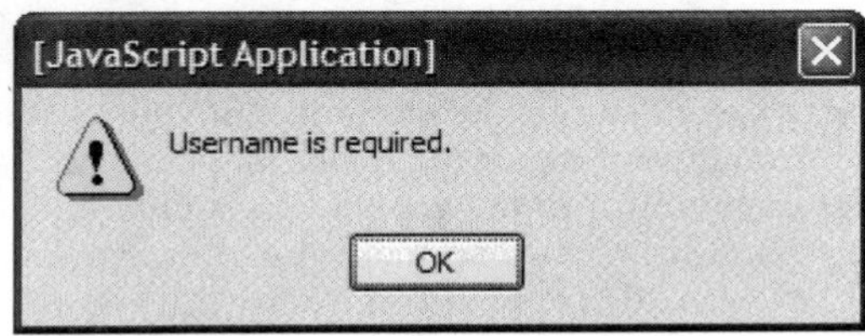

When turning off JavaScript in your browser, the Validator will catch the error on the server-side and you'll get the message shown in the following screen shot. So if you don't want to use JavaScript in your application, virtually no coding is necessary, save the XDoclet tags. If you aren't using XDoclet, you'll need to configure `validation.xml` manually–I like to refer to this as *declarative validation.*

Main Menu

User Profile

Username is required.

Username

First Name Matt

Last Name Raible

You can also use the Validator to perform validation based on variables, such as validating that a zip code matches a regular expression. This is possible with a mask that contains a regular expression as its value. For regular expressions that might be used more than once, it's a good idea to define them as constants in your `validation.xml` file. Since we're using XDoclet, this can be done in a `validation-global.xml` file, which lives in our merge directory. In the `struts-resume` application, this is `metadata/web/`.

```
<constant>
  <constant-name>zip</constant-name>
  <constant-value>^\d{5}\d*$</constant-value>
</constant>
```

This regular expression says that `zip` must be five characters long and all characters must be digits. To validate a zip code in the `userForm`, you'll need to configure `validation.xml` like so:

```
<field property="postalCode" depends="required,mask">
  <msg name="required" key="errors.required"/>
  <msg name="mask" key="errors.zip"/>
```

```
    <arg0 key="userForm.postalCode"/>
    <var>
      <var-name>mask</var-name>
      <var-value>${zip}</var-value>
    </var>
  </field>
```

As mentioned earlier, the <msg> elements can be eliminated if you want to use the default values for the validators. However, the default error message key for mask is `errors.invalid`, which is simply `{0}, is invalid`. To enhance usability of the application, a different key (such as `errors.zip`) with more information is probably better (such as `The {0} field must be a 5-digit number`). To configure this for the `postalCode` field is easy with XDoclet. All you need to do is add a tag to specify the rule and the variable's name-value pair:

```
  * @struts.validator type="mask" msgkey="errors.zip"
  * @struts.validator-var name="mask" value="${zip}"
```

Advanced Validator Features

Other features of the Validator that I haven't mentioned yet include multipage validation, indexed property validation, conditional validation, and DynaFormValidation. Multipage validation allows you to spread your validation rules for a form across more than one page. This can be very helpful when you have a wizardlike form for gathering information in your application. To configure this, you need to add a hidden field to specify the page number in your JSP:

```
  <html:hidden property="page" value="1"/>
```

This is complimented by adding a `page` attribute to the field's validation rule in `validation.xml`. In the examples you've seen so far, the fields have a `property` and `depends` attribute. Add the `page` attribute and now your form can contain validation that is invoked across different JSP pages!

```
  <field property="firstName" depends="required,mask" page="1">
```

I really like this feature because it's so simple to configure.

Indexed property validation allows you to have forms contained within forms or subforms. For instance, in your application, a `ResumeForm` can contain one-to-many `SkillGroupForms`. `SkillGroups` describe a group of skills. On a technical résumé, a good `SkillGroup` might be "Java" or at an even higher level, "Programming Languages." Furthermore, `SkillGroupForms` can contain one-to-many `SkillForms`. To elaborate on the Java example, you might have `SkillForms` such as "Swing," "JDBC," and "XML." A nice user interface for editing these would allow you to view all your résumé's `SkillGroups` and their subsequent `SkillForms`.

Displaying all this isn't a big deal, because you can use a `<logic:iterate>` tag or `<c:forEach>`. However, to save them, you have to know what row (or form) the user edited. This is where indexed properties come to the rescue. You can basically add a getter/setter to your form that allows for setting/getting nested form values. Please see the section on indexed properties and their use with the nested tag library for more information. To configure the Validator to validate an indexed property, you need to add an `indexedListProperty` attribute to your `<field>` element:

```
<field property="groupName" depends="required" indexedListProperty="skills">
  <var>
    <var-name>field[0]</var-name>
    <var-value>name</var-value>
  </var>
  <var>
    <var-name>field-indexed[0]</var-name>
    <var-value>true</var-value>
  </var>
  <var>
    <var-name>field-test[0]</var-name>
    <var-value>NOTNULL</var-value>
  </var>
</field>
```

This states that the `skills` property contains a list and the required field within this skills list is the `name` property.

A new feature recently added to the Validator is an ability to conditionally require validator fields based on the value of other fields. It allows you to define logic such as "only validate this field if field X is non-null and field Y contains 'male'". The Validator has support for validating indexed properties, indicated in the previous example by the `"[0]"` indicator. However, it doesn't support dynamic indexed properties at the time of this writing. Which is to say that you must know the number of child (indexed) properties and configure the Validator accordingly. Conditionally validating can be very useful, but since I haven't used it in `struts-resume`, I recommend consulting the online documentation for more information.

Using the Validator with DynaActionForms

The final feature of the validator I would like to mention is that it can also be used with `DynaActionForms`. As you saw earlier, `DynaActionForms` are forms that are created by specifying the form's properties in `struts-config.xml`. This can save time when developing concrete forms for an application. Personally, I prefer using concrete Java classes for my forms, rather than cluttering up a configuration file with form properties. The main motivation behind `DynaActionForms` was to speed up and facilitate Struts development so developers could quickly create new forms. Using XDoclet to generate your forms is even faster, because it also (in my example) creates the persistence layer. Using XDoclet also creates the form-bean entries and `validation.xml` for you, while if you use `DynaActionForms`, you still need to manually create `validation.xml`. That said, creating a `DynaActionForm` that uses the Validator is as simple as specifying which type of bean it is. A regular `UserForm` created as a `DynaActionForm` might look as follows:

```
<form-bean name="userForm"
           type="org.apache.struts.action.DynaActionForm">
  ...
</form-bean>
```

To make this form validator-enabled, all you need to do is change the `type` attribute:

```
<form-bean name="userForm"
           type="org.apache.struts.validator.DynaValidatorForm">
  ...
</form-bean>
```

Configuring the validator might look like a lot of work; after all, you do have to add three different pieces of code to your JSP page: the form's `onsubmit` handler, the button's `onclick` handler, and the JavaScript declarations at the bottom of the form. However, it's easy to automate this process using the StrutsGen tool. I've simply modified the `ActionForm_jsp.xdt` file (located at `tools/strutsgen/src`) to include all of this validator-specific code, and now my initial forms will be generated with validator support! How sweet is that?

Performing Validation on Indexed Tags

The Validator is also capable of performing validation on indexed tags. You simply need to add a `[#]` to your `validation.xml` for the field you want to validate. As an example, if you wanted to configure the `ResumeForm` to require the first `SkillForm`'s name, you could configure the `validation.xml` file with something like the following:

```
<form name="resumeForm">
  ...
  <field property="skills[0]name"
         depends="required">
    <msg name="required"
         key="errors.required"/>

    <arg0 key="skillForm.name"/>
  </field>
```

The one problem with the Validator's support of indexed properties is that it doesn't support a dynamic number of indexed properties. That is, you must code the actual number of children: `skills[0]` to `skills[n]` for each child you want to validate. I've seen patches submitted for adding this functionality, but it hasn't been implemented at the time of this writing.

Using Built-In Struts Actions

If you've already built a Struts application, you might have found that you developed actions to follow an MVC pattern, but you really didn't need them. Or maybe you linked directly to JSP pages and bypassed the recommended "every link should go through a controller" model. I know I did–until I discovered the actions that Struts has built in. I now think of these as a bunch of eager benchwarmers saying, "put me in coach, I promise I'll make you proud!" However, you might not realize they exist. Therefore, I'll introduce these well-conditioned actions now, so you'll get a taste of their potential and maybe even let them into the game.

There are five built-in actions with Struts and the first three (`ForwardAction`, `IncludeAction`, and `SwitchAction`) require no coding at all. The last two, `DispatchAction` and `LookupDispatchAction`, are designed to promote code reduction and reuse.

ForwardAction

The `ForwardAction` can be used to redirect to a JSP page, but still utilize the built-in features of a controller–such as securing actions with the `roles` attribute. It can also be very useful when migrating a model 1 architecture (that is, JSP pages only) to Struts. In your example resume application, a `ForwardAction` is used to direct users to the Main Menu page. To configure a `ForwardAction`, you simply specify the `org.apache.struts.actions.ForwardAction` class as the type, and the JSP page (or Tiles definition) as the parameter.

```
<action path="/mainMenu"
        type="org.apache.struts.actions.ForwardAction"
        parameter=".mainMenu"/>
```

I've also created a global-forward to call this action:

```
<forward name="mainMenu"
         path="/mainMenu.do"/>
```

After configuring the action and forward, it can then be called in your application's start page (`index.jsp`):

```
<logic:redirect forward="mainMenu"/>
```

You should also note that the previous action and forward definitions are in the `metadata/web` directory in the files `struts-actions.xml` and `global-forwards.xml`, respectively. XDoclet grabs these fragments and merges them into the main `struts-config.xml` file when the `strutsconfigxml` task is executed. You'll need to define your actions and forwards in these files for all three of the "no-coding-required" actions.

IncludeAction

`IncludeAction` was developed for the same reason as `ForwardAction`. It allows you to integrate servlet-based components that utilize `RequestDispatcher.include()`. Like `ForwardAction`, it only requires that you specify `name`, `parameter`, and `type` attributes. Personally, I've never used it and I've never seen it in use, but here's how you might configure it:

```
<action path="/resumeComments"
        type="org.apache.struts.actions.IncludeAction"
        parameter="/path/to/servlet"/>
```

SwitchAction

The `SwitchAction` was designed to allow switching of application modules. Please refer to the section about modules later for a full description and how to configure it.

DispatchAction

`DispatchAction` and `LookupDispatchAction` are two great additions to the Struts framework. For the first application I developed, I ended up creating an Edit and Save action for each entity's Create, Retrieve, Update, and Delete (CRUD) classes. After writing the classes, I noticed that there was a lot of duplicate code in the Edit (used for retrieval and searching) and Save classes. `DispatchAction`, and its friendly sibling, `LookupDispatchAction`, allow you to create different methods in your action that are "dispatched" to according to a parameter.

This means that rather than writing an `execute()` method in your action, you can write methods that detail your business logic (such as `add()`, `save()`, `remove()`, `search()`). Both dispatch action classes are subclasses of `Action`, so it's still possible to use the `execute()` method, but you'll have to build your own dispatching mechanism in this method if you want the dispatch behavior. These actions use reflection (which is much faster in JDK 1.3 and 1.4) to choose and invoke the appropriate methods.

Therefore, your methods must have a public modifier or you'll get the Struts white screen of death (or whatever background color you have your browser set to!).

To use the dispatch action, you simply have to extend it rather than Action in your Action class. I usually create a BaseAction for my applications and use that to extend the appropriate Action class. What advantages does this provide? By using a BaseAction, you only have to extend Struts's Action class in one location, and you can elect to switch to a DispatchAction or LookupDispatchAction at any time. Also, I've seen cases in which developers use BaseAction to process or dispatch, but I've never had the need to do things that way. Which is to say that there is an execute() method on the BaseAction class, and it's configured as the servlet for Struts in the web.xml. To do this in struts-resume, you could simply change the following line in metadata/web/servlets.xml from

```
<servlet-class>org.apache.struts.action.ActionServlet</servlet-class>
```

to

```
<servlet-class>org.appfuse.webapp.action.BaseAction</servlet-class>
```

If you want to perform logic before dispatching to your methods, your best bet is to dig into the Struts code (good ol' open source!) and use DispatchAction or LookupDispatchAction as your base class. You can also use a preExecute() method in your base class (or in each class) that you call at the beginning of each method. I've had good success with simply using a BaseAction to hold common action methods. For instance, I've used my BaseAction to implement a convenience method, and getUserForm(session) to get a user's information from the session.

Once you've written your action, you then need to configure your <action-mappings> with a parameter appropriately named method or action–I use method to be consistent with the documentation, even though I prefer action:

```
<action path="/test" type="org.example.MyAction" name="MyForm" scope="request"
        input="/test.jsp" parameter="method"/>
```

Then you'll need to add a hidden field to your forms that call this action. For instance:

```
<html:hidden property="method" value="add"/>
```

You can also do this with a normal HTML tag if you aren't trying to grab the method property from your form:

```
<input type="hidden" name="method" id="method" value="add" />
```

It's also plausible that you won't always call your dispatch action with a form, say if editing an item from a list. For this, you can use a forward defined by the method already defined:

```
<forward name="editUser" path="/editUser.do?method=edit"/>
```

There are, however, issues with DispatchAction. For instance, if you have a form with a number of buttons (such as **Add**, **Copy**, **Save**, **Delete**) to perform different actions, you have to use JavaScript to manipulate the method hidden field. While JavaScript is a perfectly acceptable way to do this, there's an easier way—LookupDispatchAction.

LookupDispatchAction

The LookupDispatchAction class is a subclass of DispatchAction that allows you to map button captions to method names. Furthermore, it reads the button captions from your Struts ResourceBundle (ApplicationResources.properties). This means that you can easily map the key button.save to the save() method.

To implement a LookupDispatchAction in your project, you must first extend the LookupDispathAction in your class. Again, I recommend doing this in a BaseAction class, and then extending your project's actions from this one. You'll need to add a parameter to your <action-mappings>, which is very similar to DispatchAction:

```
<action path="/test"
        type="org.example.MyAction"
        name="MyForm"
        scope="request"
        input="/test.jsp"
        parameter="action"/>
```

You could set the parameter to method, but action is demonstrated in the LookupDispatchAction's Javadoc, so I've used it here to avoid confusion. The action request parameter will be used to locate the corresponding key in ApplicationResources. After configuring your struts-config.xml appropriately, or your XDoclet tags in your action class, you'll then need to implement the getKeyMethodMap() method in your subclass like so:

```
protected Map getKeyMethodMap() {

  Map map = new HashMap();

  map.put("button.add", "add");
  map.put("button.delete", "delete");

  return map;
}
```

Your ApplicationResources.properties file determines the text that appears on your buttons and therefore should contain entries for both of these keys:

```
button.add=Add Record
button.delete=Delete Record
```

Finally, you need to set the `property` attribute to `action` for your form's Submit buttons in order to pass the buttons' caption to your action:

```
<html:submit property="action">
  <bean:message key="button.add"/>
</html:submit>

<html:submit property="action">
  <bean:message key="button.delete"/>
</html:submit>
```

In the `struts-resume` application, the `BaseAction` extends `LookupDispatchAction`. I've also added my own little enhancement to the `getKeyMethodMap()` method, so that the key or value pairs are loaded from another property's file. This allows mapping new methods to buttons without recompilation. This might seem like overkill, but it only took a couple minutes to implement. One problem I've seen with this class is if you use JavaScript to disable your Submit buttons after they've been clicked, the action parameter won't be sent.

> *More information on each of these built-in actions can be found in the Struts Javadocs at http://jakarta.apache.org/struts/api/org/apache/struts/actions/package-frame.html.*

Using the Tiles Framework to Assemble the View

Tiles is a Composite View framework for assembling presentation pages from component parts. Each part, or tile, can be reused as often as needed throughout your application. You can use Tiles in any JSP or servlet application, but it was originally designed for Struts and is therefore easiest to use within Struts. Since Struts 1.1 Beta 2, the Tiles framework has been integrated into the core Struts library (`struts.jar`). Tiles is often seen as a heavyweight, configuration-intensive plug-in, when in fact it offers the same simple functionality as the (now deprecated) `struts-template` tag library.

Tiles was developed by Cedric Dumoulin, and in my opinion is one of the best things that ever happened for JSP developers. Standards like CSS and XHTML are also awesome (and have provided more structure to develop web applications that work across browsers), but Tiles has made it so much *easier.* Tiles will reduce your development time in building web applications and will also make it relatively easy to change the entire application's look. It offers the best layout framework I know of, although there are others that have fervent supporters such as SiteMesh (http://www.opensymphony.com/sitemesh) from OpenSymphony.

I've developed several JSP applications over the past few years, and I've laid them out using many different techniques. The first technique was similar to how you would develop a static website, where each JSP page contained all the layout elements of a typical HTML page. This included the `<html>` declaration, the `<head>` element, `<body>`, and any `<div>`s or `<table>`s within the body as well as the actual content. While this is generally easier for HTML developers to grasp, it's definitely the hard way. If you ever need to carry out a site redesign, chances are you'll need to meddle with every JSP file to do so. Of course, HTML editors (such as Dreamweaver, BBEdit, and HomeSite) will make this easier with their global search and replace features, but you can easily mess up your HTML at the same time.

An easier way is to *include* elements that are common to all pages. Such elements include the `<head>` element, which contains your CSS and JavaScript references, or a menu that is common to all pages.

While this approach is much easier than the first approach, you're still duplicating code between all your pages to include these external elements. It might only be three or four lines of code, but nevertheless, if you forget to include the header, chances are you won't find out until you (or your users) run your page through a browser.

If you're using Struts, I'd recommend Tiles because it offers many built-in interoperability features with Struts. Just like the Validator, it can be used on its own by simply making a servlet entry in your application's `web.xml`. However, I won't explore this configuration because this chapter focuses on Struts-based solutions. I will illustrate the templating system used in the example resume application and how I've implemented Tiles in this particular application. The architecture and techniques I'll be using have been tried and proven in production applications. Tiles can be used in many different ways for building portal sites and menuing systems as well as customization.

Detailed online documentation for Tiles can be found at http://www.lifl.fr/~dumoulin/tiles/.

Using Tiles in the Example Application

First of all, let's see how to integrate Tiles into the Struts application. With Struts 1.1, it's much like the Validator and only needs to be registered as a plug-in in your `struts-config.xml` file:

```
<plug-in className="org.apache.struts.tiles.TilesPlugin" >
  <set-property property="definitions-config"
                value="/WEB-INF/tiles-config.xml" />
  <set-property property="moduleAware" value="true" />
  <set-property property="definitions-parser-validate" value="true" />
</plug-in>
```

If you're using XDoclet, this will need to go in a `struts-plugins.xml` file in your `merge` directory. There are basically two ways to use Tile:

- The first is through a JSP page that includes other pages as a template.
- The second is to use an XML file to define the different components in a given page, also known as a **definition.**

I highly recommend the XML-configuration route because it enables you to change page definitions in one location, rather than on a page-by-page basis. It also supports inheritance so you can define a base definition with the same header and footer, and then you don't need to specify these in the child definitions. The first property, `definitions-config`, points to the file you use to define your definitions. It also supports a comma-delimited list of file paths, which might be handy if you have many pages or definitions in your application. The second property, `moduleAware`, allows Tiles to recognize modules (formerly known as subapplications). I'll describe these further in an upcoming section.

The basis of Tiles is that it allows you to define a "template" for your entire application, or several templates depending on your needs. This template will generally look like a regular HTML file, with all the basic elements, such as `<html>`, `<head>`, `<body>`, and any layout elements, such as `<div>`s or `<table>`s. If you're still using tables for laying out your web applications, I implore you to try a tableless layout with `<div>`s and CSS because it will make your pages much lighter and smaller for your clients. XHTML and CSS, and a modern browser of course, make this much easier. The following is a very simple template for Tiles:

```
<!DOCTYPE html PUBLIC "-//W3C//DTD XHTML 1.0 Strict//EN"
    "http://www.w3.org/TR/xhtml1/DTD/xhtml1-strict.dtd">

<%@ taglib uri="http://jakarta.apache.org/struts/tags/struts-tiles"
    prefix="tiles" %>
<%@ taglib uri="http://jakarta.apache.org/struts/tags/struts-bean"
    prefix="bean" %>

<html:html xhtml="true" locale="true">
  <head>
    <%-- Push tiles attributes in page context --%>
    <tiles:importAttribute />
    <title><bean:message name="title.key"/></title>
  </head>
  <body>
    <div id="header">
      <tiles:insert attribute="header"/>
    </div>
    <div id="menu">
      <tiles:insert attribute="menu" ignore="true"/>
    </div>
    <div id="content">
      <%@ include file="/common/messages.jsp" %>
      <h1><bean:message name="heading.key"/></h1>
      <tiles:insert attribute="content"/>
    </div>
    <div id="footer">
      <tiles:insert attribute="footer"/>
    </div>
  </body>
</html:html>
```

The `ignore` attribute for the `menu` attribute signifies that the menu isn't a required element in this template. Note that the Tiles tag library can be used in place of the `struts-template` tag library. It offers the same functionality, but also allows for more advanced features.

In the previous template, you can see that there are attributes that you import and attributes you insert. Basically, the `<tiles:importAttribute>` is used for the `<bean:message/>` tags. When you configure the application to use this template, you can actually tell it which key from your `ApplicationResources.properties` file to use for the `title.key` and for the `heading.key`. The `<tiles:insert />` tag is used to insert or include a JSP page, but this could also be a URL to any component within your application.

If you're inserting JSP pages into your Tiles template, you'll need to configure your JSP pages so they can be executed independently of other pages. By this, I mean to say that they could be referenced with a dynamic include (`<jsp:include>`) rather than a static include (`<%@ include />`). Therefore, you must reference the appropriate tag libraries at the top of each page. To make development easier and faster, I usually create a JSP file with all my tag library declarations, and then use a static include to include them on every page. You can see an example of this in the struts-resume application. The previous template will render a layout similar to the one you saw earlier in the chapter:

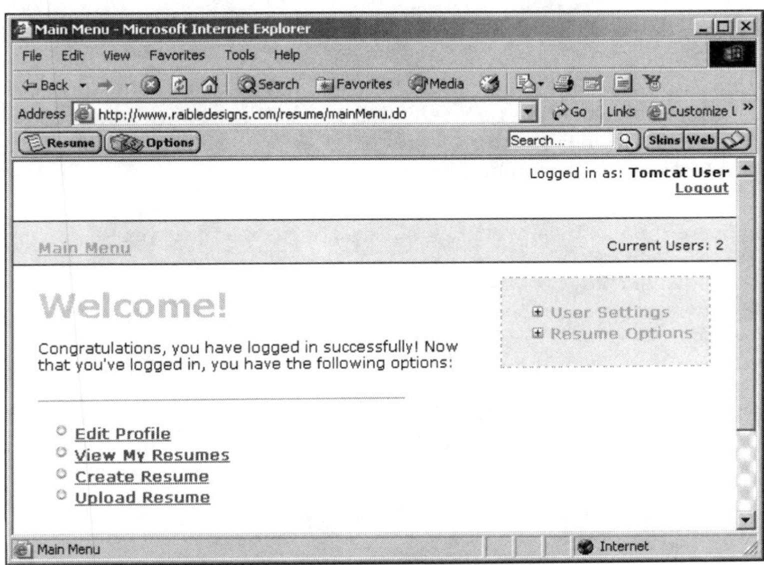

Tiles templates, also known as layouts, can be referenced using two different techniques. The first is by using a JSP page. For example, you could put all the JSP pages in a pages directory. This technique comes in handy when using JSP pages to compose Tiles pages. You can simply put all your different page sections (or **tiles**) in the pages directory, and then reference them from the root directory. For instance, this is what a login.jsp page might look like in the root directory:

```
<%@ include file="/common/taglibs.jsp"%>
<tiles:insert page="/layouts/simpleLayout.jsp" flush="true">
  <tiles:put name="title.key" value="login.title"/>
  <tiles:put name="heading.key" value="login.heading"/>
  <tiles:put name="header" value="/common/header.jsp "/>
  <tiles:put name="menu" value="/menu.html"/>
  <tiles:put name="content" value="/WEB-INF/pages/login.jsp"/>
  <tiles:put name="footer" value="/common/footer.jsp "/>
</tiles:insert>
```

The second option is to use an XML file and create **definitions** for each page. This is nice because definitions can extend each other as well as provide a central repository of your page composition information. Furthermore, definitions can still be references from a JSP page (when using a /do/* mapping) or as ActionForward paths in struts-config.xml. Let's look at the how the previous JSP code might look in a tiles-config.xml file:

```
<definition name=".login" path="/layouts/simpleLayout.jsp">
  <put name="title.key" value="login.title"/>
  <put name="heading.key" value="login.heading"/>
  <put name="header" value="/common/header.jsp"/>
```

```
    <put name="menu" value="/menu.html"/>
    <put name="content" value="/WEB-INF/pages/welcome.jsp"/>
    <put name="footer" value="/common/footer.jsp"/>
</definition>
```

One of the principal advantages of using definitions is that you can inherit properties from each other. In this way, you can create a `baseLayout` definition that all definitions inherit from, and child definitions won't need to define certain properties, such as the header and footer. The previous definition can be refactored to something like this:

```
<definition name="baseLayout" path="/layouts/baseLayout.jsp">
  <put name="title.key"/>
  <put name="heading.key"/>
  <put name="header" value="/common/header.jsp"/>
  <put name="footer" value="/common/footer.jsp"/>
</definition>

<definition name=".login" extends="baseLayout">
  <put name="title.key" value="login.title"/>
  <put name="heading.key" value="login.heading"/>
  <put name="menu" value="/menu.html"/>
  <put name="content" value="/WEB-INF/pages/welcome.jsp"/>
</definition>
```

In the previous `".login"` definition, you'll notice that I've prefixed the tile name with a period (`.`). This dot-notation is the recommended practice for naming Tiles. Since Tiles's definitions can be references in a forward's "path" attribute, this prefix makes them easier to recognize.

A definition can be referenced in a JSP page if you don't want to forward to it from an action. In `struts-resume`, I do this in the `login.jsp` page. I'm protecting all `*.do` mappings with a `<security-constraint>`, so I'm unable to access any action without authenticating. The content of the `login.jsp` page is short and simple:

```
<%@ include file="/common/taglibs.jsp"%>
<tiles:insert definition=".login" flush="true"/>
```

In the examples provided, you'll notice that messages come from `ApplicationResources.properties` for title and heading settings, but another option is available. This may be why Tiles seems so intimidating to some–there are so many options! However, I do want to show you some other options that might be more suitable for you. Rather than using the `ApplicationResources.properties` file to represent the title or heading, you can code the strings directly in your definition or JSP:

```
<put name="title" value="Login to Struts Resume"/>
```

Rather than using `<tiles:importAttributes/>` and `<bean:message key="title.key"/>`, you can use `<tiles:getAsString name="title"/>`. You might think you've lost the Internationalization (I18n) support in this process, but Tiles allows for an alternative way of achieving

I18n: creating separate XML definition files for each locale. Using this strategy, you would have a `tiles_config_en.xml` for English, `tiles_config_ru.xml` for Russian, and so on. Using the `ApplicationResources.properties` file is an easier way to internationalize your application, because then all language changes are available in one file.

Earlier I mentioned that CSS stylesheets can be used to greatly improve your layout flexibility. I've worked on many projects where we used different stylesheets for different pages or even for different users. There are two approaches that I've used to switch stylesheets, the first being on a page basis, and the second for users. The first uses Tiles definitions to set the stylesheet for any given page. While you're at it, you might as well add this same feature for including JavaScript files. First of all, you can add the files you want to include in your `baseLayout` definition:

```
<definition name="baseLayout" path="/layouts/baseLayout.jsp">
  <put name="title.key"/>
  <put name="heading.key"/>
  <put name="header" value="/common/header.jsp"/>
  <put name="footer" value="/common/footer.jsp"/>

  <!-- Default JavaScript File -->
  <putList name="scripts">
    <add value="/scripts/global.js"/>
  </putList>

  <!-- Default Stylesheet File -->
  <putList name="styles">
    <add value="/styles/default.css"/>
  </putList>
</definition>
```

Then in the `baseLayout.jsp` file you can use Tiles tags and the JSTL to get these attributes and render them as follows:

```
<%-- Get JavaScript List --%>
<tiles:useAttribute id="scriptList" name="scripts"
                    classname="java.util.List" ignore="true"/>

<c:forEach var="js" items="${scriptList}">
  <script type="text/JavaScript"
        src="<%=request.getContextPath()%><c:out value="${js}"/>">
  </script>
</c:forEach>

<%-- Get List of Stylesheets --%>
<tiles:useAttribute id="styleList" name="styles"
                    classname="java.util.List" ignore="true"/>

<c:forEach var="css" items="${styleList}">
  <link rel="stylesheet" type="text/css" media="all"
      href="<%=request.getContextPath()%><c:out value="${css}"/>" />
</c:forEach>
```

I had to add the scriptlet `<%=request.getContextPath()%>` since the `add value` inside a `putList` only renders the literal value. I didn't want to hard-code the `contextPath` in my the definitions file, so this was a simple solution. If you're using JSP 2.0, you can replace the `<c:out value="${variable}"/>` with `${variable}`. You can also replace the `<link>` tag for the stylesheet with the more modern method of importing stylesheets, using `@import`. Using this syntax, the stylesheet import would look as follows:

```
<style type="text/css" media="all">
  <c:forEach var="css" items="${styleList}">
    @import url(<%=request.getContextPath()%><c:out value="${css}"/>);
  </c:forEach>
</style>
```

This technique can be used to decrease the amount of HTML written as well as to disable stylesheets for older browsers (that is, Netscape 4.x). This may sound foolish, but why would you want to disable stylesheets for older browsers? The reason is simple. If your site is developed using CSS and `<div>`s for layout, the chances are that viewing your site without stylesheets is still readable, but it's just plain text, in black and white, with no fancy layout. This allows older browsers to still see your content, and you don't have to worry about making your CSS compatible with old browsers. Of course, this luxury is purely dependent on your customers. My advice is to drop support for older browsers–I guarantee that that alone will speed up your productivity. If you're willing to use a standards-compliant server (J2EE), why not expect a standards-compliant client? Surely most users have upgraded to newer browsers by now.

In the `struts-resume` application, I'm using the `<link>` syntax so we can use a stylesheet switcher in the future. Paul Sowden developed the stylesheet switcher I've implemented and instructions on how to implement it are documented at http://www.alistapart.com/stories/alternate/. Basically, it uses JavaScript and cookies to disable or enable your preferred stylesheets. I've used it on several projects and have found it very useful.

After you've set up the template and `baseLayout` definition to render multiple stylesheets, you can override the list in a child definition. One thing to note is `<putList>` doesn't allow extension, so you have to replace the entire thing. The means that if all you want to do is add an additional stylesheet, you also have to create include the original (`default.css`) stylesheet. In the `mainMenu` definition, you're using the **Struts-Menu** (http://www.sourceforge.net/projects/struts-menu) as your menuing system. This menu requires an additional stylesheet file as well as an additional JavaScript file. Therefore, you should replace the original lists with new ones:

```
<putList name="scripts">
  <add value="/scripts/global.js"/>
  <add value="/scripts/menuExpandable.js"/>
</putList>

<putList name="styles">
  <add value="/styles/default.css"/>
  <add value="/styles/menuExpandable.css"/>
</putList>
```

Pretty slick huh? I've used this technique for the last year and it's worked great.

Tiles, XDoclet, and Forwards

Using Tiles to assemble and define your pages can be quite handy, but how do you call these definitions? The easiest way is to reference your Tiles definitions is using an `ActionForward`. When you add the Tiles plug-in to your Struts configuration file, a smart Tiles-aware processor is used to execute requests. This processor, named `TilesRequestProcessor`, subclasses the Struts default `RequestProcessor` to intercept calls to includes and forwards to see if the specified URI (path) is a definition name.

To configure Tiles definition forwarding in your application, all you need to do is match up the "path" attribute of a <forward> with the "name" attribute of a definition. For example, in `struts-resume`, the `ResumeAction`'s `search()` method returns an `ActionForward` to a local `<forward>` named "list":

```
return mapping.findForward("list");
```

This forward is defined in `struts-config.xml` for the `ResumeAction` class as follows:

```
<action path="/editResume" type="org.appfuse.webapp.action.ResumeAction"
        name="resumeForm" scope="request" input="viewResumes"
        parameter="action" unknown="false" validate="false">

  <forward name="edit" path=".resumeDetail" redirect="false"/>
  <forward name="list" path=".resumeList" redirect="false"/>
</action>
```

In `tiles-config.xml`, the `".resumeList"` definition is a simple definition that defines a title, header, and content page.

```
<definition name=".resumeList" extends=".mainMenu">
  <put name="title.key"   value="resumeList.title" />
  <put name="heading.key" value="resumeList.heading" />
  <put name="content" value="/WEB-INF/pages/resumeList.jsp"/>
</definition>
```

In `struts-resume`, the `BaseAction` class extends `LookupDispatchAction`, and Tiles definitions are used extensively for assembling pages. The logic flow from a JSP's URL to an action's method to a Tiles definition can be somewhat confusing, especially when you bring XDoclet into the mix to define the action's mapping and local forwards. Hopefully, the following flow chart can help you understand the logical flow of it all:

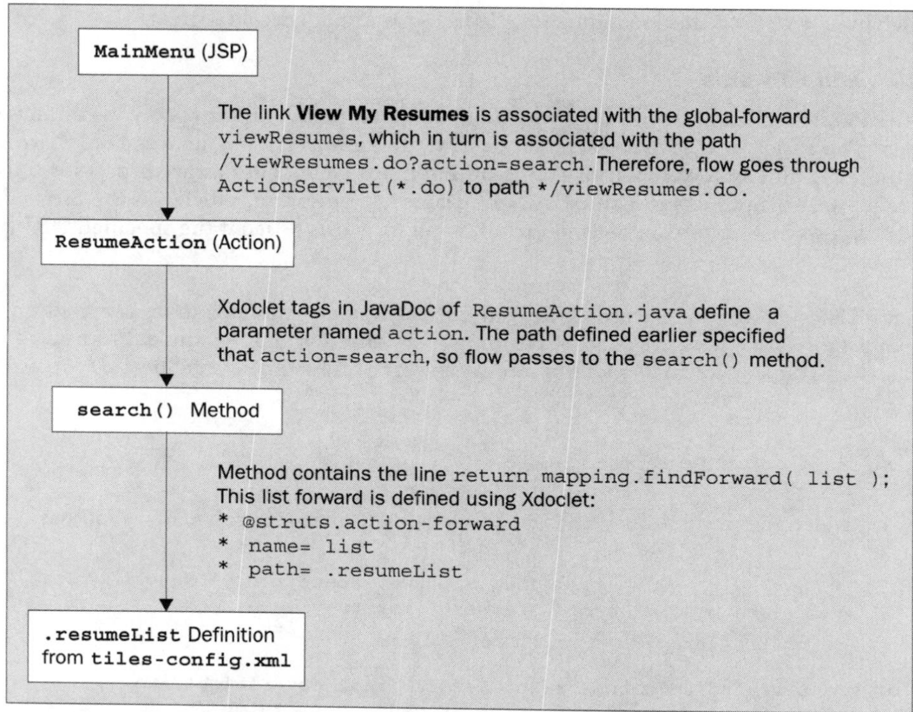

In the previous diagram, the `ResumeAction` class extends `LookupDispatchAction`. Basically, it allows you to use a parameter (action) to specify which method to call in your `Action` class. The figure shows the XDoclet tags used to create the `ResumeAction`'s mapping in the Struts configuration file as well its local forward. All of these tags are written in the class's header Javadoc comments.

Tiles Controllers

Tiles controllers can be very helpful in improving the architecture of your Tiles-enabled application. They haven't received much press in current publications, but can be a very useful feature. At its core, a Tiles controller is designed to prepare data for presentation on a tile. You might think of it as a mini-action. However, these controllers aren't designed to determine application flow; that's the responsibility of the `ActionServlet`. If you're developing a portal site or you have tiles that require their own custom data, you should definitely considering using one.

Of course it will be easier to understand if I give you an example. Therefore, I've created a feature for `struts-resume` that counts the current number of active sessions and displays it as "Current Users." I did this by first creating a `UserCounterListener` that implements `ServletContextListener` and `HttpSessionListener`. This listener increments an application-scoped variable when new sessions are created and decrements from the same variable when sessions are destroyed. This source file is located in struts-resume at `src/web/org/appfuse/webapp/listener`. I've used XDoclet's `@web:listener` tag to create a `<listener>` entry for this class in `web.xml`.

To implement a Tiles controller, I created a `UserCounterController` class that implements the `Controller` interface and its `perform()` method:

```
public final class UserCounterController implements Controller {

    /**
     * This method illustrates a simple example of using a Tiles Controller
     * to get a "current users" counter for this application.
     *
     * @param tileContext Current tile context
     * @param request Current request
     * @param response Current response
     * @param servletContext Current Servlet Context
     */
  public void perform(ComponentContext tilesContext,
                      HttpServletRequest request,
                      HttpServletResponse response,
                      ServletContext servletContext)
                      throws ServletException, IOException {
    // Get the number of current users from the application's context
    String userCounter =
        (String) servletContext.getAttribute(UserCounterListener.COUNT_KEY);

      // Add this number to the request for display
      request.setAttribute(UserCounterListener.COUNT_KEY, userCounter);
  }
}
```

You can see that the `perform()` method's signature is similar to the `Action` class's signature–except there's no `ActionMapping` or `ActionForm`. The `ComponentContext` is a scope similar to that of request or session, however it's specific to Tiles and is used to store its configuration information.

The `UserCounterController` is simply grabbing an attribute out of the application scope and putting it into the request scope. However, you could easily add more complex logic in this method. In this example, you're storing the attribute in the request attribute for simplicity, but it could also be stored in the `ComponentContext` using the following code:

```
tilesContext.putAttribute(UserCounterListener.COUNT_KEY, userCounter);
```

This would ensure that the attribute was only available for this tile. To configure `struts-resume` to use this controller, I edited `tiles-config.xml` file (in `web/WEB-INF`). I decided I wanted to display this "Current Users" counter in the header of the page–and since I only defined the header in the `"baseLayout"` definition, this was an easy change. Before the change, the header tile was simply pointing to the `header.jsp` file:

```
<definition name="baseLayout" path="/layouts/baseLayout.jsp">
...
    <put name="header" value="/common/header.jsp"/>
...
</definition>
```

To make the *header* tile controller-enabled, I created a new definition for it and pointed to it from the `baseLayout` definition:

```
<definition name="baseLayout" path="/layouts/baseLayout.jsp">
...
    <put name="header" value=".header.userCount"/>
...
</definition>

<definition name=".header.userCount" path="/common/header.jsp"
            controllerClass="org.appfuse.webapp.action.UserCounterController" />
```

This means that for each page that the `".header.userCount"` tile appears on, `UserCounterController.perform()` will be called. To display the counter in the `header.jsp`, I then added the following JSP code:

```
<%-- Check to ensure "userCounter" is in request, if not, don't display --%>
<c:if test="${requestScope.userCounter != null}">
<div id="activeUsers">
  <bean:message key="mainMenu.activeUsers"/>:
  <c:out value="${userCounter}" />
</div>
</c:if>
```

To test it, I logged into the `struts-resume` application with two different browsers, which created two different sessions:

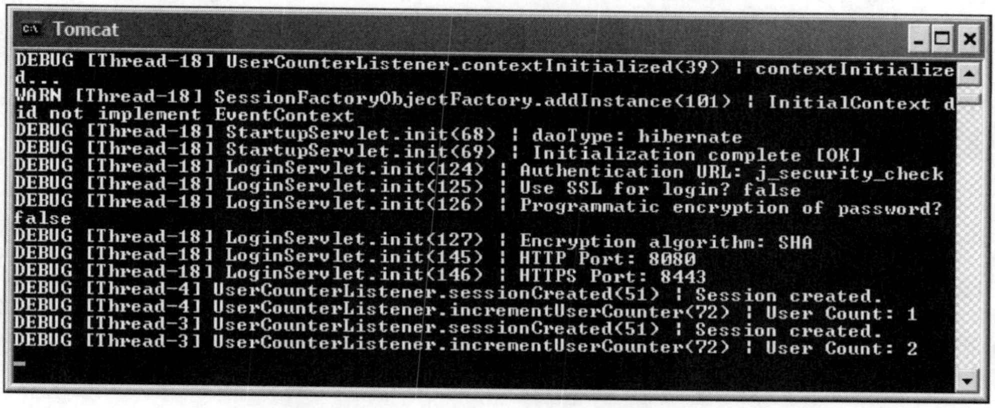

```
Tomcat
DEBUG [Thread-18] UserCounterListener.contextInitialized(39) | contextInitialize
d...
WARN [Thread-18] SessionFactoryObjectFactory.addInstance(101) | InitialContext d
id not implement EventContext
DEBUG [Thread-18] StartupServlet.init(68) | daoType: hibernate
DEBUG [Thread-18] StartupServlet.init(69) | Initialization complete [OK]
DEBUG [Thread-18] LoginServlet.init(124) | Authentication URL: j_security_check
DEBUG [Thread-18] LoginServlet.init(125) | Use SSL for login? false
DEBUG [Thread-18] LoginServlet.init(126) | Programmatic encryption of password?
false
DEBUG [Thread-18] LoginServlet.init(127) | Encryption algorithm: SHA
DEBUG [Thread-18] LoginServlet.init(145) | HTTP Port: 8080
DEBUG [Thread-18] LoginServlet.init(146) | HTTPS Port: 8443
DEBUG [Thread-4] UserCounterListener.sessionCreated(51) | Session created.
DEBUG [Thread-4] UserCounterListener.incrementUserCounter(72) | User Count: 1
DEBUG [Thread-3] UserCounterListener.sessionCreated(51) | Session created.
DEBUG [Thread-3] UserCounterListener.incrementUserCounter(72) | User Count: 2
```

After the sessions were created, the User Counter text in the header shows that there are currently two users active in the application. I realize this may not be a precise count, but it's about as accurate as it gets with web applications:

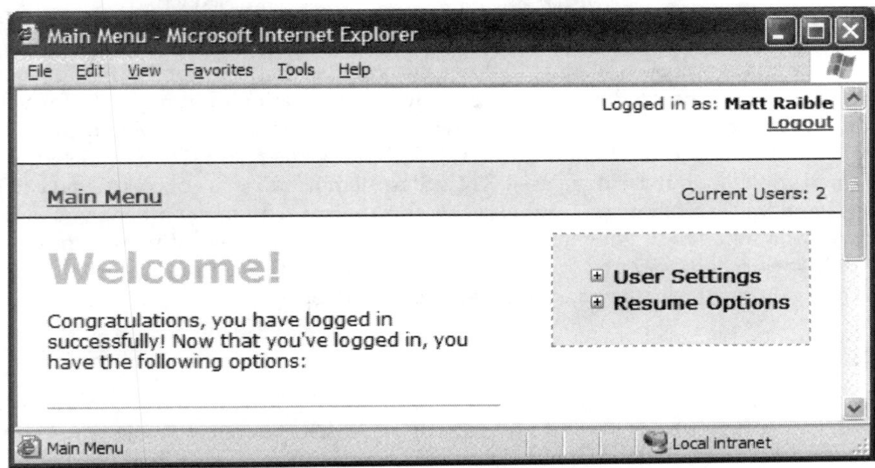

You can see that the Tiles controller can be a very valuable asset in your Struts toolbox. You can reduce the amount of code needed in your actions and move specific logic to specific tiles. You might even eliminate the need to chain actions together, using multiple tiles and controller combinations instead. You're encouraged to consider using controllers because they can greatly help organize your code and view logic. By using controllers, actions can focus on page flow rather than preparing views.

If you're developing a very small and simple application, Tiles might not be necessary. The difficult part of Tiles is finding a good example to operate from and extend. I hope that these examples, in combination with the `struts-resume` application, will make your Struts development journey easier. You should be able to use the `basicLayout.jsp` and `tiles-config.xml` files to get up and running. If you already know Struts and aren't using Tiles, you owe it to yourself (and your deadlines) to try it out.

Using IDEs and Struts Development Environments

The year 2002 seemed like the Year of the IDE to me. I used to use Macromedia's HomeSite and `vi` for all my Java editing, because I hated the bloat and RAM wastage of an IDE. Furthermore, IDEs always seemed to complicate things more than they helped. With the maturity of tools like IDEA and Eclipse, using an IDE is fun again–and worth my time (a gig of RAM doesn't hurt either).

I've never felt the need to use an IDE to help me configure my `struts-config.xml` or `web.xml` file. However, this was probably because these tools didn't exist when I first started working with Struts and web application. Now I'm glad I learned the DTDs and I feel that it's easier to do my job with this knowledge. If editing XML files by hand, I recommend XMLSpy (http://www.xmlspy.com). This is a great tool for any XML-related development because it validates your XML against a DTD and also performs auto-completion as you type. Another reason to learn the DTDs is because tools like XDoclet assemble the `struts-config.xml` file from a number of XML fragments, and most IDE tools only support editing fully assembled `struts-config.xml` files.

There are also applications that have been created simply to provide a development environment for Struts's application development. Let's take a look at a couple of these now.

Struts Console

Struts Console (found at http://www.jamesholmes.com/struts/) is a free application for managing Struts-based applications. It can be used as a stand-alone Swing application or as a plug-in for your favorite IDE. Supported IDEs are JBuilder (v4.0+), Eclipse (v1.0+), IBM WebSphere Appl. Dev. (v4.0.3+), IDEA (v3.0, build 668+), NetBeans (v3.2), Sun ONE/Forte (v3.0+), and JDeveloper (v9i+). It has support for managing all your Struts-related XML files, such as `struts-config.xml`, `tiles-config.xml`, and `validation.xml`. When using this tool, as with many others, you'll lose any formatting you've applied to the document. However, it does allow formatting within the tool to "pretty up" your XML. It also has a wizard for converting JSP and HTML pages into Struts JSP pages–a very handy feature if you're converting an existing application to Struts.

Easy Struts

The Easy Struts project (see http://easystruts.sourceforge.net/) provides a set of tools for Struts development, including a `struts-config.xml` editor, XSLT generation, tooltips from the Struts DTD, support for modules, and an input helper. Easy Struts is only available as an IDE plug-in; no stand-alone application is available. Supported IDEs are Eclipse (v2.0+) and JBuilder (v5.0+).

Using Modules in Team Development Environments

Have you ever worked on a project where many developers were working on the same codebase? Many development teams work in this type of environment, while others allocate development roles to single individuals. Let's imagine two types of teams; the first has fifteen developers and the second has three individuals. We'll pretend that both teams are developing similar applications that use Struts and EJBs for handling credit card payments for a large bank. The large team will probably divide the work among tiers, where five people work on each tier–EJBs, `ActionServlets` and business layer, and the web tier comprising JSP pages or Velocity templates. The second (smaller) team will simply assign one person to each tier.

In a team environment where many people are configuring and manipulating deployment descriptors, it can be difficult to keep your `web.xml` and `struts-config.xml` in sync. The simplest solution I've found is to use XDoclet to generate these configuration files, but there is another option–**modules**. When initially developed by the Struts development team, they were called subapplications, which is a more descriptive name. Modules allow you to separate different areas of an application out into different modules. Modules are a core feature of Struts 1.1 and can be very helpful for large projects as well as for creating pluggable features.

Since the development of modules is very similar to developing a standard Struts application, I'll show you how to set them up, and I've actually implemented an "upload" feature that uses them in the `struts-resume` application. The setup is rather simple, consisting of the following three steps:

1. Prepare a config file for your module.

2. Inform the controller of the module.

3. Use forwards or actions to switch to your new module.

We won't detail the first step here, because this is the same as creating a new Struts application. You could probably use XDoclet to create your configuration files for the different modules, but you would have to coax your Ant webdoclet task to output struts-config.xml to different directories. Of course, the purpose of submodules is to make development and configuration easier, and XDoclet already does this for you!

The second step involves adding a new init-parameter to the ActionServlet's definition in the application's deployment descriptor, web.xml. In the struts-resume application, this configuration is located at metadata/web/servlets.xml:

```
<servlet>
  <servlet-name>action</servlet-name>
  <servlet-class>org.apache.struts.action.ActionServlet</servlet-class>
  <init-param>
    <param-name>config</param-name>
    <param-value>/WEB-INF/struts-config.xml</param-value>
  </init-param>
  <init-param>
    <param-name>config/upload</param-name>
    <param-value>/WEB-INF/struts-upload.xml</param-value>
  </init-param>
  <init-param>
    <param-name>debug</param-name>
    <param-value>2</param-value>
  </init-param>
  <init-param>
     <param-name>detail</param-name>
     <param-value>2</param-value>
   </init-param>
   <load-on-startup>2</load-on-startup>
</servlet>
```

This configuration indicates that there are two modules in this application–the default module, which has no forward slash (/) in its name, and the second, our "upload" feature. The configuration files for both modules are located in the WEB-INF directory. The recommended standard for naming module configuration files is struts-*module*.xml.

While you're looking at the ActionServlet's configuration, I want to point out a few changes between 1.0 and 1.1. In 1.0, it was common practice to specify the ResourceBundle for messages as an "application" init-parameter. I used this setting, as well as the "nocache" init-parameter. In Struts 1.1, these settings have been deprecated and moved to a <controller> element in the struts-config.xml file. The following setting can be found in metadata/web/struts-controller.xml:

```
<controller nocache="true"
            inputForward="true"
            maxFileSize="2M" />
```

The nocache setting tells the controller to add HTTP headers to prevent caching of content–it's off by default. You can also specify a forwardPattern attribute, such as WEB-INF/pages/MP, where the $M variable indicates the module prefix and $P indicates the path attribute of the selected <forward> element, although it isn't used here. The inputForward attribute allows you to use local or global forwards in the input attribute of an action mapping. This is a very handy and much needed feature.

More information on optional values and their meanings can be found online at http://jakarta.apache.org/struts/userGuide/configuration.html#controller_config.

The application's ResourceBundle is now specified in a `<message-resources>` element in `struts-config.xml`. If you're using XDoclet, you can place this in a `struts-message-resources.xml` file. In the `struts-resume` application, this file is located in the same location as the rest of the Struts configuration fragments:

```
<message-resources parameter="ApplicationResources"/>
```

Since I keep this file (`ApplicationResources.properties`) directory under `WEB-INF/classes`, there is no need to specify a package name. You can also specify alternate resource bundles for the application by adding a second `<message-resources>` element and specifying a `key` attribute:

```
<message-resources parameter="CustomResources" key="custom"/>
```

This can be useful if, for instance, you're building a product using Struts and you only want to expose a minimal amount of options that customers may change. To use this ResourceBundle with the `<bean:message>` tag, you only need to specify a `bundle` attribute that matches the key:

```
<bean:message key="webapp.title.prefix" bundle="custom"/>
```

Now that you've seen how to set up modules for an application, let's see how to switch between them. For demonstration purposes, I've added an "upload" module to `struts-resume` for uploading résumés. This module doesn't demonstrate much more than file-upload and module-switching. It could be developed into a feature that allows for simple uploading of existing résumés, but not much more than that. At the time of writing, there are two basic techniques to switching modules. The first involves using a forward (global or local) with a `contextRelative` attribute set to `true`. This will tell the controller and request dispatcher to be module-sensitive, rather than simply context-sensitive:

```
<forward name="toUpload"
         contextRelative="true"
         path="/upload/index"
         redirect="true">
```

In this example, `index` is a definition in the `tiles-upload.xml` document. Adding `redirect="true"` is required to enable the switching to execute correctly. The second method is to use the built-in `SwitchAction`. Using the `SwitchAction` would result in an `<action-mappings>` such as the one you see here:

```
<action-mappings>
  <action path="/switchModule"
          type="org.apache.struts.actions.SwitchAction"/>
  ...
</action-mappings>
```

Then to change to the upload module, you could use a URL such as http://localhost:8080/struts-resume/switchAction.do?prefix=upload&page=index. I think it's much easier and cleaner to use the global-forward technique, and therefore I've configured the following forward in `metadata/web/global-forwards.xml`:

```
<forward name="uploadResume" contextRelative="true"
         path="/upload/index.do" redirect="true" />
```

One thing I noticed when building the "upload" module for `struts-resume` was that it was possible to share configuration settings between the applications. For instance, I've shared the same `basicLayout.jsp` template that I used for Tiles. The one problem I encountered was that any messages (in ApplicationResources) and any forwards that you include in your submodule have to be defined in their respective files. For instance, I had to define the error page messages, button labels, and Validator messages. I expected this, so it wasn't an issue. It's nice to see that there is clean separation of modules, but you're also allowed to share pieces of each.

Hopefully, you'll find this simple enough to consider using if you think you have need for modules in an application. The one limitation of modules at this point is that they're only supported when using extension-mapping of your `ActionServlet`. Which is to say that `*.do` is supported, but `/do/*` isn't, but consult the Struts site (http://jakarta.apache.org/struts) or mailing lists for the current status of this issue.

Testing Struts Applications

Like any good Java programmer, you will have heard of testing frameworks and you've probably used **JUnit** before. JUnit version 3.8.1 (required by `struts-resume`) can be downloaded from http://www.junit.org. Ant can be a very powerful tool for running JUnit tests. To run them, you need to have JUnit's JAR file (`junit.jar`) in the `$ANT_HOME/lib` directory.

JUnit works great for testing classes outside a servlet container, but doesn't provide the needed structure for testing what a user will actually do. For this, you've been blessed with **Cactus** from the Jakarta project. Cactus is a simple test framework for unit testing server-side Java code such as servlets, EJBs, tag libraries, and filters. It supports both in container testing and out of container testing via *mock objects*. It's pretty slick in that you can run a test (for instance "`ant test-cactus -Dtestcase=ActionFilterTest`" for the `struts-resume` application) and it will start Tomcat, run the test, and then stop Tomcat. It also integrates with **HttpUnit** for testing your JSP pages and validating that the resulting HTML is correct.

> *More information on Cactus can be found at* http://jakarta.apache.org/cactus. *You can find the HttpUnit web site at* http://httpunit.sourceforge.net.

The `struts-resume` example uses a tool called **JUnitDoclet** (http://www.junitdoclet.org) to generate JUnit-based skeleton test cases and test suites of all your Java source files. All you need to do is execute "`ant gen-test-`*`module`*" where *`module`* is `common`, `web`, or `ejb`.

JUnitDoclet is a pretty slick tool in that it will update your test cases if you add new methods, and it won't overwrite any custom code you've added to the test case. I'm saying this to warn you that there may be some test cases without any "meat in the methods." In most cases, this is because I've used the class before and I know it works, so I don't care to test it. Is this a bad practice? Maybe, but it will sure help my development time.

I'm using a different source tree for test cases, and it works really well with this approach. Unfortunately, once you've changed a test case to extend something other than JUnit (that is, Cactus's ServletTestCase), it won't update that class anymore. It will simply ignore it, which is fine with me.

Another testing framework, specific to Struts, was introduced in late 2001. Known as **StrutsTestCase for JUnit** (see http://strutstestcase.sourceforge.net/), it's an extension of the standard JUnit test case. By providing both a mock object and a Cactus approach to run the `ActionServlet`, StrutsTestCase allows testing of Struts code with or without a running servlet engine. Since it uses the controller to test code, it tests not only the implementation of `Action` objects, but also mappings, `ActionForms`, and `ActionForwards`.

StrutsTestCase is compliant with both the Java Servlet 2.2 and 2.3 specifications and supports Struts 1.02 and 1.1 and Cactus 1.4.1 and JUnit 3.8.

StrutsTestCase already provides validation methods, so it's simple to create unit test cases, as demonstrated by the following code snippet:

```
public void testEditUser() {
  setRequestPathInfo("/editUser");
  setRequestParameter("action", "edit");
  addRequestParameter("email","tomcat");
  actionPerform();
  verifyForward("success");
  assertTrue(getSession().getAttribute(Constants.USER_KEY) != null);
}
```

You could run a very comprehensive test of your application using Cactus and HttpUnit to verify your action classes and whatever view technology you happen to use in rendering your UI (JSP, XML, or Velocity). An HttpUnit test is also pretty simple, as demonstrated in the following example:

```
WebConversation wc = new WebConversation();
WebResponse resp = wc.getResponse(
                   "http://www.httpunit.org/doc/Cookbook.html");
WebLink link = resp.getLinkWith("response");
link.click();
WebResponse jdoc = wc.getCurrentPage();
```

HttpUnit also supports testing of JavaScript, and their site carries the warning that it's "very basic at present" (see http://www.httpunit.org/doc/javascript-support.html). If you're looking for a more robust JavaScript testing framework, I recommend **JsUnit** (http://www.jsunit.net). JsUnit is a unit testing framework for client-side testing of JavaScript. JsUnit tests are written in JavaScript: it's essentially a JavaScript port of JUnit, so you name your methods and such accordingly. It's important to note that these languages are drastically different and whoever writes the JavaScript should probably also write the tests.

The last testing framework I want to cover is the **WebTest** tool (http://webtest.canoo.com) from Canoo. This is a much easier testing framework to develop with because everything is simply configured in an XML file. Similar to the other testing frameworks, WebTest is run with Ant. However, the main difference is that the entire test is configured in an Ant task. For instance, this might be how you create a test for a user logging into your application:

```
<target name="login">
  <testSpec name="tomcat-login">
    <config host="${tomcat.server}" port="${tomcat.port}"
            protocol="http" basepath="${webapp.name}" verbose="true"
            resultpath="." resultfile="web-test-result.xml" summary="true"
            saveresponse="true"/>
    <steps>
      <invoke stepid="get Login Page" url="/"/>
      <verifytitle stepid="we should see the login title" text="Login"/>
      <setinputfield stepid="set user name"
                     name="j_username" value="tomcat"/>
      <setinputfield stepid="set password"
                     name="j_password" value="tomcat"/>
      <clickbutton label="Login" stepid="Click the submit button"/>
      <verifytitle text="Main Menu"
                   stepid="Home Page follows if login ok"/>
    </steps>
  </testSpec>
  <loadfile property="web-test.result"
            srcFile="web-test-result.xml"/>
  <echo>${web-test.result}</echo>
</target>
```

WebTest is a great framework for web developers, because you can easily test the path a user takes without writing any code, just XML. It also appears to use HttpUnit, so it isn't reinventing the wheel, rather just providing an easier way to develop it.

For testing your application's interactions with a database, you might want to take a look at **Dbunit** (http://www.dbunit.org). Dbunit is a JUnit extension that sets up your database in a known state so you can execute your tests with expected data. It uses XML datasets, or collections of data tables, and performs database operations before and after each test. Of course, you can also do this in your test cases, where you can insert, update, or delete an object, but since there's no guarantee of the order that these will execute–Dbunit is probably a good idea. I've had good luck with putting my tests in a particular order in a class, and then having these methods get executed in that order, but an ideal test method is autonomous.

I've included examples of Cactus tests, Struts Action tests, HttpUnit tests and even a simple Canoo WebTest example. The following table indicates which classes you can use for this and how to run them. Run `test-cactus` instead of `test-web` if you want to run these tests while Tomcat is already running.

Test Type	File Location	Ant Command
Cactus	`test/org/appfuse/webapp/action/UserAction`	`ant test-web -Dtestcase=LoginActionTest`
Struts	`test/org/appfuse/webapp/action/ResumeAction`	`ant test-web -Dtestcase=ResumeActionTest`
HttpUnit	`test/org/appfuse/webapp/action/MainMenuTest`	`ant test-web -Dtestcase=MainMenuTest`
Canoo	`web-tests.xml`	`ant test-canoo -Dtestcase=login`

Using servlet testing frameworks like StrutsTestCase and Cactus will make testing your actions much easier. It's either that or testing them through your browser, which may take you five clicks to get to. There's no need to wait for your JSP pages to compile if you really only want to hit a servlet. The `struts-resume` application makes it easy to develop and run new tests. I encourage you to use it and learn from it.

A real timesaver with JSP development is precompiling the JSP pages prior to deploying them to your servlet container. This can be done with Ant's `<jspc>` task, which uses Tomcat's Jasper compiler to generate `.java` source files. While it's great for testing, you would like use this tool to precompile your JSP pages for production use too, right? Unfortunately, to do this, you need to make an entry for every JSP in your `web.xml` file, and boy would that be a long and laborious process. If you don't do this step, Tomcat will just recompile over the top of the pages you've already compiled. Some application servers, such as WebLogic and SunONE, allow you configure precompilation of JSP pages once the application has been deployed. I'd love it if other vendors would copy this feature.

Another nice thing to do when developing JSP pages is to check that your CSS and HTML is correct. Of course, you won't be able to do this until the JSP has compiled and displayed. If you're using WebTest, it actually generates an HTML file for each request it makes, thereby recording the last viewed request. In the `struts-resume` application, these can be found in `build/test/data`. If you aren't using WebTest, you can just view source in your browser and save the HTML to a directory. Then you can upload it to the W3C's validator (http://validator.w3.org) to ensure the HTML complies with the specified DOCTYPE. I usually create a "sandbox" directory in my project's directory where I can put these HTML files for validation and other quick fixes. Sometimes it's nice to work with a static HTML version. What I do is change the absolute path for all my stylesheets, JavaScript, and images in order to use a relative path. In the struts-resume project, this would entail changing "`/struts-resume/`" to "`../web/`".

Once you've validated your application and tested it thoroughly, you'll be much more confident that it works and therefore more likely to produce quality software. Hopefully, with the examples I've put together, the hard work of writing tests is over. Writing tests might seem like a pain, but that's only if you're writing your actual code first. Try writing your test cases first next time I think you'll find them most enjoyable. There's nothing like writing an application that works the first time you run it in a browser (thanks to the unit tests of course).

Handling Exceptions in Struts Applications

Struts 1.1 has made it much easier to handle exceptions in a Struts application. A popular rule in software development is that "if something goes wrong, you should tell the user about it." This can become quite complicated in a web application that uses MVC and business objects to talk to a database. Exceptions can be thrown at any level, in your data access code, in your `Action` classes, in your business objects, or even in your JSP pages.

What I've done in the past was to use a `try...catch` in both my `Action` classes and in my business objects and then "bubble" any exceptions up to the top. This is ugly and can result in the user being presented with a message such as column street_address not found. Furthermore, in my `Action` classes, I've caught my business-level exceptions, wrapped them in a `ServletException,` and thrown them to the client. I have an error page configured in `web.xml` as well as on my JSP pages, which the client is directed to in the event of an error.

Even though I'm going to show you a better way to handle exceptions with Struts, I still think it's important to configure your JSP pages and `web.xml` to deal with uncaught exceptions. You should add an entry to `web.xml` for when the server throws a HTTP Status Code 500, the dreaded Internal Server Error:

```
<error-page>
  <error-code>500</error-code>
  <location>/error.jsp</location>
</error-page>
```

Alternatively, you can use `<exception-type>` rather than an HTTP Status Code or error-code:

```
<error-page>
  <exception-type>java.lang.Throwable</exception-type>
  <location>/error.jsp</location>
</error-page>
```

You can also add both of them, just to be safe. When using XDoclet, you can specify these entries in an `error-pages.xml` file in your `merge` directory. I usually declare an `errorPage` in my JSP pages as well:

```
<%@ page language="java" errorPage="/error.jsp" %>
```

In our the example application, this line only exists in the `common/taglibs.jsp` file. Adding these entries will basically prevent users from ever seeing a stack trace of the exception–providing that you've written your `error.jsp` appropriately. For an advanced error page, you might even configure it to e-mail an administrator when it's displayed to users (or use log4j's SMTP Logger). I've seen the 500 Internal Server Error more than I've seen the classic 404 error in recent years. Adding a pretty face onto these errors can make everyone's life a little more pleasant.

The real hope is that an error page will never be displayed. As a savvy web user, if it does get displayed, I'd like to see exactly what went wrong–the SQL details. Of course, this will depend on your application's security requirements. If your application is open for attack (resides on the Internet rather than an intranet), you might want to suppress messages that give any database information. At the same time, not all your users will want to see the nitty-gritty details of exceptions, and therefore, I recommend you aim for more user-friendly messages.

Chained Exceptions

In my opinion, a well-developed application should catch error messages, turn them into friendly messages, and then return the user to the last page they viewed successfully. At the same time, it would be nice to add a technical message as well, for those savvy users (or developers) that want to know the exact cause of the problem and may be able to avoid it. To achieve this, the first thing you can do is to use **chained exceptions**. The traditional Java exception mechanism only allows you to throw one exception. This presents a problem in a layered architecture where exceptions can occur at each layer.

Of course, you can wrap exceptions, as I've done with a `ServletException`, but this might result in a loss of detail in the end. Ted Husted described the solution best in one of his Struts Tips. Rather than trying to manipulate his words to sound like I came up with the idea, it's easiest to quote him (see http://husted.com/struts/tips/015.html):

> *"What we really need to do is "stack" or "chain" the exceptions, so that each layer can add its own viewpoint to the incident. Then, at the end, display them all, with the originating exception at the bottom of the list.*
>
> *This approach works surprisingly well in a layered architecture. The "topmost" layer is "closest" to the user, and so throws the most "user-friendly" exceptions. The "lowest" layer throws the "geek-friendly" errors that we need to solve the problem. When we chain exceptions by linking them together, the user-friendly message comes first, followed by the more detailed messages. The user is told what they need to know first, and can leave the rest to the system administrators."*

If you're using JDK 1.4, the `java.lang.Exception` class has a `getCause()` method that allows you to find the original cause of each exception. To use this properly, you'll need to throw the exceptions that occurred from each tier, rather than just catching an exception and throwing it with a message. By this, I mean to say that it's better to have this:

```
try {
  ...
} catch (Exception e) {
    throw new DAOException("Error occurred connecting to database", e);
}
```

rather than just throwing the message:

```
try {
  ...
} catch (Exception e) {
    throw new DAOException("Error occurred connecting to database");
}
```

I'm using this functionality in the `struts-resume` application, in the `ActionFilter.java` class to be precise. If you're using a JDK less than 1.4, I invite you to take a look at the Scaffold package, which includes a `ChainedException` class that works with older JDKs. The following snippet illustrates how I've implemented this functionality in the `ActionFilter.java` class (located in `src/web/org/appfuse/webapp/filters`):

```
// User authenticated, empty user object
if (username != null && userForm == null) {
  try {
    UserManager mgr =
      new UserManagerImpl(
        (String) ctx.getAttribute(Constants.DAO_TYPE));
    UserForm user = mgr.getUser(username);
    session.setAttribute(Constants.USER_KEY, user);
  } catch (Exception e) {

    // Log the message so we can read the logs and see
```

```
      //  what went wrong
      log.error("Error getting user's information " + e);

      // Print a StackTrace, always a good idea
      e.printStackTrace();

      // Set up an empty ActionErrors collection to add all
      //  the exception messages to
      ActionErrors errors = new ActionErrors();

      // Add a general message that says "The process did not complete."
      errors.add(ActionErrors.GLOBAL_ERROR,
             new ActionError("errors.general"));

      StringBuffer sb = new StringBuffer();

      // JDK 1.4 ONLY - if there are causes, loop through them and get
      //  all their messages
      if (e.getCause() == null) {
        sb.append(e.getMessage());
      } else {
        while (e.getCause() != null) {
          sb.append(e.getMessage());
          sb.append("\n");
          e = (Exception) e.getCause();
        }
      }

      // Add all the errors to a resource bundle key, defined as:
      //  errors.detail={0}
      errors.add(
        ActionErrors.GLOBAL_ERROR,
        new ActionError("errors.detail", sb.toString()));

      // Add the errors to the request so we can display them for the user
      request.setAttribute(Globals.ERROR_KEY, errors);

      // Dispatch to the error messages page
      RequestDispatcher dispatcher =
        request.getRequestDispatcher("/error.jsp");
      dispatcher.forward(request, response);
      return;
    }
  }
```

The end result is a series of error messages as follows:

```
* A required resource is not available.
* The process did not complete. Details should follow.
* Cannot connect to MySQL server localhost:3307. Is there a MySQL server running
the machine/port you're trying to connect to? (java.net.ConnectException)
```

It's easy to see how chained exceptions can give you messages that will satisfy all your users. It might even be possible to use the previous error-looping code in a declared exception for Struts, but I haven't tried this yet. After you've built all your errors, you need to direct the user to a friendly page. When using this code in an Action class, you'll most likely direct them back to where they came from.

```
return (new ActionForward(mapping.getInput()));
```

This can be problematic if you access the same ActionMapping from several different pages. I've seen this solved in a couple of different ways. The first way is to add an extra parameter to the form or URL that called the action, and then use that value to forward appropriately. The other method is one used by the Roller Weblogger open-source project (http://www.rollerweblogger.org). It uses a BreadCrumbFilter to hold a stack of the last URLs accessed by the application. This is nice in that you can simply grab the last URL off the stack and so forward back to the last viewed page.

Declaring Exceptions

New to Struts 1.1 is the concept of configurable exceptions. That is, you can declaratively specify exceptions on a global level in struts-config.xml as well as on an ActionMapping level. This concept is similar to the one you see with global forwards and with local forwards. It's easy to register an exception–the only attribute that is required is type, which states the type of the exception. Optionally, you can specify a key (to a message in your resource bundle) and the path to direct the response to. The following is an example that might be used to handle UserNotFoundException:

```
<exception key="missing.user"
           type="org.appfuse.webapp.services.UserNotFoundException"
           path="addUser"/>
```

In this example, addUser is a forward whose path references a tile's definition (in tiles-config.xml). You could easy change this to redirect to a JSP page (for instance /addUser.jsp or perhaps /editUser?action=add). Exceptions are best used at the ActionMapping level, without a defined path. If you don't define a path, Struts is smart enough to redirect to your ActionMapping's input value. Of course, if you don't have an input defined, you should probably specify the path for your exception, or you'll get the dreaded blank screen of Struts. The key in this example is used to override the key used by the exception itself.

Struts makes it easier to develop exceptions and provides built-in internationalization. Let's take a look at the code for the UserNotFoundException:

```
import org.apache.struts.util.ModuleException;

public class UserNotFoundException extends ModuleException {
  /**
   * Construct a new instance of this exception for the specified username.
   * @param username Username that was not found
   */
  public UserNotFoundException(String username) {
    super("error.user.missing", username);
  }
}
```

error.user.missing refers to a key in the default ResourceBundle, as defined in struts-config.xml. In the struts-resume application, this bundle is ApplicationResource.properties, where the key is defined as follows:

```
error.user.missing=Could not find user information for username '{0}'
```

Of course, you can change your exception's constructor to handle as many parameters as you have in your message key. If you specify a key for this exception in struts-config.xml, it will override the message that is spit out by the exception. One disadvantage to this is that you lose the ability to substitute parameters, but it can be useful for exceptions that don't use the Struts's message bundle.

A nice feature of Struts's exception handling is that messages are easily externalized in a properties file. That is, you get I18n built right into your exception handling. Furthermore, you can specify a separate ResourceBundle for your error messages by specifying the bundle attribute on your exception. Of course, you could use a ResourceBundle on your business and persistence layers with properties file, but it might not be needed if these exceptions never bubble up to the UI.

The beauty of using declared exceptions in your application is that you don't have to catch them in your Action classes. To enabled declared exceptions, you'll need to change the signature of your actions from using the Struts 1.0 perform() method to using the Struts 1.1 execute() method. The main difference between the two is that the perform() method could throw an IOException and a ServletException, whereas the execute() method only throws a top-level Exception. Since all exceptions extend Exception somewhere along the line, this makes it easy to write and throw your exceptions:

```
public ActionForward execute(ActionMapping mapping,
                             ActionForm form,
                             HttpServletRequest request,
                             HttpServletResponse response)
                             throws Exception {
```

When a registered exception is caught by Struts, it will actually create an errors object for you that can be then displayed using <html:errors/> or a syntax like that in struts-resume. The following is what the messages.jsp file uses that is included in the struts-resume application's main Tiles template:

```
<%-- Error Messages --%>
<logic:messagesPresent>
  <div class="error">
    <html:messages id="error">
      <bean:write name="error" filter="false"/><br />
    </html:messages>
  </div>
</logic:messagesPresent>

<%-- Success Messages --%>
<logic:messagesPresent message="true">
  <div class="message">
```

```
    <html:messages id="message" message="true">
      <bean:write name="message" filter="false"/><br />
    </html:messages>
  </div>
</logic:messagesPresent>
```

This could also be done with the JSTL, but I prefer the shorter method with less typing, so I'm using Struts tags. You'll notice the second half of this page is used to display success messages. I think it's important to know how to create and display success messages in an application, so I'll show you how easy it is. Essentially, all you need do is create a new `messages` object and add one or more messages to it. It's very similar to the `ActionErrors` class (it's actually its superclass), so the creation process is pretty much the same:

```
ActionMessages messages = new ActionMessages();

// execute business logic to add a new record

// add success message to the request
messages.add(ActionMessages.GLOBAL_MESSAGE, new ActionMessage("record.added");
```

While I haven't yet used declarative exception handling with Struts on any real-world projects, I've implemented it in the `struts-resume` application where it was very useful. If you have an exception framework that works for your Struts-based application, I also invite you to chime in on the `struts-dev` mailing list and suggest improvements. The `struts-resume` application gives an example of using declared exceptions, and you can also find an example in the `struts-example` application that ships with Struts.

Summary

One of the most frustrating things I've experienced in software development is reading about how to do something, but not having any examples. Design patterns are only good if they work when implemented. I believe in keeping it simple and I believe that Struts makes JSP and servlet development simpler. I know that Struts can be overwhelming at first, but its rewards are awesome. Using Struts will ultimately lead you to understand web applications better and will reduce your development time as you use it more.

Using the tools and sample applications available for Struts can also be overwhelming. The only way to truly learn what is best is to try them and learn what is best for you. If you send a message to the Struts user mailing list about something non-Struts-related (for example HTML, JavaScript, persistence), chances are you'll get a whole gamut of different responses and opinions. However, it's a very active community and chances are you'll get your questions answered. Hopefully, I've given you some guidance in what works well with Struts, and perhaps my sample application will show you how XDoclet makes generating code and other items much easier. I also invite you to download and use Dave Johnson's Roller Weblogger software–it's open source and has a lot of good Struts code in it. It also uses XDoclet and is a fairly robust application.

More information on Roller can be found at: http://www.rollerweblogger.org.

Above all, I advise not trying to reinvent the wheel with anything related to web applications. Chances are that someone has already tried to do what you're doing. Spending the time to research your problem and solutions may save you a lot of time down the road. Using mailing list archives and Google can solve a great number of problems. Open-source projects are great because you get a whole team of developers working with you and helping you use their frameworks. It helps to get involved with the technology you're using as well. If you're using Struts, subscribe to the `struts-user` mailing list and watch your Inbox fill up, or subscribe to the digest list for only a couple of e-mails per day. Remember that anything possible in a simple JSP and servlet application is possible when using Struts. *Struts just makes it easier*, as I'm sure any web-based MVC framework does. Likewise, anything that is possible on an HTML page is possible in a JSP page.

Another reason I really like using Struts is because of the tools that have appeared to automate the development process. I'm comfortable enough with developing all the components that I can check the generated code to make sure everything is fine. You wouldn't want to use a code-generator that produces spaghetti code! The Struts Roadmap includes enhanced support for these tools as well as embraces newer technologies such as JSF and the JSTL.

I'll just note a few tips here as gentle reminders of what we covered in the chapter.

- If you need validation in your Struts application, use the Validator. If you're using the Validator, use XDoclet to generate your `validation.xml`.
- If you need templating in a Struts application, use Tiles. If you're using Tiles, use definitions and use them as forwards in your `struts-config.xml`.
- Use container-managed authentication for login–then you'll have roles available to show or hide tiles and to limit access to certain actions and links.
- Use CSS rather than tables for page layout. It will reduce the size of your pages and it's easier to develop with in the long run.

JavaServer Pages Syntax Reference

This appendix describes the syntax for JavaServer Pages 2.0. The intention is to provide you with a reference that is complete and useful, but more compact than the specification.

> **JSP specifications from version 2.0 upward are available by visiting http://java.sun.com/products/jsp/.**

This appendix looks in turn at the following:

- Various preliminary details: the notation we're using, how URLs are specified in JSP code, and the various types of commenting you can use.
- The JSP **directives**: the `page`, `taglib`, and `include` directives.
- JSP **scripting elements**: declarations, scriptlets, and expressions.
- JSP's **standard actions** including the `<jsp:useBean>`, `<jsp:setProperty>`, `<jsp:getProperty>`, `<jsp:include>`, and `<jsp:forward>` actions.
- A brief review of the syntax for using **tag libraries**.
- The **implicit objects** that are available within a JSP such as `request`, `response`, `session`, and `application`. You'll examine these in more detail in "Appendix B: JavaServer Pages Implicit Objects."
- Various predefined request and application **attributes** that you may find useful.

Preliminaries

Before you get stuck into the details, here are a few miscellaneous observations.

Notation

A word on the notation used in this appendix:

- *Italics* show what you'll have to specify.
- **Bold** shows the default value of an attribute. Attributes with default values are optional, if you're using the default. Sometimes, where the default value is a little complicated, we use **default** to indicate that the default is described in the following text.
- When an attribute has a set of possible values, those are shown delimited by `|`.

```
import="package.class, package.*, ..."
session="true|false"
```

URL Specifications

URLs specified within JSP tags can be of two sorts:

- **Context-relative** paths start with a "/"; the base URL is provided by the web application to which the JSP belongs. For example, in a web application hosted at http://localhost:8080/projsp-appendixA/, the URL `/pageurl.jsp` would be equivalent to http://localhost:8080/projsp-appendixA/pageurl.jsp.
- **Page-relative** paths are relative to the JSP page in which they occur. Unlike context-relative paths, page-relative paths don't start with "/". For instance, a page application hosted at http://localhost:8080/projsp-appendixA/morespecs/urlspec.jsp might give a page as `subfolder/urlspec.jsp`, which would be equivalent to http://localhost:8080/projsp-appendixA/morespecs/subfolder/urlspec.jsp.

Comments

Two sorts of comments are allowed in JSP code–JSP and HTML:

```
<!-- HTML comments remain in the final client page.
     They can contain JSP expressions, which will be ignored by the JSP
     container.
-->

<%-- JSP comments are hidden from the final client page --%>
```

Remember too that within scriptlets (inside `<% %>`, `<%! %>`, or `<%= %>` tags), you can use standard Java comments:

```
<%
  /* This Java comment starts with a slash asterisk and continues
     until you come to a closing asterisk slash.
  */

  // Comments starting with a double slash continue to the end of the line.
%>
```

Directives

Directives are instructions to the JSP container regarding page properties, importing tag libraries, and including content within a JSP. Because directives are instructions rather than in-out processes, they cannot produce any output via the `out` stream.

The page Directive

The `page` directive specifies attributes for the page–all the attributes are optional, because the essential ones have default values, shown in bold.

```
<%@ page language="java"
         extends="package.class"
         import="package.class, package.*, ..."
         session="true|false"
         buffer="none|default|sizekb"
         autoFlush="true|false"
         isThreadSafe="true|false"
         info="Sample JSP to show tags"
         isErrorPage="true|false"
         errorPage="ErrorPage.jsp"
         contentType="TYPE|
                      TYPE; charset=CHARSET|
                      text/html; charset=ISO-8859-1"
         pageEncoding="default"
         isELIgnored="true|false"
%>
```

- The default buffer size is defined to be *at least* 8 kb.
- The `errorPage` attribute contains the relative URL for the error page to which this page should go if there's an unhandled error on this page.
- The specified error page file must declare `isErrorPage="true"` to have access to the `Exception` object.
- The `contentType` attribute sets the MIME type and the character set for the response. The default value is `text/html` when defining JSP Pages standard syntax and `text/xml` when implementing JSP Documents in XML format.
- The `pageEncoding` attribute defines the character encoding for the JSP page. The default is that specified in the `contentType` attribute, or `"ISO-8859-1"` if none was specified there.

This is an example of the code that may be used for an error page:

```
<%@ page language="java"
         isErrorPage="true" %>

<html>
  <body>
    <!-- This displays fully-qualified name of the exception -->
    <%= exception.toString() %>
    <br>

    <!-- This displays the exception's descriptive message -->
    <%= exception.getMessage() %>
  </body>
</html>
```

The page will print out the error message received.

This directive can also switch on support for scripting and the expression language (EL) in the JSP document, using the following two attributes:

- isScriptingEnabled: Sets scripting support.
- isELEnabled: Sets EL support. Settings in web.xml may influence the behavior of this attribute.

For both of these attributes, a value of true enables support and false disables it, and the default values are both true.

The taglib Directive

A tag library is a collection of tags used to extend a JSP container functional model. The taglib directive defines a tag library namespace for the page, mapping the URI of the tag library descriptor to a prefix that can be used to reference tags from the library on this page.

```
<%@ taglib uri (or tagdir)="/WEB-INF/taglib.tld" prefix="tagPrefix" %>

.
.
.

<tagPrefix:tagName attributeName="attributeValue" >
  JSP content
</tagPrefix:tagName>

<tagPrefix:tagName attributeName="attributeValue" />
```

You should assume that the tag library descriptor (TLD) defines a tagName element.

`tagdir` indicates this prefix is to be used to identify tag extensions installed in the `/WEB-INF/tags/` directory or a subdirectory. If a `tld` is present in the specified directory, it's used. Otherwise, an implicit tag library is used. A translation error must occur if the value doesn't start with `/WEB-INF/tags/`. A translation error must occur if the value doesn't point to a directory that exists. A translation error must occur if used in conjunction with the `uri` attribute.

The File Tag Directive

Most JSP directives can be used in simple tag handler code files. Note that the `page` directive itself isn't used, and instead you use the `tag` directive, which may only be used in tag files. The directives available are

- `taglib`: used just as in JSP pages
- `include`: used just as in JSP pages
- `tag`: only available in tag files
- `attribute`: only available in tag files
- `variable`: only available in tag files

Here's an example `tag` directive:

```
<%@ tag name="msg"
  display-name="Message"
  body-content="scriptless"
  dynamic-attributes="true"
  small-icon="/WEB-INF/small-icon.jpg"
  large-icon="/WEB-INF/large-icon.jpg"
  description="Simple usage of a tag directive"
%>
```

The include Directive

There are two include tags–the `include` directive and the `jsp:include` action.

The `include` directive includes a static file at translation time, adding any JSP in that file to this page for runtime processing:

```
<%@ include file="header.html" %>
```

See also the `jsp:include` action.

Scripting Elements

Scripting elements are used to include snippets of Java code within a JSP: to declare variables and methods, execute arbitrary Java code, and display the result of Java expressions.

Declarations

The following syntax allows you to declare variables and methods for the page. These are placed in the generated servlet *outside* the `_jspService()` method, in other words variables declared here will be instance variables of the servlet. Declarations don't produce any output.

Here's an example of declaring a variable:

```
<%! String  message; %>
```

The following code declares a variable and initializes it:

```
<%! String message = "variable declarared"; %>
```

You can define a method for use on the global page like so:

```
<%! public String showMessage() { return message; } %>
```

Declaration tags are mainly used in conjunction with scriptlets.

Scriptlets

Scriptlets enclose Java code (on however many lines) that is evaluated *within* the generated servlet's `_jspService()` method to generate dynamic content:

```
<%
  // Java code
%>
```

Take care when using adjacent scriptlet blocks because the following code

```
<% if(user.isLoggedIn) { %>
     <p>Hi!</p>
<% } %>
<% else { %>
     <p>Please log in first...</p>
<% } %>
```

isn't legal because we've broken the `else` block into two scriptlets.

Expressions

Expressions return a value from the scripting code as a `String` to the page:

```
<p>Hello there,
<%= userName %>
Good to see you.</p>
```

Standard Actions

The standard actions provide various facilities for manipulating JavaBeans components, including and forwarding control to other resources at request-time and generating HTML to use the Java plug-in.

<jsp:useBean>

The `<jsp:useBean>` tag checks for an instance of a bean of the given `class` and `scope`. If a bean of the specified class exists it references it with the `id`, otherwise it instantiates it. The bean is available within its `scope` with its `id` attribute.

You can include code between the `<jsp:useBean>` tags, as shown in the second example–this code will only be run if the `<jsp:useBean>` tag successfully instantiates the bean:

```
<jsp:useBean id="aBeanName"
             scope="page|request|session|application"
             typeSpecification
/>
```

or:

```
<jsp:useBean id="anotherBeanName"
             scope="page|request|session|application"
             typeSpecification
>
  <jsp.setProperty name="anotherBeanName"
                   property="*|propertyName" />
</jsp:useBean>
```

There is a lot of flexibility in specifying the type of the bean (indicated by *`typeSpecification`*). You can use

- `class="`*`package.class`*`"`
- `type="`*`typeName`*`"`
- `class="`*`package.class`*`" type="`*`typeName`*`"` (and with terms reversed)
- `beanName="`*`beanName`*`" type="`*`typeName`*`"` (and with terms reversed)

whereby

- typeName is the class of the scripting variable defined by the id attribute; that is, the class that the bean instance is cast to (whether the class, a parent class, or an interface the class implements).
- beanName is the name of the bean, as used in the instantiate() method of the java.beans.Beans class.

<jsp:setProperty>

The <jsp:setProperty> tag you used previously sets the property of the bean referenced by name using the value:

```
<jsp:setProperty name="anotherBeanName"
                 propertyExpression
/>
```

The *propertyExpression* can be any of the following:

- property="*"
- property="*propertyName*"
- property="*propertyName*" param="*parameterName*"
- property="*propertyName*" value="*propertyValue*"

whereby

- The * setting tells the tag to iterate through the request parameters for the page, setting any values for properties in the bean whose names match parameter names.
- The param attribute specifies the parameter name to use in setting this property.
- The value attribute can be any runtime expression as long as it evaluates to a String.
- Omitting value and param attributes for a property assumes that the bean property and request parameter name match.
- The value attribute String can be automatically cast to boolean, byte, char, double, int, float, long, and their class equivalents. Other casts will have to be handled explicitly in the bean's set*PropertyName*() method.

<jsp:getProperty>

The final bean-handling action is <jsp:getProperty>, which gets the named property and outputs its value for inclusion in the page as a String:

```
<jsp:getProperty name="anotherBeanName" property="propertyName" />
```

<jsp:param>

The `<jsp:param>` action is used within the body of `<jsp:forward>`, `<jsp:include>`, and `<jsp:plugin>` to supply extra name-value parameter pairs. It has the following syntax:

```
<jsp:param name="parameterName" value="parameterValue" />
```

<jsp:forward>

To forward the client request to a static resource, whether it be an HTML file, a JSP page, or a servlet class in the same context as the page, use the following syntax:

```
<jsp:forward page="relativeURL" />
```

or

```
<jsp:forward page="relativeURL" >
  <jsp:param name="parameterName" value="parameterValue" />
</jsp:forward>
```

whereby

- The `page` attribute for `<jsp:forward>` can be a runtime expression.
- The `value` attribute for `<jsp:param>` can be a runtime expression.

<jsp:include>

The `<jsp:include>` action includes a static or dynamically referenced file at runtime:

```
<jsp:include page="relativeURL" flush="true|false" />
```

or

```
<jsp:include page="relativeURL"
             flush="true" >
  <jsp:param name="parameterName" value="parameterValue"/>
</jsp:include>
```

whereby

- The `page` attribute can be the result of some runtime expression.
- The optional `flush` attribute determines whether the output buffer will be flushed before including the specified resource. The default value is `"false"`. (Note that in JSP 1.1 this attribute was mandatory and the only permissible value was `"true"`.)
- The `jsp:param` tag allows parameters to be appended to the original request, and if the parameter `name` already exists, the new parameter `value` takes precedence in a comma-delimited list.

<jsp:plugin>

The `<jsp:plugin>` action enables the JSP to include a bean or an applet in the client page. It has the following syntax:

```
<jsp:plugin type="bean|applet"
            code="class"
            codebase="classDirectory"
            name="instanceName"
            archive="archiveURI"
            align="bottom|top|middle|left|right"
            height="inPixels"
            width="inPixels"
            hspace="leftRightPixels"
            vspace="topBottomPixels"
            jreversion="1.2|number"
            nspluginurl="pluginURL"
            iepluginurl="pluginURL"
            mayscript="true|false" >
  <jsp:params>
    <jsp:param name="parameterName" value="parameterValue">
  </jsp:params>
  <jsp:fallback>Problem with plugin</jsp:fallback>
</jsp:plugin>
```

Most of these attributes are direct from the HTML spec (http://www.w3.org/TR/html4/), with the exceptions being `type`, `jreversion`, `nspluginurl`, and `iepluginurl`.

- The `name`, `archive`, `align`, `height`, `width`, `hspace`, `vspace`, `jreversion`, `nspluginurl`, and `iepluginurl` attributes are optional.
- The `<jsp:param>` tag's `value` attribute can take a runtime expression.
- The `jreversion` is the Java Runtime Environment specification version that the component requires.
- `nspluginurl` and `iepluginurl` are the URL where the Java plug-in can be downloaded for Netscape Navigator and Internet Explorer.

Tag Libraries

The syntax for using tag libraries is very similar to that for the standard actions, except of course that the tag names and attributes are defined in the tag library itself rather than by the JSP standard. Each tag library is associated with a **prefix** by using the `taglib` directive to map the prefix to a URI identifying the tag library. For example, using the Jakarta Taglibs project's `request` tag library (http://jakarta.apache.org/taglibs/doc/request-doc/intro.html):

```
<%@ taglib uri="http://jakarta.apache.org/taglibs/request-1.0" prefix="req"
  %>
```

Within the JSP, tags from the library can then be used by using the prefix defined in the `taglib` directive and the tag's name, for example:

```
<req:attributes id="loop">
  Name: <jsp:getProperty name="loop" property="name"/>
  Value: <jsp:getProperty name="loop" property="value"/>
</req:attributes>
```

The mapping between a particular URI (as used in the `taglib` directive) and the TLD can be set up in one of two ways. In JSP 1.2, it's possible to package tag libraries so that the mapping is automatic, based on settings contained in the TLD file. Alternatively, an entry can be made in the `web.xml` file to map a URI to a TLD file:

```
<taglib>
  <taglib-uri>http://jakarta.apache.org/taglibs/request-1.0</taglib-uri>
  <taglib-location>/WEB-INF/request.tld</taglib-location>
</taglib>
```

Implicit Objects

JSP defines a number of implicit objects that JSP scripting elements can make use of:

- `request`, of type `javax.servlet.http.HttpServletRequest`
- `response`, of type `javax.servlet.http.HttpServletResponse`
- `out`, of type `javax.servlet.jsp.JspWriter`
- `session`, of type `javax.servlet.http.HttpSession`
- `application`, of type `javax.servlet.ServletContext`
- `exception`, of type `java.lang.Throwable`
- `config`, of type `javax.servlet.ServletConfig`
- `page`, a reference to the implementing servlet class for the JSP
- `pageContext`, of type `javax.servlet.jsp.PageContext`

Appendix B gives details of these objects and the methods that each makes available. There are many more classes and interfaces defined by the JSP and Servlet specifications.

Predefined Attributes

The servlet and JSP specifications define a number of special request and context (application) attributes.

Security-Related Attributes

These attributes are only available when a request has been made over the Secure Sockets Layer (SSL). SSL allows you to set up secure communications between the server and a client.

javax.servlet.request.cipher_suite

`javax.servlet.request.cipher_suite` is a request attribute of type `String` containing the **cipher suite** used for an SSL request.

javax.servlet.request.key_size

`javax.servlet.request.key_size` is a request attribute of type `Integer` containing the bit size that was used for an SSL request.

Here's an example:

```
public boolean isOver128bit(HttpServletRequest request) {

  Integer reqSize = (Integer) request.getAttribute(
                              "javax.servlet.request.key_size");
  if(reqSize != null) {
    if (reqSize.intValue() < 128) {
      return false;
    } else {
      return true;
    }
  }
}
```

javax.servlet.request.X509Certificate

`javax.servlet.request.X509Certificate` is a request attribute of type `java.security.cert.X509Certificate` containing any certificate associated with an SSL request.

Inclusion-Related Attributes

These attributes apply when a servlet or JSP is accessed via a `<jsp:include>` or a `RequestDispatcher.include()` like so:

```
request.getRequestDispatcher("servelt_path/myservlet").forward(req, res);
```

javax.servlet.include.request_uri

`javax.servlet.include.request_uri` is a request attribute of type `String` containing the URI under which this included servlet or JSP is being accessed.

```
String reqURI = (String) request.getAttribute(
                         "javax.servlet.include.request_uri");
```

javax.servlet.include.context_path

`javax.servlet.include.context_path` is a request attribute of type `String` containing the context path of the URI under which this included servlet or JSP is being accessed.

```
String contextPath = (String) req.getAttribute(
                          "javax.servlet.include.context_path");
```

javax.servlet.include.path_info

`javax.servlet.include.path_info` is a request attribute of type `String` containing the path info of the URI under which this included servlet or JSP is being accessed.

```
String pathInfo = (String) req.getAttribute(
                      "javax.servlet.include.path_info");
```

javax.servlet.include.servlet_path

`javax.servlet.include.servlet_path` is a request attribute of type `String` containing the servlet path of the URI under which this included servlet or JSP is being accessed.

```
String pathInfo;

if(req.getAttribute("javax.servlet.include.servlet_path") != null) {
  pathInfo = (String)req.getAttribute("javax.servlet.include.path_info");
}
```

javax.servlet.include.query_string

`javax.servlet.include.query_string` is a request attribute of type `String` containing the query string of the URI under which this included servlet or JSP is being accessed.

```
String reqQueryString = req.getAttribute(
                    "javax.servlet.include.query_string");
```

Servlet Error Page Attributes

These attributes are only available within an error page declared in `web.xml`.

javax.servlet.error.status_code

`javax.servlet.error.status_code` is a request attribute of type `Integer` containing the status code of the servlet or JSP that caused the error.

```
Integer statusCode = (Integer) req.getAttribute(
                          "javax.servlet.error.status_code");
String error = "HTTP Status Code - " + statusCode.intValue();

return error;
```

javax.servlet.error.exception_type

`javax.servlet.error.exception_type` is a request attribute of type `Class` that contains the type of the exception thrown by the servlet or JSP. It's now redundant with the introduction of the `javax.servlet.error.exception` attribute.

```
Exception e = (Exception) req.getAttribute(
                           "javax.servlet.error.exception_type");
```

javax.servlet.error.message

`javax.servlet.error.message` is a request attribute of type `String` containing the message contained within the exception thrown by the servlet or JSP. It's now redundant with the introduction of the `javax.servlet.error.exception` attribute.

```
String statusCode = (String) req.getAttribute(
                              "javax.servlet.error.status_code");

String message= (String)req.getAttribute("javax.servlet.error.message");

if message == null) {
  message = "Unknown error";
}
```

javax.servlet.error.exception

`javax.servlet.error.exception` is a request attribute of type `Throwable` containing the exception thrown by the servlet or JSP.

```
public void doGet(HttpServletRequest req, HttpServletResponse res)
                               throws ServletException, IOException {

PrintWriter out = res.getWriter();

Throwable throwable = (Throwable) req.getAttribute(
                       "javax.servlet.error.exception");

.
.
.

if (throwable != null)
  throwable.printStackTrace(out);
.
.
.
```

javax.servlet.error.request_uri

`javax.servlet.error.request_uri` is a request attribute of type `String` containing the URI of the request that caused the servlet or JSP to throw an exception.

```
String reqErrorUri = (String) req.getAttribute("
                              javax.servlet.error.request_uri");
```

JavaServer Pages Error Page Attribute

This attribute is available within error pages declared in a JSP `page` directive.

javax.servlet.jsp.jspException

`javax.servlet.jsp.jspException` is a request attribute of type `Throwable` containing the exception thrown by the JSP page.

```
<%
  .
  try {
    InputStream in = pageContext.getServletContext()
                     .getResourceAsStream(fileName);

    if(in == null) {
      throw new JspException( "Error while opening file: '"+ fileName + "'");
    }
  } catch(Exception ex ) {
    .
    .
    .
  }
%>
```

Temporary File Directory Attribute

This attribute allows a web application to make use of a temporary working directory.

javax.servlet.context.tempdir

`javax.servlet.context.tempdir` is a context attribute of type `java.io.File` referencing a temporary working directory that can be used by the web application.

```
File tempDir = (File) getServletContext()
                      .getAttribute("javax.servlet.context.tempdir");
```

JavaServer Pages Implicit Objects

JSP defines a number of implicit objects that scripting elements can make use of. This appendix gives details of these objects and the methods that each of them exposes. There are many more classes and interfaces defined by the JSP and Servlet specifications.

> *This appendix lists **all** the methods available for each object (except those defined in `java.lang.Object`), irrespective of which class or interface defines the methods.*

The implicit objects are as follows:

- `request`
- `response`
- `out`
- `session`
- `application`
- `exception`
- `config`
- `page`
- `pageContext`

The request Object

The `request` object is an instance of a class that implements the `javax.servlet.http.HttpServletRequest` interface. It represents the request made by the client, and makes the following methods available:

```
public Object getAttribute(String name)
```

`getAttribute()` returns the value of the specified request attribute name. The return value is an `Object` or subclass if the attribute is available to the invoking `ServletRequest` object or `null` if the attribute isn't available.

```
public java.util.Enumeration getAttributeNames()
```

`getAttributeNames()` returns an `Enumeration` containing the attribute names available to the invoking `ServletRequest` object.

```
public String getAuthType()
```

`getAuthType()` returns the name of the authentication scheme used in the request or `null` if no authentication scheme was used. It returns one of the constants `BASIC_AUTH`, `FORM_AUTH`, `CLIENT_CERT_AUTH` or `DIGEST_AUTH` or `null` if the request was not authenticated.

```
public String getCharacterEncoding()
```

`getCharacterEncoding()` returns a `String` object containing the character encoding used in the body of the request or `null` if there is no encoding.

```
public int getContentLength()
```

`getContentLength()` returns the length of the body of the request in bytes or –1 if the length is not known.

```
public String getContentType()
```

`getContentType()` returns a `String` object containing the MIME type (`"text/plain"`, `"text/html"`, `"image/gif"`, etc.) of the body of the request or `null` if the type isn't known.

```
public String getContextPath()
```

`getContextPath()` returns the part of the request URI that indicates the context path of the request. The context path is the first part of the URI and always begins with the "/" character. For servlets running in the root context, this method returns an empty `String`. For example if there is an incoming request from request: http://localhost/guide/suburbs/index.jsp then `getContextPath()` would return "/guide".

```
public Cookie[] getCookies()
```

getCookies() returns an array containing any Cookie objects sent with the request or null if no cookies were sent.

```
public long getDateHeader(String name)
```

getDateHeader() returns a long value that converts the date specified in the named header to the number of milliseconds since midnight January 1, 1970 Greenwich Mean Time (GMT). This method is used with a header that contains a date and returns -1 if the request doesn't contain the specified header.

```
public String getHeader(String name)
```

getHeader() returns the value of the specified header expressed as a String object or null if the request doesn't contain the specified header. Here is an example HTTP request:

```
GET /search?index=servlets+jsp HTTP/1.1
Accept: image/gif, image/jpg, */*
Accept-Encoding: gzip
Connection: Keep-Alive
Cookie: userID=id66589
Host: www.mycompany.com
Referer: http://www.mycompany.com/getproducts.html
User-Agent: Mozilla/4.6 [en] (WinXP; U)
```

For example, if the usage is getRequest("Connection"), it would return "Keep-Alive":

```
public java.util.Enumeration getHeaderNames()
```

getHeaderNames() returns an Enumeration containing all of the header names used by the request.

```
public java.util.Enumeration getHeaders(String name)
```

getHeaders() returns an Enumeration containing all of the values associated with the specified header name. The method returns an empty enumeration if the request doesn't contain the specified header.

```
public ServletInputStream getInputStream() throws java.io.IOException
```

getInputStream() returns a ServletInputStream object that can be used to read the body of the request as binary data.

```
public int getIntHeader(String name)
```

getIntHeader() returns the value of the specified header as an int. It returns -1 if the request doesn't contain the specified header and throws a NumberFormatException if the header value cannot be converted to an int. This method was made for convenience when the Header type is known to be an integer; this way it can be absorbed by the code without any conversion.

```
public java.util.Locale getLocale()
```

getLocale() returns the preferred locale of the client that made the request.

```
public java.util.Enumeration getLocales()
```

getLocales() returns an Enumeration containing, in descending order of preference, the locales that are acceptable to the client machine.

```
public String getMethod()
```

getMethod() returns the name of the HTTP method used to make the request. Typical return values are "GET", "POST", or "PUT".

```
public String getParameter(String name)
```

getParameter() returns a String object containing the value of the specified parameter or null if the parameter doesn't exist.

```
public java.util.Map getParameterMap()
```

getParameterMap() returns a Map containing the request parameters.

```
public java.util.Enumeration getParameterNames()
```

getParameterNames() returns a Enumeration containing the parameters contained within the invoking ServletRequest object.

```
public String[] getParameterValues(String name)
```

getParamterValues() is used when a parameter may have more than one value associated with it. The method returns a String array containing the values of the specified parameter or null if the parameter doesn't exist.

```
public String getPathInfo()
```

getPathInfo() returns any additional path information contained in the request URL. This extra information will be after the servlet path and before the query string. It returns null if there is no additional path information. For example, in the incoming request from http://localhost/guide/suburbs/innersuburbs/ then getContextPath() would return "/innersuburbs".

```
public String getPathTranslated()
```

getPathTranslated() returns the same information as the getPathInfo() method, but translated into a real path.

```
public String getProtocol()
```

`getProtocol()` returns the name and version of the protocol used by the request. A typical return `String` would be `"HTTP/1.1"`.

```
public String getQueryString()
```

`getQueryString()` returns the query string that was contained in the request URL without any decoding from the container or `null` if there was no query string.

```
public java.io.BufferedReader getReader() throws java.io.IOException
```

`getReader()` returns a `BufferedReader` object that can be used to read the body of the request as character data.

```
public String getRemoteAddr()
```

`getRemoteAddr()` returns a `String` object containing the IP address of the client machine that made the request.

```
public String getRemoteHost()
```

`getRemoteHost()` returns a `String` object containing the name of the client machine or the IP address if the name cannot be determined.

```
public String getRemoteUser()
```

`getRemoteUser()` returns the login of the user making the request or `null` if the user hasn't been authenticated.

```
public RequestDispatcher getRequestDispatcher(String path)
```

`getRequestDispatcher()` returns a `RequestDispatcher` object that acts as a wrapper around the resource located at the specified path. The path must begin with "/" and can be a relative path.

```
public String getRequestedSessionId()
```

`getRequestedSessionId()` returns the session ID that was specified by the client or `null` if the request didn't specify an ID.

```
public String getRequestURI()
```

`getRequestURI()` returns a subsection of the request URL, from the protocol name to the query string.

```
public StringBuffer getRequestURL()
```

`getRequestURL()` reconstructs the URL used to make the request including the protocol, server name, port number, and path, but excluding the query string.

```
public String getScheme()
```

`getScheme()` returns the scheme (`"http"`, `"https"`, `"ftp"`, and so on) used to make the request.

```
public String getServerName()
```

`getServerName()` returns a `String` object containing the name of the server that received the request.

```
public int getServerPort()
```

`getServerPort()` returns the port number that received the request.

```
public String getServletPath()
```

`getServletPath()` returns the part of the request URL that was used to call the servlet, without any additional information or the query string.

```
public HttpSession getSession(boolean create)
public HttpSession getSession()
```

`getSession()` returns the `HttpSession` object associated with the request. By default, if the request doesn't currently have a session calling this method will create one. Setting the `boolean` parameter `create` to `false` overrides this.

```
public boolean isRequestedSessionIdFromCookie()
```

`isRequestedSessionIdFromCookie()` returns `true` if the session ID came in from a cookie.

```
public boolean isRequestedSessionIdFromURL()
```

`isRequestedSessionIdFromURL()` returns `true` if the session ID came in as part of the request URL.

```
public boolean isRequestedSessionIdValid()
```

`isRequestedSessionIdValid()` returns `true` if the session ID requested by the client is still valid.

```
public boolean isSecure()
```

`isSecure()` returns `true` if the request was made using a secure channel, for example HTTPS.

```
public boolean isUserInRole(String role)
```

isUserInRole() returns true if the authenticated user has the specified logical role or false if the user isn't authenticated.

```
public void removeAttribute(String name)
```

removeAttribute() makes the specified attribute unavailable to the invoking ServletRequest object. Subsequent calls to the getAttribute() method for this attribute will return null.

```
public void setAttribute(String name, Object o)
```

setAttribute() binds a value to a specified attribute name. Note that attributes will be reset after the request is handled.

```
public void setCharacterEncoding(String env)
        throws java.io.UnsupportedEncodingException
```

setCharacterEncoding() overrides the character encoding used in the body of this request.

```
public static final String BASIC_AUTH
public static final String FORM_AUTH
public static final String CLIENT_CERT_AUTH
public static final String DIGEST_AUTH
```

These String constants are used to identify the different types of authentication that may have been used to protect the servlet. They have the values BASIC, FORM, CLIENT_CERT, and DIGEST, respectively.

```
public String getRealPath(String path)
public boolean isRequestedSessionIdFromUrl()
```

These methods are deprecated and should not be used in new code–they exist for compatibility with existing code. Use ServletContext.getRealPath(java.lang.String) instead of getRealPath(String path) and use ServletContext.isRequestedSessionIdFromURL() instead of isRequestedSessionIdFromUrl().

The response Object

The response object is an instance of a class that implements the javax.servlet.http.HttpServletResponse interface. It represents the response to be made to the client and makes the following methods available:

```
public void addCookie(Cookie cookie)
```

addCookie() adds the specified cookie to the response (more than one cookie can be added).

```
public void addDateHeader(String name, long date)
```

`addDateHeader()` adds a response header containing the specified header name and the number of milliseconds since midnight January 1, 1970 GMT. This method can be used to assign multiple values to a given header name.

```
public void addHeader(String name, String value)
```

`addHeader()` adds a response header with the specified `name` and `value`. This method can be used to assign multiple values to a given header name.

```
public void addIntHeader(String name, int value)
```

`addIntHeader()` adds a response header with the specified name and `int` value. This method can be used to assign multiple values to a given header name.

```
public boolean containsHeader(String name)
```

`containsHeader()` returns `true` if the response header includes the specified header name. This method can be used before calling one of the `set()` methods to determine if the header value has already been set.

```
public String encodeRedirectURL(String url)
```

`encodeRedirectURL()` encodes the specified URL or returns it unchanged if encoding isn't required. This method is used to process a URL before sending it to the `sendRedirect()` method.

```
public String encodeURL(String url)
```

`encodeURL()` encodes the specified URL by including the session ID or returns it unchanged if encoding isn't needed. All URLs generated by a servlet should be processed through this method to ensure compatibility with browsers that don't support cookies.

```
public void flushBuffer() throws java.io.IOException
```

`flushBuffer()` causes any content stored in the buffer to be written to the client. Calling this method will also commit the response, meaning that the status code and headers will be written.

```
public int getBufferSize()
```

`getBufferSize()` returns the buffer size used for the response or `0` if no buffering is used.

```
public String getCharacterEncoding()
```

`getCharacterEncoding()` returns a `String` object containing the character encoding used in the body of the response. The default is `"ISO-8859-1"`, which corresponds to Latin-1.

```
public java.util.Locale getLocale()
```

`getLocale()` returns the locale that has been assigned to the response. By default, this will be the default locale for the server.

```
public ServletOutputStream getOutputStream() throws java.io.IOException
```

`getOutputStream()` returns a `ServletOutputStream` object that can be used to write the response as binary data.

```
public java.io.PrintWriter getWriter() throws java.io.IOException
```

`getWriter()` returns a `PrintWriter` object that can be used to write the response as character data.

```
public boolean isCommitted()
```

`isCommitted()` returns `true` if the response has been committed, meaning that the status code and headers have been written.

```
public void reset()
```

`reset()` clears the status code and headers and any data that exists in the buffer. If the response has already been committed, calling this method will cause an exception to be thrown.

```
public void resetBuffer()
```

`resetBuffer()` clears the content of the response buffer without clearing the headers or status code. It will throw an `IllegalStateException` if the response has been committed.

```
public void sendError(int sc, String msg) throws java.io.IOException
public void sendError(int sc) throws java.io.IOException
```

`sendError()` sends an error response back to the client machine using the specified error status code. A descriptive message can also be provided. This method must be called before the response is committed (in other words, before the status code and headers have been written).

```
public void sendRedirect(String location) throws java.io.IOException
```

`sendRedirect()` redirects the client machine to the specified URL. This method must be called before the response is committed (in other words, before sending it to the client).

```
public void setBufferSize(int size)
```

`setBufferSize()` requests a buffer size to be used for the response. The actual buffer size will be at least this large.

```
public void setContentLength(int len)
```

`setContentLength()` sets the length of response body.

```
public void setContentType(String type)
```

`setContentType()` sets the content type of the response sent to the server. The `String` argument specifies a MIME type and may also include the type of character encoding, for example `"text/plain; charset=ISO-8859-1"`.

```
public void setDateHeader(String name, long date)
```

`setDateHeader()` sets the time value of a response header for the specified header name. The time is the number of milliseconds since midnight January 1, 1970 GMT. If the time value for the specified header has been previously set, the value passed to this method will override it.

```
public void setHeader(String name, String value)
```

`setHeader()` sets a response header with the specified `name` and `value`. If the value for the specified header has been previously set, the value passed to this method will override it.

```
public void setIntHeader(String name, int value)
```

`setIntHeader()` sets a response header with the specified name and `int` value. If the `int` value for the specified header has been previously set, the value passed to this method will override it.

```
public void setLocale(java.util.Locale loc)
```

`setLocale()` specifies the locale that will be used for the response.

```
public void setStatus(int sc)
```

`setStatus()` sets the status code and should be one of SC_ACCEPTED, SC_OK, SC_CONTINUE, SC_PARTIAL_CONTENT, SC_CREATED, SC_SWITCHING_PROTOCOLS, or SC_NO_CONTENT.

```
public static final int SC_CONTINUE
public static final int SC_SWITCHING_PROTOCOLS
public static final int SC_OK
public static final int SC_CREATED
public static final int SC_FOUND
public static final int SC_ACCEPTED
public static final int SC_NON_AUTHORITATIVE_INFORMATION
public static final int SC_NO_CONTENT
public static final int SC_RESET_CONTENT
public static final int SC_PARTIAL_CONTENT
public static final int SC_MULTIPLE_CHOICES
public static final int SC_MOVED_PERMANENTLY
public static final int SC_MOVED_TEMPORARILY
public static final int SC_SEE_OTHER
```

```
public static final int SC_NOT_MODIFIED
public static final int SC_USE_PROXY
public static final int SC_BAD_REQUEST
public static final int SC_UNAUTHORIZED
public static final int SC_PAYMENT_REQUIRED
public static final int SC_FORBIDDEN
public static final int SC_NOT_FOUND
public static final int SC_METHOD_NOT_ALLOWED
public static final int SC_NOT_ACCEPTABLE
public static final int SC_PROXY_AUTHENTICATION_REQUIRED
public static final int SC_REQUEST_TIMEOUT
public static final int SC_CONFLICT
public static final int SC_GONE
public static final int SC_LENGTH_REQUIRED
public static final int SC_PRECONDITION_FAILED
public static final int SC_REQUEST_ENTITY_TOO_LARGE
public static final int SC_REQUEST_URI_TOO_LONG
public static final int SC_UNSUPPORTED_MEDIA_TYPE
public static final int SC_REQUESTED_RANGE_NOT_SATISFIABLE
public static final int SC_EXPECTATION_FAILED
public static final int SC_INTERNAL_SERVER_ERROR
public static final int SC_NOT_IMPLEMENTED
public static final int SC_BAD_GATEWAY
public static final int SC_SERVICE_UNAVAILABLE
public static final int SC_GATEWAY_TIMEOUT
public static final int SC_HTTP_VERSION_NOT_SUPPORTED
```

These constants represent the status codes defined in the HTTP specification. (Go to http://www.w3.org/TR/html401/ for more information.)

```
public String encodeUrl(String url)
public String encodeRedirectUrl(String url)
public void setStatus(int sc, String sm)
```

These methods are deprecated and should not be used in new code–they exist for compatibility with existing code.

The out Object

The out object is an instance of the `javax.servlet.jsp.JspWriter` class. It's used to create the content returned to the client and has the following useful methods available:

```
public abstract void clear() throws java.io.IOException
```

`clear()` clears the contents of the buffer; it throws an exception if some data has already been written to the output stream.

```
public abstract void clearBuffer() throws java.io.IOException
```

`clearBuffer()` clears the contents of the buffer, but doesn't throw an exception if some data has already been written to the output stream.

```
public abstract void close() throws java.io.IOException
```

`close()` flushes and then closes the output stream.

```
public abstract void flush() throws java.io.IOException
```

`flush()` flushes the output buffer and sends any bytes contained in the buffer to their intended destination. `flush()` will flush all the buffers in a chain of `Writers` and `OutputStreams`.

```
public int getBufferSize()
```

`getBufferSize()` returns the size in bytes of the output buffer.

```
public abstract int getRemaining()
```

`getRemaining()` returns the number of bytes still contained in the buffer. It will return 0 if output is unbuffered.

```
public boolean isAutoFlush()
```

`isAutoFlush()` returns `true` if the buffer flushes automatically when an overflow condition occurs.

```
public abstract void newLine() throws java.io.IOException
```

`newLine()` writes a newline character to the output stream.

```
public abstract void print(boolean b) throws java.io.IOException
public abstract void print(char c) throws java.io.IOException
public abstract void print(int i) throws java.io.IOException
public abstract void print(long l) throws java.io.IOException
public abstract void print(float f) throws java.io.IOException
public abstract void print(double d) throws java.io.IOException
public abstract void print(char[] s) throws java.io.IOException
public abstract void print(String s) throws java.io.IOException
public abstract void print(Object obj) throws java.io.IOException
```

`print()` prints the specified primitive data type, `Object` or `String` to the client.

```
try {
  boolean b = false;
  out.print(b);
  JspWriter out = pageContext.getOut();
  out.print(b);
} catch(IOException ioe) {
  // Catch error.
}
```

The output is as follows:

false

```
public abstract void println() throws java.io.IOException
public abstract void println(boolean x) throws java.io.IOException
public abstract void println(char x) throws java.io.IOException
public abstract void println(int x) throws java.io.IOException
public abstract void println(long x) throws java.io.IOException
public abstract void println(float x) throws java.io.IOException
public abstract void println(double x) throws java.io.IOException
public abstract void println(char[] x) throws java.io.IOException
public abstract void println(String x) throws java.io.IOException
public abstract void println(Object x) throws java.io.IOException
```

`println()` prints the specified primitive data type, `Object` or `String` to the client, followed by a newline character at the end. The no-argument version simply writes a newline character. For example:

```
try {
  JspWriter out = pageContext.getOut();
  out.println("<html><title>Page Title</title></html>");
} catch(IOException ioe) {
  // Catch error.
}
```

The session Object

The `session` object is an instance of a class that implements the `javax.servlet.http.HttpSession` interface. It can be used to store session state for a user and makes the following methods available:

```
public Object getAttribute(String name)
```

`getAttribute()` returns the `Object` bound to the specified `name` in this session or `null` if it doesn't exist.

```
public java.util.Enumeration getAttributeNames()
```

`getAttributeNames()` returns an `Enumeration` of `String` objects containing the names of all the objects bound to this session.

```
public long getCreationTime()
```

`getCreationTime()` returns the time when the session was created in milliseconds since midnight Jan 1, 1970 GMT.

```
public String getId()
```

`getId()` returns a `String` object containing a unique identifier for this session.

```
public long getLastAccessedTime()
```

getLastAccessedTime() returns the last time a client request associated with the session was sent. The return value is the number of milliseconds since midnight Jan 1, 1970 GMT.

```
public int getMaxInactiveInterval()
```

getMaxInactiveInterval() returns the number of seconds the server will wait between client requests before the session is invalidated. A negative return value indicates the session will never time out.

```
public void invalidate()
```

invalidate() invalidates the session and unbinds any objects bound to it.

```
public boolean isNew()
```

isNew() returns true if the server has created a session that hasn't yet been accessed by a client.

```
public void logout()
```

logout() logs out the current client from the web server and invalidates all existing sessions connected with this client.

```
public void removeAttribute(String name)
```

removeAttribute() removes the Object bound to the specified name from this session.

```
public void setAttribute(String name, Object value)
```

setAttribute() binds an Object to the specified attribute name, in this session. If the attribute name already exists, the Object passed to this method will replace the previous Object.

```
public void setMaxInactiveInterval(int interval)
```

setMaxInactiveInterval() specifies the number of seconds the server will wait between client requests before the session is invalidated. If a negative value is passed to this method, the session will never time out.

```
public HttpSessionContext getSessionContext()
public Object getValue(String name)
public String[] getValueNames()
public void putValue(String name, Object value)
public void removeValue(String name)
```

These methods are deprecated and should not be used in new code–they exist for compatibility with existing code.

The application Object

The `application` object is an instance of a class that implements the `javax.servlet.ServletContext` interface and allows the page to obtain and set information about the web application in which it is running. It makes available the following methods:

```
public Object getAttribute(String name)
```

`getAttribute()` returns the value of the specified attribute `name`. The return value is an `Object` or subclass if the attribute is available to the invoking `ServletContext` object or `null` if the attribute isn't available.

```
public java.util.Enumeration getAttributeNames()
```

`getAttributeNames()` returns an `Enumeration` containing the attribute names available to the invoking `ServletContext` object.

```
public ServletContext getContext(String uripath)
```

`getContext()` returns the `ServletContext` object for the resource at the specified path on the server. The path argument is an absolute URL beginning with "/".

```
public String getInitParameter(String name)
```

`getInitParameter()` returns a `String` object containing the value of the specified initialization parameter or `null` if the parameter doesn't exist.

```
public java.util.Enumeration getInitParameterNames()
```

`getInitParameterNames()` returns an `Enumeration` containing the initialization parameters associated with the invoking `ServletContext` object.

```
public int getMajorVersion()
```

`getMajorVersion()` returns the major version of the Java Servlet API that the server supports. For servers supporting version 2.3 of the Servlet specification, this method will return 2.

```
public String getMimeType(String file)
```

`getMimeType()` returns the MIME type of the specified file or `null` if the MIME type cannot be ascertained. Typical return values will be `"text/plain"`, `"text/html"`, or `"image/jpg"`.

```
public int getMinorVersion()
```

`getMinorVersion()` returns the minor version of the Java Servlet API that the server supports. For servers supporting version 2.3 of the Servlet specification, this method will return 3.

```
public RequestDispatcher getNamedDispatcher(String name)
```

`getNamedDispatcher()` returns a `RequestDispatcher` object that will be wrapped around the named servlet.

```
public String getRealPath(String path)
```

`getRealPath()` returns a `String` object containing the real path, in a form appropriate to the platform on which the servlet is running, corresponding to the given virtual path. An example of a virtual path might be `"/blah.html"`.

```
public RequestDispatcher getRequestDispatcher(String path)
```

`getRequestDispatcher()` returns a `RequestDispatcher` object that acts as a wrapper around the resource located at the specified path. The path must begin with "/" and is interpreted relative to the current context root.

```
public java.net.URL getResource(String path)
        throws java.net.MalformedURLException
```

`getResource()` returns a `URL` object that is mapped to the specified path or `null` if there is no resource mapped to the path. The path must begin with "/" and is interpreted relative to the current context root.

```
public java.io.InputStream getResourceAsStream(String path)
```

`getResourceAsStream()` returns the resource at the specified path as an `InputStream` object.

```
public java.util.Set getResourcePaths()
```

`getResourcePaths()` returns all the paths to resources held in the web application as `Strings` beginning with a "/".

```
public String getServerInfo()
```

`getServerInfo()` returns a `String` object containing information on the server on which the servlet is running. At a minimum, the `String` will contain the servlet container name and version number.

```
<% out.print(application.getServerInfo()); %>
```

The output is as follows:

Apache Tomcat/5.0.0

```
public String getServletContextName()
```

getServletContextName() returns the name of the web application, as specified in the <display-name> element in web.xml.

```
public void log(String msg)
public void log(String message, Throwable throwable)
```

log() is used to write a message to the servlet engine's log file. The second version writes both an explanatory message and a stack trace for the specified Throwable exception to the log file.

```
public void removeAttribute(String name)
```

removeAttribute() makes the specified attribute unavailable to the invoking ServletContext object. Subsequent calls to the getAttribute() method for this attribute will return null.

```
public void setAttribute(String name, Object object)
```

setAttribute() binds a value to a specified attribute name.

```
public Servlet getServlet(String name) throws ServletException
public java.util.Enumeration getServlets()
public java.util.Enumeration getServletNames()
public void log(Exception exception, String msg)
```

These methods are deprecated and should not be used in new code–they exist for compatibility with existing code.

The exception Object

The exception object is an instance of the java.lang.Throwable class. It's available in error pages only and represents the exception that occurred that caused control to pass to the error page. Its most useful methods are as follows:

```
public String getLocalizedMessage()
```

getLocalizedMessage() returns a localized description of this Throwable object. In many cases, this will return the same result as getMessage().

```
public String getMessage()
```

getMessage() returns the error message string of this Throwable object.

```
public void printStackTrace()
public void printStackTrace(PrintStream ps)
public void printStackTrace(PrintWriter pw)
```

`printStackTrace()` prints information about this `Throwable` object, along with a listing of the method calls that led to the error condition arising. The output can be directed to the standard error stream or to a specified `PrintStream` or `PrintWriter` object.

```
public String toString()
```

`toString()` returns a short description of this `Throwable` object. If an error message was supplied when the object was created, the result is the `Throwable` class's name, followed by a colon and a space, followed by that message. For example:

```
<%
  try {
    throw new Exception("Here's my Exception");
  } catch(Exception e) {
    out.print(e.toString());
  }
%>
```

The output is as follows:

java.lang.Exception: Here's my Exception

The config Object

The `config` object is an instance of the `javax.servlet.ServletConfig` interface. It's used to make initialization parameters available and has the following methods:

```
public String getInitParameter(String name)
```

`getInitParameter()` returns the value of the specified initialization parameter or `null` if the parameter doesn't exist.

```
public java.util.Enumeration getInitParameterNames()
```

`getInitParameterNames()` returns an `Enumeration` of `String` objects containing the names of all of the servlet's initialization parameters.

```
public ServletContext getServletContext()
```

`getServletContext()` returns the `ServletContext` object associated with the invoking servlet. A `ServletContext` object contains information about the environment in which the servlet is running.

```
public String getServletName()
```

`getServletName()` returns the name of the servlet. If the servlet is unnamed, the method will return the servlet's class name.

The page Object

The `page` object is a reference to the `servlet` object that implements this JSP page. JSP page authors don't often use this object, because it's very expensive memory-wise.

The pageContext Object

The `pageContext` object is an instance of the `javax.servlet.jsp.PageContext` class and is used by the container-generated servlet code for your JSP page to access the various scopes available within the JSP page. JSP page authors don't often use this object, because it was intended to be generated by the container; it's important when writing tag libraries.

```
HttpSession thisSession = pageContext.getSession();
```

Index

Symbols

A

B

C

D

E

F

H

I

J

K

L

M

N

O

P

Q

R

S

T

U

V

W

X